www.wadsworth.com

wadsworth.com is the World Wide Web site for Wadsworth and is your direct source to dozens of online resources.

At *wadsworth.com* you can find out about supplements, demonstration software, and student resources. You can also send email to many of our authors and preview new publications and exciting new technologies.

wadsworth.com
Changing the way the world learns®

Introduction to Research in Education

SIXTH EDITION

Donald Ary
Northern Illinois University

Lucy Cheser Jacobs
Indiana University

Asghar Razavieh
Shiraz University, Shiraz, Iran

WADSWORTH
™
THOMSON LEARNING

Australia • Canada • Mexico • Singapore • Spain • United Kingdom • United States

WADSWORTH

THOMSON LEARNING

Education Editor: Dan Alpert
Development Editor: Tangelique Williams
Editorial Assistant: Alex Orr
Marketing Manager: Becky Tollerson
Project Manager, Editorial Production: Trudy Brown
Print/Media Buyer: Tandra Jorgensen
Permissions Editor: Bob Kauser
Production Service: Matrix Productions

Text Designer: Cecile Kaufman
Copy Editor: Linda Purrington
Cover Designer: Denise Davidson
Cover Image: © Simon Osbourne, Wonderfile
Compositor: Thompson Type
Text and Cover Printer: Phoenix Color Corp

Printed in the United States of America
3 4 5 6 7 04 03

**Library of Congress
Cataloging-in-Publication Data**
Ary, Donald.
   Introduction for research in education/Donald Ary,
Lucy Cheser Jacobs, Asghar Razavieh.—6th ed.
   p. cm.
Includes bibliographical references and index.
ISBN 0-534-24665-6
   1. Education—Research. I. Ary, Donald. II. Jacobs,
Lucy Cheser. III. Razavieh, Asghar. IV. Title.

LB1028.A7 2002
370′.7′2—dc21   2001033156

Wadsworth/Thomson Learning
10 Davis Drive
Belmont, CA 94002-3098
USA

For more information about our products, contact us:
Thomson Learning Academic Resource Center
1-800-423-0563
http://www.wadsworth.com

International Headquarters
Thomson Learning
International Division
290 Harbor Drive, 2nd Floor
Stamford, CT 06902-7477
USA

UK/Europe/Middle East/South Africa
Thomson Learning
Berkshire House
168-173 High Holborn
London WC1V 7AA
United Kingdom

Asia
Thomson Learning
60 Albert Street, #15-01
Albert Complex
Singapore 189969

Canada
Nelson Thomson Learning
1120 Birchmount Road
Toronto, Ontario M1K 5G4
Canada

To Sheila, Marion, and Nasrin

CONTENTS

PART SIX ▪ Communicating Research

PREFACE

Our goal while preparing the first edition of *Introduction to Research in Education* in 1972 was to provide a book that would enable readers to master the basic competencies necessary to (1) understand and evaluate the research of others, and (2) plan and conduct original research with a minimum of assistance. The continued acceptance of this book through five editions indicates success in reaching that goal.

As research in education has evolved and matured, we have adapted each new edition to provide our readers with the knowledge required to keep abreast of these changes. The focus of this edition remains to provide a text designed for use in an introductory course in educational research. Its aim is to provide a framework for evaluating existing research and to familiarize the beginning researcher with procedures for conducting an original research project. We focus on typical and practical problems encountered in research, beginning with formulation of questions and continuing through preparation of a final report.

The sequence of topics we discuss in this book begins with general descriptions of the quantitative and qualitative approaches to the search for knowledge. We assume that our readers are not familiar with the concepts, assumptions, and terminology of these approaches; therefore, we explain these as we introduce them. This introduction is followed by suggestions for translating general problems into specific questions amenable to disciplined inquiry. We emphasize the identification of the population and variables of interest.

Next we describe the role of previous research and theory in the planning of a research project. We have updated the sources of related literature, giving particular emphasis to databases that provide efficient access to relevant research and theory and how these databases can be accessed. We then proceed to investigate the ways in which theory, experience, observations, and related literature lead to hypothesis formation.

Sampling procedures and the more widely used descriptive and inferential statistical procedures are described. We deleted some of the computational procedures included in previous editions and have given more emphasis to the role of statistics in the research process and to the uses and the interpretation of statistics. The role of systematic observation and measurement is explored, and examples of useful measurement procedures are included. We have revised and updated the chapter on reliability and validity.

Then we discuss the various types of research that have proven useful in education, pointing out the advantages and disadvantages of various approaches without espousing any particular one as superior to the others. In this edition, we have expanded the section on qualitative research and have added a chapter on analyzing qualitative research.

We conclude by presenting the general rules for interpreting the results of research and the accepted procedures for reporting such results. We have updated the section on ethical and legal considerations.

In addition to the study questions at the end of each chapter, multiple-choice questions are available in the instructor's manual. We also include questions linked to *InfoTrac College Edition,* a Wadsworth exclusive, which offers students 24-hour access to full-text articles from hundreds of scholarly and popular publications.

Although *Introduction to Research in Education* is directed toward the beginning student in educational research, we hope that others who wish to learn more about the philosophy, tools, and procedures for systematic inquiry in education will also find it useful. The principal criterion used in determining what to include has been the potential usefulness of various aspects of educational research to the educational practitioner.

To all those teachers who used the first five editions and have made very valuable suggestions for improving and updating the sixth edition, we are deeply grateful. We are also grateful to the following reviewers whose comments and suggestions helped shape this revision: Susan Kushner Benson, University of Akron; Ben Layne, Georgia State University; Larry E. Miller, Ohio State University; Clyde Paul, Southwest Missouri State University; Bruce G. Rogers, University of Northern Iowa; Marlene Schommer-Aikins, Wichita State University; Christine Sorensen, Northern Illinois University; Hoi K. Suen, Pennsylvania State University; Marilyn Ann Verna, St. Francis College; Aimin Wang, Miami University; Claudia R. Wright, California State University, Long Beach; and Suzanne Young, University of Wyoming. We appreciate the thorough and scholarly work Jennie Ver Steeg and Samuel Huang have done to produce a comprehensive and up-to-date chapter on reviewing the related literature.

We are grateful to Longman Group UK Ltd., on behalf of the literary executor of the late Sir Ronald A. Fisher, F.R.S., and Dr. Frank Yates, F.R.S., for permission to reprint Tables III, IV, and VII from *Statistical Tables for Biological, Agricultural and Medical Research* (6th ed., 1974).

Chapter 1

The Nature of Scientific Inquiry

INSTRUCTIONAL OBJECTIVES

After studying this chapter, the student will be able to

1 List five major sources of knowledge and comment on each source.

2 Describe the characteristics of the scientific approach.

3 State the assumptions underlying science and the characteristic attitudes of scientists.

4 Specify the purpose and characteristics of scientific theory in the behavioral sciences.

5 Indicate the limitations involved in the application of the scientific approach in the social sciences.

6 Define educational research and give examples.

Educators are, by necessity, decision makers. Daily they face the task of deciding how to plan learning experiences, teach, guide students, organize a school system, and myriad other matters. Unlike unskilled workers, who are told what to do and how to do it, professionals must plan for themselves. People assume that professionals have the knowledge and skills necessary to make valid decisions about what to do and how. Alexander & Dochy (1995, p. 416) write that "Knowledge encompasses all a person knows or believes to be true. . . ." How are educators to know what is true? How do they acquire reliable information? Although there are other sources of knowledge, such as experience, authority, and tradition, scientific knowledge about the educational process makes the most valuable contribution to decision making in education. Educators can turn to this source for reliable information and suggestions to be used in a decision-making situation. This fund of knowledge has been made available to educators by scientific inquiry into educational problems. However, education has not always been influenced by the results of such careful and systematic investigations. In fact, the development of an educational science is at a comparatively early stage.

SOURCES OF KNOWLEDGE

Before we further pursue the role of scientific inquiry in education, let us review some of the ways in which human beings throughout history have sought knowledge. The major sources of knowledge can be categorized under five headings: (1) experience, (2) authority, (3) deductive reasoning, (4) inductive reasoning, and (5) the scientific approach.

Experience

Experience is a familiar and well-used source of knowledge. After trying several routes from home to work, you learn which route takes the least time or is the most free of traffic or is the most scenic. By personal experience you can find the answers to many of the questions you face. Much wisdom passed from generation to generation is the result of experience. If people were not able to profit from experience, progress would be severely retarded. In fact, this ability to learn from experience is a prime characteristic of intelligent behavior.

Yet for all its usefulness, experience has limitations as a source of knowledge. How you are affected by an event depends on who you are. Two people will have very different experiences in the same situation. The same forest that is a delightful sanctuary to one person may be a menacing wilderness to another. Two supervisors observing the same classroom at the same time could truthfully compile very different reports if one focused on and reported the things that went right and the other focused on and reported the things that went wrong.

Another shortcoming of experience is that you so frequently need to know things that you as an individual cannot learn by experience. A child turned loose to discover arithmetic alone might figure out how to add, but would be unlikely to find an efficient way to compute square roots. A teacher could learn through experience the population of a classroom on a particular day but could not personally count the population of the United States.

Authority

For things difficult or impossible to know by personal experience, people frequently turn to authority; that is, they seek knowledge from someone who has had experience with the problem or has some other source of expertise. People accept the word of recognized authorities. To learn the size of the U.S. population, you can turn to reports by the U.S. Bureau of the Census. A student can look up the accepted pronunciation of a word in a dictionary. A superintendent can consult a lawyer about a legal problem at school. A beginning teacher asks an experienced one for suggestions, and may try a certain technique for teaching reading because the supervisor suggests that it is effective.

Throughout history you can find examples of reliance on authority for knowledge, particularly during the Middle Ages when people preferred ancient scholars, such as Plato and Aristotle, and the early Fathers of the church as sources of information—even over direct observation or experience. Although authority is a very useful source of knowledge, you must always ask, How does authority know? In earlier days people assumed an authority was right simply because of the position he or she held, such as king, chief, or high priest. Today people are reluctant to rely on an individual as an authority merely because of position or rank. They are inclined to accept the assertions of an authority only when that authority bases its assertions on experience or other recognized sources of knowledge.

Closely related to authority are custom and tradition, on which people depend for answers to many questions related to professional, as well as everyday problems. In other words, people often ask, "How has this been done in the past?" and then use the answer as a guide for action. Custom and tradition have been especially prominent influences in the school setting, where educators often rely on past practices as a dependable guide. However, an examination of the history of education reveals that many traditions that prevailed for years were later found to be erroneous and had to be rejected. It is wise to appraise custom and tradition carefully before you accept them as reliable sources.

As a source of knowledge, authority has shortcomings that you must consider. In the first place, authorities can be wrong. Also, you may find that authorities disagree among themselves on issues, indicating that their authoritative statements are often more personal opinion than fact.

Deductive Reasoning

Ancient Greek philosophers made perhaps the first significant contribution to the development of a systematic approach for gaining knowledge. Aristotle and his followers introduced the use of **deductive reasoning,** which can be described as a thinking process in which you proceed from general to specific statements using prescribed rules of logic. You go from general knowledge to specific knowledge through logical argument.

An argument consists of a number of statements standing in relation to one another. The final statement is the conclusion, and the rest, called *premises,* offer supporting evidence. A major kind of deductive reasoning is the syllogism. A syllogism consists of a major premise and a minor premise followed by a conclusion. For example, "All men are mortal" (major premise); "The king is a man" (minor premise); "Therefore, the king is mortal" (conclusion). In deductive reasoning, if the premises are true, the conclusion is necessarily true. Deductive reasoning lets you organize premises into patterns that provide conclusive evidence for a conclusion's validity. Mystery fans will recall that Sherlock Holmes frequently would say, "I deduce . . ." as he combined previously unconnected facts in such a way as to imply a previously unsuspected conclusion.

However, deductive reasoning does have limitations. To arrive at true conclusions, you must begin with true premises. The conclusion of a syllogism can never exceed the content of the premises. Because deductive conclusions are necessarily elaborations on previously existing knowledge, you cannot conduct scientific inquiry through deductive reasoning alone, because it is difficult to establish the universal truth of many statements dealing with scientific phenomena. Deductive reasoning can organize what people already know and can point out new relationships as you proceed from the general to the specific, but it is not sufficient as a source of new knowledge.

Despite its limitations, deductive reasoning is useful in research because it provides a way to link theory and observation. It lets researchers deduce from existing theory what phenomena they should observe. Deductions from theory can help build hypotheses, which are a vital part of scientific inquiry.

Inductive Reasoning

As noted, the conclusions of deductive reasoning are true only if the premises on which they are based are true. But how are you to know if the premises are true? In the Middle Ages people often substituted dogma for true premises, so they reached invalid conclusions. It was Francis Bacon (1561–1626), who first called for a new approach to knowing. He held that thinkers should not enslave themselves by accepting premises handed down by authority as absolute truth. He believed that an investigator should establish general conclusions on the basis of facts gathered through direct observation. Bacon advised the seeker of truth to observe nature directly and to rid his or her mind of prejudice and preconceived ideas, which Bacon called "idols." For him, obtaining knowledge required that the thinker observe nature itself, gather particular facts, and formulate generalizations from these findings. You can see the importance of observation in the following anecdote, attributed to Bacon:

> In the year of our Lord 1432, there arose a grievous quarrel among the brethren over the number of teeth in the mouth of a horse. For 13 days the disputation raged without ceasing. All the ancient books and chronicles were fetched out, and wonderful and ponderous erudition, such as was never before heard of in this region, was made manifest. At the beginning of the 14th day, a youthful friar of goodly bearing asked his learned superiors for permission to add a word, and straightway, to the wonderment of the disputants, whose deep wisdom he sore vexed, he beseeched them to unbend in a manner coarse and unheard-of,

and to look in the open mouth of a horse and find an answer to their questionings. At this, their dignity being grievously hurt, they waxed exceedingly wroth; and, joining in a mighty uproar, they flew upon him and smote him hip and thigh, and cast him out forthwith. For, said they, surely Satan hath tempted this bold neophyte to declare unholy and unheard-of ways of finding truth contrary to all the teachings of the fathers. After many days more of grievous strife the dove of peace sat on the assembly, and they as one man, declaring the problem to be an everlasting mystery because of a grievous dearth of historical and theological evidence thereof, so ordered the same writ down. (Mees, 1934, pp. 113–119)

The youth in this story was calling for a new way of seeking truth: namely, seeking the facts rather than depending on authority or on sheer speculation. This became the fundamental principle of all science.

In Bacon's system, the investigator made observations on particular events in a class (or category) and then, on the basis of the observed events, made inferences about the whole class. This approach, known as **inductive reasoning,** is the reverse of the deductive method. You can see the difference between deductive and inductive reasoning in the following examples:

Deductive: Every mammal has lungs.
              All rabbits are mammals.
              Therefore, every rabbit has lungs.

Inductive: Every rabbit that has ever been observed has lungs.
              Therefore, every rabbit has lungs.

Note that in deductive reasoning you must know the premises before you can reach a conclusion, but in inductive reasoning you reach a conclusion by observing examples and generalizing from the examples to the whole class or category. To be absolutely certain of an inductive conclusion, the investigator must observe all examples. This is known as **perfect induction** under the Baconian system; it requires that the investigator examine every example of a phenomenon. In the preceding example, to be absolutely sure that every rabbit has lungs, the investigator would have to have observations on all rabbits currently alive, as well as all past and future rabbits. Clearly this is not feasible; you generally must rely on imperfect induction based on incomplete observation.

Inductive conclusions can be absolute only when the group about which you assert them is small. For example, you may observe that all the red-haired pupils in a particular class make above-average grades in spelling and thus you might legitimately assert that the red-haired children currently enrolled in the class have above-average spelling grades. But you could not draw legitimate conclusions concerning the spelling grades of red-haired children in other classes or in future classes.

Because people can make perfect inductions only on small groups, they commonly use **imperfect induction,** a system in which you observe a sample of a group and infer from the sample what is characteristic of the entire group. An example of a conclusion based on imperfect induction is the present thinking concerning the physical characteristics of very intelligent children. For many years people generally believed that exceptionally bright children tended to be poor physical specimens. Even today cartoonists usually portray the bright child as a scrawny creature with thick spectacles. Terman, a pioneer in the field of mental testing, was interested in the characteristics of exceptionally bright youngsters (Terman, 1926). He intensively studied more than 1000 California children who scored above 140 on the Stanford-Binet intelligence test. He found the average height, weight, and general physical health of these children to be slightly above average for children of their age. From this and subsequent studies of the phenomenon, researchers have concluded that bright children, far from being scrawny, are a little more likely to be above average in physical development than children with average IQ scores. Note that this conclusion has not been positively proved. It is simply highly probable. To be positively sure about this conclusion, you would need physical measures for *all* children with IQ scores of 140 or more on the Stanford-Binet. Even then you could only be positive about the characteristics of such children today and could not be 100 percent sure that the same would be true of such children in the future. Although imperfect induction does not lead to infallible conclusions, it can provide reliable information about what is likely to be true and on which you can make reasonable decisions.

The Scientific Approach

Exclusive use of induction often resulted in the accumulation of isolated knowledge and information that made little contribution to the advancement of knowledge. Furthermore, people found that many problems could not be solved by induction alone. In the 19th century scholars began to integrate the most important aspects of the inductive and deductive methods into a new technique, namely the inductive-deductive method, or the scientific approach. This approach differs from inductive reasoning in that it uses hypotheses. A **hypothesis** is a statement describing relationships among variables that is tentatively assumed to be true. It identifies observations to be made to investigate a question. For example, a researcher interested in increasing student on-task behavior might hypothesize that positive teacher feedback increases on-task behavior. All hypotheses indicate specific phenomena to be observed (the variables), in this case positive teacher feedback and on-task behavior.

Charles Darwin, in developing his theory of evolution, is generally recognized as the first to apply this method in the pursuit of knowledge. Darwin reported that he spent a long time making biological observations, hoping to establish some generalizations concerning evolution. In the following passage, he describes how he arrived at a new approach:

> My first note-book (on evolution) was opened in July 1837. I worked on true Baconian principles, and without any theory collected facts on a wholesale scale, more especially with respect to domesticated productions, by printed enquiries, by conversation with skillful breeders and gardeners, and by extensive reading. When I see the list of books of all kinds which I read and abstracted, including whole series of Journals and Transactions, I am surprised at my industry. I soon perceived that selection was the keystone of man's success in making useful races of animals and plants. But how selection would be applied to organisms living in a state of nature remained for some time a mystery to me. In October 1838, that is, fifteen months after I had begun my systematic enquiry, I happened to read for amusement "Malthus on Population," and being well prepared to appreciate the

struggle for existence which everywhere goes on from long-continued observation of the habits of animals and plants, it at once struck me that under these circumstances favourable variations would tend to be preserved, and unfavourable ones to be destroyed. The result of this would be the formation of new species. Here then I had at last got a theory by which to work. (Darwin, 1899, p. 68)

Darwin's procedure, involving only observation, was unproductive until reading and further thought led him to formulate a tentative hypothesis to explain the facts that he had gathered through observation. He then proceeded to test this hypothesis by making deductions from it and gathering additional data to determine whether these data would support the hypothesis. From this method of inquiry, Darwin was able to develop his theory of evolution. This use of both inductive and deductive reasoning is characteristic of modern scientific inquiry, which is regarded as the most reliable method for obtaining knowledge.

The **scientific approach** is generally described as a process in which investigators move inductively from their observations to hypotheses and then deductively from the hypotheses to the logical implications of the hypotheses. They deduce the consequences that would follow if a hypothesized relationship were valid. If the deduced implications are compatible with the organized body of accepted knowledge, researchers then further test them by gathering empirical data. On the basis of the evidence, they accept or reject the hypotheses.

The use of hypotheses is a principal difference between the scientific approach and inductive reasoning. In inductive reasoning, you make observations first and then organize the information gained. In the scientific approach you reason what you would find if a hypothesis were true and then you make systematic observations to confirm (or fail to confirm) the hypothesis.

An Example of the Scientific Approach

Award-winning author Robert Pirsig provides a vivid and succinct description of the scientific approach by comparing it to the process of maintaining a motorcycle in good working order:

Two kinds of logic are used, inductive and deductive. Inductive inferences start with observations of the machine and arrive at general conclusions. For example, if the cycle goes over a bump and the engine misfires, and then goes over another bump and the engine misfires, and then goes over another bump and the engine misfires, and then goes over a long smooth stretch of road and there is no misfiring, and then goes over a fourth bump and the engine misfires again, one can logically conclude that the misfiring is caused by the bumps. That is induction: reasoning from particular experiences to general truths.

Deductive inferences do the reverse. They start with general knowledge and predict a specific observation. For example, if, from reading the hierarchy of facts about the machine, the mechanic knows the horn of the cycle is powered exclusively by electricity from the battery, then he can logically infer that if the battery is dead the horn will not work. That is deduction.

Solution of problems too complicated for common sense to solve is achieved by long strings of mixed inductive and deductive inferences that weave back and forth between the observed machine and the mental hierarchy of the machine found in the manuals. The correct program for this interweaving is formalized as scientific method.

Actually I've never seen a cycle-maintenance problem complex enough really to require full-scale formal scientific method. Repair problems are not that hard. When I think of formal scientific method an image sometimes comes to mind of an enormous juggernaut, a huge bulldozer—slow, tedious, lumbering, laborious, but invincible. It takes twice as long, five times as long, maybe a dozen times as long as informal mechanic's techniques, but you know in the end you're going to *get* it. There's no fault isolation problem in motorcycle maintenance that can stand up to it. When you've hit a really tough one, tried everything, racked your brain and nothing works, and you know that this time Nature has really decided to be difficult, you say, "Okay, Nature, that's the end of the *nice* guy," and you crank up the formal scientific method.

For this you keep a lab notebook. Everything gets written down, formally, so that you know at all times where you are, where you've been, where you're going and where you want to get. In scientific work and electronics technology this is necessary because otherwise the problems get so complex you get lost in them and confused and forget what you know and what you don't know and have to give up. In cycle maintenance things are not that involved, but when confusion starts it's a good idea to hold it down by making everything formal and exact. Sometimes just the act of writing down the problems straightens out your head as to what they really are.

The logical statements entered into the notebook are broken down into six categories: (1) statement of the problem, (2) hypotheses as to the cause of the problem, (3) experiments designed to test each hypothesis, (4) predicted results of the experiments, (5) observed results of the experiments, and (6) conclusions from the results of the experiments. This is not different from the formal arrangement of many college and high-school lab notebooks but the purpose here is no longer just busywork. The purpose now is precise guidance of thoughts that will fail if they are not accurate.

The real purpose of scientific method is to make sure Nature hasn't misled you into thinking you know something you don't actually know. There's not a mechanic or scientist or technician alive who hasn't suffered from that one so much that he's not instinctively on guard. That's the main reason why so much scientific and mechanical information sounds so dull and so cautious. If you get careless or go romanticizing scientific information, giving it a flourish here and there, Nature will soon make a complete fool out of you. It does it often enough anyway even when you don't give it opportunities. One must be extremely careful and rigidly logical when dealing with Nature: one logical slip and an entire scientific edifice comes tumbling down. One false deduction about the machine and you can get hung up indefinitely.

In Part One of formal scientific method, which is the statement of the problem, the main skill is in stating absolutely no more than you are positive you know. It is much better to enter a statement "Solve Problem: Why doesn't cycle work?" which sounds dumb but is correct, than it is to enter a statement "Solve Problem: What is wrong with the electrical system?" when you don't absolutely *know* the trouble is *in* the electrical system. What you should state is "Solve Problem: What is wrong with cycle?" and *then* state as the first entry of Part Two: "Hypothesis Number One: The trouble is in the electrical system." You think of as many hypotheses as you can, then you design experiments to test them to see which are true and which are false.

This careful approach to the beginning questions keeps you from taking a major wrong turn which might cause you weeks of extra work or can even hang you up completely. Scientific questions often have a surface appearance of dumbness for this reason. They are asked in order to prevent dumb mistakes later on.

Part Three, that part of formal scientific method called experimentation, is sometimes thought of by romantics as all of science itself because that's the only part with much visual surface. They see lots of test tubes and bizarre equipment and people running around making discoveries. They do not see the experiment as part of a larger intellectual process and so they often confuse experiments with demonstrations, which look the same. A man conducting a gee-whiz science show with fifty thousand dollars' worth of Frankenstein equipment is not doing anything scientific if he knows beforehand what the results of his efforts are going to be. A motorcycle mechanic, on the other hand, who honks the horn to see if the battery works is informally conducting a true scientific experiment. He is testing a hypothesis by putting the question to Nature. The TV scientist who mutters sadly, "The experiment is a failure; we have failed to achieve what we had hoped for," is suffering mainly from a bad scriptwriter. An experiment is never a failure solely because it fails to achieve predicted results. An experiment is a failure only when it also fails adequately to test the hypothesis in question, when the data it produces don't prove anything one way or another.

Skill at this point consists of using experiments that test only the hypothesis in question, nothing less, nothing more. If the horn honks, and the mechanic concludes that the whole electrical system is working, he is in deep trouble. He has reached an illogical conclusion. The honking horn only tells him that the battery and horn are working. To design an experiment properly he has to think very rigidly in terms of what directly causes what. This you know from the hierarchy. The horn doesn't make the cycle go. Neither does the battery, except in a very indirect way. The point at which the electrical system *directly* causes the engine to fire is at the spark plugs, and if you don't test here, at the output of the electrical system, you will never really know whether the failure is electrical or not.

To test properly, the mechanic removes the plug and lays it against the engine so that the base around the plug is electrically grounded, kicks the starter lever and watches the spark-plug gap for a blue spark. If there isn't any he can conclude one of two things: (a) there is an electrical failure or (b) his experiment is sloppy. If he is experienced he will try it a few more times, checking connections, trying every way he can think of to get that plug to fire. Then, if he can't get it to fire, he finally concludes that *a* is correct, there's an electrical failure, and the experiment is over. He has proved that his hypothesis is correct.

In the final category, conclusions, skill comes in stating no more than the experiment has proved. It hasn't proved that when he fixes the electrical system the motorcycle will start. There may be other things wrong. But he does know that the motorcycle isn't going to run until the electrical system is working and he sets up the next formal question: "Solve Problem: What is wrong with the electrical system?" He then sets up hypotheses for these and tests them. By asking the right questions and choosing the right tests and drawing the right conclusions the mechanic works his way down the echelons of the motorcycle hierarchy until he has found the exact specific cause or causes of the engine failure, and then he changes them so that they no longer cause the failure.

An untrained observer will see only physical labor and often get the idea that physical labor is mainly what the mechanic does. Actually the physical labor is the smallest and easiest part of what the mechanic does. By far the greatest part of his work is careful observation and precise thinking. That is why mechanics sometimes seem so taciturn and withdrawn when performing tests. They don't like it when you talk to them because they are concentrating on mental images, hierarchies, and not really looking at you or the physical motorcycle at all. They are using the experiment as part of a program to expand their hierarchy of knowledge of the faulty motorcycle and compare it to the correct hierarchy in their mind. They are looking at underlying form. (Pirsig, 1974, pp. 107–111)

In Pirsig's narrative, we see five steps that are typical in scientific inquiry:

1. *Identification of the problem.* The first step is the realization that a problem exists. The problem may involve a question about something, a discrepancy in findings, or a gap in knowledge. In the foregoing example, the fact that the motorcycle did not start constituted the problem.

2. *Statement of the problem.* The next step is the clarification of the problem. The investigator states more precisely the nature and scope of the problem that has been identified.

3. *Formulation of hypotheses.* The investigator formulates hypotheses about possible solutions of the problem. In the current example, the first hypothesis was that the motorcycle didn't start because of trouble in the electrical system.

4. *Prediction of consequences.* The investigator next predicts the consequences of each hypothesis; that is, what should result if the data support the hypothesis.

5. *Testing of hypotheses.* The researcher gathers objective data to evaluate the adequacy of each hypothesis formulated. If the data support the hypothesis, it is accepted as a reasonable explanation. If the data do not support the hypothesis, it is rejected.

THE NATURE OF SCIENCE

We should mention at this point that all sciences, although they may differ from one another in subject matter or in specialized techniques, have in common this general method for arriving at reliable knowledge. This method of inquiry determines whether a discipline is a science. Perhaps science is best described as a *method of inquiry* that permits investigators to examine the phenomena of interest to them. In addition to the method scientists follow as they seek reliable knowledge, there are certain other aspects of the scientific approach, which we will examine briefly. These are (1) assumptions made by scientists, (2) attitudes of scientists, and (3) formulation of scientific theory.

Assumptions That Scientists Make

A fundamental assumption scientists make is that the events they investigate are lawful or ordered—no event is capricious. Science is based on the belief that all natural phenomena have antecedent factors. This assumption is sometimes referred to as **universal determinism.** Primitive people proposed supernatural causes for most of the events they observed. Modern science did not develop until people began to look beyond supernatural explanations and to depend on the observation of nature itself to provide answers.

This assumption underlies any statement that declares that under specified conditions certain events will occur. For example, the chemist can state that when a mixture of potassium chlorate and manganese dioxide is heated, the process will produce oxygen. Behavioral scientists likewise assume that the behavior of organisms is lawful and predictable. Related to this first assumption is the belief that the events in nature are, at least to a degree, orderly and regular and that people can discover this order and regularity of nature through the scientific method.

A second assumption is that reliable knowledge can ultimately derive only from direct and objective observation. Reliance on empirical observation differentiates science from nonscience. The scientist does not depend on authority as a source of knowledge but insists on studying empirical evidence. In the history of science we find many examples of scientists who rejected the prevailing notions of their day and proceeded with their observations and experimentation. Galileo's early experiments with falling bodies resulted in new knowledge that contradicted notions held by the authorities of his day. A corollary of this assumption is the belief that only phenomena that are subject to observation lie within the realm of scientific investigation.

Attitudes of Scientists

Scientists recognize certain characteristic attitudes that they acquire as they pursue their work:

1. *Scientists are essentially doubters, who maintain a highly skeptical attitude toward the data of science.* Scientists investigate questions concerning the relationships among natural phenomena. Their findings are regarded as tentative, however, and are not accepted by themselves or other scientists unless further investigations can verify them. Verification occurs when repeated observations yield the same or similar results. Verification thus requires scientists to make their research measurements and procedures known so that others may replicate the study and verify, or fail to verify, the findings.

2. *Scientists are objective and impartial.* In conducting observations and interpreting data, scientists are not trying to prove a point. They take particular care to collect data in such a way that any personal biases they may have will not influence their observations. They seek knowledge and accept the findings even when those results are contrary to their own opinions. If the accumulated evidence upsets a favorite theory, then they either discard that theory or modify it to agree with the findings.

3. *Scientists deal with facts, not values.* They do not indicate any potential moral implications of their findings; they do not make decisions for other people about what is good or what is bad. Scientists provide data concerning the relationships among events, but you must go beyond scientific data if you want a decision

about whether a certain consequence is desirable. Thus, although the findings of science may be of key importance in solving a problem about a value decision, the data themselves do not furnish that value judgment.

4. *Scientists are not satisfied with isolated facts but seek to integrate and systematize their findings.* They want to put the things known into an orderly system. Thus scientists aim for theories that seek to bring together empirical findings into a meaningful pattern. However, they regard these theories as tentative or provisional, subject to revision as new evidence appears.

Scientific Theory

The last aspect of the scientific approach we consider here is the construction of theory. The ultimate goal of science is theory formation. Scientists, through empirical investigation, gather many facts; but facts by themselves are of limited usefulness. As facts accumulate, scientists must integrate, organize, and classify to make the isolated findings meaningful. They must identify and explain significant relationships in the data. That's where theory comes into play. Scientists formulate theories to summarize and order the existing knowledge in a particular area. A **theory** may be defined as "a set of interrelated constructs (concepts), definitions, and propositions that presents a systematic view of phenomena by specifying relations among variables, with the purpose of explaining and predicting the phenomena" (Kerlinger, 1986, p. 9).

Theories knit together the results of observations, enabling scientists to make general statements about variables and the relationships among variables. Theories range from a few simple generalizations to complex formulations of laws. For example, you can observe that if you hold pressure constant, hydrogen gas expands when its temperature increases from 20°C to 40°C. You can observe that if you hold pressure constant, oxygen gas contracts when its temperature decreases from 60°C to 50°C. A familiar theory, Charles's law, summarizes the observed effects of temperature changes on the volumes of all gases: When pressure is held constant, as the temperature of a gas increases, its volume increases; and as the temperature of a gas decreases, its volume decreases. The theory not only summarizes previous information but predicts other phenomena by telling you what to expect of any gas under any temperature change.

Purposes of Theories

Theories serve a useful function in the development of science. In the first place, a theory organizes the findings from many separate observations and investigations into a framework that provides explanations of phenomena. A theory explains by showing what variables are related and how they are related. A theory of learning, for example, might explain the relationships among the speed and efficiency of learning and such variables as motivation, reinforcement, practice, and so on. Researchers have developed useful theories to explain motivation, intellectual and cognitive development, moral development, social development, and so on. From the explanatory framework of a theory, scientists can proceed to prediction and, finally, to control. As soon as a statement (theory) was made about the relationship between the *Anopheles* mosquito and malaria in humans, scientists could (1) *explain* why malaria was endemic in some areas and not in others, (2) *predict* how changes in the environment would entail changes in the incidence of malaria, and (3) *control* malaria by changing the environment.

Researchers state and test hypotheses deduced from theories, which results in the development of new knowledge. Deductions from a theory permit predictions of phenomena, some as yet unobserved. For example, from theory astronomers predicted the existence of the outermost planets long before they were actually observed. Testing the deductions from a theory serves to confirm and elaborate the theory. If, however, research findings do not support the theory, scientists revise it and then collect more data to test the revised theory.

Criteria for Theories

To serve its purpose in science, a theory should satisfy certain criteria. The following are some of the characteristics of a sound theory:

1. *A theory should be able to explain the observed facts relating to a particular problem.* It should be able to propose the "how" and "why" concerning the phenomena under consideration. This explanation of the events should take the simplest form possible. Scientists favor a theory that has fewer complexities and assumptions over a more complicated one. This rule is called the **principle of parsimony.**

2. *A theory should be consistent with observed facts and with the already established body of knowledge.* Scientists build on what has already been found. They look for the theory that provides the most probable or the most efficient way of accounting for the accumulated facts.

3. *A theory should provide means for its verification.* Scientists achieve this for most theories by making deductions in the form of hypotheses stating the consequences that you can expect to observe if the theory is valid. Scientists can then investigate or test these hypotheses empirically to determine whether the data support the theory. We must emphasize that it is inappropriate to speak of the "truth" or "falsity" of a theory. The acceptance or rejection of a theory depends primarily on its *utility,* or usefulness. A theory is useful or not useful depending on how efficiently it leads to predictions concerning observable consequences, which are then confirmed when the empirical data are collected. Even then, any theory is tentative and subject to revision as new evidence accumulates.

   You may recall the old theory of formal discipline, which stated that the mind is like a muscle that can be strengthened through exercise. Certain subjects such as logic, Latin, and Greek were once included in the curriculum because educators believed them to be best for strengthening the mind. This theory of formal discipline prevailed until the early 20th century, when E. L. Thorndike, William James, and Charles Judd challenged it. When their studies independently refuted this theory, educators abandoned it.

4. *A theory should stimulate new discoveries and indicate further areas in need of investigation.*

The goal of theory formation has been achieved to a far greater extent in the physical sciences than in the social sciences, which is not surprising because they are older sciences. In the early days of a science, the emphasis typically is on empiricism; scientists are concerned with collecting facts in particular areas. Only with maturity does a science begin to integrate the isolated knowledge into a theoretical framework.

Although there are marked differences in the number and power of the theories that have been established in the physical and social sciences, theory has the same role to play in the progress of any science. Regardless of the subject matter, theory works in essentially the same way. It serves to summarize existing knowledge, to explain observed events and relationships, and to predict the occurrence of unobserved events and relationships. Theories represent the best efforts to understand the basic structure of the world in which we all live.

Limitations of the Scientific Approach in the Social Sciences

Despite their use of the scientific approach and accumulation of a large quantity of reliable knowledge, education and the other social sciences have not attained the scientific status typical of the natural sciences. The social sciences have not established generalizations equivalent to the theories of the natural sciences in scope of explanatory power or in capacity to yield precise predictions. Frequently researchers in the social sciences disagree on what the established facts are or what explanations are satisfactory for the assumed facts. Perhaps the social sciences will never realize the objectives of science as completely as the natural sciences. Certainly we must stress that using the scientific approach is not in itself a sufficient condition for scientific achievement. Several limitations hinder the application of the scientific approach in education and the other social sciences.

Complexity of Subject Matter

A major obstacle is the inherent complexity of subject matter in the social sciences. Natural scientists deal with physical and biological phenomena. A limited number of variables that can be measured precisely are involved in explaining many of these phenomena, and it is possible to establish universal laws. For example, Boyle's law, summarizing the influence of pressure on gas volume, a law that deals with relatively uncomplicated variables, formulates relations among phenomena that are apparently unvarying throughout the universe.

In contrast, social scientists deal with the human subject. They are concerned with the subject's behavior and development, both as an individual and as a member of a group.

You must consider many variables, acting independently and in interaction, in any attempt to understand complex human behavior. Each individual is unique in the way he or she develops, in mental ability, in social and emotional behavior, and in total personality. The behavior of humans in groups and the influence of the behavior of group members on an individual must also be dealt with by social scientists. A group of first-graders in one situation will not behave like first-graders in another situation. There are learners, teachers, and environments, each with variations that contribute to the behavioral phenomena observed in a setting. Thus researchers must be extremely cautious about making generalizations, because the data from one group or in one situation may have limited validity for other groups and other settings.

Difficulties in Observation

Observation, the sine qua non of science, is more difficult in the social sciences than in the natural sciences. Observation in the social sciences is often less objective, because it more frequently involves interpretation on the part of the observers. For example, the subject matter for investigation is often a person's responses to the behavior of others. Motives, values, and attitudes are not open to inspection. Observers must make subjective interpretations when they decide that behaviors observed indicate the presence of any particular motive, value, or attitude. The problem is that social scientists' *own* values and attitudes may influence both what they choose to observe and their assessment of the findings on which they base their conclusions. Natural scientists study phenomena that require less subjective interpretation.

Difficulties in Replication

The chemist can objectively observe the reaction between two chemicals in a test tube. The findings can be reported and the observations can be easily replicated by others. Replication is much more difficult to achieve in the social sciences. An American educator cannot reproduce the conditions of a Russian educator's experimental teaching method with the same precision as that with which an American chemist can replicate a Russian chemist's experiment. Even within a single school building one cannot reproduce a given situation in its entirety and with precision. Social phenomena are singular events and cannot be totally repeated for purposes of observations.

Interaction of Observer and Subjects

An additional problem is that mere observation of social phenomena may produce changes that might not have occurred otherwise. Researchers may think that X is causing Y, when in fact their own observation of X may cause Y. For example, in the well-known Hawthorne experiments changes in worker productivity stemmed not from the varying working conditions but from the mere fact that the workers knew they had been singled out for investigation. Investigators are human beings, and their presence as observers in a situation may change the behavior of their human subjects. The use of hidden cameras and tape recorders may help minimize this interaction in some cases, but much social science research includes the responses of human subjects to human observers.

Difficulties in Control

The range of possibilities for controlled experiments on human subjects is much more limited than in the natural sciences. The complexities involved in research on human subjects present control problems that have no parallels in the natural sciences. In the latter, rigid control of experimental conditions is possible in the laboratory. Such control is not possible with human subjects; the social scientists must deal with many variables simultaneously and must work under conditions that are much less precise. They try to identify and control as many of these variables as possible, but the task is sometimes very difficult.

Problems of Measurement

Systematic research must provide for measurement of the variables involved. The tools for measurement in the social sciences are much less perfect and precise than the tools of the natural sciences. Social science has nothing that can compare with the precision of the ruler, the thermometer, or the numerous laboratory instruments. We have already pointed out that an understanding of human behavior is complicated by the large number of determining variables acting independently and in interaction. The multivariate statistical devices available for analyzing data in the social sciences take care of relatively few of the factors that obviously are interacting. Furthermore, these devices permit you to attribute the variance only to factors operating at the time of measurement. Factors that have influenced development in the past are not measurable in the present, even though they may have significantly influenced the course of development. Because the complexity and difficulty of observation, replication, and measurement complicate social science research, researchers must exercise great caution in generalizing from their studies. It is often necessary to conduct several studies in an area before attempting to formulate generalizations. If they consistently confirm initial findings, then researchers can be more confident in making broad generalizations.

Despite the handicaps, education and the social sciences have made great progress, and their scientific status can be expected to increase as scientific investigation and methodology become more systematic and rigorous.

◼ THE NATURE OF RESEARCH

Scientific research is the application of the scientific approach to studying a problem. It is a way to acquire dependable and useful information. Its purpose is to discover answers to meaningful questions by applying scientific procedures. To be classified as scientific research, an investigation must involve the approach we described in the previous section. Although it may take place in different settings and may use different methods, scientific research is universally a systematic and objective search for reliable knowledge.

Educational Research

Educational research is the application of the scientific approach to the study of educational problems. Educational research is the way in which people acquire dependable and useful information about the educative process. Educators usually conduct research to find a solution to some problem or to gain insight into an issue they don't understand. The ultimate goal is to discover general principles or interpretations of behavior that people can use to explain, predict, and control events in educational situations—in other words, to formulate scientific theory.

The acceptance of the scientific approach in education and the other social sciences has lagged far behind its acceptance in the physical sciences. In 1897 J. M. Rice, a pioneer in educational research, found himself in a situation similar to that described by the quotation attributed to Bacon earlier in this chapter. Rice asked the educators at the annual meeting of the National Education Association's Department of Superintendence if it would be possible to determine whether students who are given 40 minutes of spelling each day learn more than students given 10 minutes each day. He reported,

> . . . to my great surprise, the question threw consternation into the camp. The first to respond was a very popular professor of psychology engaged in training teachers in the West. He said, in effect, that the question was one which could never be answered; and he gave me a rather severe drubbing for taking up the time of such an important body of educators in asking them silly questions. (Rice, 1912, pp. 17–18)

Rice did, in fact, collect empirical evidence on his question and found that the differences in achievement between those spending 10 minutes a day and those spending 40 minutes a day were negligible. He also pointed out that many words children were required to learn how to spell had little practical value. His work led other investigators, such as Edward L. Thorndike, to use documentary analysis to determine the frequency of use of words in the English language. Their work in turn led to improvements in language arts texts and curricula.

Although educational research is a young science, it has continued to progress since its beginnings in the late 19th century. As a science, educational research uses investigative methods consistent with the basic procedures and operating conceptions of scientific inquiry. Educational researchers conduct different types of studies and use a range of methods to obtain reliable information about educational problems. We consider these in the next chapter.

SUMMARY

Human beings have sought to acquire knowledge through experience, authority, deductive reasoning, inductive reasoning, and the scientific approach. The scientific approach is widely regarded as the single most reliable source of new knowledge.

The scientific approach rests on two basic assumptions: (1) People can derive truth from observation, and (2) phenomena conform to lawful relationships.

Scientific inquirers seek not absolute truth but rather theories that explain and predict phenomena in a reliable manner. They seek theories that are parsimonious, testable, and consistent, as well as theories that are themselves stimuli for further research. The scientific approach incorporates self-correction, inasmuch as every theory is tentative and may be set aside if a new theory better fits the criteria.

Investigators have used the scientific approach to explain, predict, and control physical phenomena for centuries but have only used it in education relatively recently. The complexity of educational variables and difficulties in making reliable observations have impeded scientific inquiry in education. However, since the beginning of the movement early in the 20th century, scientific inquiry in education has enjoyed increasing acceptance and increasing success both in theoretical and practical research.

REFERENCES

Alexander, P. A., & Dochy, F. (1995). Conceptions of knowledge and beliefs: A comparison across varying cultural and educational communities. *American Educational Research Journal, 32,* 413–442.

Darwin, F. (Ed.). (1899). *The life and letters of Charles Darwin* (Vol. 1). New York: Appleton.

Kerlinger, F. N. (1986). *Foundations of behavioral research,* 3rd ed. New York: Holt, Rinehart, and Winston.

Mees, C. E. K. (1934). Scientific thought and social reconstruction. *General Electric Review, 37,* 113–19.

Pirsig, R. M. (1974). *Zen and the art of motorcycle maintenance: An inquiry into values.* New York: Morrow.

Rice, J. M. (1912). *Scientific management in education.* New York: Hinds, Noble and Eldredge.

Terman, L. M. (1926). The mental and physical traits of a thousand gifted children. In *Genetic studies of genius* (Vol. 1). Stanford, CA: Stanford University Press.

KEY CONCEPTS

deductive reasoning	inductive reasoning	scientific approach
hypothesis	perfect induction	theory
imperfect induction	principle of parsimony	universal determinism

EXERCISES

1. Identify the source of knowledge—*deductive reasoning, inductive reasoning,* or the *scientific approach*—most prominently used in the following examples:

a. After extensive observation of reactions, Lavoisier concluded that combustion is a process in which a burning substance combines with oxygen. His work was the death blow to the old phlogiston theory of burning.

b. Dalton, after much reflection, concluded that matter must consist of small particles called *atoms*. His early assumptions became the basis for the atomic theory.

c. Later scientists took Dalton's assumptions, made deductions from them, and proceeded to gather data that confirmed these assumptions. They found support for the atomic theory.

d. Knowing that radioactive substances constantly give off particles of energy without apparently reducing their mass, Einstein developed the formula $E = mc^2$ for converting matter into energy.

e. Accepting Einstein's theory, Fermi carried on experimentation that resulted in splitting the atom.

f. After studying reinforcement theory, a teacher hypothesizes that using a tutorial computer program will lead to superior achievement in arithmetic. She devises a study in which the tutorial is used with two sixth-grade classes, while conventional materials are used with two other sixth-grade classes.

2. What is the role of theory in scientific inquiry?

3. What is the difference between an inductive theory and a deductive theory?

4. Give examples of the use of authority and experience as sources of knowledge.

5. Evaluate the following deductive arguments:
   a. All graduating seniors with high GPAs study Latin.
   John is a senior with a high GPA.
   Therefore, John studies Latin.
   b. All vertebrates have backbones.
   This animal has a backbone.
   Therefore, this animal is a vertebrate.

6. Evaluate the following inductive arguments:
   a. This animal has a backbone.
   Animals with backbones are vertebrates.
   I am reasonably certain that this animal is a vertebrate.
   b. This is a student who studies very hard.
   Students who make good grades tend to study hard.
   This student probably makes good grades.

7. Which characteristic attitudes of scientists are violated in the following statements?
   a. This study was undertaken to prove that the use of marijuana is detrimental to academic achievement.
   b. It proved conclusively that this is the case.
   c. The results show that marijuana is evil.

8. What are the characteristics of a useful theory?

ANSWERS

1. a. Inductive reasoning
   b. Deductive reasoning
   c. Scientific approach
   d. Deductive reasoning
   e. Scientific approach
   f. Scientific approach

2. Theory integrates findings, summarizes information, provides leads for new research, and enables people to explain and predict phenomena.

3. An inductive theory serves to explain previous observations, whereas a deductive theory is developed before extensive observations have been made.

4. Answers will vary.

5. a. The argument is flawed; the major premise is not valid.
    b. The argument is correct.
6. a. The argument is correct.
    b. The argument is flawed; cannot say that because the student studies hard, he or she makes good grades.
7. a. The scientist is objective and impartial.
    b. The scientist is skeptical and regards findings as tentative.
    c. The scientist deals with facts, not values.
8. A useful theory explains the phenomena in the simplest form possible, is consistent with observation and the established body of knowledge, provides means for its verification, and stimulates new investigation.

 INFOTRAC COLLEGE EDITION

Use the keywords *deductive reasoning* or *inductive reasoning* to find an article that discusses either of these approaches in scientific thought. Compare the discussion in this article with the textbook discussion of deductive/inductive reasoning.

Chapter 2

The Scientific Approach in Education

INSTRUCTIONAL OBJECTIVES

After studying this chapter, the student will be able to

1 Describe the major research methodologies used in educational investigations.

2 Distinguish between the philosophical approaches underlying quantitative and qualitative research.

3 List the specific types of research that fall into the broad categories of quantitative and qualitative research.

4 Give an example of a research problem that would be investigated by quantitative methodology and one for which qualitative methodology would be most appropriate.

5 Identify the research methodology used in given examples of both quantitative and qualitative research.

6 List the steps involved in the research process.

7 Distinguish between the characteristics of basic and applied research.

8 Explain the terms *concept, construct,* and *variable.*

9 Distinguish among various types of variables: categorical versus continuous, independent versus dependent, and active versus attribute.

10 Describe various types of definitions: constitutive versus operational and measured operational versus experimental operational.

Educational research is typically divided into two broad categories: quantitative and qualitative research. Each approach has its own terminology, methods, and techniques. **Quantitative research** uses objective measurement and statistical analysis of numeric data to understand and explain phenomena. It generally requires a well-controlled setting. **Qualitative research,** in contrast, focuses on understanding social phenomena from the perspective of the human participants in the study. The data are collected in natural settings, and the research aims at generating theory rather than testing theory.

Historically, quantitative methodology has dominated education research, but in recent years qualitative research has become more popular. Qualitative research emerged because researchers sometimes found quantitative methods inadequate for investigating many problems in education. For example, if you wished to study children's aggressive behavior in the school setting, it would not be enough to merely record the nature and number of incidents. You would also want to observe and interview aggressive children and try to uncover reasons for the aggression. How do such children perceive the teacher and other children at school? How do other children react to them? How does the teacher handle aggressive behavior? Qualitative research lets you gain insight into the context, to better understand the behavior.

Quantitative and qualitative research stem from different philosophical assumptions that shape the ways researchers approach problems and collect and analyze data. Quantitative research originated in **positivism,** a philosophic view formulated in the 19th century. Positivists believe that general principles or laws govern the social world as they do the physical world. Researchers can discover these general principles and then apply them to predict human behavior. Positivists thus emphasize measurement and gathering data with objective techniques as the best way to answer questions and to explain and predict behavior. Positivism is often considered the traditional scientific approach, first used in the natural sciences and later extended to education and the social sciences. It typically involves testing theories and hypotheses and generalizing findings to a larger population. The result is research that is systematic and open to replication by other investigators.

Qualitative research is rooted in **phenomenology,** which sees social reality as unique. The phenomenologic approach sees the individual and his or her world as so interconnected that essentially the one has no existence without the other. Thus the researcher can only understand human behavior by focusing on the meanings that events have for the people involved. You must look not only at what people do but also at how they think and feel, and must experience what happens to them. The result of a phenomenologic study is a narrative report so comprehensive that you can understand the social reality experienced by the participants. Furthermore, because researchers don't know in advance how naturally occurring events will unfold or what variables may be important, they do not begin a study with hypotheses.

There has been considerable debate over the merits of qualitative research as compared with quantitative. Some scientists see the qualitative approach as less rigorous and thus less acceptable as a way of doing research. Our position is that both methodologies are valuable in educational research. Which method researchers choose depends not on their preference for methods but on the nature of the question they are asking. Which approach you decide to use depends on the suitability of the particular method to a particular research problem. As Walker (1985, p. 16) wrote, "Certain questions cannot be answered by quantitative methods, while others cannot be answered by qualitative ones." We should note that some writers no longer view the quantitative–qualitative distinction as useful. There has been a trend toward rapprochement, which manifests in research where the same study uses both approaches. Hammersley (1996) writes that researchers can combine the two approaches in three ways: using one to verify the findings of the other; using one as the groundwork for the other; and using them in complementary fashion, to explore different aspects of the same research question. Astor, Meyer, and Behre (1999) used both quantitative and qualitative approaches in studying violence in a high school. They gathered data on the incidence of violent acts and also on the times and the locations within the school where violence occurred. They then interviewed students and teachers to learn why these specific locations and times were more dangerous. The interviews also gathered the perspectives of students, teachers, and administrators on the school's organizational response to the violence. Finally, these researchers came up with a socioenvironmental theoretical perspective on school violence.

Table 2.1 summarizes the major characteristics of the quantitative and qualitative research approaches.

We will now look at some specific types of research included in the broad categories of quantitative and qualitative research.

Table 2.1	Comparison of Quantitative and Qualitative Research	
	QUANTITATIVE	QUALITATIVE
Purpose	To study relationships, cause and effect	To understand social phenomena
Design	Developed prior to study	Evolves during study
Approach	Deductive; tests theory	Inductive; generates theory
Tools	Uses standardized instruments	Uses face-to-face interaction
Sample	Uses large samples	Uses small samples
Analysis	Statistical analysis of numeric data	Narrative description and interpretation

QUANTITATIVE RESEARCH

Quantitative research may be further classified as either experimental or nonexperimental.

Experimental Research

Experimental research involves a study of the effect of the systematic manipulation of one variable on another variable. The manipulated variable is called the experimental treatment or the **independent variable.** The observed and measured variable is called the **dependent variable.** For example, assume a university researcher wanted to investigate the effect of providing on-line feedback to students immediately following course examinations. Using two sections of economics taught by the same professor, the researcher would randomly select one section to receive on-line feedback about student performance on test questions; the other section would receive the traditional type of feedback provided in the classroom. The researcher would compare the two sections based on students' exam scores and the final grades they received in the course (dependent variables). If test scores and final grades were significantly higher in the section receiving on-line feedback, the researcher could tentatively conclude that there is evidence the on-line feedback (treatment) contributed to increased learning.

In experiments, you seek to control all other variables that might influence the dependent variable so that alternative explanations of the findings can be eliminated. In the foregoing example, the researcher would attempt to make sure that both groups had the same instructor; that both sections met at the same time of day but on different days; that lecture notes, readings, and exams were the same; and so forth. The researcher might also check on the ability level and background of the students in the two sections to make sure one section was not superior or better prepared than the other.

To have a "true" experiment, subjects must be randomly assigned to the experimental treatments. Sometimes, however, researchers cannot randomly assign subjects to experimental treatments for a study. Instead, as in the preceding example, the experimenter must use already assembled groups such as classes. In this case, the research is called *quasi-experimental*. We discuss experimental research more thoroughly in Chapter 10.

Nonexperimental Research

In nonexperimental quantitative research, the researcher identifies variables and may look for relationships among them, but does not manipulate the variables. Major forms of nonexperimental research are ex post facto, correlational, and survey research.

Ex post facto research (also called *causal comparative research*) is similar to an experiment, except the researcher does not manipulate the independent variable, which has already occurred in the natural course of events. The researcher then compares groups differing on the independent variable to determine its effect on the dependent variable. For example, to answer the question "Do first-grade children from single-parent homes have more difficulty in school than children from two-parent homes?" would require the ex post facto method. The experimenter could not manipulate the backgrounds of children by making some one-parent families and others two-parent families, but instead would identify the children from one-parent homes and compare their achievement with that of children from two-parent homes. Because researchers lack control over many factors, you must be especially careful in interpreting the results of ex post facto investigations. Despite its name, causal-comparative research does not establish a simple causal relationship among the variables of a study. We look at ex post facto or causal-comparative research in Chapter 11.

Correlational research seeks to examine the strength and direction of relationships among two or more variables. The extent of relationship is expressed as a numeric index. Examples of correlational research questions are "Is there a relationship between the quality of writing samples produced by incoming college freshmen and their performance during the freshman year?" and "What are the relationships among certain noncognitive variables such as academic self-concept, motivation, and leadership and college freshmen's academic achievement?" We discuss correlational research in Chapter 12.

Survey research uses instruments such as questionnaires and interviews to gather information from groups of subjects. Surveys permit the researcher to summarize the characteristics of different groups or to measure their attitudes and opinions toward some issue. Researchers in education and the social sciences use surveys widely. For example, an educational researcher might ask a group of parents about what kind of sex education program, if any, they believe schools should provide for middle school students. A survey of teachers could reveal their attitudes toward the inclusion of disabled children in the regular classroom. Opinion polls are surveys that researchers conduct to determine whom people are likely to vote for or what positions they take on certain issues. We discuss surveys in Chapter 13. Figure 2.1 summarizes the major types of quantitative research.

QUALITATIVE RESEARCH

Qualitative researchers seek to understand a phenomenon by focusing on the total picture rather than breaking it down into variables. The goal is a holistic picture and depth of understanding, rather than a numeric analysis of data. For example, social scientists have long observed that differences in educational background alone do not seem to account for the difficulties black students encounter in a predominantly white university. Researchers could explore the question "How do black students perceive their academic experience in a white university?" using qualitative methodology. The researcher would focus on a few black students and study them in great detail through observation and in-depth interviews. There are many different types of qualitative research; we will consider briefly just eight of the most widely used approaches: ethnography, case studies, document analysis, naturalistic observation, focused interviews, phenomenologic studies, grounded theory, and historical studies. We discuss qualitative research more extensively in Chapters 14 and 15.

Ethnography

Ethnography is an in-depth study of naturally occurring behavior within a culture or social group. Social scientists sometimes call ethnography *field research,* because it is conducted in a natural setting or "field." The researcher observes behavior as it occurs natu-

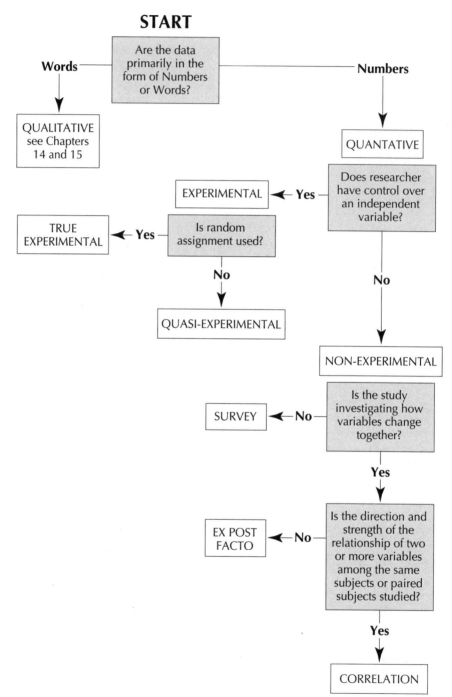

FIGURE 2.1
Major Types of Quantitative Educational Research

rally, without any simulation or imposed structure. Ethnography requires a variety of data-gathering procedures, such as prolonged observation of the setting, interviewing members of the culture, and studying documents and artifacts. Researchers interpret the data in the context of the situation in which they gathered the data.

Ethnography is rooted in anthropology. Educational researchers use ethnography, for example, to learn about education in suburban schools or inner-city schools.

Case Studies

A case study is an in-depth study of a single unit, such as one individual, one group, one organization, one program, and so on. The goal is to arrive at a detailed description and understanding of the entity. In addition, a case study can result in data from which generalizations to theory are possible (Eisenhardt, 1999, p. 135). Freud, for example, used the case study extensively in building theory. Case studies use multiple methods, such as interviews, observation, and archives to gather data. Education and psychology researchers have used the case study widely. For example, you might conduct a case study of an inner-city school where the students have achieved at a high level on standardized tests.

Document or Content Analysis

Content analysis focuses on analyzing and interpreting recorded material within its own context. The material may be public records, textbooks, letters, films, tapes, diaries, themes, reports, and so on. When using such documentary sources, the researcher must establish the authenticity of the document itself, as well as the validity of its contents. Education researchers for example, have used content analysis, to study textbooks for their readability or to determine the coverage given to certain topics.

Naturalistic Observation

In naturalistic observation, the investigator seeks to make entirely unobtrusive observations of a setting without altering the situation in any way. The goal is to observe and study behavior as it normally occurs. Researchers use hidden cameras, one-way mirrors, and other unobtrusive techniques so that people being observed are unaware of the investigation. Piaget used naturalistic observation in his research on cognitive development in children.

Focused Interviews

Focused interviews ask questions designed to draw out subjects' responses on a topic of interest. Subjects are free to answer in their own words rather than having to choose from predetermined options, as in a survey. The unstructured, open-ended format permits greater flexibility and responsiveness to emerging issues for the participants. An educational researcher might conduct a focused interview study of a group of high school students about relationships among the racial groups in their school.

Phenomenologic Studies

Phenomenologic studies begin with the assumption that multiple realities are rooted in subjects' perspectives. Thus an experience has different meanings for each person. Through unstructured interviews, the investigator explores the subject's thoughts and feelings to elicit the essence of an individual's experience. A phenomenologic study might be conducted to answer the questions "What is the relationship between a beginning teacher and his or her mentor really like? What does the experience mean to the beginning teacher?"

Grounded Theory

The grounded theory type of study is designed to develop a theory of social phenomena based on the field data collected in a study. Experience with the data generates insights, hypotheses, and questions, which researchers pursue with further data collection.

From an inductive analysis of the data, the researcher constructs concepts. He or she then forms a theory by proposing plausible relationships among the concepts. The theory is thus said to be grounded in the data. For example, a researcher interested in mainstreaming in elementary school might observe a number of classrooms and conduct interviews with teachers and students. Analysis of the data could lead to a theory about mainstreaming in the elementary school.

Historical Research

Historical research analyzes documents and artifacts to gain insight into what has happened in the past. Its success depends on the accuracy and completeness of these records. An educational researcher might want to investigate the trends in kindergarten education in a particular school district from its beginnings to the present.

Table 2.2 summarizes the major types of qualitative research.

Table 2.2 *Types of Qualitative Research*	
TYPE	MAJOR QUESTION
Ethnography	What are the culture and perspectives of this group of people in its natural setting?
Case Study	What are the characteristics of this individual, organization, or group?
Document Analysis	What can be learned about this phenomenon by studying these documents?
Naturalistic Observation	What can be learned by unobtrusively observing behavior as it naturally occurs?
Focused Interview	What can be learned about a particular topic by interviewing members of this group?
Phenomenological Study	What does this experience mean for the participants in the experience?
Grounded Theory	What theory can be derived inductively about a phenomenon from the data collected in this particular setting?
Historical	What insights or conclusions can be reached about this past event?

TYPICAL STAGES IN RESEARCH

All researchers engage in a number of activities regardless of the particular methodology chosen for the research. We focus on these activities in greater detail in later chapters; here, we briefly summarize the steps involved.

1. **Selecting a problem.** The first step is to select the problem to investigate. The problem should be consequential enough to warrant investigation. Also, the answer to the problem is not already available, but the means for finding answers are available. Quantitative researchers typically state the problem in the form of a specific question about the relationship between variables. For example, "Do children who are taught reading through the whole-language approach score higher on reading achievement than children who are taught reading through phonics?" or "Do parents in Bloomington want mandatory school uniforms for children in elementary school?" Qualitative researchers begin with a general topic of interest. The problem statement may ask the "why" or "how" of certain phenomena. For example, "How do elementary classroom teachers deal with aggressive children?" or "How do high school students become alienated from their peers?"

2. **Reviewing the literature on the problem.** Researchers should thoroughly review the relevant literature to gain more understanding and insight into the problem and to determine what research may already have been done. The beginning researcher will likely turn to the literature for help in locating and formulating a researchable problem.

3. **Designing the research.** The investigator next plans how to conduct research to answer the question. The design is the researcher's plan for the study, which includes the method to be used, what data will be gathered, where, how, and from whom. Quantitative researchers maintain that once this research plan is set forth, it must be followed. Unhypothesized observed relationships among variables may be reported and proposed as topics for future research, but they should not replace the original intent of the study. In qualitative research the design is flexible and may change during the investigation if appropriate. The design of qualitative research is thus often described as "emergent."

4. **Collecting the data.** The next step involves executing the research plan. Quantitative researchers use a wide variety of instruments to gather data, including tests, questionnaires, ratings, attitude scales, and so on. Qualitative researchers also have a toolbox of data-gathering techniques, including in-depth interviewing, participant observation, and document analysis.

5. **Analyzing the data.** The data collected in research must be analyzed. Quantitative data are usually in the form of numbers that researchers analyze using various statistical procedures. The analysis provides evidence that supports or fails to support the hypothesis of the study. Qualitative data generally take the form of words (descriptions, observations, impressions, recordings, and the like). The

researcher must organize and categorize or code the large mass of data so that they can be described and interpreted. Although the qualitative researcher does not deal with statistics, analyzing qualitative data is not easy. It is a time-consuming and painstaking process.

6. **Interpreting the findings and stating conclusions.** The researcher next tries to interpret the findings in terms of the research problem. The quantitative researcher makes statements about the probability that such a finding is due to chance and reaches a conclusion about the hypothesis. Qualitative researchers present their interpretations and explanations in narrative form. They do not talk about probability, but try to emphasize the *trustworthiness* and *credibility* of the findings.

7. **Reporting results.** Researchers must make their procedures, findings, and conclusions available in a form intelligible to others who may be interested. This involves clearly and concisely presenting the steps in the study in sufficient detail so that another person can replicate it.

We discuss in detail each of the foregoing stages of a research study in later chapters. It is probably rare for researchers to follow precisely the sequence as we have described in the preceding discussion. These activities often overlap, and researchers may move back and forth from one stage to another.

QUESTIONS THAT EDUCATIONAL RESEARCHERS ASK

The specific question chosen for research, of course, depends on the area that interests the researchers, their background, and the particular problem they confront. However, we may classify questions in educational research as theoretical (having to do with fundamental principles) or as practical (designed to solve immediate problems of the everyday situation).

Theoretical Questions

Questions of a theoretical nature are those asking, "What is it?" or "How does it occur?" or "Why does it occur?" Educational researchers formulate "what" questions more specifically as "What is intelligence?" or "What is creativity?" Typical "how" questions are "How does the child learn?" or "How does personality develop?" "Why" questions might ask, "Why does one forget?" or "Why are some children more achievement-oriented than other children?"

Research with a theoretical orientation may focus on either developing theories or testing existing theories. The former involves a type of study in which researchers seek to discover generalizations about behavior, with the goal of clarifying the nature of relationships among variables. They may believe that certain variables are related and thus conduct research to describe the nature of the relationship. From the findings they may begin to formulate a theory about the phenomenon. Theories of learning have been developed thus, because investigators have shown the relationships among certain methods, individual and environmental variables, and the efficiency of the learning process.

Probably more common in quantitative educational research are studies that aim to test already existing theories. It may be overly ambitious, especially for beginning researchers in education, to take as a goal the development of a theory. It is usually more realistic to seek to deduce hypotheses from existing theories of learning, personality, motivation, and so forth, and to test these hypotheses. If the hypotheses are logical deductions from the theory, and the empirical tests provide evidence that supports the hypotheses, then this evidence also provides support for the theory itself.

Practical Questions

Many questions in educational research are direct and practical, aimed at solving specific problems that educators may encounter in everyday activities. These questions are relevant for educational research because they deal with actual problems at the level of practice. Such questions are, for example, "How effective is peer tutoring in the elementary school classroom?" or "How does teaching children cognitive strategies affect their reading comprehension?" or "What is the relative effectiveness of the problem discussion method as compared with the lecture method in teaching high school social studies?" The answers to such questions may be quite valuable in helping teachers make practical decisions.

These practical questions can be investigated just as scientifically as the theoretical problems. The two types of questions differ primarily on the basis of the goals they help achieve rather than on the study's level of sophistication.

BASIC AND APPLIED RESEARCH

Another system of classification concerns whether research is basic or applied. **Basic research** is research aimed at obtaining empirical data used to formulate and expand theory. Basic research is not oriented in design or purpose toward the solution of practical problems. Its essential aim is to expand the frontiers of knowledge without regard to practical application. Much early psychological investigation of reinforcement was basic research. Later, social scientists found that the reinforcement theory resulting from that research had educational applications.

Applied research aims to solve an immediate practical problem. It is research performed in relation to actual problems and under the conditions in which they appear in practice. Through applied research, educators can often solve their problems at the appropriate level of complexity; that is, in the classroom teaching–learning situation. Although applied research may solve some specific question, it may not provide the general knowledge to solve other problems. For example, an elementary school teacher may study the effect of a new method of teaching fractions. She or he conducts the research to answer a practical question, not necessarily to make broad generalizations or to help develop a theory.

This classification of research is not always distinct, however, because there are varying degrees on the basic–applied continuum. Research along this basic–applied dimension is usually classified on the degree to which the findings are directly applicable to solving a practical problem. Basic research often has more practical benefits in the long run than does applied research. For example, advances in the practice of medicine depend on basic research in biochemistry, microbiology, and genetics. Likewise, progress in educational practice has related to progress in discovering general laws through basic psychological, educational, and sociological research.

Actually, in recent years basic and applied research has tended to merge in education and psychology. The trend has been for basic research to move more toward classroom studies, because the findings of applied research may help basic researchers complete theoretical formulations. Researchers developing general theories of learning, for example, often go into classrooms, because to understand how children learn investigators must consider variables such as context and social structure that are not present in the artificial environments of the laboratory. Once the theories are formulated, they can be tested through further research in the classroom.

THE LANGUAGE OF RESEARCH

Any scientific discipline needs a specific language for describing and summarizing observations in that area. Scientists need terms at the empirical level to describe particular observations; they also need terms at the theoretical level for referring to hypothetical processes that may not be subject to direct observation. Scientists may use words taken from everyday language, but they often ascribe to them new and specific meanings not commonly found in ordinary usage. Or perhaps they must introduce new terms that are not a part of everyday language, but are created to meet special needs. One of these terms is *construct*.

Constructs

To summarize their observations and to provide explanations of behavior, scientists create constructs. **Constructs** are abstractions that cannot be observed directly, but are useful in interpreting empirical data and in theory building. For example, people can observe that individuals differ in what they can learn and how quickly they can learn it. To account for this observation, scientists invented the construct called *intelligence*. They hypothesized that intelligence influences learning and that individuals differ in the extent to which they possess this trait. Other examples of constructs in educational research are motivation, reading readiness, anxiety, underachievement, creativity, and self-concept.

Specification of Meaning

Defining constructs is a major concern for researchers. The further removed constructs are from the empirical facts or phenomena they are intended to represent, the greater the possibility for misunderstanding and the greater the need for precise definitions. Constructs may be defined in a way that gives their general meaning, or they may be defined in terms of the operations by which they will be measured or manipulated in a particular study. The former type of definition is called a *constitutive definition;* the latter is known as an *operational definition.*

Constitutive Definition

A **constitutive definition** is a formal definition in which a term is defined by using other terms. It is the dictionary type of definition. For example, intelligence may be defined as the ability to think abstractly or the capacity to acquire knowledge. This type of definition helps convey the general meaning of a construct, but it is not precise enough for research purposes. The researcher needs to define constructs so that readers know exactly what is meant by the term and so that other investigators can replicate the research. An operational definition serves this purpose.

Operational Definition

An **operational definition** ascribes meaning to a construct by specifying operations that researchers must perform to measure or manipulate the construct. Operational definitions may not be as rich as constitutive definitions but are essential in research because investigators must collect data in terms of observable events. Scientists may deal on a theoretical level with such constructs as learning, motivation, anxiety, or achievement, but before studying them empirically scientists must specify observable events to represent those constructs and the operations that will supply relevant data. Operational definitions help the researcher bridge the gap between the theoretical and the observable.

There are two types of operational definitions: measured and experimental. A **measured operational definition** details the operations by which investigators measure a construct. For example, intelligence may be defined operationally as scores on the Stanford-Binet Intelligence Scale; creativity may operationally refer to scores on the Minnesota Test of Creativity. When the researcher defines constructs in terms of how they are measured, you know precisely what the researcher means by the term. An **experimental operational definition** details the steps a researcher takes to produce certain experimental conditions. For example, the operational definition of frustration in a research study may take the form of preventing subjects from reaching a goal; cognitive dissonance may be defined operationally as requiring the subjects of a study to make public statements contrary to their private beliefs.

Although investigators are guided by their own experience and knowledge and the reports of other investigators, the operational definition of a concept is to some extent arbitrary. Often they choose from a variety of possible operational definitions those that best represent their own approach to the problem. Certainly an operational definition does not exhaust the full scientific meaning of any concept. It is very specific in meaning; its purpose is to delimit a term, to ensure that everyone concerned understands the particular way a term is being used. Operational definitions are considered adequate if their procedures gather data that constitute acceptable indicators of the constructs they are intended to represent. Often it is a matter of opinion whether they have achieved this result.

Operational definitions are essential to research because they permit investigators to measure abstract constructs and permit scientists to move from the level of constructs and theory to the level of observation, on which science is based. By using operational definitions, researchers can proceed with investigations that might not otherwise be possible. It is important to remember that, although researchers report their findings in terms of abstract constructs and relate these to other research and to theory, what they have actually found is a relationship between two sets of observable and measurable data that they selected to represent the constructs. In practice, an investigation of the relation between the construct creativity and the construct intelligence relates scores on an intelligence test to scores on a measure of creativity.

Variables

Researchers, especially quantitative researchers, find it useful to think in terms of variables. A **variable** is a construct or a characteristic that can take on different values or scores. Researchers study variables and the relationships existing among variables. Height is one example of a variable; it can vary in an individual from one time to another, among individuals at the same time, among the averages for groups, and so on. Social class, gender, vocabulary level, intelligence, and spelling test scores are other examples of variables. In a study concerned with the relation of vocabulary level to science achievement among eighth-graders, the variables of interest are the measures of vocabulary and the measures of science achievement. There are different ways to measure science achievement. The researcher could use a standardized achievement test, a teacher-made test, grades in science class, or evaluations of completed science projects. Any of these measures could represent the variable "science achievement."

Types of Variables

There are several ways to classify variables. Variables can be categorical or they can be continuous. When researchers classify subjects by sorting them into groups, the attribute on which they base the classification is termed a **categorical variable.** Home language, county of residence, father's principal occupation, and school in which enrolled are examples of categorical variables. The simplest type of categorical variable has only two mutually exclusive classes and is called a **dichotomous variable.** Male–female, citizen–alien, and pass–fail are dichotomous variables. Some categorical variables have more than two classes; some examples are educational level, religious affiliation, and state of birth.

When an attribute has an infinite number of values within a range, it is a **continuous variable.** As a child grows from 40 inches to 41 inches, he or she passes through an infinite number of heights. Height, weight, age, and achievement test scores are examples of continuous variables.

The most important classification of variables is on the basis of their *use* within the research under consideration, when they are classified as independent variables or dependent variables. **Independent variables** are antecedent to dependent variables and are known or are hypothesized to influence the **dependent variable,** which is the outcome. In experimental studies the treatment is the independent variable and the outcome is the dependent variable. In an experiment in which freshmen are randomly assigned to a "hands on" unit on weather forecasting or to a textbook-centered unit and are then given a common exam at the end of the study, the method of instruction ("hands on" versus textbook) antecedes the exam scores and is the independent variable in this study. The exam scores follow and are the dependent variable. The experimenter is hypothesizing that the exam scores will partially depend on how the students were taught weather forecasting. In this case, freshman status is a constant.

In nonexperimental studies, a variable that inevitably precedes another variable in time is an independent variable. For example, Okagaki and Frensch (1998) compared the expectations for children's ideal educational attainment held by Asian-American, Latino, and European-American parents of fourth- and fifth-grade students. In this instance, attitudes could partly depend on parents' ethnicity but ethnicity could not depend on expectations. Thus ethnicity is the independent variable and expectation is the dependent variable. The researchers found that Asian-American parents held the highest ideal educational attainment expectations for their children, whereas Latino and European-American parents' expectations were similar. In other cases it is not possible to tell which variable is antecedent and which follows. In a study of the relationship between self-confidence and popularity in high school students, either variable could be considered independent or dependent. It is possible for a variable to be an independent variable in one study and a dependent variable in another. Whether a variable is independent or dependent depends on the purpose of the study. If you investigate the effect of motivation on achievement, then motivation is the independent variable. However, if you wish to determine the effect of testing procedures, classroom grouping arrangements, or grading procedures on students' motivation, then motivation becomes the dependent variable. Intelligence is generally treated as an independent variable because educators are interested in its effect on learning, the dependent variable. However, in studies investigating the effect of nursery school experience on the intellectual development of children, intelligence is the dependent variable.

A classification of independent variables can be made on the basis of whether the independent variable is one that the investigators can manipulate. According to this classification, there are two types of independent variables, active and attribute. An **active independent variable** is defined as one that the researcher can manipulate directly. For instance, method of teaching, method of grouping, and reinforcement procedures are all variables that can be manipulated and are thus called active variables. An **attribute independent variable** is one that the researcher cannot actively manipulate. Such variables, sometimes called *assigned variables,* are individuals' characteristics that cannot be manipulated at will. For example, aptitude, gender, race, age, and social class are typical

START

Is this description true of all subjects in the study? — **Yes** → LABEL CONSTANT

No ↓

LABEL VARIABLE

Is this variable assumed to depend on another antecedent variable? — **Yes** → LABEL DEPENDENT VARIABLE

No ↓

LABEL INDEPENDENT VARIABLE

Can researcher directly manipulate this variable? — **Yes** → LABEL ACTIVE INDEPENDENT VARIABLE

No ↓

LABEL ATTRIBUTE INDEPENDENT VARIABLE

Can independent/ dependent variable take on an infinite number of values within a range? — **Yes** → ADD LABEL "CONTINUOUS" TO VARIABLE DESCRIPTION

No ↓

ADD LABEL "CATEGORICAL" TO VARIABLE DESCRIPTION

FIGURE 2.2

Flow Chart for Classifying Variables and Constants

attribute variables. Investigators can incorporate attribute variables into their research by assigning subjects to groups on the basis of such preexisting variables.

Constants

The opposite of variable is constant. A **constant** is a fixed value within a study. If all subjects in a study are eighth-graders, then grade level is a constant. In a study comparing the attitudes toward school of high school girls who plan professional careers with those who do not plan professional careers, high school girls constitute a constant; whether they plan professional careers is the independent variable, and their attitudes constitute the dependent variable. Figure 2.2 illustrates a process for classifying variables and constants.

SUMMARY

The two broad research methodologies in education are quantitative and qualitative. Quantitative research deals with questions of relationship, cause and effect, or current status that researchers can answer by gathering and statistically analyzing numeric data. It can be further classified as experimental and nonexperimental. Qualitative research focuses on understanding social phenomena and providing rich verbal descriptions of settings, situations, and participants. The qualitative approach includes a number of different methods, such as ethnography, case study, naturalistic observation, focused interviews, and historical. Both qualitative and quantitative methodologies are important in educational research. The method chosen depends on the nature of the research question.

The typical steps in educational research are (1) selecting a problem; (2) reviewing the literature; (3) selecting research strategy and developing instruments; (4) collecting, analyzing, and interpreting data; and (5) communicating the findings by reporting the results of the study.

Based on the objective, educational research can be classified into two major categories: basic and applied. The primary concern of basic research is to expand the frontiers of knowledge and to discover general laws. The main goal of applied research is to solve immediate practical problems.

At a theoretical level, educational scientists use terms such as *intelligence, creativity, problem-solving ability,* and *motivation,* which are abstractions from observation of certain behaviors. These are referred to as *constructs.* In quantitative research, constructs are quantified and take on different values. Thus they are referred to as *variables.* There are two major types of variables: independent and dependent. If a variable is antecedent to another variable, it is called an *independent variable;* but if it is the consequence of another variable, it is the *dependent variable.*

In quantitative research, variables must be operationally defined. There are two ways of defining variables operationally: (1) by specifying how they will be measured or (2) by listing the steps taken in an experiment to produce certain research conditions. The first type is referred to as a *measured operational definition,* and the second is an *experimental operational definition.*

REFERENCES

Astor, R. A., Meyer, H. A., & Behre, W. J. (1999). Unowned places and times: Maps and interviews about violence in high schools. *American Educational Research Journal, 36,* 3–42.

Eisenhardt, K. M. (1999). Building theories from case study research. In A. Bryman and R. G. Burgess (Eds.), *Qualitative research* (Vol. 1, pp. 135–159). Thousand Oaks, CA: Sage.

Hammersley, M. (1996). The relationship between qualitative and quantitative research: Paradigm loyalty versus methodological eclecticism. In J. T. E. Richardson (Ed.), *Handbook of Qualitative research methods for psychology and the social sciences.* Leicester, England, BPS Books.

Okagaki, L., and Frensch, P. A. (1998). Parenting and children's school achievement: A multiethnic perspective. *American Educational Research Journal, 35,* 123–144.

Walker, R. (1985). An introduction to applied qualitative research. In R. Walker (Ed.), *Applied qualitative research,* pp. 3–26. Aldershot, England: Gower.

KEY CONCEPTS

active independent variable
applied research
attribute independent variable
basic research
categorical variable
constant
constitutive definition

construct
continuous variable
dependent variable
dichotomous variable
experimental operational
definition
hypothesis

independent variable
measured operational definition
operational definition
qualitative research
quantitative research
variable

EXERCISES

1. Based on the title of each study, classify the following research as *basic* or *applied:*
   a. "The Effect of RNA (Ribonucleic Acid) Injections on the Transfer of Skills from Trained Animals to Untrained Animals"
   b. "Outcomes of a Remedial Arithmetic Program"
   c. "Conditioning as a Function of the Interval between the Conditioned and Original Stimulus"
   d. "Teaching Geometry to Cultivate Reflective Thinking: An Experimental Study"

2. Using the designations "active," "attribute," or "may be either," classify the following variables:
   a. Amount of drug administered
   b. Physical disability
   c. Anxiety
   d. Teaching method

3. In a study designed to determine the effect of varying amounts of sleep deprivation on

the learning of nonsense syllables, identify the following:
   a. What is the independent variable?
   b. What is the dependent variable?

4. Classify the following variables as *categorical* or *continuous:*
   a. Achievement
   b. Phonics method of reading versus look–say method of reading
   c. Spanish speaking, English speaking, French speaking
   d. Muscle prowess
   e. Music aptitude

5. What are the characteristics of operational definitions?

6. Which kind of operational definition (*measured* or *experimental*) is better suited for each of the following variables?
   a. Reinforcement
   b. Achievement
   c. Attitude
   d. Teaching method

7. You are a teacher who has been concerned about the amount of aggressive behavior you observe among the children. You have interviewed parents about their child-rearing practices (use of punishment, rewards, and the like) and the amount of TV viewing and video games the children engage in. You have collected a great deal of data, but you feel that there is no unifying theme. According to the scientific approach, what would your next step most likely be?

8. Which research method (*experimental, ex post facto,* or *survey*) would most effectively give you answers to each of the following questions?
   a. Do children who eat breakfast make better grades in school?
   b. Does a unit on proper nutrition change children's breakfast-eating habits?
   c. How many children in school report that they do not have breakfast at home?
   d. Does the institution of a free breakfast program at school make a difference in the achievement of students?

9. Based on the titles, classify each of the following studies according to the research methodology most likely used:
   a. "Gender-Based Differential Item Performance in Mathematics"
   b. "Effects of 'On-Line' Test Feedback on the Seriousness of Subsequent Errors"
   c. "College Students' Views and Ratings of an Ideal Professor"
   d. "Effect of Early Absence of Father on Scholastic Aptitude"
   e. "An Alternative High School: An In-Depth Study"

10. Give an example of how basic research in the biological sciences has improved the practice of medicine.

11. Give an example of how basic research in learning has improved the practice of teaching.

12. Give an example of applied research completed in your field of interest. List other areas where additional research needs to be done in your field. What variables might be investigated in such studies?

13. What research methodology do you believe would be the most appropriate for investigating each of the following research questions?
   a. How do parents conduct home schooling?
   b. Does collaborative learning promote learning in the college classroom?
   c. What is the relationship between vocabulary and reading achievement in the primary grades?
   d. Do parents support character education in the middle school curriculum?
   e. What is the relationship between teachers' undergraduate background (education versus liberal arts) and certain measures of competence in the classroom?

f. How did educational reforms of the junior high school lead to development of the middle school?

g. What is the influence of family composition on children's conformity to the student role?

h. What kind of education do students receive in a church-sponsored Christian high school?

14. How would you operationally define science achievement?

ANSWERS

1. a. Basic
   b. Applied
   c. Basic
   d. Applied

2. a. Active
   b. Attribute
   c. May be either
   d. Active

3. a. Amount of sleep deprivation
   b. Number of nonsense syllables learned

4. a. Continuous
   b. Categorical
   c. Categorical
   d. Continuous
   e. Continuous

5. Acceptable definitions state a clear-cut procedure for creating or for determining the existence of the phenomenon and its extent.

6. a. Experimental
   b. Measured
   c. Measured
   d. Experimental

7. Formulate a theory of aggression in children

8. a. Ex post facto (causal-comparative)
   b. Experimental
   c. Survey
   d. Experimental

9. a. Ex post facto
   b. Experimental
   c. Survey
   d. Ex post facto
   e. Qualitative

10. Answers will vary.

11. Answers will vary.

12. Answers will vary.

13. a. Qualitative
    b. Experimental
    c. Correlational
    d. Survey
    e. Ex post facto
    f. Historical
    g. Ex post facto
    h. Qualitative

14. Answers may vary; an example: "Science achievement is the score on the science subtest of the Iowa Test of Basic Skills."

 ## INFOTRAC COLLEGE EDITION

Use the keyword *independent variable* to locate an article that discusses the use of variables in quantitative research in general, or in a particular research study.

Chapter 3

The Research Problem

INSTRUCTIONAL OBJECTIVES

After studying this chapter, the student will be able to

1. Define a research problem.

2. Identify potential sources of problems for educational research.

3. State the criteria to use for evaluating a research problem.

4. Evaluate a given problem for research using the accepted criteria.

5. Take a general problem in an area of interest in education and state it in a specific form ready for empirical investigation.

6. Distinguish between the types of problem statements used in quantitative research and qualitative research.

7. Define terms such as *population* and *variables* as used in a quantitative research study.

8. Identify the population and the variables in a given study.

Systematic research begins with a **research problem.** John Dewey (1933) spoke of the first step in the scientific method as the recognition of a felt difficulty, an obstacle or problem that puzzles the researcher. Selecting and formulating a problem is one of the most important aspects of doing research in any field. Beginning researchers are often surprised to find that this initial stage often takes up a large part of the total time invested in a research project. There is no way to do research until a problem is recognized, thought through, and formulated in a useful way.

A researcher must first decide on the general problem area. The researcher should have knowledge or experience in the area in order to ask questions that research can answer. We often hear students in difficult courses say, "I don't know enough to ask questions." Similarly, unless a researcher has knowledge or experience in an area, he or she does not know what additional knowledge is needed or how to obtain it through empirical investigation.

Furthermore, the problem area chosen for investigation should hold deep interest or be one about which the researcher is really curious. The choice must necessarily be very personal or else the researcher may find it difficult to muster the motivation to carry the research through to its end. For example, an elementary school teacher may be interested in finding a more effective way to teach reading. A high school biology teacher may want to know if using computer simulations would improve students' problem-solving skills. An elementary school principal may want to know if a mentoring program would improve the effectiveness of beginning teachers.

Once having chosen the general subject, the researcher then narrows it down to a specific statement of the research problem. Most beginning researchers find this task of formulating a researchable problem or question difficult. The difficulty is not caused by a shortage of researchable problems in education. In fact, so many questions beg for answers that researchers usually have trouble choosing. The difficulty is that the researcher must select a problem and formulate a question very early, when the beginner's understanding of how to do research is most limited. In addition, uncertainties about the nature of research problems, isolation of a problem, criteria for acceptability, and how to solve the problem often seem overwhelming. Even experienced researchers usually must make several attempts before arriving at a research problem that meets generally accepted criteria. A first selection or formulation may on closer examination prove infeasible or not worth doing. Skill in doing research is to a large extent a matter of making wise choices about what to investigate. The skill takes time and repeated effort to develop but the willing beginner can do so. Unlikely as it may seem, once the researcher has selected a problem area and clearly formulated a question or statement, he or she has accomplished one of the most difficult phases of the research process.

THE SOURCES OF PROBLEMS

The first question most students ask is "How do I find a research problem?" Although there are no set rules for locating a problem, certain suggestions can help. Three important **sources for research problems** are experience, deductions from theory, and related literature.

Experience

Among the most fruitful sources for beginning researchers are their own experiences as educational practitioners. A geometry teacher may notice that certain teaching methods seem to get better results than others and may plan a quantitative research study systematically comparing the methods. An elementary school teacher may want to investigate the influence of one-parent families on the achievement and adjustment of children. A high school social studies teacher may want to determine what high school seniors know about the process through which political parties select candidates for U.S. President. Some qualitative research problems that may arise from experience are "How do new faculty members become socialized into the total faculty group?" "How does 'pecking order' among high school students evolve over time?" or "What does education mean in the families of my minority students?"

Observations of certain relationships for which no satisfactory explanations exist are yet another source of problems for investigation. A teacher may notice an increase in overt signs of anxiety in students at certain times. To investigate this, the teacher can structure various tentative explanations of the origin of the anxiety and then proceed to test them empirically. This investigation may not only solve the immediate problem but also may contribute to understanding the causes of classroom anxiety.

Similarly, educators must make decisions about practices that have become routine in the school situation and are in some instances based mainly on tradition or authority, with little or no support from scientific research. Why not evaluate some of these practices—for instance, the annual testing program? Is the program beneficial? Would alternative tests be more valid for the purpose intended than those the schools now use?

Educators' everyday experiences can yield worthwhile problems for investigation, and, in fact, most research ideas that beginning educational researchers develop tend to come from their personal experiences. They may have hunches about new relationships or about alternative ways of accomplishing certain objectives and thus, through an intuitive process, arrive at ideas for research. These studies will be mainly of a type leading to solution of an immediate problem, but sometimes such problems are nevertheless more appropriate and meaningful for beginning researchers than those logically deduced from theory. In addition, studies derived from teachers' classroom experiences can significantly contribute to the improvement of educational practice.

There is currently a great need for research that focuses on how to improve educational practice. American schools face a number of critical problems, such as incorporating increasing numbers of educationally disadvantaged students into the educational mainstream (Pallas, Natriello, & McDill, 1989) and preparing students for an increasingly competitive and technologically advanced workplace (U.S. Department of Labor, 1991). Findings from practitioners' research studies can play an important role in solving these problems and improving U.S. schools. A recent report of the National Academy of Education (1991, p. 19) said, "Current efforts to implement broad-based school reforms without adequate research to guide the direction of change will fail."

Deductions from Theory

The deductions that the researcher can make from various educational and behavioral theories with which he or she is familiar provide an excellent source of problems. Theories involve general principles whose applicability to specific educational problems is only hypothetical until research empirically confirms them. Only through research can you determine whether the generalizations embodied in theories can translate into specific recommendations for improving educational practice.

From a theory, the researcher can generate hypotheses stating the expected findings in a particular practical situation; that is, the researcher asks, "What relationships between variables will appear if the theory correctly summarizes the state of affairs?" and then conducts systematic inquiry to ascertain whether the empirical data support the hypothesis and hence the theory.

Theory not only provides many ideas for research problems but also ties ideas into existing knowledge. A beginning researcher can find summaries of theories in journals and textbooks, or can read primary sources. Then, the researcher can make deductions or predictions based on the theory: If "this" is true, then you should expect to make "this" observation. The researcher might also try to see if the theory holds or can be applied in situations different from the one in which it was developed.

The validity, scope, and practicality of cognitive theories, motivational theories, developmental theories, attribution theories, and many others can be profitably tested in educational situations. Reinforcement theory may be a particularly useful starting point for classroom research. Consider the implications for classroom testing that could be deduced from just one postulate of reinforcement theory—namely, that reinforcing responses increases response rate and strength. This theory has stimulated a great deal of research already, but there are still many deductions to be made and tested under classroom conditions. For instance, not enough research has been done on the effect of *lack* of overt reinforcement or of nonreinforcement on correct student responses in classroom situations. Scientists know from experimental laboratory studies with animals that each withholding of reinforcement decreases the probability of that response and eventually extinguishes it. Can research extrapolate this finding to the classroom? In other words, can the teacher assume that correct student responses that are not overtly reinforced will weaken and become extinct? At the present time educators do not have sufficient classroom research testing the applicability of this principle.

Many researchers are trying to understand the roots of youth violence that has occurred in U.S. high schools. Erik Erikson's theory (1959) of personality development may be relevant to understanding this problem. Erikson describes psychosocial development in terms of stages throughout the life span, each of which involves a critical issue or conflict that the person must resolve. Adolescence, one of these stages, has as its major task the development of a positive self-concept or, to use Erikson's term, a strong sense of identity. Forming a strong personal identity is difficult because competing roles and values face the young person. Achieving a solid personal identity leads to social competence and a stable adult personality. But if the adolescent does not resolve the identity crisis, a sense of inferiority and personal alienation may result. It is interesting that students who have committed violent acts often report feelings of alienation. Marcia (1980) who has elaborated Erikson's theory reports that adolescents who have achieved a sense of identity are more independent, better able to cope with stress, and have a higher self-esteem. Erikson's theory could become the foundation for research into school violence. For example, what school practices may contribute to feelings of inferiority, mistrust, and isolation among some students? What are some positive things the school can do to help young people solve the identity crisis? You might want to look at the relationship of gender or ethnicity to the adolescent task of forming a sense of identity, for example.

A theory-based approach to research problems results in studies that are easily integrated because they all stem from a common theory. Such interrelated research is especially productive as a means for expanding knowledge in a particular area.

Related Literature

Another valuable source of problems is the literature in your own area of interest. In reading about previous research, you encounter examples of research problems and the way in which research is conducted. There are several ways in which the review of previous research can help in formulating new research problems.

1. *Review of previous research helps people formulate research questions that are the next logical step from previous investigations.* The outcomes of one piece of research very often lead to new questions. In the concluding section of their research reports, some researchers describe new questions that have arisen. A productive way to extend studies is to introduce new variables for further control and for detecting interaction effects between variables. Many multivariate studies are extensions of earlier single-variable investigations.

2. *Review of previous research may stimulate a researcher to see whether the procedures employed can be adapted to solving other problems, or whether a similar study could be conducted in a different field or subject area or with different groups of subjects.* For example, you may read a study investigating the effectiveness of a multimedia approach in teaching chemistry. Perhaps you could conduct a similar study in biology or in another subject area. A study involving secondary school students might serve as a guide to the elementary teacher who is interested in determining whether the same relationships between variables prevail at the elementary level. Or you might repeat, using a sample of students with learning disabilities as the subjects, a study on the effectiveness of using computers in teaching reading to a regular group of first-graders.

3. *Reviewing previous research may suggest the desirability of replication to confirm previous findings.* An essential characteristic of a scientific research study is that it should be replicable, so that researchers can verify the findings. Replication of a study with or without variation may be a profitable activity for a beginning researcher. Repeating a study increases the extent to which the research findings can be generalized and provides additional evidence of the validity of the findings. In

many educational experiments it is not possible to select subjects at random; rather, you must use classroom groups as they are already organized. Of course, this limits the extent to which the findings can be generalized. However, as experiments are repeated at different times and in different places with the expected relations supported in each study, educators can place increasing confidence in the scientific validity of the findings.

Mere repetition of other studies is not the most challenging research activity, but in most cases replications are not exact. Variation is introduced to clarify some aspect of the findings, to test how far the findings can be generalized, or to investigate factors not included in the original study. For example, in other countries researchers have conducted numerous replications of Piaget's studies (1932) of the development of moral judgment in children. These studies have used Piaget's basic approach but have investigated the development of moral judgment in children of different socioeconomic classes, in children of the same chronological age but differing in intelligence level, in children differing in the extent of their participation in their own age groups, in children differing in the nature of parental discipline, and in both boys and girls. Recently other investigators have used techniques that differed from Piaget's in their attempts to confirm his findings and conclusions. In general, the large body of research stemming from Piaget's investigations has supported his original conclusions. Thus, a single research study, if it deals with a significant problem and if its findings are exciting, can inspire many other studies.

4. *Reviewing research studies previously undertaken may raise the question of the applicability of their findings to other cultures.* Conclusions from research done in a given culture do not automatically apply to other cultures. This is one reason why in recent decades investigators have placed considerable emphasis on cross-cultural research. In such areas as child and adolescent psychology, social learning, cognitive and language development, achievement motivation, personality development, and educational practices, numerous examples of cross-cultural research appear. The growing number of international students in American universities has both increased interest in this kind of research and facilitated the collection of cross-cultural data. A number of theses and dissertations by these students are of this type and provide basis for further cross-cultural studies.

5. *Reviewing previous research may result in detecting inconsistencies and contradictions or in dissatisfaction with the conceptualization, methodology, measuring instruments, and statistical analysis used.* Researchers can often find something to improve on in previous research. For example, Hartshorne and May (1928) challenged the existing theory that honesty was a unified character trait. They investigated the behavior of several thousand schoolchildren in various temptation situations. They concluded from the low correlations among the temptation measures that honesty was not a general inner trait; rather, it was specific and influenced by the situation in which individuals were placed.

Burton (1963) replicated this study because he questioned Hartshorne and May's emphasis on situational factors in honesty behavior. Burton used a factor analysis approach and found evidence for intraindividual consistency across the tasks presented to the children. He concluded that there probably was an underlying trait of honesty that a person shows in resisting temptation situations, but he agreed with Hartshorne and May in rejecting an "all-or-none" formulation about a person's character.

Hunt (1965) replicated Burton's study but used analysis of variance instead of factor analysis as the statistical technique. Hunt argued that personality differences, situations, and the interaction between persons and situations should be considered as sources of variation in honesty behavior and found support for the interaction hypothesis.

Nelsen, Grinder, and Mutterer (1969) replicated and extended all the above studies. They compared the alternative methodological approaches to the problem and concluded that temptation behavior is only moderately consistent across a variety of tasks. Thus their findings agree with the early Hartshorne and May study despite a time difference of more than forty years in the data collection periods of the two studies, and despite different populations, tasks, and methodological procedures.

Another example of research inspired by previous studies is the research that investigates the effects of ability grouping on student achievement. Since the early years of the last century, hundreds of studies have been done on this problem, yet it is still a topic for research (Gamoran, 1993; George, 1993; Schmidt, 1993).

When reading the organized knowledge in a particular area, you may become aware of information gaps. You can plan research to help fill these gaps and result in more reliable knowledge. For students, conferences with professors in their major field of study may help with this step. With some critical analysis of published research in their field and a bit of creativity, students should be able to find several potentially researchable problems. An understanding of the theoretical and empirical aspects of the subject area should enable you to read critically and choose a good problem.

Noneducation Sources

Experiences and observations in the world at large, as well as professional activities, can be fruitful sources of research problems. You can adapt theories or procedures you encounter in other fields to apply to education. Often movements that originate outside a profession lead people to new paths of research. The women's movement has led researchers to study gender stereotyping in educational materials, the influence of schools on the learning of sex roles, gender differences in achievement and personality, and so forth. The civil rights movement led to many studies about the education of minority children. The prevalence of the AIDS epidemic in this country has stimulated a great deal of research on the best procedures and materials to use to acquaint young people in school with the danger of the disease and how best to protect themselves from it. The inspiration for much valuable research in education has come from such noneducation sources.

EVALUATING THE PROBLEM

After you have tentatively selected a problem, you must evaluate it. A researcher must be confident that the problem area is of sufficient importance to warrant investigation, although this is not always easy to determine. Judging the worth of a problem is often a matter of individual values and subjective opinion. However, you should use certain criteria in evaluating the significance of a problem.

1. *Ideally, the problem should be one whose solution will contribute to the body of organized knowledge in education.* The researcher should show that the study is likely to fill in gaps in present knowledge or help resolve some of the inconsistencies in previous research. Perhaps the study can improve on earlier studies in such a way that it makes more reliable knowledge available. Most scholars agree that problems rooted in theory have greater potential for satisfying this criterion. The investigator might ask whether the study will yield knowledge about new relationships or will replicate previously established findings.

    Experienced researchers are more likely to focus on theory, but beginners should probably pick a problem that would have an impact on educational practice. Popham, a veteran educational researcher, offered this advice: "Beginning researchers will do well to look at what's currently happening in schools. Or, even better, if it can be discerned, what's *likely to happen*" (1991, p. 18). Researchers should be able to answer the question "So what?" with respect to their proposed study. Would the solution of the problem make any difference to educational practice? Would other educators be interested in the findings? Would the findings be useful in an educational decision-making situation?

    Sometimes, in their effort to locate a problem, students select a question involving rather trivial relationships. For example, "What is the relationship between popularity with peers and reading speed?" would be considered a trivial problem because it has little or no significance for educational practice, has little relationship to other studies, and has no consequences for theory. The answers to some questions are obvious. A question such as "What is the correlation between verbal aptitude and reading achievement?" would also be considered trivial because educators already have sufficient data on this relationship and additional research is probably unnecessary. There is no need to "reinvent the wheel."

2. *The problem must be researchable.* Although this criterion would seem self-evident, in practice many problems do involve questions that cannot be subjected to scientific investigation. To be researchable, a problem must be one that can be attacked empirically; that is, it should be possible to gather data that answer the question. Many interesting questions in education cannot be subjected to empirical research but must be investigated through philosophic inquiry. Such questions as "Is it good to have sex education in the elementary schools?" or "Should we offer more vocational training in the high school?" or "Should schools give more attention to character education?" are philosophic issues and cannot be

answered by scientific investigation. Although these questions as worded cannot be attacked empirically, they might be reformulated into workable research questions. For instance, you might restate the first question above as "What is the effect of sex education in the elementary schools on the attitudes of junior high school students toward premarital sex?" Researchers could design a study to obtain information on this type of question. Although philosophical questions as such are not appropriate for scientific research, people can use the information provided by research to develop solutions to philosophical and ethical questions; that is, the data compiled through scientific research on a problem can be useful to educators as they make decisions involving rights and values.

The researcher must also give some attention to the definition and measurement of the variables involved in the question. A problem such as "What is the effect of changes in national priorities on the future of American education?" would not be appropriate for research. It would be difficult to define the terms "changes in national priorities" and "the future of American education" in such a way that they could be measured.

3. *The problem should be one that will lead to new problems and so to further research.* If researchers begin by linking their problem to organized knowledge and consider the type of study that might logically follow their own, they are much more likely to satisfy this criterion. A good study, while arriving at an answer to one question, usually generates a number of other questions that need investigation. This has been true of the studies dealing with reinforcement theory in the classroom. In contrast, much survey research fails to satisfy this second criterion. In connection with this criterion, we suggest that the beginning student in research consider selecting a problem that could possibly be expanded or followed up later in a master's thesis or even a doctoral dissertation. It is helpful if students familiarize themselves with the research efforts of their professors, who not only can suggest related problems needing investigation, but may also later serve as a mentor or a doctoral committee member.

4. *The problem must be suitable for the particular researcher.* The problem may be excellent from the point of view of the criteria mentioned but inappropriate for the individual. First, the problem should be one in which you, the researcher, have a genuine interest and about which you can be enthusiastic. It should be a problem whose solution is personally important because of what it could contribute to your own knowledge or to improving your performance as an educational practitioner. Unless the problem is meaningful and interesting, it is doubtful whether you would be willing to expend the time and energy to do a thorough job.

Furthermore, the problem should be in an area in which you have both knowledge and some experience. To identify a worthwhile problem, you need to be familiar with the existing theories, concepts, and established facts. Also, you should consider whether you have the necessary skills that you may need to carry the study through to completion. You may have to develop and validate instruments, or do complex statistical analyses.

Another consideration is whether researching the problem is actually feasible in your situation. Are the data necessary to answer the question available, or will they be? You must make sure that the necessary subjects will be available or that the appropriate school records will be accessible. School administrators are quite often opposed to having research conducted in their schools. So unless you are employed in a school situation at the time, you are quite likely to be left without the means to solve the research problem. One of the authors of this book found it necessary to visit four school systems before getting permission to conduct an educational experiment.

Also, is the problem one that you can investigate and complete in the allotted time? Don't select a problem that is too big or too involved, and allow adequate time for constructing the instruments, administering the instruments, analyzing the data, and writing the report.

5. *The problem should be ethically appropriate.* The problem should be one that you can investigate without violating ethical principles. Unlike researchers in the physical sciences, educational researchers are dealing with human subjects with feelings, sensitivities, and rights who must be treated ethically. We will discuss ethics in greater detail in Chapter 14. At this point, we will just mention briefly three issues the researcher should consider:

   a. *Consent.* Researchers need to obtain consent from the intended subjects. Subjects should be able to choose whether they wish to participate in the study. Obtain consent from subjects after taking steps to ensure that they have a complete understanding of the procedures to be used, any risks involved, and any demands that will be placed on them. Obtain parental consent if minor children are to be involved in the study.

   b. *Protection from harm.* Do not plan research that may bring physical harm or psychological harm such as stress, discomfort, or embarrassment that could have lasting adverse effects. Fortunately, most educational research does not involve great risk of harm to subjects.

   c. *Privacy.* A researcher should invade the privacy of subjects as minimally as possible. For example, a researcher may plan to use an inventory that asks adolescents questions about sexual experiences, religious beliefs, attitudes toward parents, or other sensitive topics. In this case, the researcher should not attach names or even identifying numbers to the inventories. Subjects have the right to expect that their anonymity will be preserved. Most educational researchers are interested in group data rather than individual responses; the scores or responses of individuals are generally pooled and reported as group averages, which tends to minimize the risk of invading privacy.

STATING THE PROBLEM

After the problem has been selected and its significance evaluated, there is still the task of formulating or stating the problem in a form amenable to investigation.

The Problem in Quantitative Research

The following are **criteria for research problem statements** in quantitative inquiry:

1. *It clarifies exactly what is to be investigated.* You do this by specifying the variables involved in the problem, stating those variables typically in question form, and operationally defining the variables. We cannot overemphasize the importance of a clear, concise statement of the problem. Beginning researchers often have a general idea of what they want to do but have trouble formulating it as a workable research problem. They find that their initial general ideas, although adequate for communication and understanding, are not specific enough to permit an empirical attack on the problem. They cannot make progress until they can state unambiguously what they are going to do.

   To illustrate, suppose a beginning researcher states that he or she is interested in studying the effectiveness of the new science curriculum in the secondary schools. As the problem is stated, you could understand in a broad sense what he or she wants to do and could communicate about it in a general way. But the researcher must specify the problem with much greater clarity if a method for investigating it is to be found.

   An essential step involves a definition of the terms involved. What is meant by *effectiveness, science curriculum,* and *secondary schools?* The definitions required for research are not usually supplied by a dictionary. For example, a dictionary defines effectiveness as "producing the intended or expected result." This definition describes the general construct *effectiveness* but is not sufficiently precise for research purposes. You need to specify exactly what indicator of effectiveness you will use or what you will do to assess the presence or absence of the phenomenon denoted by the concept *effectiveness.* The same is true for the other terms. In other words, you must operationally define the variables of the problem. As mentioned earlier, an operational definition defines a concept in terms of the operation or processes that will be used to measure or to manipulate the concept.

   In this study the researcher might choose to define effectiveness as the improvement made in scores on a test of critical thinking or on a standardized science test. The term *curriculum* would be defined as the computer-assisted biology course offered to high school sophomores. *Secondary schools* might refer to those high schools that have certain specified characteristics such as size, type, and so on. The problem in the example given now might become "What is the effect of the computer-assisted biology course on the comprehension of biological concepts in beginning biology students at the sophomore level?" The operational definitions serve to focus the scope of a general question to specific observable variables.

   Now that the work is indicated with some clarity and focus, the researcher can proceed to design an experimental study that compares the scores made on pretests and posttests of comprehension of biological concepts by students having the computer-assisted biology course with those of similar students having an alternative biology curriculum. The researcher can now begin to gather some objective evidence concerning a particular curriculum in a particular situation that will shed light on the more general original question.

2. *The problem asks about a relationship between two (or more) variables stated in the form of a question or implied question.* Although quantitative research problems generally focus on the relationship among two or more variables, this does not mean that the *exact* words "What is the relationship between . . ." and . . . ? have to appear in the statement. The statement *may* appear in that form, or the relationship may only be implied. Neither must you state the problem in the form of a question. Students are often confused on this point. For instance, compare the declarative statement "This study examines the relative effectiveness of Reading Methods A and B in teaching slow learners" with the question "What is the relative effectiveness of Reading Method A as compared with Method B in teaching slow learners?" Both focus on the "relationship between variables" but without using those precise words, and both are acceptable ways to present the research problem. Some researchers prefer the question form simply because it is straightforward and psychologically seems to orient the researcher to the task at hand— namely, to plan a method of finding the answer to the question. In some cases both a declarative statement and a question are presented; a more general declarative statement may be followed by one or more very specific questions.

3. *The problem should be stated in such a way that research into the question is possible;* that is, so that one can collect data to answer the question. For this reason, avoid philosophical issues, as well as value or judgmental questions that empirical investigation cannot answer.

The development of a workable problem is an evolutionary process involving many attempts to sharpen concepts, define operations, and consider ways of collecting data.

IDENTIFYING POPULATION AND VARIABLES

A good strategy for shaping a felt problem—or a vague notion of what you want to investigate—into a researchable problem is to think in terms of population and variables.

For example, let us consider Ms. Burke, an elementary school principal whose felt difficulty is "Does individual tutoring by upper-grade students have a positive effect on below-average readers?" It is usually easiest to identify the **population,** those people about whom you wish to learn something. The population is below-average readers. Reading ability is not a variable in this question, because all the children being considered have been diagnosed as below-average readers. Having identified below-average readers as the population in the original statement, Ms. Burke should now ask herself if that is really the population she wants. She will probably decide that "below-average readers" is too broad a category and she should confine herself to a particular age. So she selects below-average second-grade readers.

Now she is ready to look for variables in the remainder of her original statement. "Individual tutoring" can be made into a variable either by varying the type of tutoring used or by varying the amount of tutoring time or by having some children receive the tutoring while others do not. Ms. Burke decides that the last alternative concerns what she really wants to know, so she rewrites the relevant part of the question to "Does receiving a specified amount of individual tutoring versus no tutoring . . . ?" Thus tutoring is the **independent variable** because it is antecedent to reading achievement, and the principal is predicting that the tutoring will have an effect on reading achievement, the **dependent variable.** Recall that the dependent variable is the outcome of interest, and the independent variable is hypothesized to influence the dependent variable. Now it becomes obvious that the word *tutoring* is too general. Unless all subjects receive the same type and amount of tutoring, the results of the study will be meaningless. Ms. Burke decides to use word flash drill as the specific type of tutoring and to specify 15 minutes per day as the amount of time.

The phrase "have a positive effect on" is quite vague until she looks at it in terms of her independent variable. Does word flash drill have an effect on . . . what? She knows it has an effect on word flash recall, but she wants to study its effects on other aspects of reading behavior that might be observed: expressive oral reading, silent reading, positive feelings toward reading, number of books read, comprehension, and so forth. But she is afraid that teachers might rate good word callers as comprehending more and being more positive toward reading, whereas they view the poorer word callers as more inferior on these variables than they really are. She wants a dependent variable that is independent of teacher judgment and decides to use reading scores from the California Achievement Test (CAT) as the dependent variable.

Ms. Burke's revised statement of the problem now reads "Among below-average second-grade readers, is there a difference in CAT reading scores between those who have received 15 minutes per day of individual word flash drill by upper-grade students and those who have received no word drill?" This question tells whom she is studying, what will be done differently for some students, and what she expects differential treatment to influence. Note also that the value judgment "positive effect" has dropped out of the question.

It is often useful to follow this procedure in a formal manner similar to that used for diagramming a sentence. You can begin by drawing a vertical line and writing *Population* to the left and *Variables* to the right. Then list these elements in the study below the horizontal line. For the preceding example, the diagram would be as follows:

Population	Variables
Below-average second-grade readers	Word flash drill for 15 minutes daily by upper-grade students versus no word flash drill (independent)
	Reading scores on CAT (dependent)

Let's take another question: "What is the effect of having experienced versus not having experienced a preschool program on the reading achievement of first-graders?"

Population	Variables
First-graders	Having experienced versus not having experienced a preschool program (independent)
	Reading achievement (dependent)

This question is complete in that it has an identified population and both the independent and dependent variables. Because "preschool program" precedes "reading achievement of first-graders," the former can be identified as the independent variable and the latter as the dependent variable.

Let's look at another example: "Does high school driver education do any good?" As it stands, the question has neither a population nor variables. An investigator starting with this question might first decide to compare 19-year-old drivers who have had high school driver education with those who have not. You now have a population statement and an independent variable. Now you can turn your attention to selecting a dependent variable. What effect might having versus not having driver education have on 19-year-old drivers? Let's say you decide that "accident rate" would be a suitable dependent variable. Putting these elements into a diagram, you now have the following:

Population	Variables
19-year-old drivers	Have had versus have not had high school driver education (independent)
	Accident rate (dependent)

You can now state a complete question: "Do 19-year-old drivers who have had high school driver education have a lower accident rate than 19-year-old drivers who have not had high school driver education?"

The question "What is the relationship of dogmatism to political attitudes among college freshmen?" illustrates another point. Consider this diagram:

Population	Variables
College freshmen	Dogmatism
	Political attitudes

This question is complete with a population and two variables. But you cannot label the variables as independent and dependent, because it cannot be determined which is antecedent to the other.

If you conduct a study to investigate status quo rather than a relationship between variables, it may be complete with only one variable. For example, you might study the opinions of college seniors concerning legalization of marijuana. In this case the population is college seniors and the single variable is their opinions on the subject.

The Journal Article

Identifying the population and the independent and dependent variables provides a framework for analyzing published quantitative research reports. The following journal article by Marsh (1984) illustrates the elements usually found in a report of an experiment. The introduction gives the rationale for the study and briefly summarizes previous thought and research on the topic. The methods section has several elements: (1) the sample (10 classes from five universities) is drawn to represent the population of interest (university students); (2) the independent variable (take-home versus in-class exams) is described and operationally defined; (3) the dependent variables (responses to a survey asking students how much they were motivated to study and learn in preparation for each type of exam, and scores on a surprise test of comprehension and application of the course material) are described and operationally defined; (4) the procedures are described in sufficient detail to enable another researcher to replicate the experiment with a different sample. The results section gives the data generated by the experiment and the results of the statistical tests. The conclusion section gives Marsh's interpretation of these results.

A Comparison of Take-Home versus In-Class Exams

This study was an effort to determine whether the take-home test was as good a vehicle or a better one for learning than the traditional in-class test. The results of this experiment are important because instructors are increasingly deleting the in-class tests (Gay and Gallagher, 1976), and there seems to be no empirical basis for the belief that the take-home test is as effective. Thus, the current trend toward eliminating formal written tests may actually operate against one of education's major goals: student retention of learned concepts.

Probably the major concern over classroom exams is that they cause debilitating anxiety. However, research on this claim is inconsistent. For example, it has been demonstrated that in a test situation anxiety has a negative effect (Sarason, Davidson, Lighthall, Waite, and Ruebush, 1960), a positive effect (Castaneda, McCandless, and Palermo, 1964), and no effect (Denny, Paterson, and Feldhusen, 1964) on test performance.

Some authors have hypothesized that it is the amount of anxiety that affects test performance. Anastasi (1976) argues that testing has a total positive effect if accomplished properly. She states that the relationship between anxiety and test performance is probably nonlinear and that some anxiety is good, while too much is detrimental. Many practices have been designed to dispel anxiety in the classroom test environment, but she points out that "the examiner's own manner and a well-organized, smoothly running testing operation will contribute toward the same goal" (Anastasi, 1976).

Although students experience different levels of anxiety before exams, it is probably not a good idea to eliminate testing for that reason alone. Our aim should not be to completely avoid stress, which is not possible in our world, but to learn how to recognize our typical response to stress and then try to adjust our coping style accordingly (Selye, 1978).

There is a paucity of specific literature comparing take-home and in-class exams. There is evidence that oral and written testing are equally effective and that either method is better than no testing at all (Calhoun, 1962). Also, studies show that academic achievement of undergraduate students is lower under a pass/fail grading system than under the standard grading system (Bain, Hales, and Rand, 1973; Gold, Reilly, Silbeman, and Lehr, 1971). In 1976 a study (Gay and Gallagher, 1976) was performed in which a large basic class of undergraduates was randomly divided into three sections. One section was given periodic take-home exercises; the second section was given periodic tests; and the third group was given a choice. It is interesting to note that no one in the third group elected to take tests. Except for these different treatments, all students were treated as equally as possible. At the end of the course a surprise exam was given, identical in all three sections. The results of the tests showed that the group that was given tests scored significantly higher than the other two.

This study differs from the preceding one in several ways. First, it included a variety of classes in the arts and behavioral and applied fields of study. Therefore, the results are likely to be generalizable to a wider audience. The study attempted to measure specific levels of learning as defined by the Bloom Hierarchy of Cognitive Learning (Bloom, Engelhart, Furst, Hill, and Krathwohl, 1956). Finally, an attempt was made to identify causality with regard to the results of the experiment.

Methods

Ten classes from five different universities were recruited as participants. There were 258 students in the total sample, which included classes in psychology, statistics, education, research, and history. Early in the academic semester each participating instructor was given a full verbal briefing on the procedures and a packet with instructions to be given verbatim. The students were told that one half would receive a take-home exam, that this was a scientific experiment, no one would be hurt by its results, and anyone who was not satisfied with his or her grade would have the option of taking another exam. It was expected that this procedure would have a neutralizing effect on the anxiety factor.

About two weeks before the midterm, the classes were randomized into two equal groups, A and B. In each class, randomly selected members of Group A were given a take-home test to be returned one week later. Members of Group B were given an identical in-class test. All tests used in this study were the multiple-choice type. The A Group submitted their completed exams at the same time that the B Group took their test in class. One week later a surprise exam was given to both groups during the regular class period. The latter covered the same material upon which they had been tested the previous week. Since members of both groups were taught by the same teachers under identical conditions, the experimental and control subjects received as equivalent an exposure as was possible with a classroom type of experiment. Only the treatment (type of test) differed for each class.

The surprise test had 50 multiple-choice questions, 25 of which measured knowledge and 25 measured a combination of comprehension and application of the course material. The latter categories included the first three levels of cognitive learning in Bloom's Hierarchy (Bloom et al., 1956). A survey was also attached to assist in determining the extent to which the students were motivated to study and learn in preparation for each type of exam. There was a 96.1 percent response rate to the questionnaire. Finally, a two-way analysis of variance was used. Because there were two groups in ten different classes, it was a 2×10 design (Ary and Jacobs, 1976).

Results

Group B (in-class exam) scored significantly higher than did Group A (take-home exam) in all categories of the surprise test. The subjects exhibited significantly more total learning, more knowledge, and more comprehension and application of the subject matter. The statistical analysis for each category thus revealed that the independent variable (type of test) and the dependent variable (learning) were highly related.

On the survey that was attached to the surprise test, one of the questions asked, "If you were a teacher and you wanted your students to really learn the subject matter, which type of test would you give?" Participant response was that 25.8 percent would give a take-home exam, 59.1 percent would give an in-class exam, and 15.1 percent were not sure. They appeared to say that the in-class exam was more effective, by a better than two-to-one margin.

Two questions were devised to determine participant attitudes toward preparing for a particular type of exam. The first question asked the student to place him-/herself on a continuum of one through ten, indicating the amount of effort put into studying the material covered on the teacher-made test given the week prior to the surprise test. The second question, also with a continuum of one through ten, asked how much study effort the student would have made had the other type of test (take-home or in-class) been assigned.

The A Group scored significantly lower on the first question. Thus, in effect, the students said that they would have studied harder had they been given an in-class exam. Conversely, the B Group scored significantly lower on the second question. One can interpret this as saying that they would have studied less had they been given a take-home exam. One conclusion that would explain the difference in learning between the groups is that those students who had the in-class test expended more effort, by their own admission.

Conclusion

These data present evidence in favor of an in-class test as opposed to a take-home test for a variety of college students enrolled in psychology, statistics, research, education, and history courses. In this experiment the type of test utilized had an effect on the amount of learning by the student on the first three levels of Bloom's Hierarchy of Cognitive Learning: knowledge, comprehension, and application. Clearly the in-class test was the superior treatment, and the students seemed to agree.

But, for many reasons, one cannot say that the classic in-class exam is the only valid method by which to promote effective learning. More research is needed, with emphasis on the goals and purposes of exams and on ways to measure and compare levels of learning in the affective domain.

THE PROBLEM IN QUALITATIVE RESEARCH

Qualitative researchers also begin with a problem, but they state it much more broadly than in quantitative research problem. A qualitative problem is a statement or question that indicates the *general* purpose of the study. Formulation of a qualitative problem begins with the identification of a general topic or an area you want to know more about. This general topic of interest is sometimes referred to by qualitative researchers as the "focus of inquiry." This initial broad focus provides the framework but allows for changes as the study proceeds. As the researcher gathers data and discovers new meanings, the general problem narrows to more specific topics and new questions may arise. For example, Villaume (2000) wanted to know more about the part that teachers play in the success of a school district's language arts reform effort. She felt that successful reform is more than just training teachers to use the new instructional programs, but rather links to the abilities and the willingness of teachers to accept and act on the uncertainty that accompanies change. From this general problem, she stated the specific problem: "The primary purpose of this study was to describe how teachers responded to the uncertainty inherent in language arts reform" (p. 18). She investigated the problem in a case study of one school system.

Whereas the quantitative researcher always states the problem before collecting data, the qualitative researcher may formulate problems after beginning to collect data. In fact, the researcher often does not present the final statement of the problem—which typically specifies the setting, subjects, context and aim of the study—until he or she has collected at least some data.

Sources of Qualitative Problems

Just as was true for quantitative researchers, beginning qualitative researchers can look to their personal experiences and interests, to the professional literature, or to current social issues and real-world concerns to find a potential problem. You need to identify an area or a topic about which you have a real interest. For example, a student might be interested in learning-disabled students and their integration into regular high school classrooms. You might look at adults who return to college—how do their experiences compare with those of young students just out of high school? What is adolescence like for young people with chronic health problems? What kind of relationship do school superintendents have with school board members? How do elementary school principals and assistant principals spend their time?

Once researchers have selected the initial focus of inquiry, they need to identify exactly what they want to know about that topic. The focus of inquiry is thus narrowed to the aspect of the phenomenon that will be explored in the research study. The focus of inquiry just mentioned can be stated as follows: "How do other students treat learning-disabled students? How do the learning-disabled respond? Although the qualitative researcher intuitively arrives at hunches about the phenomenon, he or she does not formulate an initial hypothesis that the study tests. Suppose you are interested in the general topic of violence in the schools. The researcher may have a theory that school violence results when students become alienated over a long period of time. Could this alienation begin in the early years of elementary school? Elementary teachers have long observed that some students are bullies and others become their victims. A qualitative researcher might use naturalistic observation to investigate this behavior in an elementary classroom over a period of time. The investigator could use videocameras and remote microphones to record instances of children being exposed repeatedly to negative verbal or physical actions on the part of one or more classmates. The researcher would want to interview the bullies to find out what they are thinking and what their motives and goals are. The victims would also be interviewed to learn about their feelings. The researcher might also look at gender differences in bullying behavior and the reaction of peers to this behavior.

Criteria for a Qualitative Problem

The following criteria guide the selection and statement of a qualitative problem:

1. The problem should be stated clearly at least in a general way.

2. It should be a problem that has some conceptual/theoretical framework. The problem should have some significance in relation to educational theory or to practice.

3. Investigation of the problem should be feasible. Will the researcher have access to a group of people or to a site? Can he or she complete the study in a reasonable time? Are financial resources adequate?

4. The problem should be one in which the researcher has a great deal of interest and experience. The researcher must also have the knowledge and skills necessary to collect the data and to analyze and interpret the results.

SUMMARY

The first task facing researchers is selecting and formulating a problem. To find a researchable problem, investigators may look to their personal experiences, to theories from which questions may be deduced, or to the current literature in some area of interest. They must evaluate the significance of the proposed problem in terms of specific criteria, asking questions such as "Will the problem contribute to the present body of knowledge? Does it have potential for leading to further research? Is it testable—that is, can the variables be observed and measured? How appropriate is the problem with respect to my interests, experience, and knowledge in the area? Do I have access to the data required by the problem, and are instruments available, or could they be constructed, to measure the variables? Can the data be analyzed and interpreted within the time available?" The question should not directly involve philosophical issues, nor should it be so general that a research undertaking is impossible. A quantitative research question asks about the relationship between certain variables. The statement of the question should identify the population of interest and the variables to be investigated. A qualitative research question indicates the general purpose of the study. There are criteria that the qualitative researcher follows in selecting and stating a problem for investigation. (See Chapter 14)

REFERENCES

Burton, R. V. (1963). Generality of honesty reconsidered. *Psychological Review, 70,* 481–499.

Dewey, J. (1933). *How we think.* Boston: Heath.

Erikson, E. H. (1959). *Identity and the life cycle: Selected papers.* Psychological Issue Monograph Series, 1(1). New York: International Universities Press.

Gamoran, A. (1993). Is ability grouping equitable? *Education Digest, 58,* 44–46.

George, P. S. (1993). Tracking and ability grouping in the middle school: Ten tentative truths. *Middle School Journal, 24,* 17–24.

Hartshorne, H., & May, M. A. (1928). *Studies in the nature of character: Studies in deceit.* New York: Macmillan.

Hunt, J. McV. (1965). Traditional personality theory in the light of recent evidence. *American Scientist, 53,* 80–96.

Marcia, J. E. (1980). Identity in adolescence. In J. Adelson (Ed.), *Handbook of adolescent psychology.* New York: Wiley.

Marsh, R. (1984). A comparison of take-home versus in-class exams. *Journal of Educational Research, 78,* 111–113.

National Academy of Education. (1991). Research and the renewal of education: Executive summary and recommendations. *Educational Researcher, 206,* 19–22.

Nelsen, E. A., Grinder, R. E., & Mutterer, M. L. (1969). Sources of variance in behavioral measures of honesty in temptation situations: Methodological analysis. *Developmental Psychology, 1,* 265–279.

Pallas, A. M., Natriello, G., & McDill, E. L. (1989). The changing nature of the disadvantaged population: Current dimensions and future trends. *Educational Researcher, 18*(5), 16–22.

Piaget, J. (1932). *The moral judgment of the child.* Glencoe, IL: Free Press.

Popham, J. (1991). A slice of advice. *Educational Researcher, 20*(9), 18, 35.

Schmidt, P. (1993). Debate over ability grouping gains high profile. *Education Week, 12,* 23.

U.S. Department of Labor, Secretary's Commission on Achieving Necessary Skills. (1991). *What work requires of schools.* Washington, DC.

Villaume, S. K. (2000). The necessity of uncertainty: A case study of language arts reform. *Journal of Teacher Education, 51,* 18–25.

KEY CONCEPTS

criteria for research problem statements

dependent variable

independent variable

population

research problem

sources for research problems

EXERCISES

1. In the Marsh article, identify (a) the active independent variable (b) the dependent variable(s), and (c) the constant.

2. Find a quantitative research report published in a journal, and answer the following questions based on your reading:

    a. What problem is investigated in the study?

    b. What is (are) the hypothesis(es)?

    c. What are the independent and dependent variables?

    d. Where did you find the problem and hypothesis(es) stated in the report?

    e. Were the problem and hypothesis(es) stated with sufficient clarity so that you knew exactly what was being investigated in the study?

3. Find a qualitative research report published in a journal and identify the
    a. Problem
    b. Methodology
    c. Findings
    d. Conclusions

4. Select a broad area in which you might be interested in doing research. Choose a particular aspect of this broad area and then identify a research problem that you would be interested in pursuing. State this problem in a form for research.

5. The following examples are inadequate statements of research problems. Restate each so that it becomes a specific question suitable for research.
    a. Coaching and performance on the Scholastic Assessment Test (SAT)
    b. Academic self-concept of learning-disabled adolescents
    c. Adolescents with diabetes
    d. Predicting achievement in the first year of law school
    e. Effectiveness of method X in the teaching of mathematical concepts
    f. Gender differences and mathematical reasoning abilities of talented preadolescents
    g. High school principals and the expulsion of students

6. Evaluate the following research problems:
    a. Have permissive child-rearing philosophies had an adverse effect on American education?

    b. What is the relationship between the preferred method of leg crossing and the intelligence of American college women?

    c. Considering recent empirical studies on math achievement, should "modern" mathematics be abandoned in the elementary school and replaced by traditional math?

    d. How do students perceive the role of the principal at Central Middle School?

    e. Should we allow prayer in the public schools?

7. State the most likely independent and dependent variables in the following studies:
    a. What is the effect of multiage classrooms on achievement in grades 1–3?
    b. What is the relative effectiveness of the whole-language and phonics approaches on reading comprehension of second-graders?
    c. What are the correlates of racial prejudice?
    d. Does taking Latin in high school have an effect on students' SAT-verbal scores?

8. List sources of research problems used by researchers and give an example of each.

9. What is the effect of children's reading of good books on their reading skills? Is this question researchable? If not, how would you suggest changing it so that it could be investigated empirically?

10. Classify the following studies as most likely being quantitative or qualitative. If quantitative, classify according to the methodology that would be used.
    a. "Adolescent Life and Ethos in a U.S. High School"
    b. "University Professors' Perspectives on Teaching"
    c. "Gender Differences in Performance on Standardized Mathematics Tests"
    d. "The Effect of Listening Skills Training on Reading Comprehension of Third-Graders"
    e. "Attitudes of Voters in Community X Toward the Use of Vouchers for School Tuition"

ANSWERS

1. a. Take–home versus in-class tests
    b. Scores on the surprise test and responses to the questionnaire items
    c. Subjects' status as university students

2. Answers will vary.

3. Answers will vary.

4. Answers will vary.

5. a. What is the effect of specific coaching for the SAT versus no coaching on students' performance on the SAT?
    b. How would you describe the academic self-concepts of a group of learning-disabled adolescents?
    c. What is life like for an adolescent with diabetes?
    d. What is the relationship of certain specified variables (such as undergraduate GPA or LSAT [Law School Aptitude Test] scores) and grades in the first year of law school?
    e. What is the effect of teaching Method X compared to an alternative method on the learning of mathematical concepts among first-graders?
    f. What is the relationship between gender and mathematical reasoning in talented preadolescents?
    g. How do high school principals reach decisions about expelling students?

6. a. This question involves a value judgment that is impossible to investigate empirically.
    b. This question is trivial, and answering it would make little contribution to knowledge.

    c. Research cannot answer questions of value; it can only provide information on which decisions can be based.
    d. Although the question could be researched, it is local in scope. Generalization to other situations would be problematic.
    e. This question involves a value judgment and as stated cannot be investigated empirically.

7. a. *Independent:* use or non-use of multiage classroom; *dependent:* measures of achievement in different areas
    b. *Independent:* whole-language and phonics approaches to teaching reading; *dependent:* measures of reading comprehension
    c. *Independent:* certain specified variables such as intelligence, age, education, socioeconomic background; *dependent:* racial prejudice
    d. *Independent:* having taken Latin or not; *dependent:* students' SAT-verbal scores

8. Educators' everyday experience; deductions from theory; related literature; noneducation sources

9. The terms *good books* and *reading skills* need to be defined. Restate as "What is the effect of children's reading of four designated classics on their vocabulary growth?"

10. a. Qualitative
    b. Qualitative
    c. Quantitative (ex post facto)
    d. Quantitative (experimental)
    e. Quantitative (survey)

 INFOTRAC COLLEGE EDITION

Use the keywords *theory* + *research* to locate research where the problem involved testing a deduction from an educational or psychological theory.

Chapter 4

Reviewing the Literature

After studying this chapter, the student will be able to

1 discuss the main functions that the review of the literature serves in research.

2 differentiate among major reference sources in education.

3 describe ERIC and other education-related indexes, explaining their similarities and differences.

4 explain how to use *SSCI* (*Social Sciences Citation Index*) in a review of the literature.

5 describe how to use the Mental Measurement Yearbooks as a source of information on tests and measuring devices.

6 detail a systematic progression of steps in organizing the literature, explaining the purpose of each step.

7 Understand the criteria to use in judging the merit of information on the World Wide Web.

8 Use Boolean operators to execute a search for research articles in ERIC or another on-line index.

Once having defined a problem, the investigator is naturally eager for action. How-ever, it is a mistake to rush headlong into planning and carrying out research in an area of interest. The topic must be related to relevant knowledge in the field. It is impor-tant for educators and others engaged in research to know how to locate, organize, and use the literature in their field. This chapter discusses (1) the role of related literature in a quantitative research project, (2) reference sources in education, and (3) the task of orga-nizing the related literature for presentation in the report.

THE ROLE OF RELATED LITERATURE IN A RESEARCH PROJECT

In quantitative research, the search for related literature should be completed before the actual conduct of the study begins. Qualitative research also involves a literature search, which may occur in another phase of the research (for example, the qualitative researcher may collect data, or observe phenomena, in order to develop a question or perspective that may then lead to a literature review); however, the researcher must always review the literature. This literature review stage serves several important functions:

1. *A knowledge of related research enables investigators to define the frontiers of their field.* To use an analogy, an explorer might say, "We know that beyond this river there are plains for 2000 miles west, and beyond those plains a range of mountains, but we do not know what lies beyond the mountains. I propose to cross the plains, go over the mountains, and proceed from there in a westerly direction." Like-wise, the researcher in a sense says, "The work of A, B, and C has discovered this much about my question; the investigations of D have added this much to our knowledge. I propose to go beyond D's work in the following manner."

2. *A thorough review of related theory and research enables researchers to place their ques-tions in perspective.* You should determine whether your endeavors are likely to add to knowledge in a meaningful way. Knowledge in any given area consists of the accumulated outcomes of numerous studies that generations of researchers have conducted, and of the theories designed to integrate this knowledge and to explain the observed phenomena. You should review the literature to find links between your study and the accumulated knowledge in your field of interest. Studies with no link to the existing knowledge seldom make significant contri-butions to the field. Such studies tend to produce isolated bits of information that are of limited usefulness.

3. *Reviewing related literature helps researchers to limit their research question and to clarify and define the concepts of the study.* A research question may be too broad to be

This chapter was revised and updated with the assistance of Jennie E. Ver Steeg, Founders Memorial Library, Northern Illinois University, DeKalb, Illinois; and Samuel T. Huang, Main Library, University of Arizona, Tucson, Arizona.

carried out or too vague to be put into concrete operation; for example, "What do parenting practices have to do with mental health?" A careful review of the literature can help researchers revise their initial questions so that the final questions can be investigated. The literature review also helps in clarifying the constructs involved in the study and in translating these constructs into operational definitions. Many educational and behavioral constructs—such as stress, creativity, frustration, aggression, achievement, motivation, and adjustment—need to be clarified and operationally defined. These, as well as many other educational and behavioral constructs, do not lend themselves to scientific research until they can be quantified. In reviewing literature, you become familiar with previous efforts to clarify these constructs and to define them operationally. Successful reviews often result in the formation of hypotheses regarding the relationships among variables in a study. These hypotheses can provide direction and focus for the study.

4. *A critical review of related literature often leads to insight into the reasons for contradictory results in an area.* Contradictory results are not uncommon. You may find the causes of inconsistencies in the kinds of approaches adopted for solving the problem or in the kinds of instruments employed, methodologies used, or analyses made. Comparing the procedures of these studies may explain the inconsistent findings. To resolve such contradictions is a challenge, but it can also provide a significant contribution to the knowledge in your field of interest.

    For example, in researching previous studies Bardwell (1984) found some literature supporting the contention that failure debilitates learning, and others supporting the contradictory view that failure facilitates learning. She hypothesized that failure is more debilitating for those who perceive that they have failed than for those who do not perceive that they have failed. She designed a study to test this hypothesis. First she gave college students thirty unsolvable perceptual judgment problems, then asked them if they thought they had succeeded or failed. Then she gave the subjects thirty similar but solvable problems. Contrary to her hypothesis, those who said they failed on the unsolvable problems scored *higher* on the subsequent solvable problems than those who said they had succeeded. Bardwell's tentative explanation for these results was that failure facilitated learning among students who perceived that they had failed on the unsolvable problems, by motivating them to try harder on the subsequent solvable problems. Subjects who thought they had succeeded on the unsolvable problems were not motivated to try harder on the subsequent solvable problems.

5. *Through studying related research, investigators learn which methodologies have proven useful and which seem less promising.* The investigator develops increasing sophistication after digging through the layers of research that the related literature represents. As you delve into your topic, you soon see that the quality of research varies greatly. Eventually, you should begin to notice that not all studies in any one field are necessarily equal. You will soon be critiquing studies and noticing ways in which they could be improved. For example, early studies in any one particular field may seem crude and ineffective, because research methodology

and design are constantly being refined with each new study. Even so, many research projects fail because they use inappropriate procedures, instruments, research designs, or statistical analyses. Becoming proficient at evaluating research to determine its worth, helps the investigator discover the correct research path.

6. *A thorough search through related research avoids unintentional replication of previous studies.* Frequently a researcher develops a worthwhile idea only to discover that a very similar study has already been made. In such a case the researcher must decide whether deliberately to replicate the previous work or to change the proposed plans and investigate a different aspect of the problem.

7. *The study of related literature places researchers in a better position to interpret the significance of their own results.* Becoming familiar with theory in the field and with previous research prepares researchers for fitting the findings of their research into the body of knowledge in the field.

REFERENCE SOURCES IN EDUCATION

It is clearly essential for scholars and researchers to know how to find previous work in their areas. To do this, you should know (1) sources for finding previous work, (2) what agencies collect and organize such information, (3) what forms the resulting databases take, and (4) efficient ways of finding the information you need. To use these sources, you must become familiar with available library facilities and services. Typically academic and larger public libraries have on-line or printed guides describing their services and regulations and can schedule orientation tours. It is especially important to learn how the library catalog, whether a card or an on-line catalog, is organized. Most research libraries have converted the traditional card catalog to an on-line catalog. As a general rule, libraries offer instruction in using various library resources, on-line or on CD-ROM, either in a formal class or in a one-on-one meeting with a librarian. Also, find out the library's policies and procedures for obtaining books and other materials, such as dissertations and periodical articles, from other institutions through interlibrary loan. Although most academic, public, and school libraries do have some method to obtain materials from other libraries, you will find that libraries vary on which materials may be ordered, who may order them, and whether a charge is involved.

Basic Guides

To begin a search of research studies, it is useful to consult basic guides to the research literature to gain a sense of the breadth of resources available. This is particularly true if you are engaged in research that may pull in the literature of more than one field or school, such as psychology, sociology, and women's studies. One of these helpful guides is *A Bibliographic Guide to Educational Research* (Berry, 1990). This guide is intended "as a concise guide to assist the student in education courses to make effective use of the resources of the library of his or her college or university." It provides an annotated listing of more than 700 major research sources arranged by types of materials, such as periodicals, research studies, government publications, reference materials, and tests. The reference materials include yearbooks, directories, bibliographical sources, and handbooks on the methodology of educational research and on form and style for writing research papers. O'Brien and Fabiano's *Core List of Books and Journals in Education* (1991) helps readers find authoritative information about education in the traditional formats of monographs and journals. Arranged by topic, it selects, describes, and in many cases evaluates sources for educational research. Balay, Carrington, and Martin's *Guide to Reference Books* (1996) briefly describes and evaluates several thousand reference sources from various subject fields, including education. This work is updated by means of biennial supplements. Wynar's *American Reference Books Annual (ARBA)*, published since 1970, covers the reference book output (including reprints) of the previous year in all subjects and provides descriptive and evaluative notes.

Reviews of Education-Related Literature

Reviews that integrate and summarize research studies on specific topics can help get you started on a literature search. They serve as very densely cited overviews of selected subjects in depth, and can provide an excellent way to extend your search by locating the sources the authors used to prepare their entries. There are several basic reviews that you can consult.

Alkin's *Encyclopedia of Educational Research* (1992), designed to present "a critical synthesis and interpretation of reported educational research," contains signed articles with bibliographies providing well-documented discussions of recent trends and developments, as well as traditional topics. This four-volume encyclopedia includes approximately 200 topics. It is a good basic source for preliminary overviews of research in various areas.

Walberg and Haertel's *International Encyclopedia of Educational Evaluation* (1990) has become one of the definitive works in the field of educational evaluation. The volume is divided into eight broad sections that cover evaluation studies, curriculum evaluation, measurement theory, measurement applications, types of tests and examinations, research methodology, and educational policy and planning. This is an essential work in locating scholarly discussions on fundamental concepts in all areas of educational evaluation.

Dejnozka and Kapel's *American Educators' Encyclopedia* (1991) consists of about 2000 short entries for names and terms frequently found in the literature of professional education. Husen and Postlethwaite's *International Encyclopedia of Education: Research and Studies* (1994) presents "an up-to-date overview of scholarship brought to bear on educational problems, practices, and institutions all over the world." It covers scholarly and professional work in education in the broad sense, surveying current developments in the various branches of education, the availability of scientifically sound and valid information relating to these developments, and the types of further research needed.

An impressive anthology dealing with international higher education, Altbach's *International Higher Education: An Encyclopedia* (1991) consists of 67 essays about major issues, themes, nations, and regions. A more comprehensive set is the ten-volume *International Encyclopedia of Higher Education* (Knowles, 1978), which includes 282 articles on contemporary topics in higher education written by educational leaders all over the world. Another similar source, Clark and Neave's *Encyclopedia of Higher Education* (1992), contains more than 300 articles and essays contributed by scholars from many countries and attempts "a far-reaching, extensive integration" of "the current international knowledge about higher education."

Recently, the influential *International Encyclopedia of Education* and the *Encyclopedia of Higher Education* have been made available together on a CD-ROM the publishers have titled *Education: The Complete Encyclopedia*. The CD version is searchable across both titles, searching for both works by subject, title, theme, contributor name, and authors cited within encyclopedia entries. It can be searched full text as well. An added feature that researchers may find useful is the linkage of references to full-text ERIC documents, where they are available.

Another useful review source is the *Handbook of Research on Teaching* (Gage, 1963; Travers, 1973; Wittrock, 1985). Three different editions, published about ten years apart, list, summarize, and critically analyze research in the field of teaching. Each edition contains authoritative articles by specialists on selected topics in the field. Comprehensive bibliographies are included, by selected topics. Among the topics in the third edition are "Measurement of Teaching," "Quantitative Methods in Research on Teaching," "Qualitative Methods in Research on Teaching," "Observation as Inquiry and Method," "Syntheses of Research on Teaching," "The Teaching of Learning Strategies," "Teacher Behavior and Student Achievement," and "Research on Teaching Arts and Aesthetics." A work similar in scope and authority, the *Handbook of Educational Psychology* (Berliner & Calfee, 1996), is an influential one-volume work summarizing the theory, methods, practice, and research in educational psychology.

Reynolds and Fletcher-Janzen's new *Encyclopedia of Special Education* (second edition, 2000) provides basic information for many disciplines and professions concerned with the education of exceptional children and with their special characteristics, needs, and problems. This three-volume encyclopedia contains more than 2000 topics. This second edition is arranged alphabetically, the various subjects grouped conceptually into seven major areas: biographies, educational and psychological tests, interventions and service delivery, handicapping conditions, related services, legal issues, and miscellaneous. Current handbooks similar in scope include the *Handbook of Research on Multicultural Education* (Banks & Banks, 1997) and the *Handbook of Research on Educational Administration* (Murphy & Lewis, 1999). The former consists of forty-seven chapters critically discussing major theory and research in the relatively new area of multicultural education. The authors discuss history, issues involved, and research problems in such areas as education of ethnic groups, immigration, and academic achievement. In the latter book, sponsored by the American Educational Research Association, eminent scholars discuss, in a cross-disciplinary approach, the last decade of research in the field of leadership and administration. Keogh's *Advances in Special Education,* published annually since 1980, presents comprehensive examinations of major fields and brief, more restricted evaluations of special areas in special education.

The *Review of Educational Research* is a publication of the American Educational Research Association (AERA). Since 1931 this quarterly has been publishing "integrative reviews and interpretation of education research literature on both substantive and methodological issues." Seeking to provide summaries of research within broad subject areas in the profession, AERA launched the series *Review of Research in Education,* published annually since 1973. This series aims to identify what research has been done, is being done, and needs to be done in the field. For instance, Volume 22 (1997) is organized around three major double themes: politics and policy, race and education, and teaching and research. It includes reviews of issues in professional development schools, markets and education, action research, and a history of race theory.

Psychological studies play an important role in education research. The *Annual Review of Psychology,* published since 1950, employs subject specialists to report on and evaluate research literature, identify trends and new developments in all aspects of psychology for each year, and indicate neglected areas. The now standard *Encyclopedia of Psychology* (Corsini, 2000), a four-volume set, contains 2500 entries, including biographies, and examines ten areas of psychology, including cognitive, developmental, and educational psychology. Its 500 expert contributors, 350-page bibliography, and extensive indexing make it a valuable source for researchers.

Periodical Indexes, Abstracting Sources, and Citation Indexes

Having established a broad base of relevant research, theory, and opinion on a particular topic of interest, you can begin to locate additional material not cited in the encyclopedic review sources just discussed, moving instead to the primary literature. You can efficiently access primary literature through **periodical indexes** and **abstracting sources.** These index and abstract sources enable you to locate more specific and usually more recently published literature on your topic of interest. Issued in successive parts at regular intervals, they serve as guides for finding information that is widely dispersed in journals and other sources. The publishers of these periodicals employ professional reviewers who survey and classify papers in published and unpublished sources. These papers are assigned several subject headings, from the thesaurus of descriptors used by the publishing agency, presenting researchers with a fairly comprehensive, reasonably up-to-date and easily searched listing of work in their areas. The abstracting periodicals publish abstracts of the works they include, also including descriptors which allow for searching of the collections.

The ERIC Database

The most important indexing system for educational literature is produced by the Educational Resources Information Center (ERIC), which the U.S. Department of Education (USDE) established in 1966 to collect, store, and disseminate information on education. Before the ERIC system was established, reports submitted to the Department of Education by its contractors and grantees received an initial scattered distribution and then disappeared, as did reports from other sources. Such materials, as reports from nongovernmental organizations, documents emanating from a school district, or papers presented at professional conferences, are examples of literature that tend to disappear. Not published in books or journals, they were thus infrequently indexed. ERIC was intended to correct this chaotic situation, to collect and preserve unpublished so-called fugitive material of interest to educators, and to make this store of information available to the public.

The **ERIC system,** funded by the National Library of Education and the U.S. Department of Education's Office of Educational Research and Improvement, gathers, indexes, and abstracts information for inclusion in the ERIC system through a central processing facility and a network of sixteen subject-oriented clearinghouses and twelve adjunct clearinghouses located at various universities and professional organizations across the country. Each clearinghouse is responsible for a specific educational area. The Education Resources Information Center's *Directory of ERIC Resource Collections* (http://www.ed.gov/BASISDB/EROD/eric/SF) lists institutions that provide microfiche access to nonjournal literature indexed in ERIC. A list of the clearinghouses and links to the Web sites of the clearinghouses can be found at http://www.accesseric.org/sites/barak.html. As ERIC, and the rest of the world, becomes more wired, each clearinghouse has begun to provide more services and publications on-line, through their Web sites.

When ERIC began, the ERIC abstracts were made available as paper periodicals, similar to the paper versions of, for example, *Reader's Guide to Periodical Literature,* in two sets, the *Current Index to Journals in Education (CIJE)* index, which indexes articles in education-related journals, and the *Resources in Education (RIE)* index, which indexes fugitive documents. These publications are still available, but it is now more typical to search both parts as a single ERIC database. Some on-line database providers still refer to the *CIJE* and *RIE* when they offer the option of limiting to journal articles (*CIJE*) or ERIC documents (*RIE*).

Articles from more than 800 journals are classified and indexed. Currently, more than 500,000 journal articles are indexed, and more than 400,000 documents are now included. The ERIC database contains over 980,000 records. The sources ERIC covers include scholarly journals, professional magazines, reports of all federally funded educational research plus abstracts, pamphlets, curriculum guides, significant papers from the proceedings of learned societies and institutes, bibliographies, exemplary course-related materials, teachers' guides and program outlines, as well as various other research proposals and project reports. With such far-ranging coverage it is clear that the documents in the ERIC collections are of vital interest to practitioners, as well as researchers in education.

Each piece of literature indexed in ERIC is assigned several subject headings (similar to those used in a card catalog) unique to the ERIC system, called ERIC *descriptors.* The *Thesaurus of ERIC Descriptors* (Houston, 1998) is available in most academic libraries. The vocabulary of the ERIC thesaurus is deliberately limited to provide a more systematic indexing system, so you may not be able to find a particular word or topic. In that case, you should look under synonyms for the topic. Figure 4.1 shows a thesaurus entry

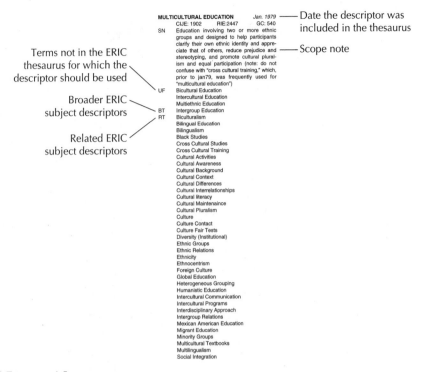

FIGURE 4.1

Example of an ERIC Thesaurus Entry

for the descriptor "multicultural education," demonstrating the breadth of subjects ERIC treats, and the type of descriptors assigned. It tells us that "multicultural education" was added to the thesaurus in January 1979, and that there are 1902 related articles in *CIJE* and 2447 related ERIC documents in *RIE*. The scope note gives the thesaurus definition of the phrase. Phrases that are not ERIC subject descriptors, for which the descriptor "multicultural education" is used, are listed under UF (use for), and related terms that are ERIC thesaurus descriptors are listed under RT (related terms).

Figure 4.2 shows a typical ERIC record to illustrate the type of information included in each entry. The abstract is particularly useful because, as in the example in Figure 4.2, the title alone gives only a partial idea of what the article is about. Each record is assigned its own accession number for the purpose of identification and for either ordering copies of the original documents from ERIC, if available, or for locating the microfiche, on-line, or hard copy of the ERIC document (depending on the resources of the library used).

Libraries may obtain individual microfiche copies of most original documents, or a standing order may be placed with ERIC to receive all documents as they become available.

Go to ... Help | Logoff

Available? ... Search ILLINET Online for library copy & volume info | Locate ERIC Document depository libraries in Illinois.
[Click "ILLINET Online" above and a new browser window will open. Standard numbers from your Ovid citation will be searched, in the IO location that corresponds to your Ovid signon. Press ALT-TAB to move between browser windows. Subsequent links from Ovid will reuse the open IO window.]

❏ **Citation 16**

Accession Number
> EJ496492

Author
> Silins, Halia C.

Title
> **Leadership** Characteristics and School Improvement.

Source
> Australian Journal of Education. v38 n3 p266–81 Nov 1994.

ERIC Subject Headings
> *Administrator Characteristics
> *Educational Change
> *Educational Improvement
> Elementary Secondary Education
> Foreign Countries
> ***Leadership** Qualities
> *Outcomes of Education
> *Principals
> Program Effectiveness

Identifiers
> Canada.

Abstract
> A study investigated the relationship between school principals' **leadership** behaviors and school outcomes in Canadian schools undertaking reform efforts. Results indicate **transformational leadership** behaviors were more effective than transactional **leadership** in enhancing school, teacher, program, instructional, and student outcomes. These findings support the importance of **leadership** in effective reform. (Author/MSE)

Publication Type
> REPORTS - Research/Technical. JOURNAL ARTICLES.

ISSN
> 0004 9441

Language
> English

Clearinghouse Code
> Higher Education.

Entry Month
> 199505

▒ FIGURE 4.2
Example of a CIJE Record

Most academic libraries have such an arrangement with ERIC, thus making available to their users the entire document collection in a convenient location. When a publication indexed by ERIC is under copyright, ERIC will give contact information for its source, but does not provide copies of the document. ERIC is invaluable for the field of education because it collects and abstracts, from a wide range of sources, relevant material for educational research, much of which was previously almost impossible to obtain. The ERIC clearinghouses also prepare annotated bibliographies on selected topics, create pathfinders (lists of sources designed to help researchers find information about a specific topic), and prepare digests of primary and secondary research on topics of current interest. Before preparing your own bibliography, it is a good idea to visit the Web site of the clearinghouse dealing with your field of interest to see if its staff already has such compilations that will be of value in conducting your literature search.

A more complete description of the ERIC system and how to use it, *All About Eric,* is accessible on the Web at http://www.accesseric.org/resources/allabout/toc.html. The clearinghouses of the ERIC network wish to make their collections as comprehensive as possible and therefore ask educators to submit relevant materials. If you have prepared a report, speech, or paper that you would like to have considered for national dissemination through ERIC, send a copy to the ERIC Processing and Reference Facility Acquisition Department, 1100 West St. 2nd Floor, Laurel, MD 20707-3598, or to the individual clearinghouse responsible for the relevant subject area. More complete information on submitting documents to ERIC can be found at http://ericfac.piccard.csc.com/submitting.html.

A generation ago a thorough search of relevant journals and documents for material related to a given research problem was a task of major proportions. Today, computerized access to the ERIC system makes it possible to conduct such searches efficiently by means of personal computer. The ERIC database is available on CD-ROM and on the World Wide Web, either by accessing it through one of the clearinghouse Web sites or through a commercial database made available by a research library. For example, to identify journal articles and documents that deal with the use of computer-based tutorials for ESL (English as a Second Language) students, the computer can be instructed to identify all documents and journal articles that have been given both the descriptor "English (second Language)" and the descriptor "Computer-assisted instruction." Electronic access to the ERIC system is increasingly the rule at institutions of higher learning and in school systems.

As a general rule, the following steps are components of a successful ERIC search.

1. Determine the key words under which articles relevant to your study might be listed. These key words will typically include the population and the variables you have identified in your problem statement.

2. Check the *Thesaurus of ERIC Descriptors* to find which of your key words are used as descriptors. You may need to find synonyms for the key words you have listed.

3. Perform the search and copy or print out the entire reference given for any title that may be useful. This procedure simplifies the task of finding the original articles.

4. Search out the articles in their journals at your own institution or through inter-library loan, or ask a librarian about the possibility of obtaining the articles on-line, either through your library or through other commercial sources.

5. Read the abstract first—if one accompanies the journal article—to determine whether it will be useful to read the entire article. If there is no abstract, start with the summary and conclusion sections.

A search of the ERIC system is an important step in the quest for related literature, but the researcher cannot assume that when this step is finished the quest is completed. Material relevant to your question may not have been included in the ERIC indexes.

Indexes of Dissertations and Theses

Master's theses and doctoral dissertations are very useful sources of information for researchers. They provide extensive bibliographies of possible sources, possible study procedures, instruments, or hypotheses that may serve as examples to either emulate or avoid. In addition to the periodical indexes and abstract journals that list some dissertations and theses, such as ERIC and *Psychological Abstracts,* several specialized guides and **indexes of dissertations and theses** can be very useful. *Dissertation Abstracts International (DAI),* published monthly since 1938, contains abstracts of more than a million doctoral dissertations submitted to University Microfilms International by cooperating universities (about 795 in 1999), going back to 1861. *DAI* is divided into three sections: humanities and social sciences, the sciences and engineering, and European universities. Electronic searches of *DAI* are available through several major on-line database vendors. A similar publication is *American Doctoral Dissertations.* It consolidates into one list the dissertations for which doctoral degrees were granted in the United States during the academic year covered, as well as those available on microfilm from University Microfilms. It includes a number of dissertations that are not included in *DAI. American Doctoral Dissertations* is arranged by subject and institution and has an author index, but no abstracts are provided. *Masters Abstracts International* (1986–) contains abstracts on microfilm of a selected list of master's theses from various U.S. universities and colleges. For a listing of master's theses from U.S. colleges and universities specific to the field of education, a good source is Silvey's *Master's Theses Directories,* which list theses written in participating U.S. and Canadian institutions in the previous year. Issued annually, it does not include abstacts but does provide bibliographical information for each thesis listed.

Social Sciences Citation Index

When you have found relevant and important articles, you can use a **citation index** to "move forward in time." For example, if you have read a particularly useful article published in 1986, through subsequent indexes you can identify more recent articles that cite this article and list it in their references. Many such articles describe continuations, expansions, or modifications of the original work of interest. You can see from the citation record of a given article how influential the article has been.

Most articles are cited heavily for five years after publication; articles that have a pattern of citation lasting much longer, or a burst of citations after several years of being infrequently cited, may be those you will want to examine to see why they have been cited or why there is renewed interest. From articles that are cited more often, you can also get a sense of the more influential journals.

Social Sciences Citation Index (*SSCI*), published by the Institute for Scientific Information since 1973 in three volumes a year, identifies which authors have been cited during the year in all areas of social science, including education, and what has been written in various areas. It also includes the necessary bibliographic information for both cited and citing authors. This information is made available by way of four indexes:

1. The *Source Index* is an alphabetical list of all authors published in the journals covered by *SSCI* during the year. Complete bibliographic information is provided for the articles published by these authors, followed by an alphabetical list of the first authors of each of the sources cited in each article. The *Source Index* is cross-referenced to secondary authors.

2. The *Citation Index* presents an alphabetic list of the first authors of all works cited in the articles included in the *Source Index,* followed by the year, journal, volume, and first page for each of that author's cited articles. For each article, the *Citation Index* lists the names of other authors who cited that article, followed by the journal, volume, first page, and year of the article in which the citation occurred. Thus the *Citation Index* lets you follow work in a particular area or of a particular author forward in time. For example, Huessy and Cohen's 1976 article, "Hyperkinetic Behaviors and Learning Disabilities Followed over Seven Years," an early longitudinal study, found a significant positive relationship between hyperactivity and learning disabilities. Its citation pattern illustrates both a common trend and the article's influence. It was cited frequently (eight times) in 1979 and 1980, with one or two citations a year after that. However, in the 1985 *SSCI,* we find this article was cited most frequently—nine times—in 1984–1985, nine years after its publication. This dramatic increase in citation apparently corresponded with increasing interest in and research examining the phenomenon of hyperkinetic behaviors. The article has been cited once or twice a year since 1985. Figure 4.3 shows the 1985 *SSCI* citation index entry for author H. R. Huessy (only the first author is included in *SSCI*). One of the article's most recent citations is in "Arithmetic Disabilities and ADD Subtypes" (Marshall, Schafer, & O'Donnell) in the May 1999 issue of *Journal of Learning Disabilities.* They found that hyperactive children who also had attention-deficit disorder (ADD) did less well on calculation and letter–word identification tests than did hyperactive children without ADD. Most articles are most heavily cited in the first couple of years after publication, becoming less frequently cited as time goes by.

First author ——— **HUESSY HR**

**UNPUB ATTENTION DEFI

BLOOMING.LM	PSYCHIAT J	9	175	84

66 MENTAL HLTH LIMITED

WELLS MH	PSYCH CL N	8	597	85

67 ACTA PAEDOPSYCHIATR   34   130

BERRY CA	PEDIATRICS	76	801	85
HOLBOROW PL	J LEARN DI	17	411	84
SATIN MS	J AM A CHIL	24	756	85
WALLANDE JL	ADV CL CH P R	8	113	85

69 J AM MED ASSOC 208 1613

GOODMAN WK	J CLIN PSY R	46	6	85

70 ACTA PAEDOPSYCHIATR   37   194

RANCUREL MD	PSYCHIAT AN	15	88	85

70 ACTA PAEDOPSYCHIATR   37   243

HOLBOROW PL	J LEARN DI	17	411	84
SHEKIM WO	J AM A CHIL	24	765	85

72 PROGR COMMUNITY MENT   206

POOLE DL	SOCIAL WORK	30	338	85

73 DRUG THERAPY SEP   52

EICHLSED W	PEDIATRICS	76	176	85

74 ACTA PAEDOPSYCHIATRY   40   230

Work being cited with year, journal, volume and page

GUALTIER CT	CLIN NEUROP	8	343	85

——— **76 PEDIATRICS   57   4**

GUALTIER CT	CLIN NEUROP	8	343	85
HOWELL DC	PEDIATRICS	76	185	85
HUESSY HR	PSYCHIAT J	10	114	85
LERNER JA	J AM A CHIL	24	42	85
WALLANDE.JL	ADV CL CH P R	8	113	85

Citing authors with journal, volume, page and year

79 CLIN EXPLORATIONS AD   19

GUALTIER CT	CLIN NEUROP	8	343	85

79 PSYCHIATRIC ASPECTS

BROWN RT	PSYCHOPH B	21	192	85
HOWELL DC	PEDIATRICS	76	185	85

80 THERAPEUTIC COMMUNIT

WELLS MH	PSYCH CL N	8	597	85

81 HOSP COMMUN PSYCHIAT   32   351

REATIG N	PSYCHOPH B R	21	329	85

84 ATTENTION DEFICIT DI   1

BLOOMING LM	PSYCHIAT J	9	175	84

84 PSYCHIAT J U OTTAWA   9   56

REATIG N	PSYCHOPH B R	21	329	85

85 J THER COMMUNITIES

WELLS MH	PSYCH CL N	8	597	85

FIGURE 4.3

SSCI Citation Entry (from 1985)

3. The *Permuterm Subject Index* takes every significant word and pairs it with every other significant word in each title. Each word in a title is then listed as a primary term combined with each of the other terms as co-terms. An alphabetical listing of the names of authors whose titles contain the words is provided for

each paired primary term and co-term. You can then find bibliographic information for each author in the *Source Index*.

4. The *Corporate Address Index* is an alphabetical listing of organizations with which authors publishing during the year are affiliated. Under each corporate entry is a list of authors with complete bibliographic information.

Social Sciences Citation Index (SSCI) is available in both paper and on-line formats. Neither is entirely efficient for the researcher. The conventional paper version is cumbersome and difficult to search, and the on-line or CD-ROM versions are expensive enough that relatively few academic libraries provide access to them. (That's the classic problem of using on-line information sources; you get what you—or your library—pays for!)

Government Publications

The federal government, a major source of education information, sponsors more research, conducts more surveys, and collects more statistics of all kinds than any other organization in the United States. The U.S. Department of Education (USDE) disseminates a vast number of publications, including research reports, surveys, administrative actions, and program descriptions.

For locating specific U.S. government publications, the U.S. Superintendent of Documents's *Monthly Catalog of U.S. Government Publications* (or its on-line counterpart *GPO Monthly Catalog,* published by the U.S. Government Printing Office, or GPO) is the prime index to consult. Its main section lists documents published by each agency, and it also includes title, author, subject, and title–key word indexes. Annual compilations by title and subject were included in each December issue until 1975; since 1976 there are six-month compilations. There are also five-year cumulative indexes for faster searching back through the years. The on-line GPO catalog has become very prevalent in academic libraries, because it is easy to search. It goes back to 1976.

You can locate publications of state departments of education and other state agencies through the home pages of each state's department of education Web site (a good resource to use in locating these Web sites is the National Association of State Boards of Education's linked list at http://www.nasbe.org/educationlinksbody.html#statelinks). Older publications can be located using the Library of Congress's *Monthly Checklist of State Publications,* which ceased publication in 1994.

As is true of nearly all indexes useful to scholars, most government indexes are now available on the World Wide Web or on CD-ROM. The gateways for government information and publications on education are the U.S. Department of Education Web site at http://www.ed.gov, and the National Center for Educational Statistics at nces.ed.gov. From these sites, you can find links to reports on current research, policy papers, and the searchable text of past and current popular paper resources, such as the *Digest of Education Statistics, Projections of Education Statistics,* and the *Condition of Education.* The purpose of the *Digest* is to provide a compilation of statistical information covering the broad field of American education from kindergarten through graduate school. The 1998 *Digest* includes 428 tables from many different data sources. *Projections of Education Statistics to 2009* provides projections for key education statistics. It includes statistics on enrollment, graduates, classroom teachers, and expenditures in elementary and secondary schools, and institutions of higher education. The tables, figures, and text contain data on enrollment, teachers, graduates, and expenditures for the past fourteen years and projections to the year 2009. The *Condition of Education* describes the current status and recent progress of education in the United States. The 1999 compendium features an overview essay and sixty indicators in five major substantive areas of education.

Test Sources

A test or measuring device is often required for conducting research, but few researchers have such extensive knowledge of the tests and instruments available to them that they can choose one without consulting expert **test sources.** *Mental Measurements Yearbooks* (*MMY*) (Impara & Plake, eds.) are important reference sources that list and provide critical reviews of some length. Published since 1938, these books are specifically designed to help users in education, psychology, and industry use standardized tests more intelligently. Each yearbook is arranged in the same pattern and is meant to supplement rather than supersede the earlier volumes. Tests are grouped by subject, and descriptions of each test are followed by critical reviews and references to studies in which the tests have been used. Each volume has cross-references to reviews, excerpts, and bibliographic references in earlier volumes. The volumes include aptitude and achievement tests in various subject areas, personality and vocational tests, and intelligence tests. Complete information is provided for each test, including cost and ordering information. *Tests in Print V* (Murphy, Impara, & Plake, 1999) serves as an index and supplement to the first thirteen *Mental Measurements Yearbooks.* The Buros Institute of Mental Measurements and other commercial database providers also offer on-line and CD-ROM access to the *MMY.*

Maddox's *Tests: A Comprehensive Reference for Assessments in Psychology, Education and Business* (1997), along with its supplements, is a standard reference work that includes more than 3000 tests available in English. Each test has been given a primary classification and is described in detail in one of the sections and may be cross-referenced in a second category.

Since 1984, Keyser and Sweetland's *Test Critiques* has provided general descriptions and critiques of measurement instruments and also has included a useful cumulative subject index of tests by type of variables. Specialized guides to tests include Compton's *Guide to 75 Diagnostic Tests for Special Education* (1984), Ostrow's *Directory of Psychological Tests in the Sport and Exercise Sciences* (1996), *Tests in Microfiche: Annotated Index* (1975–1994), and the *Educational Testing Service Test Collection Catalog* (1986–1993).

Information about tests may also be found in periodical indexes, ERIC, *Education Index, Exceptional Child Education Resources* (*ECER*), and *Psychological Abstracts,* where tests are listed under their specific name in the subject index. You can also search under such subject headings as "Tests" and "Test Reviews." A *Consumer's Guide to Tests in Print* (Hammill, 1992) fills a gap in the literature of test criticism, in that it is the only source in which all tests covered are reviewed by means of a standardized evaluation form. You can use this book to select an appropriate test, to teach the process of test evaluation, and to improve the quality of tests.

Dictionaries

Almost every academic discipline has its own specialized vocabulary. It is the function of a subject dictionary to briefly explain the words—whether terms or names—that make up a particular discipline's jargon. There are several basic **specialized dictionaries** in the field of education. Good's *Dictionary of Education* (1973) is a scholarly dictionary of more than 33,000 words and terms that have special meaning in the educational field. Educational terms used in Canada, England, and Wales are defined in separate sections at the end of the dictionary. Although Good's dictionary is dated, it is considered a classic in the field. A somewhat more recent work, *The International Dictionary of Education* (Page, Thomas, & Marshall, 1980), includes more than 10,000 entries covering expressions and terms, international organizations, major national institutions and associations, educators, and the like.

The first volume of Husen and Postlethwaite's *International Encyclopedia of Higher Education* (1985) also includes brief definitions of acronyms and a glossary of terms. More recent general education dictionaries are *The Cyclopedic Education Dictionary* (Spafford, Pesce, & Groser, 1998), providing over 10,000 definitions, including World Wide Web and legal terminology, and the *Dictionary of Multicultural Education* (Grant & Ladson-Billings, 1997), which provides more in-depth coverage of 150 terms and contextual examples. In the area of special education, the *Special Education Dictionary* (Gorn, 1997) is a current, high-quality, short-entry comprehensive work.

Statistical Sources

For educational statistics, the federal government, followed by states and local governments, accounts for the greatest number of statistical documents. *Statistics Sources* (O'Brien & Wasserman, 2000), a basic **statistical sources** reference work, is an alphabetic guide to sources of information on over 20,000 subjects, with 10,000 citations from over 2000 sources, print and nonprint, in print and out of print, U.S. and international. It is a subject guide to data on various topics, including education, for the United States and other nations. The 2000 edition of this work also includes listings of the Federal Statistical Databases and Federal Statistical Telephone contacts. Several other commonly known reference works—such as *World Almanac and Book of Facts, Information Please Almanac,* and *Statistical Abstract of the United States*—contain statistics from educational fields and other subjects. In general, the data are reliable and sources for many of the statistics are also given.

Three indexes to statistics published by the Washington-based Congressional Information Service are the *American Statistics Index (ASI), Statistical Reference Index (SRI),* and *Index to International Statistics (IIS).* The ASI indexes and abstracts almost every statistical source issued by the federal government, and the SRI indexes and abstracts state documents. The latter also includes many nongovernmental statistics, ranging from those issued by private concerns and businesses to nonprofit organizations and associations. The IIS includes major governmental statistics from around the world. It is an excellent source of U.N. statistical data. These three indexes are also available in CD-ROM and on-line. Besides these three indexes, *Education Index* and *Education Abstracts* are also valuable sources for locating educational statistics.

Since 1962, the *Digest of Education Statistics* has covered the broad field of American education from kindergarten through graduate school. This publication includes a selection of data from many sources, both government and private, and draws especially on the results of surveys and activities carried out by the National Center for Education Statistics (NCES). As noted previously, the full text of the digest and other important statistical publications are searchable through the NCES Web site (http://nces.ed.gov).

Other Periodical Indexes

There are many other periodical indexes in the field of education that are useful for locating up-to-date information on research, as well as contemporary opinion. *Exceptional Child Education Resources (ECER)* is a quarterly publication that contains abstracts of resources in special and gifted education. It uses the same thesaurus, indexing and abstracting rules that ERIC does, and there is considerable overlap in resources indexed by ERIC and ECER.

One of the standard indexes for the field is the *Education Index,* which has been published regularly since 1929. This index lists articles in 478 periodicals, yearbooks, bulletins, proceedings, and monographic series. Ninety-two of these 478 periodicals are not indexed by ERIC. *Education Index* is the best source for locating journal articles published prior to the establishment of ERIC, as well as for very recent articles, as it typically lists articles about six months before ERIC does. A disadvantage of the *Education Index* is that it has few annotations. *Education Abstracts,* an electronic version of the *Index,* contains abstracting and indexing coverage for all 478 periodicals included in *Education Index,* as well as 133 additional periodicals.

In addition to these general indexes, a number of useful specialized indexes are available to the researcher. *Psychological Abstracts* lists the world's literature in psychology and related disciplines. Published since 1927 (indexing materials back to the 1890s), this index includes books, doctoral dissertations, and periodical articles, with a summary of each, enabling the reader to determine the relevance of the material. *Child Development Abstracts and Bibliography,* also published since 1927, provides an author and subject approach to the areas of infancy, clinical medicine and public health, counseling, and developmental, comparative, and experimental psychology. *Educational Administration Abstracts* provides an author and subject approach to specialized journals in the field of educational administration. *Higher Education Abstracts* is a compilation of abstracts from journals, conference proceedings, and research reports relating to college students and student services. Topics covered include counseling and housing, financial aid, and testing and measurement.

There are specialized indexes for every discipline, including business education, industrial arts, and medicine, to name only a few. Some are available electronically and some in paper; many are available through both. The availability of either format depends on the library and its users' needs, the quality of the electronic version of the index, cost, and other factors. Consulting the basic guides to the literature or consulting a librarian will give researchers the names of the specialized indexes in other fields that they may need.

Using Electronic Indexes and Abstracts

Nearly all medium and large academic libraries, and most smaller institutions, provide on-line access to indexes and catalogs. Many offer brief training sessions to teach users how to do their own searches or provide FAQs (lists of frequently asked questions) or training materials on the library's Web page. Most of the sources cited in this chapter have been incorporated into on-line databases, including *Education Index,* the *ERIC Indexes, Exceptional Child Education Resources, Psychological Abstracts, Social Sciences Citation Index, Dissertation Abstracts International,* and Impara and Plake's *Mental Measurements Yearbooks* (MMY). In addition, there are many other useful on-line databases, such as the *AIDSLINE* database, *Educational Testing Service Test Collection Catalog* (ETS), and *Sociological Abstracts.* One extraordinary database that is invaluable to researchers in nearly any field is *WorldCat,* an on-line database of nearly 32 million books, journals, music scores, videorecordings, films, newspapers, maps, dissertations, manuscripts and more, in 400 languages. The index includes all the holdings of most academic libraries of size, larger public libraries and specialized collections, and the national libraries of France, Great Britain, Canada, and the U.S. Library of Congress, to name a few. Although no abstracts are given, the libraries that hold each item are listed as part of the item records; this can be helpful information for either the researcher or the interlibrary loan staff to use in obtaining an item.

A large, complex index such as *WorldCat* would not be possible without on-line searching and indexing capabilities. No book or multivolume set could ever be that large! In fact, on-line searching affords several advantages, no matter the size of the index. First of all, it saves time. When there are several synonymous or analogous terms for the concept(s) involved, (such as *attention-deficit disorder, ADD, ADHD, hyperactivity, attention deficit*), in only seconds the computer can retrieve and print information, thus eliminating hours or even days for a manual search. Second, it is current. On-line databases are frequently updated weekly or biweekly and thus are usually more up-to-date than printed indexes. Third, it allows combined searching. When the research topic combines two or more subjects, the database software can search more than one topic at the same time. Fourth, computer searching allows greater precision than human searching. When a subject cannot be easily identified in printed indexes, the computer provides access by searching titles, words in the abstract, journal title, key words, subject codes, or additional subject headings that paper indexes do not offer. On-line computer searching can also bypass superfluous information by specifying parameters such as date and type of publication, publication type, or language of publication. A fifth benefit is uniqueness. Some

Shaded areas represent what is retrieved
by each logical statement.

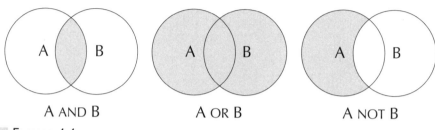

A AND B   A OR B   A NOT B

FIGURE 4.4
Boolean Logic

databases provide information that is not available in printed sources. Sorting functions are another important advantage. On-line searches can sort retrieved information according to publication date (descending or ascending order), or alphabetically by author or by title.

For most contemporary researchers, using electronic sources is the research method of choice. In a manual search you must examine numerous periodical indexes for a particular topic, follow the topic through the indexes, and find a few relevant entries that combine the selected term with another of interest. Computer searching, however, can search for many topics at the same time and combine them, using logical concepts known as **Boolean logic** (from the logic system developed by the 19th-century English mathematician George Boole). Figure 4.4 illustrates this concept. Using Boolean operators, "A AND B" asks for those items that have both key terms. For example, in August 1999 a search of the ERIC database using the Firstsearch interface found 8407 items with the major descriptor "adult students" and 6219 items with the major descriptor "mathematics education." Twenty-one item records that contain both descriptors were identified. If the researcher requests "A OR B," the computer searches for items that have either or both of the key terms. For example, a request for mathematics education or mathematics achievement would yield items that contain either or both of these terms. A typical search will use both these strategies. For instance, an adult educator interested in mathematics education would use OR statements to include various key terms that might cover the domain of adult education and OR statements to include various items that might cover the domain of mathematics education, together with an AND statement to link the two domains (factors).

More important than the mere existence of Boolean searching is the fact that searching on-line or CD-ROM indexes requires the use of a kind of logic that many students and researchers do not use frequently or really think about elsewhere in their research. It can be difficult to think of terms, possible synonyms for those terms, or how best to construct a search without first gaining experience or seeking the help of an expert, be it a collection of FAQs or a librarian. As well, the searching software used by these sources evolves, so that one mode of searching a database, such as ERIC, may provide a very different way of combining terms than another mode of accessing it, such as using pull-down menus, typing the Boolean operators manually, or using a mapping function to enter the on-line thesaurus directly. There will always be a librarian or other expert who can help researchers learn to get the most out of any database they may need to use.

The Internet

The statistics on the magnitude of Internet usage are both astonishing and conflicting, ranging from 75 to 154 million users worldwide in 1998. Nearly 85 percent of incoming freshmen in a 1998 University of California study reported using the Internet for research (Honan, 1999), and in 1996 the American Library Association reported that 87 percent of doctorate-granting universities' libraries had Web pages from which to access resources or get library information (Lynch, 1996). The **Internet,** originally developed in the 1960s by the U.S. Department of Defense and further developed by the science community for use as a communication medium, is a network of networks. Prior to the development of the **World Wide Web,** which uses hyperlinking and graphical interfaces (enabling searchers to click rather than remember the addresses of every site they want to access), few people aside from scientists used the Internet, which was used primarily for file transfer, archiving, and e-mail. Since the Web has been available to consumers, the growth in Internet use, and in the variety of uses, both legitimate and suspect, has been unprecedented. By linking information, computer resources and human insight, the Internet can help researchers access different databases on various subjects around the world. For example, to obtain information on assessment, you can use the Internet to access the databases of the ERIC Clearinghouse on Assessment and Evaluation (ERIC/AE) at the University of Maryland (http://www.ericae.net). Resources available through this clearinghouse include the Educational Testing Service (ETS) Test Collection database, which provides a system for searching more than 9500 test descriptions, and citations to the *Mental Measurements Yearbooks'* descriptions and reviews of specific tests (see Impara & Plake, 1998).

The strength of the Internet, however, namely its size and comprehensiveness, can work against the beginning researcher, and may confound even the most experienced researcher. The old problem of not finding enough information has now been replaced by the equally vexing problem of finding far too much information, and needing to be able to determine the relative quality of the information.

Many new researchers are surprised to find out that search engines such as Yahoo!, Northern Light, or Google do not search for information in the same way a periodical index or on-line library catalog does—even though the resulting list of "hits" you get searching the former looks very much like the result of a search of the latter. Whereas searching ERIC, for example, usually includes searching by ERIC subject descriptors—created by ERIC and assigned by ERIC to each record—few search engines use what is called a "controlled vocabulary." Instead, the search engine may search the entire document for the term or terms typed in, may search the titles, Web addresses, internal metadata tags, page headings, or may search them all and employ a kind of weighting system to construct a list of results. According to Danny Sullivan (2000), Internet consultant and author of *Search Engine Watch* (www.searchenginewatch.com), search engines may also check to see if the search term appears near the top of a Web document, the frequency of a particular key word, even the number of sites with links to the page to determine relevancy and assign a weighted score, putting a given Web page higher in the list of results the search engine provides. Although you nearly always find *something* when searching the World Wide Web using a search engine, the likelihood that what you find is useful is considerably lower than if an unsuspecting novice researcher were searching an index with a "controlled vocabulary."

Also, because there is no real "publication cycle" for Internet materials, there are no editors, fact checkers, proofreaders, and no accurate way for the reader to determine the authority of the author, as there is in traditional publishing. A huge amount of information exists on the Internet, some erroneous, outdated, slanted, and even harmful. The Web sites of hate groups, Holocaust revisionists, conspiracy theorists, and other biased authors are the more extreme examples, but one can also find such things as a free on-line Webster's Dictionary—copyright 1913!

It is often more difficult to determine the worth of a Web site than that of a paper source, because many personal sites look every bit as professional and authoritative as a governmental or educational site. Many libraries and organizations provide lists of subject-specific Web sites for researchers. They usually serve as excellent starting points, such as the American Federation of Teachers' Research Related Web Sites page (http://www.aft. org/research/rel_site.htm) or the Illinois State University library's Education Resources page (http://www.mlb.ilstu.edu/ressubj/subject/educat/home.htm). Eventually, however, the researcher will need to branch out.

When you begin to evaluate a source on the Internet, you first need to consider what the Internet is—and what it isn't. The Internet is not created equal; that is, even though all the information found on the Web appears on the computer desktop, some is provided by authoritative sources, using the technology to serve as the medium for the message, and some is not. The on-line version of ERIC or *Psychological Abstracts* is free to a student, and the student can access it from home and can download or e-mail portions of the database, but the information comes from an established provider, or has been purchased for use by the university library. It is thus a credible, authoritative source, using the Internet as a publication medium. This is one reason why it is important to pay careful attention to the address of the Web sites used, and their authors and sponsors, because saying, "I found it on the Internet" is rather like saying "I read it on a piece of paper." (Was it an authoritative piece of paper?)

You can also find many Web pages on education-related topics by using a search engine such as Google, Northern Light, or Hotbot. You can find a great deal of information on nearly any topic by doing this global kind of search. An August 1999 search for the term "Ebonics" using the Yahoo! search engine results in two category matches, seventeen site matches, and 6049 Web pages. Examination of the first page of Web page results found letters to the editor to on-line newspapers, an Ebonics parody of *the Night Before Christmas,* interviews, archived listserv messages and statements of philosophy on school district web pages—but little, if any, primary research. Because the Internet is a means by which information of such varying quality can be presented—the worthy and suspect side by side—it is important that the researcher has criteria by which to judge Internet sources. For example, determining the quality of a given nonelectronic journal's articles has traditionally focused on such criteria as

Reputation of the journal

Stringency of its editorial policies

Reporting of primary research, as opposed to feature articles synthesizing or summarizing bodies of research for the lay audience

Use of blind reviews

Reputation of its reviewers

Journal's affiliation with distinguished learned societies

Presence or absence of advertising

Audience for which the journal is intended, scholarly versus the lay audience

All these criteria have been used as ways to determine the relative worth of a particular journal source. These criteria help a novice researcher determine whether the article he or she is looking at is likely to be of high quality. However, when accessing research from Web versions of formerly paper-based journals, journals that exist solely in electronic form, or accessing the full text of articles from a variety of sources using a database such as ERIC as a gateway to full text content, these criteria become less easily applied, even irrelevant. A Web-based magazine for the general reader may look as professional and authoritative as a governmental or educational site, and the standards used or editorial policies can be difficult to determine. In particular, it is increasingly common to access articles through aggregated databases such as ERIC, in which the database provider removes the traditional quality markers, so that an article from the popular *Psychology Today* is presented exactly like one from the scholarly *Journal of Developmental Psychology*. In these cases, it becomes especially important that the student look beyond the traditional "markers" to judge the substance, the content, and the source material.

Authority

Is the author of the resource identified? Is a "snail mail" address or e-mail address given so that you can contact him or her? Is the author affiliated with a university, professional organization, or community organization? Is there a link to the sponsoring group's home page, a description of the group, or contact information? For information found on the Web, what is the site extension? Web addresses end in a suffix such as ".edu" or ".com." This suffix gives the researcher an idea of who is hosting the Web site, as follows:

.com	A commercial site
.edu	A college or university
.gov	The U.S. government
.us	Usually a state government, community college or school district site
.org	An organization
.net	A community network or Internet service provider

Although you cannot be assured of the quality of information in any kind of site, educational and governmental sites usually contain authoritative information. Information provided by companies may be slanted to sell the company's products. In fact, it may be hard to distinguish between an advertisement and a source of objective information.

Accuracy

Is the resource part of an edited publication; has it been selected by a reviewer or editor? Are factual statements supported with bibliographies, endnotes, links to the sources used? Are statistics given dates or are the sources cited?

Timeliness

Is it clear when the information was originally published? For Web-based information, is there a date listed when the page was last updated? If there are links given to outside Web pages, are the links still active, or are they linking to sites that have moved or changed address?

Useful introductions to the Internet include *The Whole Internet: The next generation: A Completely New Edition of the First and Best User's Guide to the Internet* (Krol & Conner-Sax, 1999), and *The Internet for Dummies* (Levine, Baroudi, & Young, 2000). Academic libraries frequently offer assistance in learning to assess the quality of Web information, or provide handouts.

ORGANIZING THE RELATED LITERATURE

Once you are satisfied that you have carried out a reasonably comprehensive search of the literature in the field, you can proceed to the task of organizing it. A useful approach is to arrange the studies by topic and determine how each of these topics relates to your own study.

Avoid the temptation to present the literature as a series of abstracts. Rather, it should lay a systematic foundation for the study. Present the literature in such a way as to justify carrying out your study by showing what is known and what remains to be investigated in the topic of concern. The hypotheses provide a framework for such organization. Like an explorer proposing an expedition, the researcher maps out the known territory and points the way to the unknown territory to be explored. If your study includes several facets or investigates more than a single hypothesis, the organization process is done separately for each one.

It is almost inevitable that a number of the reports you have carefully studied and included in your notes will, on reflection, prove only peripherally related to the topic. It is neither necessary nor desirable to include in a proposal every study encountered in the search through the literature. Your readers will not be impressed by mere quantity. Relevance and organization of the material are of prime importance.

The researcher who fails to approach the task of assembling the related literature in a systematic manner from the beginning can become very disorganized. The following suggestions may be of assistance. Your university, department or research adviser may offer help sessions or minicourses, and the librarians at most institutions can also provide helpful suggestions.

1. *Begin reading the most recent studies in the field and then work backward through earlier volumes.* An obvious advantage of this approach is that you start with studies that have already incorporated the thoughts and findings of previous research. Earlier misunderstandings have been corrected, and unprofitable approaches have been identified. Another advantage is that these studies include references to earlier works and therefore direct you to sources you might not otherwise encounter. Obviously, limits must be set to the process of gathering related research. On the one hand, laying meaningful groundwork for a study entails including all the important works in the field. On the other hand, devoting excessive time to this endeavor could result in boring the readers of your own report with super- fluous detail. Make sure the related literature serves, but does not dominate, your own work.

2. *Read the abstract or summary sections of a report first to determine whether it is relevant to the question.* Doing so can save much time that might be wasted reading un- helpful articles.

3. *Before taking notes, skim the report quickly to find those sections that are related to the question—another way to save reading time.*

4. *Make notes, either on file cards, in a word processing program, or in some format that can be accessed easily, or moved around to cluster with other notes on related research; this begins to organize the review.*

5. *Write out a separate complete bibliographic reference for each work. For the sake of record- keeping, include the reference in the bibliography list and with the individual "notecard" with the notes on the source.* A bibliography typically includes author, title, pub- lisher, year, issue and volume numbers, and/or the Universal Resource Locator (URL) or Web address, the date you accessed an electronic source, and other information depending on the type of sources. Follow the most recent edition of the chosen style manual for citing references. There are Web sites that provide help in using the American Psychological Association (APA) and Turabian style manuals (see Chapter 17), which may be good places to begin. Add the library call number, location of the terminal, or URL of the source, to facilitate finding the work again, should it be necessary.

6. *To facilitate sorting and organizing, do not put more than one reference on each page, entry, or card.* It is not possible to arrange references alphabetically or in any other way unless they are recorded singly.

7. *Be sure to indicate which parts of the notes are direct quotations from the author and which are your own paraphrases.* Failure to make this distinction can lead to inad-

vertent plagiarism. It is also wise to clearly separate the author's evaluation of his or her research from your own conclusions.

8. *If you have searched on-line databases, keep the search strategies (often called "search histories") on file. Typically, any given database will give the option of printing out a search history, the list of searches typed in, along with the results.* This information will help retrieve information and reduce cost and time in case an update is needed.

SUMMARY

If the researcher covers the avenues to information in his or her area as suggested, the result should provide a reasonably complete picture of the place the study occupies within the field. Table 4.1 summarizes important sources and contents of related literature in education.

REFERENCES

AIDSLINE. (1980–). Available: Internet Grateful Med at http://igm.nlm.nih.gov

Alkin, M. C. (Ed.). (1992). *Encyclopedia of educational research* (6th ed., 4 vols.). New York: Macmillan.

Altbach, P. G. (Ed.). (1991). *International higher education: An encyclopedia* (2 vols.). Hamden, CT: Garland.

American Doctoral Dissertations. (1957–). Ann Arbor, MI: University Microfilms.

American Statistics Index. (1973–). Bethesda, MD: Congressional Information Service.

Annual Review of Psychology. (1950–). Stanford, CA: Annual Reviews.

Balay, R., Carrington, V. F., & Martin, M. S. (Eds.). (1996). *Guide to reference books* (11th ed.). Chicago: American Library Association.

Banks, J. A. & Banks, C. A. (Eds.). (1995). *Handbook of research on multicultural education.* New York: Macmillan.

Bardwell, R. (1984). Failure: Facilitating or debilitating? *Journal of Experimental Education, 52,* 192–194.

Berliner, D. C., & Calfee, R. C. (1996). *Handbook of educational psychology.* New York: Macmillan.

Berry, D. M. (1990). *A bibliographic guide to educational research* (3rd ed.). Metuchen, NJ: Scarecrow Press.

Child Development Abstracts and Bibliography. (1927–). Lafayette, IN: Purdue University, Society for Research in Child Development.

Clark, B. R., & Neave, G. R. (Eds.). (1992). *The encyclopedia of higher education* (4 vols.). Tarrytown, NY: Pergamon Press.

Compton, C. (1984). *Guide to 75 diagnostic tests for special education.* Belmont, CA: Fearon Education.

Table 4.1 Important Sources of Related Literature in Education

SOURCE	CONTENT
Child Development Abstracts and Bibliography	Abstracts of journal articles in the field of child development
Current Index to Journals in Education	Citations of journal articles related to education, with annotations where needed. Indexed by subject, by author, and by journal; no abstracts
Dissertation Abstracts International	Abstracts of doctoral dissertations in the United States, Canada, and Europe
Education Index / Education Abstracts	Citations of journal articles related to education. The *Index,* the paper version, is indexed by subject and title. No abstracts. The *Abstracts,* an on-line version, contains abstracting and indexing coverage for all 478 periodicals included in *Education Index* and 133 additional periodicals. Fully searchable.
Educational Resources Information Center (ERIC) main page (www.accesseric.org).	Access to the Web pages of all ERIC clearinghouses, with access to links and on-line documents
Encyclopedia of Educational Research	Summaries and evaluations of published research at the end of each decade
Exceptional Child Education Resources	Abstracts of journal articles and other sources in special education
Mental Measurements Yearbooks	Information and evaluations of commercially available tests
Monthly Catalog of Government Publications	Subject listing of U.S. federal government publications
National Center for Educational Statistics (nces.ed.gov)	Provides links to all major educational statistics collected by the U.S. government
Psychological Abstracts	Abstracts of journal articles in psychology
Resources in Education	Abstracts of research reports and other documents acquired by ERIC clearinghouses
Review of Educational Research	Reviews on various topics in each quarterly issue
Social Sciences Citation Index	Bibliographic information for cited authors and topics
Test Critiques	Reviews of measurement instruments, including critiques of tests, and technical aspects
Tests in Print V	Index and supplement to the first 13 *Mental Measurements Yearbooks*
Thesaurus of ERIC Descriptors	Terms for classifying and indexing ERIC documents
U.S. Department of Education Web site (www.ed.gov)	Collection of information about federal initiatives, grant opportunities, offices, and full text and ordering information for publications, research, and statistics

Condition of Education. (1975–). Washington, DC: National Center for Educational Statistics. Also available: National Center for Educational Statistics, *Encyclopedia of ED Stats* link: http://nces.ed.gov

Corsini, R. J. (2000). *Encyclopedia of psychology* (3rd ed.). New York: Wiley.

Current Index to Journals in Education. (1969–). Phoenix, AZ: Oryx Press.

Cumulative Index to Nursing and Allied Health Literature (CINAHL). (1982–). Ann Arbor, MI: Bell & Howell.

Dejnozka, E. L., & Kapel, D. E. (1991). *American educators' encyclopedia.* Westport, CT: Greenwood Press.

Digest of educational statistics (1962–). Washington, DC: National Center for Educational Statistics. Also available: National Center for Educational Statistics, *Encyclopedia of ED Stats:* http://nces.ed.gov

Dissertation Abstracts International. (1938–). Ann Arbor, MI: University Microfilms.

Education Abstracts. (1986–). New York: H. W. Wilson.

Education Index. (1929–). New York: H. W. Wilson.

Educational Administration Abstracts. (1966–). Beverly Hills, CA: Sage.

Education: The complete encyclopedia. (1998). [CD-ROM] Available: New York: Pergamon Press.

Education Resources Information Center (ERIC). (2001, February). *All about ERIC* [On-line]. Available: http://accesseric.org/resources/allabout/toc.html

———. (2000, June). *Directory of ERIC resource collections* [On-line]. Available: http://www.ed.gov/BASISDB/EROD/eric/SF

———. (2001, March). *ERIC sites* [On-line]. Available: http://www.accesseric.org/sites/barak.html

———. (2001, March). *Submitting documents to ERIC: Frequently asked questions (FAQs)* [On-line]. Available: http://ericfac.piccard.csc.com/submitting.html

Educational Testing Service Test Collection Catalog. (1986–1993). Phoenix, AZ: Oryx Press.

Exceptional Child Education Resources. (1969–). Reston, VA: Council for Exceptional Children.

Gage, N. L. (Ed.). (1963). *Handbook of research on teaching.* Chicago: Rand McNally.

Good, C. V. (Ed.). (1973). *Dictionary of education* (3rd ed.). New York: McGraw-Hill.

Gorn, V. (1997). *Special education dictionary.* Horsham, PA: LRP Publications.

GPO Monthly Catalog. (1895–). [On-line]. Available: OCLC Firstsearch. Firstsearch home page at http://www.oclc.org/oclc/menu/fs.htm.

Grant, C. A., & Ladson-Billings, G. (1997). *Dictionary of multicultural education.* Phoenix, AZ: Oryx Press.

Hammill, D. D. (1992). *A consumer's guide to tests in print* (2nd ed.). Austin, TX: Pro-Ed.

Higher Education Abstracts. (1984–). Claremont, CA: Claremont Institute for Administrative Studies.

Honan, W. H. (1999, June 25). College freshmen's Internet use a way of life. *New York Times* Late Edition, Section A, p. 11.

Houston, J. E. (Ed.). (1998). *Thesaurus of ERIC descriptors* (14th ed.). Phoenix, AZ: Oryx Press.

Huessy, H. R., & Cohen, A. H. (1976). Hyperkinetic behaviors and learning disabilities followed over seven years. *Pediatrics, 57,* 4–10.

Husen, T., & Postlethwaite, T. N. (Eds.). (1994). *The international encyclopedia of education* (*2nd ed*). New York: Pergamon Press.

————. (1985). *The international encyclopedia of education: Research and studies.* New York: Pergamon Press.

Impara, J. C., & Plake, B. S. (Eds). (1998). *The thirteenth mental measurements yearbook.* (13th ed.). Lincoln, NE: Buros Institute of Mental Measurements, University of Nebraska.

Index to International Statistics. (1982–). Bethesda, MD: Congressional Information Service.

Information Please Almanac. (1947–). Boston: Houghton Mifflin.

Keogh, B. K. (1980–). *Advances in Special Education: A Research Annual.* Greenwich, CT: JAI Press.

Keyser, D. J., & Sweetland, R. C. (Eds.). (1984–). *Test Critiques* (Vol. 1–). Kansas City, MO: Test Corporation of America.

Knowles, A. S. (Ed.). (1978). *The international encyclopedia of higher education* (10 vols.). San Francisco: Jossey-Bass.

Krol, E., & Conner-Sax, K. (1999). *The Whole Internet: The next generation: A completely new edition of the first and best user's guide to the Internet.* Sebastopol, CA: O'Reilly.

Levine, J. R., Baroudi, C., & Young, M. L. (2000). *The Internet for dummies* (7th ed.). Foster City, CA: IDG Books Worldwide.

Lynch, M. J. (1996). *Electronic services in academic libraries: ALA survey report.* Chicago: American Library Association.

Maddox, T. (1997). *Tests: A comprehensive reference for assessments in psychology, education and business* (4th ed.). Austin, TX: Pro-Ed.

Marshall, R. M., Schafer, V. A., & O'Donnell, L. (1999). Arithmetic disabilities and ADD subtypes: Implications for DSM-IV. *Journal of Learning Disabilities, 32,* 239–247.

Masters Abstracts International. (1986–). Ann Arbor, MI: University Microfilms.

Murphy, J., & Louis, K. S. (Eds.). (1999). *Handbook of research on educational administration: A project of the American Educational Research Association.* New York: Jossey-Bass.

Murphy, L. L., Impara, J. C., & Plake, B. S. (Eds.). (1999). *Tests in print V: An index to tests, test reviews and literature on specific tests.* Lincoln, NE: Buros Institute of Mental Measurements, University of Nebraska.

O'Brien, J. W., & Wasserman, S. R. (Eds.). (2000). *Statistics sources* (23rd ed., 2 vols.). Detroit: Gale Research.

O'Brien, N. P., & Fabiano, E. (1991). *Core list of books and journals in education.* Phoenix, AZ: Oryx Press.

Ostrow, A. C. (1996). *Directory of Psychological Tests in the Sport and Exercise Sciences* (2nd ed.). Morgantown, WV: Fitness Information Technology.

Page, G. T., Thomas, J. B., & Marshall, A. R. (1980). *International dictionary of education.* Cambridge, MA: MIT Press.

Projections of Education Statistics. (1975–). Washington, DC: National Center for Educational Statistics. Also available: National Center for Educational Statistics, *Encyclopedia of ED Stats:* http://nces.ed.gov/

Psychological Abstracts. (1927–). Lancaster, PA: American Psychological Association.

PsycInfo (1887–). Washington, DC: American Psychological Association. Available through www.ovid.com.

Readers' guide to periodical literature. Minneapolis: H. W. Wilson Co., (1905–).

Resources in Education. (1968–). Phoenix, AZ: Oryx Press.

Review of Educational Research. (1931–). Washington, DC: American Educational Research Association.

Review of Research in Education. (1973–). Washington, DC: American Educational Research Association.

Reynolds, C. R., & Fletcher-Janzen, E. (2000). *Encyclopedia of special education: A reference for the education of the handicapped and other exceptional children and adults* (2nd ed.) New York: Wiley.

Silvey, H. M. (1951–). *Master's Theses Directories.* Cedar Falls, IA: Research Publications.

Social Sciences Citation Index. (1973–). Philadelphia: Institute for Scientific Information.

Sociological Abstracts. (1953–). San Diego, CA: Sociological Abstracts.

Spafford, C. S., Pesce, A. J., & Grosser, G. S. (1998). *The cyclopedic education dictionary.* Albany, NY: Delmar.

Statistical Abstract of the United States. (1878–). Washington, DC: U.S. Bureau of the Census.

Statistical Reference Index. (1980–). Bethesda, MD: Congressional Information Service.

Sullivan, D. (2001). *Search Engine Watch* [On-line]. Available: http://www.searchenginewatch.com

Sweetland, R. C., & Keyser, D. J. (Eds.). (1991). *Tests: A comprehensive reference for assessments in psychology, education and business* (3rd ed.). Austin, TX: Pro-Ed.

Tests in Microfiche (1975–1994). Princeton, NJ: Educational Testing Service.

Travers, R. (Ed.). (1973). *Second handbook of research on teaching* (2nd ed.). Chicago: Rand McNally.

U.S. Library of Congress, Exchange and Gift Division. (1910–1994). *Monthly Checklist of State Publications.* Washington, DC: U.S. Government Printing Office.

U.S. Superintendent of Documents. (1895–). *Monthly Catalog of U.S. Government Publications.* Washington, DC: U.S. Government Printing Office.

Walberg, H. J., & Haertel, G. D. (Eds.). (1990). *The international encyclopedia of educational evaluation.* Elmsford, NY: Pergamon Press.

Wynar, B. S. (Ed.). (1970–). *American Reference Books Annual.* Littleton, CO: Libraries Unlimited.

Wittrock, M. C. (Ed.). (1985). *Handbook of research on teaching* (3rd ed.). New York: Macmillan.

World Almanac and Book of Facts. (1868–). New York: Newspaper Enterprise Association.

WorldCat. (1991–). [On-line]. Available: OCLC Firstsearch at http://firstsearch.oclc.org/.

KEY CONCEPTS

Boolean logic
citation index
ERIC system
index of dissertations and theses

Internet
periodical index
specialized dictionary
statistical source

test sources
World Wide Web

EXERCISES

1. Which of the following are recommended strategies for organizing a literature search?
   a. Organize studies by topic.
   b. Begin with early articles and work forward in time.
   c. Read the abstract or summary sections of a report first.
   d. Skim the report to find those sections that are related to the chosen questions.
   e. Write out a complete bibliographic reference for each work.

2. According to the text, what are three important roles of incorporating related literature in a research project? In your opinion, which role seems most important to you in your current or future research?

3. Conduct a search on the same general topic in both ERIC (focusing on CIJE items) and in *Education Index*. Compare the usefulness of ERIC and *Education Index* in finding related research on your topic. Compare and contrast two of the following: the quality of abstracts, the journals covered, and the subject terms or descriptors used by the index. Which index do you predict would be the most useful in finding research on your topic?

4. Explain the organization and the purpose of the *Mental Measurements Yearbook* (see Impara & Plake, 1998). How does the information differ from that in *Tests* (Maddox, 1997) or *Test Critiques* (Sweetland & Keyser, 1991)?

5. What purposes might searching the *Social Science Citation Index* serve? In addition to information about an article's citation record, what conclusions might the *SSCI* help you draw about an author or about a journal itself?

6. What conclusion could be drawn regarding a work, published in 1959, which was cited in twenty articles listed in the 1999 *SSCI?*

7. If you were interested in the effect of teachers' stereotyping on the achievement of girls in math classes, what are some terms you might search on? Illustrate how you might combine them into on-line search statements with Boolean operators AND, OR, or NOT.

8. Describe the differences among the purposes and content of handbooks, encyclopedias, and yearbook sources. For which audiences are they intended, what kind of information do they seem to provide, and at what point would they be most useful to the researcher?

9. If you wanted more information on the concept of multiple intelligence, which type of source might you consult to get an overview of the concept? Where would you go to see the more current research on the topic?

10. Find two Web resources on an education-related topic of your choice, one from a commercial site and one from an educational (.edu) site. Evaluate them using the criteria of authority, accuracy, and timeliness. Are there notable differences between the sources? (Explain.)

ANSWERS

1. a, c, d, and e.

2. Knowledge of related research enables the researcher to define the frontiers of the field, place the question in perspective, and avoid unintentional replication of previous studies. Defining the frontiers of research is especially important for a relatively inexperienced researcher, but any well-reasoned choice is acceptable.

3. Both provide a means to locate relevant journal articles. *Education Index* covers journals from 1929 on and lists new articles more quickly than *CIJE. CIJE* includes more journals. Begun in 1966, it indexes articles using the ERIC thesaurus of subject descriptors and provides annotations. *Education Index,* though older, does not index unpublished literature, though there are still periodicals that only *Education Index* covers, which tend to be newsletters, and so on. As *Education Abstracts,* the electronic version of the index, tends to have shorter abstracts and also uses a controlled vocabulary that is less specific than the ERIC descriptors, most students will consider ERIC more useful, unless the student is doing historical research.

4. The editions of *MMY* provide the most comprehensive listing and description of standardized tests available, given its long publication history and the length and authority of its reviews. The critical reviews of the tests assist one in selecting an appropriate test. *Test Critiques* (Sweetland & Keyser, 1991) is easier to use and may be better for a layperson or a beginner who only wants to read a description of a test, and *Tests* (Maddox, 1997) serves as a listing of tests in print and does not offer much evaluative content.

5. The *SSCI* provides a way to see what subsequent research has followed a particular article. You can draw tentative conclusions about the influence of an author by looking at how often his or her work has been cited, and in turn, you can draw conclusions about the influential journals in a field by seeing how often those articles that are heavily cited seem to come from a cluster of important journal titles.

6. If an older article becomes heavily cited several years later, there may be several explanations; the research may have been treated by a noted scholar in a new way, a seminal piece of research may have recently been disproved, or the field of study may be experiencing a surge of interest because of a news event or finding.

7. Answers will vary, but terms mentioned would include *Females* (not *Girls*) AND *Teacher Attitudes* (not *Teacher Stereotypes,* which refers to stereotypes of teacher behavior and attributes) AND *Mathematics Instruction, Mathematics Education,* or *Mathematics. Sex Discrimination* or *Sex Stereotypes* might also be used successfully.

8. An encyclopedia or handbook would give a more or less detailed overview, usually with history, the names of major researchers, and so on. Encyclopedias tend to offer more brief and general information, and handbooks tend to assume that the audience is not made up of casual readers, but of students and researchers. Handbooks tend to focus on more specific topics. Yearbooks and yearbook-type sources (such as, for example, *Review of Research in Education* or the *Educational Media and Technology Yearbook*) focus on "hot topics" and more recent research, although they are of course secondary sources. These reference sources could be used at many points in the research process; students will usually use them in the beginning while formulating a research question, or during the literature review to introduce themselves to related topics. However, periodical indexes, which give access to more

recent primary works, would be the best source to look for recent research on the topic.

9. Students may pick up on the fact that this topic will be present in both psychology and education indexes, and that it has appeared in the news media, making it possible to find some periodical sources on the topic in general interest databases. ERIC, the *Cumulative Index* to *Nursing and Allied Health Literature, PsycInfo,* and so forth, would all be good places to look for the more recent research on the topic. Sources such as the *Encyclopedia of Educational Research* or the *Handbook of Educational Psychology* would be good places to find overview information.

10. Answers will vary.

 ## INFOTRAC COLLEGE EDITION

Use InfoTrac College Edition to search for references useful for writing the related literature section of a required paper for a research methods class or for another class. Look for different kinds of references on your topic such as research articles, discussions, books, and so on.

Chapter 5

The Hypothesis

After studying this chapter, the student will be able to:

1 Define *hypothesis.*

2 Explain the role of the hypothesis(es) in quantitative and qualitative research.

3 Distinguish between an inductive and a deductive hypothesis.

4 State the criteria used to evaluate hypotheses for research.

5 Define *operational definition,* and give an example.

6 Identify a testable hypothesis from given examples.

7 Define *null hypothesis,* and explain its purpose in a research study.

8 Write a research hypothesis and a null hypothesis for a research study.

9 Distinguish between a directional and a nondirectional hypothesis.

10 Describe the steps in testing a hypothesis.

11 State the purpose of the research plan, and list the elements to be included.

12 State the purpose of a pilot study.

After stating the problem and examining the literature, the quantitative researcher is ready to state a hypothesis. Recall that the quantitative problem asks about the relationship between two (or more) variables. The hypothesis states the expected answer to the research question. It presents the researcher's expectations about the relationship between variables within the problem. Hence it is put forth as a suggested solution to the problem, with the understanding that the ensuing investigation may lead either to its tentative retention or its tentative rejection.

The hypothesis is a powerful tool in scientific inquiry. It enables researchers to relate theory to observation and observation to theory. Today the use of hypotheses enables people, in the search for knowledge, to employ both the ideas of the inductive philosophers, with their emphasis on observation, and the logic of the deductive philosophers, with their emphasis on reason. The use of hypotheses has united experience and reason to produce a powerful tool for seeking knowledge.

For instance, you may begin with the question "What is the role of children's perceptions of themselves in the process of learning to read?" You might then hypothesize that there is a positive relationship between children's perceptions of themselves and their achievement in reading in the first grade. Or you may begin with a question such as "What is the effect of preschool training on the achievement of culturally disadvantaged children in first grade?" The hypothesis might read "Culturally disadvantaged children who have had preschool training achieve at a higher level in first grade than culturally disadvantaged children who have not had preschool training." In both examples you can see that the hypothesis is a proposition relating two variables. In the first hypothesis the variables are self-perception and reading achievement; in the second, the variables are having or not having preschool training and achievement in first grade.

Although hypotheses are recommended and, as you will see, serve several important purposes, they are not absolutely essential in all research studies. Hypotheses are tools in the research process, not ends in themselves. Studies are often undertaken in areas where there is little accumulated background information. If an investigator lacks insight into the scope of a problem, the major variables that influence a phenomenon, or the settings in which the variables occur, then it is very difficult to state a meaningful hypothesis. For example, surveys that seek to describe the characteristics of particular phenomena, or to ascertain the attitudes and opinions of groups, often proceed without hypotheses. In qualitative research, hypotheses are rarely formulated at the beginning of the research. They are usually generated as data accumulate and the researcher gains more insight and understanding about the phenomenon under investigation.

Two reasons for stating a hypothesis before the data-gathering phase of a quantitative study are (1) a well-grounded hypothesis indicates that the researcher has sufficient knowledge in the area to undertake the investigation, and (2) the hypothesis gives direction to the collection and interpretation of the data; it tells the researcher what procedure to follow and what type of data to gather and thus may prevent a great deal of wasted time and effort on the part of the researcher.

PURPOSE OF THE HYPOTHESIS

Principal purposes served by the hypothesis include the following:

1. *The hypothesis brings together information to enable the researcher to make a tentative statement about how the variables in the study are related.* By integrating information based on experience, related research, or theory, the researcher states the hypothesis that provides the most accurate prediction or the best solution to a problem.

2. *Because hypotheses propose tentative explanations for phenomena, they stimulate a research endeavor that results in the accumulation of new knowledge.* They permit investigators to validate or fail to validate theory and thus extend knowledge.

3. *The hypothesis provides the investigator with a relational statement that is directly testable in a research study.* That is, it is possible to collect and analyze data that will confirm or disconfirm the hypothesis. Questions cannot be tested directly. An investigation begins with a question, but only the proposed relationship between the variables can be tested. For instance, you do not test the question "Do teachers' comments on students' papers cause a significant improvement in student performance?" Instead, you test the hypothesis that the question implies: "Teachers' comments on students' papers result in a significant improvement in performance"; or more specifically, "The performance scores of students who have had teacher comments on previous papers will exceed those of students who have not had teacher comments on previous papers." You then proceed to gather data about the relationship between the two variables (teachers' comments and student performance).

4. *The hypothesis provides direction to the research.* The hypothesis posits a specific relationship between variables and thus determines the nature of the data needed to test the proposition. Very simply, the hypothesis tells the researcher what to do. Facts must be selected and observations made because they have relevance to a particular question, and the hypothesis determines the relevance of these facts. The hypothesis provides a basis for selecting the sampling, measurement and research procedures to use, as well as the appropriate statistical analysis. Furthermore, the hypothesis helps keep the study restricted in scope, preventing it from becoming too broad or unwieldy.

   For example, consider again the hypothesis concerning preschool training of culturally disadvantaged children and their achievement in first grade. This hypothesis indicates the research method required and the sample to use, and it even directs the researcher to the statistical test that would be necessary for analyzing the data. It is clear from the statement of the hypothesis that the researcher will conduct an ex post facto study that compares the first-grade achievement of a sample of culturally disadvantaged children who went through a preschool program and a similar group of disadvantaged children who did not have preschool training. Any difference in the mean achievement of the two groups could be analyzed for statistical significance by the t-test or analysis-of-variance technique. (We discuss these procedures in Chapter 7.)

5. *The hypothesis provides a framework for reporting the findings and conclusions of the study.* The researcher will find it very convenient to take each hypothesis separately and state the conclusions that are relevant to it; that is, the researcher can organize this section of the written report around the provision of answers to the original hypotheses, thereby making a more meaningful and readable presentation.

SUGGESTIONS FOR DERIVING HYPOTHESES

As explained in Chapter 3, a study might originate in a practical problem, in some observed behavioral situation in need of explanation, in previous research, or even more profitably in some educational, psychological, or sociological theory. Thus, researchers derive hypotheses inductively from observations of behavior or deductively from theory or from the findings of previous research.

Inductive Hypotheses

In the inductive procedure, the researcher formulates an **inductive hypothesis** as a generalization from apparent observed relationships—that is, the researcher observes behavior, notices trends or probable relationships, and then hypothesizes an explanation for this observed behavior. He or she should accompany this reasoning process by examining previous research to determine what findings other investigators have reported on the question. The inductive procedure is a particularly fruitful source of hypotheses for classroom teachers. Teachers observe learning and other student behavior every day and try to relate it to their own behavior, to the behavior of other students, to the teaching methods used, to changes in the school environment, and so on. On the basis of their experience and knowledge of behavior in a school situation, teachers may inductively formulate a generalization that seeks to explain the observed relationship. This tentative explanation can become the hypothesis in a scientific investigation.

Perhaps a teacher has observed that classroom tests arouse a high degree of anxiety, and believes this adversely affects student performance. Furthermore, the teacher has noted that when students receive an opportunity to write comments about objective questions, their test performance seems to improve. The teacher reasons that this freedom to make comments must somehow reduce anxiety and, as a result, the students score better. This observation suggests a hypothesis: Students who are encouraged to write comments about test items on their answer sheets will make higher test scores than students who have no opportunity to make comments. The teacher could then design an experiment to test the validity of this hypothesis. Note that the hypothesis expresses the teacher's belief concerning the relationship between the two variables (writing comments about test items and performance on the test). Note also that the variable *anxiety* that was part of the reasoning chain leading to the hypothesis is not part of the final hypothesis. Therefore, the results of the investigation would provide information concerning only the relation between writing comments and test performance. The relationships between anxiety and comments, and anxiety and test performance, could be subjects for subsequent hypotheses to investigate. Frequently an original idea involves a series of relationships that you cannot directly observe. You then reformulate the question to focus on relationships that are amenable to direct observation.

The following are some other examples of hypotheses that might result from a teacher's observations:

Students' learning of computer programming in the middle grades increases their development of logical thinking skills.

Using advance organizers increases high school students' learning from computer-assisted instruction in chemistry.

There are positive relationships among academic self-concept, expectancy of success, and academic achievement.

Students trained to write summaries of a lecture will perform better on an immediate posttest on lecture comprehension than will students who simply take notes.

Children score higher on final measures of first-grade reading achievement when they are taught in small groups rather than large groups.

The cognitive and affective development of first-grade children is influenced by the amount of prior preschool experience.

In the inductive process, the researcher makes observations, thinks about the problem, turns to the literature for clues, makes additional observations, and then formulates a hypothesis that seeks to account for the observed behavior. The researcher (or teacher) then tests the hypothesis under controlled conditions to examine scientifically the assumption concerning the relationship between the specified variables.

Deductive Hypotheses

In contrast to hypotheses formulated as generalizations from observed relationships, some are derived by deduction from theory. These hypotheses have the advantage of leading to a more general system of knowledge, because the framework for incorporating them meaningfully into the body of knowledge already exists within the theory itself. A science cannot develop efficiently if each study results in an isolated bit of knowledge. It becomes cumulative by building on the existing body of facts and theories. A hypothesis derived from a theory is known as a **deductive hypothesis.**

Theory

A **theory** may be defined as a set of interrelated constructs and propositions that specify relations among variables to explain and predict phenomena (Kerlinger, 1986, p. 9). Theories are proposed as general explanations that apply to a wide range of phenomena. From the interrelationships proposed in the theory, you can state specific consequences that could logically be assumed to follow. A scientific theory must imply conclusions that can be verified through empirical investigation; that is, from the theory you should be able to predict certain events that will or will not be observed. These deduced consequences become the hypotheses that are subjected to empirical investigation. As the hypotheses derived from a theory receive support in research, the theory also receives support. Hypotheses thus direct people to seek the evidence that supports, expands, contradicts, or leads to revision of the theories from which they derived. We should emphasize that although research can disprove a theory, it cannot ever prove the theory true. This is because theories are generalizations that apply to all possible instances of the phenomena they are trying to explain; it is not possible to test a theory against all possibilities. But the more support the theory gets in a variety of research studies, the more confidence you can have that the theory is valid and useful.

Going from Theory to Hypothesis

Theories are more general in content than hypotheses, and one theory may give rise to a number of hypotheses to investigate in several separate studies. You may begin a study by selecting one of the theories in your own area of interest. The particular theory that you choose is determined, of course, by the purpose of the research and the contribution that the theory can make to understanding the problem. To gain a thorough understanding of the theory, read not only textbook summaries but also some primary sources on the theory. Another important consideration in choosing a theory is that it should be testable. Not all theories are equally useful to a beginning researcher; some are very complex and difficult to understand. The theory chosen should be one from which the researcher can make a concise prediction that can be verified through empirical observation.

Next you use deductive reasoning to arrive at the logical consequences of the theory. These deductions then become the hypotheses in the research study. Marsh and associates (1995) used Festinger's social comparison theory (1954) as the basis for an interesting study on the effects of placement in gifted and talented (G&T) programs on students' academic self-concepts. This theory suggests that the formation of academic self-concepts requires students to compare their self-perceived academic accomplishments to some standard or frame of reference. Because individuals have different frames of reference, the same academic accomplishments can lead to different academic self-concepts.

Marsh reasoned that students compare their own academic ability to the academic abilities of their classmates (the standard) and use this social comparison as the basis for forming their own academic self-concepts. Thus, G&T students would be expected to have lower academic self-concepts as a result of comparing themselves to more able students in selective settings and higher academic self-concepts as a result of comparing themselves to less able students in mixed ability settings. Marsh referred to this as the big-fish–little-pond effect.

Marsh administered students a well-developed multidimensional instrument containing three academic self-concept scales, four nonacademic self-concept scales, and a global self-esteem scale, as well as standardized achievement tests in reading and mathematics. On the basis of achievement test scores and teachers' recommendations, Marsh and associates selected a group of students for the G&T class; a matched comparison group was placed in regular classes. The researchers compared students and evaluated changes over a two-year period for both groups.

The research hypothesis was "G&T children in special G&T programs will experience a decline in academic self-concept in comparison to matched students in regular, mixed-ability classes." This hypothesis was supported in two separate studies that found that students in the special G&T programs experienced significant declines in three domains of academic self-concept over time when compared to the matched comparison students. This pattern of results was consistent across gender, age, and initial ability. A second aspect of both studies found no significant effect of G&T programs on students' nonacademic self-concepts.

This study is interesting because the findings seem to contradict conventional wisdom that G&T programs benefit participants. Marsh cautions, however, that the results do not indicate that G&T programs are bad but merely that participation may have an unanticipated, negative effect on one outcome—academic self-concept. Much more research is needed in this area. What is the effect of these programs on academic achievement as opposed to academic self-concept? Would the effect be the same in G&T programs that encourage students to pursue their own areas of interest so that outcomes are not so easily compared as opposed to competitively oriented programs that encourage social comparisons?

A useful theory from which an educational researcher might make deductions is Piaget's classic theory on the development of logical thinking in children. Piaget (1968) suggested that children pass through various stages in their mental development, one of which is the stage of concrete operations, which begins at age 7 or 8 and marks the transition from dependence on perception to an ability to use some logical operations. These operations are on a concrete level but do involve symbolic reasoning. Using this theory as a starting point, you might therefore hypothesize that the proportion of 9-year-old children who will be able to answer correctly the transitive inference problem "Frank is taller than George; George is taller than Robert; who is the tallest?" will be greater than the proportion of 6-year-olds who are able to answer it correctly. Such research has implications for the importance of determining students' cognitive capabilities and structuring educational tasks that are compatible with their developmental level.

Piaget's cognitive theory also emphasizes that learning is a highly active process in which learners must construct knowledge. This tenet that knowledge must be constructed by learners rather than simply being ingested from teachers is the basis for much of the research on discovery-oriented and cooperative learning.

In a study designed to test a deduction from a theory, it is extremely important to check for any logical gaps between theory and hypothesis. The researcher must ask, "Does the hypothesis logically follow from the theory?" If the hypothesis does not really follow from the theory, then the researcher cannot reach valid conclusions about the adequacy of the theory. If the hypothesis is supported, but not rigorously deduced from the theory, the researcher cannot say that the findings furnish credibility to the theory. Conversely, if the data do not support the hypothesis, the theory from which it originated will not necessarily be any less credible.

It is true that many hypotheses that can be deduced from the better-known theories have already been tested, but many such deductions remain to be made and tested. Also, a previously researched deduction can be used to generate hypotheses in varied circumstances, to extend the application of the theory.

■ CHARACTERISTICS OF A USABLE HYPOTHESIS

After tentatively formulating the hypothesis, but before attempting any actual empirical testing, you must assess the potential of the hypothesis as a research tool. A hypothesis must meet certain criteria of acceptability. The final worth of a hypothesis cannot be judged prior to empirical testing, but there are certain **criteria for evaluating hypotheses,** and the researcher should use them to judge the adequacy of the proposed hypothesis.

A Hypothesis Must State the Expected Relationship between Variables

A hypothesis should conjecture the relationship between two or more variables. For example, suppose you attempt to start your car and nothing happens. It would be unprofitable to state, "The car will not start and it has a wiring system," because no relationship between variables is specified, and so there is no proposed relationship to test. A fruitful hypothesis would be "The car will not start because of a fault in the wiring system." This criterion may seem patently obvious, but consider the following statement: "If children differ from one another in self-concept, they will differ from one another in social studies achievement." The statement appears to be a hypothesis until you note that there is no statement of an expected relationship. An expected relationship could be described as "Higher self-concept is a likely antecedent to *higher* social studies achievement." This hypothesis would then be stated as "There will be a *positive* relationship between self-concept and social studies achievement." If the opposite is predicted—that is, higher self-concept leads to *lower* social studies achievement—then the hypothesis would be "There will be a *negative* relationship between self-concept and social studies achievement." Either statement would meet this first criterion.

A Hypothesis Must Be Testable

The most important characteristic of a "good" hypothesis is testability. A testable hypothesis is verifiable; that is, deductions, conclusions, or inferences can be drawn from the hypothesis in such a way that empirical observations either support or not support the hypothesis. If the hypothesis is on target, then certain predictable results should be manifest. A testable hypothesis enables the researcher to determine by observation and data collection whether consequences that are deductively implied actually occur. Otherwise, it would be impossible either to confirm or not to confirm the hypothesis. In the preceding example, the hypothesis "The car's failure to start is a punishment for my sins" is apparently untestable in this world.

Many hypotheses—or propositions, as they may initially be stated—are essentially untestable. For instance, the hypothesis "Preschool experience promotes the all-around adjustment of the preschool child" would be hard to test because of the difficulty of operationalizing and measuring "all-around adjustment." To be testable, a hypothesis must relate variables that can be measured. If no means are available for measuring the variables, then no one could gather the data necessary to test the validity of the hypothesis. We cannot emphasize this point too strongly. Unless you can specifically define the indicators of each variable and subsequently can measure these variables, then you cannot test the hypothesis.

The indicators of the variables are referred to as *operational definitions*. An operational definition, as explained earlier, is one that defines a variable by stating "operations," or procedures, necessary to measure that variable. For instance, consider this hypothesis: "There is a positive relationship between a child's self-esteem and his or her reading achievement in first grade." For this hypothesis to be testable, you must define the variables operationally. You might define *self-esteem* as the scores made on the Coopersmith Self-Esteem Scale (Coopersmith, 1981), and reading achievement as scores on the California Reading Test, or as first-grade teachers' ratings of reading achievement.

A primary consideration in formulating a hypothesis is to make sure the variables can be given operational definitions. Avoid the use of constructs for which it would be difficult or impossible to find adequate measures. Constructs such as *creativity, authoritarianism, democracy,* and the like have acquired such diverse meanings that reaching agreement on operational definitions of such concepts would be difficult, if not impossible. Remember that the variables must be defined in terms of identifiable and observable behavior.

It is important to avoid value statements in hypotheses. A statement such as "A counseling program in the elementary school is desirable" cannot be investigated in a research study. However, you could test the hypothesis "Elementary pupils who have had counseling will verbally express greater satisfaction with their school than those who have not had counseling." You can measure verbal expressions of satisfaction, but whether they are desirable is a value judgment.

A Hypothesis Should Be Consistent with the Existing Body of Knowledge

Hypotheses should not contradict previously well-established knowledge. The hypothesis "My car will not start because the fluid in the battery has changed to gold" satisfies the first two criteria but is so contrary to what is known about the nature of matter that you would not pursue it. The hypothesis "The car will not start because the fluid in the battery has evaporated to a low level" is consistent with previous knowledge and therefore is worth pursuing. It would probably be unprofitable to hypothesize an *absence* of relationship between the self-concept of adolescent boys and girls and their rate of physical growth because the preponderance of evidence supports the *presence* of such a relationship. Historians of science find that people such as Einstein, Newton, Darwin, and Copernicus developed truly revolutionary hypotheses that conflicted with what was accepted knowledge in their time. But remember that the work of such pioneers was not really so much a denial of previous knowledge as a reorganization of the knowledge into more satisfactory theory. In most cases, and especially for the beginning researcher, it is safe to suggest that the hypothesis should agree with knowledge already established in the field. Again, this points up the necessity for a thorough review of the literature so that hypotheses are formulated on the basis of previously reported research in the area.

A Hypothesis Should Be Stated as Simply and Concisely as Possible

A hypothesis should be presented in the form of a concise declarative statement. A complete and concisely stated hypothesis makes clear what the researcher needs to do to test it. It also provides the framework for presenting the findings of the study. If a researcher is exploring more than one relationship, he or she will need to state more than one hypothesis. The general rule is to state only one relationship in any one hypothesis. For example, if you were investigating the effect of a new teaching method on student achievement and student satisfaction, you would state two hypotheses. You need not worry about the verbal redundancy inevitable in stating multiple hypotheses. Remember that the goals of testability and clarity will be served better by more specific hypotheses.

The terms used in the hypothesis should be the simplest acceptable for conveying the intended meaning; avoid ambiguous or vague constructs. Use terms in the way that is generally accepted for referring to the phenomenon. When two hypotheses are of equal explanatory power, prefer the simpler one, because it will provide the necessary explanation with fewer assumptions and variables to be defined. Remember that this principle of parsimony is important in evaluating hypotheses.

The following excerpt provides an example of a study with hypotheses deduced from a theory (Davis, 1988).

The Effect of Time of Day of Instruction on Achievement

Research Problem

What is the effect of time of day of instruction on eighth-grade students' English and mathematics achievement?

Theory

A theory involving short-term memory (STM) and long-term memory (LTM) suggests that tasks that involve mainly the use of STM are learned and performed better in the morning; tasks that involve mainly the use of LTM are learned and performed better in the afternoon. Two physiological factors account for time-of-day differences in learning: (*a*) basal arousal rises from a low level in the morning to a peak in the evening, and the use of STM and LTM are associated with it, respectively; (*b*) diurnal rhythms in plasma and hormone levels influence the way people encode, store, and retrieve information and are associated with better LTM processing later in the day and better STM processing earlier in the day.

Hypothesis

Because reading involves connecting the printed information to prior knowledge and experience, it was hypothesized: Students will achieve more in reading when instruction is provided in the afternoon. And because instruction in math skills involves more mental manipulation of data and use of STM, it was hypothesized: Students will achieve more in arithmetic when instruction is provided in the morning than in the afternoon.

Methods

Eighty eighth-grade students were randomly assigned to the following treatment groups: (1) first-period English, (2) last-period English, (3) first-period math, (4) last-period math. The same English teacher and the same math teacher taught the first-period and last-period sections of the courses using the same methods and materials. The Comprehensive Test of Basic Skills (CTBS) was administered at the beginning (pretest) and the end of the school year (posttest) to measure achievement. The tests were given on the same day for each content area, as well as during the middle of the school day for all groups in order to control the potential influence of time of day of output effects.

Analysis

The respective sets of English and math scores were each analyzed through the analysis of covariance (ANCOVA), with the pretest scores serving as the covariate. ANCOVA takes into account the variation that exists between pupils' pretest scores and adjusts the posttest scores in relation to them so that valid comparisons can be made.

Results

The afternoon English group achieved at a significantly higher level than the morning English group. There was no significant difference in the math achievement of the morning and afternoon math groups.

Conclusions

It was concluded that learners would benefit more from afternoon instruction than from morning instruction in eighth-grade English. Time of day of instruction made no difference in eighth-grade math achievement. The researcher concluded that the hypothesis concerning math should be subjected to further investigation. Perhaps the STM and LTM functions found in previous research are not very representative of those required in math reasoning; or perhaps math reasoning involves a fairly balanced use of STM and LTM.

TYPES OF HYPOTHESES

The Research Hypothesis

The hypotheses we have discussed thus far are called *research,* or substantive, *hypotheses.* They are the hypotheses developed from observation, the related literature, and/or the theory described in the study. A research hypothesis is a statement about the relationship one expects to find as a result of the research. It may be a statement about the expected *relationship* or the expected *difference* between the variables in the study. A hypothesis about children's IQ and anxiety in the classroom could be stated "There is a positive relationship between IQ and anxiety in elementary school children," or "Children classified as having high IQs will exhibit more anxiety in the classroom than children classified as having low IQs." Research hypotheses may be stated in a **directional** or **nondirectional** form. A directional hypothesis specifies the direction of the predicted relationship or difference. The preceding two hypotheses about IQ and anxiety are directional. A nondirectional hypothesis, in contrast, states that a relationship or difference exists but without specifying the direction or nature of the expected finding—for example, "There is a relationship between IQ and anxiety in children."

The Null Hypothesis

It is impossible to test research hypotheses directly. The only way you can judge the credibility of a research hypothesis is to state a null hypothesis (symbolized H_0) and assess the probability that this null hypothesis is true. It is called the **null hypothesis** because it states that there is *no* relationship between the variables in the population. A null hypothesis states a negation (not the reverse) of what the experimenter expects or predicts. A researcher may hope to show that, after an experimental treatment, two populations will have different means, but the null hypothesis would state that after the treatment the populations' means will *not* be different.

What is the point of the null hypothesis? A null hypothesis lets researchers assess whether apparent relationships are genuine or are likely to be a function of chance. It says, "The results of this study could easily have happened by chance." Statistical tests are used to determine the probability that the null hypothesis is true. If the tests indicate that observed relationships had only a slight probability of occurring by chance, the null hypothesis becomes an unlikely explanation. Therefore it can be rejected in favor of an alternative hypothesis. Testing a null hypothesis is analogous to the prosecutor's work in a criminal trial. To establish guilt, the prosecutor (in the U.S. legal system) must provide sufficient evidence to enable a jury to reject the presumption of innocence beyond reasonable doubt. It is not possible for a prosecutor to prove guilt conclusively, nor can a researcher obtain unequivocal support for a research hypothesis. The defendant is presumed innocent until sufficient evidence indicates that he or she is not, and the null hypothesis is presumed true until sufficient evidence indicates otherwise.

For example, you might start with the expectation that children will show the development of greater mastery of mathematical concepts through individual instruction than through group instruction. In other words, you are positing a relationship between the independent variable (method of instruction) and the dependent variable (mastery of mathematical concepts). The research hypothesis is "Students taught through individual instruction will exhibit greater mastery of mathematical concepts than students taught through group instruction." The null hypothesis, the statement of no relationship between variables, will read "The mean mastery scores (population mean μ_i) of all students taught by individual instruction will equal the mean mastery scores (population mean μ_g) of all those taught by group instruction" $H_0: \mu_i \neq \mu_g$. Note that the hypothesis "Children taught by individual instruction will exhibit less mastery of mathematical concepts than those taught by group instruction" also posits a relationship between variables and therefore is *not* a null hypothesis. It is an example of what is called an **alternative hypothesis.** In the example, if the sample mean of the measure of mastery of mathematical concepts is higher for the individual instruction students than for the group instruction students, and inferential statistics indicate that the null hypothesis is unlikely to be true, you reject the null and tentatively conclude that individual instruction results in greater mastery of mathematical concepts than does group instruction. If, in contrast, the mean for the group instruction students is higher than the mean for the individual instruction students, and inferential statistics indicate that this difference is not likely to be a function of chance, then you tentatively conclude that group instruction is superior. If inferential statistics indicate that observed differences between the means of the two instructional groups could easily be a function of chance, the null hypothesis is retained, and you decide insufficient evidence exists for concluding there is a relationship between the dependent and independent variables. The retention of a null hypothesis is *not* positive evidence that the null hypothesis is true. It indicates that the evidence is insufficient and that the null hypothesis, the research hypothesis, and the alternative hypothesis are all possible.

TESTING THE HYPOTHESIS

A quantitative study begins with a research hypothesis, which should be a simple, clear statement of the expected relationship between the variables. We explained earlier that hypotheses must be testable, that is, amenable to empirical verification. When researchers speak of testing a hypothesis, however, they are referring to the null hypothesis. Only the null hypothesis can be directly tested by statistical procedures. **Testing a hypothesis** involves the following steps:

1. State, in operational terms, the relationships that should be observed if the research hypothesis is true.
2. State the null hypothesis.
3. Select a research method that will enable the hypothesized relationship to be observed if it is there.
4. Gather and analyze the empirical data.
5. Determine whether the evidence is sufficient to reject the null hypothesis.

Many hypotheses that are formulated are rejected after empirical testing. Their predictions are not supported by the data. Many beginning researchers believe that if the data they collect do not support their hypothesis, then their study is a failure. This is not the case. In the history of scientific research, hypotheses that failed to be supported have greatly outnumbered those that have been supported. Experienced researchers realize that unconfirmed hypotheses are an expected and useful part of the scientific experience. They can lead to reconsideration or revision of theory and the generation of new hypotheses, which often brings science closer to a correct explanation of the state of affairs. "I have steadily endeavored," Darwin (1898) wrote, "to keep my mind free so as to give up any hypothesis, however much beloved (and I cannot resist forming one on every subject), as soon as facts are shown to be opposed to it. Indeed, I have had no choice but to act in this manner, for with the exception of the Coral Reefs, I cannot remember a single first-formed hypothesis which had not after a time to be given up or greatly modified."

Even though you may find support for a hypothesis, except in cases of perfect induction the hypothesis is not *proved* to be true. A hypothesis is never proved or disproved; it is only supported or not supported. Hypotheses are essentially probabilistic in nature; empirical evidence can lead you to conclude that the explanation is probably true or that it is reasonable to accept the hypothesis, but it never proves the hypothesis.

A Classroom Example of Testing a Hypothesis

A teacher is interested in investigating reinforcement theory in the classroom. From her understanding of reinforcement theory, this teacher hypothesizes that teachers' positive comments on students' papers will lead to greater achievement.

Step 1. The deduced implication is stated as follows: "Teachers' positive comments on students' papers during a specified unit will result in higher scores on the end-of-unit test for those students, compared with students who received no comments." It is the relationship between the two variables—teachers' positive comments and pupil performance on the end-of-unit test—that will be investigated.

Step 2. For statistical testing, the research hypothesis must be transformed into a null hypothesis: "The population mean achievement score for students receiving positive comments (experimental group) will be the same as the population mean achievement score for students receiving no comments (control group)."

Step 3. The teacher would randomly select a number of students to be assigned to the experimental and control groups. For those students in the experimental group, she would write positive comments on their papers, whereas the students assigned to the control group would receive no comments. (The comments to the experimental group should simply be words of encouragement such as "Excellent," "Keep up the good work," or "You're doing better." These comments should have nothing to do with content or the correction of particular errors; otherwise, any improvement could be attributed to the instructional usefulness of such comments.

Step 4. After completing the specified unit, the teacher would administer a common end-of-unit test to both groups, and derive average (mean) achievement scores on the test for each group.

Step 5. Inferential statistics (see Chapter 7) can then be used to indicate whether any difference in mean achievement scores is real or is likely to be merely a function of chance. If the difference is not likely to be a function of chance, the researcher tentatively concludes that it results from the different treatments given to the two groups.

THE RESEARCH PLAN

After identifying the problem and formulating the research hypothesis, you are ready to develop a tentative research plan. The **research plan** at this stage is only a preliminary proposal; many changes will probably be needed before the final, formal proposal is written (see Chapter 16). Developing this tentative research plan is essential because it forces you to set down ideas in a concrete form. Many initial ideas seem promising until you must spell them out in black and white; then the difficulties or the inadequacies become obvious.

Another advantage of a written plan is that you can give it to others for their comments and criticism. In a research methods class, for example, the professor would certainly need to see what research students are planning. The director of a thesis or dissertation would want to see a written plan rather early in the process. It is much easier for another person to detect flaws and problems in a proposal that is written out than in one communicated orally. Another point to keep in mind is that the more complete and detailed this initial proposal, the more useful it will be to the researcher and the more time may be saved later.

A quantitative research plan should include the following elements: the problem, the hypothesis, the research methodology, and data analysis. The following list briefly describes each component.

1. *Problem.* The plan begins with a clear statement of the research problem. A quantitative problem asks about the relationship between specified variables; a qualitative problem is stated in terms of the purpose of the study. Include the rationale for the study and a brief description of the background of the problem in theory and/or related research.

2. *Hypothesis.* A quantitative question is followed by a concise statement of the research hypothesis. Provide operational definitions of the variables. Qualitative researchers do not state hypotheses at the beginning of the study. Instead, they generate hypotheses during the process of data collection and analysis.

3. *Methodology.* This section explains how you will conduct the study. Include the proposed research design, the population of concern, the sampling procedure, the measuring instruments, and any other information relevant to the conduct of the study. The qualitative researcher will need to describe the setting for the research, the people involved, and the various data sources to be used.

4. *Data Analysis.* Indicate how you will analyze the data to test the hypothesis and/or answer the research question. Beginning quantitative researchers may find it difficult to write this section because they are not yet familiar with statistics. You might look at the related literature to see what type of statistical analysis other researchers used, or you might consult with the professor or an expert in statistics.

The Pilot Study

After the tentative research plan is approved, it may be helpful to try out the proposed procedures on a few subjects. This trial run, or **pilot study,** will, first of all, help the researcher to decide whether the study is feasible and whether it is worthwhile to continue. It provides an opportunity to assess the appropriateness and practicality of the research methodology. It permits a preliminary testing of the hypothesis, which may give some indication of its tenability and suggest whether further refinement is needed.

Unanticipated problems that appear can be solved at this stage, thereby saving time and effort later. A pilot study is well worth the time required and is especially recommended for the beginning researcher.

SUMMARY

To proceed with the confirmatory phase of a quantitative research study, it is important to have one or more clearly stated hypotheses. The hypothesis is the researcher's prediction about the outcome of the study. Hypotheses are derived inductively from observation or deductively from a known theory. Experience and knowledge in the area and familiarity with previous research are important factors in formulating a satisfactory hypothesis.

The hypothesis serves a multipurpose function in research. It provides direction to the researcher's efforts because it determines the research method and the type of data relevant to the solution of the problem. It also provides a framework for interpreting the results and for stating the conclusions of the study.

A good hypothesis must satisfy certain criteria. It must be testable, which means that it relates variables that can be measured. It must agree with the preponderance of existing data. It must be stated as clearly and concisely as possible. And it must state the expected relationship between the variables.

Once formulated and evaluated in terms of these criteria, the research hypothesis is ready to be subjected to an empirical test. The null hypothesis—the negation of what the researcher expects—is stated. It is important to remember that a research hypothesis cannot be proved or disproved, only supported or not supported. Even if it is not supported, a hypothesis may still serve a useful purpose because it can lead the researcher to reevaluate rationale and procedures and to consider other approaches to the problem.

REFERENCES

Coopersmith, S. (1981). *The antecedents of self-esteem.* San Francisco: Consulting Psychology.

Darwin, F. (Ed.). (1898). *The life and letters of Charles Darwin* (Vol. 1). New York: Appleton.

Davis, F. (1988). The effect of time of day of instruction on eighth-grade students' English and mathematics achievement. *High School Journal, 71,* 78–80.

Festinger, L. (1954). A theory of social comparison process. *Human Relations, 7,* 117–140.

Kerlinger, F. N. (1986). *Foundations of behavioral research* (3rd ed.). New York: Holt, Rinehart and Winston.

Marsh, H. W., Chessor, D., Craven, R., & Roche, L. (1995). The effects of gifted and talented programs on academic self-concept: The big fish strikes again. *American Educational Research Journal, 32,* 285–319.

Piaget, J. (1968). *Six psychological studies.* New York: Vintage Books.

KEY CONCEPTS

alternative hypothesis
criteria for evaluating hypotheses
deductive hypothesis
directional hypothesis

functions of hypotheses
inductive hypothesis
nondirectional hypothesis
null hypothesis

pilot study
research plan
testing hypotheses
theory

EXERCISES

1. What is the purpose of the hypothesis in research?

2. What is the difference between an inductive and a deductive hypothesis?

3. State a hypothesis based on each of the following research questions:
   a. What would be the effect of using the Cuisenaire method in teaching elementary arithmetic?
   b. Is there a relationship between the gender of the tutor and the gains made in reading achievement by black male elementary students?
   c. Does living in interracial housing affect attitudes toward members of another race?
   d. Is there any relationship between the type of reinforcement (tangible or intangible) and the amount of learning achieved by socioeconomically disadvantaged children?
   e. Does preschool training reduce the educational gap separating advantaged and disadvantaged children before they enter first grade?
   f. Do teacher expectations of children's intellectual performance have any effect on the children's actual performance?

4. Rewrite the following hypothesis in null form: "Children who read below grade level will express less satisfaction with school than those who read at or above grade level."

5. Evaluate the adequacy of each of the following hypotheses. If a hypothesis is inadequate, state the reason for the inadequacy and write an adequate hypothesis.
   a. "Teachers deserve higher pay than administrators."
   b. "Students who take a middle school government course will be capable of more enlightened judgments concerning local political affairs than will those who do not take the course."
   c. "Computer-based drill and practice is a better way to teach slow learners multiplication combinations than is flash cards."

   d. "If students differ in their socioeconomic status, they will differ in their English proficiency scores."
   e. "Children who show high achievement motivation will show high anxiety as measured by the Children's Manifest Anxiety Scale."
   f. "Positive verbal reinforcement of student responses by the teacher will lessen the probability of future responses."

6. Write a directional and a nondirectional hypothesis based on the research question "What is the relationship between the rate of maturation of adolescent boys and their self-concepts?"

7. Why should a hypothesis be clearly stated before a quantitative research study is initiated?

8. Label the following hypotheses as research hypotheses or null hypotheses:
   a. "Students will receive lower scores on achievement tests that measure the higher levels of Bloom's taxonomy."
   b. "There is no difference in the performance of students taught mathematics by Method A and those taught mathematics by Method B."
   c. "The mean retention scores of children receiving experimental Drug X will not differ from the scores of children who did not receive Drug X."
   d. "Students taught by laissez-faire teachers will show higher problem-solving skills than students taught by authoritarian teachers."

9. Locate a research study stating a hypothesis, and try to identify the theory from which the hypothesis originated.

10. Evaluate the following statements as possible research hypotheses:
    a. "Asian high school students are better in mathematics than American high school students."

b. "Do SAT prep courses improve students' scores on the SAT?"

c. "Students who participate in the high school volunteerism program become better adult citizens than students who do not."

11. A researcher has a theory about children's ordinal position in the family and their achievement motivation. Write a research hypothesis that might be based on existing theory. Then write the hypothesis in null form.

12. Formulate a tentative research plan for your class project.

a. What is the general research problem under consideration for investigation?

b. State the preceding general problem as a research question.

c. Explain the rationale for such a study. What are its theoretical or practical applications?

d. State the hypothesis (or hypotheses) for this study.

e. Was this hypothesis derived deductively from theory, or inductively from experience and observation? Explain.

f. Identify the variables in the study, and operationally define each.

g. What kind of research methodology will be required for this study?

h. What subjects (sample) will you select for the study?

i. Have you located any published research related to your problem? If so, briefly summarize the findings.

13. Select a theory that you find interesting and derive a research hypothesis from this theory. You might choose a learning theory, motivational theory, theory of cognitive dissonance, or any other educational or psychological theory.

ANSWERS

1. The purpose of hypotheses is to provide a tentative proposition suggested as a solution to a problem or as an explanation of some phenomenon.

2. With an inductive hypothesis, the researcher makes observations of relationships and then hypothesizes an explanation for the observed behavior. With a deductive hypothesis, the researcher formulates a hypothesis based on known theory, accompanied by a rationale for the particular proposition.

3. a. "Elementary students taught by the Cuisenaire method will score higher on an arithmetic test than students not taught by the Cuisenaire method."

b. "Black male elementary students tutored by another male will achieve higher reading scores than will black male elementary students tutored by a female."

c. "People living in interracial housing will express more favorable attitudes toward those of another race than will people living in segregated housing."

d. "Socioeconomically disadvantaged children reinforced with tangible rewards will exhibit greater learning achievement than will children reinforced with intangible rewards."

e. "Advantaged and disadvantaged children of preschool age receiving preschool training will be separated by a smaller educational gap than will advantaged and disadvantaged children of preschool age not receiving preschool training." (*Note:* The terms *advantaged* and *disadvantaged children, preschool training,* and *educational gap* would need to be defined.)

f. "Children whose teachers have high expectations of their intellectual performance will perform at a higher level than will children whose teachers have low expectations of their intellectual performance."

4. There is no difference in the satisfaction with school expressed by children who read below grade level and children who read at or above grade level.

5. a. The hypothesis is inadequate, because it is a value statement and cannot be investigated in a research study. A legitimate hypothesis would be "Teachers who receive higher pay than their administrators will express greater job satisfaction than will teachers who do not receive higher pay than their administrators."

   b. The hypothesis is inadequate because *enlightened judgments* is a value term. An acceptable hypothesis would be "Students who take a middle school government course will evidence more knowledge concerning local political affairs, and will more often arrive at inferences based on this knowledge, than will students who do not take a middle school government course."

   c. The hypothesis is inadequate because *better* is a value term and because it lacks clear and concise operational definitions. A testable hypothesis would be "Those students performing below grade level in math who practice multiplication combinations through computer drill and practice will, on average, score a higher proportion of correct answers on a criterion test than will students performing below grade level who spend the same amount of time practicing multiplication combinations with flash cards."

d. The hypothesis is inadequate because there is no statement of an expected relationship between variables. An acceptable hypothesis would be "Students classified as having high socioeconomic status will have higher scores on an English proficiency test than will students classified as having low socioeconomic status."

e. The hypothesis is inadequate because there are no independent or dependent variables. An acceptable hypothesis would be "Children who show high achievement motivation will have higher scores on the Children's Manifest Anxiety Scale than children with low achievement motivation."

f. The hypothesis is inadequate because it is inconsistent with the existing knowledge of positive reinforcement and its effect on student responses.

6. *Directional hypothesis:* "Early-maturing boys will exhibit more positive self-concepts than late-maturing boys." *Nondirectional hypothesis:* "There is a difference in the self-concepts of early- and late-maturing adolescent boys."

7. The hypothesis gives direction to the collection and interpretation of data. Clearly stating the hypothesis reveals flaws that were not apparent while developing the vague idea of the study in mind.

8. a. Research
   b. Null
   c. Null
   d. Research

9. Answers will vary.

10. a. "Better in math" needs to be operationally defined.

   b. A hypothesis is not stated in question form.

   c. It is not testable as stated. How would you define and measure "better adult citizens"?

11. *Research hypothesis:* "Achievement motivation and ordinal birth position in the family are positively related; or first-born children have greater achievement motivation than their siblings." *Null hypothesis:* "There is no relationship between children's birth position in the family and their achievement motivation."

12. Answers will vary.

13. Answers will vary.

 ## INFOTRAC COLLEGE EDITION

Use the keywords *hypothesis* + *research* to locate a research article that states a hypothesis. How was the hypothesis stated? Was the hypothesis based on deduction from a theory or was it derived inductively from observation? Were operational definitions provided for the variables in the hypothesis?

Chapter 6

Descriptive Statistics

After studying this chapter, the student will be able to

1. Identify the characteristics and limitations of four types of measurement scales—nominal, ordinal, interval, and ratio.

2. Organize research data into frequency distributions, and present them as frequency polygons and histograms and interpret polygons and histograms occurring in the professional literature.

3. Distinguish between the measures of central tendency and the situations in which each should be used, and calculate the mean, the median, and the mode for any given data. Interpret measures of central tendency.

4. Describe appropriate applications of measures of variability, and compute variance, standard deviation, and range for any given set of data.

5. Explain why z-scores have universal meaning and how this is useful in interpreting the position of a single observation in a distribution.

6 Convert a *z*-score to a stanine score, and use this to give a verbal description of the score's meaning.

7 Transform raw scores into standard scores, and determine the relative position of *z*-scores in a normal curve.

8 Identify characteristics of the normal curve.

9 Explain advantages and disadvantages of percentile ranks. Calculate percentile rank for a given score.

10 Identify appropriate applications of Pearson *r* correlation for describing the relationship between variables.

11 Compute the coefficient of correlation between two sets of interval or ratio data.

12 Describe the meaning of coefficient of determination and its application in interpreting the coefficient of correlation.

13 Identify the components of effect size and what increases and what decreases effect size.

14 Explain how effect size assesses the strength of relationships between variables.

15 Calculate effect size.

16 Calculate meta-analysis, and explain the meaning of a meta-analysis outcome.

Statistical procedures are basically methods of handling quantitative information in such a way as to make that information meaningful. These procedures have two principal advantages. First, they enable researchers to organize, summarize, and describe observations. Such techniques are called **descriptive statistics.** Second, they help determine how reliably researchers can infer that those phenomena observed in a limited group—a *sample*—will also occur in the unobserved larger population of concern from which the sample was drawn—in other words, how accurately you can employ inductive reasoning to infer that what you observe in the part will be observed in the whole. For problems of this nature you will need to employ **inferential statistics.** A knowledge of some basic statistical procedures is essential for researchers proposing to carry out quantitative research, so that they can analyze and interpret their data and communicate their findings to others. In addition, it is desirable that educators who need to keep abreast of research and to use research findings be familiar with statistical procedures so they can understand and evaluate research studies conducted by others. The proper administration and interpretation of tests used in schools also require some understanding of statistical procedures. Teachers who are unfamiliar with these procedures may have difficulty evaluating their students' abilities and performance. They also find it difficult to review research in their areas of specialization and to acquire up-to-date information.

SCALES OF MEASUREMENT

A fundamental step in the conduct of research is measurement: the process through which observations are translated into numbers. S. S. Stevens (1951) p. 1 stated, "In its broadest sense, measurement is the assignment of numerals to objects or events according to rules." Quantitative researchers first identify the variables they want to study, then use rules to determine how to express these variables numerically. The variable *religious preference* may be measured according to the numbers indicated by students who are asked to select one among (1) Catholic, (2) Jewish, (3) Protestant, or (4) other. The variable *weight* may be measured as the numbers observed when subjects step on a scale. The variable *social maturity* may be measured as scores on the Vineland Social Maturity Scale. The nature of the measurement process that produces the numbers determines the interpretation that can be made from them and the statistical procedures that can be meaningfully used with them. The most widely quoted taxonomy of measurement procedures is Stevens's Scales of Measurement, in which he classifies measurement as nominal, ordinal, interval, and ratio.

Nominal Scale

The most primitive scale of measurement is the **nominal scale.** Nominal measurement involves placing objects or individuals into categories that are qualitatively rather than quantitatively different. Measurement at this level requires only that you be able to distinguish two or more relevant, mutually exclusive categories, and know the criteria for placing an individual or object into the appropriate category. The required empirical operation at this level of measurement involves only recognizing whether an object or individual does or does not belong in a given category. The only relationship between categories is that they are *different* from each other; there is no suggestion that one category represents "more" or "less" of a characteristic. For example, classifying students according to gender constitutes nominal measurement.

Numbers may be used at the nominal level, but only when arbitrarily assigned to serve as labels to identify the categories. There is no empirical relationship between the numbers used in nominal measurement that corresponds to the actual mathematical relationship between the numbers used. For example, the numeral 0 might be used to represent males and the numeral 1 to represent females—but the 1 does not indicate more of something than the 0, and numbers could be interchanged without affecting anything but the labeling scheme used. School District 231 is not necessarily more or less of anything than School District 103. The numbers used at the nominal level do not represent either absolute or relative amounts of any characteristic, but merely serve to identify members of a given category.

The identifying numbers in a nominal scale cannot, of course, be arithmetically manipulated through addition, subtraction, multiplication, or division. You may use only those statistical procedures based on mere counting, such as reporting the numbers of observations in each category, or expressing those numbers as percentages of the total number of subjects.

Ordinal Scale

Next on the hierarchy of measurement scales is the **ordinal scale,** which ranks objects or individuals with respect to how much or how little of the attribute under consideration they possess. Objects or individuals are placed in order according to the degree to which they possess that attribute—but without indicating the degree of difference, or distance, between them. Ordinal measurement occurs, for example, when teachers rank students in a class from highest to lowest on characteristics such as social maturity, leadership abilities, or cooperativeness.

The essential requirement for measurement at this level is that the relationship must be such that if object A is greater than object B and object B is greater than object C, then object A is greater than object C and is written thus: If $(A > B)$ and $(B > C)$, then $(A > C)$. When appropriate, other wording may be substituted for "greater than"—"stronger than," "precedes," "has more of," and so on.

When numbers are assigned in ordinal measurement, they indicate only the *order* of the observations and nothing more. Neither the difference between the numbers nor their ratio has meaning. Thus if the numerals 1, 2, and 3 are used to label observations, there is no implication that the distance between ranks is equal—that is, that 1 is as much higher in rank than 2 as 2 is higher than 3. In an untimed footrace, you only know who came in first, second, and third; you have no way of knowing how much faster one runner was than any other. The difference between first and second place would not necessarily be the same as the difference between second and third, nor could you say that the runner who came in second was twice as fast as the runner who came in fourth. A ranking of students on the basis of math scores or a ranking of high school seniors on the basis of grades represents an ordinal scale.

Another good example of an ordinal scale is the scale of hardness of minerals. Geologists arrange minerals according to their ability to scratch one another. If mineral A can scratch mineral B, then mineral A is said to be harder than mineral B. On this basis a diamond is ranked as the hardest, because it can scratch all other known minerals but cannot be scratched by any others. Geologists selected a set of ten minerals ranging in hardness from the softest to the hardest as a standard and assigned them numbers from 1 to 10, with 1 indicating the softest mineral and 10 the hardest. Other minerals are assigned numbers on the basis of the scratch test. Thus this scale gives the order of hardness of minerals, but does not say how much harder one mineral is than another. You cannot assume that a mineral assigned a value of 4 is twice as hard as a mineral with a value of 2, or that the difference in hardness between minerals 2 and 4 is the same as the difference in hardness between minerals with values 1 and 3.

The statistics appropriate for an ordinal scale are limited. Because the size of the interval between the categories is unknown, you cannot appropriately use any statistical procedure that assumes equal intervals. Statistics that indicate the points below which certain percentages of the cases fall are appropriate with an ordinal scale.

Interval Scale

A more precise measurement system is the **interval scale,** which not only orders objects or events according to the amount of the attribute they represent but also has an arbitrary origin and establishes equal intervals between the units of measure. Equal differences in the numbers represent equal differences in the attribute being measured. The Fahrenheit and Centigrade thermometers are examples of interval scales.

On an interval scale, both the order and distance relationships among the numbers have meaning. You can assert that the difference between 50 and 51 degrees Centigrade is equal to the difference between 30 and 31 degrees Centigrade. You could not say, however, that 50 degrees is twice as hot as 25 degrees. This is because there is no true zero point on an interval scale. A zero point is established by convention, as in the Centigrade scale, which assigns the value 0 degrees to the freezing point of water.

Likewise, the zero point on a psychological or educational scale test is arbitrary. For example, there is no zero intelligence; there is no way in standardized intelligence tests to identify an individual of zero intelligence. A student may occasionally receive a score of 0 on a statistics test, but this does not mean that he or she has zero knowledge of statistics. If you had three students who made scores of 15, 30, and 45 on a statistics test, you could not say that the score of 30 represents twice as much knowledge of statistics as the score of 15 or that the score of 45 represents three times as much knowledge as the score of 15. To understand the reason why, let's assume that 15 very simple items are added to the test so that all three students can answer them correctly. The three scores would now become 30, 45, and 60 for the three students. If you attempted to form ratios between the values on this interval-type scale, you would (mistakenly) report that the student with a score of 60 had twice as much knowledge of statistics as the student with a score of 30—but in the earlier ratio you had already (incorrectly) assumed that the same student had three times as great a knowledge of statistics as the other student. Thus the conclusions do not agree.

Numbers on an interval scale may be manipulated by addition and subtraction, but because the zero is arbitrary, multiplication and division of the numbers are not appropriate. As noted, ratios between the numbers on an interval scale are meaningless. However, the difference between positions on an interval scale may be reported or the numbers may be added. Any statistical procedures based on adding may be used with this level scale along with the procedures appropriate for the lower-level scales. These include most of the common statistical procedures.

It is important to point out that in most academic measures, the intervals are equal in terms of the measuring instrument itself but not necessarily in terms of the performance being measured. To illustrate, consider a spelling test with the following words: *cat, dish, ball, loquacious, schizophrenia,* and *pneumonia.* Here the distance between one correct and three correct is the same as the distance between three correct and five correct. However, when considered in terms of spelling performance, the difference between three and five correct suggests a greater difference in ability than does the difference between one and three correct. Unless you can say that the distance between three and five on the spelling test represents the same amount of spelling performance as does the distance between one and three, then these scores indicate nothing more than the rank order of the students.

However, through careful construction it is possible to produce an instrument where the intervals observed between scores on the test give a reasonable approximation of ability intervals. The better intelligence tests are an example of this. The difference in ability between an IQ of 90 and an IQ of 95 may not be precisely the same as the difference between an IQ of 105 and an IQ of 110, but you will not be greatly misled if you assume that the two differences are approximately equal.

It has become common practice to treat many educational variables, such as classroom tests and grades ($A = 4$, $B = 3$, and so on), as if they were interval data, even when that assumption is not well justified. It would be difficult to maintain that the difference between $F = 0$ and $D = 1$ represents the same difference in academic achievement as the difference between $C = 2$ and $B = 3$, or to justify treating scores on our spelling test example as interval. Be cautious when interpreting interval statistics derived from such data. The statistics imply interval-level information when the information is actually somewhere between ordinal and interval.

Ratio Scale

A **ratio scale,** the highest level of measurement scale, has a true zero point, as well as equal intervals. Ratios can be formed between any two given values on the scale. A yardstick used to measure length in units of inches or feet is a ratio scale, because the origin on the scale is an absolute zero corresponding to no length at all. Thus, it is possible to state that a stick 6 feet long is twice as long as a stick 3 feet long. With a ratio scale, it is possible to multiply or divide each of the values by a certain number without changing the properties of the scale. For example, you can multiply 2 pounds by 16 to change the unit of measurement to 32 ounces, or you can multiply 6 feet by 12 to change the unit to inches. You can multiply and maintain the same ratio as before the multiplication. For example, you can multiply 4 quarts of milk and 2 quarts of milk by 2 and change the unit of measurement to pints. In pints, 8 pints is still twice as much as 4 pints.

Only a few variables of interest in education are ratio in nature. These are largely confined to motor performance and other physiological measures. Although you can say that a person 6 feet tall is twice as tall as a person 3 feet tall, because heights are ratio data, you cannot say that a person who scores 40 on a math test is twice as good at math as a person who scores 20 on a math test, because math test scores are interval data. All types of statistical procedures are appropriate with a ratio scale.

ORGANIZING RESEARCH DATA

Describing data that have not been arranged in some kind of order is very difficult, if not impossible. Therefore, organizing research data is a fundamental step in descriptive statistics. Two frequently used ways of organizing data are (1) arranging the measures into frequency distributions and (2) presenting them in graphic form.

Frequency Distributions

A systematic arrangement of individual measures from lowest to highest is called a **frequency distribution.** The use of this technique merely involves listing the individual measures in a column, with the highest measure at the top, the next highest second from the top, and continuing down until the lowest measure is recorded at the bottom of the column. Several identical scores often occur in a distribution. Instead of listing these scores separately, it is customary to add a second column where the frequency of each measure is recorded. Table 6.1 shows the scores of a group of 105 students in a statistics test. Section A of the table lists the scores in an unorganized form. Section B arranges the same scores in a frequency distribution. From a frequency distribution it is possible to examine the general "shape" of the distribution. With the scores so organized, you can determine their spread, whether they are distributed evenly or tend to cluster, and where clusters occur in the distribution. For example, looking over the frequency distribution of the scores presented in Table 6.1, it is easy to see that they range from 21 to 35, that 29 is the most frequent score, and that scores tend to cluster more near the top of the distribution than the bottom. None of this would be apparent had the scores not been organized. Organizing data into frequency distributions also facilitates the computation of various useful statistics.

Graphic Presentations

It is often helpful and convenient to present research data in graphic form. Among various types of graphs, the most widely used are the **histogram** and the **frequency polygon.** The initial steps in constructing the histogram and the frequency polygon are identical:

1. Lay out the score points on a horizontal dimension (abscissa) from the lowest value on the left to the highest on the right. Leave enough space for an additional score at both ends of the distribution.

Table 6.1 The Test Scores of 105 Students on a Statistics Test

A. UNORGANIZED SCORES

33	29	30	30	33	29	33	32	28	24	34	31	27	29	23
25	29	24	27	26	33	33	26	30	28	26	29	32	32	31
28	34	30	31	33	21	29	31	30	32	35	30	31	27	29
26	29	33	32	29	28	28	30	28	27	30	31	34	33	22
30	29	27	29	24	30	21	31	31	33	28	21	31	29	31
31	33	22	29	31	32	32	31	28	29	30	22	33	30	30
32	33	31	33	28	29	27	33	27	21	30	29	28	27	33

B. FREQUENCY DISTRIBUTION

SCORES (X)	TALLIES	FREQUENCIES (f)
35	/	1
34	///	3
33	LHT LHT LHT	15
32	LHT ///	8
31	LHT LHT ////	14
30	LHT LHT ////	14
29	LHT LHT LHT /	16
28	LHT LHT	10
27	LHT ///	8
26	////	4
25	/	1
24	///	3
23	/	1
22	///	3
21	////	4
		$N = \overline{105}$

2. Lay out the frequencies of the scores (or intervals) on the vertical dimension (ordinate), numbering up from 0.

3. Place a dot above the center of each score at the level of the frequency of that score.

From this point you can construct either a histogram or a polygon. In constructing a histogram, draw through each dot a horizontal line equal to the width representing a score, as shown in Figure 6.1. To construct a polygon, connect the adjacent dots, and connect the two ends of the resulting figure to the base (zero line) at the points representing 1 less than the lowest score and 1 more than the highest score, as shown in Figure 6.2. Histograms are preferred when a researcher wants to indicate the discrete nature of the data, such as when a nominal scale has been used. Polygons are preferred to indicate the continuous nature of the data.

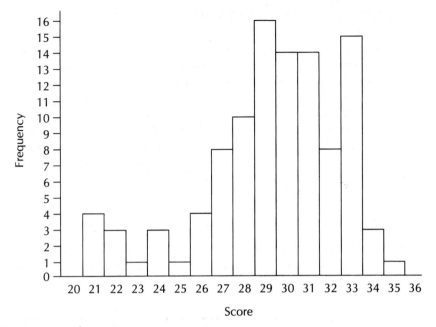

FIGURE 6.1

Histogram of 105 Test Scores from Table 6.1

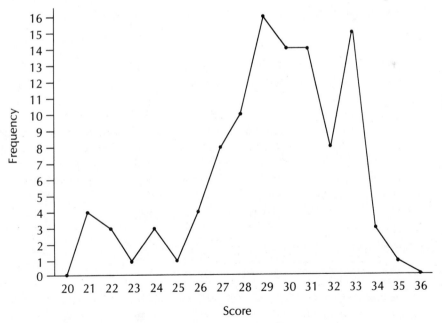

FIGURE 6.2

Frequency Polygon of 105 Test Scores from Table 6.1

◼ MEASURES OF CENTRAL TENDENCY

A convenient way of summarizing data is to find a single index that can represent a whole set of measures. For example, finding a single score that can give an indication of the performance of a group of 300 students on an aptitude test would be useful for comparative purposes. In statistics three indexes are available for such use. They are called **measures of central tendency,** or *averages*. To most laypeople, the term *average* means the sum of the scores divided by the number of scores. To a statistician, the average can be this measure, known as the *mean,* or one of the other two measures of central tendency, known as the *mode* and the *median*. Each of these three can serve as an index to represent a group as a whole.

The Mode

The **mode** is the value in a distribution that occurs most frequently. It is the simplest to find of the three measures of central tendency, because it is determined by inspection rather than by computation. Given the distribution of scores

| 14 | 16 | 16 | 17 | 18 | 19 | 19 | 19 | 21 | 22 |

you can readily see that the mode of this distribution is 19 because it is the most frequent score. In a histogram or polygon the mode is the score value of the highest point, as you can see in Figures 6.1 and 6.2, where the mode is 29. Sometimes there is more than one mode in a distribution. For example, if the scores had been

| 14 | 16 | 16 | 16 | 18 | 19 | 19 | 19 | 21 | 22 |

you would have two modes: 16 and 19. This kind of distribution with two modes is called *bimodal*. Distributions with three or more modes are called *trimodal* or *multimodal,* respectively.

The mode is the least useful indicator of central value in a distribution, for two reasons. In the first place, it is unstable. For example, two random samples drawn from the same population may have quite different modes. In the second place, a distribution may have more than one mode. In published research the mode is seldom reported as an indicator of central tendency. Its use is largely limited to inspectional purposes. A mode may be reported for any of the scales of measurement, but it is the only measure of central tendency that may legitimately be used with nominal scales.

The Median

The **median** is defined as that point in a distribution of measures below which 50 percent of the cases lie (which means that the other 50 percent will lie above this point). When there are an odd number of scores, the median is the middle score in the distribution. For example, given the following distribution of scores the median is 18.

14   15   16   17   18   19   20   21   22

When there are an even number of scores, the median is the midpoint between the two middle scores (average of the two middle scores). For example, given the distribution of scores

14   16   16   17   18   19   20   20   21   22

the point below which 50 percent of the cases fall is halfway between 18 and 19. Thus the median of this distribution is 18.5. To find this value, we first placed the ten scores of the distribution in rank order (that is, from the lowest to the highest) and then found the point below which one half of the scores lie. This point, 18.5, which exactly separates the two values 18 and 19, is called in statistical terminology the *upper limit* of the score 18 and the *lower limit* of the score 19. In computing the median, each score is thought of as representing a range, or interval, from halfway between that score and the next lowest score up to halfway between that score and the next highest score. Thus, in the example, 18 is thought of as representing an interval from 17.5 to 18.5, whereas 19 represents an interval from 18.5 to 19.5.

It is important to note that the median does not always fall on the borderline between two values. If there are tied scores at the middle of the distribution, the median is located somewhere between the upper limit and the lower limit of that score interval and you must interpolate within the interval. For the purpose of establishing the median, you must picture a recorded score as representing the range between its lower and upper limits rather than a single point. Consider the following example:

23   24   25   26   26   26   26   27

In this distribution, the median falls between two of the scores of 26. Note the frequency of the score 26. There are four of these scores in the distribution, one of which is located below the midpoint and three above the midpoint. In this case, to find the median you must subdivide the interval 25.50 to 26.50 into four parts. The distance between each of these four scores would thus be 0.25 of the interval. Each of these scores is therefore thought of as representing a range covering 0.25 of the distance between 25.50 and 26.50, which are the lower and upper limits of the score 26. The following is an illustration of this concept, showing the position and value of the median:

Notice that the median does not take into account the size of individual scores. To find it, arrange your data in rank order and find the point that divides the distribution into two equal halves. The median is an ordinal statistic because it is based on rank. You can compute a median from interval or ratio data, but in such cases the interval characteristic of the data is not being used. One circumstance in which the median may be the preferred measure of central tendency arises when there are some extreme scores in the distribution. In this case the use of a measure of central tendency that takes into account the size of each score results in either overestimation or underestimation of the typical score. The median, because of its insensitivity to extreme scores, is the appropriate index to be applied when you want to find the typical score. For illustration, consider the following distribution:

49   50   51   53   54   55   56   70   89

The score of 54, which is the median of this distribution, is the most typical score. An index that takes into account the individual values of the scores 70 and 89 will certainly result in an overestimation of the typical score.

The Mean

The most widely used measure of central tendency is the **mean,** or *arithmetic average.* It is the sum of all the values in a distribution divided by the number of cases. In terms of a formula it is

$$\overline{X} = \frac{X_1 + X_2 + X_3 + \ldots + X_n}{N} \tag{6.1}$$

which is usually written as

$$\overline{X} = \frac{\Sigma X}{N} \tag{6.2}$$

where

$$\overline{X} = \text{mean}$$
$$\Sigma = \text{sum of}$$
$$X = \text{raw score}$$
$$N = \text{number of cases}$$

Applying formula 6.2 to the following IQ scores, we find that the mean is 111:

IQ scores: 112   121   115   101   119   109   100

$$\overline{X} = \frac{112 + 121 + 115 + 101 + 119 + 109 + 100}{7} = \frac{777}{7} = 111$$

Note that in this computation the scores were not arranged in any particular order. Ordering is unnecessary for calculation of the mean.

Because the mean is an arithmetic average, it is classified as an interval statistic. Its use is appropriate for interval or ratio data but not for nominal or ordinal data.

Comparison of the Three Indexes of Central Location

Because the mean is an interval or ratio statistic, it is generally a more precise measure than the median (an ordinal statistic) or the mode (a nominal statistic). It takes into account the value of *every* score. It is also the most stable of the three measures of central tendency in that if a number of samples are randomly drawn from a parent population, the means of these samples will vary less from one another than will their medians and their modes. For these reasons the mean is more frequently used in research than the other two measures.

The mean is the best indicator of the combined performance of an entire group. However, the median is the best indicator of *typical* performance. Consider, for example, a school board whose members have the following annual incomes: $140,000, $60,000, $50,000, $40,000, and $40,000. The mean, $66,000, is the sum of their incomes divided by the number of members, but it is higher than all but one of the board members' incomes. The median, $50,000, gives a better picture of the typical income in the group.

Shapes of Distributions

Frequency distributions can have a variety of shapes. A distribution is symmetrical when the two halves are mirror images of each other. In a **symmetrical distribution** the values of the mean and the median coincide. If such a distribution has a single mode, rather than two or more modes, the three indexes of central tendency will coincide, as shown in Figure 6.3.

If a distribution is not symmetrical, it is described as a **skewed distribution,** pulled out to one end or the other by the presence of the extreme scores. In skewed distributions

FIGURE 6.3
Symmetrical Distribution

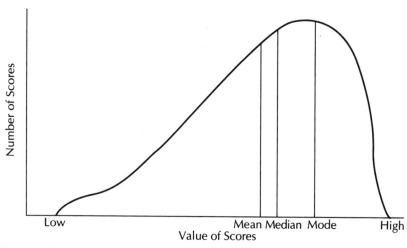

FIGURE 6.4
Negatively Skewed Distribution

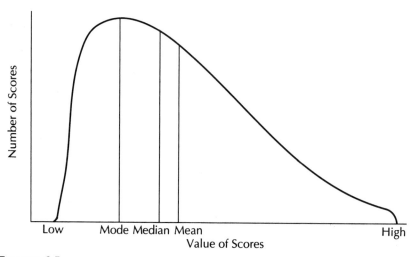

FIGURE 6.5
Positively Skewed Distribution

the values of the measures of central tendency differ. In such distributions the value of the mean, because it is influenced by the size of extreme scores, is pulled toward the end of the distribution in which the extreme scores lie, as shown in Figures 6.4 and 6.5. The effect of extreme values is less on the median because this index is influenced not by the size of scores but by their position. Extreme values have no impact on the mode because this index has no relation with either of the ends of the distribution. When the distribution is skewed toward the lower end, or negatively skewed, the mean is *always* smaller than the median and the median is *usually* smaller than the mode (Figure 6.4). When a distribution is skewed toward the higher end, or positively skewed, the mean is *always* greater than the median and the median is *usually* greater than the mode (Figure 6.5). The skew of a distribution can be identified by comparing the mean and the median without necessarily constructing a histogram or polygon.

MEASURES OF VARIABILITY

Although indexes of central tendency help researchers describe data in terms of average value or typical measure, they do not give the total picture of a distribution. The mean values of two distributions may be identical, whereas the degree of dispersion, or **variability,** of their scores might be different. In one distribution the scores might cluster around the central value; in the other, they might be scattered. For illustration, consider the following distributions of scores:

(a) 24, 24, 25, 25, 25, 26, 26 $\overline{X} = 175/7 = 25$

(b) 16, 19, 22, 25, 28, 30, 35 $\overline{X} = 175/7 = 25$

The value of the mean in both these distributions is 25, but the degree of scattering of the scores differs considerably. The scores in distribution (a) are obviously much more homogeneous than those in distribution (b). There is clearly a need for indexes that can describe distributions in terms of *variation, spread, dispersion,* or *scatter* of scores. In statistics several indexes are available for this purpose. The most commonly used are range, variance, and standard deviation.

Range

The simplest of all indexes of variability is the **range.** It is the difference between the highest and the lowest scores in a distribution, and it is found by subtracting the smallest value from the highest and adding 1. As a formula, it is

$$R = (X_h - X_l) + 1 \qquad (6.3)$$

R = range
X_h = highest value in a distribution
X_l = lowest value in a distribution

For example, 15 and 7, respectively, are the ranges in the following distributions:

2	10	11	12	13	14	16
9	10	11	12	13	14	15

Recall from a previous discussion that each score in a distribution represents an interval from halfway between that score and the next lowest score up to halfway between that score and the next highest score. For example, the number 4 represents the midpoint of the interval 3.5 to 4.5. Thus to find the range, you take the upper real limit of the highest score minus the lower real limit of the lowest score.

In the first example just given, you find the range by subtracting 1.5 (the lower limit of the lowest score) from 16.5 (the upper limit of the highest score), which is equal to 15. In the second example, the range is 15.5 − 8.5, or 7. It is simpler to use formula 6.3, and to just subtract the lower number from the higher number and add 1. In the first example, 16 − 2 + 1 = 15, and in the second 15 − 9 + 1 = 7. The range is an unreliable index of variability because it is based on only two values, the highest and the lowest. As you can readily see from the preceding distributions, it is not a stable indicator of the nature of the spread of the measures around the central value. For this reason the use of the range is mainly limited to inspectional purposes. Some research reports refer to the range of distributions, but such references are usually used in conjunction with other measures of variability, such as variance and standard deviation.

Variance and Standard Deviation

Variance and standard deviation are the most useful measures of variability. They are both based on *deviation scores*—scores that show the difference between a raw score and the mean of the distribution. The formula for a deviation score is

$$x = X - \overline{X} \tag{6.4}$$

where

$$x = \text{deviation score}$$
$$X = \text{raw score}$$
$$\overline{X} = \text{mean}$$

Scores below the mean will have negative deviation scores, and scores above the mean will have positive deviation scores. By definition, the sum of the deviation scores in a distribution is always 0. Thus, to use deviation scores in calculating measures of variability, you must find a way to get around the fact $\Sigma x = 0$. The technique used is to square each deviation score so that they all become positive numbers. If you then sum the squared deviations and divide by the number of scores, you have the mean of the squared deviations from the mean, or the **variance.** In mathematical form, variance is

$$\sigma^2 = \frac{\Sigma x^2}{N} \tag{6.5}$$

where

$$\sigma^2 = \text{variance}$$
$$\Sigma = \text{sum of}$$
$$x = \text{deviation of each score from the mean } (X - \overline{X}), \text{ otherwise known}$$
$$\quad \text{as the } deviation\ score$$
$$N = \text{number of cases in the distribution}$$

Table 6.2 *Computation of the Standard Deviation*

(1) X	(2) $x = X - \overline{X}$	(3) $x^2 = (X - \overline{X})^2$
10	+4	+16
9	+3	+9
9	+3	+9
8	+2	+4
7	+1	+1
6	0	0
5	−1	+1
3	−3	+9
2	−4	+16
1	−5	+25
$\Sigma X = 60$		$\Sigma x^2 = 90$

$$\overline{X} = \frac{60}{10} = 6 \qquad \sigma = \sqrt{\frac{90}{10}} = \sqrt{9} = 3$$

Because each of the deviation scores is squared, the variance is necessarily expressed in units that are squares of the original units of measure. For example, you might find that the variance of the heights of children in a class is 9 square inches. This would tell you that this class is more heterogeneous in height than a class with a variance of 4 square inches and more homogeneous than a class with a variance of 16 square inches.

In many cases educators prefer an index that summarizes the data in the same unit of measurement as the original data. **Standard deviation** (σ), the square root of variance, provides such an index. It is by far the most commonly used measure of variability. By definition, the standard deviation is the square root of the mean of the squared deviation scores. Rewriting this definition using symbols, you obtain

$$\sigma = \sqrt{\frac{\Sigma x^2}{N}} \tag{6.6}$$

For an illustration, consider Table 6.2. Column (1) in this table shows the distribution of vocabulary test scores of ten individuals. The mean of this distribution is 6. Column (2) presents the deviations for each of the scores. For example, the deviation of the score 8 from the mean is +2, the deviation of the score 5 from the mean is −1, and so forth. Column (3) shows the squares of each of these deviation scores. The sum of these squared deviation scores is 90. Putting this value in the formula and dividing by 10, the number of cases, you arrive at 9, which is the mean of the squared deviation scores. The square root of this value is 3, which is the standard deviation of this distribution. The foregoing procedure is convenient when the mean of the distribution is a round number, which it is not in most cases. Therefore, the following formula has been developed to eliminate

Table 6.3 *Computation of the Standard Deviation Using Formula 6.7*

X	X²	
10	100	
9	81	$\sigma = \sqrt{\dfrac{450 - \dfrac{(60)^2}{10}}{10}}$
9	81	
8	64	
7	49	$= \sqrt{\dfrac{450 - 360}{10}}$
6	36	
5	25	
3	9	$= \sqrt{9}$
2	4	$= 3$
1	1	
$\Sigma X = 60$	$\Sigma X^2 = 450$	

the tedious task of working with fractional deviation scores. Using this formula gives the same result with much less labor. Thus we recommend that students always use this formula for computing standard deviation if the computation must be done "by hand":

$$\sigma = \sqrt{\frac{\Sigma X^2 - \dfrac{(\Sigma X)^2}{N}}{N}} \qquad (6.7)$$

where

σ = standard deviation
ΣX^2 = sum of the squares of each score (that is, each score is first squared, then these squares are summed)
$(\Sigma X)^2$ = sum of the scores squared (the scores are first summed, then this total is squared)
N = number of cases

Table 6.3 shows the computation of the standard deviation of the data in Table 6.2 using formula 6.7. The first column in this table shows the scores and their sum. The second column shows the square of each score and the sum of these squares. The rest of the table shows the application of formula 6.7 to find the value of the standard deviation. Note that the resulting value is the same as that found by applying formula 6.7 to the same data.

The standard deviation belongs to the same statistical family as the mean; that is, like the mean, it is an interval or ratio statistic and its computation is based on the size of individual scores in the distribution. It is by far the most frequently used measure of variability and is used in conjunction with the mean.

Formulas 6.5, 6.6, and 6.7 are appropriate for calculating the variance and the standard deviation of a population. In the example, if you are only interested in describing the heterogeneity of the vocabulary scores of the ten individuals, the population, these formulas are appropriate. If scores from a finite group or sample, are used to estimate the heterogeneity of a population from which that group was drawn, research has shown that these formulas more often underestimate the population variance and standard deviation than overestimate them. Mathematically, to get unbiased estimates $N - 1$ rather than N should be used as the denominator. Thus the formulas become

$$s^2 = \frac{\Sigma x^2}{N - 1} \tag{6.8}$$

$$s = \sqrt{\frac{\Sigma x^2}{N - 1}} \tag{6.9}$$

$$s = \sqrt{\frac{\Sigma X^2 - \dfrac{(\Sigma X)^2}{N}}{N - 1}} \tag{6.10}$$

Following the general custom of using Greek letters for population parameters and Roman letters for sample statistics, the symbols for variance and standard deviation calculated with $N - 1$ are s^2 and s.

With the data in Table 6.2, $s^2 = \dfrac{90}{10 - 1} = 10$ and $s = \sqrt{10} = 3.16$.

Formulas 6.8, 6.9, and 6.10 are often used to calculate variance and standard deviation even when there is no intention to estimate population parameters. Many computer and calculator programs calculate variance and standard deviation this way unless instructed to do otherwise. Spread, scatter, heterogeneity, dispersion, and volatility are measured by standard deviation, in the same way that volume is measured by bushels and distance is measured by miles. A class with a standard deviation of 1.8 on reading grade level is more heterogeneous than a class with a standard deviation of 0.7. A month when the daily Dow Jones Industrial Average has a standard deviation of 40 is more volatile than a month with a standard deviation of 25. A school where the teachers' monthly salary has a standard deviation of $900 has more disparity than a school where the standard deviation is $500.

MEASURES OF RELATIVE POSITION

Measures of relative position indicate where a score falls in relation to all other scores in the distribution. Researchers often want to assess an individual's relative position in a group or to compare the relative position of one individual on two or more measures or of two or more individuals on the same measure. The most widely used statistics for these purposes are z-scores, stanines, other standard scores, and percentile rank.

z-Score

The most widely used measure of relative position is the **z-score,** which indicates the positive or negative difference between an individual score and the mean as measured in standard deviation units. It and other indexes derived from it are known as **standard scores.** The z-score is defined as the distance of a score from the mean as measured by standard deviation units. The formula for finding a z-score is

$$z = \frac{x}{\sigma} = \frac{X - \overline{X}}{\sigma} \qquad (6.11)$$

where

$$\begin{aligned}
X &= \text{raw score} \\
\overline{X} &= \text{mean of the distribution} \\
\sigma &= \text{standard deviation of the distribution} \\
x &= \text{deviation score } (X - \overline{X})
\end{aligned}$$

Applying this formula, a score exactly one standard deviation above the mean becomes a z of $+1$, a score exactly one standard deviation below the mean becomes a z of -1, and so on. A score equal to the mean will have a z-score value of 0. For illustration, suppose a student's score on a psychology test is 72 where the mean of the distribution is 78 and the standard deviation equals 12. Suppose also that the same student has made a score of 48 on a statistics test where the mean is 51 and the standard deviation is 6. If you substitute these figures for the appropriate symbols in formula 6.11, you can derive a z-score for each test:

PSYCHOLOGY

$$z_1 = \frac{72 - 78}{12} = -0.50$$

STATISTICS

$$z_2 = \frac{48 - 51}{6} = -0.50$$

Both these standard scores belong to the z-distribution, where by definition the mean is always 0 and the standard deviation is 1, and therefore they are directly comparable. It is apparent in this example that the score of 72 on the psychology test and the score of 48 on the statistics test are equivalent—that is, both scores indicate the same relative level of performance. In other words, the standing of the student who has obtained these scores is the same in both tests when compared with the performance of the other students. It would be very difficult to make such a comparison without employing the z-score technique.

Let's use another example: Suppose a student who has taken the same tests has obtained a score of 81 on the psychology test and a score of 53 on the statistics test. As before, it is difficult to compare these raw scores to show on which test this student has done better. Converting the scores to z-scores makes the comparison easy. Using formula 6.11, we find the values of z_1 and z_2 in this case to be as follows:

PSYCHOLOGY

$$z_1 = \frac{81 - 78}{12} = +0.25$$

Table 6.4	Conversion of z-Scores to Stanines	
Z-SCORE	STANINE	INTERPRETATION
Above +1.75	9	Among the very highest scores
+1.25 to +1.75	8	Quite well above average
+.75 to +1.25	7	Quite noticeably above average
+.25 to +.75	6	Above average
−.25 to +.25	5	Near dead average
−.75 to −.25	4	Below average
−1.25 to −.75	3	Quite noticeably below average
−1.75 to −1.25	2	Quite well below average
Below −1.75	1	Among the lowest scores

STATISTICS

$$z_2 = \frac{53 - 51}{6} = +0.33$$

This result shows that the score of 53 on the statistics test actually indicates a slightly better relative performance than the score of 81 on the psychology test. Compared with the other students, this student has done somewhat better in statistics than in psychology.

Because the mean of the z-scores in any distribution is zero and the standard deviation is 1, they have universal meaning. A z-score of -0.1 is slightly below average in a distribution of statistics test scores, a distribution of weights of people in a weight control program, a distribution of pork belly prices or any other distribution. A z-score of $+2.4$ is very high, whether you are talking about ACT scores, scores on a measure of depression, corn yield per acre, or any other measure.

Stanine Scores

During World War II the U.S. Army Air Corps developed a standard system of nine scores called **stanine scores** to help its personnel interpret z-scores. A stanine score of 5 represents z-scores that are average or a little above or a little below average, that is equivalent to z-scores between $-.25$ and $+.25$. From there, stanine scores go up to 9 and down to 1 in increments of .5 as shown in Table 6.4. A z-score of 0.12 (stanine 5) is just a tad above dead average. This is the case whether you are looking at a vocabulary test score, a measure of paranoia, or weight. A z-score of -1.38 (stanine 2) is very well below average whether you are looking at a quantitative reasoning test score, a geniality score, or the price of a hamburger. Stanines are standardized with the mean of 5 and a standard deviation of 2. The formula for stanines is $2z + 5$. You convert a z-score to a stanine by multiplying by 2 and adding 5. Stanines are always rounded to the nearest whole number. Whenever the result is greater than 9, the value 9 is assigned. Whenever the result is less than 1, the value 1 is assigned. Because all z-scores above 1.75 are assigned a stanine score of 9 and all z-scores below -1.75 are assigned a score of 1, stanine scores are not useful for comparing extreme scores. Stanines are widely used in school systems for reporting students' standardized test scores.

Other Standard Scores

Z-scores can also be transformed into other standard-score scales that do not involve negative numbers or decimals. One of the most common procedures is to convert to **T-scores** by multiplying the z-scores by 10 and adding 50. This results in a scale of positive whole numbers that has a mean of 50 and a standard deviation of 10. The T-score formula is

$$T = 10z + 50 = 10\left(\frac{X - \overline{X}}{\sigma}\right) + 50 \qquad (6.12)$$

Suppose a student's score on a Spanish test is 21. Given that the mean of the scores in this test is 27 and the standard deviation is 6, the z-score will be $(21 - 27)/6$, which can be inserted directly into the T-score formula as follows:

$$T = 10\left(\frac{21 - 27}{6}\right) + 50 = 40$$

The transformation of z-score into T-scores not only enables one to work with whole numbers, but it also avoids the adverse psychological implications of describing subjects' performances with negative numbers. In the preceding example, it would be easier to report that the student's score is 40 where the mean score is 50 than to report a score of -1.00 with an average of zero.

Teachers who wish to compare the standings of their students on successive tests, or to add all the scores obtained on different tests in the same course to make a general distribution, can convert the students' raw scores to z-scores or T-scores in order to give equal weight to each set of scores. Adding and averaging scores that belong to different distributions and have different means and different standard deviations, without converting them to some kind of standard score, is not statistically justified. In addition to T, there are other transformed standard-score distributions. To transform a distribution of scores to a new standardized distribution, it is only necessary to multiply the z-score by the desired standard deviation and add the desired mean. The general formula is as follows:

$$A = \sigma_A(z) + \mu_A \qquad (6.13)$$

where

$$A = \text{standard score on the new scale}$$
$$\mu_A = \text{mean for the new standard scale}$$
$$\sigma_A = \text{standard deviation for the new standard scale}$$

For example, College Entrance Examination Board scores (CEEB) have a mean of 500 and a standard deviation of 100 for its transformed distribution. If you were 1.5 standard deviations above the mean ($z = 1.5$) on the verbal section of the SAT (SAT = Scholastic Assessment Test), your score would be reported as 650 [$500 + 100(1.5) = 650$]. If your quantitative score were 500, you would have scored exactly at the mean.

The Wechsler Adult Intelligence Test (WAIS) scores are standard scores with a mean of 100 and a standard deviation of 15. So to convert a raw score on a Wechsler test to the standard scale, you would first determine its z-value, then multiply by 15 and add 100.

Transforming a set of scores to standard scores does not alter the shape of the original distribution. If a distribution of scores is skewed, the derived standard scores also produce a skewed distribution. Only if the original distribution is normal do the standard scores produce a normal distribution.

Percentile Rank

A measure of relative position that most people find easy to understand and interpret is the percentile rank. A **percentile rank** (PR) indicates the percentage of scores in a distribution that fall below a given score. It is easy to picture a score with a percentile rank of 32 as having 32 percent of the scores in its distribution below it and a score with a percentile rank of 89 having 89 percent of the scores below it. Percentile rank is defined as the percentage of scores below a specific score plus half the percentage of scores tied at that score.

Consider the following ten scores, each 10 percent of the distribution:

24   26   26   27   27   27   28   30   30   35

The score of 24 is halfway between the lower real limit (23.5) and the upper real limit of 24 (24.5) so it is assigned a percentile rank of 5. The scores of 26 have 10 percent of the distribution below them, and 20 percent tied at 26 so the percentile rank of $10\% + 20\%/2 = 20$ is assigned to both scores of 26. The percentile rank for 27 is $30\% + 30\%/2 = 45$. For 28, $PR = 65$; for 30, $PR = 80$; and for 35, $PR = 95$. The major advantages of percentile ranks are

1. They have universal meaning. A score with a percentile rank of 89 is high in any distribution. A score with a percentile rank of 32 is somewhat low in any distribution.
2. The familiar concept of zero to 100 percent applies to the interpretation of percentile rank.

The major difficulties of percentile rank are

1. Equal differences between percentile ranks do not represent equal differences between the scores in the original distribution. Note that a difference of one score point, from 26 to 27, yields a difference in percentile rank of 25, whereas a difference of 5 score points between 30 and 35 yields a difference of only 15. In most cases, original score differences nearer the center of a distribution yield

greater changes in percentile rank than the same original score differences near the top or bottom of the distribution.

2. As with other ordinal statistics, percentile ranks cannot be added or subtracted.

THE NORMAL CURVE

The distribution of many physical and psychological measures takes the shape of a bell when plotted as a frequency polygon. For example, if you measure American boys on their tenth birthday, you will find many boys whose height is near the mean and slightly fewer boys who are a bit above or a bit below the mean. The further you get from the mean, the fewer boys you will find at each height. A polygon showing this **normal distribution** closely resembles a theoretical polygon known as the *normal curve*. Tables of the ordinate and the areas of the normal curve have already been computed. The areas are shown in Figure 6.6 and in Table A.1 in the Appendix. This hypothetical polygon indicates the expected (that is, theoretical) frequencies of all possible z-scores. Z-scores near 0 will be expected to occur more frequently than other z-score values, and the farther from 0 a z-score is, the less frequently it will be expected to occur.

Inasmuch as so many naturally occurring distributions resemble the normal curve, this theoretical model has proved very useful. Whenever actual data are known or believed to resemble the normal curve in distribution, you can deduce many useful estimates from the theoretical properties of the normal curve.

Note in Figure 6.6 that the normal curve is a symmetrical distribution with the same number of cases at specified z-score distances below the mean as above the mean. Its mean is the point below which exactly 50 percent of the cases fall and above which the other 50 percent of the cases are located. The median and the mode in such a distribution are identical values and coincide with the mean. In a normal curve, most of the cases concentrate near the mean. The frequency of cases decreases as you proceed away from the mean in either direction. Approximately 34 percent of the cases in a normal distribution fall between the mean and one standard deviation above or below the mean. The area between one and two standard deviations from the mean on either side of the distribution contains about 14 percent of the cases. Only about 2 percent of the cases fall between two and three standard deviations from the mean, and only about 0.1 percent of the cases fall above or below three standard deviations from the mean.

These characteristics can be seen in Figure 6.6 and are set forth in lines beneath the curve. You can see visually that about one-sixth of the curve falls to the left of one standard deviation below the mean. Beneath the curve the cumulative percentage line tells you that 15.9 percent falls below -1σ. You can see in the percentile equivalents line that below -1σ is nearer to 20 percent than 10 percent. This line also illustrates how rapidly percentile ranks change near the mean and how slowly they change far from the mean. The following lines show the z-scores and standard scores based on z-scores including T-scores, CEEB (College Entrance Examination Board) scores, stanines, and deviation IQs. Note that 95 percent of the normal curve falls between plus and minus $z = 1.96$ and 99 percent falls between plus and minus $z = 2.58$. These boundaries will

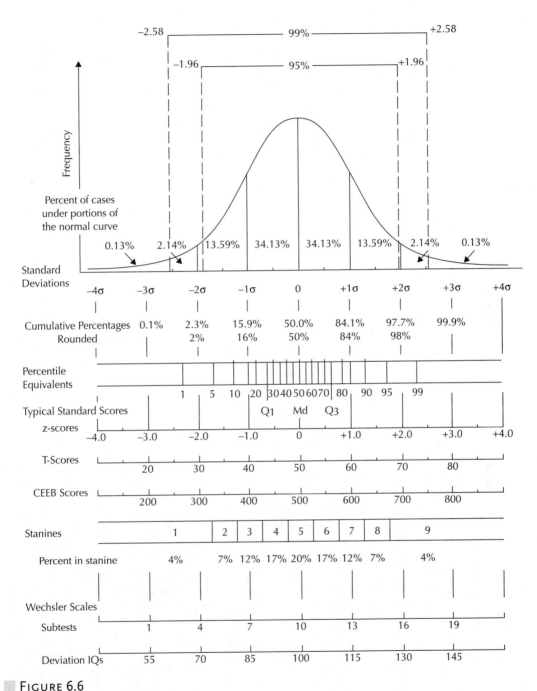

Adapted from Seashore, H. G. (Ed) "*Methods of expressing test scores*" Test service bulletin (48) New York: Psychological Corporation (p. 2)

FIGURE 6.6

Normal Curve and Equivalents

become important when we discuss inferential statistics. This distribution is illustrated in Figure 6.6.

It is possible to determine the exact percentage of the cases below and above each z-score in the normal distribution by consulting Table A.1 in the Appendix, which gives the areas of the normal curve. Column (1) of the table contains different z-values. Column (2) gives the area under the curve between the mean and each z-value. Column (3) shows the remaining area from each z-score to the end of the curve. Therefore the areas in column (2) and column (3) add up to .5000. Take as an example the z-value of $+.70$. The area between this z-value and the mean can be found in column (2); it is .2580. This figure indicates that about 26 percent of the cases fall between this z-value and the mean of the distribution. Because the mean of the normal distribution coincides with the median, 50 percent of the cases lie below the mean. Add .50 to the .2580, and the result tells you that you can expect 75.8 percent of the cases to fall below the z-value of $+.70$. Column (3) indicates that 24.2 percent of the cases fall above the z-value of $+.70$.

This procedure is reversed when the z-value is negative. Suppose you want to find the percentage of cases below the z-value of -0.70. The area between the mean and a z-score of -0.70 is .2580 or, in terms of percentage, 25.8 percent of the cases. Subtracting 25.8 from 50, you obtain 24.2. This result would indicate that only about 24 percent of the scores lie below a z-value of -0.70 in a normal distribution. This value can also be found in column (3) of the table, which gives a value of .2420 for a z-score of 0.70. The percentage of scores above -0.70 is 100 minus 24.2, or 75.8 percent. Among other applications, the normal curve can be used to help people who are unfamiliar with standard scores to interpret them. For example, how high is a score of 110 on the WAIS (Wechsler Adult Intelligence Scale)? The WAIS has a mean of 100 and a standard deviation of 15, so the z-score here is .67. Consulting Table A.1 column (2), you find .2486 of the normal curve falls between the mean and $z = .67$. Adding the 50 percent below the mean, you can say that a WAIS score of 110 exceeds the scores of 75 percent of WAIS scores. A WAIS score of 98 has a z-score of $-.13$, higher than about 45 percent of the scores.

Because it is known that the population distribution of WAIS scores closely resembles the normal curve, PR approximations based on the normal curve will be quite near to the actual PRs. With other scores, as actual distributions become less and less like the normal curve the PR approximations become less and less on target. Where the shape of a distribution is not known, it is usually reasonable to assume a distribution similar to the normal curve and to use the normal curve table to find reasonable approximations of the PRs of various z-scores. The more the actual shape differs from the normal, the less useful the approximations become.

CORRELATION

Our discussion of statistical techniques so far has been concerned with describing single distributions of scores. We will now discuss a method of indicating the relationship between pairs of scores.

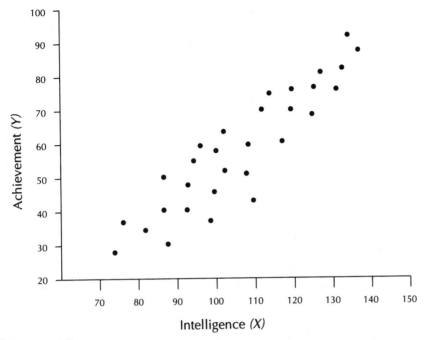

■ FIGURE 6.7
Scattergram Showing the Relationship between Intelligence and Achievement

Scattergrams

Statistical techniques for determining relationships between pairs of scores are known as **correlational procedures.** Typically measurements on two variables are available for each member of a group, and you determine if there is a relationship between these paired measurements. Correlational procedures show the extent to which change in one variable is associated with change in another variable. For example, we know that achievement and intelligence are related and so we would expect students with high IQs to earn above-average scores on achievement tests. A simple way of showing this relationship is to plot the intelligence test scores and achievement test scores of a number of individuals in a two-dimensional table called a **scattergram.** Scores on one variable are plotted on the horizontal axis, with the lowest number on the left and the highest on the right. Scores on the other variable are plotted on the vertical axis, with the lowest at the bottom and the highest at the top. The position of each individual on the two tests is then indicated by a single point in the scattergram. The achievement test scores of 30 tenth-graders are plotted against their intelligence test scores in Figure 6.7. An examination of this figure reveals that there is a tendency for achievement scores to be high when the intelligence tests scores are high.

Plotting a scattergram lets you see both the direction and the strength of a relationship. The term *direction* refers to whether the relationship is positive or negative. In Figure 6.7, the dots form a pattern going from lower left to upper right as low scores on one variable (intelligence) are associated with low scores on the other variable (achievement) and high scores on one variable are associated with high scores on the other. (By convention, scores of the independent variable [X] are plotted along the horizontal axis and scores of the dependent variable [Y] are plotted on the vertical axis.) Such a relationship between variables is said to be positive because high scores are associated with high scores and low scores with low scores.

The relationship between two variables is not always positive. Some variables are negatively related. For example, birthrate and socioeconomic level have been found to be negatively related; that is, birthrate decreases as the socioeconomic level increases. With a negative relationship, high scores on one variable are associated with low scores on the other variable and the dots on the scattergram go from upper left to lower right.

A scattergram of z-scores also reveals the *strength* of the relationship between variables. If the dots in the scattergram form a narrow band, so that when a straight line is drawn through the band the dots will be near the line, there is a strong relationship between the variables. However, if the dots in the z-score scattergram scatter widely, the relationship between variables is relatively weak. The scattergrams in Figure 6.8 show various positive and negative and strong and weak relationships, expressed mathematically by r.

Correlation Coefficients

Statistical indexes have been developed that indicate both the direction (negative or positive) and the strength of a relationship between variables. These indexes are called **correlation coefficients.** Calculations of a correlation coefficient between two variables results in a value that ranges from -1.00 to $+1.00$. A correlation coefficient of -1.00 indicates a perfect negative relationship, a value of $+1.00$ indicates a perfect positive relationship, and the midpoint of this range, 0, indicates no relationship at all. A perfect **positive correlation** results when each individual's z-score on one variable is identical in size and sign to the z-score on the other variable. A perfect **negative correlation,** in contrast, results when each individual's z-scores are the same in size but opposite in sign. A 0 correlation results when no such trends are present—that is, when positions on one variable are not associated with positions on the other. A coefficient of correlation near unity, either -1.00 or $+1.00$, indicates a high degree of relationship. Such high relationships allow accurate predictions about one variable on the basis of information about the other. A negative correlation coefficient is just as good for prediction as a positive correlation.

Figure 6.8 gives the coefficient of correlation for each of the sets of data in z-score form. Note that where the correlation is perfect, all the scores fall on a straight line. The nearer to zero the coefficient of correlation is, the greater the deviation of the scores from a straight line. In example F, illustrating zero correlation, the scores are scattered over the surface of the graph and do not take any shape in any direction.

Correlation coefficients in educational and psychological measures, because of the complexity of these phenomena, seldom reach the maximum points of $+1.00$ and

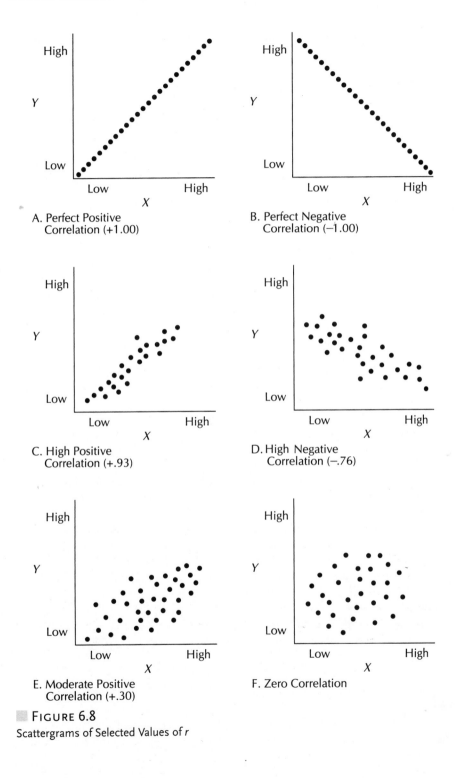

A. Perfect Positive
   Correlation (+1.00)

B. Perfect Negative
   Correlation (−1.00)

C. High Positive
   Correlation (+.93)

D. High Negative
   Correlation (−.76)

E. Moderate Positive
   Correlation (+.30)

F. Zero Correlation

FIGURE 6.8

Scattergrams of Selected Values of *r*

−1.00. For these measures, any coefficient that is greater than plus or minus .90 is usually considered to be very high.

The Pearson Product Moment Coefficient of Correlation

The **Pearson product moment coefficient** of correlation, developed by the English statistician Karl Pearson and called Pearson r, is the most commonly used correlation index. This coefficient is used when the scale of measurement is either interval or ratio. It is defined as the mean of the z-score products; that is, each individual's z-score on one variable (X) multiplied by his or her z-score on the other variable (Y). These paired z-score products are added, and the sum is divided by the number of pairs. The definition formula for Pearson r is

$$r = \frac{\Sigma z_x z_y}{N} \qquad (6.14)$$

where

$$r = \text{Pearson product moment coefficient of correlation}$$
$$\Sigma z_x z_y = \text{sum of the } z\text{-score products}$$
$$N = \text{number of paired scores}$$

Because of the way z-score are defined mathematically, when each individual has the same z-score on X that he or she has on Y the sum of the $z_x z_y$ products will be equal to the number of pairs and the mean z-score product (the Pearson product moment correlation) will be +1.00. If there is a perfect positive correspondence between z-scores, the product moment correlation will be +1.00. If z-scores are numerically identical but of opposite sign, the product will be negative and the Pearson product moment correlation will be −1.00. In both cases all the scores will fall along a straight line when plotted on a scattergram. Now let's use formula 6.14 to compute the correlation between the scores of 14 subjects on two tests, X (descriptive statistics) and Y (inferential statistics), as shown in Table 6.5.

Columns (2) and (3) present the subjects' raw scores (X) and deviation scores (x), respectively, on the descriptive statistics test. Columns (5) and (6) present the subjects' raw scores (Y) and deviation scores (y) on the inferential statistics test. Columns (4) and (7) show the squared deviation scores used for calculating the standard deviations. Columns (8) and (9) present the z-scores of the X- and Y-scores computed using formula 6.11. Column (10) shows the products of $z_x z_y$ values. The sum of these products is 11.50. It is now possible to find the Pearson product moment coefficient of correlation between the two sets of scores by applying formula 6.14:

$$r = \frac{11.50}{14} = +.82$$

The process of converting scores to z-scores becomes tedious when many cases are being used. It is possible to eliminate this step and work directly with the raw scores by

Table 6.5 *Computation of Pearson r between Two Sets of Scores (X and Y)*

(1) SUBJECTS	(2) X-SCORES	(3) x	(4) x^2	(5) Y-SCORES	(6) Y	(7) y^2	(8) z_x	(9) z_y	(10) $z_x z_y$
1	18	+3	9	28	4	16	+1.5	+1	+1.50
2	18	+3	9	30	6	36	+1.5	+1.5	+2.25
3	17	+2	4	30	6	36	+1	+1.5	+1.50
4	17	+2	4	26	2	4	+1	+0.5	+0.50
5	16	+1	1	28	4	16	+0.5	+1	+0.50
6	16	+1	1	24	0	0	+0.5	0	0
7	15	0	0	22	−2	4	0	−0.5	0
8	15	0	0	20	−4	16	0	−1	0
9	14	−1	1	26	2	4	−0.5	+0.5	−0.25
10	14	−1	1	22	−2	4	−0.5	−0.5	+0.25
11	13	−2	4	24	0	0	−1	0	0
12	13	−2	4	18	−6	36	−1	−1.5	+1.50
13	12	−3	9	20	−4	16	−1.5	−1	+1.50
14	12	−3	9	18	−6	36	−1.5	−1.5	+2.25
	210		56	336		224			11.50

$$\bar{X} = \frac{\Sigma X}{N} = \frac{210}{14} = 15 \qquad \bar{Y} = \frac{\Sigma Y}{N} = \frac{336}{14} = 24$$

$$\sigma_x = \sqrt{\frac{\Sigma x^2}{N}} = \sqrt{\frac{56}{14}} = 2 \qquad \sigma_y = \sqrt{\frac{\Sigma y^2}{N}} = \sqrt{\frac{224}{14}} = 4$$

using a computation formula that is mathematically equivalent to formula 6.14, as shown here:

$$r = \frac{\Sigma XY - \frac{(\Sigma X)(\Sigma Y)}{N}}{\sqrt{\left(\Sigma X^2 - \frac{(\Sigma X)^2}{N}\right)\left(\Sigma Y^2 - \frac{(\Sigma Y)^2}{N}\right)}} \qquad (6.15)$$

where

r = Pearson r
ΣX = sum of scores in X-distribution
ΣY = sum of scores in Y-distribution
ΣXY = sum of the products of paired X- and Y-scores
ΣX^2 = sum of the squared scores in X-distribution
ΣY^2 = sum of the squared scores in Y-distribution
N = number of paired X- and Y-scores (subjects)

Table 6.6	Computation of Pearson r Using the Raw-Score Formula				
(1) SUBJECTS	(2) X	(3) Y	(4) X²	(5) X²	(6) XY
1	18	28	324	784	504
2	18	30	324	900	540
3	17	30	289	900	510
4	17	26	289	676	442
5	16	28	256	784	448
6	16	24	256	576	384
7	15	22	225	484	330
8	15	20	225	400	300
9	14	26	196	676	364
10	14	22	196	484	308
11	13	24	169	576	312
12	13	18	169	324	234
13	12	20	144	400	240
14	12	18	144	324	216
$N = 14$	$\Sigma X = 210$	$\Sigma Y = 336$	$\Sigma X^2 = 3206$	$\Sigma Y^2 = 8288$	$\Sigma XY = 5132$

Using the same raw–score data as before, let's use formula 6.15 to compute the Pearson product moment coefficient of correlation. The necessary figures and calculations are provided in Table 6.6. Substituting the values from this table in formula 6.15, you can calculate Pearson r:

$$r = \frac{5132 - \dfrac{(210)(336)}{14}}{\sqrt{\left[3206 - \dfrac{(210)^2}{14}\right]\left[8288 - \dfrac{(336)^2}{14}\right]}} = +.82$$

Note that applying this formula not only made it unnecessary to convert the scores to z-scores, but also eliminated computation of the means and standard deviations of the two distributions.

The product moment coefficient of correlation belongs to the same statistical family as the mean. Its computation takes into account the size of each score in both distributions, X and Y. Like the mean and the standard deviation, it is an interval statistic that can also be used with ratio data. An assumption underlying the product moment coefficient of correlation is that the relationship between the two variables (X and Y) is **linear:** that is, a straight line provides a reasonable expression of the relationship of one variable to the other. If a curved line is needed to express this relationship, the relationship is said to be **curvilinear.**

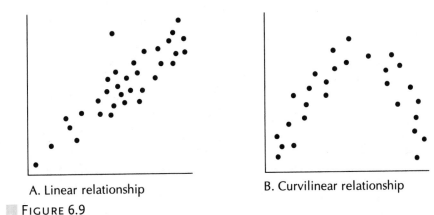

A. Linear relationship   B. Curvilinear relationship

■ FIGURE 6.9
Linear and Curvilinear Relationships

A practical way of finding out whether the relationship between two variables is linear or curvilinear is to examine the scattergram of the data. Figure 6.9 shows two diagrams, one of which (A) indicates a linear relationship and the other (B), a curvilinear one.

If the relationship between variables is curvilinear, the computation of the Pearson r will result in a misleading underestimation of the degree of relationship. In this case another index, such as the correlation ratio (η), should be applied. A discussion of the correlation ratio appears in Chapter 12.

Interpretation of Pearson r

You have seen that when two variables are highly related in a positive way, the correlation between them approaches +1.00. When they are highly related in a negative way, the correlation approaches −1.00. When there is little relation between variables, the correlation will be near 0. Pearson r provides a meaningful index for indicating relationship, with the sign of the coefficient indicating the direction of the relationship, and the difference between the coefficient and 0 indicating the degree of the relationship.

However, in interpreting the coefficient of correlation keep the following points in mind:

1. *Correlation does not necessarily indicate causation.* When two variables are found to be correlated, this indicates that relative positions in one variable are *associated* with relative positions in the other variable. It does not necessarily mean that changes in one variable are *caused* by changes in the other variable. In our example we found a correlation of +.82 between scores in a test on descriptive statistics and another test on inferential statistics. This correlation coefficient tells us that a person with an above-average score on one test will probably obtain an above-average score on the other test—but we cannot say that a high performance on one test *causes* a high performance on the other. Scores on both tests

may result from other causes, such as the numerical aptitude of the people who take these tests.

Using another example, suppose you find a high positive correlation between the wealth of families and intelligence of the children of those families. Such high correlation is by no means indicative of a cause-and-effect relationship between these two variables. Wealth does not necessarily result in intelligence, nor does intelligence necessarily create wealth for these individuals.

2. *The size of correlation is in part a function of the variability of the two distributions to be correlated.* Restricting the range of the scores to be correlated reduces the observed degree of relationship between two variables. For example, people have observed that success in playing basketball is related to height: The taller an individual is, the more probable that he or she will do well in this sport. This statement is true about the population at large, where there is a wide range of heights. However, within a basketball team whose members are all tall, there may be little or no correlation between height and success, because the range of heights is restricted. In a college that accepts students with a wide range of scores on a scholastic aptitude test, you would expect a correlation between the test scores and college grades. In a college that accepts only students with very high scholastic aptitude scores, you would expect very little correlation between the test scores and grades because of the restricted range of the test scores in this situation.

3. *Correlation coefficients should not be interpreted in terms of percentage of perfect correlations.* Because correlation coefficients are expressed as decimal fractions, people who are not trained in statistics sometimes interpret correlation coefficients as a percentage of perfect correlation. An *r* of .80 does *not* indicate 80 percent of a perfect relationship between two variables. This interpretation is erroneous because, for example, an *r* of .80 does not express a relationship that is twice as great as an *r* of .40. A way of determining the degree to which you can predict one variable from the other is to calculate an index called the *coefficient of determination.* The coefficient of determination is the square of the correlation coefficient. It gives the percentage of variance in one variable that is associated with the variance in the other. For example, if you find a correlation of +.80 between achievement and intelligence, 64 percent of the variance in achievement is associated with variance in intelligence test scores. Probably the best way to give meaning to the size of the correlation coefficient is to picture the degree of scatter implied by correlations of different sizes (as illustrated in Figure 6.8) and to become familiar with the size of correlations commonly observed between variables of interest.

4. *Avoid interpreting the coefficients of correlation in an absolute sense.* In interpreting the degree of correlation, keep in mind the purpose for which it is being used. For example, a coefficient of correlation equal to +.50 may be satisfactory when predicting the future performance of a group of individuals, but it may not be wise to use this coefficient of correlation for predicting the performance of one

person in a future task. The coefficient of $+.50$ is not an absolute value with the same implication in both cases.

Chapter 12 provides additional information on the use and interpretation of correlation.

EFFECT SIZE

Measuring **effect size** is a technique used to assess the magnitude of the difference between two groups. The most widely used measure of effect size is the difference between experimental and control group means divided by the standard deviation of the control group. As a formula,

$$\Delta = \frac{\overline{X}_e - \overline{X}_c}{s_c} \qquad (6.16)$$

where

$$\Delta = \text{effect size for a difference between means}$$
$$\overline{X}_e = \text{mean of the experimental group}$$
$$\overline{X}_c = \text{mean of the control group}$$
$$s_c = \text{standard deviation of the control group}$$

Consider an experiment in which on-task behavior is the dependent variable. The experimental group receives contingent reinforcement while the control group does not receive the contingent reinforcement. We explain this contrast more fully in Chapter 10. The control group has a mean of 90 and a standard deviation of 10. The experimental group has a mean of 96. The effect size is $\dfrac{96 - 90}{10} = .6$. Consider another experiment with the same dependent variable but with a drug versus a placebo as the independent variable. The control group has a mean of 95 and a standard deviation of 8. The experimental group has a mean of 97. The effect size here is $\dfrac{97 - 95}{8} = .25$. The evidence suggests that reinforcement has had a greater effect on on-task behavior than the drug did.

Effect sizes are interpreted in the same way that z-scores are interpreted. Effect size can be used to compare the relative magnitude of the relationships various independent variables have with a common dependent variable. In addition, it can be used to help decide whether the difference an independent variable makes on the dependent variable is strong enough to recommend its implementation in practice. Cohen (1988) has proposed the following descriptions:

.20 is small

.50 is medium

.80 is large

Another approach is to ask if a given effect size is larger or smaller than effect sizes found in other studies with the same dependent variable. Or you can assess the utility of an effect size by relating the cost in time, money, and other resources needed to implement the independent variable in relation to the importance of the dependent variable. A school of nursing would be interested in a brief, inexpensive procedure that produced an effect size of .20 on state nursing licensure exam scores. A researcher would hesitate to recommend an expensive, time-consuming independent variable with an effect size of .50 on a relatively unimportant dependent variable. Effect size is a useful statistic for assessing the strength and utility of a treatment or other independent variable.

As a form of z-scores, effect sizes have universal meaning. An effect size of $-.50$ always means that the experimental group mean was half a standard deviation below the control group mean. Effect size is important for evaluating the results of a quantitative study. The American Psychological Association (1994) publication manual encourages (p. 18) reporting of effect sizes. We hope the reporting of effect size will become more frequent in the future. Descriptions of effect sizes other than the one for differences between means can be found in Cohen's (1988) book.

META-ANALYSIS

Meta-analysis, a method for systematically combining research results from a number of studies focusing on the same question and using similar variables, is defined by Glass, McGaw, and Smith (1981) as an "analysis of analyses." Using statistics reported from a number of original studies comparing groups that got treatment (experimental groups) with groups that did not get treatment (control groups), the researcher derives a common metric that is interpreted as an overall summary of outcomes for the selected studies.

The most widely used form of meta-analysis averages effect sizes of similar studies to produce a statistic that is interpreted as an overall summary of outcomes for the selected studies. The average effect size as a formula is

$$\overline{\Delta} = \frac{\Delta_1 n_1 + \Delta_2 n_2 + \ldots + \Delta_k n_k}{N} \tag{6.17}$$

where

$$\overline{\Delta} = \text{average effect size}$$
$$\Delta_1 = \text{effect size for Group 1}$$
$$\Delta_k = \text{effect size of the last group}$$
$$n_1 = \text{number in first group}$$
$$n_k = \text{number in last group}$$
$$N = \text{total number of subjects}$$

Suppose we have four studies investigating the effect of a specific treatment on reading proficiency. Their statistics are as follows:

Study 1, effect size $= .9, n = 60$

Study 2, effect size $= .4, n = 40$

Study 3, effect size $= -.2, n = 30$

Study 4, effect size $= .1, n = 70$

The average effect size is

$$\overline{\Delta} = .9(60) + .4(40) + -.2(30) + .1(70) = \frac{54 + 16 - 6 + 7}{200} = \frac{71}{200} = .36$$

This is about halfway between what Cohen describes as a small effect size and a medium effect size. Another way of looking at it is to use the normal curve. Consulting Table A-1 in the appendix, you see that a z-score of $+.36$ has a percentile rank of 64. The mean in a treatment group is equivalent to a score with a percentile rank of approximately 64 in the control group. If treatment is relatively inexpensive, you would be inclined to recommend it in practice. If treatment is expensive and/or the dependent variable is relatively unimportant, you would not be inclined to recommend it.

Smith and Glass (1977) used meta-analysis to investigate the broad question. Does psychotherapy make a difference? A standard literature search located 1000 experiments. Experiments selected as appropriate for a complete analysis yielded a total of 833 effect sizes. The selected studies included ego, dynamic, behavioral, and humanistic treatment strategies, related experimentally to such outcome variables as self-esteem, adjustment, fear/anxiety, and school performance. The average effect size was .68; that is, the average posttreatment mean for treated subjects was equivalent to a score .68 of a standard deviation above the mean for untreated subjects. Smith and Glass concluded that the typical outcome of psychotherapy is a gain on the dependent variable equivalent to a move from the mean to the 75th percentile of the control group. (See Figure 6.10.)

Meta-analysis is also used to integrate the findings of nonexperimental studies. Hyde, Fennema, and Lamon (1990) did a meta-analysis of 100 studies comparing male and female mathematics performance on standardized tests. For the total of 3,175,188 subjects in these 100 studies, the average mean for males was only .20 of a standard deviation higher than the mean for females. When the researchers excluded studies that represented samples selected for low performance or high performance (such as college or college-bound youth), the average difference was a mere .05 higher for females. The authors concluded that in general, gender differences in mathematics performance are small.

Meta-analysis has sometimes been criticized for including the results of poorly designed, poorly conducted studies along with the results of more credible studies (criteria for evaluating research designs are in Chapter 10). This problem can be resolved by first calculating the average effect size of all studies then calculating the average effect size of well-designed studies to see if the latter agree with the former. Qin, Johnson, and Johnson (1995) did this in the meta-analysis of "studies" comparing problem-solving performance of subjects under cooperative versus competitive conditions. In fifty-five cases

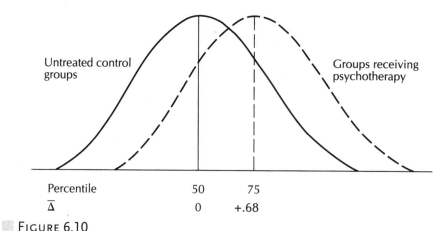

Percentile   50   75
Δ̄   0   +.68

▦ FIGURE 6.10

Estimated Average Effect Size for Therapies Compared to Untreated Groups

(data based on 40,000 treated and untreated subjects, averaging just under 20 hours of therapy with therapists averaging 2½ years of experience)

cooperation outperformed competition, whereas in eight competition outperformed cooperation. The average effect size was .55 in favor of cooperation. The average effect size of the 33 studies judged as being of high methodological quality was .68. Meta-analyses can be made for various subclasses of studies. Qin, Johnson, and Johnson found average effect sizes of .37 for linguistic problems and .72 for nonlinguistic problems. They found average effect sizes of .52 for well-defined problems and .60 for ill-defined problems. The reader is referred to Becker and Hedges (1992) for a discussion of other meta-analysis approaches and applications.

▦ CALCULATORS AND COMPUTER PROGRAMS FOR STATISTICS

Many pocket calculators have built-in programs for the statistical procedures described in this and the next chapter. Computer programs such as SPSS-X and SAS are available for statistical analysis of data. A description of statistical programs is included in Chapter 16.

▦ SUMMARY

Descriptive statistics serve to describe and summarize observations. The descriptive technique to be employed is selected according to the purpose the statistic is to serve and the scale of measurement used.

Scales of measurement are means of quantifying observations and are of four types: (1) Nominal scales classify observations into mutually exclusive categories; (2) ordinal

Table 6.7 *Summary of Descriptive Statistics Presented in This Chapter*			
	NOMINAL	ORDINAL	INTERVAL
Indexes of Central Tendency	Mode	Median	Mean
Indexes of Variability	Range	Quartile deviation	Variance and standard deviation
Indexes of Location	Label or classification	Percentile rank	z-score, T-score, and other standard scores
Correlation Indexes	Phi[a]	Spearman rho[a]	Pearson r

[a] The phi and Spearman rho correlation coefficients are described in Chapter 12.

scales sort objects or classes of objects on the basis of their relative standing; (3) interval scales use equal intervals for measurement and indicate the degree to which a person or an object possesses a certain quality; and (4) ratio scales use equal intervals for measurement and measure from an absolute zero point. Once observations are quantified, the data can be arranged into frequency distributions and shown graphically in histograms or polygons.

Measures of central tendency—the mode, the median, and the mean—provide a single index to represent the average value of a whole set of measures. The mode, which is a nominal statistic, is the least stable and least useful measure in educational research. The median is an ordinal statistic that takes into account the ranks of scores within a distribution but not the size of the individual scores. The mean, which is an interval (or ratio) statistic, is the most stable and most widely used index of central tendency. Another way of describing observations is to indicate the variation, or spread, of the values within a distribution. The range, the variance, and the standard deviation are three indexes used for this purpose. The range, a nominal statistic, is the distance between the highest and the lowest values in a distribution, plus 1. Variance is the mean of the squared deviations of values from the mean. It is an interval (or ratio) statistic. Standard deviation—the square root of the variance—is the most widely used index of variability.

Standard scores are used to indicate the position of a single score in a distribution. The most widely used is the z-score, which converts values into standard deviation units. Z-scores are often converted into stanines, T-scores, or other standard scores. An ordinal index of location that shows a score's position is percentile rank (PR), which indicates what percentage of scores fall below the midpoint of the score's interval. Using the characteristics and the areas of the normal curve, you can approximate the percentage of cases below and above each z-score in a normal distribution.

Effect size—the difference between the mean of the experimental and control groups divided by the standard deviation of the control group—is a useful measure of the strength or magnitude of the independent variable. A small effect size indicates that the effect of the independent variable is trivial. A large effect size indicates that the effect is substantial.

Meta-analysis combines data from many studies into a single index. It enables researchers to succinctly summarize results of many studies on a particular question. The most widely used index is the average effect size. Correlation techniques enable researchers to describe the relationship between two sets of measures. Product moment correlation (Pearson *r*), the most widely used index of relationship, is used with interval or ratio data. Table 6.7 summarizes correlation indexes appropriate for data of interval, ordinal, and nominal data.

REFERENCES

American Psychological Association. (1994). *Publication manual of the American Psychological Association* (4th ed.). Washington, DC: Author.

Becker, B. J., & Hedges, L. V. (Eds.) (1992). *Journal of Educational Statistics, 17*(4), 583–587.

Cohen, J. (1988). *Statistical power analysis for the behavioral sciences.* Hillsdale, NJ: Erlbaum.

Cooper, H., & Hedges, L. V. (1993). *The handbook of research synthesis.* New York: Russell Sage Foundation.

Glass, G. V., McGaw, B., & Smith, M. L. (1981). *Meta-analysis in social research.* Beverly Hills, CA: Sage.

Hedges, L. V., & Nowell, A. (1995). Sex differences in mental test scores, variability, and numbers of high scoring individuals. *Science, 269,* 41–45.

Hyde, J. S., Fennema, E., & Lamon, S. J. (1990). Gender differences in mathematics performance: A meta-analysis. *Psychological Bulletin, 107,* 139–155.

Qin, Z., Johnson, D. W., & Johnson, R. T. (1995). Cooperative versus competitive efforts and problem solving. *Review of Educational Research, 65*(2), 129–143.

Smith, M. L., & Glass, G. V. (1977). Meta-analysis of psychotherapy outcome studies. *American Psychologist, 32,* 752–760.

Stevens, S. S. (1951). Mathematics, measurement, and psychophysics. In S. S. Stevens (Ed.), *Handbook of experimental psychology* (p. 1). New York: Wiley.

KEY CONCEPTS

coefficient of determination	frequency distribution	median
correlational procedures	frequency polygon	measures of central tendency
correlation coefficient	histogram	meta-analysis
curvilinear relationship	inferential statistics	mode
descriptive statistics	interval scale	negative correlation
deviation scores	linear relationship	negatively skewed curve
effect size	mean	nominal scale

normal distribution	range	stanine score
ordinal scale	ratio scale	symmetrical distribution
Pearson product moment	scattergram	T-score
coefficient	skewed distribution	variability
percentile rank	standard deviation	variance
positive correlation	standard score	z-score

EXERCISES

1. Identify the type of measurement scale—nominal, ordinal, interval, or ratio—suggested by each statement:
   a. John finished the math test in 35 minutes, while Jack finished the same test in 25 minutes.
   b. Jack speaks French, but John does not.
   c. Jack is taller than John.
   d. John is 6 feet 2 inches tall.
   e. John's IQ is 120, whereas Jack's IQ is 110.

2. Draw a histogram and a frequency polygon for the following frequency distribution:

X	f	X	f	X	f	X	f
80	1	76	6	73	20	70	7
79	2	75	15	72	17	69	3
78	3	74	22	71	9		
77	10						

3. Provide answers as requested, given the following distribution: 15, 14, 14, 13, 11, 10, 10, 10, 8, 5.
   a. Calculate the mean.
   b. Determine the value of the median.
   c. Determine the value of the mode.

4. Briefly explain the relationship between the skewness of a distribution of scores and the resulting values of the mean, median, and mode.

5. Identify the measure—mode, mean, or median—that best suits each type of scale:

   a. Ordinal
   b. Nominal
   c. Interval

6. Identify the measure—mode, mean, or median—that each term defines:
   a. The middle score
   b. The arithmetic average
   c. The most frequently occurring score

7. Discuss the benefits and disadvantages of range and standard deviation as measures of variability of the scores.

8. a. Calculate the z-score for a score of 5 in a distribution with a mean of seven and a standard deviation of 0.5.
   b. What would the stanine score for this score be?

9. a. Using Table A-1, what is the estimated percentile rank for a z-score of $+1.20$?

10. To minimize the effect of an extreme score, should you choose the mean or median as the measure of central tendency?

11. In an analysis of National Assessment of Educational Progress scores, Hedges and Nowell (1995) found that male scores were more heterogeneous, more spread from low to high, than female scores.
    a. Which statistics would be greater for males?
    b. Which gender had more stanine scores of 9?
    c. Which gender had more stanine scores of 1?
    d. Which gender had more stanine scores of 5?

12. The mean score on a test is 40, and the standard deviation is 4. Express each of the following raw scores as a z-score:
    a. 41
    b. 30
    c. 48
    d. 36
    e. 46

13. a. What would be the T-score for the raw score of 46 in Exercise 12?
    b. What would the stanine score for the raw score of 46 be?

14. In a normal distribution, what percentage of the scores would fall below a z-score of -1.0? A z-score of 0? A z-score of $+.67$?

15. Describe the relationship shown by these scattergrams. Then estimate the correlation coefficients.

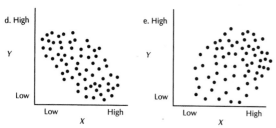

16. Five girls took a history test and a geography test, with the following results:

| | History | | Geography | |
	Raw Score	z-Score	Raw Score	z-Score
Ann	28	.5	85	1.5
Nesa	32	1.5	65	.5
Mar'a	26	0	55	0
Benazir	20	-1.5	45	-.5
Yoko	24	-.5	25	-1.5

HISTORY
$$\Sigma X = 130$$
$$\sigma = 4$$

GEOGRAPHY
$$\Sigma X = 275$$
$$\sigma = 20$$

a. What is the mean of the history test?
b. Whose performance in history is most in agreement with her performance in geography?
c. What is the correlation between the history and geography scores?

17. Given that the history test mean in Exercise 13 is lower than the geography test mean, which of the following conclusions would be correct?
    a. These girls are better in history than in geography.
    b. These girls are better in geography than in history.
    c. Their teacher has probably spent twice as much time on geography as on history.
    d. Their teacher knows more geography than history.
    e. None of the above.

18. If the coefficient of correlation between variable X and variable Y is found to be $-.98$, which of the following would be indicated?
    a. Variable X and variable Y are closely related.
    b. Variable X and variable Y are unrelated.
    c. Variable X and variable Y are perfectly related.
    d. Variable Y is a result of variable X.

19. For each of the following cases, indicate which statistic should be used—mean, standard deviation, z-score, or Pearson r.
   a. We want to know how spread out or heterogeneous the scores of a class are.
   b. We want to determine how Joe's score compares with the scores of the rest of the class.
   c. We want to know how well the class as a whole did on an examination.
   d. We want to predict the future achievement of students from their IQ.

20. Which statistical technique has been called *analysis of analyses?*

21. Define *effect size,* and tell how it is used.

22. What is the purpose of meta-analysis?

23. Interpret the following: "On the College Board exam ($\mu = 500, \sigma = 100$), the mean of this years Central High School seniors was 490, the standard deviation 110. The correlation between the exam scores and high school grade-point average was +.40."

24. Interpret the following: "Parents of Central High students were asked to rank ten problems statements from 10 = most serious to 1 = least serious. The median for the problem 'physical safety' was 5.21."

ANSWERS

1. a. Ratio
   b. Nominal
   c. Ordinal
   d. Ratio
   e. Interval

2. (Figures may be expanded or contracted vertically or horizontally or both and be correct if the relationships between scores and frequencies are maintained)

HISTOGRAM

POLYGON

3. a. Mean = 11
   b. Median = 10.5
   c. Mode = 10

4. The three measures are not equal in a skewed distribution. The mean is pulled in the direction of the skewed side. Thus in a positively skewed distribution the mean is always higher than the median, and the mode is usually

lowest in value. In a negatively skewed distribution, the mean is always lower than the median, and the mode is usually highest in value.

5. a. Median
   b. Mode
   c. Mean

6. a. Median
   b. Mean
   c. Mode

7. The range is easy to calculate and to explain. The standard deviation takes into account all the scores and is more stable.

8. a. $z = 5 - 7/.5 = -2$
   b. stanine $= 1$

9. 88 (rounded from 88.49)

10. Median because extreme scores do not influence the median.

11. a. Male scores had higher variance, standard deviation, and range.
    b. Males
    c. Males
    d. Females

12. a. .25
    b. -2.5
    c. 2
    d. -1
    e. 1.5

13. a. $T = 10z + 50 = 10(1.5) + 50 = 65$
    b. Stanine score $2 z + 5$ rounded $= (2)(1.5) + 5 = 8$

14. 16%; 50%; 75%

15. a. Perfect positive, $+1$ correlation, 0
    b. Positive, $+75$

c. Perfect negative, -1
d. Negative, $-.75$
e. No correlation, 0

16. a. 26
    b. Maria; she had the same z-score on both tests
    c. $r = \dfrac{\Sigma z_x z_y}{N} = \dfrac{3}{5} = .6$

17. e

18. a

19. a. Standard deviation
    b. z-score
    c. Mean
    d. Pearson r

20. Meta-analysis

21. Effect size (a form of z-score) is the difference between experimental and control groups divided by the standard deviation of the control group. It indicates the strength of the relationship between independent and dependent variables.

22. It combines the result of studies with similar independent and dependent variables to produce an average effect size, a mathematical summary of the results.

23. As a group the Central High seniors were slightly below the national average (effect size = .10). Their scores were a bit more heterogeneous than usual. Those with high scores tended to have high GPAs. Those with low scores tended to have low GPAs. The relationship between scores and GPAs was moderate positive.

24. Parents ranked "physical safety" about average.

 ## INFOTRAC COLLEGE EDITION

Use InfoTrac College Edition to locate a research article on a topic of interest to you. Describe the level of measurement associated with each of the measures used in the research. What descriptive statistics were used to summarize the data? Was the statistic appropriate for the level of measurement?

Chapter 7

Sampling and Inferential Statistics

INSTRUCTIONAL OBJECTIVES

After studying this chapter, the student will be able to:

1 Describe the meaning, rationale, and steps involved in sampling, and distinguish between probability and nonprobability sampling.

2 List the characteristics, uses, and limitations of each kind of probability and nonprobability sampling.

3 Explain the meaning of *sampling error* and its relationship to making statistical inferences.

4 Explain the meaning of *statistical significance.*

5 Explain how a *null hypothesis* is used in scientific research.

6 Describe Type I and Type II errors.

7 Explain the difference between directional and nondirectional tests of significance and the appropriate use of each of these tests.

8 Describe the elements to consider in determining sample size.

9 Use power formulas to calculate sample size needed in a statistical test about the mean of a population.

10 Explain the strategy employed in testing a null hypothesis.

11 Apply the *t*-test to find the significance of the difference between independent and dependent means.

12 Describe how effect size and sample size determine statistical significance.

13 Describe the purpose of the *t*-test for the Pearson *r*, and determine if a given correlation coefficient differs significantly from zero.

14 Apply the *F*-test for finding the significance of the differences between groups in one-way and two-way analysis of variance.

15 Apply the chi-square test for finding the significance of the differences between proportions in one-way and two-way classifications.

16 Select the kind of inferential statistical procedures appropriate for use in testing a given research hypothesis.

17 Demonstrate comprehension of the basic technical statistical terms used in reporting research results.

The statistics discussed in the previous chapter are used for organizing, summarizing, and describing data. In research, however, we often need to go further than describing data. After making observations of a sample, researchers employ induction or inference to generalize findings to the entire population from which the sample was drawn. To do this they need techniques that enable them to make credible inferences from samples to whole populations.

SAMPLING

An important characteristic of inferential statistics is the process of going from the part to the whole. For example, you might study a randomly selected group of 500 students attending a university in order to make generalizations about the entire student body of that university.

The small group that is observed is called a *sample,* and the larger group about which the generalization is made is called a *population.* A **population** is defined as all members of any well-defined class of people, events, or objects. For example, in a study where American adolescents constitute the population of interest, you could define this population as all American boys and girls within the age range of 12–21. A **sample** is a portion of a population. For example, the students of Arlington High School in Indianapolis constitute a sample of American adolescents. They are a portion of the large population in that they are both American citizens and within the age range of 12–21.

Statistical inference is a procedure by means of which you estimate **parameters** (characteristics of populations) from **statistics** (characteristics of samples). Such estimations are based on the laws of probability and are best estimates rather than absolute facts. In making any such inferences, a certain degree of error is involved. As we note later, inferential statistics are used to test hypotheses about populations on the basis of observations of a sample drawn from the population.

Rationale of Sampling

Inductive reasoning is an essential part of the scientific approach. The inductive method involves making observations and then drawing conclusions from these observations. If you can observe all instances of a population, you can, with confidence, base conclusions about the population on these observations (perfect induction). However, if you observe only some instances of a population, then you can do no more than infer that these observations will be true of the population as a whole (imperfect induction). This is the concept of sampling, which involves taking a portion of the population, making observations on this smaller group, and then generalizing the findings to the parent population, the larger population from which the sample was drawn.

Sampling is indispensable to the researcher. Usually the time, money, and effort involved do not permit a researcher to study all possible members of a population. Furthermore, it is generally not necessary to study all possible cases to understand the phenomenon under consideration. Sampling comes to your aid by enabling you to study a portion of the population rather than the entire population.

Because the purpose of drawing a sample from a population is to obtain information concerning that population, it is extremely important that the individuals included in a sample constitute a representative cross section of individuals in the population. Samples must be representative if you are to be able to generalize with confidence from the sample to the population. For example, the researcher may assume that the students at Arlington High School are representative of American adolescents. However, this sample may not be representative if the individuals who are included have some characteristics that differ from the target population. The location of their school, their socioeconomic backgrounds, their family situations, their prior experiences, and many other characteristics of this group may make them unrepresentative of American adolescents. This type of sample would be termed a **biased sample.** The findings on a **biased sample** in a research study cannot legitimately be generalized to the population from which it is taken.

Steps in Sampling

Researchers distinguish between the target population and the accessible population (Kempthorne, 1961). The first step in sampling is the identification of the **target population** to be represented in the study. If the researcher is interested in learning about the teachers in the St. Louis public school system, all those who teach within that system constitute the target population. In a study of the attitudes and values of American adolescents, the target population would be all American boys and girls in the age range of 12–21, given that adolescence is operationally defined as the period between ages 12 and 21.

However, because it is usually not possible to deal with the whole target population, you must identify that portion of the population to which you can have access—called the **accessible population**—and it is from this group that you will take the sample for the study. The nature of the accessible population is influenced by the time and resources of the researcher. In a typical attitude study, for example, a researcher might designate all adolescent boys and girls in California or just those in San Francisco as the accessible population.

From the accessible population, select a sample in such a way that it is representative of that population. For example, a researcher would have to sample from adolescents all over the state of California if California adolescents are identified as the accessible population. Or, if adolescents living in San Francisco are the accessible population, then the sample would be drawn from this particular group.

How safely can you generalize from a sample to the target population? If the sample selected is truly representative of the accessible population, then there is little difficulty in making this first step in the generalization process. The general principle is, If a sample has been selected so that it is representative of the accessible population, findings from the sample can be generalized to that population. For example, if you have selected a representative sample of California adolescents, then you could make generalizations concerning the attitudes and values of all adolescent boys and girls in California.

However, generalizing from the accessible population to the target population typically involves greater risk. The confidence you can have in this step depends on the similarity of the accessible population to the target population. In the preceding example, a researcher could have more confidence making generalizations about American adolescents if adolescents in several states throughout the country are designated as the accessible population, rather than adolescents in California alone. In this way all sections of the United States would be represented and a more adequate sampling of attitudes and values would be possible.

It is true that you must make an inferential "leap of faith" when estimating population characteristics from sample observations. The likelihood that such inferences will be correct is largely a function of the sampling procedure employed. Two major types of sampling procedures are available to researchers: probability and nonprobability sampling. **Probability sampling** involves sample selection in which the elements are drawn by chance procedures. The main characteristic of probability sampling is that every member or element of the population has a known probability of being chosen in the sample. **Nonprobability sampling** includes methods of selection in which elements are not chosen by chance procedures. There is no way of estimating the probability that each element has of being included in the sample. Its success depends on the knowledge, expertise, and judgment of the researcher. Nonprobability sampling is used when the application of probability sampling is not feasible. Its advantage are convenience and economy.

Probability Sampling

Probability sampling is defined as the kind of sampling in which "every element in the population has a nonzero chance of being selected" (Stuart, 1984). The possible inclusion of each population element in this kind of sampling takes place by chance and is attained through random selection. When probability sampling is used, inferential statistics enable researchers to estimate the extent to which the findings based on the sample are likely to differ from what they would have found by studying the whole population. The four types of probability sampling most frequently used in educational research are simple random sampling, stratified sampling, cluster sampling, and systematic sampling.

Simple Random Sampling

The best known of the probability sampling procedures is simple random sampling. The basic characteristic of simple random sampling is that all members of the population have an equal and independent chance of being included in the **random sample.** In other words, for every pair of elements X and Y, X's chance of being selected equals Y's chance, and the selection of X in no way affects Y's probability of selection. The steps in simple random sampling comprise the following:

1. Define the population.
2. List all members of the population.
3. Select the sample by employing a procedure where sheer chance determines which members on the list are drawn for the sample.

The most systematic procedure for drawing a random sample is to refer to a **table of random numbers,** which is a table containing columns of digits that have been mechanically generated, usually by a computer, to assure a random order. Table A.6 in the Appendix is an example. The first step in drawing a random sample from a population is to assign each member of the population a distinct identification number. Then use the table of random numbers to select the identification numbers of the subjects to include in the sample.

Let's illustrate the use of this table to obtain a sample of adolescents from the population of students attending Arlington High School. First you need to enumerate all the individuals in the population. The principal's office could supply a list of all students enrolled in the school. You would then assign a number to each individual in the population, for identification purposes. Assuming there were 800 students in the school, you might use the numbers 000, 001, 002, 003, . . . , 799 for this purpose. Then you would enter a table of random numbers to obtain numbers of three digits each, using only those numbers that are less than or equal to 799. For each number chosen, the corresponding element in the population falls in the sample. Continue the process until the desired number for the sample has been chosen. It is customary in using a table of random numbers to determine by chance the point at which the table is entered. One way is to touch the page blindly and begin wherever the page is touched.

The generally understood meaning of the word *random* is "without purpose or by accident." However, random sampling is purposeful and methodical. It is apparent that a sample selected randomly is not subject to the biases of the researcher. Rather, the researchers commit themselves to selecting a sample in such a way that their biases are not permitted to operate. They are pledging themselves to avoid a deliberate selection of subjects who will confirm the hypothesis. They are allowing chance alone to determine which elements in the population will be in the sample.

You would expect a random sample to be representative of the target population sampled. However, a random selection, especially with small samples, does not absolutely guarantee a sample that will represent the population well. Random selection does guarantee that any differences between the sample and the parent population are only a function of chance and not a result of the researcher's bias. The differences between random samples and their parent population are not systematic. For example, the mean reading achievement of a random sample of sixth-graders may be higher than the mean reading achievement of the target population, but it is equally likely that the mean for the sample will be lower than the mean for the target population. In other words, with random sampling the sampling errors are just as likely to be negative as they are to be positive.

Furthermore, statistical theorists have shown, through deductive reasoning, how much a researcher can expect the observations derived from random samples to differ from what would be observed in the population under the null hypothesis. All inferential statistical procedures have this aim in mind. Remember that characteristics observed in a small sample are more likely to differ from population characteristics than are characteristics observed in a large sample. When random sampling is used, the researcher can employ inferential statistics to estimate how much the population is likely to differ from the sample. The inferential statistics in this chapter are all based on random sampling and apply directly only to those cases in which the sampling has been random.

Unfortunately, simple random sampling requires enumeration of all individuals in a finite population before the sample can be drawn—a requirement that often presents a serious obstacle to the practical use of this method. Now let's look at other probability sampling methods that are approximations to simple random sampling and may be used as alternatives in certain situations.

Stratified Sampling

When the population consists of a number of subgroups, or strata, that may differ in the characteristics being studied, it is often desirable to use a form of probability sampling called **stratified sampling.** For example, if you were conducting a poll designed to assess opinions on a certain political issue, it might be advisable to subdivide the population into subgroups on the basis of age or occupation, because you would expect opinions to differ systematically among various age or occupational groups. In stratified sampling, you first identify the strata of interest and then randomly draw a specified number of subjects from each stratum. The basis for stratification may be geographic, or may involve characteristics of the population such as income, occupation, gender, age, year in college, or teaching level. In studying adolescents, for example, you might be interested not merely in surveying the attitudes of adolescents toward certain phenomena, but also in comparing the attitudes of adolescents who reside in small towns with those who live in medium-size and large cities. In such a case you would divide the adolescent population into three groups, based on the size of the towns or cities in which they reside, and then randomly select independent samples from each stratum.

An advantage of stratified sampling is that it enables the researcher to study the differences that might exist between various subgroups of a population. In this kind of sampling you may either take equal numbers from each stratum or select in proportion to the size of the stratum in the population. The latter procedure is known as *proportional stratified sampling,* which is applied when the characteristics of the entire population are the main concern in the study. The stratum is represented in the sample in exact proportion to its frequency in the total population. For example, if 10 percent of the voting population are college students, then 10 percent of a sample of voters to be polled would be taken from this stratum.

In some research studies, however, the main concern is with differences among various strata. In these cases the researcher chooses samples of equal size from each stratum. For example, if you are investigating the difference between the study habits of graduate and undergraduate students, you include equal numbers in both groups and then study the differences that might exist between them. You choose the procedure according to the nature of the research question. If your emphasis is on the types of differences among the strata, you select equal numbers of cases from each. If the characteristics of the entire population are your main concern, proportional sampling is more appropriate. When the population to be sampled is not homogeneous but consists of several subgroups, stratified sampling may give a more representative sample than simple random sampling. In simple random sampling, certain strata may by chance be over- or underrepresented in the sample. For example, in the simple random sample of high school students it would be theoretically possible (though highly unlikely) to obtain female subjects only. This could not happen, however, if males and females were listed separately and a random sample were then chosen from each group.

The major advantage of stratified sampling is that it guarantees representation of defined groups in the population.

Cluster Sampling

As mentioned earlier, it is very difficult, if not impossible, to list all the members of a target population and select the sample from among them. The population of American high school students, for example, is so large that you cannot list all its members for the purpose of drawing a sample. In addition, it would be very expensive to study a sample that is scattered all around the United States. In this case it would be more convenient to study subjects in naturally occurring groups, or clusters. For example, a researcher might choose a number of schools randomly from a list of schools and then include all the students in those schools in the sample. This kind of probability sampling is referred to as **cluster sampling,** because the unit chosen is not an individual but a group of individuals who are naturally together. These individuals constitute a cluster insofar as they are alike with respect to characteristics relevant to the variables of the study. To illustrate, let us assume a public opinion poll is being conducted in Atlanta. The investigator would probably not have access to a list of the entire adult population; thus it would be impossible to draw a simple random sample. A more feasible approach would involve the selection of a random sample of, say, fifty blocks from a city map and then the polling of all the adults living on those blocks. Each block represents a cluster of subjects, similar in certain characteristics associated with living in proximity. A common application of cluster sampling is the use of intact classrooms as clusters.

It is essential that the clusters actually included in your study be chosen at random from a population of clusters. Another procedural requirement is that once a cluster is selected, *all* the members of the cluster must be included in the sample. The sampling error (see discussion later) in a cluster sample is much greater than in true random sampling. It is also important to remember that if the number of clusters is small, the likelihood of sampling error is great—even if the total number of subjects is large.

Systematic Sampling

Still another form of probability sampling is called **systematic sampling.** This procedure involves drawing a sample by taking every Kth case from a list of the population.

First you decide how many subjects you want in the sample (n). Because you know the total number of members in the population (N), you simply divide N by n and determine the sampling interval (K) to apply to the list. Select the first member randomly from the first K members of the list, and then select every Kth member of the population for the sample. For example, let's assume a total population of 500 subjects and a desired sample size of 50: $K = N/n = 500/50 = 10$.

Start near the top of the list so that the first case can be randomly selected from the first ten cases; and then select every tenth case thereafter. Suppose the third name or number on the list was the first selected. You would then add the sampling interval or 10, to 3—and thus the 13th person falls in the sample, as does the 23rd, and so on—and would continue adding the constant sampling interval until you reached the end of the list.

Systematic sampling differs from simple random sampling in that the various choices are not independent. Once the first case is chosen, all subsequent cases to be included in the sample are automatically determined. If the original population list is in random order, systematic sampling would yield a sample that could be statistically considered a reasonable substitute for a random sample. However, if the list is not random, it is possible that every *K*th member of the population might have some unique characteristic that would affect the dependent variable of the study and thus yield a biased sample. Systematic sampling from an alphabetical list, for example, would probably not give a representative sample of various national groups because certain national groups tend to cluster under certain letters and the sampling interval could omit them entirely or at least not include them to an adequate extent.

Note that the various types of probability sampling that have been discussed are not mutually exclusive. Various combinations may be used. For example, you could use cluster sampling if you were studying a very large and widely dispersed population. At the same time, you might be interested in stratifying the sample to answer questions regarding its different strata. In this case you would stratify the population according to the predetermined criteria and then randomly select the cluster of subjects from among each stratum.

Nonprobability Sampling

In many research situations, the enumeration of the population elements—a basic requirement in probability sampling—is difficult, if not impossible. In these instances the researcher may use nonprobability sampling, which involves nonrandom procedures for selecting the members of the sample. The major forms of nonprobability sampling are accidental sampling, purposive sampling, and quota sampling.

Accidental Sampling

Accidental sampling, which is regarded as the weakest of all sampling procedures, involves using available cases for a study. Interviewing the first individuals you encounter on campus, using the students in your own classroom as a sample, or taking volunteers to be interviewed in survey research are various examples of accidental sampling. There is no way (except by repeating the study using probability sampling) of estimating the error introduced by the accidental sampling procedures. If you do use accidental sampling, be extremely cautious in interpreting the findings.

Purposive Sampling

In **purposive sampling**—also referred to as **judgment sampling**—sample elements judged to be typical, or representative, are chosen from the population. Researchers often use purposive sampling for forecasting national elections. In each state they choose a number of small districts whose returns in previous elections have been typical of the entire state. They interview all the eligible voters in these districts, and use the results to predict the voting patterns of the state. Using similar procedures in all states, the pollsters forecast the national results.

The critical question in purposive sampling is the extent to which judgment can be relied on to arrive at a typical sample. There is no reason to assume that the units judged to be typical of the population will continue to be typical over a period of time. Consequently, the results of a study using purposive sampling may be misleading. Because of its low cost and convenience, purposive sampling has been useful in attitude and opinion surveys. Be aware of the limitations, however, and use the method with extreme caution.

Quota Sampling

Quota sampling involves selecting typical cases from diverse strata of a population. The quotas are based on known characteristics of the population to which you wish to generalize. Elements are drawn so that the resulting sample is a miniature approximation of the population with respect to the selected characteristics. For example, if census results show that 25 percent of the population of an urban area lives in the suburbs, then 25 percent of the sample should come from the suburbs.

Here are the steps in quota sampling:

1. Determine a number of variables, strongly related to the question under investigation, to be used as bases for stratification. Variables such as gender, age, education, and social class are frequently used.

2. Using census or other available data, determine the size of each segment of the population.

3. Compute quotas for each segment of the population that are proportional to the size of each segment.

4. Select typical cases from each segment, or stratum, of the population to fill the quotas.

The major weakness of quota sampling lies in step 4, the selection of individuals from each stratum. You simply do not know whether the individuals chosen are representative of the given stratum. The selection of elements is likely to be based on accessibility and convenience. If you are selecting 25 percent of the households in the inner city for a survey, you are more likely to go to houses that are attractive rather than dilapidated, to those that are more accessible, to those where people are at home during the day, and so on. Such procedures automatically result in a systematic bias in the sample, because certain elements are not going to be represented. Furthermore, there is no basis for calculating the error involved in quota sampling.

Despite these shortcomings, researchers have used quota sampling in many projects that might otherwise not have been possible. Many feel that speed of data collection outweighs the disadvantages. Moreover, years of experience with quota samples have made it possible to identify some of the pitfalls and to take steps to avoid them.

You can find further discussion of sampling techniques in works by Cochran (1985) and Sudman (1976) that are listed in the References at the end of this chapter.

The Size of the Sample (Fundamentals)

Laypeople are often inclined to criticize research (especially research whose results they don't like) by saying the sample was too small to justify the researchers' conclusions.

How large should a sample be? Other things being equal, a larger sample is more likely to be a good representative of the population than a smaller sample. However, the most important characteristic of a sample is its representativeness, not its size. A random sample of 200 is better than a random sample of 100, but a random sample of 100 is better than a biased sample of 2,500,000.

Size alone, then, will not guarantee accuracy. A sample may be large and still contain a bias. The latter situation is well illustrated by the *Literary Digest* magazine poll of 1936, which predicted the defeat of President Roosevelt. Although the sample included approximately 2½ million respondents, it was not representative of the voters; thus the pollsters reached an erroneous conclusion. The bias resulted from selecting respondents for the poll from automobile registrations, telephone directories, and the magazine's subscription lists. These subjects would certainly not represent the total voting population in 1936, when many people could not afford automobiles, telephones or magazines. Also, because the poll was conducted by mail, the results were biased by differences between those who responded and those who did not. The researcher must recognize that sample size will not compensate for any bias that faulty sampling techniques may introduce. Representativeness must remain the prime goal in sample selection.

Later in this chapter we will introduce a procedure for determining appropriate sample size, on the basis of how large an effect size is considered meaningful and on statistical considerations. Such procedures, known as **power calculations,** are the best way to determine needed sample sizes.

The Concept of Sampling Error

When an inference is made from a sample to a population, a certain amount of error is involved because even random samples can be expected to vary from one to another. The mean intelligence score of one random sample of fourth-graders may differ from the mean intelligence score of another random sample of fourth-graders from the same population. Such differences, called *sampling errors,* result from the fact that the researcher has observed only a sample and not the entire population.

Sampling error is "the difference between a population parameter and a sample statistic." For example, if you know the mean of the entire population (symbolized μ) and also the mean of a random sample (symbolized $\overline{X}$) from that population, the difference between these two $(\overline{X} - \mu)$ represents sampling error (symbolized e). Thus, $e = \overline{X} - \mu$. For example, if you know that the mean intelligence score for a population of 10,000 fourth-graders is $\mu = 100$ and a particular random sample of 200 has a mean of $\overline{X} = 99$, then the sampling error is $\overline{X} - \mu = 99 - 100 = -1$. Because we usually depend on sample statistics to estimate population parameters, the notion of how samples are expected to vary from populations is a basic element in inferential statistics. However, instead of trying to determine the discrepancy between a sample statistic and the population parameter (which is not often known), the approach in inferential statistics is to estimate the variability that could be expected in the statistics from a number of different random samples drawn from the same population. Because each of the sample statistics is considered to be an estimate of the same population parameter, any variation among sample statistics must be attributed to sampling error.

The Lawful Nature of Sampling Errors

Given that random samples drawn from the same population will vary from one another, is using a sample to make inferences about a population really any better than just guessing? Yes, it is, because sampling errors behave in a lawful and predictable manner. The laws concerning sampling error have been derived through deductive logic and have been confirmed through experience.

Although researchers cannot predict the nature and extent of the error in a single sample, they can predict the nature and extent of sampling errors in general. Let us illustrate, with reference to sampling errors connected with the mean.

Sampling Errors of the Mean

Some sampling error can always be expected when a sample mean is used to estimate a population mean μ. Although, in practice, such an estimate is based on a single sample mean, assume that you drew several random samples from the same population and computed a mean for each sample. You would find that these sample means would differ from one another and would also differ from the population mean (if it were known). This variation among the means is caused by the sampling error associated with each random sample mean as an estimate of the population mean. Statisticians have carefully studied sampling errors of the mean and found that they follow known laws.

The Expected Mean of Sampling Errors Is Zero   Given an infinite number of random samples drawn from a single population, the positive errors can be expected to balance the negative errors so that the mean of the sampling errors will be zero. For example, if the mean height of a population of college freshmen is 5 feet 9 inches and several random samples are drawn from that population, you would expect some samples to have mean heights greater than 5 feet 9 inches and some to have mean heights less than 5 feet 9 inches. In the long run, however, the positive and negative sampling errors will balance. If you had an infinite number of random samples of the same size, calculated the mean of each of these samples, then computed the mean of all these means, the mean of the means would be equal to the population mean.

Because positive errors equal negative errors, a single sample mean is as likely to underestimate a population mean as to overestimate it. Therefore, we can justify saying that a sample mean is an unbiased estimate of the population mean and is a reasonable estimate of the population mean.

Sampling Error Is an Inverse Function of Sample Size   As the size of a sample increases, there is less fluctuation from one sample to another in the value of the mean. In other words, as the size of a sample increases, the expected sampling error decreases. Small samples are more prone to sampling error than are large ones. You would expect the means based on samples of ten to fluctuate a great deal more than the means based on samples of 100. In the height example, it is much more likely that a random sample of four will include three above-average freshmen and one below-average freshman than that a random sample of forty would include thirty above-average and ten below. As sample size increases, the likelihood that the mean of the sample is near the population mean also increases. There is a mathematical relationship between sample size and sampling error. We will show later how this relationship has been incorporated into inferential formulas.

Sampling Error Is a Direct Function of the Standard Deviation of the Population
The more spread, or variation, there is among members of a population, the more spread there will be in sample means. For example, the mean weights of random samples of 25, each selected from a population of professional jockeys, would show relatively less sampling error than the mean weights of samples of 25 selected from a population of schoolteachers. The weights of professional jockeys fall within a narrow range; the weights of schoolteachers do not. Therefore, for a given sample size, the expected sampling error for teachers' weights would be greater than the expected sampling error for jockeys' weights.

Sampling Errors Are Distributed in a Normal or Near-Normal Manner around the Expected Mean of Zero   Sample means near the population mean will occur more frequently than sample means far from the population mean. As you move farther and farther from the population mean, you find fewer and fewer sample means occurring. Both theory and experience have shown that the means of random samples are distributed in a normal or near-normal manner around the population mean. Because a sampling error in this case is the difference between a sample mean and the population mean, the distribution of sampling errors is also normal or near normal in shape.

The distribution of sample means will resemble a normal curve even when the population from which the samples are drawn is not normally distributed. For example, in a typical elementary school you will find about equal numbers of children of various ages included, so a polygon of the children's ages would be basically rectangular. If you took random samples of 40 each from a school with equal numbers of children aged 6 through 11, you would find many samples with a mean age near the population mean of 8.5, sample means of about 8 or 9 would be less common, and sample means as low as 7 or as high as 10 would be rare. Note that the word "error" in this context does not mean "mistake"—it refers to what is unaccounted for.

Standard Error of the Mean

Because the extent and the distribution of sampling errors can be predicted, researchers can use sample means with predictable confidence to make inferences concerning population means. However, you need an estimate of the magnitude of the sampling error associated with the sample mean when using it as an estimate of the population mean. An important tool for this purpose is the standard error of the mean. Sampling error manifests itself in the variability of sample means. Thus, if you calculate the standard deviation of a collection of means from random samples from a single population, you would have an estimate of the amount of sampling error. It is possible, however, to obtain this estimate on the basis of only one sample. We have noted that two things affect the size of sampling error: the size of the sample and the standard deviation in the population. When these two things are known, you can predict the standard deviation of sampling errors. This expected standard deviation of sampling errors of the mean is called the **standard error of the mean** and is represented by the symbol $\sigma_{\bar{x}}$. Deductive logic shows that the standard error of the mean is equal to the standard deviation of the population (σ) divided by the square root of the number in each sample ($\sqrt{n}$). As a formula,

$$\sigma_{\bar{x}} = \frac{\sigma}{\sqrt{n}} \qquad (7.1)$$

where

$$\sigma_{\bar{x}} = \text{standard error of the mean}$$
$$\sigma = \text{standard deviation of the population}$$
$$n = \text{number in each sample}$$

In Chapter 6 we noted that standard deviation (σ) is an index of the degree of spread among individuals in a population. In the same way, standard error of the mean ($\sigma_{\bar{x}}$) is an index of the spread expected among the means of samples drawn randomly from a population. As you will see, the interpretation of σ and $\sigma_{\bar{x}}$ is very similar.

Because the means of random samples have approximately normal distributions, you can also use the normal-curve model to make inferences concerning population means. Given that the expected mean of sample means is equal to the population mean, that the standard deviation of these means is equal to the standard error of the mean, and that the means of random samples are distributed normally, you can compute a z-score for a sample mean and refer that z to the normal-curve table to approximate the probability of a sample mean occurring through chance that far or farther from the population mean. The z is derived by subtracting the population mean from the sample mean and then dividing this difference by the standard error of the mean:

$$z = \frac{\overline{X} - \mu}{\sigma_{\bar{x}}} \qquad (7.2)$$

To illustrate, consider a college admissions officer who wonders if her population of applicants is above average on the Verbal subtest of the College Board examination. The national mean for College Board Verbal scores is 500, and the standard deviation is 100. She pulls a random sample of 64 from her population and finds the mean of the sample to be 530. She asks the question, How probable is it that a random sample of 64 with a mean of 530 would be drawn from a population with a mean of 500? Using formula 7.1, the admissions officer calculates the standard error of the mean as 12.5:

$$\sigma_{\bar{x}} = \frac{\sigma}{\sqrt{n}}$$
$$= \frac{100}{\sqrt{64}}$$
$$= 12.5$$

Calculating the z-score for her sample mean with formula 7.2, she obtains the following result:

$$z = \frac{\overline{X} - \mu}{\sigma_{\overline{x}}}$$

$$= \frac{530 - 500}{12.5}$$

$$= 2.4$$

Thus the sample mean deviates from the population mean by 2.4 standard error units. What is the probability of having a sample mean that deviates by this amount ($2.4\sigma_{\overline{x}}$) or more from the population mean? It is only necessary to refer to the normal curve in order to express this deviation (z) in terms of probability. Referring to the normal curve table, the admissions officer finds that the probability of a $z = 2.4$ or higher is .0082. This means that a z-score that great or greater would occur by chance only about 8 times in 1000. Because the probability of getting a sample mean that far from the population mean is remote, she concludes that the sample mean probably did not come from a population with a mean of 500 and therefore the mean of her population, applicants to her college, is probably greater than 500.

THE STRATEGY OF INFERENTIAL STATISTICS

Inferential statistics is the science of making reasonable decisions with limited information. Researchers use what they observe in samples and what is known about sampling error to reach fallible but reasonable decisions about populations. The statistical procedures performed before these decisions are made are called **tests of significance**. A basic tool of these statistical tests is the null hypothesis.

The Null Hypothesis

Suppose you have 100 fourth-graders available to participate in an experiment concerning the teaching of certain number concepts. Further, suppose that your research hypothesis is that Method B of teaching results in a greater mastery of these concepts than Method A. You randomly assign 50 students to be taught these concepts by Method A and the other 50 to be taught by Method B. You arrange their environment in such a way that the two groups differ only in method of instruction. At the end of the experiment you administer an examination that is considered to be a suitable operational definition of mastery of the number concepts of interest. You find that the mean for the students taught by Method B is higher than the mean for those taught by Method A. How do you interpret this difference?

Assuming you have been careful to make the learning conditions of the two groups equivalent, except for the method of teaching, you could account for the difference by declaring that (1) the method of teaching caused the difference or (2) the difference occurred by chance. Even though the subjects were randomly assigned to the treatments, it is possible that through chance the Method B group had students who were more intelligent, more highly motivated, or for some other reason were more likely to learn the number concepts than the students in the Method A group, no matter how they were taught.

The difference between the groups therefore could be a result of a relationship between the variables, method of teaching, and mastery of the concepts, or it could be the result of chance alone (sampling error). How are you to know which explanation is correct? In the ultimate sense you cannot positively prove that the method of teaching caused the difference. However, you can estimate the likelihood of chance alone being responsible for the observed difference and then determine which explanation to accept as a result of this estimate.

The chance explanation is known as the **null hypothesis,** which, as you recall from Chapter 5, is a statement that there is *no* actual relationship between the variables and that any observed relationship is only a function of chance. In the example, the null hypothesis would state that there is no relationship between teaching method and mastery of the number concepts.

Another way of stating the null hypothesis in the example is to declare that the mean for all fourth-graders taught by Method A is equal to the mean for all fourth-graders taught by Method B. In formula form, using the symbol μ for population mean, this statement becomes

$$H_0 : \mu_A = \mu_B$$

where

H_0 = null hypothesis
μ_A = mean of all fourth-graders taught by Method A
μ_B = mean of all fourth-graders taught by Method B

Note that the assumption is made that the 50 pupils taught by Method A are a random sample of the population of fourth-graders who might be taught by Method A and the 50 pupils taught by Method B are a random sample of the population who might be taught by Method B. The investigator hopes to use the data from the experiment to infer what would be expected when other fourth-graders are taught by Method A or B.

In interpreting the observed difference between the groups, the investigator must choose between the chance explanation (null hypothesis) and the explanation that states there is a relationship between variables (research hypothesis)—and must do so without knowing the ultimate truth concerning the populations of interest. This choice is based on incomplete information and is therefore subject to possible error.

Type I and Type II Errors

The investigator will either retain or reject the null hypothesis. Either decision may be right or wrong. If the null hypothesis is true, the investigator is correct in retaining it and in error in rejecting it. The rejection of a true null hypothesis is labeled a **Type I error.** If the null hypothesis is false, the investigator is in error in retaining it and correct in re-

Table 7.1 *Schematic Representation of Type I and Type II Errors*

		REAL SITUATION IN THE POPULATION	
		H_0 is true	H_0 is false
Investigator's Decision after Making Test of Significance	Rejects H_0	Type I error	Correct
	Retains H_0	Correct	Type II error

jecting it. The retention of a false null hypothesis is labeled a **Type II error.** The four possible states of affairs are summarized in Table 7.1.

Let's consider some possible consequences of the two types of errors, using the example we've been following.

Type I Error

A Type I error, symbolized by a Greek lowercase letter alpha (α), is a "false alarm"—the investigator thinks he or she has something when there is nothing there. For example, the investigator rejects the null hypothesis and declares that there is a relationship between teaching method and mastery of the numerical concepts, and therefore recommends Method B as the better method. Schools discard textbooks and other materials based on Method A and purchase materials based on Method B. In-service training is instituted to train teachers to teach by Method B. After all this expenditure of time and money, the schools do not observe an increase in mastery of the numerical concepts. Subsequent experiments do not produce the results observed in the original investigation. Although the ultimate truth or falsity of the null hypothesis is still unknown, the evidence supporting it is overwhelming. The original investigator is embarrassed and humiliated.

Type II Error

A Type II error, symbolized with a lowercase Greek letter beta (β), is a "miss"—the investigator concludes there is nothing when there really is something. In the example, the investigator concludes that the difference between the two groups may be attributed to chance and that the null hypothesis is probably true. She thus retains the null hypothesis and declares that there is insufficient evidence for concluding that one method is better than the other. Subsequent investigators conclude that Method B is better than Method A, and schools that change from Method A to Method B report impressive gains in student mastery. Although the ultimate truth still remains unknown, a mountain of evidence supports the research hypothesis. The original investigator is embarrassed (but probably not humiliated). Figure 7.1 provides a mnemonic for distinguishing Type I and Type II errors.

A FABLE FOR THE REMEMBRANCE OF TYPE I AND TYPE II ERRORS
by Donald Ary and John W. Sloan

A beautiful maiden was married to Alpha, the handsome and favorite number one son of the king. Alas, she discovered her husband was impotent. The king's ugly, despised number two son, Beta, became her lover.

In order to escape being stoned to death, she had to declare to the world that with number one, Alpha, there was a relationship when in truth there was none. Concerning number two, Beta, she had to declare that there was no relationship when in truth there was.

The Gods took pity on her and forgave both Type I and Type II errors. They promised her immortality with these words: "Our revered statisticians shall sing of your tragedy to generation after generation throughout all time to come, and the understanding of your dilemma shall cause scholars of all nations to sigh."

Source: From *The CEDR Quarterly* (1977). 10. (4) p. 19

FIGURE 7.1

Comparison of Type I and Type II Errors

Type I errors typically lead to changes that are unwarranted. Type II errors typically lead to a maintenance of the status quo when a change is warranted. The consequences of a Type I error are generally considered more serious than the consequences of a Type II error, although there are certainly exceptions.

LEVEL OF SIGNIFICANCE

Recall that all scientific conclusions are statements that have a high probability of being correct, rather than statements of absolute truth. How high must the probability be before an investigator is willing to declare that a relationship between variables exists? In other words, how unlikely must the null hypothesis be before a researcher rejects it? The consequences of rejecting a true null hypothesis, a Type I error, vary with the situation. Therefore investigators usually weigh the relative consequences of Type I and Type II errors and decide, before conducting their experiments, how strong the evidence must be before they would reject the null hypothesis. This predetermined level at which a null hypothesis would be rejected is called the *level of significance*. The probability of a Type I error is directly under the control of the researcher, who sets the level of significance according to the type of error he or she wishes to guard against.

Of course, a researcher could avoid Type I errors by always retaining the null hypothesis or avoid Type II errors by always rejecting it. Neither of these alternatives is productive. If the consequences of a Type I error would be very serious but a Type II error would be of little consequence, the investigator might decide to risk the possibility of a Type I error only if the estimated probability of the observed relationship's being caused by mere luck is one chance in a thousand or less. This is testing the hypothesis at the .001 level of significance, which is considered to be a quite conservative level. In this case the investigator is being very careful not to declare that a relationship exists when there is no relationship. However, this decision means accepting a high probability of a Type II error, declaring there is no relationship when in fact a relationship does exist.

If the consequences of a Type I error are judged to be not serious, the investigator might decide to declare that a relationship exists if the probability of the observed relationship's being caused by mere luck is one chance in ten or less. This is called "testing the hypothesis at the .10 level of significance." Here the investigator is taking only moderate precautions against a Type I error, yet is not taking a great risk of a Type II error.

The **level of significance** is the probability of a Type I error that an investigator is willing to risk in rejecting a null hypothesis. If an investigator sets the level of significance at .01, it means that the null hypothesis will be rejected if under the assumption that chance alone is responsible, the obtained probability is equal to or less than one time in a hundred. The investigator is saying that he or she is willing to limit the probability of rejecting the null hypothesis when it is true (Type I error) to 1 in 100. If the level of significance is set at .0001, the probability of making a Type I error is one in 10,000 or less. The most commonly used levels of significance in the field of education are the .05 and the .01 levels.

Traditionally, investigators determine the level of significance after weighing the relative seriousness of Type I and Type II errors, but before running the experiment. If the data derived from the completed experiment indicate that the probability of the null hypothesis being true is equal to or less than the predetermined acceptable probability, the investigators reject the null hypothesis and declare the results to be statistically significant. If the probability is greater than the predetermined acceptable probability, the results are described as nonsignificant—that is, the null hypothesis is retained.

The familiar meaning of the word *significant* is "important" or "meaningful." In statistics, this word means "less likely to be a function of chance than some predetermined probability." Results of investigations can be statistically significant without being inherently meaningful or important.

Directional and Nondirectional Tests

In testing a null hypothesis, researchers are not usually concerned with the direction of the differences in either direction. Rather, they are interested in knowing about the possible departure of sample statistics from population parameters. When comparing the ef-

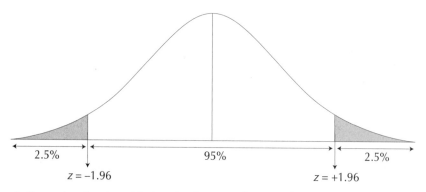

A. Curve showing the critical region for a nondirectional test (two-tailed test)

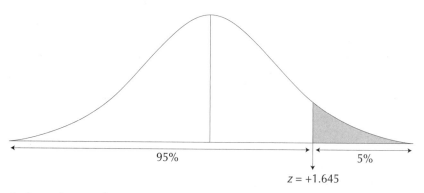

B. Curve showing the critical region for a directional test (one-tailed test)

FIGURE 7.2

Curves Showing the Critical Regions of Directional and Nondirectional Tests

fectiveness of competing treatments, an investigator usually wants to learn if treatment A is better than treatment B or if treatment B is better than treatment A. This kind of test is called **nondirectional** (two-tailed), because the investigator is interested in differences in either direction. The investigator states only that there will be a difference. Note in Figure 7.2 that the region of rejection is equally divided between the two tails of the distribution. Thus, if a sample mean is observed that is *either* sufficiently greater or sufficiently less than the hypothesized value, the null hypothesis would be rejected. The direction of the difference is not important.

However, if only one alternative to the null hypothesis is of interest, a **directional test** (one-tailed) is used. For example, an investigator studying the effects of a specific diet among obese people would only be interested in assessing the probability that the diet reduces weight. Or, if a basketball coach is investigating the effects of a practice regimen on the success rate for shooting from the foul line, he (or she) would only implement the regimen if there is reasonable evidence that it increases success. Results indicating that the regimen decreases success would lead to the same decision as would a retained null hypothesis: Forget the regimen.

If on the basis of experience, previous research, or theory the researcher chooses to state the direction of possible differences, then she or he would perform a directional test. A directional hypothesis would state *either* that the parameter is greater than *or* that the parameter is less than the hypothesized value. Thus, in directional tests the critical region is located in only one of the two tails of the distribution. For an .05 level of significance, this region in a normal curve is the point equal to $z = 1.645$. You do not, as you would in nondirectional tests, divide the 5 percent between the two sides of the curve. Rather, you place the whole 5 percent of chance error on one side of the curve. This means that the null hypothesis will be retained unless the observed difference is in the hypothesized direction. It is obvious that for rejecting a null hypothesis at a given level, a directional test requires a smaller z-value than a nondirectional test (compare $z = 1.645$ with $z = 1.96$, the z value required for a two-tailed test). So a directional test makes it easier to reject the null hypothesis and thus increases the probability that the null hypothesis will be rejected if the difference is in the hypothesized direction.

In statistical terminology, a nondirectional test is often referred to as a *two-tailed test of significance,* a directional test as a *one-tailed test*. The decision to use either a one-tailed test or a two-tailed test should be made early in the study, before any statistical tests are performed. You do not wait to see what the data look like and then select a one-tailed or two-tailed test.

The Size of the Sample (Calculation)

Now that we have considered Type I and Type II errors and level of significance, let us return to the question of the size of the sample needed in a research study. A scientific method of determining the sample size needed is to specify a meaningful effect size (Δ), then determine the sample size needed to reach a desired probability of rejecting the null hypothesis at a given level of significance. Recall that effect size is the difference between experimental and control groups divided by the standard deviation of the control group.

To illustrate, let us return to the college admissions officer who wonders if her population of applicants is above average. To determine the number of subjects needed to test her hypothesis, she first specifies what effect size would be meaningful. She decides that an effect size of .33 (one-third of a standard deviation) or more would be meaningful, but an effect size of less than .33 would not be meaningful.

The specification of what is a meaningful effect size is a judgment call. However, professionals in their fields are usually able to specify an effect size that serves as a reasonable dividing line between meaningful and trivial differences. Cohen's (1989) verbal labels for effect sizes (see Chapter 6) are useful guides for this purpose. In this example an effect size of .33 on the Verbal subtest of the College Board examination might be considered a reasonable dividing line. It is saying that a mean score of 533 or greater [$500 + (.33)(100)$] on the Verbal subtest of the College Board examination is enough to matter, whereas a smaller effect size has little or no practical importance. Consulting the normal curve table

(Table A.1 in the Appendix), we see that a z-score of .33 has 62.93 percent below it. Therefore the admissions officer is saying that if approximately 63 percent of the general population have scores less than the average for her population of applicants the difference is considered meaningful, whereas less difference would not be considered meaningful.

Next the admissions officer determines her level of significance, designated as alpha (α), and her desired probability of rejecting the false null hypothesis ($1 - \beta$). Let us say that she decides she wants a 90 percent chance of rejecting the null hypothesis with a one-tailed .05 alpha. Now she has all the ingredients needed to determine the needed sample size, as shown by the following formula:

$$N = \left(\frac{1}{\Delta}\right)^2 (z\alpha + z\beta)^2 \tag{7.3}$$

where

> N = the number needed in the sample
> Δ = the specified effect size
> $z\alpha$ = the z-score for the level of significance
> $z\beta$ = the z-score for the desired probability of rejecting the null hypothesis

In Table A.1 you can find that the z-score for a one-tailed .05 alpha is 1.645. The z-score for a one-tailed probability of 90 percent (the desired probability of rejecting the null hypothesis) is 1.28. Substituting these z-values and the specified Δ, you have the following:

$$
\begin{aligned}
N &= \left(\frac{1}{.33}\right)^2 (1.645 + 1.28)^2 \\
&= 3^2 (2.925)^2 \\
&= 9(8.56) \\
&= 77.04
\end{aligned}
$$

With a random sample of 78 subjects from her population of applicants, the admissions officer has a 90 percent chance of rejecting the null hypothesis at the one-tailed .05 level if the true effect size in her population is .33 or greater.

Note that as effect size gets smaller, the number needed gets larger. If the investigator had wanted an effect size of .10 to have a 90 percent probability of rejecting the null hypothesis at the one-tailed .05 level, she would need 856 subjects in her sample. Note also that as ($1 - \beta$), the desired probability of rejecting the null hypothesis gets larger and as alpha gets smaller (more demanding), the number of subjects needed gets larger.

Determining the number needed in a sample is really a function of how precise you want to be—that is, how large or small an effect size you want to be statistically significant, how much chance of Type I error you are willing to live with, and how much probability of rejecting a false null hypothesis you want. These are all judgment calls, but they can all be made on a rational basis. We would defend the specifications of $\Delta = .33$, $\alpha = .05$, and ($1 - \beta$) = .90 in the example as reasonable. Therefore we consider a sample size of 78 sufficient in this case.

Although it may be heresy to suggest a sample might ever be too large, it is true that as sample size increases, tinier and tinier effect sizes become statistically significant. We recommend that when planning research, both effect size and statistical significance be considered.

Formulas such as formula 7.3 are called **power formulas.** They indicate the number of subjects needed to give the investigator the desired power to reject the null hypothesis for specified effect size and level of significance. Many statistics books describe calculations for determining numbers needed when effect size is defined in terms of proportion, correlation, or other statistics. Borenstein and Cohen's *Statistical Power Analysis* (1989) provides extensive information on these procedures.

THE t-TEST

Among the more widely used methods for testing null hypotheses are the t-tests. We have shown that it is possible to make use of the normal probability curve to compare the mean of a sample with the population mean by using the z-score to see whether or not the sample mean is representative of the population mean. In the example we have been using, the college admissions officer found the standard error of the mean for the sample distribution, then used the formula $(\overline{X} - \mu)/\sigma_{\overline{x}}$. Implied in using this procedure is the appropriateness of the normal probability curve.

It has been shown mathematically, however, that the normal curve is appropriate for hypothesis testing only when the population standard deviation is known, as is the case with College Board scores. In most research situations the population standard deviation is not known, but can be estimated by the formula

$$s = \sqrt{\frac{\Sigma x^2}{n - 1}} \qquad (7.4)$$

where

$$s = \text{estimated population standard deviation}$$
$$\Sigma x^2 = \text{sum of the squared deviation scores, } \Sigma(X - \overline{X})^2$$
$$n = \text{number in the sample}$$

When this estimate (s) is substituted for the population standard deviation (σ) in the calculation of the standard error of the mean, it is customary to express formula 7.1 as

$$s_{\overline{x}} = \frac{s}{\sqrt{n}} \qquad \text{instead of} \qquad \sigma_{\overline{x}} = \frac{\sigma}{\sqrt{n}}$$

When $s_{\overline{x}}$ is used instead of $\sigma_{\overline{x}}$, each finite sample size has its own unique probability distribution. These distributions are known as the t-curves. These distributions become more and more similar to the normal curve as the size of the sample increases. A series of distributions called t-distributions has been developed for testing hypotheses concerning the population mean using small samples. When the sample size is infinite, the t-distribution is the same as the normal distribution. As the sample size becomes smaller,

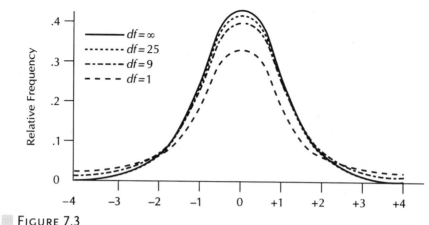

■ FIGURE 7.3

t-Curves for Various Degrees of Freedom

the *t*-distribution becomes increasingly different from the *z*-distribution. For our purposes it is not necessary to know how to calculate *t*-distributions because the most frequently needed results of these calculations are to be found in Table A.2 in the Appendix. The *t*-curve does not approach the baseline as rapidly as does the normal curve. Some of the *t*-curves are shown in Figure 7.3 along with the normal curve, the solid line labeled *df* = ∞.

The *t*-curves are labeled according to their degrees of freedom, abbreviated *df*. Before further discussion of the characteristics of *t*-curves, let us turn our attention to the concept of degrees of freedom.

Degrees of Freedom

The number of **degrees of freedom** (*df*) is the number of observations free to vary around a constant parameter. To illustrate the general concept of degrees of freedom, suppose a teacher asks a student to name any five numbers that come into his or her mind. The student would be free to name any five numbers he or she chooses, so we would say that the student has 5 degrees of freedom. Now suppose the teacher tells the student to name five numbers but to make sure that the mean of these five numbers is 20. The student now is free to name any numbers for the first four, but for the last number must name the number that will make the total for the five numbers 100 in order to arrive at a mean of 20. If the student names, as the first four numbers, 10, 16, 20, and 35, then the fifth number must be 19. The student has five numbers to name and one restriction, so his or her degrees of freedom are 5 − 1 = 4. We can show this as a formula:

$$df = n - 1$$
$$= 5 - 1$$
$$= 4$$

Now suppose the teacher asks the student to name seven numbers in such a way that the first three have a mean of 10 and all seven have a mean of 12. Here we have seven numbers and two restrictions, so

$$df = n - 2$$
$$= 7 - 2$$
$$= 5$$

When the unknown population standard deviation is estimated from the sample standard deviation $\left(s = \sqrt{\dfrac{\Sigma x^2}{N-1}} \right)$, one degree of freedom is lost. The one df is lost because the sample statistic (s) is derived from the deviations about the sample mean that must always sum to 0. Thus, all but one of the deviations is free to vary, or $df = N - 1$.

The concept of degrees of freedom is involved in most of the procedures in inferential statistics. An appropriate method of computing the degrees of freedom is associated with each procedure. Often, the number of degrees of freedom on which a sample statistic is based depends on the sample size (N) and the number of sample statistics used in its calculation.

The *t*-Test for Independent Samples

Research workers often draw two random samples from a population and assign a different treatment to each group. After exposing the two groups to these treatments, the researchers compare them with respect to the dependent variable(s) to assess the effect of the treatments. A difference observed between the two groups after such treatments may be statistically nonsignificant—that is, easily attributable to chance—and researchers must determine whether this is the case. The index used to find the significance of the difference between the means of the two samples for this purpose is called the *t*-test for independent samples. These samples are referred to as *independent* because they are drawn independently from a population without any pairing or other relationship between the two groups.

Let's use an example. Suppose a researcher is interested in finding out whether stress affects problem-solving performance. The first step is to randomly assign the students in a course to two groups. Because the members of the two groups are assigned randomly, the mean performances of the two groups in a problem-solving task should not significantly differ prior to the treatment. After the treatment, however, the mean performances of the two groups should differ significantly if stress is actually related to problem-solving performance.

Table 7.2 shows the posttreatment problem-solving scores (X), deviation scores (x), and squared deviation scores (x^2) of the members of the two groups, one of which worked under stress conditions and the other under relaxed (nonstress) conditions. The mean

Table 7.2	*Computing the t-Value for Two Sample Means*				
	GROUP 1 NONSTRESS CONDITION			GROUP 2 STRESS CONDITION	
X_1	x_1	x_1^2	X_2	x_2	x_2^2
18	+4	16	15	+5	25
17	+3	9	13	+3	9
16	+2	4	12	+2	4
16	+2	4	12	+2	4
16	+2	4	11	+1	1
15	+1	1	11	+1	1
15	+1	1	11	+1	1
15	+1	1	10	0	0
14	0	0	10	0	0
14	0	0	10	0	0
13	−1	1	9	−1	1
12	−2	4	8	−2	4
11	−3	9	6	−4	16
10	−4	16	6	−4	16
8	−6	36	6	−4	16

$$\frac{\Sigma X_1}{n_1} = \frac{210}{15} \qquad \Sigma x_1^2 = 106 \qquad \frac{\Sigma X_2}{n_2} = \frac{150}{15} \qquad \Sigma x_2^2 = 98$$

$$\overline{X}_1 = 14 \qquad\qquad\qquad\qquad \overline{X}_2 = 10$$

performance score of the subjects in the stress group is 10 and the mean performance score of the nonstress group is 14. Clearly, there is a difference: 4 score points between the means of the two groups.

If we designate the nonstress condition as the control group the effect size is $\overline{x}_e - \overline{x}_c / S_c = 4/\sqrt{106/15} - 1 = 4/2.75 = 1.45$. This is a very large effect size. However, an impressive-looking effect size can easily occur by chance when sample sizes are small. To determine the likelihood that this effect size or a larger one could be a function of chance alone, we first calculate the "standard error of the difference between two means" $(s_{\overline{x}_1 - \overline{x}_2})$, and then the t value.

The formula for $s_{\overline{x}_1 - \overline{x}_2}$ is

$$s_{\overline{x}_1 - \overline{x}_2} = \sqrt{\frac{\Sigma x_1^2 + \Sigma x_2^2}{n_1 + n_2 - 2}\left(\frac{1}{n_1} + \frac{1}{n_2}\right)} \qquad (7.5)$$

where

$$s_{\bar{x}_1 - \bar{x}_2} = \text{standard error of the difference between two means}$$
$$n_1 = \text{number of cases in Group 1}$$
$$n_2 = \text{number of cases in Group 2}$$
$$\Sigma x_1^2 = \text{sum of the squared deviation scores in Group 1}$$
$$\Sigma x_2^2 = \text{sum of the squared deviation scores in Group 2}$$

The standard error of the difference between two means is sometimes referred to as the "error term for the independent t-test." In the example, this would be calculated as follows:

$$s_{\bar{x}_1 - \bar{x}_2} = \sqrt{\frac{106 + 98}{15 + 15 - 2}\left(\frac{1}{15} + \frac{1}{15}\right)}$$

$$= \sqrt{\frac{204}{28}\left(\frac{2}{15}\right)}$$

$$= \sqrt{0.9715}$$

$$= .99$$

This calculation tells you the average difference that would be expected through chance alone if the null hypothesis were true. In other words, the value 0.99 is the mean difference you would expect between the mean performance scores for the two groups if they were drawn at random from a common population and were *not* subjected to different treatments. Given an infinite number of samples in such circumstances, you would expect to observe a difference of less than 0.99 (plus or minus) in 68 percent of the calculations of the differences between such random groups and a value of more than 0.99 (plus or minus) in the other 32 percent. (It is beyond the scope of this text to discuss the reason why the application of the formula for the standard error of the difference between means yields the appropriate estimated difference that would be due to chance. For a discussion of the rationale of this procedure, see Ary and Jacobs (1976). In the example for the data in Table 7.2, you should expect an average difference of 0.99 through chance under a true null hypothesis. A difference of 4.0 was observed. Is the observed difference sufficiently greater than the expected difference to enable you to reject the null hypothesis?

To answer this question, first make a ratio of the two numbers. This ratio, called the t-ratio, is expressed by the following formula:

$$t = \frac{\overline{X}_1 - \overline{X}_2}{s_{\bar{x}_1 - \bar{x}_2}} \tag{7.6}$$

where

$$t = t\text{-ratio}$$
$$\overline{X}_1 - \overline{X}_2 = \text{observed difference between two means}$$
$$s_{\bar{x}_1 - \bar{x}_2} = \text{standard error of the difference between two means (expected}$$
$$\text{difference between the two means when the null hypothesis is true)}$$

You can write the *t*-ratio formula in more complete form by including the formula for the standard error for the difference between two means:

$$t = \frac{\overline{X}_1 - \overline{X}_2}{\sqrt{\left(\dfrac{\Sigma x^2 + \Sigma x_2^2}{n_1 + n_2 - 2}\right)\left(\dfrac{1}{n_1} + \dfrac{1}{n_2}\right)}} \qquad (7.7)$$

In the example, then, the value of the *t*-ratio is

$$\frac{14 - 10}{0.99} = 4.04$$

The observed difference is 4.04 times as large as the difference expected under a true null hypothesis. Is this large enough to reject the null hypothesis at the .05 level? To answer this, calculate the degrees of freedom and consult the *t*-table.

The degrees of freedom for an independent *t*-test are the number of cases in the first group plus the number of cases in the second group minus 2, or

$$df = n_1 + n_2 - 2$$

In the example you have $15 + 15 - 2 = 28$ degrees of freedom. Now you can use Table A.2 in the Appendix to determine the significance of your results. The first column in this table is labeled *df* (degrees of freedom). Find the appropriate row in the table by locating the degrees of freedom in your study. For your example, consult the row for 28 degrees of freedom. The remaining columns show the *t*-values associated with certain probabilities for directional and nondirectional tests. Because the independent variable in your example could affect problem solving in either a positive or negative direction, you need to perform a nondirectional test. In the row for 28 degrees of freedom, you find 1.701 in the column labeled .10 for a nondirectional test, which tells you that with a true null hypothesis and 28 degrees of freedom, a *t*-ratio of $+1.701$ or more or -1.701 or less will occur by chance one time in ten. The number 2.048 in the column labeled .05 indicates that under a true null hypothesis and 28 degrees of freedom, a *t*-ratio of $+/- 2.048$ or more will occur by chance 5 percent of the time.

Your observed ratio of 4.04 is greater than 2.048, which means that the difference between your groups is greater than the value required to reject the null hypothesis at the .05 level of significance. The estimated probability of the null hypothesis being true is less than 5 percent ($p < .05$). Thus, you would reject the null hypothesis. Although you do not know for certain that the variables stress and problem–solving performance are related, the evidence is significant enough according to your previously set criteria to enable you to conclude that the observed relationship is probably not just a chance occurrence. If the observed *t*-ratio had been less than 2.048, you would have concluded that the evidence was not good enough to lead you to declare that a relationship exists between the variables. In other words, you would have retained the null hypothesis.

Notice that as you proceed from left to right in the *t*-table you find the *t*-values required for rejecting the null hypothesis at increasingly rigorous levels of significance. For 28 degrees of freedom, a value of 2.763 or greater would lead to the rejection of a null hypothesis at the .01 level. A value of 3.674 or greater would lead to the rejection of the null hypothesis at the .001 level. So your value of 4.08 is significant not only at the .05 level ($p < .05$) but also at the .01 level ($p < .01$) and the .001 level ($p < .001$).

Because the denominator is a measure of how much apparent difference can be expected through chance alone, it is called the **error term** of the t-test. If the ratio of observed difference (numerator) divided by error term (denominator) equals or exceeds the value indicated in Table A.2, you can reject the null hypothesis at the indicated level of significance.

Formula 7.7 is the definition formula for the independent t-ratio. The denominator, the spread within groups (Σx_1^2 and Σx_2^2) adjusted for the number in the sample indicates the theoretical average difference that you would expect when the null hypothesis is true. The numerator ($\overline{X}_1 - \overline{X}_2$) shows the actual difference observed. The larger the ratio of numerator to denominator, the less likely it is that the observed difference between means is a function of chance alone.

In practice the calculation of Σx_1^2, and Σx_2^2 is very tedious unless the means are a whole number (which seldom occurs except in textbook examples). The computation is much simpler if the calculation formula (formula 7.8) is used:

$$t = \frac{\overline{X}_1 - \overline{X}_2}{\sqrt{\dfrac{\Sigma X_1^2 - (\Sigma X_1)^2/n_1 + \Sigma X_2^2 - (\Sigma X_2)^2/n_2}{n_1 + n_2 - 2}\left(\dfrac{1}{n_1} + \dfrac{1}{n_2}\right)}} \tag{7.8}$$

The Logic of the t-Test

The numerator of the t-test is the actual difference that has been observed between two groups. The denominator ($s_{\overline{x}_1 - \overline{x}_2}$), or error term, is an estimate of how much these two groups would be expected to differ by chance alone; that is, it indicates the difference to be expected between two groups selected by a random procedure from a single parent population. This denominator is based on (1) the number in the samples, $n_1 + n_2$ (the larger the number, the fewer random differences to be expected between sample means); and (2) the variation within the groups, s_1 and s_2 (the greater the variation *within* groups, the greater the random differences to be expected between groups).

If the ratio of observed difference (numerator) divided by error term (denominator) equals or exceeds the value indicated in the table of t-values, you can reject the null hypothesis at the indicated level of significance.

The t-Test for Dependent Samples

So far, our discussion has centered on comparing the means obtained from two independent samples. In an independent sample, each member is chosen randomly from the population and the composition of one group has no bearing on the composition of the other group. Sometimes, however, investigators may wish to match the subjects of their two groups on some qualities that are important to the purpose of their research, or they may wish to compare the means obtained by the same group under two different experimental conditions. In such cases the groups are no longer independent, inasmuch as the composition of one group is related to the composition of the other group. You would expect the dependent variable scores to be correlated. Therefore, the **t-test for dependent, or correlated, samples** must be used. This test is also known as the correlated, or nonindependent or paired observations, t-test. The measure to be analyzed by the dependent t-test is the mean difference between the paired scores.

Let's consider an example. Suppose you wish to know whether taking a research course affects the attitudes of the students toward research. To investigate this, you select a research class and obtain attitude measures toward research from the students on the first and last days of class. Let's suppose you have collected such data and the results are as presented in Table 7.3. Columns (2) and (3) show the scores of each student in the first and second measures. Column (4) presents the difference between the first and second scores of each student. The sum of these differences amounts to +30. The mean of the differences, +2, is found by dividing +30 (ΣD) by the number of paired observations, or 15. Column (5) shows the squares of the differences.

The standard deviation of the difference scores S_D is

$$s_D = \sqrt{\frac{\Sigma D^2 - \frac{(\Sigma D)^2}{n}}{N - 1}} \tag{7.9}$$

In the example, this is

$$s_D = \sqrt{\frac{164 - \frac{(30)^2}{15}}{15 - 1}} = \sqrt{\frac{164 - 60}{14}} = \sqrt{\frac{104}{14}} = \sqrt{7.4286} = 2.7255$$

Effect size, the mean difference divided by the standard deviation $\left(\Delta = \frac{\overline{D}}{s_D}\right)$, is 2 / 2.7255 = .7338. By Borenstein & Cohen's (1989) definition, this is nearer a "large" (.8) than a "moderate" (.6) effect size.

To determine the likelihood that the effect size is a function of chance, first calculate a t-ratio by multiplying effect size by the square root of the number of pairs:

$$t = \Delta\sqrt{N} \tag{7.10}$$

In this example the t is .7338 · $\sqrt{15}$ = .7338 · 3.87 = 2.84

With the dependent t-test, it is easy to see the relationship of effect size and number on the one hand and the statistical significance on the other. The larger the effect size, the larger the t and the more likely the results are statistically significant. The larger the number, the larger the t and the more likely the results are statistically significant.

The t-ratio tells you that the observed difference is 2.84 times as great as the difference that would be expected under a true null hypothesis. Now consult the table of t-values

Table 7.3 *Before-and-After Attitude Scores of 15 Students in an Introduction to Research Class*

(1) SUBJECT NUMBER	(2) PRETEST	(3) POSTTEST	(4) D	(5) D^2
1	10	12	+2	+4
2	9	13	+4	+16
3	8	12	+4	+16
4	11	9	−2	+4
5	10	8	−2	+4
6	7	9	+2	+4
7	10	12	+2	+4
8	9	11	+2	+4
9	8	10	+2	+4
10	6	10	+4	+16
11	10	12	+2	+4
12	7	13	+6	+36
13	10	6	−4	+16
14	9	13	+4	+16
15	10	14	+4	+16
			$\Sigma D = +30$	$\Sigma D^2 = 164$

(Appendix Table A.2) to determine the statistical significance of the observed ratio. A more commonly used formula for the dependent *t*-test is:

$$t = \frac{\overline{D}}{\sqrt{\dfrac{\Sigma D^2 - \dfrac{(\Sigma D)^2}{N}}{N(N-1)}}} \qquad (7.10a)$$

where

$$
\begin{aligned}
t &= t\text{-ratio}\\
\overline{D} &= \text{average difference}\\
\Sigma D^2 &= \text{different scores squared then summed}\\
(\Sigma D)^2 &= \text{difference scores summed then squared}\\
N &= \text{number of pairs}
\end{aligned}
$$

   The number of degrees of freedom for the dependent *t*-test equals $N - 1$, N being the number of pairs of observations. In the example you have $15 - 1 = 14$ degrees of freedom. In the table of *t*-values you find that with 14 degrees of freedom a *t*-value of 2.145 is needed for the *t* to be significant at the .05 level, and a *t*-value of 2.977 for significance at the .01 level when a nondirectional test is performed. Your obtained value of 2.84 exceeds the given value for the .05 level but does not reach the given value for the .01 level. This means that the difference between the two means is significant at the .05 level but not at the .01 level. If you had set your level of significance at .05, you could conclude that the attitude of the students toward research had changed.

The *t*-Test for Pearson *r* Correlation Coefficients

Another important use for the *t*-test is in testing hypotheses concerning a population correlation (ρ). The most common null hypothesis in such cases is that the population correlation is zero and that the correlation observed in the sample (*r*) is a function of chance. For example, an investigator might draw a sample of twenty-seven college freshmen, administer vocabulary and spatial orientation tests to them, and find a Pearson *r* of .20 between the two measures. The next step is to decide whether this observed correlation coefficient could easily be a result of chance in a population where the true correlation in the population (ρ) is zero. To test the hypothesis that the population correlation is zero, you do not have to calculate a *t*-test. These calculations have been done for various sample sizes and sample correlations and are shown in Table A.5 in the Appendix.

Whereas with the dependent *t*-test the degrees of freedom are the number of paired observations minus 1, it has been shown mathematically that with the Pearson *r* the degrees of freedom are the number of paired observations minus 2. A significant *r* is equal to or larger than the tabled value with $N - 2$ degrees of freedom, where $N =$ the number of *pairs* of scores. Table A.5 indicates that with *df* = 25 (the number in the sample minus 2) when a two-tailed test is performed, an observed Pearson *r* above $+.3809$ or less than $-.3801$ is required to reject the null hypothesis at the two-tailed .05 level. Thus, the correlation of .20 obtained in the study involving college freshmen is not significant at that level of significance.

With a reasonably large number of cases, a coefficient of correlation may be relatively low in value and yet be statistically significant. For example, Jackson and Lahaderne (1967), with a sample of 292 sixth-graders, found a correlation of $+.25$, a correlation statistically significant at the .01 level, between the students' response on a questionnaire measuring students' satisfaction with school and their teachers' prediction of how these students would respond to the questionnaire. The findings indicate that in the population represented by the sample, the correlation is not likely to be 0. However, recall that the coefficient of determination (r^2) indicates the extent of relationship between variable.s Only $.25^2$ or 6.25 percent of the variance of teachers' predictions is in common with the girls' actual responses. Although teachers can predict student satisfaction at greater than chance level, the teachers' predictions of satisfaction have only a weak relationship with actual student satisfaction.

The *t*-test can also be used to test hypotheses about population correlations other than zero. You can also use it to test the hypothesis that the correlations observed in two samples could have arisen from the same population. Because this is an introductory text, we have chosen not to include such tests here. A useful description of these tests may be found in Glass and Hopkins (1984) and in various other texts.

ANALYSIS OF VARIANCE

In **analysis of variance (ANOVA)**, as in the *t*-test, a ratio comparing observed differences to the error term is used to test hypotheses about differences among groups. This ratio, called the **F-ratio,** employs the variance (σ^2) of group means as a measure of observed differences among groups. This means that ANOVA is a more versatile technique than the *t*-test. A *t*-test can be used only to test a difference between *two* means. ANOVA can test the difference between *two or more* means. Some statisticians never use the *t*-test because ANOVA can be used in any situation where a *t*-test can be used and, moreover, can do many things the *t*-test cannot do.

The general rationale of ANOVA is that the *total variance* of all subjects in an experiment can be subdivided into two sources: *variance between groups* and *variance within groups.* Variance between groups is incorporated into the numerator in the *F*-ratio. Variance within groups is incorporated into the error term or denominator, as it is in the *t*-test. As variance between groups increases, the *F*-ratio increases. As variance within groups increases, the *F*-ratio decreases. The number of subjects influences the *F*-ratio: The larger the number, the larger the numerator becomes. When the numerator and denominator are equal, the differences between group means are no greater than would be expected by chance alone. If the numerator is greater than the denominator, you consult the table of *F*-values (Table A.3 in the Appendix) to determine whether the ratio is great enough to let you reject the null hypothesis at the predetermined level.

Computing the *F*-Ratio (Simple Analysis of Variance)

Suppose you have the three experimental conditions of high stress, moderate stress, and no stress, and you wish to compare the performance of three groups of individuals, randomly assigned to these three conditions, on a simple problem-solving task. Assume that the data presented in Table 7.4 summarize your observations of the performance of these three groups and that you are now going to test the null hypothesis that there is no significant difference among these observations at the .01 level.

The means can be seen to differ from one another and from the overall mean for all thirty subjects ($\overline{\overline{X}}$, the *grand mean*). Are the differences among these means great enough to be statistically significant, or is it likely that they occurred by chance? To answer this, compute the *F*-ratio.

The first step is to find the sum of the squared deviation of each of the individual scores from the grand mean. This index is called the "total sum of squares" and reflects all treatment effects and sampling error. It is expressed by the following formula:

$$SS_t = \Sigma x_t^2 = \Sigma X_t^2 - \frac{(\Sigma X_t)^2}{N} \qquad (7.11)$$

In this example, this value is

$$SS_t = 6830 - \frac{(444)^2}{30} = 258.8$$

Table 7.4 *Measures Obtained in Three Random Samples after Performance of a Task under Conditions of High Stress, Moderate Stress, and No Stress*

GROUP 1 HIGH STRESS		GROUP 2 MODERATE STRESS		GROUP 3 NO STRESS	
X_1	X_1^2	X_2	X_2^2	X_3	X_3^2
19	361	22	484	15	225
18	324	20	400	14	196
17	289	19	361	14	196
16	256	18	324	13	169
15	225	17	289	13	169
15	225	16	256	12	144
14	196	16	256	12	144
13	169	15	225	11	121
12	144	14	196	11	121
11	121	12	144	10	100
$\Sigma X_1 = 150$	$\Sigma X_1^2 = 2310$	$\Sigma X_2 = 169$	$\Sigma X_2^2 = 2935$	$\Sigma X_3 = 125$	$\Sigma X_3^2 = 1585$

$$\overline{X}_1 = 15.0 \qquad \overline{X}_2 = 16.9 \qquad \overline{X}_3 = 12.5 \qquad \overline{\overline{X}} = 14.8$$

$$\Sigma X_t = 444 \qquad \Sigma X_t^2 = 6830$$

Next find the part of the total sum of squares that is caused by the deviations of the group means from the grand mean. This index is called the "sum of the squares between groups." (To be grammatically correct, we should say "the sum of squares *among* groups" when more than two groups are involved. However, it is a long-standing tradition to use the term "sum of squares between groups," and to be consistent with other texts we are retaining this usage here.) This index is found by applying the formula

$$SS_b = \Sigma x_b^2 = \frac{(\Sigma X_1)^2}{n_1} + \frac{(\Sigma X_2)^2}{n_2} + \ldots - \frac{(\Sigma X)^2}{N} \tag{7.12}$$

In the problem, this value is

$$SS_b = \Sigma x_b^2 = \frac{(150)^2}{10} + \frac{(169)^2}{10} + \frac{(125)^2}{10} - \frac{(444)^2}{30} = 97.4$$

Then you find the part of the total sum of squares that is caused by the deviations of each individual score from its own group mean. This index, called the "sum of the squares within groups," is found by applying the raw-score formula for the sum of squared deviations to each group and then summing across groups ($SS_w = SS_1 + SS_2 + SS_3$):

$$SS_w = \Sigma x_w^2 = \left[\Sigma X_1^2 - \frac{(\Sigma X_1)^2}{n_1} \right] + \left[\Sigma X_2^2 - \frac{(\Sigma X_2)^2}{n_2} \right] + \ldots \tag{7.13}$$

Table 7.5   *Summary of the Analysis of Variance of the Three Groups*

(1)	(2)	(3)	(4)	(5)	(6)
					LEVEL OF
SOURCE OF VARIANCE	SS	df	MS	F	SIGNIFICANCE
Between Groups	97.4	2	48.70	8.14	0.01
Within Groups	161.4	27	5.98		
Total	258.8	29			

In the problem, this value is

$$SS_w = \Sigma X_w^2 = \left[2310 - \frac{(150)^2}{10} \right] + \left[2935 - \frac{(169)^2}{10} \right] + \left[1585 - \frac{(125)^2}{10} \right] = 161.4$$

The sum of the squares within groups could also be found by subtracting the sum of squares between groups from the total sum of the squares, expressed as follows:

$$SS_w = SS_t - SS_b \text{ or } \Sigma x_w^2 = \Sigma x_t^2 - \Sigma x_b^2 \tag{7.14}$$

In the present case,

$$SS_w = 258.8 - 97.4 = 161.4$$

You can consider the sum of squares between groups as systematic variation, possibly due to effects of treatment. Dividing the between groups sum of squares (97.4) by the total sum of squares, you get .376. Therefore, 37.6 percent is associated with differences between group means systematic variation. The other 161.4 / 258.8 = 62.4 percent is associated with spread within groups (error variation).

The F-Test of Significance

Table 7.5 summarizes the results of the calculations so far, together with the results of further calculations. Column (1) of the table lists the three sources of variation: between-groups variance, within-groups variance, and total variance. Column (2) contains the sums of squares, which you have already calculated. Column (3) lists the number of degrees of freedom associated with each source of variance. The number of degrees of freedom for between-groups variance is equal to $(G - 1)$, G being the number of groups. In our example this value is $3 - 1 = 2$. The degrees of freedom for within-groups variance is $n_1 - 1 + n_2 - 1 + \ldots$ (or $[N - G]$, total number of scores $[N]$ minus the number of groups $[G]$). In our example this value is $10 - 1 + 10 - 1 + 10 - 1 = 27$, or $30 - 3 = 27$. The number of degrees of freedom for total variance equals $N - 1$; in our example $30 - 1 = 29$. This last value could also be obtained by adding the between-groups and within-groups degrees of freedom.

The next step, then, is to calculate the two population variance estimates known as the *between-groups mean square* and the *within-groups mean square*. These values are obtained by dividing the between–groups and within–groups sums of squares by their respective degrees of freedom. The resulting values are the mean squares. It has been shown mathematically that if the null hypothesis is true, the population variance estimates mean square between and mean square within will be approximately equal and a ratio MS_b/MS_w will be approximately 1. As differences among group means increase, the value of MS_b increases. As number of subjects increase, the value of MS_w decreases. Therefore, as the ratio MS_b/MS_w (called the F-ratio) increases the likelihood that group differences were a function of chance decreases. In the example, the mean square between groups is 97.4 / 2 = 48.7 and the mean square within groups is 161.4 / 27 = 5.98. The mean square within groups is the error term for your F-ratio. By applying the following formula, you finally arrive at the end product of the analysis-of-variance procedure, the F-ratio:

$$F = \frac{MS_b}{MS_w} = \frac{SS_b/df_b}{SS_w/df_w} \tag{7.15}$$

In your example, this value is

$$F = \frac{48.70}{5.98} = 8.14$$

Now consult Table A.3 in the Appendix to determine whether the F-ratio is statistically significant. You find the column headed by the between–groups (numerator) degrees of freedom and go down this column to the row entry corresponding to the number of within–groups (denominator) degrees of freedom. At this point in the column you find two values, one in lightface type and one in boldface type. If the F-ratio is equal to or greater than the value given in lightface, it is significant at the .05 level. If the obtained F-ratio is equal to or greater than the value given in boldface, it is also significant at the .01 level. In the example, with 2 and 27 degrees of freedom you need an F-ratio of 3.35 to reject the null hypothesis at the .05 level and an F-ratio of 5.49 to reject the null hypothesis at the .01 level. Because the obtained F-ratio is greater than both of these values, it is significant at the .01 level and the null hypothesis is rejected at that level. When the null hypothesis is rejected as a result of this analysis-of-variance procedure, you cannot say more than that the measures obtained from the groups involved differ and that the differences are greater than you would expect to exist by chance alone.

A significant F-ratio does not necessarily mean that all groups differ significantly from all other groups. The significant F may be a result of a difference between one group and the rest of the groups. For instance, in your problem it might be that group 3 is significantly different from group 1 and group 2, but groups 1 and 2 do not differ significantly from each other. Several statistical tests can be applied to find the location of significant differences. The Glass and Hopkins text (1984) describes several of these tests and their applications.

In your example you selected the three groups randomly from the same population and thus you can assume that they did not differ beyond the chance expectation prior to your experimental treatments. The significance of the F-ratio indicates that the differences found between these groups *after* treatment are beyond chance expectation. You tentatively attribute this to the experimental treatment and conclude that the level of stress affects the performance of individuals in simple problem-solving tasks. This is as far as you can go in interpreting this F-ratio. If you need further statistical analysis, you can use other tests to determine the significance of difference between specific groups or combinations of groups. Suppose that before the experiment you had designated the no-stress group as the control group and planned to follow the F-test with tests of the significance of differences between this control group and the other two groups. The Glass and Hopkins text (1984) tells us that the Dunnett method is appropriate for these contrasts. The effect size for the difference between the moderate-stress and no-stress groups is $(15.0 - 12.5) / 1.60 = 1.56$ (formula 5.16). The Dunnett test indicates that this is not significant at the two-tailed .05 level. The effect size for the moderate-stress versus no-stress groups is $(16.9 - 12.5) / 1.60 = 2.75$. The Dunnett test indicates that this is significant at the two-tailed .05 level.

Multifactor Analysis of Variance

You may want to investigate the combined effect of stress level and achievement need on performance in a problem-solving task. To investigate this problem you will vary both the level of stress and the achievement need. The layout for an experiment investigating the combined effects of two or more independent variables is called a **factorial design,** and the results are analyzed by means of a "**multifactor analysis of variance.**"

Let's assume that you have carried out this experiment using five subjects in each group and that the data shown in Table 7.6 represent a summary of your observations of the performance of the subjects. Applying multifactor analysis of variance will enable you to learn (1) whether there is a significant difference between the performance of all the subjects under a high-stress condition and all those under a low-stress condition, (2) whether there is a significant difference between the performance of all the subjects with high achievement need and all those with low achievement need, and (3) whether the difference between performance under high- and low-stress conditions is the same for both subjects with high need for achievement and subjects with low need for achievement. The effects investigated by the first and second analyses are called **main effects,** whereas the third is referred to as the **interaction effect.** The end products of these analyses will be three F-ratios, two of which indicate the significance of the two main effects and the third, that of the interaction effect.

The computation of these F-ratios involves the following steps:

1. Find the total sum of squares, the sum of squares between groups, and the sum of squares within groups, using the same procedures and formulas applied in

Table 7.6 *Measures on Problem-Solving Tasks of Subjects with Low and High Achievement Need under High and Low Conditions of Stress*

		Stress			
		High	**Low**		
Achievement Need	**High**	20 20 Group 1 19 19 $\overline{X} = 19$ 17 $\Sigma X\,95$	23 22 Group 3 21 20 $\overline{X} = 21$ 19 $\Sigma X\,105$	$\Sigma X_{r_1} = 200$ $\overline{X}_{r_1} = 20.0$	
	Low	22 21 Group 2 20 19 $\overline{X} = 20$ 18 $\Sigma X\,100$	18 16 Group 4 15 14 $\overline{X} = 15$ 12 $\Sigma X\,75$	$\Sigma X_{r_2} = 175$ $\overline{X}_{r_2} = 17.5$	
		$\Sigma X_{c_1} = 195$ $\overline{X}_{c_1} = 19.5$	$\Sigma X_{c_2} = 180$ $\overline{X}_{c_2} = 18.0$	$\Sigma X\,\text{Total} = 375$ $\overline{\overline{X}}$ (grand mean) $= 18.75$	

simple analysis of variance. These values, derived from the data in Table 7.6, are as follows:

$$SS_t = 7181 - \frac{(375)^2}{20} = 149.75$$

$$SS_b = \frac{(95)^2}{5} + \frac{(100)^2}{5} + \frac{(75)^2}{5} + \frac{(105)^2}{5} - \frac{(375)^2}{20} = 103.75$$

$$SS_w = 149.75 - 103.75 = 46.00$$

2. Break down the sum of the squares between groups into three separate sums of squares—(a) the sum of squares between columns, (b) the sum of squares between rows, and (c) the sum of squares for interaction between columns and rows—as shown next:

a. The between-columns sum of squares represents the sum of the squared deviations caused by the difference between the column means and the grand mean. Find it by using the formula

$$SS_{bc} = \frac{(\Sigma X_{c_1})^2}{n_{c_1}} + \frac{(\Sigma X_{c_2})^2}{n_{c_2}} + \ldots - \frac{(\Sigma X)^2}{N} \qquad (7.16)$$

With this formula, the sum of squares between the columns for the data shown in Table 7.6 is

$$SS_{bc} = \frac{(195)^2}{10} + \frac{(180)^2}{10} - \frac{(375)^2}{20} = 11.25$$

b. The between-rows sum of squares is the sum of the squared deviations caused by the difference between the row means and the grand mean. Find it by applying the formula

$$SS_{br} = \frac{(\Sigma X_{r_1})^2}{n_{r_1}} + \frac{(\Sigma X_{r_2})^2}{n_{r_2}} + \ldots - \frac{(\Sigma X)^2}{N} \qquad (7.17)$$

For the data presented in Table 7.6, this value is

$$SS_{br} = \frac{(200)^2}{10} + \frac{(175)^2}{10} - \frac{(375)^2}{20} = 31.25$$

c. The sum-of-squares interaction is the part of the deviation between the group means and the overall mean that is due neither to row differences nor to column differences. Expressed as a formula, it becomes

$$SS_{int} = SS_b - (SS_{bc} + SS_{br}) \qquad (7.18)$$

Expressed in words, the interaction sum of squares is equal to the between-groups sum of squares minus the sum of the between-columns sum of squares and the between-rows sum of squares.

For the data presented in Table 7.6, this interaction sum of squares is

$$SS_{int} = 103.75 - (11.25 + 31.25) = 61.25$$

3. Determine the number of degrees of freedom associated with each source of variation. They are found as follows:

df for between-columns sum of squares $= C - 1$

df for between-rows sum of squares $= R - 1$

df for interaction $= (C - 1)(R - 1)$

df for between-groups sum of squares $= G - 1$

df for within-groups sum of squares $= N - G$

df for total sum of squares $= N - 1$

where

C = number of columns
R = number of rows
G = number of groups
N = number of subjects in all groups

Table 7.7   Summary of a 2 × 2 Multifactor Analysis of Variance

SOURCE OF VARIANCE	SS	df	MS	F	LEVEL OF SIGNIFICANCE
Between Columns (stress)	11.25	1	11.25	3.913	—
Between Rows (achievement need)	31.25	1	31.25	10.869	.01
Columns by Rows (interaction)	61.25	1	61.25	21.304	.01
Between Groups	103.75	3	34.583		
Within Groups	46.00	16	2.875		
Total	149.75	19			

4. Find the mean-square values by dividing each sum of squares by its associated number of degrees of freedom.

5. Compute the *F*-ratios for the main and the interaction effects by dividing the between-groups mean squares by the within-groups mean square for each of the three components.

The results of the calculations based on the data presented in Table 7.6 are summarized in Table 7.7. Three *F*-ratios are listed in this table. To find the significance of each of these values, consult Table A.3 (the table of *F*-values) as before. To enter this table, use the number of degrees of freedom associated with each *F*-ratio (*df* for the numerator) and the number of degrees of freedom associated with the within-groups mean square (*df* for the denominator). For example, the between-columns *F*-ratio is 3.913. Consulting the table, you see that, with 1 and 16 degrees of freedom, an *F*-ratio of 4.49 or more is needed for significance at the .05 level. Because the *F*-ratio is smaller than the value shown in the table, you can conclude that the high-stress versus low-stress difference is not statistically significant.

Because the between-rows degrees of freedom are the same as the degrees of freedom between columns, the same levels of 4.49 (.05 level) and 8.53 (.01 level) apply. Because the obtained value of 10.869, exceeds both of these values, it is significant at the .01 level.

In the example, the degrees of freedom for interaction are the same (1 and 16). Therefore the same values of *F* are required. The *F*-value of 21.304 is greater than 8.35, therefore the interaction is significant at the .01 level. You can reject the null hypothesis—that the difference between the high-stress minus low-stress group means among the subjects with low need for achievement is the same as the difference between the high-stress minus low-stress group means among the subjects with high need for achievement.

Interpreting the F-Ratios

The first *F*-ratio (between columns) in Table 7.7 is not significant and shows that the stress conditions do not differ significantly from one another in their effect on the performance of the subjects in the experiment. This analysis is a comparison of the combined performance of Groups 1 and 2 ($\overline{X} = 19.5$) with the combined performance of Groups 3 and 4 ($\overline{X} = 18.0$). You could have arrived at the same conclusion by using the *t*-test procedure.

The second *F*-ratio (between rows), which is significant at the .01 level, is based on comparing the performance of the subjects in Groups 1 and 3 ($\overline{X} = 20.0$) with those in Groups 2 and 4 ($\overline{X} = 17.5$). From the significance of this *F*-ratio you can infer that the difference between the performance of those subjects with high achievement need and those with low achievement need is beyond chance expectation. Because you have a significant *F*-ratio for the difference, you conclude that under conditions similar to those of your experiment, a higher level of task performance can be expected from people with higher achievement need.

The third *F*-ratio shows the interaction effect between the two variables: stress level and achievement need. The significance of the *F*-ratio in this case means that the effect of stress level on performance in a problem–solving task depends on the degree of achievement need. You can see this phenomenon more clearly if you compare the observed results with the results that would be expected if there had been no interaction between the two independent variables.

Now calculate what you would expect the means of the four groups to be if there had been no interaction. The mean for all subjects is 18.75. The mean for the ten subjects under high stress, 19.5, is .075 greater than this figure, whereas the mean of the ten subjects under low stress is 0.75 less. The mean for the ten subjects with high achievement need, 20, is 1.25 greater than the mean for all subjects, whereas the mean for the ten subjects with low achievement need is 1.25 less.

For each group you can calculate the mean that would be expected for this group if there had been no interaction. Do this by adding to the grand mean the difference for the column that group is in and the difference for the row that group is in. If there had been no interaction, what would you expect the mean of Group 1 to be? Beginning with the total mean, 18.75, you would add 0.75 because the subjects were under high stress and another 1.25 because they had high achievement need. This gives a total of 20.75.

Following this procedure for each of the four groups, you would obtain the following expected values:

	Overall Mean +	Stress Difference +	Achievement Need Difference =	Expected Value
Group 1	18.75	+0.75	+1.25	20.75
Group 2	18.75	+0.75	−1.25	18.25
Group 3	18.75	−0.75	+1.25	19.25
Group 4	18.75	−0.75	−1.25	16.75

Now compare the actual group means with these expected group means:

	Actual High	Low	
High	Group 1 $\bar{X} = 19$	Group 3 $\bar{X} = 21$	$\bar{X} = 20$
Low	Group 1 $\bar{X} = 20$	Group 4 $\bar{X} = 15$	$\bar{X} = 17.5$
	$\bar{X} = 19.5$	$\bar{X} = 18.0$	$\bar{\bar{X}} = 18.75$

	Expected High	Low	
High	Group 1 $\bar{X} = 20.75$	Group 3 $\bar{X} = 19.25$	$\bar{X} = 20$
Low	Group 3 $\bar{X} = 18.25$	Group 4 $\bar{X} = 16.75$	$\bar{X} = 17.5$
	$\bar{X} = 19.5$	$\bar{X} = 18.0$	$\bar{\bar{X}} = 18.75$

(Note that you could use the differences between expected and observed values to compute the sum of squares for interaction directly. Each group differs from its expected mean by 1.75. Square this value and multiply by the number of cases to get $1.75^2 \times 20 = 61.25$.)

You can see that Group 1 actually did less well than you would expect, knowing they were under high stress and had high achievement need. Group 2, having low achievement need and being under high stress, did better than you would expect. Considering the groups under low stress, you find that Group 3, with high achievement need, did better than expected, whereas Group 4, with low achievement need, did less well than expected. Because your F-test indicated that the interaction was significant, you can conclude that high stress produces higher scores when combined with low achievement need than when combined with high achievement need, whereas low stress produces higher scores when combined with high achievement need than when combined with low achievement need.

Multifactor analysis has been of great value in educational research because many questions educators need to investigate are inherently complex in nature. These techniques enable educators to analyze the combined effects of two or more independent variables in relation to a dependent variable. For example, a simple comparison of the dependent variable means of two groups of pupils taught by different methods may yield insignificant results. But if you incorporate intelligence into the experiment as a measured independent variable, you may find that one method works better with the less intelligent pupils whereas the other works better with the more intelligent pupils. (We present more on interpreting factorial analysis of variance in Chapter 10.)

Multifactor analysis of variance is not limited to two independent variables as in our example. Any number of independent variables may be incorporated in this technique. Several intermediate statistics books, including Glass and Hopkins (1984), explain the computation and interpretation of these procedures.

THE CHI-SQUARE TEST OF SIGNIFICANCE

Sometimes researchers need to find the significance of differences among the *proportions* of subjects, objects, events, and so forth, that fall into different categories. A statistical test used in such cases is called the chi-square (χ^2) test. In the **chi-square test,** two sets of frequencies are compared: **observed frequencies** and **expected frequencies.** Observed frequencies, as the name implies, are the actual frequencies obtained by observation. Expected frequencies are theoretical frequencies, which are used for comparison.

The One-Variable Chi-Square (Goodness of Fit)

Consider the hypothesis that the proportion of male and female students in statistics courses is different from that of male and female students in a school of education as a whole. If you know that 40 percent of the total enrollment in the school is male and that 300 students are enrolled in statistics courses, the expected frequencies of male and female students enrolled in statistics will be

$$\left.\begin{array}{ll}\text{Male students} & 120 \\ \text{Female students} & 180\end{array}\right\} 300$$

Now suppose that the observed frequencies are found to be

$$\left.\begin{array}{ll}\text{Male students} & 140 \\ \text{Female students} & 160\end{array}\right\} 300$$

To determine whether the difference between the expected and observed frequencies is statistically significant, apply the chi-square formula:

$$\chi^2 = \Sigma\left[\frac{(f_o - f_e)^2}{f_e}\right] \tag{7.19}$$

where

$$\begin{array}{l}\chi^2 = \text{value of chi-square} \\ f_o = \text{observed frequency} \\ f_e = \text{expected frequency}\end{array}$$

Applying this formula to the data, you obtain

$$\chi^2 = \frac{(140 - 120)^2}{120} + \frac{(160 - 180)^2}{180} = 5.55$$

Table 7.8   *The Observed Frequencies of Responses of 120 Undergraduate Students on Their Preference for Living Accommodations*

SUBJECTS	DORMITORY	TOWN	NO PREFERENCE	TOTAL
Undergraduate students	40	50	30	120

To determine whether this chi-square value is significant, consult the table of χ^2 values in the Appendix (Table A.4). The first column in this table shows the number of degrees of freedom involved in any given chi-square problem. The remaining columns present the values needed for different levels of significance. The number of degrees of freedom, as we have discussed previously, is based on the number of observations that are free to vary once certain restrictions are placed on the data. When you have a fixed number of observations divided into only two categories, as soon as the number falling into one category has been determined, the other is fixed. Thus, when you find that the number of male students is 140, the number of female students in the total of 300 must be 160. In this example, there is only 1 degree of freedom. In the one-variable chi-square, the number of degrees of freedom equals $K - 1$, where K is the number of categories used for classification. By consulting the table of χ^2 values, you find that your observed value of 5.55 is statistically significant at the .05 (and .02) level.

Interpreting this result, you can now state that the proportion of males who take statistics courses is significantly greater than the proportion in the entire college of education at the .05 level of confidence. The significance level of .05 means that there are less than five chances in a hundred of observing such a difference between the proportions of male and female students through chance alone. Thus the data lend support to your research hypothesis that the proportions of male and female students who take statistics courses is significantly different from the proportion of males and females in the entire school of education.

The use of the chi-square test is not limited to situations in which there are only two categories of classification; this test can also be used to test a null hypothesis stating that there is no significant difference between the proportion of the subjects falling into any number of different categories. Suppose, for example, you asked a sample of 120 undergraduate students whether they prefer to live in a dormitory or in town or have no preference, with the results shown in Table 7.8.

If there were no difference between the three categories of response, you would have 40 responses in each category. These would be your expected frequencies, as shown in Table 7.9.

A comparison of the two sets of frequencies presented in Tables 7.8 and 7.9 shows that there are differences between your expected and observed data. To determine whether they are significant, apply the chi-square test. The value of χ^2 for these data, using formula 7.19, would be

$$\chi^2 = \frac{(40 - 40)^2}{40} + \frac{(50 - 40)^2}{40} + \frac{(30 - 40)^2}{40} = 5.00$$

Table 7.9 The Expected Frequencies of Responses of 120 Undergraduate Students on Their Preference for Living Accommodations				
SUBJECTS	DORMITORY	TOWN	NO PREFERENCE	TOTAL
Undergraduate Students	40	40	40	120

The degrees of freedom, again, equal the number of categories minus 1 $(K - 1)$ or, in this case, $3 - 1 = 2$. Referring to the table of χ^2 values, you can see that with 2 degrees of freedom, a χ^2 value of 5.991 or greater is required for significance at the .05 level. However, your obtained χ^2 value is smaller than this value and therefore is not statistically significant. This means that the observed differences between categories could easily have happened by chance. Consequently, the null hypothesis—that there is no significant difference between the frequencies of the three categories—cannot be rejected. In other words, if the proportions of preferences for the three categories in the entire undergraduate population were equal, you would expect to observe sample differences as great as those in your sample more often than five times in a hundred through chance.

The Two-Variable Chi-Square (Chi-Square Test of Independence)

So far we have only considered examples in which observations were classified along a single dimension. Sometimes, however, researchers wish to use more than one dimension for classification. The two-variable chi-square design uses two independent variables, each with two or more levels, and a dependent variable in the form of a frequency count. The purpose of the test is to determine whether or not the two variables in the design are independent of one another. Suppose, for example, you add another dimension to the previous problem and ask both graduate and undergraduate students to state their preferences as to their living accommodations. Assume the frequencies shown in Table 7.10 were the result.

In this case the null hypothesis is that the preference for living accommodations is the same for graduates as it is for undergraduates—that is, the variables "student status" and

Table 7.10 The Observed Frequencies of Responses of 200 Undergraduate and Graduate Students on Their Preference for Living Accommodations				
SUBJECTS	DORMITORY	TOWN	NO PREFERENCE	TOTAL
Undergraduate Students	40	50	30	120
Graduate Students	20	40	20	80
Total	60	90	50	200

Table 7.11 *The Expected Frequencies of Responses of 200 Undergraduate and Graduate Students as to Their Preference with Respect to Living Accommodations*

SUBJECTS	DORMITORY	TOWN	NO PREFERENCE	TOTAL
Undergraduate Students	36	54	30	120
Graduate Students	24	36	20	80
Total	60	90	50	200

"preference for living accommodations" are unrelated, or independent. The null hypothesis in this *chi-square test of independence* is always that the variables are independent in the population. Your observations show that 30 percent of all students prefer dormitories, 45 percent prefer town, and 25 percent state no preference. If the null hypothesis is true, you would expect to find these same proportions among both graduates and undergraduates. You can compute expected cell frequencies by multiplying the row frequency associated with a cell by the column frequency associated with that cell, then dividing this product by the grand total ($E = f_r f_c / N$). For example, the expected frequency of response for undergraduate students who want to live in a dormitory is $120 \times 60 \div 200 = 36$; for those undergraduate students who prefer to live in town, it is $120 \times 90 \div 200 = 54$; and for graduate students who want to live in a dormitory, it is $80 \times 60 \div 200 = 24$. Using this approach, you can find the expected frequencies for each cell as shown in Table 7.11.

Note that all the row and column totals in Table 7.11 are exactly the same as those shown in Table 7.10. Now you ask if the observed frequencies differ enough from the expected frequencies to enable you to reject the likelihood that these differences could have occurred merely by chance. Applying the formula, you obtain

$$\chi^2 = \frac{(40-36)^2}{36} + \frac{(50-54)^2}{54} + \frac{(30-30)^2}{30} + \frac{(20-24)^2}{24} + \frac{(40-36)^2}{36} + \frac{(20-20)^2}{20}$$

$$\chi^2 = 1.8518$$

The number of degrees of freedom for a two-way table is found by applying the formula

$$df = (C-1)(R-1) \tag{7.20}$$

where

$$df = \text{number of degrees of freedom}$$
$$C = \text{number of columns}$$
$$R = \text{number of rows}$$

Applying this formula to the problem under consideration, you obtain

$$df = (3-1)(2-1) = 2$$

Referring to Table A.4, you can see that with 2 degrees of freedom, a χ^2 value of 5.991 is needed for significance at the .05 level. But your obtained χ^2 value of 1.8518 is smaller than this tabled value and is therefore not significant. This means that the differences between expected and observed frequencies are not beyond what you would expect by chance. In other words, you do not have reliable evidence that there is a relationship between the variables "student status" and "living accommodation preference" in the population from which your sample was drawn. The null hypothesis cannot be rejected.

Assumptions of Chi-Square

Chi-square is so easy to use that researchers may forget that there are assumptions that must be met if valid interpretations are to be made.

1. Observations must be independent—that is, the subjects in each sample must be randomly and independently selected.

2. The categories must be mutually exclusive: Each observation can appear in one and only one of the categories in the table.

3. The observations are measured as frequencies.

USING COMPUTERS IN STATISTICS

A number of computer packages are available for calculating the statistics presented in this chapter and in Chapter 6. The calculations we have presented in these chapters are to illustrate how the statistics work rather than to serve as a map for the calculations, because computers can perform these calculations faster and more accurately.

SUMMARY

Investigators hope to form generalizations about populations by studying groups of individuals selected from populations. These generalizations will be sound only if the selected groups (the samples) used in these studies are representative of the larger groups (the populations) from which they are chosen.

Statisticians distinguish between two major types of sampling procedures: probability sampling and nonprobability sampling. Probability sampling is characterized by random selection of population elements. In nonprobability sampling, the researcher's judgment replaces random selection. Simple random sampling, stratified sampling, cluster sampling, and systematic sampling are forms of probability sampling. In simple random sampling, all members of a population have an equal chance of being included within the sample. In stratified sampling, researchers select independent samples from different subgroups, or strata, of a population. In cluster sampling, researchers randomly select naturally occurring groups, or clusters, from a population; then they use as the sample all individuals within the selected clusters. Finally, in systematic sampling, researchers take as the sample every *K*th case from a list of the population. Forms of nonprobability sampling are accidental sampling, purposive sampling, and quota sampling. In accidental sampling, researchers use the available cases as the sample. In purposive sampling, cases judged as typical of the population of interest constitute the sample. Finally, in quota sampling, quotas are assigned to various strata of a population; then cases judged to be typical of each stratum are selected.

Inferential statistics provide tools by means of which researchers can estimate how confident they can be in inferring that phenomena observed in samples will also appear in the populations from which the samples were drawn. In other words, inferential statistics enable you to estimate how reliable your observations may be.

A basic strategy in inferential statistics is to compute the difference among observations that would be likely to arise by chance alone. The result of this computation is called the *error term*. Then the observed differences among observations are compared with the error term. If the observed differences are similar to the differences that could arise by chance, the researcher cannot reject the likelihood that the observed differences were merely a function of chance. If the observed differences are greater than the error term, the researcher consults the tabled values of the statistic to determine whether the ratio of observation to error is great enough to reject the chance explanation at a predetermined level of significance. Effect size and sample size determine statistical significance.

Power calculations determine the sample size needed to give a specified probability of rejecting the null hypothesis at a specified level of significance for a given effect size.

The indexes most commonly used in inferential statistics are the *t*-test, analysis of variance (ANOVA), and the chi-square test. The *t*-test is used to determine whether the difference between two sample means is statistically significant. There are three types of *t*-tests: (1) the *t*-test for independent groups, which is used to compare two sample means when the samples have been drawn independently from a population; (2) the *t*-test for dependent groups, which is employed with two samples in which the subjects are matched or with two repeated measures obtained from the same subjects; and (3) the *t*-test for Pearson product moment correlation.

Analysis of variance is used to compare the means of two or more samples and to test the null hypothesis that no significant differences exist between the means of these samples. Multifactor analysis of variance enables researchers to test the effect of more than one independent variable and the interaction effect of such variables.

The chi-square statistic is an index employed to find the significance of differences between proportions of subjects, objects, events, and so forth that fall into different categories, by comparing observed frequencies and frequencies expected under a true null hypothesis.

REFERENCES

Ary, D., & Jacobs, L. C. (1976). *Introduction to statistics.* New York: Holt, Rinehart and Winston.

Borenstein, M., & Cohen, J. (1989). *Statistical power analysis.* Hillsdale, NJ: Erlbaum.

Cochran, W. C. (1985). *Sampling Techniques* (2nd ed.). New York: Wiley.

Glass, G. V., & Hopkins, K. D. (1984). *Statistical methods in education and psychology* (2nd ed.). Englewood Cliffs, NJ: Prentice Hall.

Jackson, P. W., & Lahaderne, H. M. (1967). Scholastic success and attitude toward school in a population of sixth graders. *Journal of Educational Psychology, 58,* 15–18.

Kempthorne, O. (1961). The design and analysis of experiments with some reference to educational research. In R. O. Collier & S. M. Elam (Eds.), *Research design and analysis: Second annual Phi Delta Kappa symposium on educational research,* pp. 97–133. Bloomington, IN: Phi Delta Kappa.

Stuart, A. (1984). *The ideas of sampling* (3rd ed.). New York: Macmillan.

Sudman, S. (1976). *Applied sampling.* New York: Academic Press.

KEY CONCEPTS

accessible population
accidental sampling
analysis of variance (ANOVA)
biased sample
chi-square test
cluster sampling
degrees of freedom
directional test
error term
expected frequency
factorial design
F-test
interaction effect
level of significance
main effect

multifactor analysis of variance
nondirectional test
nonprobability sampling
null hypothesis
observed frequency
one-tailed test
parameter
population
power calculation
power formulas
probability sampling
purposive (judgment) sampling
quota sampling
random sample
sampling error

standard error of the mean
statistic
stratified sampling
systematic sampling
table of random numbers
target population
test of significance
t-test for dependent samples
t-test for independent samples
t-test for Pearson *r*
two-tailed test
Type I error
Type II error
unbiased samples

EXERCISES

1. Does the accuracy of a sample in representing the characteristics of the population from which it was drawn always increase with the size of the sample? Explain.

2. You have been asked to determine whether teachers in the Central School District favor the "year-round school" concept. Because the district is rather large, you are asked to contact only 500 teachers. Determine the number you would choose from each of the following levels to draw a proportional stratified random sample:

Level	Total number
Elementary	3500
Middle School	2100
High School	1400
Total	7000

3. You are asked to conduct an opinion survey on a college campus with a population of 15,000 students. How would you proceed to draw a representative sample of these students for your survey?

4. A national magazine has one million subscribers. The editorial staff wants to know which aspects of the magazine are liked and which are not. The staff decides that a personal interview is the best method to obtain the information. For practical and economic reasons, only 500 people in five cities will be surveyed. In this situation, identify the following:
   a. The target population
   b. The accessible population
   c. The sample

5. Which of the following are probability samples? Which are nonprobability samples?
   a. Random sample
   b. Accidental sample
   c. Cluster sample
   d. Stratified sample
   e. Purposive sample
   f. Quota sample
   g. Systematic sample

6. Investigators wish to study the question "Do blondes have more fun?"
   a. What is the null hypothesis in this question?
   b. What would be a Type I error in this case?
   c. What would be a Type II error in this case?
   d. If one investigator uses a .05 level of significance in investigating this question and another investigator uses a .001 level of significance, which would be more likely to make a Type I error?
   e. If one investigator uses a .05 level of significance in investigating this question and another investigator uses a .001 level of significance, which would be more likely to make a Type II error?

7. Inferential statistics enable researchers to do which of the following?

   a. Reach infallible conclusions
   b. Reach reasonable conclusions with incomplete information
   c. Add an aura of legitimacy to what is really sheer guesswork

8. What two conditions are necessary for a Type I error to occur?

9. Which of the following statements describes the role of the null hypothesis in research?
   a. It enables researchers to determine the probability of an event occurring through chance alone when there is no real relationship between variables.
   b. It enables researchers to prove there is a real relationship between variables.
   c. It enables researchers to prove there is no real relationship between variables.

10. A Type II error occurs when a researcher does which of the following?
   a. Rejects a false null hypothesis
   b. Rejects a true null hypothesis
   c. Has already made a Type I error
   d. Retains a false null hypothesis
   e. Retains a true null hypothesis

11. The phrase "level of significance" refers to which of the following situations?
   a. The probability of an event being due to chance alone, which is calculated after the data from an experiment are analyzed
   b. The probability of a Type I error that an investigator is willing to accept
   c. The actual probability of a Type II error
   d. The probability of a Type II error that an investigator is willing to accept

12. How do you determine the level of significance to use in an experiment?

13. A cigarette manufacturer has employed researchers to compare the rate of occurrence of lung cancer among smokers and nonsmokers. Considering the results of previous research on this question, the manufacturer would probably urge the researchers to be especially careful to avoid making a Type I error or a Type II error?

14. What is indicated when the results of a study are not statistically significant?

15. Compare stratified sampling with quota sampling.

16. What are the three elements to consider in determining sample size?

17. How large a sample would be needed for an effect size of .10 or greater to have an 80 percent chance of being statistically significant at the two-tailed .05 level of significance?

18. Find the chi-square value for the following set of data. Then indicate if the obtained value of chi-square is significant at the .05 level of significance.

2	8	10
6	4	10
8	12	

19. You have the responses of two groups of students (education and noneducation majors) to an item in an attitude scale. Find the chi-square value for this problem, and indicate whether your obtained chi-square value is statistically significant.

	Strongly Agree	Agree	Unde-cided	Dis-agree	Strongly Disagree
Education Students	7	8	10	9	6
Noneduca-tion Students	8	10	7	8	7

20. For testing each of the following hypotheses, indicate which of the following statistical procedures would be appropriate.

　　t-test for independent means
　　t-test for nonindependent means
　　Factorial analysis of variance
　　Chi-square one variable or goodness of fit test
　　Chi-square test of independence

a. The proportion of students in the class who receive A's will be the same as the proportion of students who receive B's.

b. The mean score of the 1 P.M. section on the final examination will be significantly higher than the mean score of the 7 P.M. section.

c. Attending the evening class instead of an afternoon class is an advantage, grade-wise, for female students and a disadvantage for male students.

d. If the same statistics quiz that was given to students on the first day of class were administered on the last day of class, students would show a significant gain in achievement.

e. There is a relationship between a student's passing or failing the class and whether that student expresses satisfaction or dissatisfaction with the course.

f. Any differences among the mean scores of the fall semester classes and the summer session classes of the same instructor can easily be accounted for by chance.

g. There is a significant interaction effect between teaching experience and research experience and success in a research course.

21. A directional test differs from a nondirectional test in that in a directional test the researcher is interested in changes that take place in which of the following ways:
a. Only in a positive direction
b. Only in a negative direction
c. In both positive and negative directions
d. Either in a positive or negative direction, but not both

22. Two randomly selected groups have been used in an experiment in which Group I received treatment and Group II received no treatment. The researcher's hypothesis is that the mean performance of Group I will be higher than the mean performance of Group II. Apply the t-test to the following information, and state if the researcher's hypothesis could be confirmed.

	$\overline{X}$	N	Σx^2
Group I	45.32	30	382.02
Group II	41.78	30	264.32

23. A researcher wants to test the hypothesis that the correlation between variable A and variable B is significantly greater than zero. He has obtained an $r = .21$ between the two variables using twenty-two subjects. Use Table A.5 to find if the hypothesis can be rejected at the .05 level (two-tailed).

24. The following data are for a 2×3 experimental design. Apply the multifactor analysis of variance to test the significance of the main effects and the interaction effect.

Rows		Columns	
	A	B	C
A	25, 23, 20,	22, 20, 18,	20, 18, 16,
	17, 15	16, 14	14, 12
B	16, 14, 12,	18, 16, 14,	19, 18, 16,
	10, 8	12, 10	14, 13

Provide a table in which the sums of squares (SS), degrees of freedom (df), mean squares (MS), and F-values are shown. Then answer the following questions:
a. Which F-values are significant and at what level?
b. How many null hypotheses are being tested in this problem?
c. How many of these hypotheses can the researcher reject?

25. Explain the logic of the t-test.

26. You have a list of high school pupils who have been assigned a number from 1 to 1000. Use the table of random numbers in the Appendix to select a sample of 50 from the hypothetical list. List the numbers selected for the sample.

ANSWERS

1. A larger *randomly* drawn sample is more likely to be representative of the population than is a smaller *random* sample. A large sample obtained with a method that permits systematic bias will not be any more representative than a small biased sample.

2. To obtain a proportional stratified sample, divide the 500 teachers in proportion to their representation in the population, as follows:
    Elementary 3500 / 7000 $\times$ 500 = 250
    Middle school 2100 / 7000 $\times$ 500 = 150
    High school 1400 / 7000 $\times$ 500 = 100
    Total sample 500

3. Number a list of all students, then select a random sample of a given number by using a table of random numbers. Starting at a random point in the table, go up or down the column and include those students whose numbers are drawn.

4. a. All subscribers to the magazine
   b. The subscribers in the five cities
   c. Five hundred individuals who are interviewed

5. Probability samples: a, c, d, g
   Nonprobability samples: b, e, f

6. a. There is no relationship between hair color and how much fun a person has.
   b. The investigators make a Type I error if they declare that blondes have more fun than nonblondes or that blondes have less

fun than nonblondes, when in fact the two groups have an equal amount of fun.

c. The investigators make a Type II error if they fail to conclude that blondes have more fun or less fun, when in fact they do.

d. The investigator with the .05 level of significance

e. The investigator with the .001 level of significance

7. b

8. The null hypothesis must be true, and the investigator must reject it.

9. a

10. d

11. b

12. By weighing the consequences of Type I and Type II errors

13. A Type I error

14. The results could easily be a function of chance: the evidence is insufficient to justify a conclusion.

15. In stratified sampling, representativeness in each stratum is achieved through randomization, whereas in quota sampling representativeness in various strata is attained by way of judgment.

16. (1) The effect size considered to be the boundary between a meaningful and a nonmeaningful difference, (2) level of significance, and (3) desired probability of rejecting a false null hypothesis

17. $N = (1 / .10)^2 (1.96 + .84)^2$
    $= 100 (7.84)$
    $= 784$
(Note that with a small effect size a large number is required.)

18. 3.33—nonsignificant

19. 0.954—nonsignificant

20. a. Chi-square one variable or goodness of fit test
    b. *t*-Test for independent means
    c. Factorial analysis of variance
    d. *t*-Test for dependent means
    e. Chi-square test of independence
    f. *t*-Test for independent means
    g. Factorial analysis of variance

21. d

22. $t = 4.11$, *df* $= 58$, significant at .001 level

23. With 20 degrees of freedom, an *r* of .4227 or greater is needed to reject the null hypothesis. Therefore the null hypothesis is retained.

24.

Source of Variance	SS	df	MS	F
Between Columns	0	2	0	0
Between Rows	120	1	120	11.34
Interaction	80	2	40	3.78
Between Groups	200	5	40	3.78
Within Groups	254	24	10.58	—

a. Between rows at .01 and interaction at .05
b. Three
c. Two

25. Sample statistics are used to determine the difference between two means that is expected due to pure chance when the null hypothesis is true. The observed difference is compared to this expected difference to determine the likelihood that the observed difference is due only to chance.

26. Answers will vary.

 INFOTRAC

Use the keywords *probability sampling* or *nonprobability sampling* and locate a research study that used either of these sampling techniques. What was the population sampled? If a nonprobability sample was used, why did the researcher use it instead of a probability sampling technique?

Chapter 8

Tools of Research

After studying this chapter, the student will be able to:

1 Explain the role of measurement in research.

2 Use the *Mental Measurements Yearbooks* to obtain data necessary in evaluating standardized tests and other measuring instruments.

3 State the difference between a test and a scale.

4 Distinguish between norm-referenced and criterion-referenced tests.

5 Distinguish between measures of aptitude and achievement.

6 Distinguish between ceiling effect and floor effect, and discuss why these may be of concern.

7 Describe the steps to follow in preparing a Likert scale for measuring attitudes.

8 Define *performance assessment,* and discuss its advantages and disadvantages.

9 Describe the characteristics of a semantic differential scale.

10 State the kinds of errors that are common to rating scales.

11 State advantages and disadvantages of self-report personality measures.

12 List at least five guidelines that a researcher should follow when using direct observation as a data-gathering technique.

13 Define a situational test, and tell when it might be used in research.

14 State the essential characteristic of a projective technique and name at least two well-known projective techniques.

One aim of quantitative research is to obtain greater understanding of relationships among variables in populations. For example, you might ask, What is the relationship between intelligence and creativity among 6-year-olds? You cannot directly observe either intelligence or creativity. Nor can you directly observe all 6-year-olds. But this does not mean that you must remain in ignorance about this and similar questions. There are indicators that approximate the constructs of intelligence and of creativity; that is, there are observable behaviors that are accepted as being valid indexes of these constructs. Using indicators to approximate constructs is the measurement aspect of research.

Some measurement is very straightforward, using a single indicator to represent a variable. For example, you could measure a person's educational background by asking about the highest grade he or she had completed. Similarly, such variables as grade level, nationality, marital status, or number of children could be measured by a single indicator simply because these variables refer to phenomena that are very clear and for which a single indicator provides an acceptable measure. Other variables, however, are more complex and much more difficult to measure. In these cases using a single indicator is not appropriate.

One of the researcher's most important tasks is to select or develop scales and instruments that can measure such complex characteristics as intelligence, achievement, personality, motivation, attitudes, aptitudes, interests, self-concept, and so on. There are two basic ways to obtain these measures: Use one that has already been developed or construct your own.

To select a measuring instrument, the researcher should look at the research that has been published on his or her problem to see what other researchers have used to measure the construct of interest. These reports will generally indicate whether the instrument worked well or whether other procedures might be better. Other useful sources for identifying published instruments for one's research purposes are the *Mental Measurements Yearbooks* and *Tests in Print,* described in Chapter 4. Another good source of information about both published and unpublished tests is the Educational Testing Service (ETS) Test Collection. The ETS Test Collection is a library of more than 17,000 commercial and research tests and other measuring devices designed to provide up-to-date test information to educational researchers. It is available on the World Wide Web. A useful addition to this series is *The Cumulative Index to Tests in Microfiche, 1975–87,* which indexes the research tests by author, title, and subject. In the subject index, there are more than 750 headings, covering everything from abstract reasoning to work attitudes.

If researchers cannot find a previously developed instrument, then they must develop their own. The procedure involves identifying and using behavior that can be considered an indicator of the presence of the construct. To locate these indicators, researchers should turn first to the theory behind the research. A good theory generally suggests how the construct will manifest itself and the changes that can be observed; that is, it suggests ways to measure the construct(s). Researchers can also use their own experience and expertise to decide on the appropriate indicators of the construct. In this chapter, we briefly discuss some of the kinds of measuring instruments that are used in educational research.

TESTS

Tests are valuable measuring instruments for educational research. A **test** is a set of stimuli presented to an individual in order to elicit responses on the basis of which a numerical score can be assigned. This score, based on a representative sample of the individual's behavior, indicates the extent to which the subject has the characteristic being measured.

The utility of these scores as indicators of the construct of interest is in large part a function of the objectivity, validity, and reliability of the tests. Objectivity is the extent of agreement among scorers. Some tests, such as multiple choice and true-false tests, are described as objective because the scoring is done by comparing students' answers with the scoring key and scorers need make no decisions. Essay tests are less objective because scores are influenced by the judgment and opinions of the scorers. In general, validity is the extent to which a test measures what it claims to measure. Reliability is the extent to which the test measures accurately and consistently. We discuss validity and reliability in Chapter 9.

Achievement Tests

Achievement tests are widely used in educational research, as well as in school systems. They measure mastery and proficiency in different areas of knowledge by presenting subjects with a standard set of questions involving completion of cognitive tasks.

Standardized Tests

Achievement tests are generally classified as **standardized** and teacher or researcher made. Standardized tests are published tests that have resulted from careful and skillful preparation by experts and cover broad academic objectives common to the majority of school systems. These are tests for which comparative norms have been derived, their validity and reliability established, and directions for administering and scoring prescribed. The directions are contained in the manuals provided by the test publishers. To establish the norms for these tests, their originators administer them to a relevant and representative sample. The norm group may be chosen to represent the nation as a whole or the state, city, district, or local school. The *mean* for a particular grade level in the sample becomes the norm for that grade level. It is important to distinguish between a norm and a standard. A *norm* is not necessarily a goal or a criterion of what should be. It is a measure of what *is.* Test norms are based on the actual performance of a specified group, not on standards of performance. The skills measured are not necessarily what "ought" to be taught at any grade level, but the use of norms does give educators a basis for comparing their groups with an estimate of the mean for all children at that grade level.

Standardized tests are available for individual school subjects, such as mathematics and chemistry, and also in the form of comprehensive batteries measuring several areas of achievement. For example, the California Achievement Test (CAT) contains tests in the areas of reading, language, and arithmetic. The Sequential Tests of Educational Progress (STEP) include tests in seven areas.

In selecting an achievement test, researchers must be careful to choose one that is reliable and is appropriate (valid) for measuring the aspect of achievement in which they are interested. The test must also be valid and reliable for the type of subjects included in the study. Sometimes a researcher is not able to select the test but must use what the school system has already selected. The *Mental Measurements Yearbooks* present a comprehensive listing, along with reviews of the different achievement tests available. Other references for commercially available tests are listed in Chapter 4.

If an available test measures the desired behavior and if the reliability, validity, and the norms are adequate for the purpose, then there are advantages in using a standardized instrument. In addition to the time and effort saved, investigators realize an advantage from the continuity of testing procedures—the results of their studies can be compared and interpreted with respect to those of other studies using the same instrument.

Researcher-Made Tests

When using standardized tests of achievement is not deemed suitable for the specific objectives of a research study, research workers may construct their own tests. It is much better to construct your own test than to use an inappropriate standardized one just because it is available. The advantage of a researcher-made test is that it can be tailored to the specific research question. For example, suppose a teacher wants to compare the effects of two teaching methods on students' achievement in mathematics. Although there are excellent standardized tests in mathematics, they are generally designed to measure broad objectives and may not focus sufficiently on the particular skills the teacher wishes to measure. It would be wise in this case for the teacher to construct the measuring instrument, paying particular attention to evidence of its validity and reliability. The teacher should administer a draft of the test to a small group who will not participate in the study, but who are similar to those who will participate. An analysis of the results enables the teacher to check on the test's validity and reliability, and to detect any ambiguities or other problems before employing the test. For suggestions on achievement test construction, refer to specialized texts in measurement, such as those by Gronlund and Linn (1999), Mehrens and Lehmann (1991), and Hopkins (1998).

Norm-Referenced and Criterion-Referenced Tests

On the basis of the type of interpretation made, standardized and teacher-made tests may be further classified as **norm referenced** or **criterion referenced.** Norm-referenced tests permit researchers to compare individuals' performance on the test to the performance of other individuals. An individual's performance is interpreted in terms of his or her relative position in a specified reference group known as the *normative group.* Performance is reported in terms of percentiles, standard scores, and similar measures.

In contrast, criterion-referenced tests enable researchers to describe what a specific individual can do, without reference to the performance of others. Performance is reported in terms of the level of mastery of some defined content or skill domain. Typically, the level of mastery is indicated by the percentage of items answered correctly. Predetermined cutoff scores may be used to interpret the individual's performance as pass–fail.

Before measuring instruments are designed, you must know the type of interpretation that is to be made. In norm-referenced tests, items are selected that will yield a wide range of scores. A researcher must be concerned with the difficulty of the items and the power of the items to discriminate among individuals. In criterion-referenced tests, items are selected solely on the basis of how well they measure a specific set of instructional objectives. They may be easy or difficult, depending on what is being measured. The major concern is to have a representative sample of items measuring the stated objectives so that individual performance can be described directly in terms of the specific knowledge and skills that these people are able to achieve.

Test Performance Range

One aspect of achievement tests that researchers should consider is the range of performance that the test permits. Ideally, researchers want a test designed so that the subjects can perform fully to their ability level without being restricted by the test itself. For example, gifted students would most likely all score near the top on a national standardized test and thus show little variability. This restriction in range at the upper end, which prevents subjects from performing to their maximum ability, represents a **ceiling effect** (Drew, Hardman, & Hart, 1996).

Ceiling Effect

A test with a low ceiling is one that is too easy for some of the subjects to whom it was administered. No one can know what their scores might have been if there had been a higher ceiling. Why is this a problem? In experimental research, for example, the effect

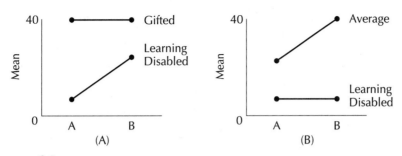

■ FIGURE 8.1

Graphs showing Ceiling Effect (A) and Floor Effect (B)

of a treatment could be underestimated because the test used doesn't measure subjects' achievement accurately at the upper end of the range.

Assume a researcher wishes to compare the effect of two teaching methods A and B with two different populations of students—a gifted group and a learning-disabled group. A test composed of forty questions is used as the measure of the learning that has occurred. The possible score range is thus 0–40. Assume the researcher calculates the mean score on the test for each group taught by each method. The results are graphed in Figure 8.1A.

Figure 8.1A apparently shows that method B is more effective than method A with learning-disabled students, but that there is no difference in effectiveness for gifted students. But note that the mean for the gifted students is very near the maximum score of 40; thus a large number of those students must have gotten all forty items answered correctly. The researcher doesn't know how many correct responses they might have made if there had not been a ceiling. Consequently, the researcher doesn't know whether methods A and B are really equally effective for gifted students or whether the range on the test was so restricted that gifted students could not perform to their maximum ability. Researchers can easily reach incorrect conclusions if they ignore this ceiling effect.

Floor Effect

Likewise, performance may be restricted at the lower end of the range, resulting in a **floor effect.** Floor effect is influenced by the difficulty of the test. On a very difficult test, you can't get real evidence about how subjects could perform, because the difficulty of the test itself rather than subjects' ability determines their performance. Consider the hypothetical data shown in Figure 8.1B. In this case, it appears that Method B is more effective than Method A for average students, but are equally effective for learning-disabled students. Is this really the case, or was the test so difficult that these students all tended to score near the bottom (zero)? If a less difficult test had been used, the students would probably have shown more variability in performance and there would not have been a floor effect. When selecting a test, a researcher should look for an instrument that permits a wide range of performance. Standardized test manuals often provide information about ceiling and floor effects, because much data on subjects' performance have been gathered during the test standardization process. Researchers who construct their own tests can try them out with various groups and look at the results for evidence of ceiling and floor effect. If it appears that performance range is restricted, then the researcher needs to revise the test.

Performance Assessments

Another way to classify achievement tests is whether they are paper-and-pencil or **performance tests.** The most common achievement tests are paper-and-pencil tests measuring cognitive objectives. Everyone is familiar with this format that requires the person to compose answers or choose responses on a printed sheet. In some cases, however, a researcher may want to measure performance—what an individual can *do* rather than what he or she *knows*. Performance assessment is a popular alternative to traditional tests among educators. A performance test is a technique in which a researcher directly observes and assesses an individual's performance of a certain task and/or judges the finished product of that performance. The test taker is asked to carry out a *process* such as playing a musical instrument or tuning a car engine, or to produce a *product* such as a written essay. The performance or product is judged against established criteria. An everyday example of a performance test is the behind-the-wheel examination taken when applying for a driver's license. A paper-and-pencil test covering knowledge of signs and rules for driving is not sufficient to measure driving skill. Stiggins (1992), an early advocate of performance assessment, defines it in terms of four components: (1) a reason for the assessment, (2) a particular performance to be evaluated, (3) exercises that elicit the performance, and (4) systematic rating procedures. In investigating a new method of teaching science, for example, you would want to know the effect of the method not only on students' cognitive behavior but also on their learning of various laboratory procedures and techniques or their ability to complete experiments. In this case, the researcher's test would require the students to perform a real task or use their knowledge and skills to solve a science problem. Performance assessment is important in areas such as art, music, home economics, public speaking, industrial training, and the sciences, which typically involve individuals' ability to do something or produce something. Portfolios that contain a collection of student work such as poetry, essays, sketches, musical compositions and so on are a popular tool in performance assessment.

Constructing a Performance Test

When a performance assessment is desired, the researcher should follow three basic steps in constructing the test.

1. Begin with a clear statement of the objectives or what individuals should do on the test and the conditions under which the task will be performed. A set of test specifications listing the critical dimensions to be assessed will lead to a more comprehensive coverage of the domain. State whether there will be time limits, whether reference books will be available, and so on.

2. Provide a problem or an exercise that gives students an opportunity to perform—either a simulation or an actual task. All individuals should be asked to perform the same task.

3. Develop an instrument (checklist, rating scale, or something similar) that lists the relevant criteria to use in evaluating the performance and/or the product. To maximize objectivity, the instrument should ensure that the same criteria are used for each individual's performance or product.

Performance tests provide a way to measure abilities and skills that cannot be measured by paper-and-pencil tests. They are, however, time intensive and thus more expensive to administer and score.

Aptitude Tests

Aptitude tests differ from achievement tests in that the former attempt to measure general ability, whereas the latter attempt to measure skills and knowledge in specific areas. Aptitude tests attempt to measure the subject's ability to perceive relationships, solve problems, and apply knowledge in a variety of contexts.

Aptitude tests were formerly referred to as *intelligence tests,* but the latter term has declined in use because of controversy over the definition of intelligence and because people tend to associate intelligence with inherited ability. Aptitude tests should *not* be considered as measures of innate (or "pure") intelligence. Performance on such tests partly depends on the background and schooling of the subject.

Educators have found aptitude tests useful and generally valid for the purpose of predicting school success. In fact, many of the tests are referred to as **scholastic aptitude tests,** a term pointing out specifically that the main function of these tests is to predict school performance. Well-known aptitude tests are the ACT (American College Testing Assessment) and the SAT (Scholastic Assessment Test) for high school students, and the GRE (Graduate Record Exam) and MAT (Miller Analogies Test) for college seniors.

Researchers also use aptitude tests extensively. Aptitude or intelligence is often a variable that needs to be controlled in educational experiments. To control this variable, the researcher may use the scores from a scholastic aptitude test. Of the many tests available, some have been designed for use with individuals and others for use with groups.

Individual Aptitude Tests

The most widely used individually administered instruments for measuring aptitude are the Stanford–Binet and the three Wechsler tests. The Stanford–Binet currently in use is the outcome of several revisions of the device first developed in France in 1905 by Alfred Binet and Theodore Simon, who wished to identify children who were not likely to benefit from normal classroom instruction. This test was originally used for measuring an individual's *mental age.* Later the concept of *intelligence quotient* (*IQ*) was introduced. This quotient is derived by dividing mental age (MA) by chronological age (CA) and multiplying the result by 100. The present revision of the Stanford–Binet yields mental ages but does not employ the MA/CA ratio for determining IQ. Instead, the IQ is found by comparing an individual's performance (score) with norms obtained from his or her age group through the use of standard scores (see Chapter 6). A major characteristic of the Stanford–Binet test is that it gives a general measure of aptitude. It does not attempt to measure separate abilities, as do some other tests.

The tests David Wechsler developed to measure aptitude now come in several forms: the Wechsler Intelligence Scale for Children–Third Edition (WISC–III), the revised Wechsler Adult Intelligence Scale (WAIS–R), and the revised Wechsler Preschool and Primary Scale of Intelligence (WPPSI–R), which was introduced for the 4- to 6½ age group. An important characteristic of the Wechsler tests is that they are divided into subtests, which enable the examiner to obtain two scores for each subject, one for verbal IQ and the other for nonverbal IQ. These subtests are further divided into subscales, which indicate the examinee's performance on specific tasks.

Group Tests of Aptitude

A Stanford–Binet or Wechsler test must be given by a trained psychometrician to an individual subject, a procedure expensive in both time and money. They are impractical as aptitude measures for large groups of individuals. In this situation, group tests are used. The first group test of mental ability was developed during World War I for measuring the ability of men in military service. One form of this test, the Army Alpha, was released for civilian use after the war and became the model for a number of group tests. Today many group tests of mental aptitude are available. Among the most widely used are the California Test of Mental Maturity (CTMM), the Cognitive Abilities Test (CAT), and the Otis–Lennon School Ability Test (OLSAT).

▮ MEASURES OF PERSONALITY

Obtaining measures of personality is another area of concern to educational research workers. There are several different types of personality measures, each reflecting a different theoretical point of view. Some reflect trait and type theories, whereas others have their origins in psychoanalytic and motivational theories. Researchers must know precisely what they wish to measure and then select the instrument, paying particular attention to the evidence of its validity. The two most widely used types of personality measures in research are inventories and projective techniques.

Inventories

In an **inventory,** researchers present subjects with an extensive collection of statements describing behavior patterns and ask them to indicate whether or not each statement is characteristic of their behavior by checking *yes, no,* or *uncertain.* Their score is computed by counting the number of responses that agree with a trait the examiner is attempting to measure. For example, paranoids would be expected to answer *yes* to the statement "People are always talking behind my back" and *no* to the statement "I expect the police to be fair and reasonable." Of course, similar responses to only two items would not indicate paranoid tendencies. However, such responses to a large proportion of items could be considered an indicator of paranoia.

Some of the self-report inventories measure only one trait, such as the California F-Scale, which measures authoritarianism. Others, such as Cattell's Sixteen Personality Factor Questionnaire, measure a number of traits. Other well-known inventories in research are the Minnesota Multiphasic Personality Inventory, the Guilford-Zimmerman Temperament Survey, the Mooney Problem Check List, the Edwards Personal Preference Schedule, the Myers-Briggs Type Indicator, the Strong Interest Inventory, and the Coopersmith Self-Esteem Inventory.

Inventories have been used in educational research to obtain trait descriptions of certain defined groups, such as underachievers, dropouts, and so forth. They are useful for finding out about students' self-concepts, their concerns or problems, and their study skills and habits. Inventories have also been used in research concerned with interrelationships between personality traits and such variables as aptitude, achievement, and attitudes.

Inventories have the advantages of economy, simplicity, and objectivity. Most of the disadvantages are related to the problem of validity. Inventories are self-report instruments, thus their validity depends in part on the respondents' being able to read and understand the items, their understanding of themselves, and especially their willingness to give frank and honest answers. As a result, the information obtained from inventories may be superficial or biased. This possibility must be taken into account when using results obtained from such instruments.

Projective Techniques

Projective techniques are measures in which an individual is asked to respond to an ambiguous or unstructured stimulus. They are called *projective* because a person is expected to project into the stimulus his or her own needs, wants, fears, anxieties, and so forth. On the basis of the subject's interpretation and responses, the examiner attempts to construct a comprehensive picture of the individual's personality structure.

Projective methods are used mainly by clinical psychologists for studying and diagnosing people with emotional problems. They are not frequently used in educational research because of the necessity of specialized training for administration and scoring and the expense involved in individual administration. Furthermore, many researchers feel that their validity has not been satisfactorily established. The two best known projective techniques are the Rorschach and the Thematic Apperception Test (TAT). The Rorschach uses ink blots as the stimulus, and in the TAT the respondent is shown pictures and asked to tell a story about each one.

ATTITUDE SCALES

Scales are used to measure attitudes, values, opinions, and other characteristics that are not easily measured by tests or other measuring instruments. A **scale** is a set of categories or numeric values assigned to individuals, objects, or behaviors for the purpose of measuring variables. The process of assigning scores to those objects in order to obtain a measure of a construct is called *scaling*. Scales differ from tests in that the results of these instruments, unlike those of tests, do not indicate success or failure, strength or weakness. They measure the degree to which an individual exhibits the characteristic of interest. For example, a researcher may use a scale to measure the attitude of college students toward religion or any other topic. A number of scaling techniques have been developed over the years.

Attitude scales which we will discuss first, use multiple responses—usually responses to questions—and combine the responses into a single scale score. Rating scales, which we discuss a little later in this chapter, use judgments—made by the individual under study or by an observer—to assign scores to individuals or other objects to measure the underlying constructs.

Attitudes of individuals or groups are of interest to educational researchers. An attitude may be defined as a positive or negative affect toward a particular group, institution, concept, or social object. The measurement of attitudes presumes the ability to place individuals along a continuum of favorableness–unfavorableness toward the object.

One source of information for research on attitude scales is *Scales for the Measurement of Attitudes* (Shaw & Wright, 1967). This book contains a collection of attitude measures developed for research purposes. It provides reliability and validity information for each measure, if information is available. Other references are *Measures of Social Psychological Attitudes* (Robinson & Shaver, 1973), and *Measures of Personality and Social Psychological Attitudes* (1991) by Robinson Shaver, & Wrightsman.

If researchers cannot locate an existing attitude scale on their topic of interest, they must develop their own scales for measuring attitudes. On the following pages we discuss two types of attitude scales: summated or Likert scales (pronounced *Lik'ert*) and semantic differential scales.

Likert Scales: Method of Summated Ratings

The Likert scale (1932) is one of the most widely used techniques to measure attitudes. A **Likert scale** (a **summated rating scale**) assesses attitudes toward a topic by presenting a set of statements about the topic and asking respondents to indicate for each whether they strongly agree, agree, are undecided, disagree, or strongly disagree. The various agree–disagree responses are assigned a numeric value, and the total scale score is found by summing the numeric responses given to each item. This total score represents the individual's attitude toward the topic.

A Likert scale is constructed by assembling a large number of statements about an object, approximately half of which express a clearly favorable attitude and half of which are clearly unfavorable. Neutral items are not used in a Likert scale. It is important that these statements constitute a representative sample of all the possible opinions or attitudes about the object. It may be helpful to think of all the subtopics relating to the attitude object and then write items on each subtopic. To generate this diverse collection of items, the researcher may find it helpful to ask people who are commonly accepted as having knowledge about and definite attitudes toward the particular object to write a number of positive and negative statements. Editorial writings about the object are also good sources of potential statements for an attitude scale. Figure 8.2 shows items from a Likert scale designed to measure attitudes toward capital punishment.

The statements, along with five response categories arranged on an agreement–disagreement continuum, are presented to a group of subjects. This group should be drawn from a population that is similar to the one in which the scale will be used. The statements should be arranged in random order so as to avoid any response set on the part of the subjects.

The subjects are directed to select the response category that best represents their reaction to each statement: *strongly agree* (SA), *agree* (A), *undecided* (U), *disagree* (D), or *strongly disagree* (SD). There has been some question of whether the undecided option should be included in a Likert scale. Most experts in the field recommend that the researcher include a neutral or undecided choice because some respondents actually feel that way and do not want to be forced into agreeing or disagreeing.

To score the scale, the response categories must be weighted. For favorable or positively stated items, the numeric values 5, 4, 3, 2, and 1, respectively, are assigned to the response categories beginning at the favorable end. For example, *strongly agree* with a favorable statement would receive a weight of 5, *agree* would receive a 4, and *strongly disagree* a weight of 1. For unfavorable or negatively stated items, the weighting is reversed, because disagreement with an unfavorable statement is psychologically equivalent to agreement with a favorable statement. Thus for unfavorable statements *strongly agree* would receive a weight of 1 and *strongly disagree* a weight of 5. (The weight values do not appear on the attitude scale presented to respondents.) Consider these examples selected from a scale measuring attitudes toward mathematics:

	SA	A	U	D	SD
Mathematics is my favorite subject in school. (+)	5	4	3	2	1
I dislike mathematics in any form. (−)	1	2	3	4	5

A person with a favorable attitude toward mathematics would agree with the positive item and disagree with the negative item; a person who disliked mathematics would agree with the negative item and disagree with the positive item. If the subject marked A for the first statement just given and D for the second, the summated score would be 8 or (4 plus 4) for these two items. The sum of the weights of all the items checked by the subject would represent the individual's total score. This weighting system means that a high scale score (SA to favorable items; SD to unfavorable items) indicates a positive attitude toward the object. The highest possible scale score is $5 \times N$ (the number of items); the lowest possible score is $1 \times N$.

Item Analysis After administering the attitude scale to a preliminary group of respondents, the researcher does an item analysis to identify the best-functioning items. The item analysis typically yields three statistics for each item: (1) an item discrimination index, (2) the number and/or percentage of respondents marking each choice to each item, and (3) the item mean and standard deviation. The item discrimination index shows

1. Capital punishment serves as a deterrent to premeditated crime.

    SA   A   U   D   SD

*2. Capital punishment is morally wrong.

    SA   A   U   D   SD

3. The use of capital punishment is the best way for society to deal with hardened criminals.

    SA   A   U   D   SD

*4. I would sign a petition in favor of legislation to abolish the death penalty.

    SA   A   U   D   SD

*5. Capital punishment should not be used because there is always the possibility that an innocent person could be executed.

    SA   A   U   D   SD

6. Capital punishment reduces the use of tax monies for the care of prison inmates.

    SA   A   U   D   SD

*7. Only God has the right to take a human life.

    SA   A   U   D   SD

8. If more executions were carried out, there would be a sharp decline in violent crime.

    SA   A   U   D   SD

*9. Capital punishment should only be considered after all rehabilitation efforts have failed.

    SA   A   U   D   SD

10. I believe murder deserves a stronger penalty than life imprisonment.

    SA   A   U   D   SD

*11. Capital punishment should be abolished because it is in conflict with basic human rights.

    SA   A   U   D   SD

*12. I would be willing to participate in an all-night vigil to protest the execution of a criminal in my state.

    SA   A   U   D   SD

*These are negative items, agreement with which is considered to reflect a negative or unfavorable attitude toward capital punishment.

FIGURE 8.2
Example of a Likert Scale

Source: These items were taken from an attitude scale constructed by a graduate student in an educational research class.

the extent to which each item discriminates among the respondents in the same way as the total score discriminates. If high scorers on an individual item have high total scores and if low scorers on this item have low total scores, then the item is discriminating in the same way as the total score. The item discrimination index is calculated by correlating item scores with total-scale scores, a procedure usually done by computer. To be useful, an item should correlate at least .25 with the total score. Items that have very low correlation or negative correlation with the total score should be eliminated because they are not measuring the same thing as the total scale and hence are not contributing to the measurement of the attitude. The researcher will want to examine those items that are found to be nondiscriminating. The items may be ambiguous or double barreled (containing two beliefs or opinions in one statement), or they may be factual statements not really expressing feelings about the object. Revising these items may make them usable. The other statistics from the item analysis (2 and 3) indicate the extent to which the respondents have used the various options. Items on which the respondents are spread out among the response categories are preferred over items on which the responses are clustered in only one or two categories.

After selecting the most consistent items as indicated by the item analysis, the researcher should then try out the revised scale with a different group of subjects and again check the items for discrimination.

Validity

Validity concerns the extent to which the scale really measures the attitude construct. It is often difficult to locate criteria to be used in obtaining evidence for the validity of attitude scales. Some researchers have used observations of actual behavior as the criterion for the attitude being measured, but this procedure is not often used, because it is difficult to determine what behavior would be the best criterion for the attitude and also because it is difficult to secure measures of the behavior.

One of the easiest ways to gather validity evidence is to determine the extent to which the scale is capable of discriminating between two groups whose members are known to have different attitudes. To validate a scale that measures attitudes toward organized religion, a researcher would determine if the scale discriminated between active church members and people who do not attend church or have no church affiliation. A scale measuring attitudes toward abortion should discriminate between members of pro-life groups and members of pro-choice groups. By "discriminate," we mean that the two groups would be expected to have significantly different mean scores on the scale. Another method of assessing validity is to correlate scores on the attitude scale with those obtained on another attitude scale measuring the same construct and whose validity is well established.

Reliability

The reliability of the new scale must also be determined. Reliability is concerned with the extent to which the measure would yield consistent results each time it is used. The

School

a. bad	:	:	:	:	:	: ✓	good
b. fast	: ✓ :	:	:	:	:		slow
c. dull	:	:	:	:	: ✓ :		sharp
d. pleasant	✓ :	:	:	:	:		unpleasant
e. light	:	: ✓ :	:	:	:		heavy
f. passive	:	:	:	:	:	: ✓	active
g. worthless	:	:	:	:	: ✓ :		valuable
h. strong	:	:	: ✓ :	:	:		weak
i. still	:	:	:	: ✓ :	:		moving

FIGURE 8.3

Semantic differential scale showing responses of one subject toward the concept "School"

first step in ensuring reliability is to make sure that the scale is long enough—that it includes enough items to provide a representative sampling of the whole domain of opinions about the attitudinal object. Other things being equal, the size of the reliability coefficient is directly related to the length of the scale. Mueller (1986) states, however, that if the items are well constructed, scales having as few as twenty to twenty-two items will have satisfactory reliability (often above .80). The number of items needed depends partly on how specific the attitudinal object is; the more abstract the object, the more items are needed.

You would also want to calculate an index of reliability. The best index to use for an attitude scale is coefficient alpha (see Chapter 9), which provides a measure of the extent to which all the items are positively intercorrelated and working together to measure one trait or characteristic (the attitude). Computer programs such as SPSS (Statistical Package for the Social Sciences) and SAS (Statistical Analysis System) routinely calculate coefficient alpha as a measure of reliability.

Semantic Differential Scales

Another approach to measuring attitudes is the **semantic differential scale,** a type developed by Osgood, Suci, and Tannenbaum (1967). It measures the meaning associated with an object or concept by asking individuals to rate the object or concept on a series of scales anchored at each extreme by bipolar adjectives. Figure 8.3 shows a semantic differential designed to measure attitude toward school.

Respondents are asked to indicate how they feel toward school by placing a check mark on the seven-point scale for each of the pairs of adjectives. Notice in Figure 8.3 that the respondent checked the extreme right position for item a and the extreme left position for item d. The adjective pairs making up a semantic differential are listed in both directions; on some pairs the rightmost position is the most positive response, and on other pairs the leftmost position is the most positive. This is done to minimize a response set or a tendency to favor certain positions in a list of options. An individual might have a tendency to choose the extreme right end and would check that position for each item. However, if the direction of the scale is changed in a random way so that the right end is not always the more favorable response, then the individual is forced to read each item and respond in terms of its content rather than in terms of a positional preference. The responses are scored by converting the positions checked into ratings (1 to 7). Seven represents the most positive, and 1, the least positive response on each scale.

Osgood and associates found through factor analysis (see Chapter 12) that three dimensions of meaning are measured by a semantic differential: *evaluation* (good–bad or valuable–worthless), *potency* (strong–weak or heavy–light), and *activity* (fast–slow or active–passive).

Each of the dimensions can be measured by using at least three separate sets of bipolar adjectives that have been shown to be measures of that dimension. Responses on the adjective pairs that make up each dimension are summed separately to provide an overall score on each of the dimensions, or an average can be calculated for each dimension. In Figure 8.3, items a, d, and g measure evaluation and the measurements on this scale are 7, 7, 6 respectively, which can be averaged $(7 + 7 + 6) / 3 = 6.67$ to arrive at a score on the evaluation dimension. This high score on the evaluative dimension indicates a positive attitude toward school. For the activity scale (items b, f, and i), the average score is $(6 + 7 + 5) / 3 = 6.00$; and for the potency scale (items c, e, and h), the average is $(6 + 3 + 4) / 3 = 4.33$.

The major problem with the semantic differential format is determining which of the three dimensions a given pair of adjectives is measuring. You may sometimes know intuitively what dimension is being measured, but the determination is made most reliably through factor analysis. You don't have to do a factor analysis, however, every time you want to use a semantic differential. A number of researchers (for example, Osgood, Suci, Tannenbaum, (1967)) have factor-analyzed many adjectives and determined their dimensions. It is recommended that if one wants to construct a semantic differential scale, he or she should consult one of these sources for a list of adjectives.

In practice, most semantic differential scales focus solely on the evaluative dimension because research has shown that the evaluative dimension is not only the strongest factor measured but also has the most significance for attitude measurement. Thus, when we measure attitudes toward a concept or object, we will select adjective pairs that measure the evaluative dimension because we want to know the value that respondents attach to those concepts.

The semantic differential is a very flexible approach to measuring attitudes. A researcher can use it to investigate attitudes toward any concept, person, or activity in a school or other type setting. It is also much easier and less time consuming to construct than a Likert scale. Instead of having to come up with twenty or so statements, you need only select four to eight adjective pairs. It is also easy to administer, because very little reading time is required on the part of the participants.

	Low	Medium	High
Personal Appearance	_____
Social Acceptability	_____
Speaking Skills	_____

FIGURE 8.4
Example of a Graphic Scale

RATING SCALES

One of the most widely used measuring instruments is the **rating scale.** Rating scales present a number of statements about a behavior, an activity or a phenomenon with an accompanying scale of categories. Observers or respondents are asked to indicate their assessment or judgment about the behavior or activity on the rating scale. For example, a teacher might be asked to rate the leadership ability of a student. The teacher would indicate his or her assessment of the student's characteristic leadership behavior by checking a point on a continuum or choosing a response category. It is assumed that raters are familiar with the behavior they are asked to assess. A numeric value may be attached to the points or categories so that an overall score could be obtained.

There are several different formats used for rating scales. One of the most widely used is the **graphic scale,** in which the rater indicates the rating by placing a check at the appropriate point on a horizontal line that runs from one extreme of the behavior in question to the other. Figure 8.4 is a typical example of a graphic scale. The rater can check any point on the continuous line.

Some graphic scales assign numeric values to the descriptive points. Such scales are referred to as *numeric rating scales.* The speaking skills item in Figure 8.4 could look like this in a numeric scale:

1	2	3	4	5	6	7
one of the poorest speakers			an average speaker			one of the very best speakers

A second type of rating scale is the **category scale,** which consists of a number of categories that are arranged in an ordered series. Five to seven categories are most frequently used. The rater picks the one that best characterizes the behavior of the person being rated. Suppose a student's abilities are being rated and one of the characteristics being rated is creativity. The following might be one category item:

How creative is this person? (check one)

exceptionally creative	_____
very creative	_____
creative	_____
not creative	_____
not at all creative	_____

Area of Competency (to be rated)	Unusually low	Poorer than most students	About average among students	Better than most	Really superior	Not able to judge
1. Does this person show evidence of clear-cut and worthy professional goals?						
2. Does this person attack problems in a constructive manner?						
3. Does he or she take well-meant criticism and use it constructively?						

FIGURE 8.5

Example of a Comparative Rating Scale

To provide greater meaning, brief descriptive phrases are sometimes used to make up the categories in this type of scale. Clearly defined categories contribute to the accuracy of the ratings. For example,

How creative is this person? (check one)

always has creative ideas _____
has many creative ideas _____
sometimes has creative ideas _____
rarely has creative ideas _____

In using the graphic and category scales, raters make their judgments without directly comparing the person being rated to other individuals or groups. In **comparative rating scales,** in contrast, raters are instructed to make their judgments with direct reference to the positions of others with whom the individual might be compared. The positions on the rating scale are defined in terms of a given population with known characteristics. A comparative rating scale is shown in Figure 8.5.

Such a scale might be used in selecting applicants for admission to graduate school. Raters are asked to judge the applicant's ability to do graduate work as compared with all the students the rater has known. If the rating is to be valid, the judge must understand the range and distribution of abilities in the total group of graduate students.

Errors in Rating

Because ratings depend on the perceptions of human observers, who are susceptible to various influences, rating scales are subject to considerable error. Among the most frequent systematic errors in rating people is the **halo effect,** which occurs when raters allow a generalized impression of the subject to influence the rating given on very specific aspects of behavior. This general impression carries over from one item in the scale to the next. For example, a teacher might rate a student who does good academic work as also being superior in intelligence, popularity, honesty, perseverance, and all other aspects of personality. Or, if you have a generally unfavorable impression of a person, you are likely to rate the person low on all aspects.

Another type of error is the **generosity error,** which refers to the tendency for raters to give subjects the benefit of any doubt; that is, when raters are not sure, they are likely to speak favorably about the people they are rating. In contrast, there is the **error of severity,** which is a tendency to rate all individuals too low on all characteristics. Another source of error is the **error of central tendency,** which refers to the tendency to avoid either extreme and to rate all individuals in the middle of the scale.

One way of reducing such errors is to train the raters thoroughly before they are asked to make ratings. They should be informed about the possibility of making these "personal bias" types of errors and how to avoid them. It is absolutely essential that raters have adequate time to observe the individual and his or her behavior before making a rating. Another way to minimize error is to make certain that the behavior to be rated and the points on the rating scale are clearly defined. The points on the scale should be described in terms of overt behaviors that can be observed, rather than in terms of behaviors that require inference on the part of the rater.

The accuracy or reliability of ratings is usually increased by having two (or more) trained raters make independent ratings of an individual. These independent ratings are pooled, or averaged, to obtain a final score. A reseacher may also correlate the ratings of the two separate raters in order to obtain a coefficient of **interrater reliability.** The size of the coefficient indicates the extent to which the raters agree. An interrater reliability coefficient of .70 or higher is considered acceptable for rating scales.

▇ DIRECT OBSERVATION

In many cases, systematic **direct observation** of behavior is the most desirable measurement method. Observation is used in both quantitative and qualitative research. When observations are made in an attempt to get a comprehensive picture of a situation, and the product of those observations is notes or narratives, the research is qualitative. In Chapter 14 we discuss the use of observation in qualitative research. The present chapter focuses on observation in quantitative research where the product of using the various observational instruments is numbers. The purpose of direct observation is to determine the extent to which a particular behavior(s) is present. An investigator identifies the behavior of interest and devises a systematic procedure for identifying, categorizing, and recording the behavior in either a natural or a contrived situation. Systematic observation has been used extensively in research on infants and preschool children. In educational research, one of the most common uses of direct observation is in studying classroom behavior. For example, if you were interested in investigating the extent to which elementary teachers use positive reinforcement in the classroom, you could probably obtain more accurate data by actually observing classrooms rather than asking teachers about their use of reinforcement. Or if you wanted to study students' disruptive behavior in the classroom and how teachers deal with it, direct observation would provide more accurate data than reports from students or teachers.

There are five important preliminary steps to take in preparing for quantitative direct observation:

1. *Select the aspect of behavior to be observed.* Because it is not possible to collect data on everything that happens, the investigator must decide beforehand which behaviors to record and which not to record.

2. *Clearly define the behaviors falling within a chosen category.* The observers must understand what actions will be classified as, for instance, cooperative behavior or disruptive behavior.

3. *Develop a system for quantifying observations.* The investigator must decide on a standard method for counting the observed behaviors. For instance, establish beforehand whether an action and the reaction to it are to count as a single incident of the behavior observed or as two incidents. A suggested approach is to divide the observation period into brief time segments and to record for each period—say, 10 seconds—whether the subject showed the behavior or not.

4. *Develop specific procedures for recording the behavior.* The memory of most observers is usually not reliable enough for meaningful research. The best solution is a coding system that allows the immediate recording of what is observed, using a single letter or digit. A coding system is advantageous in terms of the observers' time and attention.

5. *Train the people who will carry out the observations.* Training and opportunity for practice are necessary in order that the investigator can rely on the observers to follow an established procedure in observing and in interpreting and reporting observations. Having the observers view a videotape and then discussing the results is a good training technique.

Devices for Recording Observations

Researchers use checklists, rating scales, and coding sheets to record the data collected in direct observation.

Checklists

The simplest device used is a checklist, which presents a list of the behaviors that are to be observed. The observer then checks whether each behavior is present or absent. A checklist differs from a scale in that the responses do not represent points on a continuum but nominal categories. For example, a researcher studying disruptive behavior would prepare a list of disruptive behaviors that might occur in a classroom. An observer would then check items such as "Passes notes to other students" or "Makes disturbing noises" each time the behavior occurs. The behaviors in a checklist should be operationally defined and readily observable.

Rating Scales

Rating scales, which we discussed in a previous section, are often used by observers to indicate their evaluation of an observed behavior or activity. Typically, rating scales consist of three to five points or categories. For example, an observer studying teachers' preparation for presentation of new material in a classroom might use a scale with the points: 5 (*extremely well prepared*), 4 (*well prepared*), 3 (*prepared*), 2 (*not well prepared*), or 1 (*totally unprepared*). A three-point scale might include 3 (*very well prepared*), 2 (*prepared*), or 1 (*not well prepared*). Scales with more than five rating categories are not recommended, because it is too difficult to accurately discriminate among the categories.

Coding Systems

Coding systems are used in observational studies to facilitate the categorizing and counting of specific, predetermined behaviors as they occur. The researcher does not just indicate whether a behavior occurred as with a checklist, but uses agreed-on codes to record what actually occurred. Whereas rating scales can be completed after an observation period, coding is completed at the time the observer views the behavior. Both rating scales and coding systems result in measures.

Tuckman (1999) lists two kinds of coding systems that are typically used by researchers (p. 227) *Sign coding* uses a set of behavior categories; each time one of the behaviors occurs, the observer codes the happening in the appropriate category. If a coding sheet used in classroom observational research listed "summarizing" as a teacher behavior, the observer would code a happening every time a teacher summarized material.

A classic coding system widely used for recording classroom observations was developed by Flanders (1970). Flanders's system provides the following categories of teacher talk: (1) *accepts feelings;* (2) *praises or encourages;* (3) *accepts ideas of students;* (4) *asks questions;* (5) *lectures;* (6) *gives directions;* (7) *criticizes or justifies authority.* Trained observers can very quickly record each of these categories of behavior as a single digit. The chain of digits produced can easily be analyzed to provide not only a record of the proportions of teacher verbal behavior falling into each category, but also a picture of which behaviors preceded or followed which other behaviors. There are also categories in Flander's system for coding pupil talk.

Urban's classic study "Behavior Changes Resulting from a Study of Communicable Diseases" (1943) is a good example of the use of coding in an observational study. Observers coded children's behavior as desirable or undesirable from a health standpoint. For example, they recorded the number of instances of undesirable behavior, such as putting fingers or other objects in the mouth, and the number of desirable behaviors, such as using a handkerchief when coughing or sneezing. Then an experimental group was selected and taught a six-week course on communicable diseases, designed to change their overt behavior as well as to provide them with factual information and understanding. At the end of the course, the behaviors were again observed and recorded. The researchers found that the undesirable behaviors had been dramatically reduced and the desirable behaviors dramatically increased in the experimental group, whereas there was little change in the control group, which had not had the course. Observations 12 weeks later found these differences between the control and experimental groups persisting.

In the second type of coding called *time coding,* the observer identifies and records all predetermined behavior categories that occur during a given time period. The time period might be 5 seconds, 10 seconds, or 5 minutes. In a classroom study, Rollins, McCandless, and Thompson (1974) used systematic observation before and after a training period during which teachers learned and were encouraged to use positive reinforcement procedures. Observations were made to determine the extent to which teachers used positive reinforcement and the effect of the positive reinforcement on the behavior of pupils. Observation was carried out in five-minute cycles: During the first cycle, observers counted the positive and negative reinforcing behaviors of the teacher; during the second, they counted disruptive behaviors by pupils; during the third, they observed and counted the attentive behaviors of pupils. The researchers found that teachers who had been trained showed approximately four times as many positive reinforcements per student and had to use far fewer punishments than did teachers in control classes. Observations of the trained teachers' pupils showed a marked decrease in disruptive behaviors and an increase in attentive behaviors. Furthermore, the students in the experimental classes made a greater average gain in reading test grade equivalent over an eight-month period. In this study, systematic observation was used very effectively to document the changes in classroom behaviors that were associated with marked changes in pupil achievement.

Coding has the advantages of recording observations at the time the behavior occurs and it may yield somewhat more objective data than do rating scales. The disadvantage is that a long training period may be required for observers to learn to code behavior reliably.

A number of standardized coding systems and observation forms are available. Beginning researchers should check references such as the ETS Test Collection Database for a suitable one before attempting to construct their own.

Evaluation of Direct Observation

As with other types of measures, the value of direct observation is related to its validity and reliability. The best way to enhance validity is to carefully define the behavior to be observed and to train the people who will be making the observations. Observers must be aware of two sources of bias that affect validity: observer bias and observer effect. **Observer bias** occurs when the observer's own perceptions, beliefs, and biases influence the way he or she observes and interprets the situation. Having more than one person make independent observations helps to detect the presence of bias. **Observer effect** occurs when people being observed behave differently just because they are being observed. One-way vision screens may be used in some situations to deal with this problem. In many cases, however, after an initial reaction the subjects being observed come to pay little attention to the observer, especially one who operates unobtrusively.

The accuracy or reliability of direct observation is investigated by having at least two observers independently observe the behavior and by then checking the extent to which the observers' records agree. Reliability is enhanced by providing extensive training for the observers so that they are competent in knowing what to observe and just how to record the observations.

CONTRIVED OBSERVATIONS

In **contrived observations,** the researcher arranges for the observation of subjects in simulations of real-life situations. The circumstances have been arranged so that the desired behaviors are elicited.

One form of contrived observation is the *situational test*. A classic example of a situational test—although not labeled as such at the time—was used in a series of studies by Hartshorne and May (1928) for the Character Education Inquiry (CEI). These tests were designed for use in studying the development of such behavior characteristics as honesty, self-control, truthfulness, and cooperativeness. Hartshorne and May observed children in routine school activities but also staged some situations to focus on specific behavior. For example, they gave vocabulary and reading tests to the children, collected the tests, and without the children's knowledge made duplicate copies of their answers. Later the children were given answer keys and were asked to score their original papers. The difference between the scores the children reported and the actual scores obtained from scoring the duplicate papers provided a measure of cheating. Another test asked the children to make a mark in each of ten small, irregularly placed circles, while keeping their eyes shut. Previous control tests under conditions that prevented peeking indicated that a score of more than 13 correctly placed marks in three trials was highly improbable. Thus, a score above 13 was recorded as evidence that the child had peeked.

Hartshorne and May found practically no relationship between cheating in different situations, such as on a test and in athletics. They concluded that children's responses were situationally specific—that is, whether students cheated depended on the specific activity, the teacher involved, and other situations rather than on some general character trait.

DATA COLLECTION IN QUALITATIVE RESEARCH

Qualitative researchers also have a number of data-gathering tools available for their investigations. The most widely used tools in qualitative research are interviews, document analysis, and observation. We discuss these methods in Chapter 14.

SUMMARY

Because a research study can be no better than the instruments used to collect the data, one of the most important tasks of researchers in the behavioral sciences is the selection and/or development of dependable measuring instruments. A variety of tests, scales, and inventories is available for gathering data in educational research, especially for quantitative studies. Researchers need to be aware of the strengths and limitations of these data-gathering instruments so that they can choose the one(s) most appropriate for their particular investigation. If an appropriate standardized instrument is available, the researcher would be wise to choose it because of the advantage in terms of validity, reliability and time saved.

A test is a set of stimuli presented to an individual to elicit responses on the basis of which a numerical score can be assigned. Achievement tests measure knowledge and proficiency in a given area and are widely used in educational research. Standardized achievement tests permit the researcher to compare performance on the test to the performance of a normative reference group. Tests may be classified as paper-and-pencil or as performance tests, which measure what someone can *do,* rather than what he or she *knows.* Aptitude tests are used to assess an individual's verbal and nonverbal capacities. Personality inventories are designed to measure the subject's personal characteristics and typical performance.

Attitude scales are tools for measuring individuals' beliefs, feelings, and reactions to certain objects. The major types of attitude scales are Likert-type scales and the semantic differential.

Rating scales permit observers to assign scores to the assessments made of observed behavior or activity. Among the types of rating scales are the graphic scale, the category scale, and comparative rating scales.

Rating scales, checklists, and coding systems are the most common procedures used to record the data in direct observation research. In coding systems, behavior can be categorized according to individual occurrences (sign coding) or occurrences during a specified time period (time coding).

REFERENCES

Drew, C. J., Hardman, M. L., & Hart, A. W. (1996). *Designing and conducting research: Inquiry in education and social science* (2nd ed.). Boston: Allyn and Bacon.

Flanders, N. A. (1970). *Analyzing teacher behavior.* Boston: Addison-Wesley.

Hartshorne, H., & May, M. A. (1928). *Studies in the nature of character: Studies in deceit* (Vol. 1). New York: Macmillan.

Hopkins, K. D. (1998). *Educational and psychological measurement and evaluation* (8th ed.) Boston: Allyn and Bacon.

Likert, R. (1932). A technique for the measurement of attitudes. *Archives of Psychology,* no. 140.

Linn, R. L., & Gronlund, N. E. (1999). *Measurement and assessment in teaching* (8th ed.). Upper Saddle River, NJ: Merrill.

Mehrens, W. A., & Lehmann, I. J. (1991). *Measurement and evaluation in education and psychology* (4th ed.). Fort Worth, TX: Holt, Rinehart and Winston.

Mueller, D. J. (1986). *Measuring social attitudes: A handbook for researchers and practitioners.* New York: Teachers College Press.

Osgood, C. E., Suci, G. J., & Tannenbaum, P. H. (1967). *The measurement of meaning.* Urbana: University of Illinois Press.

Robinson, J. P., & Shaver, P. R. (1973) *Measures of Social Psychological Attitudes* Ann Arbor, MI: Survey Research Center, Institute for Social Research.

Robinson, J. P., Shaver, P. R., & Wrightsman L. S. (1991). *Measures of personality and social psychological attitudes.* San Diego: Academic Press.

Rollins, H. A., McCandless, B. R., & Thompson, M. (1974). Project success environment: An extended application of contingency management in inner-city schools. *Journal of Educational Psychology, 66,* 167–178.

Sax, G. (1997). *Principles of educational and psychological measurement and evaluation* (4th ed.). Belmont, CA: Wadsworth.

Shaw, M. E., & Wright, J. M. (1967). *Scales for the measurement of attitudes.* New York: McGraw-Hill.

Stiggins, R. J. (1992). High quality classroom assessment: What does it really mean? *Educational Measurement, 11,* 35–39.

Tuckman, B. W. (1999). *Conducting educational research* (5th ed.). Fort Worth: Harcourt Brace College Publishers.

Urban, J. (1943). Behavior changes resulting from a study of communicable diseases. In *Teachers College contributions to education* (No. 896). New York: Teachers College Press, Columbia University.

KEY CONCEPTS

achievement test

aptitude test

attitude scale

category scale

ceiling effect

coding system

comparative rating scales

contrived observation

criterion-referenced test

direct observation

error of central tendency

error of severity

floor effect

generosity error

graphic scale

halo effect

interrater reliability

inventory

Likert scale

norm-referenced test

observer bias

observer effect

performance test

projective technique

rating scale

scale

scholastic aptitude test

semantic differential scale

standardized test

summated rating scale

test

EXERCISES

1. What is the meaning of the term *standardized* when applied to measuring instruments?

2. What is the difference between comparative rating scales and graphic and category scales?

3. List some of the common sources of bias in rating scales.

4. What type of instrument would a researcher choose in order to obtain data about each of the following?

   a. How college professors feel about the use of technology in their teaching

   b. The potential of the seniors at a small college to succeed in graduate school

   c. To see if high school chemistry students can analyze an unknown chemical compound

   d. How well the students at Brown Elementary School compare to the national average in reading skills

   e. The advising-style preferences of a group of college freshmen

   f. How well students perform in a public speaking contest

   g. How middle school students feel about a school's new dress code

   h. The general verbal and nonverbal abilities of a student with attention-deficit disorder

   i. The extent to which elementary teachers use negative reinforcement in the classroom, and the effect of that reinforcement on students' behavior

   j. The problems faced by minority students during the first year at a large research university

   k. How parents in a school system feel about moving the sixth grade from the elementary school to the middle school

5. What is the main measurement use of the semantic differential scale?

6. What are some procedures for increasing the accuracy of direct-observation techniques?

7. Construct a five-item Likert scale for measuring peoples' attitudes toward the electoral college system used in presidental elections.

8. What are the main advantages of a semantic differential scale over a Likert scale for measuring attitudes?

9. Construct a five-item semantic differential scale for measuring middle school students' attitudes toward school sports programs.

10. Intelligence tests can most accurately be described as
    a. Measures of innate mental capacity
    b. Academic achievement measures
    c. Reading tests
    d. Scholastic aptitude tests

11. List and briefly describe the instruments available for recording data in observational research.

ANSWERS

1. *Standardized* refers to instruments for which comparative norms have been derived, their reliability and validity have been established, and directions for administration and scoring prescribed.

2. In judging an individual on a comparative rating scale, the rater must have knowledge of the group with which the individual is being compared. In judging an individual on graphic and category scales, raters do not make a direct comparison of the subject with other people.

3. Raters may be less than objective in judging individuals when influenced by such tendencies as the halo effect, the generosity error,

the error of severity, or the error of central tendency.

4. a. Attitude scale
    b. Aptitude test (group)
    c. Performance test
    d. Standardized achievement test
    e. Inventory
    f. Rating scale (performance test)
    g. Attitude scale
    h. Aptitude or intelligence test (individual)
    i. Direct observation
    j. Inventory
    k. Attitude scale

5. The semantic differential scale is used to measure the connotative meaning that a person attaches to an object.

6. The behaviors to be observed must be specified; behaviors falling within a category must be defined; a system for quantification must be developed; and the observers must be trained to carry out the observations according to this established procedure.

7. Answers will vary.

8. The main advantage is that the semantic differential scale is easier and less time consuming to construct. It is very flexible and can even be used with young children.

9. Answers will vary.

10. d.

11. Checklists indicate the presence or absence of certain behaviors. Rating scales and coding schemes both yield quantitative measures. In ratings, the person indicates his/her judgment of the behavior on a continuum. Ratings are sometimes completed in retrospect. Coding schemes are used to categorize observed behavior as it occurs.

INFOTRAC COLLEGE EDITION

Use InfoTrac College Edition and locate a quantitative research article on a topic that interests you. What measuring instruments (tests, scales, etc.) were used to gather the data in this study? Were the instruments standardized or researcher-made? Did the researcher believe that the tools were satisfactory for the purpose?

Chapter 9

Validity and Reliability

After studying this chapter, the student will be able to:

1 Distinguish between validity and reliability.

2 List the major sources of evidence used to support the valid interpretation of test scores.

3 Define *construct underrepresentation* and *construct-irrelevant variance,* and explain their relevance to the validity of test scores.

4 Distinguish between convergent and discriminant designs in gathering data on test–criterion relationships.

5 Discuss the relationship of social consequences and test validity.

6 Distinguish between random and systematic errors of measurement and their relationship to validity and reliability of test scores.

7 State the different sources of error in educational and psychological measures.

8 Describe the different procedures (test-retest, equivalent forms, split-half, Kuder-Richardson, and others) for estimating the reliability of a measure.

9 Compute reliability coefficients from given data.

10 Define *interobserver reliability*, and explain how it is calculated.

11 Apply the Spearman-Brown formula to determine the effect of lengthening a test on test reliability.

12 Explain the factors affecting the size of a reliability coefficient.

13 Compute the standard error of measurement and interpret score bands as indications of reliability.

14 Compute indexes to show the reliability of a criterion-referenced test.

Quantitative research always depends on measurement. There are two essential criteria of the quality of any measuring instrument: *validity* and *reliability*. Validity is the extent to which scores on a test enable one to make meaningful interpretations. Reliability indicates how consistently a test measures whatever it does measure. Researchers must inquire into the validity and reliability of the scores derived from instruments used in a study and must include this information in the research report. If a researcher's data are not obtained with valid and reliable instruments, one can have little faith in the results obtained or in the conclusions based on the results.

VALIDITY

Validity is the most important consideration in developing and evaluating measuring instruments. Historically, **validity** was defined as the extent to which an instrument measured what it claimed to measure. The focus of recent views of validity is not on the instrument itself but on the interpretation and meaning of the scores derived from the instrument. The new *Standards for Educational and Psychological Testing* (1999), prepared by the American Educational Research Association (AERA), defines validity as "the degree to which evidence and theory support the interpretations of test scores entailed by proposed uses of tests" (p. 9).

Assessing validity is important to the researcher because most instruments used in educational and psychological investigations are designed for measuring hypothetical constructs. Recall that constructs such as intelligence, creativity, anxiety, critical thinking, motivation, self-esteem, attitudes, and the like represent abstract variables derived from theory or observation. Researchers have no direct means of measuring these constructs such as exist in the physical sciences for the measurement of characteristics like length, volume, and weight. To measure such constructs, you must move from the theoretical domain surrounding the construct to an empirical level that operationalizes the construct. You do this by selecting specific sets of observable tasks believed to serve as indicators of the particular theoretical construct. Then you assume that performance (scores) on the tasks reflects the particular construct of interest as distinguished from other constructs. Tests may be imprecise measures of the constructs they are designed to assess because they either leave out something that theory says should be included or else include something that should be left out, or both. Messick (1995) identified two problems that threaten the interpretation (validity) of test scores: construct underrepresentation and construct-irrelevant variance. The term **construct underrepresentation** refers to assessment that is too narrow and fails to include important dimensions of the construct. The test may not adequately sample some kinds of content or some types of responses or psychological processes and thus fails to adequately represent the theoretical domain of the construct. For example, a test designed to measure general self-concept might measure only social self-concept and not academic and physical components of self-concept.

The term **construct-irrelevant variance** refers to the extent to which test scores are affected by processes that are extraneous to the construct. Construct-irrelevant variance could lower scores on a science achievement test for individuals with limited reading skills or limited English skills. Reading comprehension is thus a source of construct-irrelevant variance in a science achievement test.

Evidential Basis of Test Interpretation

Numerous studies may be required to build a body of evidence to support (or fail to support) a particular interpretation of test scores. The proposed interpretation is the construct of interest. The *Standards* (1999) state that the evidence for validity may be based on "test content," "response processes," "internal structure," and "relations to other variables." Using these categories does not imply that there are distinct types of validity but rather, that different types of evidence may be gathered to support the intended use of a test.

Evidence Based on Test Content

Evidence based on test content involves the test's content and its relationship to the construct it is intended to measure. The researcher seeks evidence that the test represents a balanced and adequate sampling of all the relevant skills and dimensions. This type of evidence is especially important in evaluating achievement tests. Validation of an achievement test, for instance, would look at the material covered, the wording of the questions, and the adequacy of the sample of items to measure the achievement in question.

A researcher who wished to develop a test in fourth-grade mathematics for a particular school system would need to determine what kinds of content (skills and objectives) are covered in fourth-grade classes throughout the system. After examining textbooks and talking with teachers, the researcher would prepare an outline of the topics, skills, and performances that make up fourth-grade mathematics (content domain) in that system, along with an indication of the emphasis given to each. Using the outline as a guide, the researcher would write a collection of test items that cover each topic and each objective in proportion to the emphasis given to each in the total content domain. The result should be a representative sample of the total domain of knowledge and skills included in that school system's fourth-grade math classes.

If the test were designed to be used nationally, the researcher would need to examine widely used textbooks, curriculum guides, syllabi, and so on across the country to determine what content is included in fourth-grade math. Subject matter experts could be asked to judge the adequacy of the test for measuring fourth-grade math achievement. If you were developing a test to select among applicants for a particular job, you would need to specify all the major aspects of the job and then write test items that measure each aspect. Again, qualified experts would look at the test content to judge the appropriateness and representativeness of the items making up the test.

Evidence based on content is thus mainly the result of a logical analysis. Publishers of standardized achievement tests provide extensive validity evidence of this type. However, we must stress again that an achievement test may have high validity for the purposes defined by the test maker but not be valid for a user who defines the content domain in a different way. Only the user of a test can ultimately judge its validity for his or her own purpose. For example, assume that a literature teacher emphasized an understanding of the ideas of selected authors and the relevance of those ideas in the twenty-first century. If the test the teacher later administered to measure achievement of these objectives contained mostly items asking students to match authors' names with their works and to recall their birth dates, pen names, and so forth, the teacher has failed to obtain a representative sample of the content domain and the test would have little validity for its intended purpose.

Evidence Based on Response Processes

Another way to obtain evidence about how well a test is measuring the construct of interest is to look at the **evidence based on response processes** of individuals actually taking the test. Questioning test takers about the mental processes and skills that they use when responding to the items of a test can provide information about what construct is being measured. Individuals might be asked to "think aloud" as they work through a verbal reasoning test, for instance. This procedure may reveal that the test is measuring verbal reasoning, or it may reveal that other factors such as vocabulary or reading comprehension are being measured. Examining response processes may indicate certain construct-irrelevant factors that differentially influence the performance of different subgroups. Thus it provides evidence about whether the test scores have the same meaning or can be interpreted in the same way across different subgroups.

Evidence Based on Internal Structure

Analyzing the internal structure of a test is another source of evidence relevant to validity. Using **evidence based on internal structure** looks at the intercorrelations among the items to determine whether the test is measuring a single construct or more than one. You then decide if the observed intercorrelations conform to the theory behind the construct being measured. Does the theory suggest a single construct or several components? The extent to which the observed item intercorrelations agree with the theoretical framework provides insight concerning the dimensions of the construct.

Evidence Based on Relations to Other Variables

A widely used source of validity evidence is the study of the relationship of the test scores to selected external variables. These external variables may be indicators of the criterion the test is believed to predict, as well as other tests believed to measure the same construct or tests measuring related or different constructs.

This **evidence based on relations to other variables** may be classified as *convergent* and *discriminant*. "Relationships between test scores and other measures intended to assess *similar* constructs provide convergent evidence, whereas relationships between test scores and measures purportedly of *different* constructs provide discriminant evidence" (AERA, 1999, p. 14). In the former case, the researcher tries to show that the intended construct is being measured; in the latter, he or she shows that the the wrong construct is not being measured. A mathematical reasoning test would be expected to correlate with grades in mathematics or with other math reasoning tests (convergent evidence). The math test and these other measures correlate because they all converge on the same construct. Conversely, the scores on the math reasoning test would be expected to have little or no relationship (discriminant evidence) with measures of other skills, such as reading. If a substantial correlation is found, then the test is being affected by reading ability, and, instead of measuring math reasoning, it is really measuring reading ability.

Test–Criterion Relationship

Evidence of a relationship between a test and a relevant criterion focuses on the question "How accurately can criterion performance be predicted from scores on the test?" The criterion is some outcome important to the test user. The choice of the criterion and its measurement are crucial. The worth of the whole procedure depends first and foremost on the *relevance* of the criterion. The criterion must well represent the attribute being measured or else it would be meaningless to use. For example, GPA is considered a relevant measure of success in college and is generally chosen as the criterion for validation studies of scholastic aptitude tests. A relevant criterion for a test designed to select salespeople might be the dollar value of sales made in a specified time.

It is sometimes difficult to find a relevant criterion measure, as in the validation of measures designed to predict teacher effectiveness. With neither an agreed-on description of teacher effectiveness nor an effective method of measuring that variable, it is extremely difficult to validate such instruments.

The criterion must also be *reliable*, which means that it is a consistent measure of the attribute over time or from situation to situation. If the criterion itself is not consistent, you would not expect it to relate consistently to any tests. The criterion should also be free from bias, which means that the scoring of the criterion measure itself should not be influenced by any factors other than actual performance on the criterion. For example, if ratings are used as the criterion, it is essential that the raters be trained and be very careful not to let any factors other than actual performance influence their ratings. The criterion may also be biased through contamination, which occurs when scores on the criterion are influenced by the scorer's knowledge of the individuals' predictor test scores. For example, assume that the criterion used to validate an art aptitude test is grades in art class. If the teachers who grade the students' work are aware of the students' scores on the aptitude test, this awareness may influence the teachers' evaluation of the students and hence the grades. Contamination of the criterion can be prevented by not permitting the person who grades or rates the criterion to see the original scores on the test. Historically, two designs have been distinguished for studying test–criterion relationships: predictive and concurrent. The distinction is made on the basis of the time the criterion data are collected. A predictive study gathers evidence about the relationship between scores on a test and criterion scores available at a future time. A concurrent study looks at the relationship between test scores and criterion scores obtained at the same time.

For example, in a predictive study of a foreign language aptitude test you would look at the relationship between scores on the test and the end-of-semester grades students eventually earned in the foreign language course. If you found a substantial correlation, you would have evidence that the aptitude test could be used to predict foreign language achievement. A concurrent design would look at the relationship between the aptitude test scores and any class test scores or grades already available. Predictive studies are widely used in education and industry, where tests are used for selection purposes. An extensive body of evidence supports the use of the SAT for predicting first-semester GPA in college. Concurrent studies are preferred for tests used for classification, certification, or diagnosis. For example, a new psychiatric screening device might be validated by looking at its correlation with a well-established instrument already available.

Validity Coefficient

The coefficient of correlation between test scores and criterion is called a *validity coefficient* (r_{xy}). Like any correlation coefficient, the size of a validity coefficient is influenced by the strength of the relationship between test and criterion and the range of individual differences in the group. As usual, the nearer the coefficient is to 1.00 (+ or −), the stronger the evidence is that the test is useful for the stated purpose.

Students often ask, "How high does a validity coefficient need to be?" Whether high or low, useful or not useful, depends on the purpose of the test and the context in which it is to be used. A correlation coefficient of .40 could be very helpful in cases for which no predictive instrument has previously been available. In other cases a correlation of .65 might be considered low and unsatisfactory if other predictors are available that have a higher relationship with the criterion. In general, an instrument has "good" validity as a selection device if evidence shows it has a higher correlation with the criterion than do competing instruments.

Accumulating predictive evidence requires time and patience. In some cases researchers must wait for several years to determine whether performance on a measure is useful for predicting success on a criterion.

Another procedure that is somewhat related to gathering convergent and discriminant evidence is the *known-groups technique,* in which the researcher compares the performance of two groups known to differ on the construct being measured. If the expected differences are found, that evidence supports the intended interpretation and use of the scores. You would expect that scores on a musical aptitude test, for instance, would differ for students currently enrolled in a school of music and an unselected group of college students. If an inventory measures psychological adjustment, the scores of a group previously identified as adjusted and a group previously identified as maladjusted should be markedly different on the inventory.

Another procedure is to apply an experimental manipulation and see if the scores change in the hypothesized way. You would expect the scores on a scale designed to measure anxiety to increase if individuals are put into an anxiety-provoking situation. The scores of a control group not exposed to the experimental manipulation should not be affected. If anxiety were manipulated in a controlled experiment and the resulting scores change in the predicted way, you have evidence that the scale is measuring anxiety.

Let's look at a historical example that illustrates the use of the various types of evidence important in the validation process. Doll (1935) designed the Vineland Social Maturity Scale to measure the abstract construct *social maturity.* Doll first defined the construct *social maturity* as a combination of interrelated elements of self-help, self-direction, locomotion, occupation, communication, and social relations. Reviewers of the first revised version of the test in Buros's *Mental Measurements Yearbook* (1949) tended to agree that these elements are aspects of the construct that should be incorporated in a test of social maturity. The next step in the validation process was to examine the items to see if they were appropriate for assessing the various elements of social maturity (evidence based on test content). For example, the parent of a 6-year-old is asked if the subject uses skates, sled, wagon (occupation); goes to bed unassisted (self-help); prints simple words (communication); plays simple table games (locomotion); and is trusted with money (self-direction). If the original scale had included items concerning the child's preference for certain foods or whether he or she is right-handed, these items would have been deleted, as they are not directly related to the elements in the construct. The internal structure of the scale was examined to see if it conformed to the definition of the construct (evidence based on internal structure). Doll showed that Vineland scores for occupation, self-help, and so forth correlated positively with one another. These observations provided internal support for the theory that the construct *social maturity* consists of interrelated elements and provided evidence that the Vineland scale was measuring these interrelated elements.

Another source of validity evidence was the relationship of scores to other variables external to the scale. Doll and others have shown that scores on the Vineland scale do correlate with chronological age, mental age, and with independent assessments of social maturity.

Sometimes researchers disagree on what the elements of a construct are. For example, if you think of the construct *intelligence* as primarily a combination of skills that enable an individual to cope with an academic environment, you would expect such skills to be measured in an intelligence test. If you define *intelligence* as a set of skills that are no more related to school environments than to other environments, you would not want school-specific skills incorporated into the test.

Application of the Validity Concept

Validity is always specific to the particular purpose for which the instrument is being used. "It is incorrect to use the unqualified phrase 'the validity of the test.' No test is valid for all purposes or in all situations" (AERA, 1999, p. 17). A test that has validity in one situation and for one purpose may not be valid in a different situation or for a different purpose. A teacher-made achievement test in high school chemistry might be valid for measuring end-of-year achievement in chemistry, but might not be valid for predicting achievement in college chemistry. A German proficiency test might be valid for placing undergraduates in German classes at a university, but not be a valid exit exam for German majors. Thus validation is always a responsibility of the test user as well as of the test developer.

Validity Generalization

A concern in validity studies of educational and employment tests is the extent to which evidence of validity based on test–criterion relationships can be generalized to new settings without further investigations of validity in the new setting. Research shows that test–criterion correlations may vary greatly from time to time and place to place because of the type of criterion measure used, the way the predictor is measured, the type of test takers, and the time period involved.

Validity generalization studies have used meta-analysis, which provides statistical summaries of past validation studies in similar situations. Research provides support for validity generalization in cases where the meta-analytic database is large, where the data adequately represent the type of situation to which a researcher wishes to generalize, and where there is a consistent pattern of validity evidence. In other circumstances where the findings of the meta-analytic studies are less consistent and where there are more differences between the new and old settings, it is more risky to generalize. Local validation studies providing situation-specific evidence would be more valuable.

Evidence Based on Consequences of Testing

An issue debated in recent years is the merging of evidence about the intended and unintended social *consequences* of test use into the concept of validity. Messick (1995) believes that a consideration of the social consequences of test use and interpretation is definitely an aspect of validity. Messick distinguishes adverse consequences that result from valid descriptions of individual and group differences from adverse consequences that stem from construct underrepresentation and construct-irrelevant variance (p. 744). The latter adverse consequences should be investigated in the validation process, whereas the former consequences represent problems of social policy. Researchers need to ensure that low scores do not occur because "the assessment is missing something relevant to the construct that, if present, would have permitted the affected persons to display their competence. Moreover, low scores should not occur because the measurement contains something irrelevant that interferes with the affected persons' demonstration of competence" (p. 746).

Wiley (1991), however, argued that although considering adverse consequences or what he calls "use errors" may be socially important, it "would needlessly complicate the conception and definition of test validity" (p. 88). Popham (1997) agreed that test use consequences should be addressed, but should not be considered an aspect of measurement validity. He wrote, "Social consequences of test use are important, but must not be confused with the validity of interpretation based on examinee's performance" (p. 9).

Agreeing with Messick, the *Standards* (AERA, 1999) states that evidence about consequences may be directly relevant to validity when it can be traced to a source such as construct underrepresentation or construct-irrelevant components. "Evidence about consequences that cannot be so traced—that in fact reflects valid differences in performance—is crucial in informing policy decisions but falls outside the technical purview of validity" (AERA, p. 16). For example, assume that you find different hiring rates for members of different groups as a consequence of using an employment test. If the difference is caused by an unequal distribution of the skills being measured, and if in fact those skills are crucial contributors to job performance, then the finding of group differences does *not* imply any lack of validity for the intended interpretation and use of the test. If, however, the test measured skill differences unrelated to job performance, validity would be an issue. For example, if an employment test requiring a high reading level were used to select applicants for a job that required only a minimal level of reading proficiency, then validity would be called into question.

In summary, test developers should try to make sure that no adverse social consequences can be traced to any sources of test invalidity such as construct underrepresentation and construct-irrelevant variance. Beyond this rule, it is probably unrealistic to include unanticipated consequences in the evaluation of test validity. The entire issue of *Educational Measurement: Issues and Practice* (17 [2]) of summer 1998 is devoted to a discussion of consequential aspects of validity. Interested readers may wish to consult this reference.

RELIABILITY

As we mentioned at the beginning of this chapter, the **reliability** of a measuring instrument is the degree of consistency with which it measures whatever it is measuring. This quality is essential in any kind of measurement. A post office will soon take action to repair a scale if users find that the scale sometimes underestimates and sometimes overestimates the weight of packages. Psychologists and educators are equally concerned about the consistency of their measuring devices when they attempt to measure such complex constructs as scholastic aptitude, achievement, motivation, anxiety, and the like. They would not consider a scholastic aptitude test worthwhile if it yielded markedly different results each time it was used with the same subjects. People who use such measuring instruments must identify and use techniques that will help them determine to what extent their measuring instruments are consistent and reliable.

Theory of Reliability

As a way of distinguishing the reliability concept from the validity concept, it is useful to identify *random errors of measurement* and *systematic errors of measurement*. Random error is error that is a result of pure chance. Random errors of measurement may inflate or depress any subject's score in an unpredictable manner. For example, one element in a physical fitness test for elementary students is the baseball throw. Subjects are instructed to throw a baseball as far as they can, and the distance of the throw is measured. Although the object of the test is to get a score that is typical of a subject's performance, certainly if you had a single subject throw a baseball on several occasions, you would find that the child does not throw it the same distance every time.

Assume you had each student make a throw on two consecutive days. If you then compared the two scores (distance thrown) for each student, you would find that they were almost never exactly the same. Most of the differences would be small, but some would be moderately large and a few, quite large. The results are inconsistent from one day's throw to the next. One throw is not completely reliable as a measure of a student's throwing ability. Three types of chance, or random, influences lead to inconsistency between scores achieved on the two days:

1. *The student may actually change* from one day to the next. On one day he or she may feel better than on the other. On one day the student may be more motivated or less fatigued. Perhaps the student's father, hearing about the task, begins coaching the child in throwing a baseball.

2. *The task itself may change* for the two measurements. For example, the ball used one day may be firm, whereas on the second day it may be wet and soggy. One day perhaps the examiner permits the students to take a running start up to the throwing line, whereas on the second day they are permitted only a couple of steps. These changes may help some students more than others.

3. *The limited sample* of behavior results in an unstable score. A small sample of behavior is subject to many kinds of chance influences. Maybe there is a gust of wind as the ball is thrown. Maybe the student loses balance when starting to throw the ball, or maybe his or her fingers slip while gripping the ball.

Reliability is concerned with the effect of such random errors of measurement on the consistency of scores. But some errors involved in measurement are predictable or systematic. Using the example of the baseball throw, imagine a situation in which the instructions for the throw are given in English—but not all the subjects understand English.

The scores of the non-English-speaking subjects could be systematically depressed because the subjects do not comprehend what they are expected to do. Such systematic errors of measurement are a validity problem. The validity of a test is lowered whenever scores are systematically changed by the influence of anything other than what you are trying to measure (irrelevant variance). In this instance you are measuring not only baseball-throwing ability but also, in part, English comprehension.

To decide whether you are dealing with reliability or validity, you determine whether you are considering random errors or systematic errors. If a class is being given the baseball throw test and two balls are being employed, one firm and one soggy, and it is purely a matter of chance who gets which ball, the variation caused by the ball used is a reliability problem. The variation caused by the ball represents random error that affects the consistency of the measurements. If class members are called to take the test in alphabetical order and it is a rainy day and the one baseball provided gets wetter with each successive throw, the variation caused by the increasing wetness of the ball is a validity problem. Scores in this case are increased for those near the beginning of the alphabet and decreased for those near the end. The validity of the baseball throw scores is lessened because the scores reflect not only baseball-throwing prowess but alphabetical order as well. This is an instance of systematic error that affects the validity of the measurement.

Reliability is concerned with how consistently you are measuring whatever you are measuring. It is not concerned with the meaning and interpretation of the scores—that is the validity question. A measuring instrument can be reliable without being valid. However, it cannot be valid unless it is first reliable. For example, someone could decide to measure intelligence by determining the circumference of the head. The measures might be very consistent from time to time (reliable), but this method would not be considered valid because circumference of the head does not correlate with any other criteria of intelligence, nor is it predicted by any theory of intelligence.

Reliability is affected by random errors, which are any factors that will result in discrepancies between individuals' scores in repeated administrations of a single measuring instrument or from one set of items to an equivalent set.

Random errors arise from a number of sources. Errors may be inherent in the instrument itself. Brevity of a test is a major source of unreliability. For example, if a test is very short, those subjects who happen to know the few answers required will get higher scores than they deserve, whereas those who do not know those few answers get lower scores than they deserve. For example, if a test is given to assess how well students know the capitals of the fifty states, but only five questions are asked, it is possible that a student who knows only ten capitals could get all five correct, whereas a student who knows forty could get none correct. In a short test, luck is more of a factor than in a long test. If a test is so easy that everyone knows most of the answers, the subjects' relative scores again depend on only a few questions and luck is a major factor. If questions are ambiguous, "lucky" subjects respond in the way the examiner intended, whereas "unlucky" subjects respond in another equally correct manner, but their answers are scored as incorrect. The scoring procedure also affects reliability. Objectivity and precise scoring procedures enhance reliability, whereas subjectivity and vague scoring procedures depress it.

Errors may be inherent in the administration of the instrument. An inexperienced person may depart from standardized procedures in administering or scoring the test. Testing conditions such as light, heat, ventilation, and the presence of distractions may affect performance. Instructions for taking the test may be ambiguous. There is also pupil error—that is, fluctuations in examinees' motivation, interest, fatigue, physical condition, anxiety, and other mental and emotional factors affect the test results. A pupil's breaking a pencil point on a timed test would increase the error component in the results.

Equations for Reliability

It is generally accepted that all measurements of human qualities contain random error. Although scientists cannot remove all this error, they do have ways to assess the aggregate magnitude of measurement errors. Reliability procedures are concerned with determining the degree of inconsistency in scores caused by random error.

When you administer a test to a student, you get a score, which can be called the *observed score*. If you had tested this student on some other occasion with the same instrument, you probably would not have obtained exactly the same observed score, because of the influence of random errors of measurement. Assuming that test scores have an error component implies that there is a hypothetical error-free score for an individual that would be obtained if the measurement were perfectly accurate. This error-free value is called the individual's *true score* on the test. The true score is conceptualized as "the hypothetical average score resulting from many repetitions of the test or alternate forms of the instrument" (AERA, p. 25). We conclude, therefore, that every test score consists of two components: the *true score* plus some *error of measurement*. As we noted earlier, this error component may be caused by any one, or a combination, of a number of factors associated with variations within the examinee from time to time or with the test and its administration.

The reliability of a test is expressed mathematically as the best estimate of what proportion of the total variance of scores on the test is true variance. As we explained in Chapter 5, variance is an index of the spread of a set of scores. If you administer a test to a group of students, some of the spread (variance) of the students' scores is due to true differences among the group and some of the spread (variance) is due to errors of measurement.

The idea of error component and true component in a single test score may be represented mathematically by formula 9.1:

$$X = T + E \qquad (9.1)$$

where

$$X = \text{observed score}$$
$$T = \text{true score component}$$
$$E = \text{error-of-measurement component}$$

The true-score component may be defined as the score an individual would make under conditions in which a perfect measuring device is used. The error-of-measurement component can be either positive or negative. If it is positive, the individual's true score will be overestimated by the observed score; if it is negative, the person's true score will be underestimated. Because researchers assume that an error of measurement is just as likely to be positive as it is to be negative, then researchers can conclude that the sum of the errors and the mean of the errors would both be 0 if the same measuring instrument or an equivalent form of the instrument were administered an infinite number of times to a subject. Under these conditions, the true component would be defined as the individual's mean score on an infinite number of measurements. The true score is a theoretical concept, because an infinite number of administrations of a test to the same subject is not feasible.

In the usual research situation, the investigator has one measure on each of a group of subjects. In other words, the researcher has a single set of test scores to consider. Each observed score has a true-score component and an error-score component. It has been shown mathematically that the variance of the observed scores of a large group of subjects (σ_x^2) is equal to the variance of their true scores (σ_t^2) plus the variance of their errors of measurement (σ_e^2) or

$$\sigma_x^2 = \sigma_t^2 + \sigma_e^2 \qquad (9.2)$$

Reliability may be defined theoretically as the ratio of the true-score variance to the observed-score variance in a set of scores, as expressed by the following formula:

$$r_{xx} = \frac{\sigma_t^2}{\sigma_x^2} \qquad (9.3)$$

where

$$r_{xx} = \text{reliability of the test}$$
$$\sigma_t^2 = \text{variance of the true scores}$$
$$\sigma_x^2 = \text{variance of the observed scores}$$

Reliability is the proportion of the variance in the observed scores that is free of error. This notion can be expressed in the following formula, derived from formulas 9.2 and 9.3:

$$r_{xx} = 1 - \frac{\sigma_e^2}{\sigma_x^2} \qquad (9.4)$$

The *coefficient of reliability* r_{xx} can range from 1, when there is no error in the measurement, to 0, when the measurement is all error. (When there is no error in the measurement, σ_e^2 in the preceding equation is 0 and $r_{xx} = 1$. If measurement is all error, $\sigma_e^2 = \sigma_x^2$ and $r_{xx} = 0$.) This degree of error is indicated by the degree of departure of the reliability coefficient from 1. A coefficient of .80 on a test, for example, indicates the best estimate is that 80 percent of the observed variance in the scores is true variance and 20 percent is error. Thus the greater the error, the more the reliability coefficient is depressed below 1 and the lower the reliability. Conversely, if the reliability coefficient is near 1, the instrument has relatively little error and high reliability.

Approaches to Reliability

A test is reliable to the extent that the scores made by an individual remain nearly the same in repeated measurements. There are two approaches to expressing the reliability of a set of measurements.

The first approach indicates the amount of variation to be expected within a set of repeated measurements of a *single* individual. If it were possible to weigh an individual on 200 scales, you would get a frequency distribution of scores to represent his or her weight. This frequency distribution would have an average value, which you could consider the "true" weight. It would also have a standard deviation, indicating the spread. This standard deviation is called the **standard error of measurement,** because it is the standard deviation of the "errors" of measuring the weight for one person. With psychological or educational data, researchers do not often make repeated measurements on an individual. Time would not permit such repetition, and in addition, the practice and fatigue effects associated with repeated measurement would have an influence on the scores. Thus, instead of measuring one person many times, researchers measure a large, diverse group on two occasions. Using the pair of measurements for each individual, they can estimate what the spread of scores would have been for the average person had the measurement been made again and again. Reliability of measurement from the second approach indicates the extent to which each individual maintains the same relative position in the group. With a reliable test, the person who scores highest on a test today should also be one of the highest scorers the next time the same test is given. Each person in the group would stay in approximately the same relative position. The more individuals shift in relative position, the lower the test's reliability. You can compute a coefficient of correlation between two administrations of the same test to determine the extent to which the individuals maintain the same relative position. This coefficient is called a *reliability coefficient* (r_{xx}). A reliability coefficient of 1.00 indicates that each individual's relative position on the two admnistrations remained exactly the same and the test would be perfectly reliable.

Thus the consistency of a measure is indicated by its standard error of measurement or by its reliability coefficient.

The Reliability Coefficients

There are three broad categories of reliability coefficients: (1) coefficients derived from correlating individuals' scores on the same test administered on different occasions (test-retest coefficients); (2) coefficients derived from correlating individuals' scores on different sets of equivalent items (alternate-form coefficient); and (3) coefficients based on the relationship among scores derived from individual items or subsets of items within a test (internal-consistency coefficients). The internal consistency coefficient requires only a single administration of a test, whereas the other coefficients require two administrations.

Test-Retest Reliability

An obvious way to estimate the reliability of a test is to administer it to the same group of individuals on two occasions and correlate the paired scores. The correlation coefficient obtained by this procedure is called a **test–retest reliability coefficient.** For example, a physical fitness test may be given to a class during one week and the same test given again the following week. If the test has good reliability, each individual's relative position on the second administration of the test will be near his or her relative position on the first administration of the test.

The test-retest reliability coefficient, because it indicates consistency of subjects' scores over time, is sometimes referred to as a *coefficient of stability.* It tells you whether you can generalize from the score a person receives on one occasion to a score that person would receive if the test had been given at a different time.

A test-retest coefficient assumes that the characteristic being measured by the test is stable over time, so any change in scores from one time to another is caused by random error. The error may be caused by the condition of the subjects themselves or to testing conditions. The test-retest coefficient also assumes there is no practice effect or memory effect. For example, students may learn something just from taking a test and thus will react differently on the second taking of the test. These practice effects from the first testing will not likely be the same across all students, thus lowering the reliability estimate. If the interval of time is short, there may also be a memory effect; students may mark a question the same way they did previously just because they remember marking it that way the first time. This memory effect tends to inflate the reliability estimate, but it can be controlled somewhat by increasing the time between the first test and the retest. However, if the time between testings is too long differential learning may be a problem—that is, students will learn different amounts during the interval, which would affect the reliability coefficient.

Because of these problems, the test-retest procedure is not usually appropriate for tests in the cognitive domain. Use of this procedure in schools is largely restricted to measures of physical fitness and athletic prowess.

Alternate-Forms Reliability

Researchers use the **alternate-forms technique** of estimating reliability, which is also referred to as the *equivalent-forms* or *parallel-forms technique,* when it is probable that subjects will recall their responses to the test items. Here, rather than correlating the results of two administrations of the same test to the same group, the researcher correlates the results of alternate (equivalent) forms of the test administered to the same individuals. If the two forms are administered at essentially the same time (in immediate succession), the resulting reliability coefficient is called the **coefficient of equivalence.** This measure reflects variations in performance from one specific set of items to another. It indicates whether you can generalize a student's score to what the student would receive if another form of the same test had been given. The question is, To what extent does the student's performance depend on the particular set of items used in the test?

If subjects are tested with one form on one occasion and with an equivalent form on a second occasion and their scores on the two forms are correlated, the resulting coefficient is called the **coefficient of stability and equivalence.** This coefficient reflects two aspects of test reliability: variations in performance from one time to another, as well as variations from one form of the test to another. A high coefficient of stability and equivalence indicates that the two forms are measuring the same performance and measuring consistently over time. This is the most demanding and the most rigorous measure available for determining the reliability of a test.

Designing alternate forms of a test that are truly equivalent is the major problem with this technique of estimating reliability. If a successful design is not achieved, then the variation in scores from one form to another could not be considered error variance. Alternate forms of a test are independently constructed tests that must meet the same specifications—that is, they must have the same number of items, instructions, time limits, format, content, range, and level of difficulty—but the actual questions are not the same. Ideally you should have pairs of equivalent items and assign one of each pair to each form. In a world geography test, for example, Form A might ask, "On what continent is the Nile River?" while Form B asks, "On what continent is the Amazon River?" Form A might ask, "What is the capital of Italy?" and Form B, "What is the capital of France?" The distribution of the test scores must also be equivalent.

The alternate-forms technique is recommended when you want to avoid the problem of recall or practice effect and in cases when you have available a large number of test items from which to select equivalent samples. Researchers generally consider that the equivalent-forms procedure provides the best estimate of the reliability of academic and psychological measures.

Internal-Consistency Measures of Reliability

Other reliability procedures are designed to determine whether all the items in a test are measuring the same thing. These are called the **internal-consistency procedures** and require only a single administration of one form of a test.

Split-Half Reliability

The simplest of the internal consistency procedures, known as the *split-half,* artificially splits the test into two halves and correlates the individuals' scores on the two halves. Researchers administer the test to a group, and later divide the items into two halves; obtain the scores for each individual on the two halves, and calculate a coefficient of correlation. This **split-half reliability coefficient** is like a coefficient of equivalence because it reflects fluctuations from one sample of items to another. If each subject has a very similar position on the two halves, the test has high reliability. If there is little consistency in positions, the reliability is low. The method requires only one form of a test, there is no time lag involved, and the same physical and mental influences will be operating on the subjects as they take the two halves. A problem with this method is in splitting the test to obtain two comparable halves. If, through item analysis, you establish the difficulty level of each item, you can place each item into one of the two halves on the basis of equivalent difficulty and similarity of content. The most common procedure, however, is to correlate the scores on the odd-numbered items of the test with the scores on the even-numbered items.

The correlation coefficient computed between the two halves systematically underestimates the reliability of the entire test. If everything else is equal, longer tests are more reliable than shorter tests. Therefore, the correlation between the 50 odd-numbered and 50 even-numbered items on a 100-item test is a reliability estimate for a 50-item test, not a 100-item test. To transform the split-half correlation into an appropriate reliability estimate for the entire test, the **Spearman-Brown prophecy formula** is employed:

$$r_{xx} = \frac{2r_{1/2\ 1/2}}{1 + r_{1/2\ 1/2}} \tag{9.5}$$

where

r_{xx} = estimated reliability of the entire test
$r_{1/2\ 1/2}$ = Pearson r correlation between the two halves

For example, if we find a correlation coefficient of .65 between two halves of a test, the estimated reliability of the entire test, using the Spearman-Brown formula, would be

$$r_{xx} = \frac{(2)(.65)}{1 + .65} = .79$$

The Spearman-Brown procedure is based on the assumption that the two halves are parallel. As this assumption is seldom exactly correct, in practice the split-half technique with the Spearman-Brown correction tends to overestimate the reliability that would be obtained with test-retest or equivalent-forms procedures. Bear this in mind when evaluating the reliabilities of competing tests.

Split-half reliability is an appropriate technique to use when time-to-time fluctuation in estimating reliability is to be avoided and when the test is relatively long. For short tests the other techniques, such as test-retest or equivalent-forms, are more appropriate. The split-half procedure is not appropriate to use with speed tests, because it yields spuriously high coefficients of equivalence in such tests. A speed test is one that purposefully includes easy items so that the scores mainly depend on the speed with which subjects can respond. Errors are minor, and most of the items are correct up to the point where time is called. If a student responds to fifty items, his or her split-half score is likely to be 25–25; if another student marks sixty items, his split-half score is likely to be 30–30, and so on. Because individuals' scores on odd- and even-numbered items are very nearly identical, within-individual variation is minimized and the correlation between the halves would be nearly perfect. Thus other procedures are recommended for use with speed tests.

Homogeneity Measures

Other internal-consistency measures of reliability do not require splitting the test into halves and scoring each half separately. These procedures assess the inter-item consistency, or *homogeneity,* of the items. They reflect two sources of error: (1) the content sampling as in split-half and (2) the heterogeneity of the behavior domain sampled. The more heterogeneous the domain, the lower the inter-item consistency and, conversely, the more homogeneous the domain, the higher the inter-item consistency.

Kuder-Richardson Procedures　　Kuder and Richardson (1937) developed procedures that have been widely used to determine homogeneity. Probably the best known index of homogeneity is the **Kuder–Richardson formula** 20, which is based on the proportion of correct and incorrect responses to each of the items on a test.

$$r_{xx} = \frac{K}{K-1}\left(\frac{s_x^2 - \Sigma pq}{s_x^2}\right) \qquad \text{K-R 20 (9.6)}$$

where

r_{xx} = reliability of the whole test
K = number of items on the test
s_x^2 = variance of scores on the total test (squared standard deviation)
p = proportion of correct responses on a single item
q = proportion of incorrect responses on the same item

The product pq is computed for each item, and the products are summed over all items to give Σpq. Kuder-Richardson 20 is applicable to tests whose items are scored dichotomously (that is, as either right or wrong). Many machine-scoring procedures for tests routinely provide a K-R 20 coefficient along with a split-half coefficient.

Another formula (Kuder-Richardson 21) is computationally simpler but requires the assumption that all items in the test are of equal difficulty. This assumption is often unrealistic.

$$r_{xx} = \frac{Ks_x^2 - \overline{X}(K - \overline{X})}{s_x^2(K - 1)} \qquad \text{K-R 21 (9.7)}$$

where

r_{xx} = reliability of the whole test
K = number of items in the test
s_x^2 = variance of the scores
$\overline{X}$ = mean of the scores

This method is by far the least time consuming of all the reliability estimation procedures. It involves only one administration of a test and employs only easily available information. As such, it can be recommended to teachers for classroom use.

For example, suppose a teacher has administered a fifty-item test to a class and has computed the mean as 40 and the standard deviation as 6. Applying formula 9.7, the reliability could be estimated as follows:

$$r_{xx} = \frac{(50)6^2 - 40(50 - 40)}{6^2(50 - 1)} = \frac{1800 - 400}{1764} = .79$$

Because the Kuder-Richardson procedures stress the equivalence of all the items in a test, they are especially appropriate when the intention of the test is to measure a single trait. For a test designed to measure several traits, the Kuder-Richardson reliability estimate is usually lower than reliability estimates based on a correlational procedure.

Analysts have shown through deductive reasoning that the Kuder-Richardson reliability for any test is mathematically equivalent to the mean of the split-half reliability estimates computed for every possible way of splitting the test in half. This fact helps explain the relationship between the two procedures. If a test is of uniform difficulty and is measuring a single trait, any one way of splitting that test in half is as likely as any other to yield similar half scores. Therefore, the Spearman-Brown and Kuder-Richardson methods will yield similar estimates. If a test has items of varying difficulty and is measuring various traits, the Kuder-Richardson estimate is expected to be lower than the split-half estimate. For example, suppose a secretarial skills test samples typing, shorthand, spelling, and English grammar skills. In applying the split-half method, the test maker would assign equal numbers of items from each subtest to each half of the test. If the test is doing a good job of measuring this combination of skills, the split-half reliability will be high. The Kuder-Richardson method, which assesses the extent to which all the items are equivalent to one another, would yield a considerably lower reliability estimate.

Coefficient Alpha Another widely used measure of homogeneity is **coefficient alpha,** also called **Cronbach alpha** after Lee Cronbach (1951). Coefficient alpha has wider applications than the K-R 20 formula. When items are scored dichotomously, it yields the same result as the K-R 20, but it can also be used when items are not scored dichotomously. The formula for alpha is as follows:

$$\alpha = \left(\frac{K}{K - 1}\right)\left(\frac{s_x^2 - \Sigma s_i^2}{s_x^2}\right) \tag{9.8}$$

where

K = number of items on the test
Σs_i^2 = sum of variances of the item scores
s_x^2 = variance of the test scores (all K items)

The formula for alpha is similar to the K-R 20 except that the Σpq is replaced by Σs^2, the sum of the variances of item scores. To calculate, you determine the variance of all the scores for *each* item and then add these variances across all items to get Σx_i^2.

Researchers use Cronbach alpha when measures have items that are not scored simply as right or wrong, such as attitude scales or essay tests. The item score may take on a range of values as, for example, on a Likert attitude scale the individual may receive a score from 1 to 5 depending on which option was chosen. Similarly, on essay tests a different number of points may be assigned to each answer. Many computer programs for

Table 9.1 *Summary of Reliability Coefficients*

		NUMBER OF TEST FORMS REQUIRED	
		One	Two
NUMBER OF ADMINISTRATIONS REQUIRED	One	Split-half K-R 20 Coefficient alpha	Equivalent-forms (no time lapse)
	Two	Test-retest	Equivalent-forms (time lapse)

reliability, such as the one included in SPSS, provide a coefficient alpha as the index of reliability.

If the test items are heterogeneous—that is, they measure more than one trait or attribute—the reliability index as computed by either coefficient alpha or K-R 20 will be lowered. Furthermore, these formulas are not appropriate for timed tests, because item variances will be accurate only if each item has been attempted by every person.

Table 9.1 presents a summary of the different types of reliability coefficients arranged according to the number of forms and number of administrations required.

Interpretation of Reliability Coefficients

The interpretation of a reliability coefficient should be based on a number of considerations. Certain factors affect reliability coefficients, and unless these factors are taken into account, any interpretation of reliability will be superficial.

1. *The reliability of a test is in part a function of the length of the test.* The longer the test, the greater its reliability. A test usually consists of a number of sample items that are, theoretically, drawn from a universe of test items. You know from what you have studied about sampling that the greater the sample size, the more representative it is expected to be of the population from which it is drawn. This is also true of tests. If it were possible to use the entire universe of items, the score of a person who takes the test would be his or her true score. A theoretical universe of items consists of an infinite number of questions and is obviously not a practical possibility. You therefore construct a test that is a sample from such a theoretical universe. The greater the length of this test (that is, the greater the number of items included in the test), the more representative it should be of the true scores of the people who take it. Because reliability is the extent to which a test represents the true scores of individuals, the longer the test, the greater its reliability, provided that all the items in the test belong in the universe of items.

2. *Reliability is in part a function of group heterogeneity.* The reliability coefficient increases as the spread, or heterogeneity, of the subjects who take the test increases. Conversely, the more homogeneous the group is with respect to the trait being measured, the lower will be the reliability coefficient. One explanation of reliability is that it is the extent to which researchers can place individuals, relative to others in their groups, according to certain traits. Such placement is easier when you are dealing with measures that fall in a large range rather than those that fall in a small range. It does not take a sensitive device to determine the placement of children in a distribution according to their weights when the age range of these children is from 5 to 15. In fact, this placement is possible with some degree of accuracy even without using any measuring device. It does take a sensitive device, however, to carry out the same placement if all those who are to be compared and placed in the distribution are 5 years old. Thus the heterogeneity of the group with whom a measuring instrument is used is a factor that affects the reliability of that instrument. The more heterogeneous the group used in the reliability study, the higher the reliability coefficient. Keep this fact in mind when selecting a standardized test. The publisher may report a high reliability coefficient based on a sample with a wide range of ability. However, when the test is used with a group having a much narrower range of ability, the reliability will be lower.

3. *The reliability of a test is in part a function of the ability of the individuals who take that test.* A test may be reliable at one level of ability but unreliable at another level. The questions in a test may be difficult and beyond the ability level of those who take it—or the questions may be easy for the majority of the subjects. This difficulty level affects the reliability of the test. When a test is difficult, the subjects are guessing on most of the questions and a low reliability coefficient will result. When it is easy, all subjects have correct responses on most of the items and only a few difficult items are discriminating among subjects. Again, we would expect a low reliability. There is no simple rule by which you can determine how difficult, or how easy, a test should be. That depends on the type of test, the purpose, and the population for which it is being constructed.

4. *Reliability is in part a function of the specific technique used for its estimation.* Different procedures for estimating the reliability of tests result in different coefficients of reliability. The alternate-forms with time lapse technique gives a lower estimation of reliability than either test-retest or split-half procedures because in this technique form-to-form as well as time-to-time fluctuation is present. The split-half method, in contrast, results in higher reliability coefficients than do its alternatives because in most tests some degree of speed is involved, and to that extent the reliability coefficient is overestimated. Thus, in evaluating the reliability of a test, you would give preference to a test whose reliability coefficient has been estimated by the alternate-forms technique, rather than by other techniques, when the reported reliabilities are similar. Standardized test manuals

report reliability coefficients based on test-retest and alternate forms techniques, but teachers generally do not use these procedures for estimating reliability. Repeated testing and alternate forms are not feasible in most classroom situations. Instead, teachers use the split-half, the Kuder-Richardson, or one of the other measures of internal consistency as a measures of reliability.

5. *Reliability is in part a function of the nature of the variable being measured.* Some variables of interest to researchers yield consistent measures more often than do other variables. For instance, because academic achievement is relatively easy to measure, most established tests of academic achievement have quite high reliability (coefficients of +.90 or higher). Aptitude tests that are designed to predict future behavior—a more difficult task—have somewhat lower reliability (.80 or lower). Reliable measures of personality variables are most difficult to obtain; thus these measures typically have only moderate reliability (.60 to .70).

What is the minimum reliability acceptable for an instrument? Perhaps the best response to this question is that a good reliability is one that is as good as or better than the reliability of competing measures. A spelling achievement test with a reliability of .80 is unsatisfactory if competing tests have reliability coefficients of .90 or better. A coefficient of .80 for a test of creativity would be judged excellent if other tests of the same construct have reliabilities of .60 or less.

The degree of reliability you need in a measure depends to a great extent on the use you will make of the results. The need for accurate measurement increases as the consequences of decisions and interpretation become more important. If the measurement results are to be used for making a decision about a group or for research purposes, or if an erroneous initial decision can be easily corrected, scores with modest reliability (coefficients in the range of .50 to .60) may be acceptable. But if the results are to be used as a basis for making decisions about individuals, especially important or irreversible decisions (such as rejection or admission of candidates to a professional school or the placement of children in special education classes), only instruments with the highest reliability are acceptable. Nunnally (1967) stated that in such situations a reliability of .90 is the minimum that should be tolerated, and a reliability of .95 should be the desired standard.

Standard Error of Measurement

As we explained earlier in this chapter, the reliability, stability, or dependability of a test may also be expressed in terms of the standard error of measurement, which provides an estimate of the range of variation in a set of repeated measurements of the same thing. Returning to the example of the baseball throw, you would expect with repeated administration, by chance, to obtain a number of different scores for the same individual. You would have a frequency distribution of scores. This frequency distribution has a mean, which is the best approximation of the true score. The distribution also has a standard deviation, indicating the extent of the variation in the scores. Because this standard deviation is the standard deviation of the errors of measurement, it is called the *standard error of measurement*. If you were to construct a frequency polygon showing this distribution of scores, its shape would approximate that of the normal curve. Measurement errors are normally distributed; there may be many small errors, but there will be few large ones. The standard deviation of this distribution of errors (standard error of measurement, s_M) would give an estimate of how frequently errors of a given size might be expected to occur when the test is used.

In many situations you do not have repeated measures, but you can get an estimate of the standard error of measurement by using the reliability coefficient:

$$s_M = s_x \sqrt{1 - r_{xx}}$$

where

$$s_M = \text{standard error of measurement}$$
$$s_x = \text{standard deviation of test scores}$$
$$r_{xx} = \text{reliability coefficient}$$

If an aptitude test has a reliability coefficient of .96 and a standard deviation of 15, then

$$s_M = 15\sqrt{1 - .96} = 15\sqrt{.04} = 3.$$

The standard error of measurement is an index of the expected variability of obtained scores around the true score. The s_M can be interpreted as the standard deviation of the error score associated with an observed score and can be interpreted like any other standard deviation. Given a student's obtained score, you use the s_M to determine the range of score values that will, with a given probability, include the true score. This range of scores is referred to as a *confidence interval*. If it can be assumed that the errors of measurement are normally distributed about a given score and equally distributed throughout the score range, you could be 68 percent confident that a person's true score lies within one s_M on either side of the observed score. For example, if a subject has an observed score of 110 on an aptitude test where the standard error of measurement is 3, you could infer at the 68 percent confidence level that the subject's true score lies somewhere between 107 and 113. Or you can state at the 95 percent confidence level that the true score will fall within $\pm 1.96\ s_M$ of the obtained score (between 104 and 116). You can also use the standard error of measurement to determine how much variability could be expected on retesting the individual. If the subject could be retested on the same aptitude test a number of times, you could expect that in about two-thirds of the retests the scores would fall within a range of 6 points, and in 95 percent of retest scores they would fall within a range of 12 points.

The standard error of measurement (s_M) and the reliability coefficient (r_{xx}) are alternative ways of expressing test reliability. How precise an estimate of the true score any obtained score will be is indicated by the size of the standard error of measurement and the reliability coefficient. Look for a low standard error of measurement or a high reliability coefficient as indicators of a test's reliability. No one method of estimating reliability is optimal in all situations. The standard error of measurement is usually recommended for use when interpreting individual scores and the reliability coefficient for use when comparing the consistency of different tests. You always want scores that are sufficiently consistent and accurate to justify anticipated uses and interpretations.

It is meaningless, however, to make a general statement that a test is "reliable." You must report the methods used to estimate the reliability index, the nature of the group from which data were derived, and the conditions under which data were obtained. Potential users of a test then must take responsibility for determining if the reliability data would apply to their population.

Reliability of Criterion-Referenced Tests

Developing satisfactory methods for assessing the reliability of criterion-referenced tests has been more difficult. Recall that criterion-referenced tests are used to determine an individual's status with respect to a well-defined set of content objectives. Reliability of this type of test is concerned with the consistency with which this status is estimated. Does the individual have the same level of proficiency on the two administrations of the test? The traditional reliability procedures, such as correlation and K-R 20, are not considered appropriate for criterion-referenced tests, because these procedures depend on the variability of the individuals for which they are computed. On criterion-referenced tests, there is typically little or no variability in scores because training continues until the skill is mastered or nearly mastered. The restricted variability, or spread, of scores will result in low or near-zero estimates of reliability, even though the test may be internally consistent and highly stable.

Several procedures have been suggested for estimating the reliability of criterion-referenced tests. A relatively simple procedure involves administering two equivalent forms of the test, or the same test, on two occasions and finding the consistency of the decisions reached. Researchers determine the consistency of the results by finding the percentage of people for whom the same decision (mastery or nonmastery) is made on both administrations. This index is referred to as the **agreement coefficient** p_0.

For example, the results displayed in Table 9.2 were obtained when two equivalent forms of a criterion-referenced test were administered to a sample of 100 students. In this situation, 70 students were consistently classified as masters and 14 students were consistently classified as nonmasters. The agreement coefficient is the proportion of the total subjects consistently classified on the two administrations of the test, or

$$p_0 = \frac{a + d}{N} = \frac{70 + 14}{100} = \frac{84}{100} = .84 \tag{9.10}$$

where

p_0 = agreement coefficient
a = number classified as masters on both administrations
d = number classified as nonmasters on both administrations
N = total number of subjects

Table 9.2   *Decisions Based on Forms 1 and 2*

		FORM 1		
		Master	Nonmaster	
FORM 2	Master	(a) 70	(b) 10	80
	Nonmaster	(c) 6	(d) 14	20
		76	24	100 (N)

Thus 84 percent of the subjects were classified consistently and .84 is the reliability index of this test. If classifications as master or nonmaster are consistent for all examinees on both administrations, the agreement coefficient equals 1, the maximum value.

Some agreement in classifications as master or nonmaster between two administrations is expected merely by chance; that is, even if classifications were made randomly, some individuals would be expected to fall in cells (a) and (d) in the example. Some writers (Swaminathan, Hambleton, & Algina, 1974) therefore suggested using coefficient kappa, κ, a statistic that takes *chance agreement* into consideration. The kappa coefficient refers to the proportion of consistent classifications observed *beyond* that expected by chance.

The rationale of kappa coefficient is straightforward. First calculate the percentage of cases expected to have consistent classification even if there were no genuine relationship between the tests—that is, if the classification on the two administrations were completely independent. This index is referred to as the *expected chance agreement, ρ_c*. The expected chance agreement is subtracted from the observed agreement $\rho_o - \rho_c$ to obtain the actual increase over chance consistency; this quantity is then divided by $1 - \rho_o - \rho_c$, the maximum possible increase in decision consistency beyond chance, to yield κ, the kappa coefficient. Thus the expected chance agreement is shown by the following formula:

$$\rho_c = \frac{(a + b)(a + c) + (c + d)(b + d)}{N^2} \tag{9.11}$$

where

$$\rho_c = \text{proportion of agreement expected by chance}$$

$$\kappa = \frac{\rho_o - \rho_c}{1 - \rho_c} \tag{9.12}$$

where

κ = proportion of agreement *above* that expected by chance
ρ_o = observed agreement coefficient
ρ_c = expected chance agreement

Using the data in the preceding example,

$$\rho_c = \frac{(80)(76) + (20)(24)}{100^2} \qquad\qquad \kappa = \frac{.84 - .66}{1 - .66}$$

$$= \frac{6080 + 480}{10,000} \qquad\qquad\qquad = \frac{.18}{.34}$$

$$= .66 \qquad\qquad\qquad\qquad\qquad = .53$$

You can see that the kappa coefficient (.53) provides a lower estimate of reliability than the agreement coefficient (.84). This is always the case, except when agreement is perfect ($\rho_0 = 1.00$) because the kappa formula begins with ρ_0 and then adjusts for expected chance agreement. Both are often calculated because the information provided by the two indexes is different. The agreement coefficient and kappa require two administrations of a test. Huynh (1976) and Subkoviak (1976) have developed techniques for estimating these coefficients from a single test administration. The simplest procedure, however, is to use tables developed by Subkoviak (1988) that permit you to read directly the approximate value of the agreement coefficient or the kappa coefficient after just one administration of a criterion-referenced test.

Reliability of Observational Data

Reliability is also important in measuring instruments that require ratings or observations of individuals by other individuals. The researcher in these cases must determine the reliability of the ratings—whether different judges/observers have given similar scores or ratings to the same behaviors. A simple way to determine the reliability of ratings is to have two or more observers independently rate the same behaviors and then correlate the observers' ratings. The resulting correlation is called the *interrater or interobserver reliability*. If the behaviors to be observed are well defined and the observers well trained, the reliability of the observations should be positive and quite high (around .90).

Take the case of two individuals who have rated several students in a performance assessment where the ratings run from 1 (very poor) to 10 (excellent). Here reliability can be assessed through correlational procedures in the same way these procedures are used in test-retest or alternate-forms reliability. The second observer serves the same function as a retest or an alternate form in a paper-and-pencil test. When the scores are only 1 or 0 (behavior occurred versus behavior did not occur), the agreement coefficient (formula 9.10) or kappa (formula 9.12) can be used to assess the reliability of the observers' scores. These procedures are also useful when training observers. Trainees watch and score a videotape that has been scored by an experienced observer, and the agreement coefficient or kappa indicates the correspondence between a trainee and the experienced observer. The trainer can go through the tape with the trainee to determine when and why the trainee misclassified observations.

An extensive discussion of reliability procedures in behavioral observations may be found in Suen and Ary's book (1989).

VALIDITY AND RELIABILITY COMPARED

Validity is a more important and comprehensive characteristic than reliability. Because it is more difficult to measure systematic error than random error, evaluating validity is more problematic. Published research studies often report much more reliability data than validity data. Validity is not obtained as directly as reliability. Assessing validity involves accumulating a great deal of evidence to support the proposed interpretations of scores. The conceptual framework indicates the kinds of evidence that you need to collect to support the meaning and interpretation of test scores. You must answer questions about the appropriateness of test content, the adequacy of criteria, the definitions of human traits, the specification of the behavioral domain, the theory behind the test content, and so forth. All these matters involve judgment and the gathering of data from many sources.

Reliability, in contrast, can be investigated directly from the test data; no data external to the measure are required. The basic issues of reliability lend themselves easily to mathematical analysis, and reasonable conclusions about the amount of error can be stated in mathematical terms.

To be valid for a particular use, a measure must first be reliable. The reliability of an instrument determines the upper limit of its validity. Scores on a test with zero reliability are entirely random and therefore cannot correlate with any criterion. The possible correlation of an instrument with any possible criterion increases as the reliability of the instrument increases. Remember, however, that a measure can have reliability without having validity; it can consistently measure the wrong thing. Feldt and Brennan emphasize the primacy of validity in evaluating the adequacy of an educational measure by stating, "No body of reliability data, regardless of the elegance of the methods used to analyze it, is worth very much if the measure to which it applies is irrelevant or redundant" (1989, p. 143).

SUMMARY

The multiplicity of measuring instruments available to the researcher requires the use of criteria for the evaluation of these instruments. The two most important criteria for measuring devices are validity and reliability.

Validity is the extent to which theory and evidence support the proposed interpretations of test scores for an intended purpose. In the process of assessing validity, the researcher gathers supporting evidence from various sources.

The researcher must also ask, How consistently does the test measure whatever it does measure? This is the issue of reliability. No test can have validity unless it measures consistently—that is, unless it is reliable. Reliability refers to the extent to which the test is consistent in measuring whatever it does measure. Specifically, reliability refers to the extent to which an individual scores nearly the same in repeated measurements as indicated by a high reliability coefficient. Reliability coefficients can be computed in various ways, depending on the source of error being considered. The reliability coefficient shows the extent to which random errors of measurement influence scores on the test. The standard error of measurement, another index of reliability, enables researchers to employ the normal curve to estimate the limits within which a subject's true score can be expected to lie.

Different types of reliability coefficients are required for norm-referenced and criterion-referenced tests. Establishing reliability of the latter is more problematic, but two procedures that have been used for criterion-referenced tests were presented in this chapter.

REFERENCES

American Educational Research Association (AERA). (1999). *Standards for educational and psychological testing.* Washington, DC: American Educational Research Association.

Buros, O. K. (1949). *Mental measurements yearbook* (Vol. 4). Lincoln: University of Nebraska Press.

Cronbach, L. J. (1951). Coefficient alpha and the internal structure of tests. *Psychometrika, 16,* 297–334.

Doll, E. A. (1935, 1949, 1965). Vineland social maturity scale. Circle Pines, MN: American Guidance Service.

Educational Measurement: Issues and Practice. (1998, Summer). *17*(2). Whole Issue.

Feldt, L. S., & Brennan, R. L. (1989). Reliability. In R. Linn (Ed.), *Educational measurement* (pp. 105–146). New York: American Council on Education and Macmillan.

Huynh, H. (1976). On the reliability of decisions in domain-referenced testing. *Journal of Educational Measurement, 13,* 265–266.

Kuder, G. F., & Richardson, M. W. (1937). The theory of estimation of test reliability. *Psychometrika, 2,* 151–160.

Messick, S. (1995). Validity of psychological assessment. *American Psychologist, 50*(9), 741–749.

Messick, S. (1989). Validity. In R. Linn (Ed.), *Educational measurement* (pp. 13–103). New York: American Council on Education and Macmillan.

Nunnally, J. C. (1967). *Psychometric theory.* New York: McGraw-Hill.

Popham, J. (1997). Consequential validity: Right concern wrong concept. *Educational Measurement:* Issues and Practices, 16(2), 9–13.

Subkoviak, M. J. (1976). Estimating reliability from a single administration of a mastery test. *Journal of Educational Measurement, 13,* 265–276.

Subkoviak, M. J. (1988). A practitioner's guide to computation and interpretation of reliability indices for mastery tests. *Journal of Educational Measurement, 25,* 47–55.

Suen, H. K., & Ary, D. (1989). *Analyzing quantitative behavioral observation data.* Hillsdale, NJ: Lawrence Erlbaum.

Swaminathan, H., Hambleton, R. K., & Algina, J. J. (1974). Reliability of criterion-referenced tests: A decision-theoretic formulation. *Journal of Educational Measurement, 11,* 263–267.

Wiley, D. E. (1991). Test validity and invalidity reconsidered. In R. E. Snow & D. E.
Wiley (Eds.), *Improving Inquiry in the Social Sciences: A volume in honor of Lee J. Cronbach*
(pp 75–107). Hillsdale, N.J.: Erlhaum.

KEY CONCEPTS

agreement coefficient

alternate forms technique

coefficient (Cronbach) alpha

coefficient of equivalence

coefficient of stability

coefficient of stability and
equivalence

consequential validity

construct-irrelevant variance

construct underrepresentation

convergent evidence of validity

criterion

discriminant evidence of validity

evidence based on consequences
of testing

internal consistency procedures

internal structure of test as
evidence of validity

Kuder-Richardson formulas

reliability

response processes as evidence of
validity

Spearman-Brown prophecy
formula

split-half reliability coefficient

standard error of measurement

test content as evidence of validity

test-retest reliability coefficient

validity

validity coefficient

EXERCISES

1. Compare *validity* and *reliability* with respect to
the following:
   a. The meaning of each concept
   b. The relative importance of each concept
   c. The extent to which one depends on the
      other

2. Explain the statement: A measuring device may
be reliable without being valid, but it cannot
be valid without being reliable.

3. How would you propose to gather evidence to
support the use of a new scholastic aptitude
test that had been developed for use with high
school seniors?

4. You have been asked to assess the validity of
an instrument designed to measure a student's
academic self-concept (that is, the way he [or
she] sees himself as a student). How would you
go about this task?

5. What source of evidence supporting the proposed interpretation of test scores is indicated
in each of the following situations?

a. The high school language proficiency test
   scores of college dropouts and college persisters are compared in order to determine
   whether the test data correlated with the
   subjects' college status.

b. A new scholastic aptitude test is found to
   have a correlation of .93 with the SAT,
   which has been used to predict college
   success.

c. A new intelligence test has been developed.
   The author argues that the mental processes
   required by the test are congruent with the
   Z theory of intelligence. Furthermore, he
   shows that among children the average score
   on the test increases with each year of age.

d. A teacher carefully examines a standardized
   achievement test to see if it covers the
   knowledge and skills that are emphasized in
   the class.

e. The mean difference between the rankings
   of members of the Ku Klux Klan and
   members of the Americans for Democratic

Action on the liberalism scale was found to be highly significant.

f. A mathematics test is judged by a group of teachers to be an adequate and representative sample of the universe of test items.

6. Identify the type of procedure for estimating reliability that is illustrated in each of the following:

a. The same test was given twice to a certain group. The correlation between the scores on the two administrations of the test was .90.

b. The group's scores on the odd items of a test were correlated with their scores on the even items of the same test: $r_{xx} = .95$.

c. Alternate forms of the test were administered after one month, and results of the two administrations were correlated: $r_{xx} = .85$.

d. The variance, the mean, and the number of items are used to estimate reliability.

7. How would you account for the differences in the reliability coefficients in Exercise 6, assuming that the groups tested were the same?

8. How would you gather evidence for the validity of a reading readiness test?

9. What can you do to increase reliability when constructing a test?

10. Indicate the source of evidence that might be most relevant for assessing validity of the following types of tests:

a. A classroom history test

b. An instrument to measure achievement motivation

c. A measure designed to identify potential dropouts

d. A group intelligence test

e. A reading readiness test

11. Explain how a mathematics achievement test could be judged to have high validity in one mathematics class and low validity in another mathematics class.

12. Criticize the following statement: "The reliability of the intelligence test is .90. Therefore, you can assume that the test scores can be interpreted as measuring intelligence."

13. Determine the standard error of measurement for a test with a standard deviation of 16 and a reliability coefficient of $r_{xx} = .84$. How would you interpret this standard error of measurement?

14. Select a standardized achievement test that you might use in a research study and obtain the necessary validity data on this test. (You may use Buros *Mental Measurements Yearbook* and the manual that accompanies the test you select.)

15. Check the test manual for the achievement test being used in your school. What type of reliability data are reported there?

16. The following data were obtained when two forms of a criterion-referenced test in mathematics were given to a group of elementary school children. There were fifty items on each form. To pass, a student had to get 80 percent correct on each form. Express the reliability of this test in terms of the agreement coefficient (ρ) and the kappa coefficient (κ).

Examinee	Form 1	Form 2
1	45	47
2	43	48
3	45	31
4	39	39
5	39	48
6	34	37
7	46	46
8	48	49
9	43	38
10	36	46
11	45	48
12	38	39
13	44	45
14	31	34
15	42	48

17. Criticize the following procedures used to gather validity evidence:

a. A high school English teacher developed a writing test for identifying talented high school students and administered the test to her senior English classes. On the basis of high scores, students were permitted to enroll in an English class at the local university. At the end of the semester the teacher correlated the original test scores with the grades the students earned in the college English class. The teacher was surprised to find a negligible correlation. What was the problem?

b. A school counselor developed a scale to measure need for academic achievement in elementary school children. The scale was administered to two classes of elementary school children, and the results were given to the teachers of these children. The teachers were asked to observe these children carefully for one semester, after which they were asked to rate the children on their need for achievement. The teachers' ratings were then correlated with the scores the children received on the scale. The correlation was quite high, so the counselor concluded that the scale had high validity for measuring need for achievement. Do you agree with the counselor's conclusion?

18. Assume that you wanted to investigate teacher "burnout." Suggest some indicators of this construct that you might use in developing a scale for this purpose.

19. A true-false test was administered to ten students. A 1 indicates a correct answer; a 0 indicates an incorrect answer. The results are as follows:

	Items										
Students	1	2	3	4	5	6	7	8	9	10	Total
A	1	1	1	1	1	1	1	1	0	0	8
B	1	1	1	1	0	1	0	1	0	0	6
C	1	1	1	1	1	0	0	0	0	0	5
D	1	1	1	0	0	0	0	1	1	0	5
E	1	1	1	1	1	1	1	1	0	0	8

	Items										
Students	1	2	3	4	5	6	7	8	9	10	Total
F	1	1	1	1	1	1	1	1	1	1	10
G	1	1	1	1	1	1	1	1	1	0	9
H	1	1	1	0	0	0	0	0	0	0	3
I	1	1	1	1	0	0	0	0	0	0	4
J	1	1	1	1	0	1	1	1	1	1	9

Calculate the split-half reliability coefficient of this test by dividing the test into odd- and even-item subtests.

20. What type of reliability estimate would be most appropriate for the following measuring instruments?

a. A multiple-choice achievement test will be used as the dependent variable in an experimental study.

b. A researcher will study changes in attitude and will administer one form of an attitude scale as both the premeasure and the postmeasure.

c. A researcher has two forms of an achievement test; she administered one form at the beginning of the study and the other at the conclusion of the study. She wants to determine the reliability of the test.

21. A 100-item test was split into two halves, and the split-half coefficient of correlation was found to be .60. Calculate the reliability coefficient for the full-length test.

22. Using a ten-point scale, two judges gave the following ratings to the essays written by a group of students. Calculate an index that indicates the reliability of this rating procedure.

	Judge 1	Judge 2
Kata	10	9
Ashok	8	7
Mary	7	10
Kwaku	9	8
Anil	6	5
Ester	4	3

23. Indicate whether each of the following practices would increase or decrease reliability?

   a. The teacher decides to give a weekly quiz instead of one big test at the end of the grading period.

   b. Jane Smith brags about her difficult tests where a large percentage of students fail.

   c. On Friday afternoon, Miss Jones postponed the big exam until the following Monday when she heard about the big football game after school that day.

   d. The teacher decided to add ten easy test items that everyone could answer correctly.

   e. The teacher wrote items having a wide range of difficulty, with most items answered correctly by 40–70 percent of students.

   f. To save time, Ms. White had the students do only two of the subtests from a standardized test instead of taking the complete test.

   g. The teacher decided to give 25 spelling words on the weekly test instead of ten.

24. The following are some comments often heard from students following exams. To what test characteristic are the comments most directly related?

   a. The test measured minute details, not the important concepts emphasized in class.

   b. The test was too long for the time available.

   c. That material was not even covered in class.

   d. The reading level was so complex that the test was really a measure of reading comprehension, not math.

   e. Many students were observed to be cheating.

   f. What does this test have to do with choosing students for the advanced chemistry class?

ANSWERS

1. Validity is the extent to which an instrument measures what it is designed to measure. Reliability is the extent to which an instrument is consistent in measuring. Validity is considered a more important aspect than reliability because lack of validity implies lack of meaning. However, an instrument cannot be valid without first being reliable.

2. A measure may produce consistent scores (reliability), yet may bear no relationship to other accepted measures of the construct or not be able to predict behavior associated with the construct (validity). Scores on a test with zero reliability are entirely random and therefore cannot correlate with any criterion. The extent of reliability sets an upper limit on possible validity.

3. You first must define what is meant by *aptitude*. If you wish to measure general academic ability, gather evidence about its content by examining the test items for representativeness.

Do they assess the basic academic skills of reading, spelling, math, and so on? Gather evidence about the correlation between the test scores and senior-year GPA, freshman-college GPA, and other criteria. Correlation with other validated aptitude test scores could also be done.

4. The items of the scale or questionnaire would need to cover aspects of the student behavior that would logically be a part of the construct *academic self-concept* (for example, I intend to go to college). Criterion measures could be personal interviews with students or independent assessment by teachers. Assuming academic self-concept is related to achievement, self-concept scores could be correlated with GPA and/or achievement test scores.

5. a. Evidence based on correlation with other variables

   b. Evidence based on correlation with other variables

c. Evidence based on response processes

d. Evidence based on content

e. Evidence based on response processes

f. Evidence based on content

6. a. Test-retest reliability

b. Split-half reliability

c. Alternate-forms with time lapse reliability

d. Internal consistency (Kuder-Richardson formula 21)

7. Split-half reliabilities tend to be higher than test-retest reliabilities because subject variability due to maturation, increase in testing skill, and other random factors is less. Equivalent-forms reliability is lower than same-test reliability because (a) it is impossible to construct exactly equivalent forms and (b) there is an added source of variability when non-identical forms are used. The internal consistancy reliability will be depressed if the test is not homogeneous.

8. You would first identify which specific skills (for example, letter recognition, left-to-right orientation) comprise reading readiness and then determine if the test incorporated these skills in appropriate proportions. When subjects who have taken the test have begun their reading programs, you would determine how scores on the test and on subtests correlate with reading test scores, teachers' ratings, and other criteria.

9. Rewriting ambiguous items, using items of appropriate difficulty, and clarifying instructions will increase reliability. Making a test longer by including additional items drawn from the same universe increases reliability, as does testing on a more heterogeneous group.

10. a. Evidence based on content

b. Evidence based on internal structure of test, correlation with other criteria of achievement motivation, and performance of contrasted groups

c. Evidence based on relationship with some criteria

d. Evidence based on internal structure of the test and relationships with appropriate criteria

e. Evidence based on internal structure of the test and relationship with appropriate criteria of reading achievement

11. A mathematics test that covered only computation would have little validity in a class that stressed concepts and reasoning. If content and emphasis of a different class match the content and emphasis of the test, the test will have high validity in that class.

12. A test can be reliable without measuring what it intends to measure. To determine validity, you need to look at content, constructs, and relations with other measures of the same construct as well as relations with measures of behavior assumed to be correlated with the construct.

13. By formula 9.9, you interpret the standard error of measurement as a standard deviation. Thus, you can say that there are two chances in three that the individual's true score will fall in the range of ± 6.4 score points from the observed score.

$$
\begin{aligned}
s_M &= s_x \sqrt{1 - r_{xx}} \\
&= 16 \sqrt{1 - .84} \\
&= 16(.4) \\
&= 6.4
\end{aligned}
$$

14. Answers will vary.

15. Answers will vary.

16. A score of 40 represents mastery ($50 \times .80 = 40$).

		Form 1		
		Master	Nonmaster	
Form 2	Master	(a) 7	(b) 2	9
	Nonmaster	(c) 2	(d) 4	6
		9	6	15

$$P_0 = \frac{7 + 4}{15} = \frac{11}{15} = .73$$

(73% of the students were classified consistently)

$$P_c = \frac{(9)(9) + (6)(6)}{15^2} = \frac{81 + 36}{225} = \frac{117}{225} = .52$$

$$\kappa = \frac{.73 - .52}{1 - .52} = \frac{.21}{.48} = .44$$

17. a. Selecting just high scorers restricted the variability. The restricted variability lowered the coefficient of correlation.
    b. There was criterion contamination. Letting the teachers see the results of the original measurement of need for achievement contaminated their ratings of the children on need for achievement.

18. There are a number of possible indicators of teacher burnout. You could look at absenteeism from school, lower evaluations by supervisors, incidences of hostility toward students or supervisors, and incidences of challenging of school policies. You might also develop a scale to measure attitudes toward their work; from teachers' own responses to appropriate questions, you might infer the presence of burnout.

19.

Student	Odd	Even	Total
A	4	4	8
B	2	4	6
C	3	2	5
D	3	2	5
E	4	4	8
F	5	5	10
G	5	4	9
H	2	1	3
I	2	2	4
J	4	5	9

The correlation between the odd and even items is $r = .72$. (Calculate the coefficient of correlation, using the raw-score formula with N in the denominator.) Using the Spearman-Brown formula, the reliability estimate for the full-length test is .84.

$$r_{xx} = \frac{2(.72)}{1.72} = .84$$

20. a. You would be interested in the internal consistency of this one form of the test. A split-half, alpha, or Kuder-Richardson reliability coefficient would be appropriate.
    b. With one form to be used as both a pre- and postmeasure, you would compute a coefficient of stability.
    c. With two forms and two administrations, you would compute the coefficient of stability and equivalence.

21.
$$r_{xx} = \frac{2(.60)}{1 + .60} = .75$$

22. Pearson r = .78

23. a. Increase
    b. Decrease
    c. Increase
    d. No effect
    e. Increase
    f. Decrease
    g. Increase

24. a. Validity
    b. Reliability
    c. Validity
    d. Validity
    e. Reliability
    f. Validity

INFOTRAC COLLEGE EDITION

Use the keywords *validity* + *construct* to locate an article that focuses on the construct validity of some measuring instrument. What procedures were used to investigate construct validity? What conclusions were reached about the validity of that instrument for measuring the construct under consideration?

Chapter 10

Experimental Research

After studying this chapter, the student will be able to:

1. Describe characteristics of experimental research.

2. Distinguish between the independent variable and levels of the independent variable.

3. Explain the concept of control and its importance in experimental research.

4. Distinguish between true control groups and comparison groups in experimental research.

5. Define internal and external validity.

6. Identify threats to internal validity and strategies for avoiding or minimizing them.

7. Identify internal-validity problems in research proposals and reports.

8. Identify threats to external validity and strategies for avoiding them.

9 Identify external-validity problems in research proposals and reports.

10 Describe the difference between random selection and random assignment, and show how they are related to internal and external validity.

11 Describe the most common true experimental designs, and state the advantages of each.

12 Define *factorial design,* and state its advantage.

13 Describe single-subject experimental research and its uses.

An **experiment** is a scientific investigation in which the researcher manipulates one or more independent variables, controls any other relevant variables, and observes the effect of the manipulations on the dependent variable(s). An experimenter deliberately and systematically introduces changes and then observes the consequences of those changes. Because the experiment involves control and careful observation and measurement, this research method provides the most convincing evidence of the effect that one variable has on another.

Early scientists learned the value of observation in the study of our environment but soon realized that nature's complexity could not always be understood through simply observing its many events. They found that events occurring in their "natural" state were often so complicated by irrelevant factors that the operation of the factor they wished to study was obscured. They solved the difficulty by controlling the conditions under which it occurred, so that the irrelevant factors were eliminated. Then they could deliberately manipulate the independent variables of interest and measure the changes in the dependent variables that result from changes in the independent variables. In other words, they began to perform experiments.

Because the application of experimental methods was fruitful in investigating the physical world, investigators applied these methods to other fields. The nineteenth century saw these methods introduced into the biological sciences, and great advances were made in zoology, physiology, and medicine. Toward the end of the nineteenth century, scholars began to apply the same methods to psychological problems, thus beginning experimental psychology. In the 1890s the experimental method was first used to study an educational problem. Rice's (1897) investigation of spelling achievement in the schools marks the first attempt at educational field experimentation. Thorndike (1924) and other early investigators extended the experimental method to education.

In its simplest form an experiment has three characteristics: (1) an independent variable is manipulated; (2) all other variables that might affect the dependent variable are held constant; and (3) the effect of the manipulation of the independent variable on the dependent variable is observed. Thus, in an experiment the two variables of major interest are the independent variable and the dependent variable. The *independent variable* is manipulated (changed) by the experimenter. The variable on which the effects of the changes are observed is called the *dependent variable,* which is observed but not manipulated by the experimenter. The dependent variable is so named because its value is hypothesized to depend on, and vary with, the value of the independent variable. For example, to examine the effect of different teaching methods on achievement in reading, an investigator would manipulate method (the independent variable) by using different teaching methods in order to ascertain their effect on reading achievement (the dependent variable).

CHARACTERISTICS OF EXPERIMENTAL RESEARCH

There are three essential ingredients with which an investigator is actively involved in conducting an experiment: control, manipulation, and observation.

Control

Control of variables is the essence of the experimental method. When a study is completed, researchers want to attribute the results to the experimental treatment. To do this, researchers must eliminate all other possible explanations.

That is, they must *control* or hold constant all influences except the one under investigation. Without control it is impossible to evaluate unambiguously the effects of an independent variable or to make inferences about causality. Let us examine briefly this concept of control in experimentation.

Basically, the experimental method of science rests on two assumptions regarding variables (Mill, 1846): (1) If two situations are equal in every respect except for a variable that is added to or deleted from one of the situations, any difference appearing between the two situations can be attributed to that variable. This statement is called the **law of the single independent variable.** (2) If two situations are not equal, but it can be demonstrated that none of the variables except the independent variable is significant in producing the phenomenon under investigation, or if significant variables other than the independent variable are made equal, then any difference occurring between the two situations after introducing a new variable (independent variable) to one of the systems can be attributed to the new variable. This statement is called the **law of the single significant variable.**

The purpose of control in an experiment is to arrange a situation in which the effect of variables can be investigated. The conditions underlying the law of the single variable are more likely to be fulfilled in the physical sciences than in education. For example, Robert Boyle was able to apply this principle in formulating his law about the effect of pressure on the volume of a gas: When temperature is held constant, the volume of a gas varies inversely with the pressure on it. Likewise, Jacques Charles formulated a law dealing with the effect of temperature: When pressure is held constant, the volume of a gas varies directly with the temperature. Because educational research is concerned with human beings, many variables are always present. To attempt to reduce educational problems to the operation of a single variable is not only unrealistic but perhaps even impossible. Fortunately such rigorous control is not absolutely essential, because many aspects in which situations differ are irrelevant to the purpose of the study and thus can be ignored. It is sufficient to apply the law of the single *significant* independent variable. For example, in a study of the different effects of two methods of teaching arithmetic, an experimenter would wish to have two groups of children who are identical in every respect except the way in which they are taught arithmetic. Because it is impossible to have two absolutely identical groups of children, the experimenter seeks to establish two groups that are as similar as possible with respect to the variables that are related to arithmetic achievement, such as reading ability, motivation, general intelligence, and the like. Other variables that are highly unlikely to be related to arithmetic, such as athletic ability, height, shoe size, or color of hair, are ignored. Although the law of the single variable cannot be followed absolutely, the experiment endeavors to approximate it as closely as possible in all relevant variables. Therefore, in experimental studies in education you need procedures that permit you to compare groups on the basis of significant variables. A number of methods of control have been devised to make such comparisons possible.

Let's assume that you wish to test the hypothesis that children taught by the inductive method (Group A) show greater gains in learning scientific concepts than children taught by the deductive method (Group B). To draw a conclusion concerning the relationship between teaching method (independent variable) and the learning of scientific concepts (dependent variable), you must control for the effects of any extraneous variables. An **extraneous variable** is a variable that is not related to the purpose of the study but may affect the dependent variable. In this experiment, aptitude is a factor that certainly affects the learning of scientific concepts; therefore, it would be considered a relevant extraneous variable that you must control. Otherwise, if the children in Group A had more aptitude than those in Group B, the greater gains in learning by Group A could be attributed to aptitude and therefore you could not properly evaluate the effects of the teaching method on learning. Aptitude has confounded the relationship between the variables in which you are interested. The term **confounding** refers to the "mixing" of the variables extraneous to the research problem with the independent variable(s) of the research study in such a way that their effects cannot be separated. It could not be clearly stated whether the relation found is (1) between the independent variable and the dependent variable of the study, (2) between the extraneous variables and the dependent variable, or (3) a combination of (1) and (2). Confounding is eliminated by controlling for the effect of relevant extraneous variables.

In the preceding experiment, the best way to control for aptitude is to randomly assign subjects to the two groups. You could put the names of all the available subjects in a hat and randomly draw one name at a time, assigning the first to Group A and the second to Group B, the third to A, the fourth to B, and so on. Random assignment increases the probability that the two groups of subjects will be similar on any relevant extraneous variables such as aptitude, gender composition, socioeconomic level, motivation, and so on. The two groups will differ only in their exposure to the independent variable.

Manipulation

The **manipulation of an independent variable** is a deliberate operation performed by the experimenter. In educational research and other behavioral sciences, the manipulation of an independent variable involves setting up different *treatment* groups or conditions. The different treatment conditions administered to the subjects in the experiment are the *levels* of the independent variable. In a study on the effect of using computer simulations on the learning of science concepts, you have one independent variable with two levels: computer simulation and no computer simulation. Do not confuse one independent variable having two levels for two independent variables. The levels represent two or more values of an independent variable and may involve differences in *degree* or differences in *kind,* depending on the nature of the manipulation. An independent variable whose levels differ in degree or amount involves manipulation in the extent of the independent variable. In contrast, manipulation may involve independent variables with levels that differ in kind. For example, assume an experimenter is interested in the effects of a stimulant on college students' learning of nonsense syllables. The researcher would begin by specifying the stimulant to be used and the amount to be administered. If the researcher is interested in the effect of the stimulant amount on learning, he or she would perhaps set up three levels of the independent variable: high, medium, and low dosage. Or the researcher could compare the effects of one stimulant with another stimulant, or with nothing at all. In this case, the levels differ in kind.

Other examples of independent variables where the levels might differ in amount are sleep deprivation or money used as an incentive. Independent variables, such as different teaching methods (lecture versus discussion) or different instructions given to subjects, would have levels differing in kind. The number of levels of an independent variable will equal the number of treatment conditions the experimenter has set up.

A researcher may manipulate more than one independent variable in a single study.

Observation

After the researcher has applied the experimental treatment, he or she must observe to determine if the hypothesized change has occurred. Researchers use various means of measuring the change in the dependent variable. Some changes can be observed directly while other changes are measured indirectly. Learning, for example, is often the dependent variable in educational research. Note that researchers cannot measure learning directly. They can only estimate learning through scores on an achievement test or other measures chosen according to the operational definition. Therefore, strictly speaking, the dependent variable is observed scores rather than learning per se.

▪ EXPERIMENTAL COMPARISON

An experiment begins with an experimental hypothesis, a prediction that the treatment will have a certain effect. The hypothesis expresses expectations as to results from the changes introduced—that the treatment and no-treatment groups will differ because of the treatment's effects. The experiment is planned and carried out to gather evidence relevant to the stated hypothesis. For the simplest experiment, you need two groups of subjects: the **experimental group** and the **control group.** The original definitions designated the experimental group as the one receiving a specific treatment, whereas the control group receives no treatment. Using a control group enables the researcher to discount many alternative explanations for the effect of treatment. For example, a fertilized field might yield a bumper crop only because of benign weather or for other reasons. If equivalent adjacent unfertilized fields yield less, the effect of fertilizer on yield becomes credible.

More common, however, than comparing a treatment group to a group receiving no treatment (*true control group*) is the situation where researchers compare groups receiving different treatments. These are called **comparison groups.** The majority of educational experiments study the difference in the results of two or more treatments rather than the difference in the results of one treatment versus no treatment at all. For example, it would be pointless to compare the spelling achievement of an experimental group taught by Method A with a control group that had no spelling instruction at all. Instead, researchers compare groups receiving Method A and Method B treatments. Comparison of groups receiving different treatments provides the same control over alternative explanations as does comparison of treated and untreated groups. To simplify subsequent discussions, we will use the term *control group* to refer both to groups with no treatment and to groups with alternative treatments. Comparisons are essential in scientific investigation. Comparing a group receiving treatment with either an equivalent group receiving no treatment or an equivalent group or groups receiving alternative treatment makes it possible to draw well-founded conclusions from the results.

The experimental and control groups must be equivalent in all variables that may affect the dependent variable; they differ only in exposure to the independent variable. After the experimenter has imposed the different conditions on the subjects, he or she measures each subject on the dependent variable.

Evaluation follows measurement. Is there a difference between the two groups? Is the effect of Treatment A different from that of Treatment B? This question implies and requires a comparison of the measures of the dependent variable in the first group with the measures of the dependent variable in the other group. The comparison should tell the experimenter whether differences on the dependent variable are associated with differences on the independent variable as represented by the two conditions, A and B.

■ EXPERIMENTAL DESIGN

The term **experimental design** refers to the conceptual framework within which the experiment is conducted. It is the researcher's plan for carrying out the experiment. Experimental designs differ in various ways. First, designs differ in the number of independent variables that are manipulated. Some experimental designs have only one independent variable; other designs have two or more. Second, designs differ in the method of assigning subjects to different treatments. In the true experiment, subjects are randomly assigned to the groups; in other cases, the design uses preexisting groups, or each subject may receive all the treatments. Third, designs also differ in how often dependent variable measures are made and whether all subjects receive all treatments or not. An experimental design serves two functions: (1) It establishes the conditions for the comparisons required to test the hypotheses of the experiment; and (2) it enables the experimenter, through statistical analysis of the data, to make a meaningful interpretation of the results of the study. If a design is to accomplish these functions, the experimenter, when selecting it, must keep in mind certain general criteria. Descriptions of various types of experimental design follow the discussion of these general criteria.

The most important criterion is that *the design must be appropriate* for testing the particular hypotheses of the study. The mark of a sophisticated experiment is neither complexity nor simplicity but rather appropriateness. A design that will do the job it is supposed to do is the right design. Thus the first task for the experimenter is to select the design that best arranges the experimental conditions to meet the needs of the particular experimental problem.

A second criterion is that *the design must provide adequate control* so that the effects of the independent variable can be evaluated as unambiguously as possible. Unless the design controls extraneous variables, you can never be confident of the relationship between the variables of the study. As you will see, **randomization** is the single best way to achieve the necessary control. Therefore, the best advice is to select a design that uses randomization in as many aspects as possible. A very significant contribution to the evaluation of research designs was made by Campbell and Stanley (1966), who suggested that there are two general criteria of research designs: *internal validity* and *external validity*, which we will now discuss. ‾

Internal Validity of Research Designs

Campbell and Stanley (1966) stated that internal validity is the basic requirement if one is to draw correct conclusions from an experiment. **Internal validity** is the extent to which the changes observed in a dependent variable are, in fact, caused by the independent variable(s) in a particular experimental situation rather than by some extraneous factors. Internal validity is concerned with such questions as, Did the experimental treatment really bring about a change in the dependent variable or was some other factor working? and Did the independent variable really make a difference? These questions of internal validity cannot be answered positively by the experimenter unless the design provides adequate control of extraneous variables. If the design provides control of variables, you can eliminate alternative explanations of the observed outcome and interpret it as showing an intrinsic relationship between variables. Internal validity is essentially a problem of control. The design of appropriate controls is a matter of finding ways to eliminate extraneous variables that could lead to alternative interpretations. Anything that contributes to the control of a design contributes to its internal validity.

Campbell and Stanley (1966) identified eight extraneous variables that frequently represent threats to the internal validity of a research design. These variables are called *threats* because, unless they are controlled, they may very well produce an effect that could be mistaken for the effect of the experimental treatment.

Threats to Internal Validity

1. *History.* Specific events or conditions, other than the experimental treatment, may occur in the environment between the first and second measurements and may produce changes in the dependent variable. Such events are referred to as the **history effect.** In this case, *history* does not refer to past events, but to events occurring *at the same time* that the experimental treatment is being applied. The longer the period of time between the pre- and postmeasurements on the subjects, the greater this threat becomes.

    Assume that a study in the spring of 1999 involved the use of films to change high school students' attitudes toward gun control. The researchers administer a pretest to gauge attitudes, show a series of films over a two-week period, and then give a posttest to see what changes may have occurred. During those two weeks, the tragic school shootings in Littleton, Colorado, occur. The effect of the films on students' attitudes would be confounded with the effects of this event, so that the researcher does not know whether the change in attitudes occurred as a result of the films or because of the shootings, and the subsequent extensive media coverage. Or, for example, during an experiment to measure the effectiveness of a unit on how the stock market works, let's say the stock market drops precipitously and the media devote considerable attention to the stock market. The investigator cannot determine whether the students' greater knowledge at the conclusion of the unit is caused by the unit or by the students' exposure to the media coverage. The effects of the unit and of the students' exposure to the media coverage are confounded, and it is impossible to know how much of the students' learning is caused by the unit and how much by events outside the experiment. In this case, history threatens the internal validity of the research.

2. *Maturation.* The term **maturation** refers to changes (biological or psychological) that may occur within the subjects simply as a function of the passage of time. These changes may produce effects that could mistakenly be attributed to the experimental treatment. Subjects may perform differently on the dependent variable measure simply because they are older, hungrier, more fatigued, or less motivated than they were at the time of the first measurements. For example, it can be difficult to assess the effects of treatments for articulation problems among preschoolers, because young children often naturally outgrow such problems.

3. *Pretesting.* Exposure to **pretesting** administered before the experimental treatment may affect the subjects' performance on a second test, regardless of the treatment. People may do better on a posttest, because they have learned subject matter from a pretest, have become familiar with the format of the tests and the testing environment, have developed a strategy for doing well on the tests, or are

less anxious about the test the second time around. In research using achievement tests, pretesting is a problem when the same content appears on both the pre- and posttest. We thus recommend using equivalent forms rather than the very same test.

With attitude and personality inventories, taking a pretest may sensitize the subjects so that they think about the questions and issues raised and subsequently give different responses on the posttest (**pretest sensitization**). For example, assume a researcher administers an attitude scale toward an ethnic group, introduces a diversity awareness program, and then gives a posttest to determine whether attitudes changed. The attitude scale itself may stimulate subjects to think about their attitudes; this self-examination rather than the program itself may lead to improvements in attitudes.

4. *Measuring instruments.* The **measuring instruments** threat to internal validity is a result of the unreliability of the measuring instruments or a change in the instruments used during the study. The measurement process itself rather than the treatment may bring about the observed differences. Changes may involve the type of measuring instrument, the difficulty level, the scorers, the way the tests are administered, using different observers for pre- and postmeasures and so on. In classroom research, for example, a teacher should not use a multiple-choice pretest and an essay posttest. The posttest should not be easier or more difficult than the pretest.

   Some of the threats are more subtle. For example, if observers recording a dependent variable know which subjects have received treatment and which have not, they may unconsciously overestimate the performance of the treatment group and underestimate it for the control group.

5. *Statistical regression.* The term **statistical regression** refers to the well-known tendency for subjects who score extremely high or extremely low on a pretest to score closer to the mean (regression toward the mean) on a posttest, regardless of the treatment. Statistical regression is a threat when a subgroup is selected from a larger group on the basis of the subgroup's extreme scores (high or low). When tested on subsequent measures, the subgroup will have a mean score closer to the mean of the original group. For example, let us assume that the lowest fourth of the scorers on an English proficiency test are selected for a special experimental program in English. The mean of this group will tend to move up toward the mean of the original population on a second test whether or not an experimental treatment is applied. Similarly, high initial scorers would tend to go down toward the population mean on a second testing.

   Let us illustrate regression with a scattergram (Figure 10.1) that shows the pattern we would get if the correlation of fourth-grade reading test scores and fifth-grade reading test scores is $r = .7$. Each dot represents both z-scores for an individual. If you select individuals with a particular z-score on the fourth-grade reading test and look at their scores on the fifth-grade reading test, you find that few have the same z-score on both tests. If the fourth-grade z-score for this

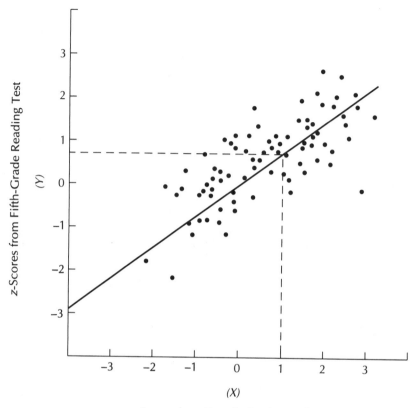

z-Scores from Fourth-Grade Reading Test

FIGURE 10.1

Scattergram for Fourth- and Fifth-Grade Reading Test Scores

subgroup is above the mean, we find that a few of the students score farther above the mean in fifth grade than they did in fourth grade, but the majority of them have z-scores closer to the mean and some even fall below the mean.

For the subgroup with a z-score one standard deviation above the mean on X, the mean on Y is +.7; for the subgroup with z-scores two standard deviations below the mean on X, the mean on Y is −1.4; the group with a z-score of +2 on X has a mean z-score of + 1.4 on Y, and so forth. The slanted line on the scattergram connects these means on Y for various scores on X. Note that for each group with scores above the mean on the fourth-grade reading test, the mean score on Y is *lower* on the fifth-grade reading test. For each group with scores below the mean on the fourth-grade reading test, the mean score is *higher* on the fifth-grade reading test. In other words, the average scores for each group move closer to the mean—which is the result of regression.

Regression inevitably occurs when the correlation between two variables is less than perfect. Because practically none of the variables of interest in education are perfectly correlated, you must always be aware of the effect of regression in designing your experiments. An aspect of regression is captured in the adages "When you are at the bottom, you have nowhere to go but up" and "When you are on top, you have nowhere to go but down."

For example, a school establishes a remedial mathematics program and assigns those middle school students who score two years or more below grade level on a standardized mathematics test to this program. After a semester the students are given an equivalent form of the standardized test. The majority of them score nearer their grade equivalent and appear to have benefited from the remedial program. Before attributing the gains to the program, remember that when you are at the bottom, you have nowhere to go but up. The lowest scorers on the pretest include those whose scores were depressed because of temporary ill health, emotional problems, inattention, or other random errors of measurement. The majority of these cases would be expected to score better in a subsequent test. Conversely, if those who score highest on any measure are assigned to a special treatment, such as an enrichment program, a posttreatment measure may make it appear that the treatment had a deleterious effect. Those on top have nowhere to go but down.

6. *Differential selection of subjects.* **Differential selection** is a threat when there are important differences between the experimental and control groups even before the application of the experimental treatment. This situation is most likely to occur when the researcher cannot assign subjects randomly but must use intact groups. An intact group is a preexisting group such as a class or a group set up independently of the planned experiment. In a learning experiment, if the experimental group is more intelligent than the control group, the former would be expected to perform better on the dependent variable measure even without the experimental treatment. As you will see later, there are ways to control this threat so that intact classes can be used in research.

Selection bias may also occur when volunteers are used. People who volunteer for a study may differ in some important respects from nonvolunteers. If the researcher then compares volunteers with nonvolunteers following the experimental treatment, the researcher does not know if the differences are caused by the treatment or by preexisting differences between the two groups.

7. **Experimental mortality.** The mortality threat occurs when there is differential loss of participants from the comparison groups. If a particular type of subject drops out of one group during the course of the experiment, this differential loss may affect the outcome of the study. If, for example, several of the lowest scorers on a pretest gradually drop out of the experimental group, this group will have a higher mean performance on the final measure, not because of the experimental treatment but because the low-scoring subjects are absent when the posttest is administered.

Assume a counselor wanted to compare the effectiveness of two different marital counseling procedures. She administered a pretreatment measure of marital adjustment to couples who had enrolled in her program, then randomly assigned each couple to Procedure A or Procedure B. With Procedure A, which involved considerable soul-searching and confrontation, only eleven of twenty couples persisted in the program and were available for the posttreatment measure. With Procedure B, which was relaxed and less demanding, eighteen of twenty couples persisted and were available for the posttreatment measure. The posttreatment mean of Procedure A was higher than the mean of the Procedure B group. This may be evidence that Procedure A is more effective, but it may also be evidence that only those couples who were highly motivated to improve their marriage persisted in the program, whereas the posttreatment scores for Procedure B included less motivated couples.

Mortality is not usually a serious threat unless the study goes on for a long time or unless the treatment is so demanding that it results in low-performing subjects' dropping out.

8. **Selection-maturation interaction.** Some of these threats may interact to affect internal validity. For example, selection and maturation may interact in such a way that the combination results in an effect on the dependent variable that is mistakenly attributed to the effect of the experimental treatment. Such interaction may occur in a quasi-experimental design where the experimental and control groups are not randomly selected but instead are preexisting intact groups, such as classrooms. Even though a pretest may indicate that the groups are equivalent at the beginning of the experiment, the experimental group may happen to have a higher rate of maturation than the control group, and the increased rate of maturation accounts for the observed effect. More rapidly maturing students are "selected" into the experimental group, and the selection-maturation interaction may be mistaken for the effect of the experimental variable.

A group who elected to take a freshman honors English class, for instance, may show more vocabulary growth than a group in a regular freshman English class because their vocabulary growth was at a higher rate both before and during their freshman year. A comparison of pretest and posttest differences of the honors and the regular classes might lead you to conclude erroneously that the independent variable was responsible for a difference in gain that is really only caused by selection-maturation interaction. This problem also frequently arises when volunteers are compared with nonvolunteers. The volunteers may be more motivated to make gains on the dependent variable than are the nonvolunteers, and this difference in gains may be mistakenly attributed to the independent variable—as can happen even when the groups are equivalent on a pretest. Although Campbell and Stanley (1966) originally listed only eight threats to internal validity, Cook and Campbell (1979) suggest that at least three more should be considered.

9. *Experimenter effect.* The threat of **experimenter effect** involves unintentional effects that the researcher him- or herself has on the study. Personal characteris-

tics of the researcher such as gender, race, age, and position can affect the performance of subjects. Sometimes the actual implementation of the experiment inadvertently gives the experimental group an unplanned advantage over the control group. For example, in an experiment comparing the effectiveness of two teaching methods, the more capable teacher may be assigned to the experimental group. Internal validity is threatened if the experimenter has expectations or a personal bias in favor of one method over another. These preferences and expectancies on the part of the experimenter may be unconsciously transmitted to subjects in such a way that their behavior is affected.

Assume an experimenter is investigating the effectiveness of a new teaching technique that he or she has developed and believes to be superior. If this experimenter is in a position to influence the experiment, he or she may unintentionally behave in a way that improves the performance of the experimental group but not of the control group. An impartial researcher would not necessarily obtain the same findings. Bias could also result if the experimenter who knows which subjects are in which group is asked to rate the performance of these subjects. The experimenter might unintentionally rate the performance of the experimental group higher. Rosenthal (1985) has extensively investigated the experimenter bias effect. He showed that rats labeled "bright" outperformed "dull" ones simply by convincing experimenters that the labels were correct. The higher scores for the "bright" rats were caused by experimenter bias rather than any genuine differences between the rats. We should emphasize, however, that this bias effect does not result from any deliberate action on the part of the experimenter to alter data or to get the experiment to come out a certain way. The best way to deal with experimenter effect is to let other trained individuals (rather than the investigator him- or herself) work directly with the participants in the study. He or she should also refrain from communicating to the people running the experiment that one experimental treatment is thought to be better than another.

10. *Subject effects.* Subjects' attitudes developed in response to the research situation called *subject effects* can be a threat to internal validity. For instance, in a study of the effects of various levels of lighting on worker productivity at the Hawthorne, Illinois, plant of the Western Electric Company, researchers observed that both increases and decreases in light intensity resulted in increased productivity. The researchers concluded, however, that the attention given to the employees and the employees' knowledge that they were participating in an experiment— rather than any changes in lighting—were the major factors leading to the production gains. This tendency for subjects to change their behavior just because they are participating in an experiment has subsequently been referred to as the **Hawthorne effect.**

This effect can be a problem in educational research that compares exciting new teaching methods with conventional methods. Sometimes subjects may react to what they perceive to be the special *demands* of an experimental situation. That is, subjects react not as they normally might, but as they think the more "important" researcher wants them to act. Research has shown, for instance, that subjects knowing they are in an experiment tolerate more stress or administer more stress to others than they normally would.

The opposite of the Hawthorne effect is the **John Henry effect.**★ This effect, also called **compensatory rivalry,** refers to the tendency of control group subjects who know they are in an experiment to exert extra effort and hence to perform above their typical or expected average. They may perceive that they are in competition with the experimental group and they want to do just as well or better. Thus the difference (or lack of difference) between the groups may be caused by the control subjects' increased motivation rather than by the experimental treatment. This effect is likely to occur in classroom research in which a new teaching technique is being compared to a conventional method that may be replaced by the new method. The students in the conventional classroom may want to show that they can do just as well as the students being taught by the new method. Furthermore, the teacher in the control classroom may want to show that the old method is just as good and is motivated to make a special effort. For example, early research on televised classroom instruction showed that the teachers in the regular classroom (control group) made a special effort, so that their students' performance matched or exceeded the performance of students receiving televised instruction (experimental group). Teachers in the conventional classroom probably felt threatened by this innovation and wanted to show that they could teach better than television.

Another subject effect, called **compensatory demoralization,** occurs when subjects feel they are receiving less desirable treatment or are being neglected. Consequently, they may become resentful or demoralized and put forth less effort than the members of the other group. There may also be a *novelty effect* where subjects react with increased enthusiasm and motivation simply because the experiment involves something new and different.

11. **Diffusion.** Diffusion occurs when participants in one group (typically the experimental group) communicate information about the treatment to subjects in the control group in such a way as to influence the latter's behavior on the dependent variable. Assume the subjects in the experimental group being taught math by an innovative method get so excited about the project that they share information with their friends in the control group. Later the groups may perform similarly on the dependent variable, not because the new method was ineffective, but because its effects were disseminated to the control group as well. Diffusion can be controlled by deemphasizing the fact that an experiment is going on involving differences between the groups.

Researchers must systematically examine how each of the preceding threats to internal validity may have influenced the results. If the threats can be elimi-

---

★This effect is named for John Henry, the legendary railroad worker, who died trying to show that he could drive steel railroad spikes as fast as a machine. The experiment was testing the machine as a replacement for human workers.

Table 10.1	*Threats to Internal Validity*
History	Unrelated events that occur between pre- and posttests affect the dependent variable.
Maturation	Changes occur within the participants just as a function of time.
Pretesting	Exposure to pretest affects posttest.
Instrumentation	Unreliability or a change in the measuring instrument affects result.
Regression	Extremely high or low scorers on a pretest regress toward mean on a posttest.
Differential Selection of Subjects	Because of selection methods, subjects in the comparison groups are not equivalent prior to study.
Selection-Maturation interaction	Subjects with different maturation rates are selected into treatment groups.
Mortality	A differential loss of participants from the groups affect dependent variable.
Experimenter Effect	Unintentional bias or behavior of experimenter affects results.
Subject Effect	Attitudes developed during the study affect performance on dependent variable.
Diffusion	Participants in experimental group communicate information about treatment to control group, which may affect the latter's performance.

nated, researchers can have confidence that the observed results were caused by the different treatments. Table 10.1 summarizes the threats to internal validity.

DEALING WITH THREATS TO INTERNAL VALIDITY

An experiment should be designed to avoid or at least minimize the effect of threats to internal validity. The researcher's first efforts must be directed toward controlling for any relevant preexisting differences between subjects used in an experiment. Only in this way can you be fairly confident that any postexperimental differences can be attributed to the conditions of the experiment rather than to preexisting subject differences. Six basic procedures are commonly used to increase equivalence among the groups that are to be exposed to the various experimental situations: (1) random assignment, (2) randomized matching, (3) homogeneous selection, (4) building variables into the design, (5) analysis of covariance, and (6) use of subjects as their own controls.

Random Assignment

Consider the experimenter's task. There is an available supply of subjects who for experimentation must be divided into two groups that will be treated differently and then compared. In assigning subjects to groups for the experiment, the experimenter needs a system that operates independently of personal judgment and of the characteristics of the subjects themselves. For example, the known high scorers must not all be assigned to Group A and the low scorers to Group B. A system that satisfies this requirement is random assignment. **Random assignment** is the assignment of subjects to groups in such a way that, for any given placement, every member of the population has an equal probability of being assigned to any of the groups. Chance alone determines whether subjects are placed in the experimental or the control group. The term **randomization** is often used as a synonym for *random assignment*.

Random assignment is not the same thing as random selection. Random selection (see Chapter 7) is the use of a chance procedure to select a sample from a population. Random assignment is the use of a chance procedure to assign subjects to treatments. For example, Ms. Brown has 1000 subjects available for an experiment but only has sufficient facilities to include 100 in her experiment. To randomly select the subjects to include in the experiment, Ms. Brown could number all the available subjects and then use a table of random numbers to select the 100 participants. Thus she avoids creating systematic differences between the subjects in the experiment and the population from which they were selected. She would then randomly assign 50 of the 100 subjects to one group and 50 to the other group. A coin flip would determine which of the two groups is to get Treatment A and which is to get Treatment B.

When subjects have been randomly assigned to groups, the groups can be considered statistically equivalent. **Statistical equivalence** does not mean the groups are absolutely equal, but it does mean that any difference between the groups is a function of chance alone and not a function of experimenter bias, subjects' choices, or any other factor. A subject with high intelligence is as likely to be assigned to Treatment A as to Treatment B. The same is true for a subject with low intelligence. For the entire sample, the effects of intelligence on the dependent variable will tend to balance or randomize out. In the same manner, subjects' differences in political viewpoints, temperament, achievement motivation, socioeconomic level, and other characteristics will tend to be approximately equally distributed between the two groups. The more subjects in the original subject pool, the more likely that randomization will result in approximately equivalent groups.

When random assignment has been employed, any pretreatment differences between groups are a function of chance alone. When this is the case, the researcher can use inferential statistics to determine how likely it is that posttreatment differences are due to chance alone.

Note that not only *known* extraneous variables, but also other relevant extraneous variables unknown to or unimagined by the experimenter, can be expected to randomize out.

Randomized Matching

An alternative procedure for assigning subjects to groups is to match individual subjects on as many extraneous variables as one thinks might affect the dependent variable, and then to use some random procedure to assign one member of each matched pair to Treat-

ment A and the other to Treatment B. This procedure is called **randomized matching.**
If the groups are adequately matched on these variables, then there is reasonable assurance
that any postexperimental differences can be attributed to the experimental treatment.

Although matching is a method for providing partial control of intersubject differences, you may encounter several difficulties. The first of these is determining what vari-
able(s) to use for matching. Variables such as IQ, MA, socioeconomic status (SES), age,
gender, reading score, or pretest score may be used. The variables on which subjects are
matched must be substantially correlated to the dependent variable or else the matching
is useless. As a general rule, we suggest that unless the variable correlates .50 or higher
with the dependent variable, the variable should not be employed for the matching procedure because it would do little to increase the precision of the study. Ideally, the experimenter would like to match on two or more variables that correlate well with the
dependent variable and do *not* correlate significantly with each other. However, when an
experimenter tries to match on more than two variables, it becomes almost impossible
to find subjects who are well matched on these several variables. Subjects are lost because no match can be found for them.

Another question that arises is how closely to match the subjects on the variable(s).
Matching closely increases the precision of the method, but it also increases the number
of subjects who cannot be matched. This, of course, reduces the sample size and introduces sampling bias into the study. Subjects for whom matches cannot be found are usually those with high or low scores. Therefore, these subjects would be underrepresented.

The researcher must decide what matching procedure is feasible in each particular
situation. The usual method is to use a person-to-person procedure, in which an effort is
made to locate two people from among the available subjects who score within the prescribed limits. For example, if the matching variable is IQ, then the researcher locates
two subjects who are within, say five points of each other on the IQ scale and then randomly assigns one subject to Treatment A and the matching subject to Treatment B. It
would not be too difficult to match subjects on just the IQ variable. But if gender and
social class were also relevant variables, then it would become extremely difficult to find
pairs who match on all three variables. The experimenter loses those subjects for whom
no match can be found.

Another method of matching is to place all subjects in rank order on the basis of
their scores on the matching variable. The first two subjects are selected from the rank
order list (regardless of the actual difference in their scores) to constitute the first pair.
One subject of this pair is then randomly assigned to Treatment A and the other to Treatment B. The next two subjects on the list are selected, and again one is randomly assigned to A and the other to B. This process is continued until all subjects have been
assigned. It is somewhat simple to match according to this procedure, but it is less precise
than the person-to-person method. Note that randomized matching requires that the
subjects be matched first and then randomly assigned to treatments. A study where subjects who are already experiencing one treatment are matched with subjects who are already experiencing another treatment cannot be classified as an experimental study. Such
studies (discussed in Chapter 11) where matching is present, but random assignment to
groups is not present, can lead researchers to erroneous conclusions.

Homogeneous Selection

Another method that can make groups reasonably comparable on an extraneous variable is to select samples that are as homogeneous as possible on that variable. This is called **homogeneous selection.** If the experimenter suspects that age is a variable that might affect the dependent variable, he or she would select only children of a particular age. By selecting only 6-year-old children, for instance, the experimenter would control for the effects of age as an extraneous independent variable. Similarly, if intelligence is likely to be a variable affecting the dependent variable of the study, then subjects would be selected from children whose IQ scores are within a restricted range, say IQ, 100–110. This procedure has controlled the effects of IQ. Then the experimenter randomly assigns individuals to groups from the resulting homogeneous population and can be confident that they are comparable on IQ. Beginning with a group that is homogeneous on the relevant variable eliminates the difficulty of trying to match subjects on that variable.

Although homogeneous selection is an effective way of controlling extraneous variables, it has the disadvantage of decreasing the extent to which the findings can be generalized to other populations. If a researcher investigates the effectiveness of a particular method with such a homogeneous sample, say, of children with average IQs, the results could not be generalized to children in other IQ ranges. The effectiveness of the method with children of low intelligence or very high intelligence would not be known, and the experiment would have to be repeated with subjects from different IQ strata.

As with matching, a true experiment requires that the subjects be selected first and then assigned randomly to treatments.

Building Variables into the Design

Some variables associated with the subjects themselves can be built into the experimental design and thus controlled. For example, if you want to control gender in an experiment and you choose not to use the homogeneous selection technique just discussed, you could add gender as another independent variable. You would include both males and females in the study, and then use analysis of variance to determine the effects of both gender and the main independent variable on the dependent variable. This method not only controls the extraneous gender variable, but also yields information about its effect on the dependent variable, as well as its possible interaction with the other independent variable(s).

Analysis of Covariance

Analysis of covariance (ANCOVA) is a statistical technique used to control for the effect of an extraneous variable known to be correlated with the dependent variable. For example, consider an experiment to study the effects of two methods of teaching reading on reading achievement, the dependent variable. Subjects' reading ability before the experiment would be a variable that would certainly be related to the dependent variable of the study. You would expect that those who are good readers to begin with would score well on the reading posttest, whereas those who are poor readers would tend to score more poorly. After randomly assigning half of the subjects to Method A and half to Method B, you would administer a reading pretest to both groups. At the end of the experiment, analysis of covariance would statistically adjust the mean reading posttest scores for any initial differences between the groups on the pretest. The ANCOVA technique removes the portion of each subject's posttest score that is in common with his or her pretest score. The resulting F value can then be checked for statistical significance. The variable used in ANCOVA to adjust scores (in this case, the reading pretest) is called the **covariate.**

Using this technique, you are not considering a subject's posttest score per se. Instead, you analyze the difference between posttest scores and what you would expect the posttest score to be, given the score on the pretest and the correlation between pretest and posttest.

By removing that portion of the dependent-variable score variance that is systematically associated with pretest variance, the precision of the experiment improves. With part of the variance in the posttest scores that is *not* caused by treatment removed, difference caused by treatment stands out more clearly. Using a covariate that is related to the dependent variable reduces the likelihood of Type II error.

Achievement pretest scores are often used as covariates, but other measures such as aptitude or attitude scores can also be used. In the example, aptitude test scores or perhaps grade-point average could be used. To be useful, a covariate must be correlated with the dependent variable. In the example, baseball throw scores or shoe sizes would not be useful covariates, as they would be expected to have negligible correlation with the reading posttest.

Using Subjects as Their Own Controls

Still another procedure involves **using subjects as their own controls**—assigning the same subjects to all experimental conditions and then obtaining measurements of the subjects, first under one experimental treatment and then under another. For example, the same subjects might be required to learn two different lists of nonsense syllables, one list with high association value and the other with low association value. The difference in learning time between the two lists is found for each subject, and the average difference in learning time for all subjects then can be tested for significance.

This method of control is efficient when feasible, but in some circumstances it cannot be used. In some types of studies, exposure to one experimental condition would make it impossible to use the subjects for the other experimental condition. You cannot, for example, teach children how to divide by fractions one way and then erase their memory and teach it another way.

In the foregoing experiment, where one group of subjects was used to investigate the relative ease of learning high-association and low-association nonsense syllables, there could be a "learning to learn" effect, and thus whichever list appeared second would have an advantage over the first. Conversely, fatigue or interference effects might result in poorer performance on the second list. In either case you cannot separate the effect of the independent variable and the effect of order on the dependent variable. A useful strategy for this experiment would be to randomly divide the subjects into two groups: one group learning the high-association syllables first, the other learning the low-association syllables first. This would "balance out" the effects of learning to learn or fatigue. However, if learning high-association syllables first helps subjects to learn low-association syllables later, and the reverse is not true, this can confound the interpretation of the results.

Controlling Situational Differences

The methods discussed in the preceding section are used to control intersubject differences that threaten internal validity. In addition, extraneous variables may operate in the experimental setting to create situational differences that can threaten internal validity. If these extraneous situational variables are not controlled in an experiment, you cannot be sure whether it is the independent variable or these incidental differences operating in the groups that are producing the difference in the dependent variable. These uncontrolled extraneous variables whose effects may mistakenly be attributed to the independent variable are called *confounding* or *contaminating* variables. For instance, let us assume that an experimenter is interested in the effectiveness of a film in producing changes in attitude toward some issue. One group of children is selected at random from a classroom and sent off to see the film, leaving a comparable group in the classroom. Unknowingly, the experimenter may have set in motion a large number of forces. The children in the control group may be resentful or feel rejected or inferior to the others. Any of these factors could affect the outcome of the study. The difference that the experimenter wants to attribute to the use of the film could really be caused by one of these incidental features. In this case steps must be taken to ensure that the control subjects also see a film of some sort and that both groups, or neither group, know that they are taking part in an experiment. This precaution is necessary in order to control subject effects, such as the Hawthorne effect or compensatory demoralization.

It is very important to control subjects' attitudes in experiments on drugs. For example, in studying the effect of a drug on the performance of a manipulative skill, all subjects must think they are taking the drug. This is managed by using a *placebo,* which is a chemically inert or neutral substance given to subjects to make them believe they are receiving the actual experimental drug. The experimenter gives every subject a substance that appears to be the same. For some subjects this is the drug under investigation and for the remainder it is the placebo. Thus the expectation of a drug effect is held constant between experimental and control subjects and is therefore eliminated as a confounding variable. Otherwise, just the knowledge that they had been given a drug might lead the experimental subjects to be either extra cautious or quite reckless—and the experimenter would not know whether it was the effect of the drug or the subjects' behavior, or both, that produced the result.

The use of a placebo as just described illustrates what is called a *single-blind experiment*. The subjects are unaware of the treatment condition they are in, although the researcher does know. Sometimes, however, it is necessary to hold the attitudes of the researcher constant for different independent variable levels. This is done by using a *double-blind experimental procedure,* in which neither the experimenter nor the subjects knows which kind of treatment the subjects are getting. Double-blind experiments are more difficult to carry out, because the nature of the treatment often makes it obvious which is the experimental group. Another consideration is that in a double-blind situation the experimenter must depend on other people to set up the groups, administer the treatment, and record results.

Methods of Controlling Situational Variables

Three methods are commonly used to control potentially contaminating situational variables: hold them constant, randomize them, or manipulate them systematically and separately from the main independent variable. Holding extraneous variables constant means that all subjects in the various groups are treated exactly alike except for their exposure to the independent variable. For instance, in a reading experiment you would need to control the size of the groups because size of group is known to be a factor affecting reading achievement. You must see that the experimental and control groups have the same number of subjects. And you must also control the teacher variable, because teacher efficiency and enthusiasm may affect the outcome of any learning experiment. Thus the same teacher should be used with two teaching methods that are to be compared. In an experiment, the various assistants must follow the same procedures: Use the same instructions, apparatus, and tests, and try to assume the same attitudes with all groups. All groups should meet at the same time of day and in the same type of room. You would not want the experimental group to meet during the first period in the morning of a school day and the control group during the last period of the day. Environmental conditions—such as temperature, light intensity, humidity, furniture in the room, and the presence or absence of distracting noises—should be the same for all groups. If you cannot hold conditions constant, as the experimenter you must attempt to randomize or balance out certain situational variables. For instance, if it is not possible to have the same teacher for both treatments, you might randomly assign half of the available teachers to use Method A and half to use Method B. You could do the same with other experimental conditions, such as apparatus. In this way you randomize situational variables; a variety of extraneous conditions is represented but not allowed to affect the dependent variable systematically.

Another way to control extraneous situational variables is by manipulating them systematically. Many educational experiments must use a sequence of experimental and control conditions to control progressive effects, such as practice and fatigue effects. Experimenters do this by controlling the order in which experimental conditions are presented, through counterbalancing; half the subjects may receive an AB order and the other half a BA order. In this case an extraneous variable is being systematically manipulated. This procedure not only controls the potentially contaminating effect of order but can also estimate the size of the order effect by determining whether the average A and B values obtained in the two sequences are different.

If a researcher believes that class size may influence the effectiveness of a new instructional method, he or she can control that variable by building it into the design as a second independent variable. The design would provide for two levels of the method variable and two levels of class size, as shown here:

		Class Size	
		Small	Large
Method	A		
	B		

The researcher could then determine the effect of the instructional method itself, the effect of class size, and any interaction effect between method and class size. This method for controlling extraneous variables amounts to the same thing as adding more independent variables to the experiment. Although it increases the complexity of the study, the method has the advantage of furnishing additional information about the effect of relevant variables on the dependent variable and their interaction with the main independent variables. The use of this method of control has been increasing since the introduction of computers to handle data analysis in complex studies. Two-way analysis-of-variance designs and more complex analysis-of-variance designs permit the simultaneous investigation of a number of variables considered singly and in interaction—the latter often being the most significant aspect of the study.

EXTERNAL VALIDITY OF RESEARCH DESIGNS

The second criterion of a research design is **external validity,** which refers to the generalizability or representativeness of the findings. The experimenter asks questions such as, Would the same results occur with other subjects, in other settings, and at other times? and To what populations, settings, experimental variables, and measurement variables can these findings be generalized? Any single study is necessarily performed on a particular group of subjects, with selected measuring instruments and under conditions that are in some respects unique. Yet researchers want the results of a study to furnish information about a larger realm of subjects, conditions, and operations than were actually investigated. To make generalizations from the observed to the unobserved, researchers need to assess how well the sample of events actually studied represents the larger population to which results are to be generalized. To the extent that the results of an experiment can be generalized to different groups, settings, and measuring instruments, the experiment possesses external validity.

Smith and Glass (1987) identified three types of external validity: population external validity, ecological external validity, and external validity of operations. **Population ex-**

ternal validity concerns identifying the population to which the results of an experiment are generalizable. It asks the question, What population of subjects can be expected to behave in the same way as did the subjects in the sample? **Ecological external validity** is concerned with generalizing experimental effects to other environmental conditions. It asks the question, In what settings can the same results be expected? **External validity of operations** is concerned with how well the operational definitions and the experimental procedures represent the constructs of interest, asking, Would the same relationships be seen if a different researcher were investigating the same question with different operations?

Population External Validity

Population external validity is related to the way subjects are selected for a study. Appropriate sampling procedures must be used so that the participants selected for a study accurately represent the population to which the findings are to generalize. For example, let's assume that a researcher, having discovered an apparently effective new method of teaching reading to a sample of first-graders, would like to conclude that this method is superior for other groups of first-graders, perhaps all first-graders in the United States. To be able to make valid generalizations of the sample experimental results to the larger population, the researcher must show that the sample correctly represents that population.

Relevant to this problem is Kempthorne's (1961) distinction between the *experimentally accessible population* and the *target population,* referred to in Chapter 7. The experimentally accessible population is the population of subjects accessible or available to the researcher for his or her study. The target population is the total group of subjects to whom the researcher wants to apply the conclusions from the findings. In the foregoing example, the experimentally accessible population would likely be all the first-graders in the local school district. The target population would be all first-grade students in the United States.

The researcher's generalizations would occur in two stages: (1) from the sample to the experimentally accessible population and (2) from the accessible population to the target population. If the researcher has randomly selected the sample from the experimentally accessible population (all first-graders in the school district), then the findings can be generalized to this larger group with no difficulty. Inferential statistics indicate the likelihood that what was true of the sample is also true of the population from which it was drawn. In the second stage, the researcher wants to generalize from the accessible to the target population (all first-graders in the United States). This type of generalizing cannot be made with the same degree of confidence as the former type. To make such an inference requires a thorough knowledge of the characteristics of both populations. The more nearly similar the accessible and target populations are, the more confidence the researcher has in generalizing from the one to the other. Generalizing from the accessible population to the target population cannot be done statistically—it is a matter of judgment. The researcher must describe the accessible population as thoroughly as possible and point out any ways this population differs from the target population. Then the researcher and the readers of the research report can make intelligent judgments about how likely the results are to generalize to the target population or to other populations.

Threats to Population External Validity

The major threat to population external validity is the possibility of interaction between subject characteristics and treatment. This interaction occurs because participants for the study are not randomly selected from a target population. Assume that the experimentally accessible population for a study of reading is the first-graders enrolled in an affluent suburban school district. Would an experimenter using first-graders in a rural school district as the accessible population expect to obtain the same results? When two experimentally accessible populations are not representative of the same target population, seemingly similar studies can lead to entirely different results. A relationship between the treatment and the dependent variable may occur with one group that would not occur in another group with different characteristics. Thus the findings from one group may not be valid for another group or for the broader population, and it would be hazardous to generalize the findings.

A teaching method that works with college students may not work with high school students. Counseling Method A may produce better results than Method B in inner-city schools, whereas Method B is superior in affluent suburban schools. The best method for teaching quantitative reasoning among second-graders may be the worst method among eighth-graders. As the old saying goes, "One man's meat is another man's poison." Again, a thorough description of the accessible population will help other educators judge whether a particular treatment is likely to be "meat or poison" for their populations of interest.

Using volunteers also presents an external validity problem, because volunteers are known to have special characteristics that may not be typical of the population to which generalizations are to be made. No one knows how nonvolunteers would be affected by the experimental treatment.

Ecological External Validity

Experimenters are also concerned with generalizing the results of their research to other situations. Before generalizing results, consider the environment in which the research was done. If the experimental environment is very different from the environment to which the results are to generalize, then the generalization is weakened. Anything that reduces the generalizability of an experiment reduces its external validity.

Obviously, the first requirement for ecological validity is that the experimenter furnish a complete description of the experimental setting involved in the study. Any artificiality in the research setting that would not be present in other situations limits the generalizability of the results. Experiments are often done in settings where variables such as lighting, noise, and other distractions can be tightly controlled. Such control is desirable for enhancing internal validity, but may reduce external validity because it makes the setting unrepresentative of the subjects' real world environment.

Even in classroom research without any artificiality, unique features in the setting may influence generalizability of findings. Size and type of school, technology available to the students, library facilities, and so on would influence generalizing to schools with different characteristics. For example, would results found in a spacious, well-equipped classroom generalize to a crowded, ill-equipped classroom? It is important that researchers sufficiently describe the setting so that readers can reasonably judge the generalizability of results.

Threats to Ecological External Validity

Any interaction of the treatment with the experimental setting threatens ecological external validity.

1. *Using a pretest, for instance, may increase or decrease the experimental subjects' sensitivity or responsiveness to the experimental variable and thus make the results obtained for this pretested population unrepresentative of the effects of the experimental variable on the unpretested population from which the experimental subjects are selected.* In this case you could generalize to pretested groups but not to unpretested ones. Assume that you give a group of seventh-graders a questionnaire concerning their dietary habits and randomly divide the group into experimental and control groups. You expose the experimental group to a series of film presentations concerning good eating habits, whereas the control group sees a series of health films unrelated to eating habits (placebo). The dependent variable is derived by observing the children's food selections in an actual free-choice situation. If the experimental group shows a significantly greater preference for healthful foods, you would like to conclude that the films are effective. Before reaching a conclusion, you must consider the possibility that the pretest caused the students to think about their eating habits and "set them up" to respond to the films. The same effect might not have been observed in an unpretested group.

2. *Attitudes and feelings of the participants that develop during a study may influence the generalizability of the findings to other settings.* This threat is also called the *reactive effect,* because subjects are reacting to the experimental arrangements or to the experience of participating in an experiment. For example, the Hawthorne effect described earlier as an internal validity problem can also be an external validity problem. Subjects' knowledge that they have been selected for an experiment and are being treated in a special way may affect the way they respond to the treatment. This effect weakens generalization to situations where people do not regard themselves as special. Likewise, the John Henry effect results in atypical behavior on the part of control groups that may affect the application of results.

3. *There may be a novelty effect in which a new treatment produces positive results simply because it is novel—or, of course, the opposite can occur.* A new instructional method may appear more successful than an old one, when in fact they are equally

effective, because teachers and students in the new program may feel they are special and develop enthusiasm for what they are doing, whereas those in the control group feel left out. Or the new method may appear *less* effective than the old one because teachers and students are using unfamiliar materials and procedures and haven't yet learned to employ them effectively by the time the dependent variable measure is taken. For example, when Schoen (1976) summarized the outcomes of prior research comparing the results of individualized versus group instruction in elementary school mathematics, he found seventeen studies with statistically significant results favoring group instruction, eleven that retained the null hypothesis, and only eight with statistically significant differences favoring individualized instruction. Most of the investigators had hypothesized that individualized instruction would be more effective. This may be evidence that for most populations, group instruction is more effective. However, it is also possible that students with group instruction did better because they and their teachers already knew how to cope with group instruction, whereas with individualized instruction they had to learn a new way of proceeding, as well as the content of the arithmetic unit.

Another threat to ecological validity is the experimenter effect, which occurs when the experimenter consciously or unconsciously provides cues to subjects that influence their performance. Sometimes the presence of observers during an experiment may so alter the normal responses of the participating subjects that you could not generalize about the effect of the experimental variable on people exposed to it in a nonexperimental setting.

External Validity of Operations

Individual investigators conduct research with specific operational definitions of the independent and dependent variables and specific procedures. The question about external validity of operations asks if similar results would be expected from different investigators with different operational definitions and/or different measurement procedures.

One aspect to consider, then, is the operational definitions of the independent and dependent variables. In some experiments anxiety has been induced by electric shock, in others by verbal instructions to the subjects. How much can findings from a study with one definition generalize to another? Is frustration produced by barring children from desirable toys the same as frustration produced by giving them unsolvable problems? If an objective test is used to measure the dependent variable, can the experimenter say that the same effect would be observed if an essay test were used as the measuring instrument? How well do scores on the Torrance Test of Creative Thinking represent the construct of creativity as an English or art teacher would define it? The reader of a research report assesses this aspect by first asking how explicitly the independent and dependent variables have been defined. For all practical purposes, reports with vague definitions are worthless. Next the reader must assess the reliability and validity of these definitions and judge how well the operational definitions fit the definitions of the constructs that have meaning for him or her. Table 10.2 summarizes the threats to external validity.

Table 10.2 *Threats to External Validity*

Selection-Treatment Interaction	Subjects are not selected randomly, which limits generalizability.
Pretest-Treatment Interaction	Pretest sensitizes subjects to treatment to produce an effect not generalizable to an unpretested population.
Setting-Treatment Interaction	Artificiality or uniqueness of experimental setting limits generalizability.
Subject Effects	Subjects' attitudes developed during the study affect the generalizability of results.
Experimenter Effects	Researchers' deliberate or unintentional actions influence results.
Operational Definitions	Operational definitions of variables influence the generalizability of results.

Dealing with Threats to External Validity

Controlling the threats to external validity is not as straightforward as with internal validity. With the latter, the research design is the significant factor. Before you can assume external validity, you need to examine carefully and logically the similarities and differences between the experimental setting and the target setting with respect to subjects, treatment, operational definitions, and so on. A review of the literature would reveal if research on the same question had used other kinds of subjects, settings, or methodology.

The following suggestions can help control threats to external validity:

1. Randomly sample the target population to select subjects for the study and then randomly assign them to treatment groups. If this is not possible because of the population size, then select subjects randomly from the experimentally accessible population and show the similarity of the experimentally accessible population and the target population.

2. Identify the relevant characteristics of subjects in the target population, and determine the impact of these characteristics by incorporating them into the research study. For example, if you want to generalize to ethnically diverse urban high schools, you could include different ethnic groups in the study and look at the performance of each group separately to see if the experimental treatment worked equally well with all groups or if there were differences. This kind of information would help determine the groups of students to whom the results could be generalized. The same could be done with gender, age, educational levels, and other characteristics. Factorial designs enable researchers to assess the effectiveness of the treatment at different levels of other variables such as race, gender, and so on.

3. You can control problems arising from an interaction of treatment with setting by (a) choosing a design that does not use a pretest or (b) using a second control group that will experience an interaction with the researcher just like the

experimental and first control group. The interaction arranged for the second control group, however, is interesting but completely unrelated to the dependent variable of the study. If there is a reactive effect brought on by subjects' participation in a research study, then it will be evident in this second control group just as it would be with the experimental group. In a sense, you have controlled for the Hawthorne effect. If the experimental group performs better on the dependent variable measure, then you have some confidence that the effect is caused by the treatment itself and not by the Hawthorne effect.

4. Provide clearly stated operational definitions for all variables related to subjects or setting.

5. Replicate the research study in a new setting. This is a good way to determine if similar results will be found. If you find the same results with other populations and in other settings, you can have reasonable confidence that generalizations are valid.

In summary, the term *internal validity* refers to the rigor or control in an investigation. A study is internally valid to the extent that the effect of influences, beyond the experimental variable, has been removed or minimized. *External validity,* in contrast, refers to generalizability. A study is externally valid to the extent that the subjects, experimental arrangements, and procedures are representative of the target setting, thus making results generalizable. Although internal validity is the sine qua non ("without which, nothing") the experimenter seeks a design that is strong in both internal and external validity. In some cases, however, obtaining one type of validity tends to threaten the other type. As a study becomes more rigorously controlled (internally valid), its artificiality increases and it becomes less generalizable and less externally valid. However, an experiment conducted in a more natural environment such as a classroom may have greater external validity, but its internal validity may be less. Fortunately, internal and external validity are not incompatible. In fact, internal validity is a prerequisite for external validity. Unless you can show that the treatment has an unambiguous effect on the dependent variable in the experimental setting (internal validity), it is almost pointless to ask if the treatment would cause the same effect in other situations. In practice researchers try to reach a compromise between internal and external validity, which amounts to choosing a design that provides sufficient control to make the results interpretable, while preserving some realism so that the findings will generalize to the intended settings.

CLASSIFYING EXPERIMENTAL DESIGNS

In the following discussion of experimental designs, designs are classified as preexperimental, true experimental, or quasi-experimental, depending on the degree of control provided. Preexperimental designs do not have random assignment of subjects to groups or other strategies to control extraneous variables. **True experimental designs** use randomization and provide maximum control of extraneous variables. **Quasi-experimental designs** lack randomization but employ other strategies to provide some control over extraneous variables. They are used, for instance, when intact classrooms are used as the experimental and control groups. Thus true experimental designs have the greatest internal validity, the quasiexperimental somewhat less, and the preexperimental designs the least internal validity.

Before we begin discussing the experimental designs, we need to introduce the terms and symbols that we will use:

1. X represents the independent variable, which is manipulated by the experimenter; we will also refer to it as the *experimental variable* or the *treatment*.

2. Y represents the measure of the dependent variable. Y_1 represents the dependent variable *before* the manipulation of the independent variable X; it is usually a pretest of some type administered before the experimental treatment. Y_2 represents the dependent variable *after* the manipulation of the independent variable X; it is usually a posttest administered to subjects after the experimental treatment.

3. S represents the subject or participant used in the experiment; the plural is Ss.

4. E *group* is the experimental group—the group that is given the independent variable treatment.

5. C group is the control group—the group that does not receive the experimental treatment. It receives a different treatment or no treatment at all.

6. R indicates random assignment of subjects to the experimental groups and the random assignment of treatments to the groups.

7. M_r indicates that the subjects are matched and then members of each pair are assigned to the comparison groups at random.

In the paradigms for the various designs, the Xs and Ys across a given row are applied to the same people.

The left-to-right dimension indicates the temporal order, and the Xs and Ys vertical to one another are given simultaneously. A dash (—) indicates that the control group does *not* receive the X treatment.

Preexperimental Designs

This section presents two designs that are classified as **preexperimental** because they provide little or no control of extraneous variables. Unfortunately these designs are still sometimes used in educational research. It will be helpful to begin our discussion with these poor designs because they illustrate quite well the way that extraneous variables may operate to jeopardize the internal validity of a design. If you become aware of these sources of weakness in a design, you should be able to avoid them.

Design 1: One-Group Pretest-Posttest Design

The **one-group pretest-posttest design** usually involves three steps: (1) administering a pretest measuring the dependent variable, (2) applying the experimental treatment X

to the subjects, and (3) administering a posttest, again measuring the dependent variable. Differences attributed to application of the experimental treatment are then evaluated by comparing the pretest and posttest scores.

Design 1: One-Group Pretest-Posttest Design		
Pretest	Independent Variable	Posttest
Y_1	X	Y_2

To illustrate the use of this design, assume that an elementary teacher wants to evaluate the effectiveness of a new technique for teaching fourth-grade social studies. At the beginning of the school year, the students are given a standardized test that appears to be a good measure of the achievement of the objectives of fourth-grade social studies. The teacher then introduces the new teaching technique and at the end of the year administers the standardized test a second time, comparing scores from the first and second administrations of the test in order to determine what difference the exposure to the new teaching method has made.

Because Design 1 involves only one group and one teacher, it would seem to control intersubject differences and situation variables. The control is only superficial, however. The major limitation of the one-group design is that because no control group is used, the experimenter cannot assume that the change between the pretest and posttest is brought about by the experimental treatment. There is always the possibility that some extraneous variables account for all or part of the change. Thus this design lacks internal validity.

What are some extraneous variables that could produce the change noted between the pretest and posttest scores? Two obvious extraneous variables are not controlled in this design are history and maturation. The term *history* as a source of extraneous variance refers to specific events that can occur between pretest and posttest, other than experimental treatment. In the social studies example, widespread community interest in an election, increased emphasis on social studies in the school, or introducing a particularly effective teacher could increase student achievement in this area. Or an epidemic causing increased absences could depress achievement. The term *maturation* refers to changes in the subjects themselves that occur over time. Between pretest and posttest, children are growing mentally and physically, and they may have learning experiences that could affect the dependent variable. History and maturation become increasingly influential sources of extraneous variance with time intervals between Y_1 and Y_2. Attitude of subjects, implementation, and regression also present uncontrolled threats to internal validity.

Another shortcoming of Design 1 is that it affords no way to assess the effect of the pretest itself. We know there is a practice effect when subjects take a test a second time or even take an alternate form of the test—subjects do better the second time even without any instruction or discussion during the interval. This is true not only for achievement and intelligence tests but also for personality tests. In the case of personality tests, a trend toward better adjustment is generally observed. As we discussed earlier, pretesting is also a problem in research on attitude change. The pretest may result in subjects' becoming aware of issues and thinking about the topic so they become motivated to change attitudes even without the treatment.

Design 1 has little to recommend it. Without a control group to make a comparison possible, the results obtained in a one-group design are basically uninterpretable.

Design 2: Static Group Comparison

Design 2—**static group comparison**—uses two or more preexisting or intact (*static*) groups, only one of which is exposed to the experimental treatment. The subjects are not randomly assigned to the groups. The researcher just assumes the groups are equivalent in all relevant aspects and that they differ only in their exposure to X. The dependent-variable measures for the groups are compared to determine the effect of the X treatment. This design has sometimes been used in methods research in education. The achievement of students taught by a new method is compared with that of a similar class taught by the old method.

Design 2 has a control group or groups, which permits the comparison that is required for scientific respectability. However, there is a basic flaw in this design. Because neither randomization nor even matching is used to assign subjects to the experimental and control groups, we cannot assume that the groups are equivalent prior to the experimental treatment. They may differ on certain relevant variables, and these differences, rather than X, may be responsible for observed change. Because we cannot be sure that the groups are equal in respect to all factors that may influence the dependent variable, we consider this design lacking in the necessary control and must classify it as preexperimental.

Design 2: Static Group Comparison		
Group	Independent Variable	Posttest
E	X	Y_2
C	—	Y_2

True Experimental Designs

The designs in this category are called *true experiments* because subjects are randomly assigned to groups. They are the most highly recommended designs for experimentation in education because of the control they provide.

Design 3: Randomized Subjects, Posttest-Only Control Group Design

Design 3—**randomized subjects, posttest-only control group design**—is one of the simplest yet one of the most powerful of all experimental designs. It requires two randomly assigned groups of subjects, each assigned to a different condition. No pretest is used; the randomization controls for all possible extraneous variables and assures that any initial differences between the groups are attributable only to chance and therefore will follow the laws of probability. After the subjects are assigned to groups, only the experimental group is exposed to the treatment. In all other respects the two groups are treated alike. Members of both groups are then measured on the dependent variable Y_2 and the scores are compared to determine the effect of X. If the obtained means of the two groups differ significantly (that is, more than would be expected on the basis of chance alone), the experimenter can be reasonably confident that the experimental conditions are responsible for the observed result.

The main advantage of Design 3 is randomization, which assures statistical equivalence of the groups before introduction of the independent variable. Recall that as the number of subjects increases, the likelihood that randomization will produce equivalent groups increases. We recommend at least thirty subjects in each group. Design 3 controls for the main effects of history, maturation, regression, and pretesting; because no pretest is used, there can be no interaction effect of pretest and X. Thus this design is especially recommended for research on attitudes. It is also useful in studies in which a pretest is either not available or not appropriate—as, for example, in studies with kindergarten or primary grades, where it is impossible to administer a pretest because the learning is not yet manifest. Another advantage of this design is that it can be extended to include more than two groups if necessary. Possible threats to internal validity are subjects' attitudes and experimenter effects.

Design 3: Randomized Subjects, Posttest-Only Control Group Design			
	Group	Independent Variable	Posttest
(R)	E	X	Y_2
(R)	C	—	Y_2

Design 3 does not permit the investigator to assess change. If such an assessment is desired, then a design (such as Design 5) that uses both a pretest and a posttest should be chosen.

Design 4: Randomized Matched Subjects, Posttest-Only Control Group Design

Design 4—**randomized matched subjects, posttest-only control group design**—is similar to Design 3, except that it uses a matching technique, to form equivalent groups. Subjects are matched on one or more variables that can be measured conveniently, such as IQ or reading score. Of course, the matching variables used are those that presumably have a significant correlation with the dependent variable. Although a pretest is not included in Design 4, if pretest scores on the dependent variable are available, they could be used very effectively for the matching procedure. The measures are paired so that opposite members' scores are as close together as possible; one member of each pair is randomly assigned to one treatment, and the other, to the second treatment. The flip of a coin can be used to achieve this random assignment.

| Design 4: Randomized Matched Subjects, Posttest-Only Control Group Design |||
Group	Independent Variable	Posttest
(M_r) E	X	Y_2
C	—	Y_2

Matching is most useful in studies where small samples are to be used and where Design 3 is not appropriate. Design 3 depends completely on random assignment to obtain equivalent groups. With small samples the influence of chance alone may result in a situation in which random groups are initially very different from each other. Design 3 provides no assurance that small groups are really comparable before the treatments are applied. The matched-subjects design, however, serves to reduce the extent to which experimental differences can be accounted for by initial differences between the groups; that is, it controls preexisting intersubject differences on variables highly related to the dependent variable that the experiment is designed to affect. The random procedure used to assign the matched pairs to groups adds to the strength of this design.

Design 4 is subject to the difficulties that we mentioned earlier in connection with matching as a means of control. The matching of all potential subjects must be complete, and the members of each pair to the groups must be assigned randomly. If one or more subjects were excluded because an appropriate match could not be found, this would bias the sample. When using Design 4 it is essential to match every subject, even if only approximately, before random assignment. Design 4 can be used with more than two groups by creating matched sets and randomly assigning one member of each set to each group.

Design 5: Randomized Subjects, Pretest-Posttest Control Group Design

In Design 5 (**randomized subjects, pretest–posttest control group design**)—subjects are assigned to the experimental and control groups by random assignment and are given a pretest on the dependent variable, Y. The treatment is introduced only to the experimental subjects for a specified time, after which the two groups are measured on the dependent variable. The average difference between the pretest and posttest $(Y_2 - Y_1)$ scores may be found for each group, and then these average difference scores are compared to ascertain whether the experimental treatment produced a greater change than the control situation. The statistical significance of the difference in average pretest-posttest gain scores (found when the average change for the control group is subtracted from the average change for the experimental group) may be determined by a t-test or F-test. For reasons beyond the scope of this discussion, measurement experts have pointed out that technical problems arise when comparing gain scores. A more precise, statistical procedure in this case is to do an analysis of covariance (ANCOVA) with posttest scores as the dependent variable and pretest scores as the covariate to control for initial group differences on the pretest. Tuckman (1999) states that analysis of covariance "gives results preferable to those of a direct comparison of gain scores (posttest minus pretest) for the two groups" (p. 164).

Design 5: Randomized Subjects, Pretest-Posttest Control Group Design				
	Group	Pretest	Independent Variable	Posttest
(R)	E	Y_1	X	Y_2
(R)	C	Y_1	—	Y_2

The main strength of this design is the initial randomization, which assures statistical equivalence between the groups prior to experimentation; also, the fact that the experimenter has control of the pretest can provide an additional check on the equality of the two groups on the pretest, Y_1. Design 5, with its randomization, thus controls most of the extraneous variables that pose a threat to internal validity. For example, the effects of history, maturation, and pretesting are experienced in both groups; therefore, any difference between the groups on the Y measure could probably not be attributed to these factors.

Differential selection of subjects and statistical regression are also controlled through the randomization procedure. Design 5 can be used with more than two groups. The main concern in using Design 5 is external validity. Ironically, the problem stems from the use of the pretest, an essential feature of the design. As mentioned earlier, there may be an interaction between the pretest and the treatment so that the results are generalizable only to other pretested groups. Although both E and C groups take the pretest and may experience the sensitizing effect, it can cause the experimental subjects to respond to the X treatment in a particular way just because of their increased sensitivity. The crucial question is, Would the effect of X on the experimental subjects be the same without the exposure to the pretest? This problem has been particularly evident in studies of attitude change. When the first attitude scale is administered as the pretest in a study, it can arouse interest or sensitize subjects to the issues or material included in the scale. Then when the experimental treatment (a lecture, film, or the like) is administered, the subjects may be responding not so much to the X treatment as to a combination of their aroused sensitivity to the issues and the experimental treatment.

Let us consider another example. Suppose that one criterion for the success of a new teaching method in high school social studies is the number of students who report that they read newspapers such as the *New York Times*. During the course itself no special emphasis is placed on this particular source; but it, along with several other papers of somewhat less repute, is made available to students. If the study uses a pretest-posttest design, the pretest questionnaire might include an item such as "Do you read the *New York Times* for daily news?" This question alone may be enough to sensitize the experimental students to that newspaper, so when it becomes available during the course, they will be more likely to pick it out from the others. As a result, the experimental group may show greater use of the *New York Times* on the posttest than does the control group—not because of the course content only, but because of the combined effect of course content and pretest. A new class taught by the same method, but not pretested and hence not sensitized, may show no greater attentiveness to the *New York Times* than the control group.

Despite this shortcoming, Design 5 is widely used because the interaction between pretest and treatment is not a serious problem in most educational research. The pretests used are often achievement tests of some type and therefore do not significantly sensitize subjects who are accustomed to such testing. However, if the testing procedures are somewhat novel or motivating in their effect, then it is recommended that the experimenter choose a design not involving a pretest. Alternatively, whenever you suspect that the effect of the pretest might be reactive, it is possible to add a new group or groups to the study—a group that is *not* pretested. Solomon (1949) suggested two designs that overcome the weakness of Design 5 by adding an unpretested group or groups. We present these designs next.

Design 6: Solomon Three-Group Design

The first of the Solomon designs uses three groups, with random assignment of subjects to groups. You can see that the first two lines of this design are identical to Design 5. However, this **Solomon three-group design** has the advantage of employing a second control group and thereby overcoming the difficulty inherent in Design 5—namely, the interactive effect of pretesting and the experimental treatment. This second control group, labeled C_2, is *not* pretested but is exposed to the X treatment. Their Y_2 measures are then used to assess the interaction effect.

Design 6: Solomon Three-Group Design			
Group	Pretest	Independent Variable	Posttest
(R) E	Y_1	X	Y_2
(R) C_1	Y_1	—	Y_2
(R) C_2	—	X	Y_2

The interaction effect is assessed by comparing the Y_2 scores for the three groups. Only the posttest scores enter into the analysis. Even though the experimental group has a significantly higher mean on Y_2 than does the first control group (C_1), the researcher cannot be confident that this difference is caused by X. It might have occurred because of the subjects' increased sensitization after the pretest and the interaction of their sensitization and X. However, if the Y_2 mean of the second control group (C_2) is also significantly higher than that of the first control group, then you can assume that the experimental treatment, rather than the pretest-X interaction effect, has produced the difference because the second control group is not pretested. This group, although receiving the X treatment, is functioning as a control and is thus labeled C_2.

Design 7: Solomon Four-Group Design

Design 7 (**Solomon four-group design**) provides still more rigorous control by extending Design 6 to include one more control group. This fourth group receives neither pretest nor treatment. Again the third group, though receiving the X treatment, is functioning as a control group.

| Design 7: Solomon Four-Group Design | | | |
Group	Pretest	Independent Variable	Posttest
(R) E	Y_1	X	Y_2
(R) C_1	Y_1	—	Y_2
(R) C_2	—	X	Y_2
(R) C_3	—	—	Y_2

Design 7 has strength because it incorporates the advantages of several other designs along with its own unique contribution. It provides good control of the threats to internal validity. The first two lines (Design 5) control extraneous factors such as history and maturation, and the third line (Design 6) provides control over the pretest-X interaction effect. When the fourth line is added to make Design 7, you have control over any possible contemporary effects that may occur between Y_1 and Y_2. The last two lines represent Design 3, so actually you have a combination of the randomized subjects pretest-posttest control group design with the randomized subjects posttest-only control group design. In addition to the strengths of each design taken separately, you also have the replication feature provided by the two experiments. This combination takes advantage of the information provided by the pretest-posttest procedure and at the same time shows how the experimental condition affects an unpretested group of Ss.

In Design 7 you can make several comparisons to determine the effect of the experimental-X treatment. If the posttest mean of the E group is significantly greater than the mean of the first control group, C_1, and if the C_2 posttest mean is significantly greater than that of C_3, you have evidence for the effectiveness of the experimental treatment. You can determine the influence of the experimental conditions on a pretested group by comparing the posttests of E and C_1 or the pre-post changes of E and C_1. You can find the effect of the experiment on an unpretested group by comparing C_2 and C_3. If the average differences between posttest scores, $E - C_1$ and $C_2 - C_3$, are about the same, then the experiment must have had a comparable effect on pretested and unpretested groups.

Design 7 actually involves conducting two experiments, one with pretests and one without pretests. If the results of these two experiments agree, as indicated earlier, the investigator can have much greater confidence in the findings.

The main disadvantage of this design is the difficulty involved in carrying it out in a practical situation. More time and effort are required to conduct two experiments simultaneously, and there is the problem of locating the increased number of subjects of the same kind that would be needed.

Another difficulty is with the statistical analysis. There are not four complete sets of measures for the four groups. As noted, you can compare E and C_1, and C_2 and C_3, but no single statistical procedure would use the six available measures simultaneously. Campbell and Stanley (1966) suggest working only with posttest scores in a two-way analysis-of-variance design. The pretest is considered as a second independent variable, along with X. The design is as follows:

	No X	X
Pretested	Y_2, control 1	Y_2, experimental
Unpretested	Y_2, control 3	Y_2, control 2

From the column means, you can determine the main effect of X; from row means, the main effect of pretesting; and from cell means, the interaction of testing with X.

Factorial Designs

The designs presented thus far have been the classical single-variable designs in which the experimenter manipulates one independent variable to produce an effect on an dependent variable. However, in complex social phenomena several variables generally interact simultaneously, and to attempt to restrict a study to one variable may impose an artificial simplicity on a complex situation. The X variable alone may not produce the same effect as it might in interaction with another, so the findings from one-variable designs may be misleading. For instance, the effectiveness of a particular method of teaching may well depend on a number of variables, such as the ability level of the students, the personality of the teacher, the general atmosphere of the classroom, and so on. Computer-assisted instruction, for example, may be more effective with slow students than with bright ones. A classical one-variable design would not reveal this interactive effect of method and intelligence level. The information yield of an experiment can be markedly increased by ascertaining the simultaneous effects of two or more independent variables in a factorial design. In fact, some have said that the real breakthrough in educational research came with Fisher's (1925) development of factorial designs (see Chapter 7). A **factorial design** is one in which the researcher manipulates two or more variables simultaneously in order to study the independent effect of each variable on the dependent variable, as well as the effects caused by interactions among the several variables.

Factorial designs are of two types. In the first type of design, only one of the independent variables is experimentally manipulated. In this case the experimenter is primarily interested in the effect of a single independent variable but must consider other variables that may influence the dependent variable. Typically these other variables are attribute variables, such as gender, intelligence, race, socioeconomic status, achievement, and the like. Their influence can be investigated (and at the same time controlled) by building the attribute variable directly into a factorial design. The experimenter assesses the effect of the main independent variable at each of several "levels" of the one or more attribute-independent variables. The different levels of the attribute variable typically represent naturally occurring selected groups of subjects, as when a study uses bright and learning-disabled students to determine the effectiveness of an instructional technique. Building the attribute variables into a factorial design not only increases the precision of the experiment but also its generalizability. Because you can determine whether the treatment has comparable effects over all levels, the generalizability of the experimental findings is increased.

In the second type of design, all the independent variables may be experimentally manipulated. Here the experimenter is interested in several active independent variables and wishes to assess both their separate and their combined effects. For instance, an experiment might compare the effects of class size as well as the introduction of computer-assisted instruction on the learning of science concepts. In this study both variables would be manipulated; there would be two levels of the variable "method of instruction" (namely, computer-assisted versus traditional) and of the second variable, "size of class" (namely, large versus small). Such a design permits analysis of main effects for both experimental variables as well as analysis of interaction between treatments.

Design 8: Simple Factorial Design

Factorial designs have been developed at varying levels of complexity. The simplest factorial design is the 2 × 2. In this design, each of two independent variables has two levels.

Design 8: Simple Factorial Design Variable 2 (X_2)	Variable 1 (X_1) Treatment A	Treatment B
Level 1	Cell 1	Cell 3
Level 2	Cell 2	Cell 4

To illustrate, let's assume that an experimenter is interested in comparing the effectiveness of two types of teaching methods—Methods A and B—on the achievement of ninth-grade science students, believing there may be a differential effect of these methods based on the students' level of science aptitude. The experimenter stratifies the population into high- and low-aptitude scores and randomly selects sixty Ss from the high group and assigns thirty Ss to Method A and thirty Ss to Method B. This process is repeated for the low-aptitude group. Teachers are also randomly assigned to the groups. In this hypothetical experiment there are two experimental treatments and two levels of aptitude. Table 10.3 shows the 2 × 2 factorial design for measuring the effects of the two methods of instruction on the learning of students. Note that a 2 × 2 design requires four groups of subjects; subjects within each of two levels of aptitude are randomly assigned to the two treatments.

The scores in the four cells represent the mean scores of the four groups on the dependent variable, the science achievement test. In addition to the four cell scores representing the various combinations of treatments and levels, there are four marginal mean scores: two for the columns and two for the rows. The marginal column means are for the two methods, or treatments, and the marginal row means are for the two levels of aptitude.

From the data given you can first determine the *main effects* for the two independent variables. The treatment mean scores without regard to aptitude level indicate the main effect for treatments. If you compare the mean score of the two Method A groups, 67.5,

Table 10.3 *Example of a Factorial Design*

| APTITUDE (X_2) | INSTRUCTIONAL METHOD (X_1) | | MEAN |
	METHOD A	METHOD B	
High	75.0	73.0	74
Low	60.0	64.0	62
Mean	67.5	68.5	

with that of the two Method B groups, 68.5, you find that the difference between these means is only one point. Therefore you might be tempted to conclude that the method used has little effect on the dependent variable.

Now examine the mean scores for the levels, to determine the main effect of X_2, aptitude level, on achievement scores. The main effect for levels does not take into account any differential effect caused by treatments. The mean score for the two high-aptitude groups is 74, and the mean score for the two low-aptitude groups is 62; this difference, 12 points, is the effect attributable to aptitude level. The high-aptitude group has a markedly higher mean score; thus, regardless of treatment, the high-aptitude groups perform better than the low-aptitude groups.

A factorial design also permits the investigator to assess the **interaction** between the two independent variables—that is, the different effects of one of them at different levels of the other. If there is an interaction, the effect that the treatment has on learning will differ for the two aptitude levels. If there is no interaction, the effect of the treatment will be the same for both levels of aptitude.

From looking at Table 10.3, you can see that the Method A mean is higher than the Method B mean for the high-aptitude group, and the Method B mean is higher for the low-aptitude group. Thus some particular combinations of treatment and level of aptitude interact to produce greater gains than do some other combinations. This interaction effect between method and aptitude levels is shown graphically in Figure 10.2. If this interaction is statistically significant, you conclude that the effectiveness of the method depends on aptitude. Method A is more effective with the high-aptitude students; Method B is more effective with the low-aptitude group. Now examine another set of data obtained in a hypothetical 2 × 2 factorial study. Table 10.4 shows the results of a study designed to investigate the effect of two methods of instruction on achievement. Again, because the investigator anticipates that the method may be differentially effective depending on the aptitude of the subject, the first step is to distinguish two levels of aptitude. The researcher randomly assigns subjects within each level to the two methods. After the experiment, the researcher administers achievement tests and records the scores for every subject. If you compare the mean score of the two groups taught by Method B, 53, with that of the two groups taught by Method A, 45, you see that the former is somewhat higher. Therefore, Method B appears more effective than Method A. The difference between the means for the two aptitude levels, on the main effects for aptitude, is 10 (54 − 44). Regardless of treatment, the high-aptitude group performs

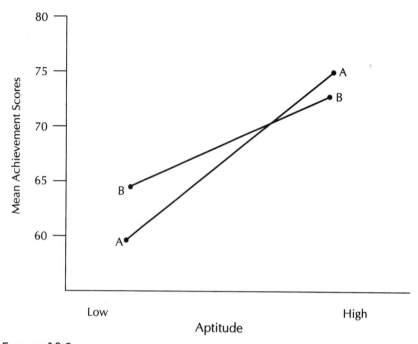

FIGURE 10.2

Illustration of Interaction between Method and Aptitude Level

better than the low-aptitude group. The data reveal no interaction between treatment and levels. Method B appears more effective regardless of the aptitude level. In other words, treatments and levels are independent of each other. The lack of interaction is illustrated graphically in Figure 10.3. It is not possible to demonstrate either the presence or absence of interaction without using a factorial design.

The factorial design can be extended to more complex experiments, in which there are a number of independent variables; the numeric values of the digits indicate the number of levels for the specific independent variables. For instance, in a $2 \times 3 \times 4$ factorial design, there are three independent variables with two, three, and four levels, respectively. Such an experiment might use two teaching methods, three ability levels, and

Table 10.4 *Example of a Factorial Design*			
	TREATMENT (X_1)		
APTITUDE (X_2)	*METHOD A*	*METHOD B*	*MEAN*
High	50	58	54
Low	40	48	44
Mean	45	53	

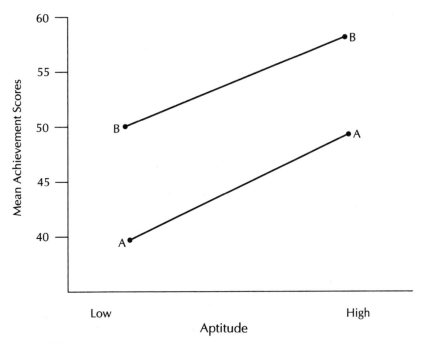

FIGURE 10.3
Illustration of Lack of Interaction between Method and Aptitude Level

four grades. Theoretically a factorial design may include any number of independent variables with any number of levels of each. However, when too many factors are manipulated or controlled simultaneously, the study and the statistical analysis become unwieldy and some of the combinations may be artificial. The number of groups required for a factorial design is the product of the digits that indicate the factorial design. In the 2 × 3 × 4 design, twenty-four groups would be required to represent all combinations of the different levels of the multiple independent variables. The mere thought of the complexities involved in arranging for large numbers of subjects under large numbers of conditions will perhaps help the reader to understand why most educational researchers attempt to answer their questions with the simplest possible designs, even though the statistical analysis can be easily handled by computer. The advantages of the factorial design are that it accomplishes in one experiment what otherwise might require two or more separate studies, provides an opportunity to study interactions that are often so important in educational research, and provides a more powerful test of hypotheses.

Quasi-Experimental Designs

Experimenters prefer designs that provide full experimental control through randomization procedures. These are the true experimental designs as presented in the previous section (Designs 3 through 8). In many situations in educational research, it is not possible to conduct a true experiment. Neither full control over the scheduling of experimental conditions nor the ability to randomize can always be realized. For instance, in educational research conducted in a school setting it may not be possible for you to assign subjects randomly to groups. In this case you must use designs that will provide as much control as possible under the existing situation. Designs that do not include random assignment are known as *quasi-experimental designs* and are used where true experimental designs are not feasible. Because the quasi-experimental design does not provide full control, it is extremely important that the researcher be aware of the threats to both internal and external validity and consider these factors in the interpretation. Campbell and Stanley stated, however, that quasi-experimental studies are "well worth employing where more efficient probes are unavailable" (1966, p. 205). These designs permit the researcher to reach reasonable conclusions even though full control is not possible.

Design 9: Nonrandomized Control Group, Pretest-Posttest Design

In a typical school situation, schedules cannot be disrupted nor classes reorganized to accommodate a research study. In such a case it is necessary to use groups as they are already organized into classes or other preexisting intact groups.

Design 9 is one of the most widely used quasi-experimental designs in educational research. You can see that it is similar to Design 5 but with one important difference; Design 9 does *not* permit random assignment of subjects to the experimental and control groups.

| Design 9: Nonrandomized Control Group, Pretest-Posttest Design | | | |
Group	Pretest	Independent Variable	Posttest
E	Y_1	X	Y_2
C	Y_1	—	Y_2

A researcher might be allowed to use two sections of freshman English at a high school for a study on vocabulary development. The researcher should select two sections that at least appear to be similar; don't choose a remedial class and an advanced class. Although subjects cannot be randomly assigned, flip a coin to determine which of the two intact groups will be the experimental and which the control group. The researcher would give a vocabulary pretest to both classes, administer a program designed to improve vocabulary to the experimental group only, and then give a vocabulary posttest to both groups. If the experimental group shows significantly greater achievement on the posttest, can the researcher conclude that the new program was effective?

Without random assignment of subjects, you do not know if the groups were equivalent before the study began. Perhaps the class designated the experimental group would have done better on the posttest without the experimental treatment. Thus there is an initial *selection bias* that can seriously threaten the internal validity of this design. The pretest, the design's most important feature, provides a way to deal with this threat. The pretest enables you to check on the equivalence of the groups on the dependent variable before the experiment begins. If there are no significant differences on the pretest, you can eliminate selection as a threat to internal validity and proceed with the study. If there are some differences, the investigator can use ANCOVA to statistically adjust the posttest scores for the pretest differences.

Because both experimental and control groups take the same pre- and posttest, and the study occupies the same period of time, other threats to internal validity such as maturation, instrumentation, pretesting, history, and regression (if groups are not selected on the basis of extreme scores) should not be serious threats to internal validity. Having the same person teach both English classes would be recommended.

There are some internal validity threats, however, that this design does not control, namely threats resulting from an interaction of selection and some of the other common threats.

Interaction of Selection and Maturation

We have stated that maturation per se is not a serious threat in this design because both groups would mature during the course of the experiment. The problem arises when the two groups differ in their propensity to maturation. If one of the selected groups is more subject to maturation than the other, you have an *interaction of selection and maturation* to threaten internal validity. Suppose Section 1 of freshman English meets at the same hour that the remedial mathematics class meets, whereas Section 3 meets at the same hour as the advanced algebra class. You would expect Section 1 as a group to show the most gain on academic performance on the posttest because many of the poorer students are in the remedial mathematics class. Section 3 would be expected to show the least gain, because many of the best students are in the advanced algebra class at the same time. The timing of the mathematics classes influences the makeup of the English sections, and because of the interaction between selection and maturation, the gain to be expected in the sections is affected.

Selection-maturation interaction can be a particularly difficult problem when volunteers are compared with nonvolunteers. For example, let's say you offer an after-school reading improvement program to those who wish it. Reading pretest means show no difference between those who volunteer for the after-school program and those who do not. If the posttreatment scores show greater gain for the treatment group than for the control group, you cannot confidently attribute the greater gain to the treatment. It is quite possible that students who were willing to participate in the after-school program were more concerned about their reading or their parents were more concerned about their reading and were therefore more likely to show greater gain in reading whether they received treatment or not.

Interaction of Selection and Regression

A selection-regression interaction could occur in this design if you drew the groups used in the study from populations having different means. Even though the groups are equivalent on a pretest, the regression toward the mean effect that occurs could result in a shift (change) from pre- to posttest that is incorrectly interpreted as an experimental effect.

Let's assume that the experimental group in a study has a mean of 75 on a pretest, which is below the mean of its parent population, whereas the control group with a pretest mean of 75 is above the mean of its population. Because each group will regress toward the mean of the parent population when retested, the experimental group will be expected to have a higher mean on the posttest, whether or not X is introduced; on the other hand, the mean of the control group will regress downward. The experimental group will appear to have made more progress during the course of the study than the control group, which will most likely be erroneously attributed to the effect of the treatment.

Interaction of Selection and Instrumentation   As we pointed out in Chapter 8, most educational tests have a ceiling, which means that range of achievement on the test is limited. This characteristic could result in changes occurring for one group that apparently do not occur for the other. The gains are limited by the difference between the posttest's ceiling and the magnitude of the pretest score. If a student answers 92 items correctly on a 100-item pretest, this student can only gain 8 points on the 100-item posttest. However, a student with a score of 42 on the pretest could make a gain of 58 points on the posttest. Thus, because of this ceiling effect, students who score high on the pretest are restricted to a low change score. They may have improved greatly, but the instrument cannot show the gain. In contrast, low-scoring students on the pretest show a large gain, because they have room to improve their scores. You might erroneously conclude that the treatment was more effective with the latter group. This illustrates the problem with change or gain scores; an analysis of covariance with the pretest scores as the covariate would be the recommended procedure for analyzing the posttest scores.

In summary, the nonrandomized control group design is a good second choice when random assignment of subjects to groups is not possible. The more similar the experimental and the control groups are at the beginning of the experiment, and the more this similarity is confirmed by similar group means on the pretest, the more credible the results of the nonrandomized control group pretest-posttest study become. If the pretest scores are similar and selection-maturation and selection-regression interactions can be shown to be unlikely explanations of posttest differences, the results of this quasi-experimental design are quite credible.

Even if the group means are noticeably different before treatment, a nonequivalent control group is better than a preexperimental design that has no control group at all. Design 9 can be extended to employ more than two groups. The threats to external validity in Design 9 are similar to those encountered with Design 5. An advantage of Design 9, however, is that the reactive effects of experimentation are more easily controlled than they are in Design 5. When intact classes are used, subjects are probably less aware of an experiment being conducted than when subjects are drawn from classes and put into experimental sessions. This contributes to the generalizability of the findings.

Design 10: Counterbalanced Design

Design 10, or **counterbalanced design,** another design that can be used with intact class groups, rotates the groups at intervals during the experimentation. For example,

Groups 1 and 2 might use Methods A and B, respectively, for the first half of the experiment and then exchange methods for the second half. The distinctive feature of Design 10 is that all subjects receive all experimental treatments at some time during the experiment. In effect, this design involves a series of replications; in each replication the groups are shifted so that at the end of the experiment each group has been exposed to each X. The order of exposure to the experimental situation differs for each group. The counterbalanced design is usually employed when several treatments are to be tested, but it also may be used with only two treatments.

Design 10: A Sample Counterbalanced Design

		Experimental Treatments		
Replication	X_1	X_2	X_3	X_4
1	Group A	B	C	D
2	Group C	A	D	B
3	Group B	D	A	C
4	Group D	C	B	A
	Column mean	Column mean	Column mean	Column mean

Each row in Design 10 represents one replication. For each replication the groups are shifted so that Group A first experiences X_1, then X_2, X_3, and finally X_4. Each cell in the design would contain the mean scores on the dependent variable for the group, treatment, and replication indicated. The mean score for each column would indicate the performance of all four groups on the dependent variable under the treatment represented by the column.

A classroom teacher could use a counterbalanced study to compare the effectiveness of two methods of instruction on learning in science. The teacher could choose two classes and two units of science subject matter comparable in the nature of the concepts; difficulty of concepts, and length. It is essential that the units be equivalent in the complexity and difficulty of the concepts involved. During the first replication of the design, Class 1 is taught Unit 1 by Method A and Class 2 is taught by Method B. An achievement test over Unit 1 is administered to both groups. Then Class 1 is taught Unit 2 by Method B and Class 2 is taught by Method A; both are then tested over Unit 2. The arrangement is shown in Table 10.5.

Table 10.5 *Example of a Counterbalanced Design*

	EXPERIMENTAL TREATMENTS	
REPLICATION	METHOD A	METHOD B
(Unit) 1	Class 1	Class 2
(Unit) 2	Class 2	Class 1
	Column mean	Column mean

After the study the column means are computed to indicate the mean achievement for both groups (classes) when taught by the method indicated by the column heading. A comparison of these column mean scores through an analysis of variance indicates the effectiveness of the methods on achievement in science.

Design 10 overcomes some of the weaknesses of Design 9; that is, when intact classes must be used, counterbalancing provides an opportunity to rotate out any differences that might exist between the groups. Because the treatments are administered to all groups, the results obtained for each X cannot be attributed to preexisting differences in the subjects. If one group should have more aptitude on the average than the other, each X treatment would benefit from this greater aptitude.

The main shortcoming of Design 10 is that there may be a carryover effect from one X to the next. Therefore, this design should be used only when the experimental treatments are such that exposure to one treatment will have no effect on subsequent treatments. This requirement may be hard to satisfy in much educational research. Furthermore, one must establish the equivalence of learning material used in various replications. It may not always be possible to locate equivalent units of material. Another weakness of the counterbalanced design is the possibility of boring students with the repeated testings this method requires.

Time Series Designs

Design 11: One-Group Time Series Design

Design 11 (**one-group time series design**) involves periodic measurement on one group and the introduction of an experimental treatment into this time series of measurements. As the design indicates, a number of measurements on a dependent variable are taken. X is introduced, and additional measurements of Y are made. By comparing the measurements before and after, you can assess the effect of X on the performance of the group on Y. A time series design might be used in a school setting to study the effects of a major change in administrative policy on disciplinary incidents. Or a study might involve repeated measurements of students' attitudes and the effect produced by introducing a documentary film designed to change attitudes.

Design 11: One-Group Time Series Design								
Y_1	Y_2	Y_3	Y_4	X	Y_5	Y_6	Y_7	Y_8

Figure 10.4 illustrates some possible patterns from time series studies into which an experimental treatment is introduced. It shows the series of measurements Y_1 through Y_8, with the introduction of the experimental treatment at point X. You can assess the effect of the X by examining the stability of the repeated measurements.

From examining the difference between Y_4 and Y_5 in Pattern A, perhaps you would be justified in assuming that X affects the dependent variable. Pattern B suggests the possibility of a temporary experimental effect of X. However, you could not assume that X produces the change in either pattern C or D. Pattern C appears to result from matura-

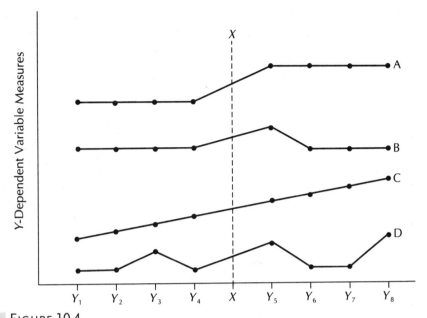

FIGURE 10.4

Illustration of Possible Outcome Patterns in a Time Design

tion or a similar influence. The erratic nature of pattern D suggests the operation of ex-traneous factors.

Design 11 is similar to Design 1 in that it uses before-and-after measures and lacks a control group. However, it has certain advantages over Design 1 that makes it more use-ful in educational research. The repeated testing provides a check on some common threats to internal validity. Maturation, testing, and regression could be ruled out as plau-sible explanations of the shift occurring between Y_4 and Y_5, if such shifts do not occur in the previous time periods under observation. It is recommended that no change in mea-suring instruments be made during the course of the time study. In this way you elimi-nate changes in instrumentation as a possible explanation of the $Y_5 - Y_4$ difference.

The major weakness of Design 11 is its failure to control history; that is, you cannot rule out the possibility that it is not X but some simultaneous event that produces the observed change. Perhaps such factors as seasonal or weather changes or such school agents as examinations could account for the change. In a study designed to assess the effect of a lecture-film treatment on student attitudes toward minorities, to what extent would the attitude measurements be affected by a nationally publicized minority riot in a dis-tant city? The extent to which history (uncontrolled contemporary events) is a plausible explanatory factor must be taken into account by the experimenters as they attempt to interpret their findings. You must also consider the external validity of the time design. Because there are repeated tests, perhaps there is a kind of interaction effect of testing that would restrict the findings to those populations subject to repeated testing. However, as long as the measurements are of a typical, routine type used in school settings, this is not likely to be a serious limitation. Further, a selection-X interaction may occur, especially if you select some particular group that may not be typical. Statistical interpretation can be a particular problem with time data. The usual tests of significance may not be appropriate with a time design. See Campbell and Stanley (1966) for a discussion of the statistical tests that may be used with this design.

Design 12: Control Group Time Series Design

Design 12 (**control group time series design**) is an extension of Design 11 to include a control group. The control group, again representing an intact class, would be measured at the same time as the E group but would not experience the X treatment. This design overcomes the weakness of Design 11—that is, failure to control history as a source of extraneous variance. The control group permits the necessary comparison. If the E group shows a gain from Y_4 to Y_5 but the C group does not show a gain, then the effect must be caused by X rather than by any contemporaneous events, which would have affected both groups.

Design 12: Control Group Time Series Design								
				Group				
E	Y_1	Y_2	Y_3	Y_4	X	Y_5	Y_6	Y_7	Y_8
C	Y_1	Y_2	Y_3	Y_4	—	Y_5	Y_6	Y_7	Y_8

Other variations of the time series design include adding more control groups, more observations, or more experimental treatments.

Validity Problems with Experimental Designs

Some sources of invalidity in the one-variable experimental designs are summarized in Table 10.6. This brief summary must not be depended on as the sole guide in selecting a design. It must be accompanied by a thorough consideration of the qualified presentation appearing in the text so that the reader understands the particular strengths and weaknesses that characterize each design.

Single-Subject Experimental Designs

The single-subject experimental design almost sounds like a contradiction in terms. How can an experiment be run with a sample size of one? Obviously there can be no random assignment or use of control groups. Yet **single-subject research** has become popular over the past twenty-five years. Proponents of this particular methodology argue that experimental control can be achieved in other than the traditional ways. After describing the two major approaches to single-subject research and the rationale behind them, we

Table 10.6 *Factors Jeopardizing the Internal Validity of Experimental Designs*

	DESIGNS[a]											
	PREEXPERIMENTAL		TRUE EXPERIMENTAL						QUASI-EXPERIMENTAL			
SOURCES OF INVALIDITY	1	2	3	4	5	6	7	8	9	10	11	12
History[b]	−	+	+	+	+	+	+	+	+	+	−	+
Maturation	−	?	+	+	+	+	+	+	+	+	+	+
Pretesting	−	+	+	+	+	+	+	+	+	+	+	+
Instrumentation	−	+	+	+	+	+	+	+	+	+	?	+
Statistical Regression	?	+	+	+	+	+	+	+	?	+	+	+
Differential Selection	+	−	+	+	+	+	+	+	−	+	+	+
Experimental Mortality	+	−	+	+	+	+	+	+	+	+	+	+
Interaction of Selection and Other Threats	−	−	+	+	+	+	+	+	−	?	+	+
Subject Effects	−	−	?	?	?	−	−	−	−	+	−	−
Experimenter Effect	−	−	?	?	?	−	−	−	−	−	−	−
Diffusion	na	−	?	?	?	?	?	?	−	?	na	?

[a]Designs are as follows:

1. One-group pretest-posttest
2. Static group comparison
3. Randomized *Ss*, posttest-only control group
4. Randomized matched *Ss*, posttest-only control group
5. Randomized *Ss*, pretest-posttest control group
6. Solomon, three groups
7. Solomon, four groups
8. Simple factorial
9. Nonrandomized control group, pretest-posttest
10. Counterbalanced
11. One-group time series
12. Control group time series

[b]A plus sign indicates that the factor is controlled; a minus sign indicates lack of control; and a question mark indicates a possible source of concern.

will examine the strengths and limitations of this type of research in comparison with the other more conventional designs.

Study of the individual has always had a place in educational and psychological research. Freud's case studies and Piaget's observations of individual children are notable examples. Although case studies (see Chapter 14) and single-subject experiments both study the individual, in a single-subject experiment, the investigator deliberately manipulates one or more independent variables, whereas in a case study the observer studies the subjects' interaction with events that occur naturally.

Single-case designs have been particularly useful in clinical applications where the focus is on the therapeutic value of an intervention for the client. A teacher of severely learning-disabled children, for example, would want information regarding the effectiveness of a specific procedure with an individual child. Some feel that studies that report mean or average differences for groups may have little meaning when treating a specific individual. Single-subject designs are basically extensions of the quasi-experimental one-group time series design (Design 11). The two most common are the ABAB and the multiple-baseline design.

ABAB Designs

The **ABAB design** consists of a period of no treatment, or baseline (A), during which the behavior of interest is repeatedly measured. Examples of such behaviors are the number of times a student with cognitive disability leaves her seat or the number of times an autistic child bangs his head. This pretreatment assessment serves as a control period with which treatment effects will be compared. After a stable picture of pretreatment behavior has been established, phase B, the treatment, is initiated. In the treatment phase the child might be given tokens (exchangeable for desired privileges) for time periods spent seated or time periods with no self-abusive action. The behavior is consistently monitored throughout the treatment phase, usually until the intervention appears to have taken effect and the rate of behavior stabilizes. Further experimental control is achieved by a second A phase. This is usually a withdrawal of treatment, but in some cases the second A phase is actually a reversal of treatment, reinforcing a behavior incompatible with the desired response. Discontinuing the giving of tokens to the girl constitutes a withdrawal of treatment, while giving her tokens when she leaves her seat is a reversal of treatment. In either case removal of treatment is expected to cause the behavior to return to the original (first baseline) level. Ending the experiment with the second A phase has the drawback of leaving the client in the same state as before the experiment started. For ethical reasons and to add strength to the design by replicating the procedure, the treatment phase (B) is again instituted. Many variations on the ABAB design are possible. More than one treatment can be tested—for instance, using an ABCACB format in which A is no treatment and B and C are alternate treatments.

Figure 10.5 illustrates an ABAB design. Mornings were often difficult for the entire family of an 8-year-old developmentally disabled boy, Curt, because he took up to two hours to get dressed in the morning. Constant reminders, pleadings, and occasional scoldings had not helped. Once during a week of baseline measurement (A) Curt did get dressed in only 4 minutes, so his parents knew he was capable of dressing himself in a reasonable time.

During the treatment (B) phase, each morning Curt's clothes were laid out in the bathroom, he was awakened, and then a kitchen timer was set for 10 minutes. Curt earned a red sticker to put on the chart on his door if he dressed himself before the timer rang. The sticker entitled him to watch TV that evening. If he did not finish within the 10 minutes, he had to stay in the bathroom until dressed and forfeit TV for the day. Curt was praised when he met the criterion, ignored when he didn't.

During the week of baseline, Curt took an average of 59 minutes to get dressed. During seventeen days of the first B phase, Curt met the criterion nine times and his average was 10 minutes. On three occasions zero minutes was recorded because he woke and dressed himself before his parents were awake.

During the following six days, Curt's clothes were laid out for him but the timer was omitted and he was allowed to watch TV no matter how long he took to dress. His dressing time averaged 23 minutes during this second A phase. When treatment was reinstituted for twelve of the next thirteen days, Curt's dressing time then averaged 8 minutes.

Because treatment was always accompanied by a change in dressing time, a credible relationship between treatment and dressing time was established. The key element in the

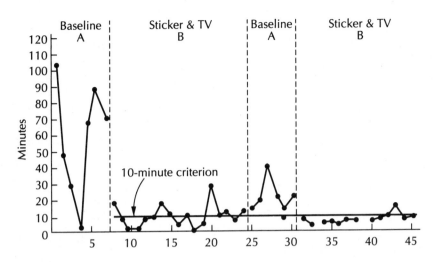

FIGURE 10.5

ABAB Design (Use of Differential Reinforcement to Decease Morning Dressing Time of an 8-year-old Boy)

From *Working with Parents of Handicapped Children* (p. 59) by W. Heward, J.C. Dardig, & A. Rossett, 1979, Columbus, OH: Merrill. Copyright 1979 by Bell & Howell Company. Reprinted by permission.

ABAB design is the return to former levels of behavior when the baseline condition is reinstated. The assumption that the intervention is the cause of the change can be quite weakened under certain circumstances. If there is considerable variability during the baseline period, you could argue that posttreatment behavior did not differ meaningfully from pretreatment behavior. If the shift from treatment (B) back to baseline (A) is equivocal, much of the power of the ABAB design is gone. The second baseline often does not show the same extreme of behavior as the first, and in some cases there is no return to previous rates. In some cases other factors, such as history or maturation, could cause the observed effect.

Kazdin (1980) argued that returning to baseline conditions may be unethical under some circumstances. Do you really want the autistic child to return to the previous levels of head-banging just to provide evidence that the treatment caused the reduction? Because of these potential problems with the ABAB design, the multiple-baseline design was developed. This design has the clinical advantage of continuing any improvement made without returning to less desired behavior.

Multiple-Baseline Designs

In a **multiple-baseline design,** measures of different behaviors are made simultaneously during the baseline condition. For example, the researcher might record the number of times a student talked in class without permission, the number of worksheets completed, and the number of times the student hit another child. Or the same behavior of several clients, such as amount of eye contact with the teacher, could be recorded for two or more children in a preschool class during the baseline phase. In both cases the treatment (B) is the same across all conditions or students. Experimental control in the multiple baseline results from starting the treatment at a different point in time for each behavior and/or person involved, rather than from returning to baseline. Thus, after the baseline is established, treatment for Behavior 1 is instituted and the baseline is continued for Behaviors 2 and 3. When treatment for Behavior 2 is instituted, treatment for Behavior 1 and baseline for Behavior 3 are continued. Finally, treatment for Behavior 3 is instituted. It is expected that each behavior will change in the desired direction at the point at which treatment is begun, not before or after.

Thus the multiple-baseline design uses the AB as its basic unit. If some outside event other than the treatment was the actual cause of the changes, it should affect all children or all behaviors at the same point in time. One assumption of this design is that treatment affects different behaviors specifically. Reinforcing one behavior (completing arithmetic problems) is not expected to increase another response (reading rate). The behaviors, or situations, must be independent (uncorrelated) for the multiple-baseline study to show interpretable effects. In actuality, independence of behavior may be difficult to attain. Modifying one behavior (such as talking in class) may influence other targeted behaviors (completing assignments on time). See Kazdin and Kopel (1975) for further exploration of multiple-baseline design problems.

Comparison of Single-Subject and Group Designs

In both single-subject and group experiments, the goal of the experimenter is to establish as unequivocally as possible the connection between the manipulation of the independent variable (treatment) and its effect on the dependent variable (behavior). In group designs, random assignment of subjects to experimental or control groups eliminates many rival explanations of differences observed after treatment. Treatment effects (between groups) can be assessed relative to intersubject variability effects (within group) by using appropriate statistical tests. These tests determine whether chance alone is a credible explanation for the results. The single-subject design uses other methods to establish credibility. The experimenter controls the amount of time in which baseline and treatment phases are in effect, and the length of the baseline period can be extended until the behavior stabilizes. For unambiguous interpretation, the baseline should be relatively flat or the trend should be in the opposite direction from that expected after treatment. One drawback to experimenter control of the length of the treatment phase is the tendency to continue treatment until "something happens." If behavior change does not closely follow the beginning of treatment, it is possible that another, nonexperimental variable is the cause of the observed change.

Single-subject experimental designs do bypass one source of error of group designs—namely, intersubject variability. Each individual serves as his or her own control, so comparability is not a problem. The major means of control is replication, a feature seldom incorporated into group designs. The ABAB design involves a single replication using the same subject, whereas the multiple-baseline design replicates more than one treatment. Replication of the multiple baseline design makes it less likely that effects attributed to treatment were in fact caused by extraneous event or subject variables (Birnbauer, Peterson, & Solnick, 1974).

Well-designed single-subject research can meet the criteria for internal validity. However, the question of external validity—the generalizability of experimental findings—is not as easily answered by designs that use only one or a few subjects. You can demonstrate that allowing a behaviorally disordered teenager to listen to rock music contingent on completing assignments increases the amount of schoolwork done by that particular teenager, but how can you determine whether this treatment will be successful with other teenagers, or all behaviorally disordered teenagers? Although any one particular single-subject study will be low in external validity, a number of similar studies that carefully describe subjects, conditions, and treatments will build the case for wide application of particular treatment effects. For a more complete discussion of single-subject designs, see Kazdin (1982).

SUMMARY

Experimentation is the most rigorous and the most desirable form of scientific inquiry. The controlled conditions that characterize the experiment make it possible to identify verified functional relationships among the phenomena of interest to educators. Experimenters who control the conditions under which an event occurs have distinct advantages over observers who simply watch or study an event without control: (1) They can manipulate or vary the conditions systematically and note the variations in results; (2) they can make the event occur at a time when they are prepared to make accurate observations and measurements; and (3) they can repeat their observations under the same conditions, for verification, and can describe these conditions so that other experimenters can duplicate them and make an independent check on the results. Research designs that represent the blueprint for carrying out the experiment are classified as preexperimental, true experimental, and quasi-experimental.

A research design should have internal and external validity. Internal validity is concerned with the question, Did the experimental treatment (independent variable) really bring about the observed changes in the dependent variable, or were they caused by some unintended variable(s)? There are a number of threats to internal validity, including selection, history, maturation, pretesting, instrumentation, regression, and the interaction effect among some of these factors. A research design has external validity if the results of the research can be generalized to other settings, operational definitions, and populations. Any factor that interferes with the generalization of experimental results to other groups or settings represents a threat to external validity. Some of the threats to external validity are selection-treatment interaction, pretest-treatment interaction, subject effects, experimenter effect, and vagueness in operationally defining the variables.

True experimental designs provide the best control of the factors that threaten internal and external validity. With these designs subjects are randomly assigned to treatments. With quasi-experimental designs the investigator can control treatment but cannot randomly assign subjects to treatments. Quasi-experimental designs that study the effect of treatment on a single subject have proven useful in behavioral research.

REFERENCES

Birnbauer, L., Peterson, C., & Solnick, J. (1974). Design and interpretation of studies of single subjects. *American Journal of Mental Deficiency, 79,* 191–203.

Campbell, D.T., & Stanley, J.C. (1966). *Experimental and quasi-experimental designs for research.* Boston: Houghton Mifflin.

Cook, T.D. & Campbell, D.T. (1979). *Quasi-experimentation: Design and analysis issues for field settings.* Chicago: Rand McNally.

Fisher, R.A. (1925). *Statistical Methods for Research Workers* (1st ed.) London: Oliver & Boyd.

Heward, W., Dardig, J.C., & Rossett, A. (1979). *Working with parents of handicapped children.* Columbus, OH: Merrill.

Kazdin, A. (1980). *Research design in clinical psychology.* New York: Harper & Row.

Kazdin, A.E. (1982). *Single case research designs: Methods for clinical and applied settings.* New York: Oxford University Press.

Kazdin, A., & Kopel, S. (1975). On resolving ambiguities of the multiple baseline design: Problems and recommendations. *Behavior Therapy, 6,* 601–608.

Kempthorne, O. (1961). The design and analysis of experiments with some reference to educational research. In R.O. Collier & S.M. Elam (Eds.), *Research design and analysis: Second annual Phi Delta Kappa symposium on Educational research,* 97–133. Bloomington, IN: Phi Delta Kappa.

Mill, J.S. (1846). *A system of logic.* New York: Harper & Brothers.

Rice, J.M. (1897). The futility of the spelling grind. *Forum, 23,* 163–172, 409–419.

Rosenthal, R. (1985). From unconscious experimenter bias to teacher expectancy effects. In J.B. Dusek (Ed.), *Teacher expectancies* (pp. 37–65). Hillsdale, NJ: Erlbaum.

Schoen, H.L. (1976). Self-paced mathematics instruction: How effective has it been? *Arithmetic Teacher, 23,* 90–96.

Smith, M.L., & Glass, G.V. (1987). *Research and evaluation in education and the social sciences.* Englewood Cliffs, NJ: Prentice Hall.

Solomon, R.L. (1949). On extension of control group design. *Psychological Bulletin, 46,* 137–150.

Thorndike, E.L. (1924). Mental discipline in high school subjects. *Journal of Educational Psychology, 15,* 1–22, 83–98.

Tuckman, B.W. (1999). *Conducting educational research.* Fort Worth, TX: Harcourt Brace College Publishers.

KEY CONCEPTS

ABAB design	compensatory demoralization	control group
analysis of covariance (ANCOVA)	compensatory rivalry	control group time series design
comparison group	confounding	control of variables

controlling situational differences
counterbalanced design
covariate
differential selection
diffusion
double-blind experiment
ecological external validity
experimental design
experimental group
experimental mortality
experimenter effect
external validity
external validity of operations
extraneous variable
factorial design
Hawthorne effect
history (as internal-validity problem)
homogeneous selection
implementation threat
interaction
internal validity
John Henry effect

law of the single independent variable
law of the single significant independent variable
manipulation of independent variable
maturation (as internal-validity problem)
measuring instruments (as internal-validity problem)
mortality
multiple-baseline design
nonrandomized control group, pretest-posttest design
novelty effect
one-group pretest-posttest design
one-group time series design
population external validity
preexperimental designs
pretest sensitization
pretesting (as internal-validity problem)
quasi-experimental designs
random assignment (randomization)

randomized matched subjects, posttest-only control group design
randomized matching
randomized subjects, posttest-only control group design
randomized subjects, pretest-posttest control group design
randomization
reactive effect
selection-maturation interaction
single-blind experiment
single-subject research
Solomon four-group design
Solomon three-group design
static group comparison
statistical equivalence
statistical regression (as internal-validity problem)
subject effects
true experimental designs
using subjects as their own controls

EXERCISES

1. From a group of students enrolled in social studies in a high school, a researcher randomly selected sixty students. The students were then divided into two groups by random assignment of thirty to Group A, the traditional social studies curriculum, and thirty to Group B, a new program designed to deal with the history of certain ethnic groups. The two groups were compared at the end of the semester on a scale designed to measure attitudes toward ethnic groups. In this study, identify the following:
    a. Independent variable
    b. Dependent variable
    c. Control group
    d. Experimental group
    e. Method(s) used to control for differences between the groups
    f. Research design used
    g. Any threats to internal validity

2. Consider the following research question: Does teaching the first year of French through an oral-aural approach, rather than the grammar-transformational method, alter pupil performance on a standardized year-end test in grammar, reading, and vocabulary?
    a. Design the *ideal* experiment to answer this question, assuming that there are no administrative or other restrictions.

b. Design the experiment that would most likely be required in the typical high school setting.

c. State the relative advantages of the ideal experimental design (Exercise 2a) as compared with the design in Exercise 2b.

3. What is the difference between random selection and random assignment? How are they related to internal and external validity?

4. Evaluate the following research designs with respect to methods used and the control provided. Make suggestions for improvements if needed.

a. A researcher wanted to ascertain if homogeneous grouping improves learning in a first course in biology. The researcher designated one of two high schools in a small city to serve as the experimental school and the other as the control. Both schools had about the same number of students in each of four sections of science. In the experimental school, pupils were grouped homogeneously on the basis of aptitude and scores on achievement tests in science. In the control school, pupils were placed in sections at random. At the end of the year, all pupils were given a standardized test in biology. Statistical tests showed the experimental group to be superior on the test. The researcher concluded that homogeneous grouping results in greater learning in biology.

b. A history teacher was concerned about her students' lack of knowledge of their state and national governments and of current events. She decided to experiment with some new materials and methods to see if she could obtain improvement. In Classes A and B she introduced the new materials and methods. In Classes C and D she used the traditional methods. Classes A and B were administered both the pretest and posttest; Classes C and D were administered only

the posttest. When comparisons were made on the posttest, Classes A and B were found to be superior. Their superior performance was attributed to the new materials and methods.

5. Design the *ideal* experiment to test the following hypothesis: Children who view films of harmonious racial interaction will show a more positive attitude toward racial minorities than will children shown films that depict racial conflict.

6. Returning to the research problem in Exercise 2, suppose you also want to know if the two methods of teaching French have differential effects for boys and girls? Outline the experimental design that would permit you to answer this question at the same time.

7. Assume an investigator had used two methods of instruction (A_1 and A_2) with two groups of students (B_1 and B_2) having varying levels of achievement motivation. The groups were compared on an achievement test at the end of the study. The means are presented below. What interpretation would you make of these results?

Level of Achievement	Method	
	A_1	A_2
Motivation B_1	35	15
B_2	15	35

8. What must occur to establish credibility of results in a single-subject design?

9. Identify the internal validity threat defined in each of the following:

a. *E* group performs better because they know they are participating in an experiment.

b. Changes occur within subjects over time that may affect the dependent variable.

c. Extraneous events occur during the research that may influence dependent variable.

d. Subjects differ on the dependent variable even before the experimental treatment.

e. Control group perceives itself in competition with the *E* group and tries harder.

f. Learning about the experiment from people in the experimental group may affect the control group's performance on the dependent variable measure.

10. Identify the threats to internal validity in each of the following experimental studies:

a. At the beginning of the school year, an elementary teacher set up reading stations in her room with supplementary reading materials in each. At the end of the year, she reported that the interest of her class in reading was higher than in any of her previous classes. She recommended that all teachers set up reading stations.

b. A researcher wanted to investigate the effectiveness of new teaching materials designed to increase students' verbal skills. One class used the new materials, and another class used conventional workbooks. Both classes were given a test of verbal skills at the end of a semester.

c. A study was conducted in three third-grade classrooms investigating the effect of three methods of teaching math. The teacher could choose the method she wanted to use, but could use only one method with her students. At the end of the semester, all the third-graders were given the same math achievement test.

11. Identify the threat to external validity in the following examples:

a. A teacher read research reporting great results from using a particular remedial reading program. She tried the program in her classroom, but did not get the same results.

b. A teacher read about a new method of instruction that was very successful with regular classes. The method did not work when she tried it with her special education students.

c. A research journal reported that a new anti-smoking film had brought about a significant change in students' attitudes. After viewing the film, students expressed many more negative attitudes toward smoking than they had on a prefilm measure. A teacher decided to use the film with his middle school students, but did not want to take time to administer the "pretest." He administered an attitude scale following the film, but did not find marked negative attitudes toward smoking.

12. A researcher wants to test the effectiveness of two different computer-based instructional methods on teaching a unit on weather in seventh-grade science. The researcher finds a teacher who will permit three of his classes to participate: Two classes use the computer-based instruction, and the third receives conventional classroom instruction. The researcher administers a pretest to all students, each class has a different method of instruction, and then a posttest as administered.

a. Specify the design of this study and represent it using the notation system used in this chapter.

b. What statistics would you choose to analyze the data?

ANSWERS

1. a. Type of social studies curriculum
   b. Scores on an ethnic attitude scale
   c. Group A, the present curriculum
   d. Group B, curriculum with ethnic history
   e. Random selection of the sample from the population and random assignment of the sample to the experimental and control groups

f. Design 3, the randomized subjects, posttest-only control group design

g. In the event that randomization does not control for initial group differences, there is no pretest to use to check if there are differences in attitudes before the study.

2. a. Use Design 3—that is, randomly assign first-year French students to either the grammar-transformational (control) or oral-aural (experimental) group. Maintain the same conditions, time spent, teachers, and classroom facilities for both groups so that only the teaching method is different. Administer test at the end of the year, and compare group achievement.

b. Randomly assign intact classes of first-year French students to the two teaching methods. Each teacher has an equal number of the two types of classes.

c. In the ideal design, threats to external and internal validity are better controlled through randomization of individual students. The design in Exercise 2b could have problems with nonequivalence of subjects before treatment is given, so that test score differences could be caused by factors other than difference in treatment.

3. Random selection is using a chance procedure to draw a sample from a population. Because it addresses the question of how well results drawn from a sample can be generalized to the population from which the sample was drawn, it is a strategy for increasing external validity. Random assignment is using a chance procedure to assign the subjects available for an experiment to treatment. It is a strategy for increasing internal validity.

4. a. Because the researcher could not assign students randomly to the high schools, there are several threats to internal validity. Students in the experimental school may have been brighter or have had more background in science than students in the control school. Differences in the quality of teaching biology in the schools have not been controlled. Because the researcher used only schools in a small city, the results of the study could not be generalized to other high schools in different settings. To improve the study, the researcher could compare initial science achievement and aptitude scores for the schools to see if the groups were equivalent before treatment. Using several high schools, with classes within each high school being randomly assigned to experimental conditions, would control for factors specific to a given school.

b. Classes not randomly assigned may not be equivalent. Pretesting could have been used to determine equivalence but was only given to the experimental groups. The pretesting of the experimental groups alone may have sensitized the groups and influenced the differences found. Classes should be randomly assigned to treatments, even if individual students cannot be randomly assigned.

5. The ideal experiment would randomly assign students to groups. The results of a posttreatment measure of attitudes toward racial minorities would be used to compare the experimental and control groups.

6. This question requires a factorial design with half of the boys and half of the girls assigned randomly to the control and experimental conditions.

7. It appears that there is an interaction between achievement motivation and type of instruction. Students with achievement motivation at level B_1 did better with Method A_1, while those at level B_2 did better with method A_2. The significance of this interaction could be tested with an F-test. There is no overall effect of motivation or instructional method, because the means for A_1 and A_2, and B_1 and B_2 are the same.

8. There must be an unambiguous change in behavior whenever there is a change in treatment.

9. a. Hawthorne effect (or subject effect)
   b. Maturation
   c. History
   d. Selection
   e. John Henry effect
   f. Diffusion

10. a. Differential selection, implementation, contemporary history, and subjects' attitudes
    b. Differential selection, implementation, contemporary history, and subjects' attitudes
    c. Without random assignment, groups may not have been equivalent at the beginning. Teachers chose the method they wanted to use; their enthusiasm rather than the method itself may have been the important factor. If one of the methods was very novel, diffusion may have occurred.

11. a. The Hawthorne effect could be a threat in this situation. The students in the original study may have felt special because they were taking part in an experiment, and thus put forth extra effort. The findings did not generalize to a nonexperimental setting.

b. The threat in this case is an interaction between selection and treatment. Certain characteristics of the students interacted with the treatment to produce an effect that did not generalize to a group with different characteristics.

c. The threat is the interaction effect of pretesting. The prefilm measure may have sensitized students so that they responded to the film differently than would a group who did not have the "pretest." It was the interaction that brought about the observed change in attitudes. Thus the results would probably generalize to other pretested populations, but not to unpretested ones. The teacher should have used the pretest.

12. a. Nonrandomized Control Group, Pretest-Posttest Design

E	Y	X	Y
E	Y	X	Y
C	Y	—	Y

b. If the groups were not significantly different on the pretest, you could use ANOVA on the posttest scores. Otherwise, ANCOVA could be used with pretest scores as the covariate.

 INFOTRAC COLLEGE EDITION

Use the keywords *quasi-experimental* + *design* to locate an article that discusses quasi-experimental research designs. What particular kinds of quasi-experimental designs were discussed? What advantages and disadvantages were discussed?

Chapter 11

Ex Post Facto Research

After studying this chapter, the student will be able to:

1 Describe ex post facto research, and compare it to experimental research.

2 State conditions needed to infer a causal relationship.

3 Describe alternative explanations in ex post facto research, and identify cases where these are or are not plausible.

4 Describe methods of partial control, and identify cases where they would be useful.

5 Design an ex post facto investigation.

6 Identify questions for which ex post facto research would be the method of choice.

As researchers probe such educational questions as "Why are some children better readers than others?" "What is the effect of single-parent homes on achievement?" and "Why do some youths become delinquent while others do not?" they find that only some questions can be investigated through experimental research. If you want to investigate the influence of such variables as home environment, motivation, intelligence, parental reading habits, ethnicity, gender, disabilities, and so forth, you cannot randomly assign students to different categories of these variables. Independent variables such as these are called **attribute independent variables.** An attribute variable is a characteristic that a subject has before a study begins.

In contrast, an independent variable that an investigator can directly manipulate is an **active independent variable.** An investigator can determine which students will have access to a computer laboratory and which will not, which will use Program A to study a unit in algebra and which will use Program B. When active independent variables are involved, an investigator can employ experimental or quasi-experimental research. When investigation involves attribute independent variables that the researcher cannot manipulate, he or she must turn to *ex post facto* research (sometimes called *causal-comparative research*). Ex post facto research is also appropriate when the variable actually could be manipulated but is not, because it would be unethical or irresponsible to do so. For example, it would not be ethical to manipulate illegal drug use or use of alcohol or cigarettes to study their effects. To study the effect of retention on subsequent achievement, you wouldn't want to randomly assign some children to be retained and others to be promoted. And you wouldn't manipulate the use of a drug such as Ritalin to study its effects on children's problem-solving behavior. But a researcher could use the ex post facto research method to study the retention question by matching retained students with non-retained students and looking at their subsequent achievement, or could compare the problem-solving behavior of a group of children already taking Ritalin with that of a matched group not taking the drug.

The designation *ex post facto,* from Latin for "after the fact," indicates that **ex post facto research** is conducted after variation in the variable of interest has already been determined in the natural course of events. This method is also called *causal comparative* because its purpose is to investigate cause-and-effect relationships between independent and dependent variables. Researchers use it, however, in situations that do not permit the randomization and manipulation of variables characteristic of experimental research.

The two basic modes of ex post facto research are (1) to begin with subjects who differ on an independent variable and try to determine the consequences of these differences, and (2) to begin with subjects who differ on a dependent variable and try to determine the antecedents (cause) of this difference. An example of the former would be investigating the effect of single-parent households versus that of two-parent households (independent variable) on truancy (dependent variable). An example of the latter would be comparing students who graduated from high school with those who drop out (dependent variable) on independent variables such as motivation, clarity of goals, and self-discipline.

EX POST FACTO AND EXPERIMENTAL APPROACHES COMPARED

In both types of research, interest is focused on discovery or establishment of relationships among the variables. Ex post facto or causal-comparative research, as well as experimental research, can test hypotheses concerning the relationship between an independent variable (X), and a dependent variable, Y. In basic logic, experimental and ex post facto approaches are similar. Thus, much of the same kind of information that an experiment provides can also be obtained through an ex post facto analysis.

However, with an experiment it is possible to obtain much more convincing evidence for **causal** (functional) **relationships** among variables than can be obtained with ex post facto studies. The effects of extraneous variables in an experiment are controlled by the experimental conditions, and the antecedent independent variable is directly manipulated to assess its effect on the dependent variable. If you observe Y to vary concomitantly with the variation in X in this controlled situation, then you have obtained evidence for the validity of the hypothesized antecedent-consequent relationship between X and Y. In an ex post facto investigation, in contrast, the researcher cannot control the independent variables by manipulation or by randomization: Changes in the variables have already taken place. Because of this lack of control, in an ex post facto study it is more hazardous to infer a genuine relationship between X and Y.

Let us illustrate the difference between ex post facto and an experimental approach by examining these two approaches to the same research question. Consider the question of the effect of students' anxiety, in an achievement-testing situation, on their examination performance. The ex post facto approach would involve measuring the already existing anxiety level at the time of the examination, then comparing the performance of "high anxious" and "low anxious" students. The weakness of such an approach is that you could not necessarily conclude that the students' anxiety produced the observed difference in achievement examination performance. Both sets of scores may have been influenced by a third factor, such as knowledge of the subject matter being examined, or general intelligence. Knowledge or aptitude may be the major cause of both the level of anxiety and the achievement test results.

In an experimental approach to the same problem, the investigator could randomly assign subjects to two exam conditions that are identical in every respect except that one is anxiety arousing and the other is neutral. The experimenter can induce anxiety by telling the subjects that their final grade depends on their performance, that the test is extremely difficult, or that the test will be used to identify the incompetent. The neutral group would merely be told that their cooperation is needed for the experiment. The investigator could randomly assign subjects to the two conditions. Then if the anxious group performed better than the neutral group, it could be concluded that the induced anxiety had a facilitating effect on test performance. Such a conclusion could be legitimately drawn because of the control provided by the random assignment of groups to treatments and by the experimenter's direct manipulation of the independent variable. Anxiety is one of the few variables that can be either an active or an attribute-independent variable. You can manipulate it actively, as described (experimental approach), or you can classify subjects on the basis of their scores on an anxiety measure (ex post facto approach).

In a sense, the ex post facto study can be viewed as a reverse approach to experimentation. Instead of taking groups that are equivalent and exposing them to different treatments, the ex post facto study starts with groups that are already different and tries to determine the consequences of or the antecedents of these differences. Such a procedure does not provide the safeguards, typical in experimentation, that are necessary for making strong inferences about causal relationships. Mistakenly attributing causation based on a relationship between two variables is called the **post hoc fallacy.** An investigator who finds a relationship between the variables in an ex post facto study has secured evidence only of some concomitant variation. Because the investigator has not controlled X or other possible variables that may have determined *why*, there is less basis for inferring a causal relationship between X and Y.

If you wish to reach a conclusion that one variable (X) is the cause of another variable (Y), three kinds of evidence are necessary:

1. That a statistical relationship between X and Y has been established
2. That X preceded Y in time
3. That other factors did not determine Y

A statistical relationship is one in which a change in one variable can be predicted from a change in the other. However, we must note that such a relationship between two variables, by itself, is not sufficient evidence of cause and effect. You must proceed to look for evidence on the other two criteria.

Therefore, the investigator must also establish the time sequence; that is, you must consider whether Y might have occurred before X and hence could not be an effect of X. If X is a cause of Y, then a change in X must precede a change in Y. Decisions about the time relationship between X and Y can be made either on a logical basis or as a result of measurements that show the groups did not differ on Y before exposure to X.

In addition to establishing the time sequence, it is also extremely important that the investigator consider whether factors other than X might have determined Y. This is the most difficult evidence to obtain. You proceed to check this possibility by introducing other relevant variables into the analysis and observing how the relationship between X and Y is affected by these additional variables. You may find that the relationship between X and Y holds up even when the other variables are introduced. In this case you have some evidence to support a causal inference. However, you may find that other variables may account for the apparent relationship between X and Y. In this case, you would conclude that the relationship between X and Y is spurious. A **spurious relationship** is one in which the two variables really have no effect on each other but are related because some other variable influences both. For example, a positive relationship between the number of churches and the number of armed robberies in the cities within a state does not mean that building more churches will increase armed robberies, nor that increasing armed robberies will cause more churches to be built. Here the extraneous variable is city size. Large cities have more churches and more armed robberies, whereas small cities have fewer armed robberies and fewer churches.

CONDUCTING AN EX POST FACTO RESEARCH STUDY

1. *The first step in an ex post facto study is to state the research problem, usually in the form of a question.* What is the relationship between variable A and variable B? Or, what is the effect of variable A on variable B? Again, in this type of research the variables involved are those that the researcher does not directly manipulate. The researcher then states a hypothesis about the expected relationship and defines the variables in operational terms.

2. *Next select the two groups to be compared.* Recall that investigators doing ex post facto or causal-comparative research achieve the variation they want, not by directly manipulating the variable itself, but by *selecting* individuals in whom the variable is present or absent, strong, or weak. Thus these two groups should differ on the variable of interest in that one group should possess the characteristic and the other group should not, but they should be similar on any relevant extraneous variables. Differential (subject) selections pose a major threat to the internal validity of ex post facto investigations because then you have no control over the selection of subjects into the two groups. They are selected because they already possess the variable of interest, for example, smoker/nonsmoker, underachiever/nonunderachiever. Whenever assignment is not random, there is always an opening for other variables to enter to explain the observed difference between the groups. The way to deal with this threat is to collect data to show that the groups are similar on any extraneous variables that might affect the variable of interest. For example, if you were looking at the effect of preschool attendance on the social maturity of kindergarteners, you would have to control any other factors that might have been shown to influence social maturity. Some of these might be age, gender, socioeconomic status, aptitude, and so on. You use logic and previous research to determine what factors need to be controlled in an ex post facto study.

3. *Choose between the basic designs for ex post facto research.*

	Independent Variables		Dependent Variables
Design 1	Subjects are already known to differ on independent variable(s).	→	Investigator tests hypothesis concerning possible dependent variable(s).
Design 2	Investigator tests hypothesis concerning possible independent variable(s).	←	Subjects are already known to differ on dependent variable(s).

a. Design 1

Design 1 looks at the consequences of differences on an independent variable. The groups differ in that one group possesses a characteristic and the other does not, or the groups may differ in the degree or extent to which they possess the characteristic. An example would be a study to compare the problem-solving performance of creative and noncreative college students. The hypothesis would read "Creative college students will exhibit greater speed and accuracy on a problem-solving task than will noncreative college students." This hypothesis clearly indicates the need for an ex post facto design, because the investigators can neither manipulate creativity nor assign students randomly to groups. They must start with two groups who already differ on the independent variable, creativity, and compare them on the dependent variable, problem-solving performance. The investigators must define "creative college student" and "noncreative college student" in precise operational terms. Creative college students might be defined as those undergraduates scoring above the third quartile both on the Guilford Test of Alternate Uses and Consequences and on an anagram test. Those students scoring below the first quartile on the tests would be defined as noncreative. The investigators should try to identify variables other than creativity that could affect the dependent variable of problem-solving performance and take steps to equate the experimental and control groups on these variables by matching or by statistical means. For example, in this study other independent variables that should be controlled are intelligence, gender, and perhaps college major or college year. A bright male sophomore in the creative group might be matched with his counterpart in the noncreative group. After formation of the matched groups, the researcher would give both groups a measure of the dependent variable, a problem-solving task. Further analysis of the data by means of a *t*-test would reveal any significant differences in the problem-solving performance of the two groups and perhaps show a relationship between creativity and problem-solving performance.

b. Design 2

Design 2 looks for the cause(s) of differences in the dependent variable. Consider ten members of a wrestling team, three of whom become ill when returning from a tournament. To investigate the cause of the illness, the doctor asks what they ate when the team stopped for dinner on their way home. She finds that every item the three ill wrestlers chose differed except for creamed chicken. The seven wrestlers who did not have creamed chicken did not become ill. She concludes that the creamed chicken caused the illness. The doctor is using philosopher John Stuart Mill's "joint method of agreement and difference":

> If two or more instances in which the phenomenon occurs have only one circumstance in common, while two or more instances in which it does not occur have nothing in common save the absence of that circumstance; the circumstance in which alone the two sets of instances differ, is the effect, or cause, or necessary part of the cause, of the phenomenon. (1846, p. 229)

An example of Design 2 is the research on gender differences in performance on standardized mathematics tests. What factors might account for observed male superiority on these tests? Royer and his colleagues (1999) found support for the hypothesis that males are faster at retrieving basic mathematical facts and hence perform at a higher level on tests. Other researchers have challenged this conclusion.

4. *Collect data on the independent and dependent variables and the relevant extraneous variables from the subjects.*

5. *Analyze and interpret the data.* The same statistics commonly used in analyzing experimental research data are used in analyzing ex post facto data. First, calculate the mean and standard deviation of each group. Then use the *t*-test to see if there is a significant difference between the means of the two groups or ANOVA if there are more than two groups. Chi square is used to determine if an event occurs more frequently in one group than another. Next the researcher states and explores alternative explanations.

Alternative Explanations in Ex Post Facto Research

When investigators can control the treatment (X) and then observe the dependent variable (Y) as in experimental research, they have reasonable evidence that X influences Y. If they cannot control (X), they may be led to inappropriate conclusions. When interpreting ex post facto research one should consider alternative explanations, such as (1) common cause, (2) reverse causality, and (3) the presence of other independent variables.

Common Cause

In an ex post facto investigation, you must consider the possibility that both the independent and dependent variables of the study are merely two separate results of a third variable—that they have a **common cause.** For example, if you use average teachers' salary as an independent variable and sales of distilled spirits as a dependent variable for each year since the repeal of Prohibition in the United States, you find a high positive correlation between the two variables. Does this mean that whenever teachers' salaries are raised they spend their money on alcohol? A more plausible explanation is that the relationship is spurious. Both teachers' salaries and sales of distilled spirits are the result of increasing affluence and inflation since 1933. It is well established that the average income of private high school graduates is much higher than the average income of public and parochial high school graduates. Does this mean that private schools better prepare students for financial success? Or is the difference due to the fact that those families with enough money to send their children to private schools are also able to finance their children's professional training, set them up in business, or buy them ambassadorships, or seats in the U.S. Senate? In city X you may find that over the last twenty years an increase in the consumption of electricity has been accompanied by a corresponding increase in cases of mental illness. Does this mean that an increase in electricity use leads to an increase in mental illness? A check of census figures shows that the population of city X has grown through the years and that the consumption of electricity and cases of mental illness are both functions of population growth.

When doing ex post facto research, you must always consider the possibilities of common cause or causes accounting for an observed relationship. In our examples fairly obvious common causes could be identified. However, in ex post facto research there is always a nagging doubt that maybe common causes no one has thought of explain a relationship. Research has shown that the injury rate of drivers who use safety belts is lower than the injury rate of drivers who do not. Is this because using safety belts reduces injury, or because cautious drivers have fewer injury-causing accidents and also use safety belts?

Reverse Causality

In interpreting an observed relationship in an ex post facto study, the researcher must consider the possibility of **reverse causality**—that the reverse of the suggested hypothesis could also account for the finding—instead of saying that X causes Y, perhaps it is the case that Y causes X. For instance, the proportion of Episcopalians listed in *Who's Who in America* is much greater than their proportion in the general population. Does this mean Episcopalianism leads to the kind of success that results in being listed in *Who's Who?* It is just as plausible, or perhaps more so, to hypothesize that successful people tend to gravitate to the Episcopal church. Similarly, if you find that college students who drink have a lower GPA than nondrinkers, you cannot automatically conclude that alcohol consumption depresses academic performance. Perhaps bad grades drive students to drink. (Or, of course, any number of common causes could lead to both drinking and poor grades.)

Investigations on the effects of child-rearing practices have revealed that children who are frequently punished show more aggressive behavior. Can you conclude that parental punishment leads to aggressive children? Or are aggressive children more likely to be punished?

The hypothesis of reverse causality is easier to deal with than the hypothesis of common cause. With the latter, numerous common causes in each case could produce a spurious relationship. With reverse causality, there is only one possibility in each case: Y caused X, instead of X caused Y.

In a situation when X always precedes Y in time, the very nature of the data rules out the possibility of reverse causality. For example, numerous studies have shown that the average annual income of college graduates is higher than the average annual income of nongraduates. You can rule out the hypothesis of reverse causality, because graduation or nongraduation precedes the subsequent annual income. You cannot rule out a variety of possible common causes.

A method of establishing the time order of variables is to obtain measurements of the same subjects at different times. Let us assume that you are interested in the relationship between employees' acceptance of the philosophy of a corporation, and job promotion within that corporation. If you merely interviewed a sample of the employees and found that those in higher positions held attitudes and opinions more in line with the company's value system, you would not know whether acceptance of company values and objectives was conducive to promotion or whether promotion increased acceptance of the company value system. To rule out reverse causality as an explanation, you could interview a group of new trainees and obtain—by means of a questionnaire, rating scale, or the like—a measure of their acceptance of the corporation philosophy. Then after a period of time, perhaps eighteen months, you could determine from company records which employees had been promoted. If the findings showed that a significantly higher proportion of employees who had expressed attitudes and opinions consistent with corporation philosophy had been promoted, as compared with those who had not, you would have better evidence that conformity with company philosophy was conducive to promotion. (You are still left with the possibility that some common cause or causes account for differences in both philosophy and promotion.)

Other Possible Independent Variables

Independent variables other than the one considered in the causal-comparative study may bring about the observed effect on the Y variable; that is, in addition to X_1, other variables, X_2 and X_3, may also be antecedent factors for the variation in the dependent variable. For example, the recorded suicide rate in Sweden is among the highest in the world. Does this mean the Swedish environment causes more people to commit suicide? Does it mean that the Swedish people are more suicide prone than others? Perhaps there is truth in one or both of these hypotheses. It is equally possible, however, that the actual independent variable is the honesty of coroners in Sweden compared with the honesty of coroners in other countries. In countries where great social stigma falls on the families of those who commit suicide, coroners may well use every conceivable means to record a death as accidental rather than suicide. Therefore, the difference between reported suicide rates may be a function of coroner behavior and nothing else.

More examples: at a governors' conference, Governor X points with pride to the low crime rate in his state. Another governor points out that the police forces in Governor X's state are seriously undermanned and the low crime rate may indicate only that very few crimes there are ever reported. An industrialist asks his personnel manager why he does not hire more Old Tuephingen University graduates, asserting that because so many of them are rapidly moving up the promotion ladder, they are obviously more competent than other graduates. The personnel manager tactfully points out that the phenomenon may not be explained by competence but rather by the fact that the industrialist is himself an Old Tuephingen University graduate and may be subconsciously favoring his fellow alumni in promotion decisions.

An obvious first task for investigators is to attempt to list all the possible alternative independent variables. Then by holding the others constant, you can test in turn each variable to determine if it is related to Y. If you can eliminate the alternative independent variables by showing that they are not related to Y, you gain support for the original hypothesis of a relationship between X and Y.

An Application of Alternative Explanations

In the following report from the National Association of Secondary School Principals (1959), the data show a relationship between automobile use and academic achievement.

Do Automobiles and Scholarship Mix?

No, says Madison HS, Rexburg, Idaho. A study made of the 4-year grade averages of a typical Madison senior class and car drivers showed the following:

No straight-A student had the use of a car.

Only 15% of the B students drove a car to school.

Of C students, 41% brought cars to school.

Of D students, 71% drove to school.

Of F students, 83% drove to school.

Action Program

As a result of the study, Rexburg's Board of Education adopted a resolution on August 11, 1958, which specified that

1. Junior and senior high school students who drive cars to school must make written application to the School Board showing the reason or need to drive their cars to school. Those granted permission will receive student permits.

2. Students driving cars to school on the student permits must park them in designated areas.

3. Students failing to comply with established rules and regulations will have their student permits revoked. If students persist in non-compliance, they will be subject to expulsion from school by action of the School Board.

Community Cooperation

The entire community has organized to support the Board of Education's regulations. The Citizen's Law Enforcement Council and the Rexburg Youth Conference have enlisted the participation of the Civic Club, Rotary Club, American Legion, newspapers, police department, and parents in their drive for high school traffic safety. Hundreds of citizens have signed a pledge to back the drive and have received membership cards issued by the Council and Conference. Madison's principal, W. G. Nelson, strongly supports the community-wide action against unrestricted car use by high school students. "We believe that restriction on automobile use will make for better attendance and closer attention to studies. We haven't 'arrived' but we certainly are on the way."

A Texas Principal

Commenting on the Rexburg program, a Texas principal said, "It has long been my opinion that there is a high correlation between rate of failure, scholarship, and ownership and operation of automobiles freely by high school youth. We are finding it difficult to obtain much interest from able-bodied boys in major athletics. So many of the boys are paying for automobiles or for their maintenance and operation by holding down part-time jobs after school hours that they don't go out for athletics. If they have money to operate their cars, they prefer to ride in them around town after school. There are a few parents who have sufficient control of and influence with their youngsters to prevent the unwise use of their own cars, but they are very scarce."

Is the conclusion that automobile use causes lower academic achievement justified? Let us consider the possible alternative hypotheses.

1. *Common cause.* Are there variables that may influence both auto use and scholarship? It is known that social class is related to scholarship. If social class also influences auto use, the apparent relationship between grades and auto use would be not a cause-effect relationship but two aspects of social class differences. Differences in student lifestyle or values could also account for the apparent relationship. If some students value driving highly and have little interest in scholarship, denying them access to cars would not necessarily increase their scholarship. You could propose a number of credible common cause hypotheses.

2. *Reverse causality.* Is it possible that poor grades are a cause of car use? You could reasonably hypothesize that students who do poorly in school look for other paths to social acceptance and that car use is one possible path.

3. *Other possible independent variables.* Could teachers perceive car users as disinterested students and assign them lower grades than they deserve?

There are so many credible alternative hypotheses that you should hesitate to interpret the data as indicating a cause-effect relationship. Asher and Schusler (1967) investigated the same issue with a design that incorporated more control than had previous studies. Instead of considering only present grades and auto use, they recorded grades of seniors at the end of the first semester and the grades of the same subjects when they were freshmen. If auto use affects scholarship, then the grades of drivers would be expected to drop between the time they were freshmen—and therefore ineligible for driver's licenses—and the time they were seniors. Asher and Schusler used the difference between freshman and senior GPA as their dependent variable. They also covaried (see Chapter 10) on IQ. They found no significant relation between auto use and change in grades. They concluded that "access to an automobile seems not to cause an established pattern of grades to decline, or for that matter, to go up."

PARTIAL CONTROL IN EX POST FACTO RESEARCH

There are strategies for improving the credibility of ex post facto research, although none can adequately compensate for the inherent weakness of such research—namely, lack of control over the independent variable. These strategies provide **partial control** of internal validity problems of common cause and other possible independent variables. Among these strategies are matching, homogeneous groups, building extraneous variables into the design, analysis of covariance, and partial correlation.

Matching

A common method of providing partial control in ex post facto investigations has been to match the subjects in the experimental and control groups on as many extraneous variables as possible. This **matching** is usually done on a subject-to-subject basis to form matched pairs. For example, if you are interested in the relationship between scouting experiences and delinquency, you could locate two groups of boys classified as delinquent and nondelinquent according to specified criteria. In such a study, it would be wise to select pairs from these groups matched on the basis of socioeconomic status, family structure, and other variables known to be related to both choosing the scouting experience and delinquency. The data from the matched samples could be analyzed to determine whether the proportion of those who participated in scouting is greater among nondelinquents than among delinquents. The matching procedure in ex post facto research presents some of the difficulties described in our discussion of its use in experimentation (Chapter 10).

In the first place, using matching in an ex post facto study assumes that you know what the relevant factors are—that is, the factors that may have some correlation with the dependent variable. Furthermore, matching is likely to greatly reduce the number of subjects that can actually be used in the final analysis. Maybe more than one variable needs to be controlled. As the number of matching variables grows, it becomes increasingly more difficult to find a match. The loss of cases inherent in the matching process is an even more serious problem in ex post facto research than in experimentation, where matching precedes the introduction of the independent variable. At least in the experimental approach there may be a possibility (although it is not recommended) of adding new cases to replace the ones that do not match. This cannot be done with ex post facto research.

An early study by Chapin (1947) shows the loss of subjects that occurs as a result of matching. Chapin was interested in the influence of high school graduation on an individual's success and community adjustment after a ten-year period. The initial data revealed that people who had completed high school were more successful than those who had not. However, examination of the high school files revealed that graduates also had higher marks in elementary school, younger ages, higher parental occupations, lived in better neighborhoods, and so on. These factors could have been the causative factors for both completing high school and later success. To partially control these common causes, Chapin examined subgroups of students matched on all these background factors and differing only in completion of high school. Matching reduced the number of cases from 1195 to 46, or 23 graduates and 23 nongraduates—fewer than 4 percent of the number interviewed.

A more serious problem than loss of subjects is the role of regression in an ex post facto matched-pairs design. Let us illustrate the point. Principal A has introduced a new reading program in the fifth grade, and after it has been in use for a year he wants to compare its effectiveness with the effectiveness of the reading program it replaced. In the same district, Principal B's school is still using the old program. Both schools give the same standardized reading test at the end of each school year. Principal A compares the mean grade-equivalent reading scores for fifth-graders in the two schools. He finds the mean grade level equivalent for his fifth-graders is 6.0, whereas the mean for Principal B's fifth-graders is 4.0. Is this dramatic evidence of the effectiveness of the new method? Principal A realizes that the difference between means could be caused by differences between the pupils when they began the fifth grade in the two schools. He obtains scores for the reading test administered when the pupils were finishing fourth grade. He finds that his students had a mean grade level equivalent of 4.8, whereas Principal B's students had a mean grade level equivalent of only 3.2. Therefore he must make an adjustment for the fact that the two groups were not at the same point when they began fifth grade.

Principal A decided to use matching as a way to control for this difference. He selected matched pairs by taking a student from his school with a fourth-grade reading score of 3.1 and matching that student with a student from Principal B's school with a fourth-grade reading score of 3.1, a student from his school with a score of 4.8 with a student from B's school with a score of 4.8 and so on. However, because the mean of the B population is lower than the mean of the A population, there will be many low-scoring B students for whom there is no match in A and many high-scoring A students for whom there is no match in the B group. The scores of all the unmatchable students will be excluded from the data analysis. For those who could be matched, the mean score for the fourth-grade reading test for Group A and Group B will be identical. Therefore, it appears the researchers have successfully created a group from School B who are the same as the group from School A in reading achievement.

This all sounds very good. Can you now attribute differences in fifth-grade reading scores to a difference in the effectiveness of the old and new methods? Alas, no! The matched pairs are basically those students with poorer fourth-grade reading scores from population A and those students with higher scores from population B. The matched A students' scores will regress *up* toward the total A mean, and the matched B students' scores will regress *down* toward the total B mean. Thus, when you compare the fifth-grade reading scores of the matched groups, you would expect the A mean to be higher than the B mean even if the new method is no more effective than the old method.

Matching looks good because it provides experimental and control groups that are equal on a pretreatment variable or variables. However, when two matched groups are drawn from different populations, regression toward the original population means will be expected to create spurious results whenever the two populations are not equal. Matching pairs from within a *single* population is often a useful strategy. Matching subjects from one population with subjects from another population is a *bad* strategy. As is the case with change scores, matching only partly adjusts for preexisting differences between groups, and this underadjustment can be misleading.

Homogeneous Groups

You may recall from the discussion of control in experimentation that it is possible to control for the effects of a variable by selecting samples that are as homogeneous as possible on that variable. A similar procedure can be followed in ex post facto research. Instead of taking a heterogeneous sample and comparing matched subgroups within it, an investigator may control a variable by including in the sample only subjects who are homogeneous on that variable. If academic aptitude is a relevant extraneous variable, the investigator could control its effect by using subjects from only one academic aptitude level. Or if gender is a variable to be controlled, you can use only males or only females in the research. This procedure serves the purpose of disentangling the independent variable in which you may be interested from other variables with which it is commonly associated, so that any effects you find can more justifiably be associated with the independent variable. Using **homogeneous groups** restricts the generalizability of the findings to that homogeneous group, thus reducing external validity of the study. Lee and Loeb (2000) used homogeneous groups in studying the effect of school size on teacher attitudes and student achievement. They avoided any influence the dimension of rural, suburban, and urban settings might have on the dependent variables by studying only schools in the City of Chicago. They found that in small schools (those with fewer than 400 students), teachers had a more positive attitude about their responsibility for students' learning and students learned more, than in medium-sized or large schools.

Building Extraneous Variables into the Design

It may be possible to build relevant extraneous independent variables into the ex post facto design and investigate their effect through the use of two-way and higher-order analyses of variance. For example, suppose an investigator wants to compare the number of truancies among students who have been through an attendance-promoting program and among students who have not been in such a program. If the investigator thinks that ethnic membership and gender influence the number of truancies, the subjects could be classified as Anglo, Hispanic, or black and as male or female. An F-test would first be used to assess the main effect of program versus no program on number of truancies. An F-test for gender would assess the truancy differences of males and females. The F-test for ethnicity by program versus no program would assess whether the effect of the program was consistent among the ethnic groups. The F-test for program by gender would assess the consistency of program effectiveness between genders. The gender by ethnicity F-test would assess the consistency of gender differences in truancy among ethnic groups. Finally, the $2 \times 3 \times 2$ higher-order interaction F-test would indicate if the treatment by ethnic group interaction was consistent between males and females. Building other variables into an ex post facto design is a partial solution, but you can never be sure that you have *all* the variables that should have been considered.

Analysis of Covariance

Analysis of covariance (ANCOVA) is sometimes used to partially adjust for preexisting differences between groups in an ex post facto design. Specifically, it adjusts scores on the dependent variable for any initial differences on the extraneous variable. However, as the adjustment is only partial, ANCOVA does not "solve" the problem of initial differences between groups, but only reduces it. When interpreting ex post facto research, it is inappropriate to assume ANCOVA has satisfactorily adjusted for initial differences.

A well-known example of the problems inherent in matching and analysis of covariance is the Cicirelli and associates (1969) ex post facto investigation of the effects of the Head Start program. This study compared the academic achievement of students who had been in the Head Start program with the achievement of those who had not been in the Head Start program. Children who had been in the program were matched with non-Head children from the same neighborhoods on gender, racial/ethnic groups, and kindergarten attendance. Analysis of covariance was used to adjust for differences in income per capita, educational level of father, and occupational level of father. The results indicated that the achievement of the non-Head Start group was greater than that of the Head Start group even when scores were adjusted for initial differences. The authors concluded that the Head Start program was harmful. Campbell and Erlebacher (1970) pointed out that because of regression, both matching and analysis of covariance underadjust for initial differences between groups. One would therefore expect adjusted posttreatment scores of a disadvantaged group to be less than adjusted posttreatment scores of a less disadvantaged group. Because the extent of the underadjustment is unknown, the Cicirelli et al. study does not determine whether the Head Start experience was harmful or beneficial or had no effect.

Partial Correlation

Partial correlation can be used to determine the extent of relationship between two variables when their relationship to other variables has been removed or "partialed out." For example, partial correlation could show the relationship between need for achievement and academic achievement in science with the influence of science aptitude removed. When both independent and dependent variables are continuous, partial correlation provides an adjustment similar to the adjustment that analysis of covariance provides when independent variable(s) are discrete. We discuss partial correlation in Chapter 12.

THE ROLE OF EX POST FACTO RESEARCH

Given the hazards involved in ex post facto research, many educational researchers feel they should not engage in this type of research at all. Basically, they contend that it is better to admit ignorance than to risk reaching incorrect conclusions. However, others contend that many variables of great interest are not amenable to experimental research. Researchers cannot randomly assign children to broken or intact homes, to high or low social class, to achievement-oriented or non-achievement-oriented peer groups, and so forth. Therefore, if they want to learn anything about relationships between such attribute variables and other variables, the ex post facto method is their only recourse. If they use appropriate methods of partial control and consider alternative hypotheses, perhaps they can be right more often than wrong.

Certainly there have been many highly credible ex post facto studies. The U.S. Surgeon General's study of the relationship between smoking and lung cancer is a well-known example. It is not possible to designate randomly a group of human subjects who are to smoke for years and a group who are not to smoke, so the study had to be done as an ex post facto investigation. The reversed-causality hypothesis that lung cancer causes people to smoke is not plausible. None of the common-cause hypotheses offered seem very likely: nervous people are prone to both smoking and lung cancer, some genetic predisposition leads to both, and so forth. The Surgeon General controlled for many alternative independent variables—for example, by analyzing separately samples from areas of high air pollution and low air pollution. Experimental evidence with animals who were made to inhale or not inhale cigarette smoke produced evidence of a cause-effect relationship. Given all this, despite the dangers inherent in ex post facto research, most would conclude that it is better to bet there *is* a cause-to-effect relationship between smoking and lung cancer among humans than to bet there is *not* such a relationship. In fact, much medical research is ex post facto in design. Researchers study diseases and try to determine the influence of factors such as eating habits, lifestyle, genes, and so on. The new science of "fetal programming" is looking at the effect of conditions and development—in utero—and adult health. Ex post facto research in education has permitted investigations of the effects variables such as home background, father absence, early experiences, disabilities, teacher competence, and others that are beyond the control of educators. In some instances, ex post facto research has discovered relationships or raised questions that can later be investigated more systematically in well-controlled experimental studies. Appropriately used and cautiously interpreted, ex post facto or causal-comparative research will continue to provide a valuable methodology for the acquisition of knowledge.

SUMMARY

Ex post facto research is used to investigate cause-and-effect relationships when the researcher cannot randomly assign subjects to different conditions or directly manipulate the independent variable. Ex post facto research begins with subjects who differ on an observed dependent variable and tries to determine the antecedents (cause) of the difference. Or the researcher begins with subjects who differ on an independent variable and tries to determine the consequences of the difference.

Although there are many disadvantages of ex post facto design, it nevertheless is frequently the only method by which educational researchers can obtain necessary information about characteristics of defined groups of students or information needed for the intelligent formulation of programs in the school. It permits researchers to investigate situations in which controlled variation is impossible to introduce. Attributes such as academic aptitude, creativity, socioeconomic status, and teacher personality cannot be manipulated and hence must be investigated through ex post facto research rather than through the more rigorous experimental approach.

The possibility of spurious relationships is always present in ex post facto research. Considering the possibilities of common cause, reversed causality, and possible alternate independent variables can help educators evaluate such research more realistically. Several partial control strategies can help researchers avoid gross errors in ex post facto designs, but none can entirely solve the problems inherent in those designs. Always exercise caution in interpreting causal-comparative results.

REFERENCES

Asher, W., & M.M. Schusler (1967). Students' grades and access to cars. *Journal of Educational Research, 60,* 10.

Campbell, D.T., & Erlebacher, A. (1970). How regression artifacts in quasi-experimental evaluations can mistakenly make compensatory education look harmful. In V. Hellmuth (Ed.), *Compensatory education: A national debate: Vol. 3. Disadvantaged child.* (pp. 597–617) New York: Brunner/Mazel.

Chapin, F.S. (1947). *Experimental designs in sociological research.* New York: Harper & Row.

Cicirelli, V., et al. (1969). *The impact of Head Start: An evaluation of the effects of Head Start on children's cognitive and affective development.* (A report presented to the Office of Economic Opportunity pursuant to contract B89-4536.) Westinghouse Learning Corporation and Ohio University. (Distributed by the Clearinghouse for Federal Scientific and Technical Information, U.S. Department of Commerce, National Bureau of Standards, Institute for Applied Technology. PB 184 328.)

Lee, V.E., & Loeb, S. (2000). School size in Chicago elementary schools: Effects on teachers' attitudes and students' achievement. *American Educational Research Journal, 37,* 1–31.

Mill, J.S. (2nd Ed) (1846). *A system of logic.* New York: Harper & Brothers.

National Association of Secondary School Principals. (1959). Do automobiles and scholarship mix? *NASSP Spotlight on Junior and Senior High Schools, 36,* 3.

Royer, J.M., Tronsky, L.N., Chan, Y., Jackson S. & Marchant, H. (1999). Math-fact retrieval as the cognitive mechanism underlying gender differences in math test performance *Contemporary Educational Psychology, 24,* 181–266.

KEY CONCEPTS

active independent variable
analysis of covariance (ANCOVA)
attribute independent variable
causal relationship
common cause

ex post facto (causal-comparative) research
homogeneous groups
matching
partial control

post hoc fallacy
reverse causality
spurious relationship

EXERCISES

1. What are the two major limitations of causal-comparative designs?

2. Classify the following independent variables as active or attribute:
   a. Kindergarten entrance age
   b. Method of teaching reading
   c. Montessori school attendance versus attendance at public school
   d. Teaching experience
   e. Use of Drug A in treating diabetes versus Drug B
   f. Learning style

3. What method would you use to investigate the following research hypothesis?
   a. High school students who work during the school year will have lower grades and lower standardized test scores than students who do not work.
   b. First-grade students who are taught reading using phonics will read at a higher level than first-grade students taught by another method.
   c. Beginning teachers who are mentored will be more effective and express more satisfaction with teaching than beginning teachers who are not mentored.
   d. Students who are in small classes (under fifteen) in grades K–3 will perform at a higher level in grades 4–6 than will students in regular-sized classes (over twenty).

4. Interpret this statement: "A statistical relationship between two variables is a necessary but not a sufficient condition for inferring a causal relationship between the variables."

5. Show the design you would use to test the hypothesis stated in Exercise 3(a).

6. What alternative hypotheses would you want to explore if your causal-comparative research indicates that there is a relationship between self-concept and achievement in school?

7. What steps would you take to avoid the post hoc fallacy in your ex post facto research?

8. In the following examples, suggest an alternative explanation for the finding:
   a. A researcher finds a relationship between use of alcohol and unemployment and concludes that using alcohol causes workers to lose their jobs.
   b. A researcher finds that the proportion of the population confined to mental hospitals for manic-depression is greater in the United States than it is in England. He concludes that the American environment is more conducive to the development of depression.
   c. A researcher finds that the increase in the use of cell phones in recent years has been accompanied by an increase in the incidence of brain tumors. He concludes that using a cell phone can result in a brain tumor.

9. Find an example of an ex post facto study in the current literature. Identify (a) the problem; (b) the operational definitions of the variables; (c) the design used; (d) the steps taken to control extraneous variables; (e) the findings; (f) the conclusions. Did the author include a caveat about the conclusion?

ANSWERS

1. The two major limitations are lack of randomization and lack of manipulation of the independent variable.

2. a. Attribute
   b. Active
   c. Attribute

d. Attribute

e. Active

f. Attribute

3. a. Ex post facto

  b. Experimental

  c. Experimental

  d. Ex post facto (it is generally not feasible to manipulate class size, although it has been done)

4. To report that one variable (X) is the cause of another variable (Y), the researcher must first show that there is a statistical relationship between the variables. But this finding by itself is not sufficient to establish a causal relationship. The researcher must examine the time $(X$ must precede $Y)$ and must show that no other variables could cause Y.

5. Use ex post facto Design 1. That is, you would select two groups of high school students, one of whom works a certain number of hours each week (X), and would compare their grades and scores on standardized tests (Y) with a comparable group of students who do not work. Or instead of studying the effect of working or not working, you could study the effect of the *extent* of work as measured by the number of hours worked each week. One group could work less than 10 hours a week, and the other group could work 20 or more hours. You would have to control a number of variables, including aptitude scores, previous grades, socioeconomic status, and gender. If

you used only one class level (only juniors or only seniors), you could control for the variable of class standing (if relevant).

6. A more positive self-concept could lead to higher achievement in school. Or the reversed causality hypothesis could account for the finding. That is, higher achievement in school could lead to a more positive self-concept. You would also want to explore a common-cause hypothesis. Perhaps another variable, such as intelligence, causes both achievement and self-concept.

7. Try to control any relevant extraneous variables that could affect the measured variable. Methods of control include (a) matching, (b) using homogeneous groups, (c) building extraneous variables into the design, and (d) using ANCOVA or other statistical means to partially control unwanted variables.

8. a. Perhaps unemployment leads to the use of alcohol.

  b. Perhaps depressed people in England receive a different type of treatment and are less likely to be hospitalized than in the United States.

  c. Perhaps there is a common cause. The stress and rapid pace of life at the turn of the century is conducive to the use of cell phones and may also influence the development of brain tumors.

9. Answers will vary.

 ## INFOTRAC COLLEGE EDITION

Use the keywords *theory* + *research* to locate a research study that used an ex post facto design. Hint: Locate the study investigating the effect of maternal child-rearing practices on preschoolers' delay of gratification behavior. Why was an ex post facto design chosen? How were the variables operationally defined? What methods of partial control were used? Were the conclusions justified?

Chapter 12

Correlational Research

After studying this chapter, the student will be able to:

1. Describe the nature of correlational research.

2. Describe the ways correlational research is used.

3. Describe the design of correlational research.

4. Distinguish between correlation and ex post facto research.

5. List different types of correlation coefficients, and state the conditions for their appropriate use.

6. Interpret correlation coefficients in terms of magnitude, statistical significance, and practical significance.

7. Test a hypothesis about a correlation coefficient, r.

8. Define *predictor* and *criterion*.

9. Define multiple correlation, and explain when it is used.

10 Define *discriminant analysis* and explain when it is used.

11 Define *factor analysis,* and explain its purpose.

12 Explain the role of correlation in factor analysis.

13 Define *partial correlation,* and explain its purpose.

14 Describe a research study in which *canonical correlation* would be appropriate.

15 Define *path analysis* and briefly explain its purpose.

Correlational research investigates how scores on one variable or variables rise and fall as scores on other variables rise or fall. It differs from experimental research in that there is usually no manipulation of the variables. It investigates the extent to which the variables are related and the direction of the relationship. Beginning researchers often confuse correlational research with ex post facto or causal-comparative research. Correlational research relates two (or more) variable measures from the *same group* of subjects, whereas ex post facto research compares two (or more) groups on the *same variable* measure. Although ex post facto research *seeks* to establish cause-effect relationships, correlational research may or may not. When correlational research finds a relationship between two variables, researchers say that the variables are *correlated*. The strength and direction of the relationship are described by means of a quantitative index called the **coefficient of correlation.** Recall from Chapter 6 that in interpreting a coefficient of correlation, one looks at both its sign and its size. The sign (+ or −) of the coefficient indicates the direction of the relationship. If the coefficient has a positive sign, this means that as one variable increases, the other also increases. For example, the correlation between height and weight is positive, because tall people tend to be heavier and short people lighter. A negative coefficient indicates that as one variable increases, the other decreases. The correlation between outdoor air temperature during the winter months and heating bills is negative.

The size of the correlation coefficient indicates the strength of the relationship between the variables. The coefficient can range in value from +1.00 (indicating a perfect positive relationship) through 0 (indicating no relationship) to −1.00 (indicating a perfect negative relationship). A perfect positive relationship means that for every z-score unit increase in one variable, there is an identical z-score unit increase in the other. A perfect negative relationship indicates that for every unit increase in one variable there is an identical unit decrease in the other. Few variables ever show perfect correlation, especially in relating human traits. Most range somewhere between 0 and ±1.00, such as +.40 for the correlation between a scholastic aptitude measure and grade-point average in high school, or −.40 for the correlation between days absent from school and spelling test scores. The correlation between aptitude scores and weight for a sample of adult subjects would be expected to be about zero.

USES OF CORRELATION

Correlational research is useful in a wide variety of studies. Major applications of correlation are classified as (1) determining relationships, (2) assessing consistency, and (3) prediction.

Determining Relationships

Correlational research methods are used to determine relationships and patterns of relationship among variables in a single group of subjects. For instance, correlational research is used to answer questions such as, Is there a relationship between math aptitude and achievement in computer science? What is the direction and strength of this relationship, if any? You would most likely predict that a positive relationship will be found between scores on a math aptitude test and grades in computer science. A correlational study would determine the extent of any relationship between these variables.

Often a correlational study is mainly exploratory; a researcher attempts to identify the pattern of relationships existing between two or more variables. Information gained from such correlational studies is especially useful when trying to understand a complex construct or to build a theory about some behavioral phenomenon. The researcher must remember, however, that the variables selected for a study of this type should be based on a theory, on previous research, or on the researcher's observations. The "shotgun" approach, in which a researcher correlates a number of variables just to see what might show up, is not recommended.

In some correlational studies, the researcher may be able to state a hypothesis about the expected relationship. For example, from phenomenological theory you might hypothesize that there is a positive relationship between first-grade children's perceptions of themselves and their achievement in reading. In other instances, the researcher may lack the information necessary to state a hypothesis.

A study by Bourke (1986) illustrates the use of the correlational method in investigating the relationships among class size, teaching practices, and student achievement. He hypothesized that the extent of the implementation of different teaching practices would be related to class size. Table 12.1 shows the variables that had significant correlations with class size.

There were more student questions in larger classes (usually seeking help or explanation), but more teacher follow-up of questions in smaller classes. A greater use of homework and assignments was typical of smaller classes. The amount of time teachers spent directly interacting with students was greater in small classes. Although the study is more involved than this illustration shows, it is possible to see how a researcher starts with correlations to help understand a complex phenomenon, in this case the possible explanations of the relationship between class size and achievement. Other complex correlational

Table 12.1   *Relationships of Teaching Practice Variables with Class Size*

VARIABLE	CORRELATION WITH CLASS SIZE
Use of whole-class teaching	−.24
Number of groups used in class	.33
Teacher directly interacting with students	−.27
Amount of noise tolerated	.34
Teacher probes after a question	−.25
Student questions	.32
Teacher waits for a response	−.20
Homework and assignments assessed	−.28
Nonacademic management	.29

procedures (such as factor analysis) may be used to study the simultaneous interrelations of many variables to give insight into the components of such constructs as attitudes toward school, leadership style, and abstract reasoning.

Assessing Consistency

In Chapter 9 we noted that the reliability (consistency) of a test can be assessed through correlating test-retest, equivalent-forms, or split-half scores. Correlation can be used to measure consistency (or lack thereof) in a wide variety of cases. For example, how consistent are the independently assigned merit ratings given by the principal and the assistant principal to teachers in a school? How much agreement is there among Olympic judges rating the performance of a group of gymnasts? When a researcher asks a group of teachers to rank the severity of disruption created by each item on a list of behavior disorders, to what extent do their rankings agree?

Prediction

If you find that two variables are correlated, then you can use one variable to predict the other. The higher the correlation, the more accurate the prediction. Prediction studies are frequently used in education. For example, correlational research has shown that high school grades and scholastic aptitude measures are related to college GPA. If a student scores high on aptitude tests and has high grades in high school, he or she is more likely to make high grades in college than is a student who scores low on the two predictor variables. Researchers can predict with a certain degree of accuracy a student's probable freshman GPA from high school grades and aptitude test scores. This prediction won't hold for every case, because other factors such as motivation, initiative, or study habits are not considered. But in general, the prediction is accurate enough to be useful to college admissions officers.

◼ DESIGN OF CORRELATIONAL STUDIES

The basic design for correlational research is straightforward. First, the researcher specifies the problem by asking a question about the relationship between the variables of interest. The population of interest is also identified at this time. In simple correlational studies, the researcher focuses on gathering data on two (or more) measures from *one* group of subjects. For example, you might correlate vocabulary and reading comprehension scores for a group of middle school students. Occasionally correlational studies investigate relationships between scores on one measure for logically paired groups such as twins, siblings, or husbands and wives. For instance, a researcher might want to look at the correlation between the SAT scores of identical twins.

An example of a typical correlational research question might be, What is the relationship between quantitative ability and achievement in science among high school students? You might state a hypothesis that the two variables are significantly related in the specified group. The hypothesis might be stated in a nondirectional form or in the directional form of a positive or negative relationship. In the preceding example, the researcher would most likely predict a significant positive relationship between students' quantitative ability and their achievement in science.

Next the researcher determines how the constructs, such as ability and achievement in the preceding example, will be quantified. He or she may already be aware of well-accepted operational definitions of the constructs, may seek definitions in sources such as those described in Chapter 4, or may develop his or her own definitions and then assess their reliability and validity. In the example, the researcher may decide that quantitative ability will be defined as scores on the School and College Ability Test, Series III (SCAT III), and science achievement will be defined as scores on the science sections of the Sequential Tests of Educational Progress (STEP III).

It is important in correlational studies to select or develop measures that are appropriate indicators of the constructs to be investigated, and it is especially important that these instruments have satisfactory reliability and are valid for measuring the constructs under consideration. The size of a coefficient of correlation is influenced by the adequacy of the measuring instruments for their intended purpose. For instance, instruments that are too easy or too difficult for the subjects of a study would not discriminate among them and would result in a smaller correlation coefficient than instruments with appropriate difficulty level. Studies using instruments with low reliability and questionable validity are unlikely to produce useful results.

Next the researcher selects the sample to represent the specified population. Typically, correlational studies do not require extremely large samples. You can assume that if a relationship exists, it will be evident in a sample of moderate size (for instance, 50 to 100). We do not recommend samples with fewer than 30 subjects. If the researcher is interested in generalizing the findings to a large population, he or she will need to draw a random sample from that population. For example, if a researcher wants to generalize the results from the correlational study of math ability and science achievement to all secondary school students in a district, then a random sample of all the secondary students in that district should be drawn.

Finally, the researcher collects the quantitative data on the two or more variables for the students in the sample and then calculates the coefficient(s) of correlation between the scores. Even before calculating the coefficient, the researcher should look at a scatterplot or a graph of the relationship between the variables. Most correlational procedures assume a linear relationship between the variables (see p. 149 and Figure 6.9). If the relationship is not linear but curvilinear, the most commonly used correlation coefficients are inappropriate because they underestimate the degree of relationship. The *eta* **correlation ratio** is appropriate in such cases.

CORRELATION COEFFICIENTS

There are many different kinds of correlation coefficients. The researcher chooses the appropriate statistical procedure primarily on the basis of (1) the scale of measurement of the measures used and (2) the number of variables.

Pearson's Product Moment Coefficient of Correlation

We introduced you in Chapter 6 to the Pearson product moment correlation coefficient, symbolized *r*, which is the most widely used descriptive statistic of correlation. You may recall that the Pearson coefficient is appropriate for use when the variables to be correlated are normally distributed and measured on an interval or ratio scale. We will briefly mention some of the other indexes of correlation without going into their computation. Interested students should consult statistics books for the computational procedures.

Spearman's Rho Coefficient of Correlation

Spearman's rho (**P**), an ordinal coefficient of correlation, is used when the data are ranks rather than raw scores. For example, assume the principal and assistant principal have independently ranked the fifteen teachers in their school from first, most effective to fifteenth, least effective, and you want to assess how much their ranks agree. You would calculate the Spearman's rho by putting the paired ranks into the Pearson *r* formula or by using a formula developed specifically for rho. Interested readers are referred to a statistics book.

Spearman's rho is interpreted the same as is Pearson *r*. Like the Pearson product moment coefficient of correlation, it ranges from -1.00 to $+1.00$. When each individual has the same rank on both variables, the rho correlation will be $+1.00$, and when their ranks on one variable are exactly the opposite of their ranks on the other variable, rho will be -1.00. If there is no relationship at all between the rankings, the rank correlation coefficient will be 0. If you have a computer or calculator program for Pearson *r*, you can calculate Spearman rho by putting the ranks into that program.

The Phi Coefficient

The **phi (Φ) coefficient** is used when both variables are genuine dichotomies scored 1 or 0. For example, phi would be used to describe the relationship between the sex of high school students and whether they are counseled to take college preparatory courses or not. Sex is dichotomized as male $= 0$, female $= 1$. Being counseled to take college preparatory courses is scored 1, not being so counseled is scored 0.

If you find the phi coefficient in School A is $-.15$, it indicates that there is a slight tendency to counsel more boys than girls to take college preparatory courses. If in School B the phi coefficient is $-.51$, it indicates a strong tendency in the same direction. As with the other correlations, the phi coefficient indicates both direction and strength of relationships.

A variety of correlation coefficients are available for use with ordinal and nominal data. These include coefficients for data that are more than just pairs; for example, assessing the agreement of three or more judges ranking the performance of the same subjects. A useful source of such correlations is Siegel and Castellan's (1988) text.

CONSIDERATIONS FOR INTERPRETING A CORRELATION COEFFICIENT

The coefficient of correlation may be simple to calculate, but it can be tricky to interpret. It is probably one of the most misinterpreted and/or overinterpreted statistics available to researchers. Various considerations need to be taken into account when evaluating the practical utility of a correlation. The importance of the numerical value of a particular correlation may be evaluated in three ways: (1) according to its absolute size and predictive utility, (2) in relation to other correlations of the same or similar variables, or (3) in terms of its statistical significance.

Absolute Size and Predictive Validity

Unsophisticated consumers of research often assume that a correlation indicates percentage of relationship; for example, that an r of .60 means the two variables are 60 percent related. No, r is the mean z-score product, not a percentage. However, when you square the Pearson r, you get an index called the **coefficient of determination, r^2,** which tells you how much of the variance of X is in common with the variance of Y. A correlation of $+.60$ or $-.60$ means that the two variables have 36 percent of their variance in common with each other. An increase in the r results in an accelerating increase in r^2. A correlation of .20 yields a coefficient of determination of .04. An r of .4 yields an r^2 of .16. An r of .8 yields an r^2 of .64, and so on. The coefficient of determination is a useful index for evaluating the meaning of size of a correlation. It also reminds one that positive and negative correlations of the same magnitude, say $r = .5$ and $r = -.5$, are equally useful for prediction and other uses, because both have the same coefficient of determination, $r^2 = .25$.

Correlation as Effect Size

The Pearson r as a measure of relationships independent of sample size is a form of effect size. Cohen (1988), employing the same logic used for describing small, medium, and large effect sizes for differences between means (see Chapter 6), has suggested the following conventions for the effect sizes of correlations:

$$r = .10 \text{ small}$$
$$r = .30 \text{ medium}$$
$$r = .50 \text{ large}$$

Obviously, a correlation of .10 with only 1 percent of the variance in common is small. Although an r of .30 with a coefficient of determination indicating only 9 percent common variance may at first seem small, the relationship and the size of the relationship can be seen in a scattergram (see Figure 6.8). Many correlation coefficients encountered in the behavioral sciences are of this order of magnitude. For example, correlation coefficients between personality tests and real life criteria typically fall around .30. Correlations within a single variable, such as two measures of the same thing, often exceed .5. Correlations of competing tests of spelling proficiency are typically about .80. Correlations between equivalent forms of a single test are often in excess of .90. However, correlations between different variables in the behavioral sciences rarely approach that level. As Cohen (p. 81) says, "Thus, when an investigator anticipates a degree of correlation between two different variables 'about as high as they come' this would by our definition be a large effect, $r = .50$." Cohen's conventions for correlations—small $r = .10$ ($r^2 = .01$), medium, $r = .30$ ($r^2 = .09$) and large $r = .50$ ($r^2 = .25$)—are approximately equal in terms of accounted-for variance to his conventions for differences between means effect sizes of .2, indicating small; .5, indicating medium; and .8, indicating large.

Comparison to Other Correlations

The magnitude of a correlation must also be assessed in relation to other correlations of the same or similar variables. For example, an r of .75 would be considered low for the relationship between the results of two equivalent forms of an achievement test, but it would be considered high for the relationship between an aptitude measure and grades for college freshmen. Over the years both the Scholastic Assessment Test (SAT) and American College Testing (ACT) tests have typically correlated with subsequent college freshman grade-point averages by about $r = .40$. A correlation of .40 is less than Cohen's definition of a high correlation. However, the 16 percent of variance in freshman grade-point averages that can be predicted from either of these tests is sufficiently helpful for making admissions decisions that their use is well justified. Anyone who could create a test for high school seniors with a correlation of .50 with college freshman grade-point average could make a fortune marketing it, because it would account for 25 percent ($.50^2$) of freshman GPA as opposed to 16 percent ($.40^2$) for ACT or SAT. A way to assess the size of a correlation is to define a high correlation as one that is higher than its competition and a low correlation as one that is lower than its competition. To help evaluate obtained correlations, the researcher should determine from a review of the literature what levels of correlation are typically found for specific types of data.

Statistical Significance

In evaluating the size of a correlation, it is important to consider the size of the sample on which the correlation is based. Without knowing the sample size, you do not know if the correlation could easily have occurred merely as a result of chance or is likely to be an indication of a genuine relationship. If there were fewer than twenty cases in the sample (which we would not recommend), then a "high" r of .50 could easily occur by chance. You should be very careful in attaching too much importance to large correlations when small sample sizes are involved; an r found in a small sample does not necessarily mean that a correlation exists in the population. To avoid the error of inferring a relationship in the population that does not really exist, the researcher should state the null hypothesis that the population correlation equals 0 and then determine whether the obtained sample correlation departs sufficiently from 0 to justify the rejection of the null hypothesis. In Chapter 7 we showed you how to use Table A.5 in the Appendix, which lists critical values of r for different numbers of degrees of freedom (df). By comparing the obtained r with the critical values of r listed in the table, you can determine the statistical significance of a product moment correlation. For example, assume a correlational study involving 92 students yields a correlation of .45. The critical value listed in Table A.5 is .27 at the .01 level and .21 at the .05 level. Because the obtained correlation of .45 exceeds the tabled values, the researcher can report that the correlation is statistically significant. The null hypothesis would be rejected, and the researcher would tentatively conclude that the two variables are related in the population.

You can see in Table A.5 that the smaller the sample, the larger the absolute size of the correlation must be to reach statistical significance. Table A.5 shows that with 22 cases ($df = 20$), a coefficient of .54 is needed to be significant at the .01 level. With 102 cases, however, a correlation of .25 is significant at the .01 level. When $N = 1000$, an r of .08 is significant at the .01 level. The larger the sample, the more likely a given correlation coefficient is to be statistically significant.

Practical Utility

Always consider the practical significance of the correlation coefficient. Even though a correlation coefficient may be statistically significant, it may have little practical utility. If a researcher had a sample of 1000, then a very small coefficient such as .10 would be statistically significant at the .01 level. But of what practical importance would this correlation be? Information on X only accounts for 1 percent of the variance in Y (r^2). In this case it would hardly be worth the bother of collecting scores on a predictor variable, X to predict another variable, Y. How worthwhile a correlation may be is partly a function of its predictive utility in relation to the cost of obtaining predictor data. A **predictor** with a high correlation that is difficult and expensive to obtain may be of less practical value than a cheap and easy predictor with a lower correlation. Also, note that a correlation coefficient only describes the degree of relationship between given operational definitions of predictor and predicted variables in a particular research situation for a given sample of subjects. It can easily change in value if the same variables are measured and correlated using different operational definitions and/or a different sample.

Thus failure to find a statistically significant relationship between two variables in one study does not necessarily mean there is *no* relationship between the variables. It only means that in that particular study, sufficient evidence for a relationship was not found. Recall from Chapter 6 that other factors, such as reliability of the measures used and range of possible values on the measures, influence the size of a correlation coefficient.

CORRELATION AND CAUSATION

In evaluating a correlational study, one of the most frequent errors is to interpret a correlation as indicating a cause-and-effect relationship. Saslow (1982) refers to this practice of interpreting correlation as causation as one of the "seven deadly sins" committed by researchers. Correlation is a necessary but never a sufficient condition for causation. For example, if a significant positive correlation is found between number of hours of television watched per week and body weight among middle school pupils, that does not prove that excessive television watching causes obesity. Recall from Chapter 11 that when the independent variable is not under the investigator's control alternate explanations must be considered. In this example, reverse causality is plausible. Perhaps the more overweight a child is, the more he or she is inclined to choose television watching instead of physical activities, games, and interacting with peers. The common-cause explanation is also plausible. Perhaps differences in family recreational patterns and lifestyle account for both differences in weight and time spent watching television.

Let us consider another example. Assume a researcher finds a relationship between measures of self-esteem and academic achievement (grades) for a sample of students. Table 12.2 summarizes the possibilities for interpreting this observed relationship.

Any number of factors could act together to lead to both self-esteem and academic achievement: previous academic experiences, parents' education, peer relationships, motivation, and so on. We must stress, however, that it is not true correlation can *never* bring evidence to bear for cause and effect. The Surgeon General's warning about the dangers of cigarette smoking are, in part, based on studies that found positive correlations between the number of cigarettes smoked per day and incidence of lung cancer and other maladies. Here, as mentioned in Chapter 11, reverse causality (cancer leads to cigarette smoking) is not a credible explanation. Various common-cause hypotheses (such as, people who live in areas with high air pollution smoke more and have higher cancer rates) have been shown not to be the case. Because the correlational studies with humans agree

Table 12.2 *Possible Interpretations of a Relationship Between Self-esteem and Academic Achievement*

Self-Esteem → Achievement (self-esteem causes achievement)

Achievement → Self-esteem (achievement causes self-esteem)

Intelligence → Self-esteem (a third factor causes both)
→ Achievement

Home Environment → Self-esteem (a third factor causes both)
→ Achievement

with the results of experimental studies with animals, the Surgeon General's warning is considered well founded.

PARTIAL AND MULTIPLE CORRELATION

The correlation techniques discussed so far are appropriate for use with two variables only. There are situations, however, when a researcher must deal with more than two variables. **Partial correlation** is a technique used to determine what correlation remains between two variables when the effect of another variable is eliminated. Correlation between two variables may occur because both of them are correlated with a third variable. Partial correlation controls for this third variable. For example, assume you are interested in the correlation between vocabulary and problem-solving skills. Both these variables are related to a third variable, chronological age. For example, 12-year-old children have more developed vocabularies than 8-year-old children, and they also have more highly developed problem-solving skills. Scores on vocabulary and problem solving will correlate with each other because both are correlated with chronological age. Partial correlation would be used with such data to obtain a measure of correlation with the effect of age removed. The remaining correlation between two variables when their correlation with a third variable is removed is called a *first-order partial correlation*. Partial correlation may be used to remove the effect of more than one variable. However, because of the difficulty of interpretation, partial correlation involving the elimination of more than one variable is not often used.

Multiple correlation also involves more than two variables. This technique enables researchers to find the best possible weighting of two or more independent variables to yield a maximum correlation with a single dependent variable. For example, Jacobs (1985) used data submitted by 4145 freshmen at a midwestern university to predict first-semester grade-point average. The predictor values were scores on the Scholastic Assessment Test subtests (SAT verbal and SAT math), along with students' relative high school rank (RHSR). Relative high school rank, found by dividing a student's rank in the high school graduating class by the size of the class, adjusts for the variation in size of graduating classes. Table 12.3 shows the simple correlations between each of the predictors and the criterion.

Table 12.3	*Correlations of Each Predictor with the Criterion*		
	SATV	SATM	RHSR[a]
GPA	0.31	0.39	−0.42

[a]The negative correlation between relative high school rank and GPA is due to the way that rank in class is measured. The highest achiever in the class has a rank of 1 (the lowest number); the lowest achiever in the class has a rank equal to the size of the class (a high number). The students with the lowest *size* rank are predicted to have the highest GPA; hence, the correlation coefficient is negative.

You can see in Table 12.3 that none of the variables has a very high correlation with freshman GPA; the best single predictor is relative high school rank. Jacobs carried out a multiple-correlation analysis to determine the correlation of the best possible weighted *combination* of the three predictor variables with GPA. The multiple correlation (R) was .50. Thus 25 percent (R^2) of the variance in GPA was accounted for by the combined SATV, SATM, and RHSR scores. The weighted combination of variables had the highest correlation with GPA and thus provided the most accurate prediction. A prediction equation was developed using the predictor variables weighted in the appropriate way.

In developing a prediction equation, each case must have a score on each of the independent (X) variables (predictors) and the dependent (Y) variable (criterion). In the future, however, the equation can be used with similar groups when only the independent variables (Xs) are known. SAT scores and relative high school ranks can be used to predict the as-yet-unknown freshman GPA for applicants to the university.

The variables should be measured on an interval scale. It is possible, however, to put categorical variables such as gender, social class, marital status, political preference, and the like into a prediction equation if they are recoded as binary variables. For instance, if the variable is gender, 1's can be assigned to females and 0's to males. Such recoded variables are referred to in multiple correlation as **dummy variables.**

Because the computations are very complex, multiple correlation is done by computer. Computer programs are available that provide not only the multiple correlation coefficient (R) and the prediction equation but also the proportion of variance in the criterion accounted for by the combination of predictors (R^2), and tests of statistical significance for the R and for the contribution of each predictor.

Several more complex techniques are available to investigate correlation of more than two variables. These analyses require more sophistication with statistics than is usually needed in a beginning research course. We will briefly describe these techniques and refer interested students to other texts.

DISCRIMINANT ANALYSIS

Discriminant analysis is a statistical procedure related to multiple correlation. It uses a number of predictor variables to classify subjects into two or more distinct groups, such as dropouts versus persisters, successful versus unsuccessful students, delinquents versus non-delinquents, and so on. The criterion in discriminant analysis is a person's group membership. The procedure results in an equation, or *discriminant function,* where the scores on the predictors are multiplied by weights to predict the classification of subjects into groups. When there are just two groups, the discriminant function is essentially a multiple-correlation equation with the group membership criterion coded 0 or 1. But with three or more groups as the criterion, discriminant analysis goes beyond multiple correlation.

For example, discriminant analysis might be used to identify predictors of success in a school of education doctoral program. You could identify the variables that discriminated membership into one of two groups: those who successfully completed doctoral study and those who did not. A number of different predictors might be used: Miller Analogies Test (MAT) scores, undergraduate GPA, graduate GPA, time lapse between the master's degree and entrance into the doctoral program, doctoral major, age at entrance, gender and marital status. Complex correlational analysis would produce an equation showing the variables that were significant in predicting the criterion, success or lack of success in a doctoral program.

Cook, Semmel, and Wilson (1999) compared the attitudes of forty-nine principals and sixty-four special education teachers regarding the placement of students with mild disabilities into regular classrooms. In their responses to seven Likert-scale items principals showed more agreement with items stating that the achievement of mildly disabled children increases when they are included in regular classrooms. Special education teachers showed more agreement with the statement that the resources devoted to the students with mild disabilities must be protected regardless of setting. Discriminant analyses of the Likert-scale item responses separated principals and special education teachers into groups with 76 percent accuracy.

FACTOR ANALYSIS

Another widely used procedure based on correlation is **factor analysis.** This procedure analyzes the intercorrelations among a large set of measures to identify a smaller number of common **factors.** Factors are hypothetical constructs assumed to underlie different types of psychological measures, such as intelligence, aptitude, achievement, personality, and attitude measures. Factor analysis indicates the extent to which tests or other instruments are measuring the same thing, enabling researchers to deal with a smaller number of constructs. Some factor analysis studies of intelligence tests, for example, have identified underlying verbal, numerical, spatial, memory, and reasoning factors.

The first steps in factor analysis involve selecting variables to be included in the analysis and developing a **correlation matrix** that shows the correlation of each measure with every other measure. There may be a very large number of correlations in the matrix. The matrix is then subjected to computations with a factor analysis computer program that produces clusters of variables that intercorrelate highly within the cluster but have low correlations with other clusters. These clusters are the factors, and the object is to identify a smaller number of separate underlying factors that can account for the co-variation among the larger number of variables. For example, consider the following hypothetical correlation matrix:

	1	2	3	4	5	6
1. Vocabulary	—	.50	.15	.12	.12	.15
2. Analogies	—	—	.12	.15	.10	.18
3. Arithmetic	—	—	—	.55	.15	.12
4. Numerical Reasoning	—	—	—	—	.20	.22
5. Picture Completion	—	—	—	—	—	.52
6. Block Design	—	—	—	—	—	—

An "inspection" factor analysis shows three clusters. The correlation between vocabulary and analogies is high (.50), but neither correlates highly with the other variables. Arithmetic and numerical reasoning correlate highly with each other, but not with the other variables. A similar pattern can be seen with picture completion and block design. Three factors appear to underlie performance on these six measures—verbal, numerical, and spatial.

It is beyond the scope of this book to cover the computational procedures of either discriminant analysis or factor analysis. The reader is referred to books such as Kim and Mueller's *Introduction to Factor Analysis* (1978), Klecka's *Discriminant Analysis* (1980), or Gorsuch's *Factor Analysis* (1983) for readable discussions of these topics.

CANONICAL CORRELATION

Canonical correlation is a generalization of multiple correlation that adds more than one dependent variable to the prediction equation. Recall that a multiple correlation coefficient shows the correlation between the "best" combination of independent variables and a single dependent variable. Canonical correlation extends the analysis to more than one dependent variable. In other words, canonical correlation is an analysis with several independent variables and several dependent variables. It takes into account the X and Y scores, the relations between the X variables, between the Y variables, and between the X and Y sets of variables. The result is a *canonical correlation coefficient* that represents the maximum correlation possible between sets of X scores and sets of Y scores. It also indicates the relative contributions of the separate independent and dependent variables to the canonical correlation, so you can see which variables are most important to the relationships between the sets. For more information on canonical correlation, see Thompson's *Canonical Correlation Analysis* (1984).

PATH ANALYSIS

Path analysis is a set of statistical procedures designed to test a hypothesized causal model about the relationships among three or more variables. Using theory and existing knowledge, the researcher proposes a causal model and then applies path analysis to determine if the causal model is consistent with the empirical data. Models inconsistent with the data are rejected, whereas those not rejected are viewed as plausible causal patterns to be subjected to further investigation.

For example, Culver, Wolfle, and Cross (1990) tested a path model of the influences affecting teachers job satisfaction early in their careers. The model hypothesized that job satisfaction is a function of a teacher's gender, age, father's education, mother's education, the teacher's academic achievement, number of years in teaching, the teacher's perceptions of the principal and coworkers, and the teacher's commitment to the teaching profession. The analysis was done separately for samples of black teachers and white teachers. For both groups, background demographic variables such as age, sex, father's education, and mother's education were found to be of little importance to job satisfaction compared to the more immediate variables of school climate and commitment to teaching. Years of teaching experience also had little influence on level of job satisfaction. In general, the path coefficients were similar for black teachers and white teachers. One exception was found when satisfaction was related to academic achievement. Lower-achieving white teachers tended to be more satisfied in their jobs than did their higher-achieving counterparts; for blacks, no such difference was found. Another observed difference occurred when satisfaction was related to gender. Black men tended to be more satisfied with their jobs than black women, but white women tended to be more satisfied than white men. The researchers concluded that the process leading to teacher job satisfaction may be different for blacks and whites. For further discussion of path analysis, see Li (1975).

SUMMARY

Correlational research is nonexperimental research that studies the direction and strength of relationships among variables. It gathers data on two or more quantitative variables from the same group of subjects (or from two logically related groups) and then determines the correlation among the variables.

Correlational procedures are widely used in educational and psychological research. They enable researchers to better understand certain phenomena and to make predictions. Correlations must be interpreted appropriately. One must look at the sample size, the magnitude of the correlation coefficient, and its statistical and practical significance. The most serious error is to interpret correlation per se as an indicator of causation.

A number of different types of correlation coefficients are used with variables that are measured on different types of scales. Multiple correlation is used to find the relationship between two or more independent variables and a dependent variable. It yields a prediction equation that the researcher can use later to predict the dependent variable for a new group of subjects, when the researcher has information on the independent variables.

Some more sophisticated correlational procedures include partial correlation, discriminant analysis, factor analysis, canonical correlation, and path analysis. It is important to know the type of research situation in which each of these techniques would be useful.

REFERENCES

Bourke, S. (1986). How smaller is better: Some relationships between class size, teaching practices, and student achievement. *American Educational Research Journal, 23,* 558–571.

Cohen, J. (1988). *Statistical power analyses for the behavioral sciences* (2nd ed.). Hillsdale, NJ: Erlbaum.

Cook, B.G., Semmel, M.I., & Gerber, M.M. (1999). *Attitudes of principals and special education teachers toward the inclusion of students with mild disabilities: critical differences of opinion. Remedial and Special Education, 20*(4), 199–207.

Culver, S.M., Wolfle, L.E. & Cross, L.H. (1990). Testing a model of teacher satisfaction for blacks and whites. *American Educational Research Journal, 27,* 323–349.

Gorsuch, R.L. (1983). *Factor analysis.* Hillsdale, NJ: Erlbaum.

Jacobs, L.C. (1985). *GPA prediction procedures and normative data for freshmen.* Bloomington: Indiana University, Bureau of Evaluative Studies and Testing.

Kerlinger, F.N. (1979). *Behavioral research: A conceptual approach.* New York: Holt, Rinehart and Winston.

Kim, J., & Mueller, C.W. (1978). *Introduction to factor analysis: What it is and how to do it.* Beverly Hills, CA: Sage.

Klecka, W.R. (1980). *Discriminant analysis.* Beverly Hills, CA: Sage.

Li, C.C. (1975). *Path analysis: A primer.* Pacific Grove, CA: Boxwood Press.

Saslow, C.A. (1982). *Basic research methods.* Reading, MA: Addison-Wesley.

Siegel, S., and Castellan, N.J., Jr. (1988). *Nonparametric statistics for the behavioral sciences.* New York: McGraw-Hill.

Thompson, B. (1984). *Canonical correlation analysis: Uses and interpretation.* Beverly Hills, CA: Sage.

KEY CONCEPTS

canonical correlation

coefficient of correlation

coefficient of determination (r^2)

correlation matrix

correlation ratio

correlational research

discriminant analysis

dummy variable

factor

factor analysis

multiple correlation

partial correlation

path analysis

phi coefficient

predictor

Spearman's Rho

EXERCISES

1. Which correlation indicates the greatest extent of relationship between two variables?
   a. +.80 or −.80
   b. +.60 or −.85
   c. +.04 or −.15

2. A state official found a correlation of .65 between the number of bars in cities in the state and the number of crimes reported in those cities. He concluded that legislation to reduce the number of bars would reduce

crime. What would you say about the official's conclusion?

3. Why are magnitude interpretations of correlation coefficients alone sometimes misleading?

4. Construct a scatter diagram for the following pairs of scores (X and Y):

X	2	3	10	6	4	9	7	3	6
Y	10	9	1	3	7	1	2	5	4

Is the relationship
   a. Linear or curvilinear?
   b. High, moderate, or low?
   c. Positive or negative?

5. A study finds a moderate positive relationship between measures of self-esteem and achievement scores for a group of middle school students. Which of the following correlation coefficients would best represent this relationship?
   a.   .94
   b.   .35
   c. −.62
   d.   .20
   e.   .62

6. A study finds almost no relationship between two physical fitness scores for a group of elementary school students. Which of the following coefficients would best represent this relationship?
   a.   .25
   b.   .75
   c. −.10
   d.   .60
   e. −.80

7. A researcher administered a series of tests to a group of entering law students at State University. At the end of the first year of law school, the researcher obtained the students' grade-point averages.
   a. What correlational technique should be used to determine the maximum relationship of these tests to first-year GPA?
   b. What assumptions would have to be made in order to generalize the findings to future

applicants to the same law school? To applicants to other law schools?

8. How would you compare the correlations .70 and .35 in terms of magnitude?

9. A researcher is interested in anxiety and how it might affect performance on scholastic aptitude tests. He has a clinical psychologist assess the anxiety of subjects by ranking them from 1 through 20. Then he administers a standardized aptitude test to each of the 20 subjects and converts their IQ scores to ranks. Which correlation coefficient should the researcher calculate for the data? Explain your answer.

10. A researcher demonstrated a correlation of +.35 between principals' ratings of teacher attire and student academic performance across 150 grade schools in his state. He concluded that encouraging teachers to be properly attired will increase academic performance. Comment on his conclusion.

11. Determine the kind of index of correlation appropriate for use in solving each of the following problems:
   a. What is the coefficient of correlation between self-esteem and aptitude scores for a group of subjects?
   b. What is the correlation between gender and being hired or not hired for a job when you have sixty men and sixty women with identical scores on a qualifying test for that job?
   c. What is the correlation between the responses of 180 students to two test items when you know the right and wrong responses of these students on both test items?
   d. What is the relationship between sociometric scores of a group of students and their academic rank in a high school class?

12. To compute a correlation coefficient between Traits A and B, which of the following must you have?
   a. One group of subjects, some of whom possess characteristics of trait A and the remainder of whom possess those of trait B

b. Measures of trait A on one group of subjects and measures of trait B on another group

c. One group of subjects, some who have both traits A and B, some who have neither trait, and some who have one trait but not the other

d. Two groups of subjects, one of which could be classified as A or not A, the other as B or not B

e. Measures of traits A and B on each subject in one group of students

13. An investigation finds a positive correlation between IQ scores and length of attention span among 10-year-olds. From this finding, which of the following would be a reasonable conclusion?

a. A long attention span is a cause of intelligence.

b. A high IQ is a cause of long attention span.

c. There is a high probability that a large sample of high-IQ 10-year-olds will have a shorter mean attention span than a large sample of low-IQ 10-year-olds.

d. One would predict longer attention spans for high-IQ 10-year-olds than for low-IQ 10-year-olds.

14. Examine the following research topics and decide whether experimental research, ex post facto research, or correlational research is the appropriate research design for each one:

a. The effect of parents' divorce on the achievement motivation of the children

b. The effect of a specific program of vocabulary instruction on social studies achievement

c. The relationship between self-esteem and grade-point average

d. The effect of phonics instruction on the reading grade level of fourth-grade students

e. The relationship between the verbal aptitude scores of identical twins

f. The relationship between preschool attendance or non attendance and academic achievement in first-graders

15. A researcher found a correlation of $-.42$ between rank in high school class and achievement in college for a sample of 1500 college freshmen. How would you interpret this coefficient in terms of direction, magnitude, and percentage of shared variance?

16. A school administrator wants to predict achievement in foreign languages. She has available scores on an intelligence test, a language aptitude test, and a reading test; she also knows the sex of the students. How would you recommend that she proceed to predict foreign language achievement?

17. Explain how it is possible for the measures of two variables to be associated in a fairly systematic way without the existence of any causal relationship between the variables?

18. A researcher is investigating the validity of an inventory designed to measure teacher stress. He wishes to know if the inventory is measuring the single construct, teacher stress, or more than one construct. What procedure would you recommend that the researcher use to answer this question?

19. A researcher wanted to predict achievement in the first year of law school. He conducted a multiple-correlation analysis with a sample size of 1000 and used six predictor variables: undergraduate GPA, undergraduate major, LSAT score, score on a a writing test, sex, and time lapse between undergraduate degree and application to law school. The resulting $R = .20$ was significant at the .01 level of significance. How would you interpret the researcher's findings?

20. A researcher wants to investigate the relationship between class size and student satisfaction in sections of beginning psychology at a university. Describe two research methodologies that might be appropriate to answer this question.

21. Distinguish between correlational research and ex post facto research.

ANSWERS

1. a. The extent of relationship is the same.
   b. −.85
   c. −.15

2. Correlation between the two variables does not indicate causation. In this case, common cause is a likely explanation. Large cities have more bars and more crime; smaller cities have fewer bars and fewer crimes.

3. To interpret the correlation, you need to know the sample size on which it is based and the magnitude of other correlations of the same variables in other studies.

4. The relationship is
   a. linear
   b. high
   c. negative

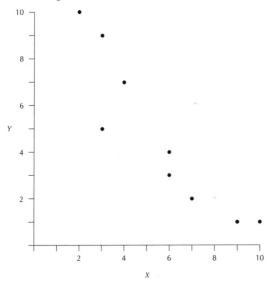

5. .35

6. −.10

7. a. Multiple correlation
   b. The researcher would have to assume that the relationship among the variables in the population of applicants to the law school remains similar over time. To apply the results to other law schools, the researcher would have to assume that the relationships among variables among applicants to other law schools are similar to these relationships among applicants to her law school.

8. An r of .70 might be described as being a very high correlation, the r of .35 as being moderate. One must *not* say that the r of .70 is twice as high as the r of .35. A good way to compare them is in terms of the coefficient of determination (r^2). With an r of .70, 49 percent of the variance is shared variance; with an r of .35, only 12 percent of the variance in Y is accounted for by variance in X. Thus the difference in magnitude of the relationship is more like four to one, instead of two to one as might have been incorrectly assumed from the absolute size of the coefficients.

9. Because the researcher has ordinal or rank-order data, he should calculate the Spearman rho correlation coefficient.

10. The researcher has no justification for inferring a causal relationship merely on the basis of correlational evidence. Principals' ratings of teacher attire and student academic performance could very well be functions of some other variable.

11. a. Pearson product moment
    b. phi coefficient
    c. phi coefficient
    d. Spearman rho

12. e.

13. d.

14. a. Ex post facto research
    b. Experimental research
    c. Correlational research
    d. Experimental research
    e. Correlational research
    f. Ex post facto research

15. The r of $-.42$ indicates a moderate negative relationship between rank in high school class and achievement in college; that is, students with a low numeric ranking would tend to have high achievement. The negative correlation is due to the way that rank in class is measured. The highest achiever in the class has a rank of 1 (the lowest number), the lowest achiever in the class has a rank equal to the size of the class (the highest number). The student with a rank of 1 in a class of 400 would be expected to have a higher GPA in college than the student with a rank of 400. An $r = -.42$ indicates that about 18 percent of the variance in college grades can be accounted for by achievement in high school as indicated by rank.

16. The school administrator would select a sample of students and obtain their scores on the three tests and their grades in foreign languages. Sex would be coded 0 or 1. The data would be entered into a multiple-correlation analysis, with the intelligence test, language aptitude test, reading test, and gender as independent variables and grades in foreign language as the dependent variable. Once the multiple-correlation equation is developed, it can be used to predict foreign language achievement of similar groups of students when only the independent variables are known.

17. Even when two variables are correlated, you cannot infer that one causes the other. Correlation does not indicate causation. A third variable, unmeasured by the researcher, may account for the observed relationship.

18. The researcher should subject the inventory to factor analysis.

19. With the large sample size, it is not surprising that a coefficient of only .20 would be statistically significant. It is only moderately useful in prediction. $R^2 = .04$; only 4 percent of the variance in law school achievement would be predictable from this combination of predictor variables.

20. You could use ex post facto methodology by selecting already existing sections with different numbers of students and comparing the satisfaction scores in the various sections. Or you could use correlational methodology by correlating class size with student satisfaction scores.

21. Both are nonexperimental quantitative research methods. Correlational research seeks to determine the relationship between two variables. It typically involves correlating two measures for one group of subjects. Ex post facto research seeks to establish a cause-effect relationship. It compares two groups on one variable measure.

INFOTRAC COLLEGE EDITION

Use the keyword *prediction* to locate an article investigating the relationship between two variables. What correlational procedures were used in the investigation? What was the extent of correlation between the variables? What was the conclusion about the prediction of one variable from the other?

In addition, use the keywords *correlation* + *causation* to locate an article that discusses the distinction between correlation and causation.

Chapter 13

Survey Research

After studying this chapter, the student will be able to:

1. State the purpose of survey research.

2. Describe the four categories of surveys classified according to their scope and focus.

3. Distinguish between longitudinal and cross-sectional surveys.

4. Describe the different types of longitudinal surveys.

5. List the steps involved in carrying out a survey.

6. Explain the importance of probability sampling in survey research.

7. Use sample data to calculate the margin of error and the confidence interval around the population parameter.

8. Calculate the sample size needed to achieve a desired margin of error in a survey.

9 List some of the factors that influence a researcher's decision about sample size.

10 State the merits of the interview as a data-gathering technique.

11 Write both open-ended and closed-ended survey questions.

12 List guidelines for conducting an interview.

13 State the advantages and disadvantages of the questionnaire as a data-gathering technique.

14 State some rules for writing items for a questionnaire.

15 List guidelines to follow relative to the format of a questionnaire.

16 Explain the advantages of field-testing a questionnaire.

17 Explain the follow-up procedures a researcher should employ with a mailed survey.

18 Write a cover letter for a questionnaire.

19 Outline procedures for dealing with nonrespondents after follow-up procedures have been used.

20 Discuss the procedures for assessing the validity and reliability of questionnaires and/or interviews.

21 Explain the data analyses that are appropriate for survey data.

22 Explain the statistics used with crosstabulations.

The survey is a research technique in which data are gathered by asking questions of a group of individuals called *respondents*. It is a widely used method of research in sociology, business, political science, and government, as well as in education. The range of topics covered by surveys and the techniques used have increased significantly in the past several years. Hardly a week goes by that you are not exposed through the news media to the results of some survey. The well-known Gallup poll, for instance, surveys public opinion on a variety of issues. Market researchers ask what products you purchase or might purchase, political pollsters ask whom you are likely to vote for, and television networks want to know what shows you watch.

Surveys are also very important in higher education. Many universities have survey research institutes, such as the University of Michigan Institute for Social Research and the UCLA Higher Education Research Institute. Annually since 1966, the latter has surveyed college freshmen in order to gather information on students' reasons for going to college and for choosing a particular college, on their anticipated major, career and graduate school plans, on their attitudes, political views, religious preferences, and many other aspects of their lives. The 1999 survey, based on the responses of 261,217 freshmen entering 462 U.S. institutions, showed that a significant percentage of the freshmen report feeling increasing levels of stress ("Student Stress," 2000). They worry about paying tuition and making ends meet and completing all the tasks confronting them. The survey also found that female students report suffering from stress at a rate nearly double that of their male counterparts. The researchers state that the data are representative of the total population of approximately 1.64 million first-time, full-time freshmen.

Many doctoral dissertations and much of the research published in educational journals involve survey methods. Public school districts also conduct surveys to gather data such as average teacher load, number of preschool children in the community, number of students who participate in extracurricular activities, opinions of parents and students and data on a myriad of other topics. For example, in August 1999, 1016 randomly selected adults in the United States were surveyed concerning ways to combat school violence. Over one-third thought that reducing violence in TV and movies was the most effective way to stop the violence. Sixty-five percent thought that police presence in the schools would reduce violence. Twenty-two percent felt that counseling teenagers was the best way to deal with the problem.

TYPES OF SURVEYS

Before initiating survey research, the investigator must determine the format that is most appropriate for the proposed investigation. Surveys are classified according to their focus and scope (census and sample surveys) or according to the time frame for data collection (longitudinal and cross-sectional surveys). Becoming familiar with the options enables the researcher to select the method that will provide the most useful data.

Surveys Classified According to Focus and Scope

A survey that covers the entire population of interest is referred to as a **census,** an example of which is the U.S. Census, undertaken by the government every ten years. In research, however, "population" does not refer to all the people of a country. The term **population** is used to refer to the entire group of individuals to whom the findings of a study apply. The researcher defines the specific population of interest. It is often difficult or even impossible for researchers to study very large populations. Hence, they select a smaller portion, a sample, of the population for study. A survey that studies only a portion of the population is known as a **sample survey.**

Surveys may be confined to simple tabulations of *tangibles,* such as what proportion of children rides school buses, and the average class enrollment. The most challenging type of survey is one that seeks to measure *intangibles,* such as attitudes, opinions, values, or other psychological and sociological constructs. In such a study you must bring to bear not only the skills involved in proper sampling but also the skills involved in identifying or constructing appropriate measures and employing the scores on these measures to make meaningful statements about the constructs involved. If you classify surveys on the basis of their scope (census versus sample) and their focus (tangibles versus intangibles), four categories emerge: (1) a census of tangibles, (2) a census of intangibles, (3) a sample survey of tangibles, and (4) a sample survey of intangibles. Each type has its own contributions to make and its own inherent problems.

A Census of Tangibles

When you seek information about a small population, such as a single school, and when the variables involved are concrete, there is little challenge in finding the required answers. If a school principal wants to know how many desks are in the school, how many children ride the school bus, or how many teachers have master's degrees, a simple count will provide the information. Because the study covers the entire population, the principal can have all the confidence characteristic of perfect induction. Well-defined and unambiguous variables are being measured, and as long as the enumeration is accurate and honest, the principal can say, without much fear of contradiction, "On the first of September there were 647 children's desks in our school" or "Sixty-five percent of the present faculty have master's degrees." The strength of a census of this type lies in its irrefutability. Its weakness lies in its confinement to a single limited population at a single point in time. The information provided by such a census may be of immediate importance to a limited group, but typically such surveys add little to the general body of knowledge in education.

A Census of Intangibles

Suppose the school principal now seeks information about pupil achievement or aspirations, teacher morale, or parents' attitudes toward school. The task will be more difficult, because this census deals with constructs that are not directly observable but must be inferred from indirect measures. The National Study of School Evaluation (NSSE) publishes an opinion inventory designed to measure student, teacher, and parent attitudes and opinions about schools. Administering the inventory to all the students, teachers, or parents in the school system would represent a census of intangibles.

Another example of this type of census is the achievement-testing program carried out by most schools. All children are tested, and the test scores are used to compare their performance with national norms, their own previous performance, and so on.

The value of a census of intangibles is largely a question of the extent to which the instruments used actually measure the constructs of interest. Reasonably good instruments are available for measuring aptitude and achievement in a variety of academic areas. Many other variables remain very difficult to measure. Because researchers lack instruments that can meaningfully measure the constructs involved, many important questions in education have not been answered. Such variables as teacher success, student motivation, psychological adjustment, and leadership have been difficult to define and measure operationally.

A Sample Survey of Tangibles

When investigators seek information about large groups, the expense involved in carrying out a census is often prohibitive. Therefore, researchers use sampling techniques and use the information they collect from the sample to make inferences about the population as a whole. When sampling is well done, the inferences made concerning the population can be quite reliable.

A well-known example of a sample survey of tangibles is the Coleman Report (1966). This study was conducted in response to Section 402 of the Civil Rights Act of 1964, which directed the Commissioner of Education to conduct a survey of inequalities in educational opportunities among various groups in the United States. The sample survey included more than 600,000 children in grades 1, 3, 6, 9, and 12 of approximately 4000 schools. The schools were considered generally representative of all U.S. public schools, although there was some intentional overrepresentation of schools with minority-group populations. From the data generated by the survey, the researchers concluded that 65 percent of blacks attended schools in which more than 90 percent of students were black and 80 percent of whites attended schools enrolling more than 90 percent white. When comparisons were made concerning class size, physical facilities, and teacher qualifications, relatively little difference was found among schools serving different racial and ethnic groups. However, these variables did differ between metropolitan and rural areas and between geographic regions. Those disadvantaged in regard to these variables appeared to be rural children and those in the South, regardless of race.

A Sample Survey of Intangibles

The public opinion polls are examples of studies measuring intangible constructs. Opinion is not directly observable but must be inferred from responses made by the subjects to questionnaires or interviews. Opinion polling began in the 1930s and has grown tremendously. Where respondents have been willing to reveal their preferences freely before elections, for instance, pollsters have been quite accurate in inferring public opinion from which they have predicted subsequent election results. These polls have provided excellent examples of the usefulness of sample statistics in estimating population parameters. However, if people who support one candidate are reluctant to reveal their preference, whereas people who support the other candidate feel free to say so, considerable error is introduced into the results of the poll. For example, people are more willing to say they will vote *against* an incumbent than *for* him or her. Before the 1948 presidential election, several polls showed Dewey leading the incumbent, Truman, but with many people indicating they were undecided. Truman won the election. Apparently most of those who indicated they were undecided actually voted for Truman. Respondents are also reluctant to reveal a choice that may appear based on self-interest, prejudice, or lack of knowledge about the issues.

How someone is going to vote is an intangible, but what is marked on a ballot is tangible. The television network news services have done very well in predicting how states will vote when only a few precincts have reported, because they can use tangible measures of a sample (that is, how some ballots have been marked) to predict the vote of a population. Therefore, the risks are only those involved in estimating population parameters from sample statistics. However, pollsters who estimate how a population *will* vote on the basis of how people *say* they will vote have the additional handicap of measuring what is intangible at the time the measurements are made. Surveys of intangibles are limited by the fact that the data researchers collect are only indirectly measuring the variables they are concerned about. The seriousness of this limitation depends on how well the observations measure the intangible variable.

The same survey may study tangibles and intangibles at the same time. The authors of the Coleman Report asked the students to answer questionnaires and administered intelligence and achievement tests in order to make inferences about social class, ability, and achievement, as well as the relationship of these variables to each other and to tangible variables in the study.

Surveys Classified According to the Time Dimension

Two types of surveys are classified according to the time of data collection: longitudinal surveys, which study changes across time, and cross-sectional surveys, which focus on a single point in time.

Longitudinal Surveys

Longitudinal surveys gather information at different points in time in order to study changes over extended periods of time. For example, a researcher studying the development of quantitative reasoning in elementary school children would select a sample of first-graders and administer a measure of quantitative reasoning. This same group would be followed through successive grade levels and tested each year to assess how quantitative reasoning abilities develop over time. Three different designs are used in longitudinal survey research: panel studies, trend studies, and cohort studies.

Panel Studies In a **panel study,** the *same* subjects are surveyed at different times over an extended period. Because the same subjects are studied over time, researchers can see the changes in the individuals' behavior and investigate the reasons for the changes. An example of a panel study is a longitudinal survey on smoking conducted at Indiana University that has followed the same group of subjects since 1980 (Chassin et al., 1998). The original study surveyed over 8000 high school students about their views on smoking. It also asked them their opinions on academics, friends, and dating. The researchers found that students who were less serious about schoolwork and were more rebellious were more likely to start smoking than their academically oriented peers. The smokers also tended to have friends who smoked. In 1987, the researchers conducted their first follow-up survey, contacting 6200 of the original group. A second follow-up started in 1993, with 73 percent of the original group participating. The researchers asked the subjects their opinion of smoking and, now that most subjects were parents, explored how having children affected their smoking. They also independently surveyed the children of the original participants, to determine if smoking behavior shows intergenerational transmission. The results (1998) showed strong evidence for the intergenerational transmission of cigarette smoking: Adolescents whose parents smoke were themselves more likely to smoke. They also found that both general parenting practices and smoking-specific discussion and punishment were significantly related to adolescents' smoking. The investigators suggested that the current peer-focused smoking prevention programs should be expanded to include parent-focused components, such as parental involvement, nurturance, and consistent behavioral control.

Trend Studies   In a **trend study,** *different* people from the same general population are surveyed at different times. For example, researchers who have studied national trends in mathematics achievement sample middle school students at various intervals and measure their math performance. Although the same individuals are not tested each time, if the samples from the population of middle school students are selected randomly, the results each time can be considered representative of the middle school population from which the student samples were drawn. Test scores from year to year are compared to see if any trends are evident. Another example of a trend study is the survey on tobacco and drug use among Indiana youth conducted annually by the Indiana Prevention Resource Center. The most recent survey based on 81,685 students in grades 6 through 12 in 281 Indiana schools found significant reductions in the rate of tobacco and drug use, especially among middle-school students (Schuckel, 1999). The survey found that 28,500 fewer youth smoked cigarettes on a monthly or more frequent basis than in 1996; two-thirds of this decrease occurred among middle-schoolers. Such trend studies permit researchers to investigate the effects over time of the increased prevention and enforcement efforts directed at the teenage population.

Cohort Studies   In a **cohort study,** a *specific* population is followed over a length of time. Whereas trend studies sample a general population that changes in membership over time, a cohort study samples a specific population whose members do not change over the duration of the survey. For example, a school system might follow the high school graduating class(es) of 2000 over time and ask them questions about higher education, work experiences, attitudes, and so on. From a list of all the graduates, a random sample is drawn at different points in time and data are collected from that sample. Thus the population remains the same during the study, but the individuals surveyed are different each time.

Cross-Sectional Surveys

Cross-sectional surveys study a cross section (sample) of a population at a single point in time. In a longitudinal study of vocabulary development, for example, a researcher would compare a measure of first-grade students' vocabulary skills in 1993 with one when they were fourth-grade students in 1996 and seventh-grade students in 1999. A cross-sectional study would compare the vocabulary skills of a sample of children from grades 1, 4, and 7 in 1999. The cross-sectional survey is the method of choice if you want to gather the data at one point in time.

Longitudinal surveys are more time consuming and expensive to conduct, because the researcher must keep up with the subjects and maintain their cooperation over a long period of time. Cross-sectional surveys, in contrast, do not require years to complete. Hence, they are less expensive. A major disadvantage of the cross-sectional method is that chance differences between samples may seriously bias the results. You may by chance draw a sample of first-graders who are more mature than average and a sample of fourth-graders who are less mature than average, with the result that the difference between the groups appears much smaller than it really is. However, researchers usually can obtain larger samples for cross-sectional studies than for longitudinal studies, and the larger samples mitigate the problem of chance differences.

THE SURVEY TECHNIQUE

The survey permits you to gather information from a large sample of people relatively quickly and inexpensively. Conducting a good survey, however, is not as easy as it might initially appear. It requires careful planning, implementation, and analysis if it is to yield reliable and valid information.

Six Basic Steps Are Involved in Survey Research

1. *Planning.* Survey research begins with a question that the researcher believes can be answered most appropriately by means of the survey method. For example, "How do elementary teachers feel about retaining students?" and "What is the extent of tobacco use among the high school students in this district?" are questions that a survey could answer. The research question in survey research typically concerns the beliefs, preferences, attitudes, or other self-reported behaviors of the people in the study. A literature review reveals what other researchers have learned about the question. The researcher also needs to decide at this time on which data-gathering technique to use.

2. *Defining the population.* One of the first important steps is to define the population under study. To whom will you distribute the survey? The population may be quite large, or it may be rather limited. For instance, the population might be all elementary teachers in the United States or all elementary teachers in the state of Indiana. Or you might further restrict the population to "all first-year male elementary teachers in the state of Indiana." Defining the population is essential for identifying the subjects appropriate to select for the study and for knowing to whom the results can be generalized.

Once the population has been defined, the researcher must obtain or construct a complete list of all individuals in the population. This list, called the **sampling frame,** can be very difficult and time consuming to construct if such a list is not already available.

3. *Sampling.* Because researchers generally can't survey an entire population, they select a *sample* from that population. It is very important to select a sample that will provide results similar to those that would have been obtained if the entire population had been surveyed. In other words, the sample must be representative of the population. The extent to which this happens depends on the way subjects are selected. The sampling procedure that is most likely to yield a representative sample is some form of probability sampling (see Chapter 7). Probability sampling permits you to estimate how far sample results are likely to deviate from the population values.

4. *Constructing the instrument.* A major task in survey research is constructing the instrument that will be used to gather the data from the sample. The two basic types of data-gathering instruments are interviews and questionnaires.

5. *Conducting the survey.* Once the data-gathering instrument is prepared, it must be field-tested to determine if it will provide the desired data. Also included in this step are training the users of the instrument, interviewing subjects or distributing questionnaires to them, and verifying the accuracy of the data gathered.

6. *Processing the data.* The last step includes coding the data, statistical analysis, interpreting the results, and reporting the findings.

Many considerations are involved in implementing the foregoing steps. The balance of this chapter discusses these considerations in detail.

Data-Gathering Techniques

There are two basic ways in which data are gathered in survey research: interviews and questionnaires. Each has two options, thus providing four different approaches to collecting data:

1. Personal interview
2. Telephone interview
3. Mailed questionnaire
4. Directly administered questionnaire

Although they all use a question-asking approach, each has certain unique characteristics, advantages, and disadvantages that you need to consider before deciding what type of instrument to use.

Personal Interviews

In a personal **interview,** the interviewer reads the questions to the respondent in a face-to-face setting and records the answers. One of the most important aspects of the interview is its flexibility. The interviewer has the opportunity to observe the subject and the total situation in which he or she is responding. Questions can be repeated or their meanings explained in case they are not understood by the respondents. The interviewer can also press for additional information when a response seems incomplete or not entirely relevant.

A greater response rate is another obvious advantage of the interview. The term **response rate** refers to the proportion of the selected sample that agrees to be interviewed or returns a completed questionnaire. With interviews, response rates are very high—perhaps 90 percent or better. Personal contact increases the likelihood that the individual will participate and will provide the desired information. With mailed questionnaires, the personal contact is missing and people are more likely to refuse to cooperate. This results in many *nonreturns* (people who do not complete and return the questionnaire). The low response rate typical for mailed questionnaires (less than 30 percent is common) not only reduces the sample size but also may bias the results (Fowler, 1993). Furthermore, the interviewer can get an answer to all or most of the questions. Missing data represent a serious problem for the mailed questionnaire.

Another advantage is the control that the interviewer has over the order with which questions are considered. In some cases it is very important that respondents not know the nature of later questions, because their responses to these questions may influence earlier responses. This problem is eliminated in an interview, where the subject does not know what questions are coming up and cannot go back and change answers previously given. For individuals who cannot read and understand a written questionnaire, interviews provide the only possible information-gathering technique.

The main disadvantage of the personal interview is that it is more expensive than other survey methods. The selection and training of the interviewers, their salary, and their travel to the interview site make this procedure costly. It takes a great deal of time to contact potential respondents, set up appointments, and actually conduct the interview. Another disadvantage is the possibility of **interviewer bias,** which occurs when the interviewer's own feelings and attitudes or the interviewer's gender, race, age, and other characteristics influence the way questions are asked or interpreted. Personal characteristics of the interviewer can influence the reaction of subjects and the way they respond. The interviewer may verbally or nonverbally encourage or reward "correct" responses that fit his or her expectations. An analysis of responses given to some surveys concerning opinions on abortion found that gender of interviewer may be a factor. Women talking to women and men talking to male interviewers tended to give more pro-choice responses to the questions than did women talking to men or men talking to women (Coughlin, 1990). Similarly, if a specific racial or ethnic group is to be interviewed, it is wise to use interviewers of the same group.

Another problem is the **social desirability bias** in which respondents want to please the interviewer by giving socially acceptable responses that they would not necessarily give on an anonymous questionnaire. For example, in preference polls in the 1989 elections involving minority candidates for mayor of New York and for governor of Virginia, the proportion of respondents who said they would vote for the minority candidates was considerably higher than the proportion of votes these candidates actually received in the election. To account for this error, researchers speculated that white voters may have feared they would appear racist if they admitted to interviewers that they preferred a white candidate (Coughlin, 1990).

Telephone Interviews

The telephone interview has become more popular, and recent studies indicate that it compares favorably with face-to-face interviewing (Wilhoit & Weaver, 1990). Its major advantages are lower cost and faster completion, with relatively high response rates. Telephone interviews can be conducted over a relatively short time span with people scattered over a large geographic area. For example, national polling organizations often use the telephone to obtain nationwide opinions among voters near election time. Large-scale surveys in major cities often use the telephone instead of sending interviewers into unsafe areas. The phone permits the survey to reach people who would not open their doors to an interviewer, but who might be willing to talk on the telephone. Another advantage is that respondents have a greater feeling of anonymity—and hence there may be less interviewer bias and less social desirability bias than with personal interviews.

The main disadvantage of the telephone interview is that there is less opportunity for establishing rapport with the respondent than in a face-to-face situation. It takes a great deal of skill to carry out a telephone interview so that valid results are obtained. The interviewer often finds it difficult to overcome the suspicions of the surprised respondents, especially when asking personal or sensitive questions. An advance letter that informs the potential respondents of the approaching call is sometimes used to deal with this problem, but the letter can induce another problem: The recipient has time to think about responses or to prepare a refusal to participate when the call comes.

Another disadvantage is that households without telephones and those with unlisted numbers are automatically excluded from the survey, which may bias results. However, a technique known as "random digit dialing" solves the problem of unlisted numbers (although it does not reach households without a telephone). In random digit dialing, a computer randomly generates a list of telephone numbers based on all possible numbers thought to be in use in an area. Because of the random determination, this technique assures that every household with telephone service has an equal chance of being included in the sample. See Fowler (1995) for a thorough discussion of random digit dialing.

Other limitations of telephone surveys arise from new technology. First, because of the increased use of telemarketing, people are bombarded with junk phone calls. When an interviewer calls, people may think it's another telemarketer and just hang up. Second, services such as caller identification, phone number blocking, and similar procedures enable residential phone customers to have much greater control over incoming calls. People may simply ignore calls from the unfamiliar number of the surveyer.

Computer-Assisted Telephone Interviewing (CATI)

Computer and telecommunications technology has been applied to telephone surveys. Wearing earphones, the interviewer sits at a computer while it randomly selects a telephone number (through random-digit dialing or from a database) and dials. When the respondent answers, the interviewer reads the first question that appears on the computer screen and types the answer directly into the computer. The computer program displays the next screen containing the next question, and so on through the entire survey. Using CATI saves a great deal of time. The surveyor can fill in forms on a computer screen or type answers to open-ended questions very quickly. The biggest advantage is that CATI software immediately formats responses into a data file as they are keyed in, which saves the researcher time usually spent in coding and manually transferring responses from paper into the computer for analysis.

Mailed Questionnaires

The direct one-on-one contact with subjects in a personal interview is time consuming and expensive. Often much of the same information can be obtained by means of a questionnaire mailed to each individual in the sample, with a request that he or she complete and return it by a given date. Because the questionnaire is mailed, it is possible to include a larger number of subjects as well as subjects in more diverse locations than is practical with the interview.

A mailed questionnaire has the advantage of guaranteeing confidentiality or anonymity, thus perhaps eliciting more truthful responses than would be obtained with a personal interview. In an interview, subjects may be reluctant to express unpopular or politically incorrect points of view or to give information they think might be used against them at a later time. The mailed questionnaire also eliminates the problem of interviewer bias.

A disadvantage of the questionnaire is the possibility of respondents misinterpreting the questions. It is extremely difficult to formulate a series of questions whose meanings are crystal clear to every reader. The investigator may know exactly what is meant by a question, but because of poor wording or different meanings of terms, the respondent makes a significantly different interpretation. Furthermore, large segments of the population may not be able to read and respond to a mailed questionnaire. Only people with considerable education may be able to complete a very complex questionnaire.

Another important limitation of mailed questionnaires is the low return rate. It is easy for the individual who receives a questionnaire to lay it aside and simply forget to complete and return it. A low response rate limits the generalizability of the results of a questionnaire study. It cannot be assumed that nonresponse is randomly distributed throughout a group. Studies have shown that there are usually systematic differences in the characteristics of respondents and nonrespondents to questionnaire studies. Response rate is often higher among the more intelligent, better educated, more conscientious, and more interested or generally more favorable to the issue involved in the questionnaires. The goal in a questionnaire study is 100 percent returns, although a more reasonable expectation may be 75–90 percent returns.

A number of factors have been found to influence the rate of returns for a mailed questionnaire. Some of these are (1) length of the questionnaire, (2) cover letter, (3) sponsorship of the questionnaire, (4) attractiveness of the questionnaire, (5) ease of completing it and mailing it back, (6) interest aroused by the content, (7) use of a monetary incentive, and (8) follow-up procedures used. We discuss these factors in more detail later.

Electronic Mail Surveys

Electronic mail (e-mail) surveys are becoming more popular. Dillman (2000) found that e-mail surveys have the advantages of prompter returns, lower item nonresponse, and more complete answers to open-ended questions. The main disadvantage is that not everyone has an e-mail address. Dillman reports that in fall 1998, only 42 percent of US households owned a computer and a total of 26 percent had e-mail connections. Because only a fraction of the U.S. population can be contacted through e-mail, . . . "there is no possibility for listing general populations and drawing a sample in which nearly every adult in the U.S. population has a known nonzero chance of being selected for participation in a survey" (p. 355). E-mail surveys have been used most successfully on college campuses with faculty and students, with companies and their employees, or with other populations having universal e-mail access. Dillman suggests combining e-mail and regular mail surveys for a maximum return rate. Research (Shaefer & Dillman, 1998) shows that some of the factors found to be important for regular mail surveys are also important in e-mail surveys. For example, people who received a prior e-mail notification about the survey were more likely to respond; also, surveys addressed individually to a person (rather than being part of a mailing list) had higher response rates.

Internet Surveys

Internet surveys are also being used and may have advantages over e-mail. Unlike e-mail surveys, Internet surveys have the same format on all users' screens. Internet surveys are also easier for the respondent to navigate.

Directly Administered Questionnaires

The directly administered questionnaire is administered to a group of people assembled at a certain place for a specific purpose. Examples include surveying the freshmen or their parents attending summer orientation at a university. Surveys at universities are often administered in classrooms or in dormitories. Jacobs (1985) used this method to gather the perceptions of freshman students concerning their academic preparation for college work. It was easy to reach a large sample of students in a variety of disciplines by administering the survey in classrooms (with the permission of professors).

The main advantage of directly administering questionnaires is the high response rate, which typically reaches 100 percent. Other advantages are the low cost and the fact that the researcher is present to provide assistance or answer questions. The disadvantage is that the researcher is usually restricted in terms of where and when the questionnaire can be administered. Also, because the sample is usually quite specific (for instance, parents of freshmen in a specific university), the findings are generalizable only to the population that the sample represents.

SELECTING THE SAMPLE

Now look again at the section in Chapter 7 on sampling techniques and the factors that influence the size of the sample selected. Some additional discussion of sample size appears in the following section.

Sample Size

How large a sample to draw is one of the early and difficult questions the researcher must answer. The general rule is the larger the sample, the better, but this rule is not specific enough to be helpful. The first step in determining sample size is to decide on the degree of accuracy or conversely the margin of error you want in the estimation of population values. You want the least sampling error, because this means that the sample data are closer to the population values you are trying to determine. You don't know the population values; if you did, there would be no need for the sample. But you can determine the probability that the sample values differ by a certain amount from the population values. This is done by calculating the **margin of error,** which indicates the range within which the true population value would be most likely to fall. Margin of error is generally given when survey results are reported. For example, in December 1999, on the basis of 899 completed surveys, *Money* magazine reported that 63 percent of Americans answered "Yes" to the question "Are you better off now than you were four years ago?" The magazine reported a margin of error of 3 percent. This means that if the sample represented the population well, there is a 95 percent probability that the population percent who would give this response is between 60 and 66 percent. In surveys conducted by the major polling organizations, a margin of error of ±3% is generally considered acceptable.

Margin of Error

How is margin of error calculated? If probability sampling is used, researchers have a basis for estimating how far sample results are likely to deviate from the population values (margin of error) for a given sample size. Using the obtained sample proportions, you can calculate the variance and then the standard error of the proportion. The variance of a proportion is *pq,* where *p* is the proportion agreeing with a given response and *q* is the proportion not agreeing. Plugging this into formula 13.1 (standard error of a proportion), you have

$$\sigma_p = \frac{\sqrt{pq}}{\sqrt{n}} \tag{13.1}$$

where

$$\sigma p = \text{standard error of a proportion}$$
$$p = \text{proportion agreeing}$$
$$q = \text{proportion not agreeing } (q = 1 - p)$$
$$n = \text{number in sample}$$

In the *Money* example,

$$\sigma_p = \frac{\sqrt{(.63)(.37)}}{\sqrt{899}} = \frac{\sqrt{.2331}}{29.9833} = \frac{.4828}{29.9833} = .0161$$

Multiplying the standard error by 1.96 to get the 95 percent confidence interval, you have .0161 × 1.96 = .0316, which rounds to the 3 percent margin of error reported.

Calculating Sample Size

We can use formula 13.2 (number required for given margin of error) to calculate the sample size needed to achieve a desired margin of error.

$$n = \left(\frac{1}{\frac{E}{\sqrt{pq}}}\right)^2 (z)^2 \qquad (13.2)$$

where

$$n = \text{sample size needed}$$
$$E = \text{desired margin of error}$$
$$pq = \text{variance of the hypothesized proportion}$$
$$z = \text{z-score of the confidence level}$$

For example, if we want a ±3 percent margin of error at the 95 percent confidence level ($z = 1.96$) for a hypothesized $p = .5, q = .5$, the required n would be

$$n = \left(\frac{1}{\frac{.03}{\sqrt{(.5)(.5)}}}\right)^2 (1.96)^2 = \left(\frac{1}{.06}\right)^2 (3.8416) = (277.7783)(3.8416)$$

$$n = 1067.1131$$

If the hypothesized population proportions are .50/.50, then 1068 subjects would be needed to yield a margin of error of ±3 percent. If a 10 percent margin of error would be acceptable, then only 97 respondents would be needed.

$$n = \left(\frac{1}{\frac{.10}{\sqrt{(.5)(.5)}}}\right)^2 (1.96)^2 = \left(\frac{1}{.2}\right)^2 (3.8416) = (25)(3.8416) = 96.04$$

Table 13.1 *Minimum Sample Sizes Required for Various Margins of Error around the Parameter Estimation at the .95 Confidence Level (sizes are shown as a function of anticipated sample proportions)*

MAXIMUM MARGIN OF ERROR	VALUE OF P		
	.10 OR .90[a]	.25 OR .75	.50
1%	3462	7212	9616
2%	866	1803	2404
3%	385	802	1069
5%	139	289	385
10%	35	73	97

[a]The sample variance, *pq,* is the same when $pq = (.10)(.90)$ as when $pq = (.90)(.10)$.

Using $p = .50$ is always a safe way to calculate the needed sample size, because pq is at its maximum possible value when p and q each equals .50 and $pq = .25$. Using population estimates of $p = q = .50$ in formula 13.2, the researcher will be confident that the margin of error will be as small as or smaller than the value specified. If there are compelling reasons to hypothesize unequal population proportions for p and $q,$ these may be substituted for .50 and .50 respectively, and the result will be a lower required number of subjects. For instance, if 20 percent of the high school boys in a school district tried out for intermural sports last year, you might use $p = .20$ and $q = .80$ in calculating the number of subjects needed for a survey of this year's boys. Note that all these statistics are based on the assumption that the sample is a random sample of the population of interest. The credibility of the results are a function of the validity of that assumption.

Table 13.1 shows the sample size needed to have a certain margin of error for a given $p.$ Note that the largest sample is required when the desired margin of error is lowest and $p = .50.$ As the acceptable margin of error increases and p varies from .50, the required sample size decreases.

As with anything else that relies on sampling, the representativeness of the sample is more important than the size of the sample. An unrepresentative sample leads to inappropriate conclusions regardless of its size. With mailed surveys, an additional consideration is how similar the respondents are to those who do not send back their responses. In the *Money* survey, researchers reported that 63 percent said they were better off financially than four years earlier. Of the 4500 households who were sent surveys, 899 returned them. The credibility of the results of this survey depends on the credibility of the assumption that the responses of the 3601 who did not return the questionnaire would be like the responses of the 899 who did.

Another factor influencing the decision about sample size is the variability of the population to be sampled. If the population is fairly homogeneous, then you can use a smaller sample than if the population is more variable. A population of college students, for example, would be expected to show less variability than a population of adults in general and thus a smaller sample could be used. Check published research studies to learn something about the variability of the population of interest and the sample size used in survey research on the population.

Also consider the statistical analysis that will be used on the survey data. Some statistics require samples of certain sizes. Chi-square, for instance, cannot be used if the sample is too small. There is also a financial consideration. Increasing the size of the sample can be expensive. Mailing of questionnaires and follow-ups is costly; interviewing is even more expensive. The researcher must consider the time and money available for the survey and select as large a sample as can be economically managed. But remember: Size alone does not guarantee a representative sample; the sampling procedure is more important in determining whether the sample is representative of the population. Another point to emphasize is that sample size does not need to be a certain percentage of the population. When random sampling is used, a sample size that is only a small percentage of the population can represent the population well. The major public opinion polls, for example, do not use really large samples. The Nielsen rating service uses a sample of only about 5000 TV-watching households in the United States to estimate the popularity of various programs. The Nielsen ratings are a major variable in determining which programs continue and which do not.

A national survey on gun control that the Associated Press conducted in April 2000 polled only 829 Americans (*The Herald-Times,* April 21, Bloomington, IN.). The survey found that a large majority of Americans want tougher gun controls. When asked what approach should be used, 42 percent of the respondents thought stricter enforcement of existing laws was the better approach; 33 percent thought that enacting tougher gun laws was better. The survey had a margin of error of plus or minus 4 percentage points.

CONSTRUCTING THE INSTRUMENT

Format of Questions

With the overall research question as a guide, the researcher's next task is to construct an instrument that will provide the desired information. Because survey data consist of peoples' responses to individual questions, it is very important to start with good questions. Two basic types of questions are used in survey instruments: closed-ended or fixed alternative and open-ended or free-response questions. Use **closed-ended questions** when all the possible, relevant responses to a question can be specified and the number of possible responses is limited. For example, in a survey of undergraduates, a question about class level would be closed-ended. The possible answers are known and are few in number: *freshman, sophomore, junior,* or *senior.* Other closed-ended questions might ask about residency status (in-state or out-of-state) or sex. **Open-ended questions** are used when there are a great number of possible answers or when the researcher can't predict all the possible answers. For example, a question about the students' reasons for selecting a particular university would probably be open-ended. A question about the college major would be open-ended because the researcher would probably not want to include the long list of possible majors. Both formats can be used in the same question—that is, a number of closed-ended responses can be followed by "Other" as the last possible response. For example, you might ask a professor a question such as

1. What type of writing assignments do you typically require in your course?
   (circle as many as apply)
   a. Reports
   b. Themes or essays
   c. Research papers
   d. Take-home essay examinations
   e. Minute papers
   f. Other (please specify)

There are advantages and disadvantages to both these question formats. The open-ended question permits a free response rather than restricting the respondent to a choice from among stated alternatives. Individuals are free to respond from their own frame of reference, thus providing a wide range of responses. Open-ended questions are easier to construct, but analyzing them is very tedious and time consuming. The researcher must read and interpret each response, then develop a coding system that will permit a quantitative analysis of the responses. Some responses may be unclear, and the researcher may be unsure how to classify or code the response. The responses to open-ended questions typically differ in length, and some respondents may give more than one response to a particular question. If asked the most important reason for choosing a certain university, a respondent might answer, "I chose University X because of its academic reputation and because it is in state and less expensive for me." The researcher must then decide whether to use both answers or only the first one, assuming the first answer is the more important one.

Closed-ended questions take more time to construct, but the responses are easier to tabulate. Responses to closed-ended questions can be coded directly on scannable sheets that can be "read" and the data entered into a computer database for analysis. Closed-ended questions can be answered more easily and quickly by respondents. A closed format also ensures that all subjects have the same frame of reference in responding and may also make it easier for subjects to respond to questions on sensitive or private topics.

A limitation of the closed-ended question is that it does not provide much insight into whether respondents really have any information or any clearly formulated opinions about an issue. It is easier for the uninformed respondent to choose one of the suggested answers than to admit to lack of knowledge on an issue. For example, in response to the question "What are the most significant benefits of the North American Free Trade Agreement (NAFTA) for the United States?" the respondent who has little knowledge of NAFTA could easily select a reasonable answer from among the alternatives provided. In contrast, respondents who have the knowledge or who have well-informed opinions on the issue may dislike being restricted to simple response categories that do not permit them to qualify their answers. It is possible to get the benefits of both open-ended and closed-ended questions. A researcher can use the open-ended format with a small sample strictly for the purpose of identifying the possible alternative responses to the questions. On the basis of the results from the sample, the researcher can design closed-ended questions for the final form of the instrument.

Structure of Questions

We have discussed the advantages and disadvantages of the closed-ended and open-ended questions in survey research. Now let's look at the ways these two formats can be used to structure questions for interviews and questionnaires.

1. *Completion,* or *fill-in, items* are open-ended questions to which respondents must supply their own answers in their own words. For example, "What is the major weakness you have observed in your students' preparation for college?"

2. **Checklists** are questions that present a number of possible answers, and the respondents are asked to check those that apply. For example,

   What type of teaching aids do you use in your classes? (check as many as apply)

   1) CHALKBOARD

   2) OVERHEAD PROJECTOR

   3) COMPUTER PROJECTOR

   4) VIDEOTAPES

   5) OTHER (please specify)

3. **Scaled items** ask respondents to rate a concept, event, or situation on such dimensions as quantity or intensity, indicating "how much"; on quality, indicating "how well"; or on frequency, indicating "how often." For example,

   How would you rate the writing skills of students you are teaching this semester? (check one)

   1) VERY POOR

   2) LESS THAN ADEQUATE

   3) ADEQUATE

   4) MORE THAN ADEQUATE

   5) EXCELLENT

   6) INSUFFICIENT INFORMATION

or

   How well prepared in basic math skills are the students who typically enroll in your course? (check one)

   1) NOT AT ALL PREPARED

   2) SOMEWHAT PREPARED

   3) VERY WELL PREPARED

   4) EXTREMELY WELL PREPARED

4. **Ranking items** ask respondents to indicate the order of their preference among a number of options. Rankings should not involve more than six options, because otherwise it becomes too difficult for respondents to make the comparisons. An example of a ranking item follows:

> Do your students have more difficulty with some types of reading than with other types? Please rank the order of difficulty of the following materials, with 1 being the most difficult and 4 the least difficult.
>
> ____ 1) TEXTBOOKS
>
> ____ 2) OTHER REFERENCE BOOKS
>
> ____ 3) JOURNAL ARTICLES
>
> ____ 4) OTHER (please specify)

5. **Likert-type items** let subjects indicate their responses to selected statements on a continuum, from *strongly agree* to *strongly disagree*. Likert-type scales were discussed in Chapter 8. An advantage of this type of item is that points can be assigned to the various responses, and thus measures of central tendency variability, correlation, and the like can be calculated. For example,

> The students who typically enroll in my course are underprepared in basic math skills. (circle one)
>
> strongly agree   agree   undecided   disagree   strongly disagree

Writing Survey Questions

Now let's examine the task of formulating good questions. Deciding how to word the questions that are asked in a survey is difficult. Before beginning to write a structured set of survey questions, it can be helpful to have focus groups discuss the questions in a non-structured form (Fowler, 1995). You do this by bringing together a few groups of five to ten people representative of the study population, to discuss the topics covered in the survey. A moderator keeps the discussion focused on a preset agenda and asks questions to clarify comments.

Focus-group discussions help the researcher understand how people talk about the survey issues, which is helpful in choosing vocabulary and in phrasing questions. Focus groups often can suggest issues, concerns, or points of view about the topic that the researcher had not considered. Emery and associates (1993) used focus groups to identify salient issues concerning college students' alcohol abuse. The researchers set up four focus groups of randomly selected students—one all men, two all women, and one with both men and women. The groups discussed the reasons for students' drinking, the reasons for not drinking, the methods for prevention, and sex differences in drinking patterns. The researchers concluded that the focus groups were a valid tool for elucidating the sensitive aspects of the issues and the relative importance of these issues to one another. Excellent sources for more in-depth information about using focus groups include Morgan (1997), Krueger (1994), and Stewart and Shamdasani (1990).

A significant body of research has shown that changes in such things as phrasing, the amount of information offered, and the choice of answers available to respondents can influence the outcome of a survey to a greater or lesser degree. In an interview with Coughlin (1990), Ballou said, "One of the rules in this business is that the question determines the answer" (p. A6). Here are basic guidelines for writing good questions:

1. *Questions should be short, simple, and direct.* Eliminate any words and phrases not essential to the clear meaning of the question. Short questions are easier to understand. A useful rule of thumb is that most of the questions should have fewer than ten words (one line), and all questions should be under twenty words (Mitchell & Jolley, 1996, p. 455).

2. *Phrase questions so that they can be understood by every respondent.* The vocabulary used should be nontechnical and should be geared to the least educated respondent. At the same time, avoid talking down to respondents or choosing words that sound patronizing. It is a good idea to have some other people, preferably ones whose background is similar to those who will be included in the study, read and give their interpretation of the content of each question. For example, questions using terms such as "authentic assessment," "distance learning," and "total quality management" may not be appropriate in a survey designed for the general public. Also, be careful not to use slang, abbreviations, or acronyms that may not be familiar to all.

3. *Phrase questions so as to elicit unambiguous answers.* The question "Did you vote in the last election?" is ambiguous because it does not specify which election. Quantify responses whenever possible. Words such as *often* and *sometimes* have different meanings for different people. For example, in a survey on how often undergraduates use the main library for studying, the responses should be quantified (*daily, five times per week, twice per week,* and so on) instead of using responses such as *usually, sometimes,* and *often.*

4. *Phrase questions so as to avoid bias that may predetermine a respondent's answer.* The wording of a question should not influence the respondent in a certain direction. For this reason, avoid stereotyped, prestige-carrying, emotionally loaded, or superlative words. Some words have such an emotional appeal in U.S. culture that they tend to bias questions regardless of how they are used. For example, the wording "Have you exercised your American right and registered to vote?" would undoubtedly bias the question. Simply asking, "Are you registered to vote?" would be preferable. Dillman (2000) says that words such as *freedom, equality, private enterprise, justice,* and *honesty* have a strong positive appeal in our culture. Words such as *bureaucratic, socialist, boss,* and *government planning* have a strong negative appeal. Avoid such words if possible. Smith (1987) gave a good example of how certain words in a question can influence response. In surveying people's attitudes about spending for welfare, Smith posed the same question in different ways. Some people were asked whether we should spend more money on "welfare"; others were asked if we should spend more on "assistance for the poor."

The question using the word *welfare* resulted in considerably more negative responses. The word *welfare* has the connotation for many people of government bureaucracy, waste, and sometimes fraud. The phrase "assistance for the poor" connotes caring, giving, and charity.

5. *Avoid questions that might mislead because of unstated assumptions.* The frame of reference for answering the questions should be clear and consistent for all respondents. If any assumptions must be made before respondents give an answer, then also include questions designed to inquire into these assumptions. For example, in a survey designed for high school seniors the question "Do you think your high school has adequately prepared you for college?" assumes the student is going to college and knows what is required in the way of preparation. The question "Have you registered to vote for the next presidential election?" assumes the high school student is 18 years of age, which may not be true.

6. *Avoid leading questions, which imply a desired response.* For example, "Why do you favor a complete overhaul of the health care system in the United States?" is a leading question.

7. *Avoid questions that may elicit embarrassment, suspicion, or hostility in the respondent.* Questions should not put the respondent on the defensive. For example, people often resent questions about their age, income, religion, or educational status. Instead of asking a subject's age, the researcher can ask for his or her year of birth. People seem less concerned about giving their year of birth than about giving their age. The question "Do you have a high school diploma?" may embarrass someone who did not graduate from high school. The question might instead ask, "What grade had you completed when you left school?" In fact, it is best to avoid personal questions entirely unless the information is essential to the research.

8. *Avoid* ***"double-barreled" questions,*** *which attempt to ask two questions in one.* For example, "Do you feel that the university should provide basic-skills courses for students and give credit for those courses?" is a double-barreled question. When a respondent answers such a question, the researcher doesn't know whether the answer applies to both parts of the question or just to one. A yes answer to the preceding question may either mean that the respondent believes the university should offer basic-skills courses and give credit for them, or that it should offer the courses but not give credit for them. You can identify a double-barreled question from noting the *and, or,* or some other conjunction in the wording.

9. *Make sure the alternatives to each questionnaire item are exhaustive—that they express all the possible alternatives on the issue.* For example, "What is your marital status?" should include not only the alternatives "married" and "single," but also "unmarried cohabiting," "widowed," "divorced," and "separated." In developing the alternatives for questionnaire items designed to identify attitudes or opinions on issues, it is a good idea first to present the questions in an open-ended form to

a small sample of respondents. Their answers can then be used as alternatives in the final product. On questions with a wide variety of possible responses, always include the alternative "other," along with a request that the respondent explain that choice. The question "What is your position in the school system?" might be followed by the alternatives "administrator," "teacher," "librarian," and "other (please specify)."

10. *Keep the questionnaire as brief as possible so that it requires a minimum of the respondents' time.* Respondents are much more likely to complete and return a short questionnaire. The researcher must make an effort to eliminate all unnecessary items, especially those whose answers are available from other sources. All the items of a questionnaire should serve a research problem function; that is, they should elicit data needed to test the hypotheses or answer the questions of the research study. For example, you can eliminate a question that asks the respondent's age in a study where this information is not needed in the data analysis.

11. *Make sure the respondents have the information necessary to answer the questions.* Avoid questions dealing with experiences or topics you know are unfamiliar to your sample.

See Fowler (1995) for additional suggestions on writing survey questions.

■ CONDUCTING THE INTERVIEW

Whether the interview is conducted in person or by telephone, the interviewer's main job is to ask the questions in such a way as to obtain valid responses and to record the responses accurately and completely. The initial task for the interviewer is to create an atmosphere that will put the respondent at ease. After introducing yourself in a friendly way, briefly state the purpose of the interview but avoid giving too much information about the study, which could bias the respondent. It is well to begin the interview with fairly simple, nonthreatening questions.

The interviewer also has the responsibility of keeping the respondent's attention focused on the task and for keeping the interview moving along smoothly. This can best be done if you are thoroughly familiar with the questions and their sequence so that you can ask the questions in a conversational tone and without constantly pausing to find what question is coming next. Of course, you must refrain from expressing approval, surprise, or shock at any of the respondent's answers.

Interviews can be more or less structured. In a less structured interview, the same questions are asked of all respondents, but the interview is more conversational and the interviewer has more freedom to arrange the order of the questions or to rephrase the questions. If comparable data are to be obtained, however, the interviewer must standardize the procedure by using a structured interview schedule. A structured interview schedule contains specific questions in a fixed order, to be asked of all respondents, along with transition phrases and **probes** (questions used to clarify a response or that push a little further into a topic). For example, if the respondent starts to hedge, digress, or give irrelevant responses, or if he or she has obviously misinterpreted the question, then the interviewer may use a fixed probe such as "Explain your answer a little further" or "Can you tell me a little more about that?" In less structured interviews, any marked deviations from the protocol should be documented so that the information can be taken into account when analyzing the interviewee's response. In using probes, take care not to suggest or give hints about possible responses. It takes less training time to teach interviewers to administer a structured interview than it does an unstructured one, because everything they need to say or do is contained in the interview schedule. For this reason, the structured interview is the most widely used format for large studies with numerous interviewers.

Training the Interviewer

It is essential that potential interviewers receive training before being sent out to conduct interviews. Quality of interviewers is probably one of the least appreciated aspects of survey research. "For a good number of common survey questions, poorly trained or supervised interviews can reduce the effective sample size by 20 or 30 percent" (Fowler, 1993, p. 145).

Topics to be covered in interviewer training should include (1) procedures for contacting respondents and introducing the study, (2) instructions on asking questions so that interviewers ask all questions in a consistent and standardized way, (3) procedures for probing inadequate answers in a nondirective way, (4) procedures for recording answers to open-ended and closed-ended questions, and (5) rules for handling the interpersonal aspects of the interview in a nonbiasing way (Fowler, 1993). To be able to answer respondents' questions, interviewers should also know the purpose of the project, the sponsorship, the sampling approach used, and the steps that will be taken with respect to confidentiality.

Interviewer trainees should be provided with written manuals on interviewing procedures. They should observe interviews being conducted by trained individuals and should be supervised in conducting practice interviews. In the practice interviews, the interviewees should be individuals drawn from the same population that will be used in the research project.

USING A MAILED QUESTIONNAIRE

As we discussed earlier, it is not always practical to obtain survey data using an interview format—in these cases questionnaires are used, and quite often they are mailed to respondents. A well-constructed questionnaire is an important factor influencing response rate. We have already offered guidelines for writing the questions. In this section, we look at the overall arrangement of the questions, the cover letter, the follow-ups, and other factors that contribute to the success of a mailed questionnaire.

Directions

It is very important to begin with precise directions that tell the respondents exactly what to do. Indicate how and where they are to mark their responses; for example, "Please indicate your response to the following questions by placing an X in the box next to the answer of your choice" or "Please use a No. 2 pencil and indicate your answers by blackening in the appropriate bubbles on the separate scannable answer sheet." If the format changes within the questionnaire, include new directions for that section.

Order of Questions

Once the questions are written, they must be arranged in an appropriate order. The order of questions is important because it can influence the respondent's interest in completing the questionnaire. The very first question should be especially interesting and easy enough for all respondents to interpret and answer. If respondents are motivated to answer the first question, they are more likely to continue with the questionnaire. The first question should seek worthwhile information that is clearly related to the topic under consideration. For this reason, never begin a questionnaire with questions relating to age, gender, education, occupation, ethnic origin, marital status, and the like. The respondents may regard these questions as irrelevant or as an invasion of privacy, and may therefore decide not to continue with the questionnaire. It could end up in the nearest wastebasket. Researchers also recommend that the first few questions be of the closed-ended type, which the respondent can complete quickly, instead of open-ended ones that may require a long, written response.

Group together questions that are similar in content. For example, in a questionnaire asking university faculty about the basic academic skills of their students, all the questions on reading would be placed together. Then questions on writing would appear together, followed later by questions related to mathematics skills. Within the content areas, group items according to the type of question. For example, the questions requiring a simple yes or no would be placed together, as would items requiring respondents to rank or to indicate the extent of agreement or disagreement.

Within each of the topic areas, arrange the questions in good psychological order. A logical or psychological arrangement contributes to better-thought-out answers on the part of the respondents. For example, first ascertain whether respondents were satisfied with working conditions before asking them to recommend changes. If both general and specific questions are asked on a topic, place the general questions first. Objective items on an issue or situation should precede the more subjective questions. Questions that are less likely to be objectionable should precede items that are more objectionable. People are sometimes reluctant to answer questions about attitudes, preferences, motives, behavior, personal feelings, and the like, but if objective questions can be used first to clarify and specify the situation, it may be easier for individuals to respond. For example, a researcher who wanted to survey students on the extent of marijuana usage might begin by asking more objective questions first, such as "How would you describe marijuana usage in our school: serious problem, moderate problem, slight problem, or no problem?" This could be followed by the questions "Do you think the frequency of marijuana smoking has increased, stayed about the same, or decreased this year?" and "Do you know students who use marijuana?" Then perhaps "Do you ever smoke marijuana?" could be asked. This principle of placing less objectionable questions before more objectionable ones implies that items dealing with demographic data such as age, gender, and occupation should be placed at the end of the questionnaire rather than at the beginning. The respondent will have fewer objections to giving this personal information after completing the questionnaire and seeing why such data would be relevant.

Matrix Sampling

A procedure called **matrix sampling** (Raghunathan & Grizzle, 1995) is sometimes used when the survey is long and the accessible population is large. This technique involves randomly selecting respondents, each of whom is administered a subset of questions, randomly selected from the total set of items. The practical advantage of using matrix sampling is the decrease in the time required for each individual to respond. This is an important advantage because one obstacle to obtaining a high response rate is the unwillingness of some individuals to take the time to answer a long questionnaire. For additional information on the concept of matrix sampling, see Raghunathan and Grizzle (1995) or the classic article by Lord (1962).

Format of the Questionnaire

The questionnaire should be formatted so that it is attractive, easy for the respondent to read and answer, and convenient for the researcher to code and score. To achieve these ends, incorporate the following suggestions into the design of the survey document:

1. *Number questions consecutively* throughout the questionnaire without any repetitions or omissions. Having a unique number for each question avoids confusion in coding responses.

2. *Differentiate questions from answer categories* by using regular type for the questions and uppercase letters for the answers. Put any specific directions for responding inside parentheses and in lowercase. For example,

    Do you favor setting standards in basic skills as a requirement for high school graduation? (check your response)

    1) NO
    2) YES

3. *Use numbers to identify the various response categories.* The numbers assigned to the options represent a form of precoding that will facilitate processing the data. You can place a blank or box in front of the response options and ask the respondent to place an *X* or check mark in the space. For example,

What is the highest level of education that you have completed? (check one)

_____ 1) GRADE SCHOOL

_____ 2) SOME HIGH SCHOOL

_____ 3) COMPLETED HIGH SCHOOL

_____ 4) SOME COLLEGE

_____ 5) COMPLETED COLLEGE

_____ 6) SOME GRADUATE WORK

_____ 7) GRADUATE DEGREE

A check or X in front of item 5 indicates that the individual has completed college, and a count can easily be made for category 5. Because of the varying lengths of the options, survey designers recommend placing the numbers for the response options at the beginning, to the left of the response categories rather than at the right, for ease of scoring.

4. *Be consistent in assigning numbers to the various answer categories.* Always use the same number for the same answer throughout the questionnaire. It is conventional to assign low numbers to the negative responses and higher numbers to the positive responses. For example, 1 is assigned to "no" and 2 is assigned to "yes"; 1 is assigned to *"unfavorable"* and 2 to *"favorable."* Whatever number scheme is chosen, use it throughout because it is confusing for a respondent to associate 1 with "no" in the first part of the questionnaire and then find 1 associated with "yes" in another part.

5. *Response categories should be arranged vertically rather than horizontally.* The vertical arrangement makes the questionnaire appear less crowded and eliminates the common error of checking the space on the wrong side of the answer, as might occur for the following:

What is your present marital status?

_____ 1) NEVER MARRIED   _____ 2) MARRIED   _____ 3) DIVORCED

_____ 4) SEPARATED   _____ 5) WIDOWED   _____ 6) UNMARRIED, COHABITING

The above confusing arrangement could be improved in the following way:

What is your present marital status? (check one)

_____ 1) NEVER MARRIED

_____ 2) MARRIED

_____ 3) DIVORCED

_____ 4) SEPARATED

_____ 5) WIDOWED

_____ 6) UNMARRIED, COHABITING

6. *Use contingency questions when not every question will be relevant to all respondents.* A **contingency question** is one whose relevancy depends on the answer to a prior question. For example, in a survey designed to assess faculty interest in using computer-assisted testing, the following question might be used:

1. Are you interested in using computer-assisted testing in your classes?

    (1) YES

    (2) NO (if NO, please go to question 6)

    (3) UNDECIDED

2. If YES: Would you use the computer-assisted testing for

    (1) QUIZZES

    (2) TESTS

    (3) BOTH

In the preceding example, the second question is a contingency question because its relevance is contingent on the answer given in the first question. Faculty members who indicated in question 1 that they were not interested in computer-assisted testing would not even have to read the next four questions, but could proceed to 6, the next relevant question. Thus contingency questions save time for the respondent and provide more accurate data for the researcher. Contingency questions can be set off by arrows, indenting, or enclosed boxes.

7. *Have the questionnaire reproduced by a high-quality printing method.* Quality printing gives the questionnaire a more professional appearance and makes a more favorable impression on respondents.

8. *Keep the questionnaire as short as possible.*

Recording Answers

The previous discussion has assumed that respondents will mark their answers directly on the questionnaire form. Whenever possible, we recommend that researchers provide scannable sheets and direct the respondents to mark all responses directly on the sheets. General-purpose scannable sheets with either five options or ten options per question are available at a nominal cost. The sheets can be read by an optical scanner and the data put on a disk or sent directly to a computer for analysis. Using scannable answer sheets saves time for the researcher and reduces human error in coding responses. Figure 13.1 shows a ten-option answer sheet. The survey questions would be printed on a separate form, and the scannable sheet included for the responses. For example,

1. How many semesters of the *same* foreign language did you have in high school?
    A. NONE (0)
    B. ONE

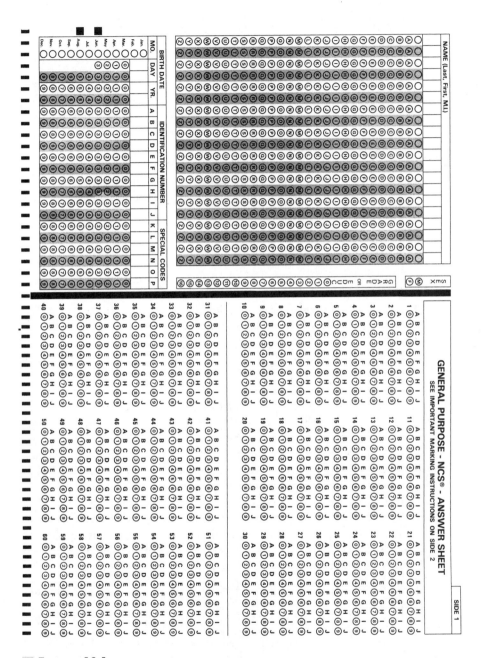

FIGURE 13.1

Example of a Scannable Sheet for Recording Responses

Source: Reproduced with permission from National Computer Systems Inc.

C. TWO
D. THREE
E. FOUR
F. FIVE
G. SIX
H. SEVEN
I. EIGHT
J. NINE

The response to the preceding question could be coded directly on the answer sheet. In some cases, it is possible to print survey questions directly on a scannable sheet. Figure 13.2 shows a sample of some survey questions used in a study of freshman students' perceptions of the adequacy of their high school preparation for college.

Field-Testing

Before the final printing, the researcher must **field-test** the instrument to identify ambiguities, misunderstandings, or other inadequacies. First it is a good idea to ask colleagues who are familiar with the study to examine a draft of the questionnaire and give their opinions on whether the instrument will obtain the desired data and whether they see any problems that may have been overlooked.

Next, administer the questionnaire personally and individually to a small group drawn from the population to be considered in the study. Respondents answer the questions one at a time and provide feedback to the researcher on any difficulties they have with the items. Pay attention to such comments as "I don't know what you mean here" and "More than one of these answers apply to me." Try to ascertain whether all respondents interpret the questions in the same way. You might even state some of the questions in different ways, to see if different responses are given to different versions of the same question. Observations made of the respondents as they fill out the questionnaire can also be enlightening. Spending an undue amount of time on a question or leaving a question blank and returning to it later can be clues that there are problems with some items.

The results of field tests can be used to clarify the items or perhaps to eliminate some. It is especially important to determine whether the questions will operate equally well in the different social classes and culture groups of the population to be studied. Some specific issues that should be addressed by field-testing include the following:

1. Do the respondents seem comfortable with the questionnaire and motivated to complete it?
2. Are certain items confusing?
3. Could some items result in hostility or embarrassment on the part of respondents?
4. Are the instructions clear?
5. How long will it take a respondent to complete the questionnaire?
6. Do all respondents interpret the items in the same way?

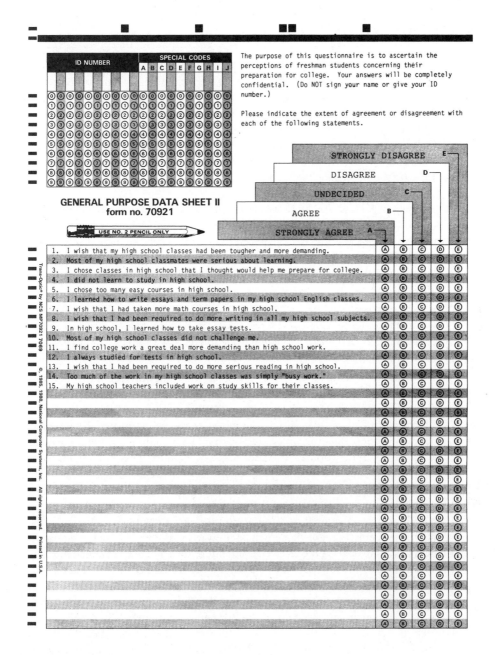

The purpose of this questionnaire is to ascertain the perceptions of freshman students concerning their preparation for college. Your answers will be completely confidential. (Do NOT sign your name or give your ID number.)

Please indicate the extent of agreement or disagreement with each of the following statements.

GENERAL PURPOSE DATA SHEET II
form no. 70921

USE NO. 2 PENCIL ONLY

STRONGLY DISAGREE   E
DISAGREE   D
UNDECIDED   C
AGREE   B
STRONGLY AGREE   A

1. I wish that my high school classes had been tougher and more demanding.
2. Most of my high school classmates were serious about learning.
3. I chose classes in high school that I thought would help me prepare for college.
4. I did not learn to study in high school.
5. I chose too many easy courses in high school.
6. I learned how to write essays and term papers in my high school English classes.
7. I wish that I had taken more math courses in high school.
8. I wish that I had been required to do more writing in all my high school subjects.
9. In high school, I learned how to take essay tests.
10. Most of my high school classes did not challenge me.
11. I find college work a great deal more demanding than high school work.
12. I always studied for tests in high school.
13. I wish that I had been required to do more serious reading in high school.
14. Too much of the work in my high school classes was simply "busy work."
15. My high school teachers included work on study skills for their classes.

■ FIGURE 13.2
Example of a Scannable Sheet with Survey Statements

Source: Reproduced with permission from National Computer Systems Inc.

Preparing the Cover Letter

Researchers may find it useful to mail an introductory letter to potential respondents in advance of the questionnaire itself. This procedure alerts the subject to the study so that he or she is not overwhelmed by the questionnaire package. In any case, a cover letter addressed to the respondent by name and title must accompany the questionnaire. One can use the "mail merge" feature of word processing packages to personalize the letter. Figure 13.3 shows a cover letter with the important parts identified. The cover letter introduces the potential respondents to the questionnaire and "sells" them on responding. The cover letter should include the following elements:

1. *The purpose of the study.* The first paragraph of the letter should explain the purpose of the study and its potential usefulness. It will be helpful to relate the importance of the study to a reference group with which the individuals may identify. For example, a cover letter with a questionnaire for graduate students should stress the importance of the data for improving graduate education at the university.

2. *A request for cooperation.* The letter should explain why the potential respondent was included in the sample and should make an appeal for the respondent's cooperation. Respondents should be made to feel they can make an important contribution to the study.

3. *The protection provided the respondent.* The letter must not only assure the respondents that their responses will be confidential but also explain how that confidentiality will be maintained. To facilitate the follow-up procedure necessary for a high return rate, use identification numbers on the questionnaires. If there is no identification, the problem of nonresponse bias is compounded because there is no way to know who has responded and who has not, and follow-up procedures become very confused. If identification numbers are used, respondents must be told that the numbers are there simply to let the researcher check the respondents' names off the mailing list when the questionnaires are returned. The respondents must be assured that their names will never be placed on the questionnaires themselves; thus there will be no way to associate particular responses with any individuals. If the researcher intends to destroy the questionnaires immediately after the responses have been rostered, this information should be conveyed in the letter, to reassure the respondents of their anonymity.

    Some researchers prefer not to use any identification system at all, especially when the topic is sensitive. In this case, it is necessary to include in the mail-out package a postcard that the respondent can mail separately to indicate that the questionnaire has also been mailed. This postcard contains a pretyped message that the questionnaire has been returned and a place for the respondent to write his or her name. In this way, a record can be kept of the returned questionnaires.

4. *Sponsorship of the study.* The signature on the letter is important in influencing the return of the questionnaire. If the study is part of a doctoral dissertation, it is

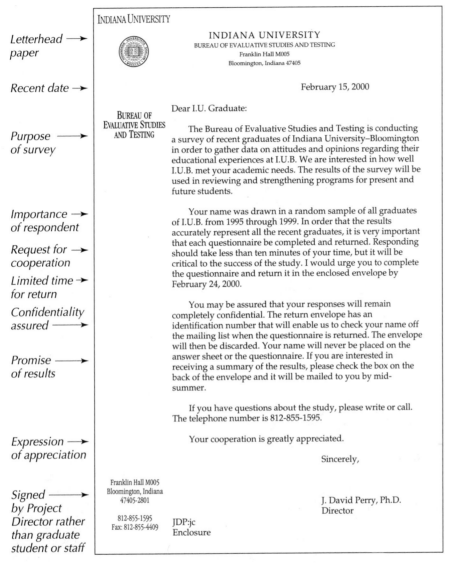

Letterhead → paper

Recent date →

Purpose → of survey

Importance → of respondent

Request for → cooperation

Limited time → for return

Confidentiality assured →

Promise → of results

Expression → of appreciation

Signed → by Project Director rather than graduate student or staff

INDIANA UNIVERSITY

INDIANA UNIVERSITY
BUREAU OF EVALUATIVE STUDIES AND TESTING
Franklin Hall M005
Bloomington, Indiana 47405

February 15, 2000

BUREAU OF
EVALUATIVE STUDIES
AND TESTING

Dear I.U. Graduate:

The Bureau of Evaluative Studies and Testing is conducting a survey of recent graduates of Indiana University–Bloomington in order to gather data on attitudes and opinions regarding their educational experiences at I.U.B. We are interested in how well I.U.B. met your academic needs. The results of the survey will be used in reviewing and strengthening programs for present and future students.

Your name was drawn in a random sample of all graduates of I.U.B. from 1995 through 1999. In order that the results accurately represent all the recent graduates, it is very important that each questionnaire be completed and returned. Responding should take less than ten minutes of your time, but it will be critical to the success of the study. I would urge you to complete the questionnaire and return it in the enclosed envelope by February 24, 2000.

You may be assured that your responses will remain completely confidential. The return envelope has an identification number that will enable us to check your name off the mailing list when the questionnaire is returned. The envelope will then be discarded. Your name will never be placed on the answer sheet or the questionnaire. If you are interested in receiving a summary of the results, please check the box on the back of the envelope and it will be mailed to you by mid-summer.

If you have questions about the study, please write or call. The telephone number is 812-855-1595.

Your cooperation is greatly appreciated.

Sincerely,

Franklin Hall M005
Bloomington, Indiana
47405-2801

812-855-1595
Fax: 812-855-4409

JDP:jc
Enclosure

J. David Perry, Ph.D.
Director

FIGURE 13.3
Example of a Cover Letter for a Survey

helpful if a person well known to the respondents, such as the head of a university department or the dean of the school, signs or countersigns the letter. Such a signature is likely to be more effective than that of an unknown graduate student. If there is a sponsor for the study, such as a foundation or some agency, mention this. Use a university or agency letterhead.

5. *Promise of results.* An offer may be made to share the findings of the study with the respondents if they are interested. Tell them how to make their request for the results. One method is to provide a place for checking on the back of the return envelope, as well as a place for the respondent's name and address.

6. *Appreciation.* Include an expression of appreciation for their assistance and cooperation with the study.

7. *Recent data on the letter.* Date the cover letter near the day of mailing. A potential respondent will not be impressed by a letter dated several weeks before receipt.

8. *Request for immediate return.* It is also important to urge immediate return of the questionnaire. If a time period such as two weeks or a month is suggested, the respondent may lay the questionnaire aside and, in spite of good intentions, forget about it. A questionnaire that fails to receive attention within a week is not likely ever to be returned.

All of the preceding elements should be included, but at the same time the cover letter should be as brief as possible. One page is the maximum recommended length. Enclose the letter in an envelope along with the questionnaire. Always include a self-addressed, stamped return envelope for the respondent's use. This is indispensable for a good return rate.

Research shows that the type of postage used on the mailing can also influence returns. Stamps increase response rate over bulk-printed postage. Evidently the stamp makes the questionnaire appear more personal and important, and less like junk mail.

Monetary Incentive

A great deal of research has shown that a token monetary incentive consistently increases response rate. A meta-analysis of the effects of monetary gratuities found that they increase response rate by about 20 percent (Hopkins & Gullickson, 1992). The gratuity offered can be a nickel, a dime, a quarter, or even a dollar. Researchers believe that the payment creates a feeling of obligation on the part of the recipient and a need to reciprocate. Monetary incentives are most effective when prepaid rather than promised, and when included with the first mailing of the questionnaire rather than with a follow-up. Zusman and Duby (1987) found that including a $1 incentive improved the response rate by 19 percent over a control group not receiving an incentive. Furthermore, a single mailing with an incentive enclosed was more effective at eliciting responses than a mailing and follow-up to an identical group not receiving the incentive. Zusman and Duby concluded that using the monetary incentive improved the overall return rate and the promptness of returns, which in turn reduced the cost of follow-ups.

Research by Singer, VanHoewyk, and Maher (1998) found that people who received a monetary incentive in the past are more likely to participate in a subsequent survey and have more favorable attitudes toward the usefulness of surveys. Of course, offering a payment is not always possible, because even a token amount can greatly increase the cost of the survey if the sample is large. It is, however, an option worth considering.

Follow-Ups

To reach the maximum percentage of returns in a mailed questionnaire survey, planned follow-up mailings are essential. Bailey (1994) presented evidence that response rate may increase by as much as 20 to 30 percent when appropriate follow-up procedures are used. Several steps are typically taken in the follow-ups and are explained here.

First Reminder

If the questionnaire has not been returned in a week or 10 days after the initial mailing, send a postcard to the respondent. This card serves as a polite reminder that a questionnaire was sent earlier and that the response is very important to the study. Urge respondents to complete and return the questionnaire immediately ("today"). Of course, express thanks to those who may have already mailed the questionnaire. An offer can be made to send another questionnaire if one is needed by people who may have misplaced or never received it. Usually the postcard reminder brings in a large number of responses.

Second Follow-Up

The follow-up, which should be sent about three weeks after the original mailing, involves a letter, another copy of the questionnaire, and an addressed return envelope. The letter should first tell the nonrespondents that their questionnaires have not been received and should reiterate the usefulness of the study. Emphasize that a replacement questionnaire is enclosed, and make a strong appeal to complete and return it. Tell the respondents not to respond a second time if they have already mailed the questionnaire.

Third Follow-Up

The third and final follow-up is sent out six to seven weeks after the initial mailing. It is similar to the second, having both a letter and a replacement questionnaire. Many researchers send this follow-up by certified mail. If a researcher has 75 to 90 percent returns after three follow-ups, he or she may be ready to terminate the survey and to declare the remaining subjects nonrespondents. The researcher must decide whether the responses obtained through further follow-up efforts would be worth the cost and time involved. Also, you do not want potential respondents to feel harassed. It is sometimes suggested that the researcher include in the third follow-up a postcard on which subjects could indicate that they do not wish to participate in the survey and will not be returning the questionnaire. Such a procedure permits definite identification of nonrespondents.

Dealing with Nonresponse

Nonresponse is a serious problem in survey research. Researchers hope that everyone surveyed will return a complete questionnaire, but this seldom happens. What does a researcher do about the nonrespondents? He or she cannot simply ignore them, if the survey is to have validity. Using information only from those who choose to respond can introduce error, because the respondents represent a self-selected group that may not represent the views of the entire sample or population.

If, after all follow-up attempts, response rate remains below about 75 percent, try to learn something about the characteristics of the nonrespondents. Research shows that respondents tend to differ from nonrespondents in characteristics such as education, intelligence, motivation, and interest in the topic of the survey. A survey with low response rate can thus be seriously biased even though the researcher started out by mailing questionnaires to a representative sample. Try to determine the extent to which respondents might differ from the nonrespondents. There are several ways to do this:

1. *Compare respondents to population.* If you have access to information on characteristics of the population—such as age, gender, education, ethnicity, socioeconomic status, and so on—you can compare the characteristics of the respondents with those of the population from which they were selected. If the respondents in general are typical of the population in important characteristics, you can assume the respondents are truly representative of the total population and thus can generalize from the respondents to the total sample. If the respondents are found to differ from the population, results must be limited to the respondents.

2. *Compare early to late respondents.* Research has shown that nonrespondents are often similar to late respondents (Goldhor, 1974). Thus, a second way to estimate the responses of nonrespondents is to look at those of the late respondents. Prior to this step, however, categorize the respondents into early and late groups and compare their responses to check for any significant differences. If no significant differences appear between early and late respondents, and late respondents are believed typical of nonrespondents, then you can assume the respondents are an unbiased sample of the recipients and can thus generalize to the total group.

3. *Compare respondents and nonrespondents.* A more systematic approach is to interview either personally or by telephone a small random sample (perhaps 10 percent) of the nonrespondents. This sample of nonrespondents drawn for comparison purposes is sometimes called a "double-dipped sample" (Miller & Smith, 1983). Using the questionnaire as an interview schedule, the investigator then gathers responses from the random sample of nonrespondents. The mean responses or the proportion of responses of the nonrespondents can be statistically compared to those of the respondents to see whether the two groups differ significantly. If no significant differences are found when the responses of the initial respondents are compared with those of the interview sample, then the researcher can reasonably assume that the respondents represent an unbiased sample of all who received the questionnaire. The data can be pooled and generalizations made to the total sample and to the population. Without such a check, you have no way of knowing if the respondents are different and therefore biased. Using a double-dipped sample is the preferred method of checking for bias, because the direction and the extent of bias that are due to nonresponse can be directly assessed. It is, however, more costly and time consuming.

Aiken (1981) shows that the extent to which the responses to survey items are representative of the responses of the total sample is a function of the sample size, proportion of returns, and proportion of respondents responding to items in a specified direction. He provides a formula for determining the minimum proportion of people who must return a survey for the researcher to feel confident that the responses represent the total sample.

If you find that certain clearly identifiable subgroups did not return the questionnaire, you may need to change the original research question to exclude these subgroups. For example, if secondary teachers showed a much lower rate of returns than did elementary teachers in a survey, a researcher might conclude that the questionnaire had little relevance or interest for secondary teachers and decide to restrict the study to elementary teachers. The research question would be restated to indicate the change.

VALIDITY

Some attention must be given to the validity of interviews and questionnaires—that is, whether they are really measuring what they are supposed to measure. The survey should have *face validity:* It should *appear* valid for its intended purpose. Subjects are more inclined to respond to questions they perceive to be relevant and meaningful than to questions whose purpose they do not comprehend. Subjects are less inclined to complete and return a questionnaire they perceive as being inappropriate. The most obvious type of scientific validity evidence is based on content, which may be gathered by having some competent colleagues who are familiar with the purpose of the survey examine the items to judge whether they are appropriate for measuring what they are supposed to measure and whether they are a representative sample of the behavior domain under investigation.

Some validity studies have looked at evidence based on the relationship of survey responses to other variables. Direct observation of behavior, for example, has been a criterion used to validate surveys. After responses were obtained, observations were made to see whether the actual behavior of the subjects agreed with their expressed attitudes, opinions, or other answers. If you find agreement between survey responses and actual behavior, you have some evidence for the validity of the survey. Other data sources, such as third parties, may also be used as criteria.

Two important variables influence the validity of a questionnaire. First, how important is the topic to the respondent? You can assume more valid responses from individuals who are interested in the topic and/or are informed about it. And second, does the questionnaire protect the respondents' anonymity? It is reasonable to assume that greater truthfulness will be obtained if the respondents can remain anonymous, especially when sensitive or personal questions are asked.

RELIABILITY

Survey data must have reliability if they are to be useful. If respondents' answers are not consistent, then the validity of the research is also questionable. One procedure for assessing reliability of questionnaires or interviews is having two different interviewers interview the same individuals to check the consistency of the results. Internal consistency may be checked by building some redundancy into the instrument—items on the same topic may be rephrased and repeated in the questionnaire or interview. The more consistent the responses, the higher the reliability.

It is also possible to repeat a questionnaire or interview with the same individuals after a period of time or to administer two different forms of the questionnaire to the same individuals. Such procedures are often expensive and time consuming, however, and somewhat impractical because it is not easy to find subjects willing to repeat the questionnaire or interview. Another problem with this approach is that some answers to questions dealing with less stable aspects of behavior may legitimately change over time.

STATISTICAL ANALYSIS IN SURVEYS

Surveys typically don't require complex statistical analyses. Data analysis may simply consist of determining the frequencies and percentages of responses for the questions of the study. For example, a survey of library resources may report the number of fiction books, the number of nonfiction books, and so on. A survey of people's attitudes on an issue may report the number and percentage of the respondents who gave each response, such as "strongly agree," "agree," "disagree," and so on. It is useful to convert numbers to percentages in order to be able to talk about the proportion responding a certain way and to be able to make comparisons. Consider the hypothetical frequency data in Table 13.2, based on a survey of 440 students concerning their opinions of a proposed increase in student activity fees at the university they attend. Looking at the raw frequencies, you might say that upperclassmen (66 juniors and seniors) and graduate students (66) are equally opposed to the increase in fees. But if you calculate *percentages* based on the total number of students *in each group,* you can see that more than twice the proportion of graduate students disapprove of the increase compared to juniors and seniors. This is because 66 of the 88 graduate students (75 percent) disapprove, compared to 66 of 192 (34 percent) juniors and seniors.

Thus, the table shows that graduate students are more likely to disapprove of the activity fee increase than undergraduates. To avoid a misinterpretation, always make sure that the total numbers for different groups are presented in tables such as this one.

Table 13.2 *Students' Attitudes toward Increase in Activity Fee*				
	APPROVE	NO OPINION	DISAPPROVE	TOTAL
Freshmen and Sophomores	60	68	32	160
Juniors and Seniors	80	46	66	192
Graduate Students	12	10	66	88
Total	152	124	164	440

Tables that show frequencies of different groups' responses are often the best way to illustrate the relationship among the variables of the survey. These tables are called crosstabulations, or **crosstabs,** because they permit comparisons across groups. The simplest crosstabs contain two variables with two categories for each variable. More complex forms are possible, however, such as 2×3, 2×4, 3×3, and so on. Crosstabulations are used most often with categorical or nominal data.

Controlling Variables in a Survey Analysis

Consider the hypothetical results of a survey of attitudes toward a new library tax for improving and expanding the county public library. Table 13.3 shows that 63 percent (150/240) of city residents favor the library tax, compared with 37 percent (96/260) of the county residents. It appears from these data that there is a relationship between place of residence and attitude toward the library tax. A chi-square test will show whether there is a statistically significant relationship between the two variables (see Chapter 7 for discussion of chi-square). Table 13.4 shows the calculation of chi-square for these data. The expected frequencies for each cell are shown in parentheses.

Referring to Table A.4 with 1 degree of freedom, you can see that the chi-square of 32.83 is highly significant (<.01). You might conclude that there is a statistically significant relationship between place of residence and attitude toward the library tax. A more cautious observer, however, might point out that the city (the location of a major state university) has a greater proportion of educated people and that it may be educational

---

Table 13.3 *Attitudes toward Library Tax by Residence*

	CITY	COUNTY	TOTAL
Favor	150	96	246
Oppose	90	164	254
Total	240	260	500

Table 13.4 *Observed and Expected Frequencies for Attitude Data*

	CITY	COUNTY	TOTAL
Favor	150 (118)	96 (128)	246
Oppose	90 (122)	164 (132)	254
Total	240	260	500

$$\chi^2 = \frac{(150 - 118)^2}{118} + \frac{(96 - 128)^2}{128} + \frac{(90 - 122)^2}{122} + \frac{(164 - 132)^2}{132}$$

$$\chi^2 = 32.83$$

Table 13.5 *Attitudes toward Library Tax Related to Education, not to Residence*

| | | COLLEGE-EDUCATED | |
	CITY	COUNTY	TOTAL
Favor	144	80	224
Oppose	36	20	56
Total	180	100	280
		NON-COLLEGE-EDUCATED	
	CITY	COUNTY	TOTAL
Favor	6	16	22
Oppose	54	144	198
Total	60	160	220

level rather than place of residence per se that accounts for the favorable attitude toward the library tax.

To explore this alternative explanation, you can control for the variable of educational level by holding it constant, and then observe whether the relationship between the first two variables continues to exist. The simplest way to hold the variable constant is to divide the subjects into separate groups, each having a different value on that variable, and to look at the crosstabs for each of these groups separately. In this case, you could categorize the 500 respondents into college-educated and non-college-educated (assuming this information is available) and look at the relationship within the two separate groups.

The data in Table 13.5 show that the alternative explanation is correct; if college education is controlled by holding it constant, there is no relationship between the variables "place of residence" and "attitude toward the tax." Among the college educated, 80 percent (144/180) of the city residents favor the tax, and so do 80 percent (80/100) of the county residents. Among the non-college-educated, 10 percent (6/60) of the city residents favor the tax, as do 10 percent (16/160) of the rural residents.

Suppose the data had been as shown in Table 13.6. Even though educational level has been held constant within each table, the relationship between the variables "residence" and "attitude" is evident. Among the college-educated, 67 percent (80/120) of the city residents favor the tax, compared with 33 percent (20/60) of the rural residents. Among the non-college-educated, 58 percent of the city residents favor the tax, compared with 38 percent of the rural residents. In this case, there *is* something about the city and county respondents, other than their education, that leads them to respond differently about the library tax.

You might also want to investigate sex differences in responses to a survey. In this case, the crosstabs would show the frequency of responses to the questions for males and females separately. Social class differences could be examined by categorizing the subjects

Table 13.6 *Attitudes toward Library Tax Related to Residence, not to Education*

	COLLEGE-EDUCATED		
	CITY	COUNTY	TOTAL
Favor	80	20	100
Oppose	40	40	80
Total	120	60	180
	NON-COLLEGE-EDUCATED		
	CITY	COUNTY	TOTAL
Favor	70	76	146
Oppose	50	124	174
Total	120	200	320

into separate groups on the basis of appropriate criteria and looking at the responses for each of the groups.

Statistics for Crosstabs

Crosstabs are a widely used way to graphically show the differences in responses among various groups, and whether or not a relationship may exist between the variables. When both variables in the crosstabulation are measured at the nominal level, the chi-square test may be used to determine whether a systematic relationship exists between the two variables. Chi-square, however, indicates *only* whether the variables are related or are independent. It does not tell the extent to which they are related. For example, the value of χ^2 for the "college-educated" versus the "non-college-educated" data in Table 13.6 is 17.09, which is statistically significant at the .01 level. Thus, you know that there is a significant relationship between place of residence and attitude toward the tax among the college educated, but you do not know how strongly the two variables are related.

To learn the extent of the relationship, you must calculate a coefficient of correlation. A coefficient that is frequently used with nominal data in 2 × 2 tables is the *phi coefficient* (Φ). The phi coefficient is a mathematical simplification of the Pearson product moment coefficient for 2 × 2 tables. Thus, phi has a value of 0 when no relationship exists, +1.00 when a perfect positive relationship exists, and −1.00 when a perfect negative relationship exists. The phi coefficient for the college-educated in Table 13.5 is .32. The phi coefficient is interpreted like any other Pearson coefficient. The .32 indicates a relatively weak positive relationship between place of residence and attitude toward the library tax among the college educated.

For tables larger than 2 × 2, an appropriate measure of relationship is the kappa statistic (κ) (Siegel & Castellan, 1988, p. 284). If there is a perfect relationship between the variables, κ will equal 1.00. If agreement between variables is exactly what would be expected through chance, κ equals 0. If agreement is less than what is expected by chance, κ will be a negative number. If the two variables in the crosstabulation are ordinal, statistics such as the Kendall coefficient of concordance (W) or the gamma statistic can be used to indicate the strength of the relationship between variables. (You can find comprehensive discussion of correlation procedures for nominal and ordinal variables in chapter 9 of Siegel and Castellan's (1988) text.

SUMMARY

The survey is a widely used research method for gathering data ranging from physical counts and frequencies to attitudes and opinions. Surveys are classified according to their focus, scope, and time of data collection. They should involve careful planning, unbiased sampling of a population, thoughtful development of data-gathering instruments, and careful analysis of the results.

If researchers use some type of probability sampling, they can infer population values from the sample results. The usual procedure is to set up an interval or range that is most likely to include the population value. The width of the interval is a function of the risk they are willing to take of being wrong and the sample size. The interval narrows as the probability of being right decreases and as sample size increases. You can also use this procedure to estimate the sample size needed for any desired margin of error.

Interviews and questionnaires are the major means of data collection for a survey. Both procedures involve asking questions of selected subjects, but each has unique advantages and disadvantages. It is important that the instruments used be valid and reliable. Various follow-up procedures have proved effective in increasing returns from mailed questionnaires.

Crosstabulations provide an excellent way to show the relationship existing among the variables in a survey.

REFERENCES

Aiken, L.R. (1981). Proportion of returns in survey research. *Educational and Psychological Measurement, 41,* 1033–1038.

Americans and their money. (1999). *Money, 28,* 143–156.

Bailey, K.D. (1994). *Methods of social research* (4th ed.). New York: The Free Press.

Cage, M.C. (1994, January 26). Beyond the B.A. *Chronicle of Higher Education, 40*(21), A29.

Chassin, L., Presson, C., Todd, M., Rose, J., & Sherman, S. (1998). Maternal socialization of adolescent smoking: the intergenerational transmission of parenting and smoking. *Developmental Psychology, 34,* 1189–1201.

Coleman, J.S., et al. (1966). *Equality of educational opportunity.* (The Coleman Report.) Washington, DC: U.S. Government Printing Office.

Coughlin, E.K. (1990, February 7). Researchers practice the science and art of public-opinion polling. *Chronicle of Higher Education, 36,* A6, A10–11.

Dillman, D.A. (2000). *Mail and internet surveys: The tailored design method* (2nd ed). New York: Wiley.

Emery, E.M., Ritter-Randolph, G.P., Strozier, A.L., & McDermott, R.J. (1993). Using focus group interviews to identify salient issues concerning college students' alcohol abuse. *Journal of American College Health, 41,* 195–198.

Fowler, F.J. (1993). *Survey research methods* (2nd ed.). Newbury Park, CA: Sage.

Fowler, F.J. (1995). *Improving survey questions: Design and evaluation.* Thousand Oaks, CA: Sage.

Goldhor, H. (1974). The use of late respondents to estimate the nature of non-respondents. Washington, DC: U.S. Office of Education. (ERIC Document ED 083 309)

Hopkins, K.D., & Gullickson, A.R. (1992). Response rate in survey research: A meta-analysis of the effects of monetary gratuities. *Journal of Experimental Education, 61,* 52–62.

Jacobs, L.C. (1985). *College freshmen view their high school preparation.* Bloomington, IN Indiana University. Indiana Studies in Higher Education, No. 53.

Krueger, R.A. (1994). *Focus groups: A practical guide.* Thousand Oaks, CA: Sage.

Lord, F.M. (1962). Estimating norms by item-sampling. *Educational and Psychological Measurement, 22,* 259–267.

Miller, L.E., & Smith, K.L. (1983). Handling nonresponse issues. *Journal of Extension, 21,* 45–50.

Mitchell, M., & Jolley, J. (1996). *Research design explained.* Fort Worth: Harcourt Brace College.

Morgan, D.L. (1997). *Focus groups as qualitative research.* Thousand Oaks, CA: Sage.

Poll: Tougher gun controls wanted. (2000, April 21). *The Herald—Times,* Bloomington, IN, p. A3.

Raghunathan, T., & Grizzle, J. (1995). A split questionnaire survey design. *Journal of the American Statistical Association, 90,* 54–63.

Schaefer, D.R., & Dillman, D.A. (1998). Development of a standard e-mail methodology: Results of an experiment. *Public Opinion Quarterly, 62*(3), 378–397.

Schuckel, Kathleen. (1999, June 28). Smoking by teens in state declines. *The Indianapolis Star,* p. A1.

Siegel, S., & Castellan, N.S. (1988). *Nonparametric statistics for the behavioral sciences* (2nd ed.). New York: McGraw-Hill.

Singer, E., VanHoewyk, J., & Maher, M. (1998). Does the payment of incentives create expectation effects? *Public Opinion Quarterly, 62,* 152–164.

Smith, T.W. (1987). That which we call welfare by any other name would smell sweeter: An analysis of the impact of question wording on response patterns. *Public Opinion Quarterly, 51,* 75–83.

Student stress is rising, especially among women. (2000, January 28). *Chronicle of Higher Education, 46,* A49–52.

Wilhoit, G.C., & Weaver, D.H. (1990). Newsroom guide to polls & surveys. Blooming-
    ton: Indiana University Press.

Zusman, B.J., & Duby, P.B. (1987). An evaluation of the use of monetary incentives in
    postsecondary survey research. *Journal of Research and Development in Education, 20*(4),
    73–78.

KEY CONCEPTS

census	interviewer bias	ranking items
checklists	Likert-type item	response rate
closed-ended question	longitudinal survey	response set
cohort study	margin of error	sample survey
contingency question	matrix sampling	sampling frame
cross-sectional survey	nonresponse	scaled items
crosstabs	open-ended question	social desirability bias
double-barreled question	panel study	trend study
field-testing	population	
interview	probe	

EXERCISES

1. Suggest a research question that can best be answered by means of a survey. Write two open-ended items, two closed-end items, and two Likert-scale items that would provide data relevant to the question.

2. What data-gathering technique would you use for each of the following surveys?
   a. A survey of a sample of high school teachers throughout the state concerning the use of mandatory competency exams for high school graduation
   b. A survey of the opinions of people in a major metropolitan area on the way juveniles who commit violent crimes are presently handled in the state's court system
   c. A survey of the opinions of a sample of professors on the campus of State University about the use of pass/fail grades instead of letter grades (You want a very high response rate.)
   d. A freshman survey of certain noncognitive characteristics that might relate to academic achievement in the first year of college
   e. A survey of 500 people from throughout the United States about their attitudes toward the administration's immigration policy

3. How does the proportion of yes/no responses influence the sample size needed?

4. The evening news on television reported the following: In a recently conducted survey of the American public, 37 percent of the respondents said they approve of the President's performance. What else would you want to know before you interpreted this report?

5. How would you interpret the following report? "A poll of 1000 randomly selected registered voters in Indiana found that 45 percent favored using state lottery profits for education. Figures from this poll are subject to a sampling

error of ± 3 percent. The confidence level is 95 percent."

6. For each of the following three sample sizes, calculate the 95% margin of error for the population proportion. Assume the sample proportion is .40 for each. What effect does an increase in sample size have on the width of the interval? Why?

    n of Sample A $= 100$

    n of Sample B $= 1000$

    n of Sample C $= 10,000$

7. A school superintendent wants to determine what proportion of the 5000 middle and high school students in the district use cigarettes. He will distribute a questionnaire to a random sample of the students. How many students will he need to sample in order to have a 95% margin of error of $\pm 5\%$ in his estimate?

8. A national polling organization wants to be able to predict the outcome of the 2004 presidential election to within ± 3 percent. How large a random sample will be needed to achieve this level of precision? Assume a 95 percent confidence level.

9. A survey had an initial response rate of 51 percent. What would you suggest to the researcher for dealing with this low response rate?

10. The administration at State University wants to estimate the incoming freshman class's interest in a computer science major. Not having the financial resources to survey all 5000 freshmen, they survey a random sample of 500. They find that 100 students report they are interested in such a major.

    a. Calculate the margin of error in this survey.

    b. What is the best estimate of the number of freshmen who would be interested in majoring in computer science?

11. Which of the following would be biased samples of the population of college students at a large university?

    a. A random sample of students entering the library on Friday evening

    b. A random sample of students registered for classes

    c. A random sample of students buying season tickets for basketball

    d. A sample composed of students who volunteered for a project after seeing a notice in the school newspaper

12. Assume you are conducting a survey to determine how elementary school teachers in a district feel about the policy of retaining students.

    a. Write two closed-ended questions for this survey.

    b. Write two open-ended questions for this survey.

    c. Write a contingency question.

13. On the basis of the time of data collection, classify each of the following surveys:

    a. Terman's study of adults who were intellectually gifted as children

    b. A comparison of math achievement in public middle schools in the United States in 1990, 1995, and 2000

    c. A follow-up of the 1995 graduates of the Indiana University School of Business

    d. A survey of reading achievement at different grade levels in a school system in 2000

14. Which of the following is an advantage of the longitudinal type of survey?

    a. More intensive individual study

    b. Providing data for different age groups at the same time

    c. Prompt data gathering

    d. No sampling errors

15. A popular weekly news magazine included a detailed questionnaire on attitudes about crime. The editors invited readers to fill out the questionnaire and return it to the magazine. The magazine subsequently printed an article on the widespread fear of crime among U.S. citizens, especially older people. How would you evaluate this survey?

16. A graduate student is planning to use a survey to gather data for her dissertation, but is

unsure whether to use mailed questionnaires or telephone interviews. Examine the following list of considerations and indicate whether a questionnaire or an interview would be more appropriate.

a. She is on a tight financial budget for her data collection.

b. Her goal is a 90 percent response rate from the sample.

c. Some of the questions may involve sensitive issues.

d. She hopes to minimize the time needed for coding and organizing data and getting it ready for computer analysis.

ANSWERS

1. Answers will vary.
   Example: How do adults in a community feel about the building of a new elementary school?

2. a. Mailed questionnaire
   b. Telephone interview
   c. Personal interview
   d. Directly administered questionnaire
   e. Telephone interview

3. The nearer the proportions are to .50–.50, the larger the sample size needed.

4. One would want to know the size of the sample, how it was drawn, the width of the interval around the estimated population parameter (the margin of error), and the confidence level.

5. The .95 confidence interval for the proportion of registered voters who favor using lottery funds for education is between 42 and 48 percent.

6. **Sample A**

$$\sigma_p = \frac{\sqrt{(.40)(.60)}}{\sqrt{100}} = \frac{\sqrt{.24}}{\sqrt{100}} = \frac{.4899}{10} = .04899$$

.04899 × 1.96 = .0960 or .10 margin of error

Sample B

$$\sigma_p = \frac{\sqrt{(.40)(.60)}}{\sqrt{1000}} = \frac{\sqrt{.24}}{\sqrt{1000}} = \frac{.4899}{31.62} = .0155$$

.0155 × 1.96 = .03 margin of error

Sample C

$$\sigma_p = \frac{\sqrt{(.40)(.60)}}{\sqrt{10,000}} = \frac{\sqrt{.24}}{\sqrt{10,000}} = \frac{.4899}{100} = .004899$$

.0049 × 1.96 = .01 margin of error

An increase in sample size decreases the width of the interval. As n increases, the sample error decreases and hence the size of the interval.

7. Use formula 13.2. Assume $p = q = .50$

$$n = \left(\frac{1}{\frac{E}{\sqrt{pq}}}\right)^2 (1.96)^2 = \left(\frac{1}{\frac{.05}{\sqrt{(.5)(.5)}}}\right)^2 (1.96)^2$$

$$= \left(\frac{1}{.10}\right)^2 (1.96)^2 = 100(3.8416) = 384$$

8. Assume $p = q = .50$

$$n = \left(\frac{1}{\frac{E}{\sqrt{pq}}}\right)^2 (1.96)^2 = \left(\frac{1}{\frac{.03}{\sqrt{(.5)(.5)}}}\right)^2 (1.96)^2$$

$$= \left(\frac{1}{.06}\right)^2 (1.96)^2 = (277.78)(3.8416) = 1067$$

9. The researcher should follow up with a post-card reminder and then another mailing or two of the questionnaire. After follow-up efforts have been completed, the researcher should try to interview some of the remaining nonrespondents to find out about their characteristics and to obtain their responses, to determine if they differ significantly from the respondents.

10. a. $p = .20$
    $q = .80$　　$\sigma_p = \frac{\sqrt{pq}}{\sqrt{n}}$

$$\sigma_p = \frac{\sqrt{(.20)(.80)}}{\sqrt{500}}$$

$$= \frac{.4}{22.36} = .0178$$

margin of error $= 1.96 \times .0178 = .03$ or $\pm 3\%$

    b. between 17–23% or between 850 and 1150 students would be interested in a computer science major

11. Samples a, c, and d would not be representative of the population of college students at a large university.

12. Answers will vary.

13. a. Longitudinal panel study
    b. Longitudinal trend study
    c. Longitudinal cohort study
    d. Cross-sectional survey

14. a.

15. Those who completed and returned the questionnaire would not be a representative sample of all U.S. citizens. A number of factors would bias this sample, such as socioeconomic level, educational level, sufficient interest in the topic to complete the questionnaire, and payment of postage to return it.

16. a. Mailed questionnaire
    b. Telephone interview
    c. Mailed questionnaire
    d. Telephone interview

 ## INFOTRAC COLLEGE EDITION

Using the key word *mailed questionnaire,* locate a survey that used this methodology for data collection. Why do you think the researcher(s) chose a mailed questionnaire rather than a personal interview? What return rate was reported? If the return rate is acceptable, identify some aspects of the survey that may have contributed to a good return. Can you think of any other techniques, such as a monetary incentive, that the researcher might have used to increase the return rate?

Chapter 14

Qualitative Research

After studying this chapter, the student will be able to:

1 Define *qualitative research,* and identify the critical aspects of this methodology.

2 Distinguish between quantitative and qualitative research.

3 Describe ways qualitative inquirers gather data.

4 List some of the different types of qualitative research.

5 Describe the major approaches to determining validity in qualitative studies.

6 Describe the major strategies for enhancing reliability in qualitative studies.

7 Distinguish between participant and nonparticipant observation.

8 Identify some ethical issues associated with qualitative research.

9 Define *content* or *documentary analysis,* and give an example of its use in educational research.

10 Define *ethnography,* and give an example of an ethnographic study in education.

11 Define *field notes,* and explain their importance in qualitative research.

12 Define *grounded theory,* and describe its role in qualitative research.

13 Explain phenomenological research and how it can be used in educational research.

14 Distinguish between primary and secondary sources in historical research.

The research methods described in Chapters 10 through 13 use numeric data to answer questions. Such procedures are classified as quantitative research because they employ such quantitative measures as frequencies, means, correlations, and *statistical* tests. In contrast, qualitative research employs words to answer questions. There has been a tremendous growth in qualitative research in recent years. More qualitative research studies appear in the literature, and the number of sessions devoted to qualitative research at meetings of educational research associations has greatly increased.

QUALITATIVE INQUIRY

The phrase **qualitative inquiry** is a generic term for a variety of educational research approaches variously labeled as ethnography, naturalistic inquiry, case studies, fieldwork, field studies, and participant observation. These approaches use different methodologies, but certain features are typical of all kinds of qualitative research. These characteristics set qualitative research apart from the quantitative approach to educational research outlined in Chapters 2, 3, and 5 and the methodology described in Chapters 10 through 13. The reader who is interested in conducting a qualitative research study is advised to consult textbooks on qualitative methodology, such as Bogdan and Biklen (1998), Marshall and Rossman (1995), and Lancy (1993).

Distinguishing Qualitative Inquiry from Quantitative Inquiry

Qualitative inquiry differs from the quantitative approach to the study of social and behavioral phenomena in rejecting the argument that the aim and methods of the social

sciences are, at least in principle, the same as the aim and methods of the natural or physical sciences.★ **Quantitative research** is based on the argument that both the natural
and social sciences strive for testable and confirmable theories that explain phenomena
by showing how they are derived from theoretical assumptions (see the discussion of scientific theory in Chapter 1). In other words, both aim at a type of scientific explanation
that includes the discovery of and appeal to laws—laws governing the behavior of the
physical world, on the one hand, and laws governing human behavior, on the other.

Qualitative inquiry begins from a different methodological assumption—namely, that
the subject matter of the social or human sciences differs fundamentally from the subject
matter of the physical or natural sciences and therefore requires a different goal for inquiry and a different set of methods for investigation. Qualitative inquirers argue that
human behavior is always bound to the context in which it occurs, that social reality (for
example, cultures, cultural objects, institutions, and the like) cannot be reduced to variables in the same manner as physical reality, and that what is most important in the social
disciplines is understanding and portraying the meaning that is constructed by the participants involved in particular social settings or events.

Qualitative inquiry seeks to understand human and social behavior from the "insider's" perspective—that is, as it is lived by participants in a particular social setting (for
example, a culture, school, community, group, or institution). It is an intensely personal
kind of research, one that freely acknowledges and admits "the subjective perception and
biases of both participants and researcher into the research frame" (Goetz & LeCompte,
1993). Defenders of qualitative approaches argue that, in contrast, quantitative inquiry is
principally concerned with the discovery of "social facts" devoid of subjective perceptions of intentions and divorced from particular social and historical contexts.

Quantitative approaches in the human sciences rely on a **hypothetico–deductive
model** of explanation. Inquiry begins with a theory of the phenomenon to be investigated. From that theory any number of hypotheses are deduced that, in turn, are subjected to a test using a predetermined procedure such as an experimental, ex post facto,
or correlational design. The ultimate goal of researchers using this hypothetico–deductive
model is to revise and support theories or lawlike statements of social and behavioral
phenomena based on the results of hypothesis testing. Theories are refined and extended
(and sometimes abandoned) to account for the results of testing their implications or instances (deductions).

Qualitative inquiry relies on a different model of explanation and argues for a different
goal of inquiry. In general, its practitioners hold that the search for generalizations (lawlike statements or theories that are invariant over time and place) is misguided. Human
behavior is always bound to a particular historical, social, temporal, and cultural context;
therefore, such researchers reject the "law and its instances" kind of explanation sought

---

★The view that the social sciences should have the same goal and methods of investigation as the natural
sciences is called *naturalism* or the "naturalistic interpretation of the social sciences." Confusion often arises
because there is a type of qualitative inquiry called *naturalistic inquiry.* In this case, the term *naturalistic* has a
different meaning; it refers to the fact that qualitative studies are conducted in a "natural" (as opposed to an
artificially constructed) setting.

in a hypothetico-deductive approach, in favor of a "cases and their interpretations" kind of explanation (Geertz, 1980). Qualitative inquirers seek to interpret human actions, institutions, events, customs, and the like, and in so doing construct a "reading," or portrayal, of what is being studied. The ultimate goal of this kind of inquiry is to portray the complex pattern of what is being studied in sufficient depth and detail so that someone who has not experienced it can understand it. When qualitative inquirers interpret or explain the meaning of events, actions, and so forth, they generally use one of the following types of interpretation: (1) construction of patterns through analysis and resynthesis of constituent parts, (2) interpretation of the social meaning of events, or (3) analysis of relationships between events and external factors (McCutcheon, 1981).

Qualitative and quantitative approaches also differ in their respective views on the role of values in inquiry. Quantitative inquirers admit that the inquirer's values may play a role in deciding what topic or problem to investigate, but that the actual investigation itself must be value free—that is, the inquirer must follow procedures specifically designed to isolate and remove all subjective elements, such as values, from the inquiry situation, so that what remains are just the "objective facts." For example, imagine an experimental study involving two different classes of third-graders in which one third-grade class is the experimental group and the other is the control group. Imagine further that observers are placed in each classroom to record interactions between teachers and students. Quantitative inquirers prefer that the observers be unaware of whether they are observing the experimental or the control group, that they be unaware of subject characteristics (their social class, IQ, previous academic achievement, and so on), and that they use highly structured observational protocols that require only low-level inferences and little, if any, interpretation about what is happening in the interactions between teacher and students. These procedures are used in quantitative inquiry to ensure that the observers' values and beliefs will not influence or contaminate the observations that they make. By following these procedures for making observations, the quantitative inquirer provides strong assurance (some might say a guarantee) that the inquiry is value free.

In contrast, the qualitative approach argues that inquiry is always value bound—it can never be considered value free—and that inquirers must be explicit about the roles that values play in any given study. Qualitative inquirers argue that inquiry is value bound in the choice of a problem to investigate, in the choice of whether to adopt a quantitative or qualitative approach to a problem, in the choice of methods used to investigate that problem, in the choice of a way to interpret results or findings, and by the values inherent in the context where the study takes place (Lincoln & Guba, 1985). Qualitative inquirers believe that it is impossible to develop a meaningful understanding of human experience without taking into account the interplay of both the inquirers' and participants' values and beliefs. Furthermore, qualitative inquirers argue that human inquiry requires frequent, continuing, and meaningful interaction between inquirers and their respondents (subjects) and that inquiry must maximize rather than minimize this kind of contact (Lincoln & Guba, 1985, p. 107). Because qualitative inquiry openly acknowledges the role of values in inquiry and demands involvement and interaction of inquirers and respondents, it is often claimed that the findings (results) of such studies are simply a matter of opinion. To counter that charge, qualitative inquirers employ a variety of techniques to demonstrate the trustworthiness of their findings. (These techniques are discussed in greater detail later in this chapter.)

MAJOR CHARACTERISTICS OF QUALITATIVE RESEARCH

Although qualitative inquirers work in many different ways, their studies have certain characteristics in common that set this approach apart from quantitative research. Some of the more important aspects of qualitative research are as follows.

Concern for Context

Qualitative inquiry shows **concern for context**—it assumes that human behavior is context-bound, that human experience takes its meaning from, and therefore is inseparable from, social, historical, political, and cultural influences. Thus inquiry is always bounded by a particular context, or setting. Proponents of qualitative inquiry argue that the quantitative approach to the study of human experience seeks to isolate human behavior from its context; it engages in "context stripping" (Mischler, 1979).

Natural Setting

Qualitative research studies real-world behavior as it occurs naturally in a classroom, an entire school, a playground, or in an organization. Qualitative inquiry takes place in the "field," in **natural settings** as they are found. It is not contrived or artificial, and there is no attempt to manipulate behavior. In addition, qualitative inquiry places no prior constraints on what is to be studied. For example, it does not identify, define, and investigate or test the relationship between independent and dependent variables in a particular setting; rather, it studies human experience holistically, taking into account all factors and influences in a given situation.

Human Instrument

One of the major characteristics that distinguishes qualitative research is the method used to collect and analyze data. In qualitative studies, the human investigator is the primary instrument for the gathering and analyzing of data. Lincoln and Guba (1985) introduced the concept of **human—as—instrument** to emphasize the unique role that qualitative researchers play in their inquiry. Because qualitative research studies human experiences and situations, researchers need an instrument flexible enough to capture the complexity of the human experience. Lincoln and Guba believed that only a human instrument was capable of this task. He or she talks with people in the setting, observes their activities, reads their documents and written records, and records this information in field notes and journals. Qualitative inquiry relies on fieldwork methods—interviewing, nonstructured observation, and document analysis—as the principal means of collecting data, avoiding the use of paper-and-pencil tests, mechanical instruments, and highly structured observational protocols.

Descriptive Data

The qualitative inquirer deals with data that are in the form of words, rather than numbers and statistics. The data collected are the subjects' experiences and perspectives; the qualitative researcher attempts to arrive at a rich description of the people, objects, events, places, conversations, and so on. From time to time some numeric data may be collected. Managing the large volume of descriptive data generated from interviews, observations, and the collection of documents is an important consideration in qualitative studies. Qualitative investigators also typically keep a personal or reflexive log or journal in which they record accounts of their thoughts, feelings, assumptions, motives, and rationale for decisions made. This is one way the qualitative inquirer addresses the issue of the inquiry being value bound.

Emergent Design

In quantitative studies, researchers carefully design all aspects of a study *before* they actually collect any data; they specify variables, measures for those variables, statistics to be used to analyze data, and so forth. This is possible because these researchers know in advance what they are looking for. They have specific hypotheses or questions in mind and can imagine what a test of the hypothesis or an answer to the question might look like. Regardless of the particular problem or phenomena being investigated, quantitative researchers insist that this careful specification of elements in a study's design is extremely important. In contrast, qualitative inquirers rarely, if ever, fully specify all aspects of a design before beginning a study; rather, the design *emerges* as the study unfolds—hence the name **emergent design.** They adjust their methods and way of proceeding (design) to the subject matter at hand. This is necessary because the qualitative inquirer is never quite sure just what will be learned in a particular setting (the investigator has not decided in advance what he or she is looking for), because what can be learned in a particular setting depends on the nature and types of interactions between the inquirer and the people and setting, and those interactions are not fully predictable, and because important features in need of investigation cannot always be known until they are actually witnessed by the investigator. Thus qualitative inquiry can only be characterized beforehand in a very general way that indicates how a study might unfold.

Inductive Analysis

In most qualitative studies, data collection and data analysis take place simultaneously. In other words, the inquirer does not wait until all the data are "in" before beginning to interpret them. From the outset of the first interview or observation, the qualitative inquirer is reflecting on the meaning of what he or she has heard and seen, developing hunches (working hypotheses) about what it means and seeking to confirm or disconfirm those hunches in subsequent interviews or observations. It is a process of **inductive data analysis**—it proceeds from data to hypotheses to theory. As the inquirer reduces and reconstructs the data through the processes of coding and categorization, he or she aims at the development of theory about the phenomena being observed that is directly tied to—*grounded*—in the data about those phenomena (Strauss & Corbin, 1998).

Janesick (1994, p. 212) summarizes the characteristics of qualitative research design as follows:

1. Qualitative design is holistic. It looks at the larger picture, the whole picture, and begins with a search for understanding of the whole.
2. Qualitative design looks at relationships within a system or culture.
3. Qualitative design refers to the personal, face-to-face, and immediate.
4. Qualitative design is focused on understanding a given social setting, not necessarily on making predictions about that setting.
5. Qualitative design demands that the researcher stay in the setting over time.
6. Qualitative design demands time in analysis equal to the time in the field.
7. Qualitative design demands that the researcher develop a model of what occurred in the social setting.
8. Qualitative design requires the researcher to become the research instrument. This means the researcher must have the ability to observe behavior and must sharpen the skills necessary for observation and face-to-face interview.
9. Qualitative design incorporates informed consent decisions and is responsive to ethical concerns.
10. Qualitative design incorporates room for description of the role of the researcher as well as description of the researcher's own biases and ideological preference.
11. Qualitative design requires ongoing analyses of the data.

DESIGNING QUALITATIVE RESEARCH

The research design is the researcher's plan of how to proceed to gain an understanding of some group or some phenomenon in its natural setting. The design begins with a general statement of a research problem or topic. Lincoln and Guba (1985) refer to this initial topic that a qualitative researcher chooses for investigation as the *focus of inquiry*. To develop the focus of inquiry, the beginning researcher needs to think about some topic in which he or she has an interest and wants to know more about. The research question may be one that comes from the investigator's observations and experiences with particular topics, settings, or groups. Qualitative problems look at the context of events, natural setting, subjects' perspectives, unfolding and uncontrolled events, reasons for the events, and phenomena needing exploration and explanation. For example, qualitative researchers may ask, How do social workers cope with the stress of their jobs? How do teachers in rural schools react to distance-learning technologies? How do chronically ill children deal with pain? What is the relationship of rural schools to their communities? What is the mentoring relationship like for a beginning teacher? What is the first-year college experience like for students who have been homeschooled?

Choosing a Problem

The following are some practical suggestions for choosing a problem (Bogdan & Biklen, 1998). Choose a problem that (1) is not only interesting to you, but also is one for which your skills are adequate; (2) is significant because it will contribute to the body of knowledge or to solving some educational problems; (3) is reasonable in size and complexity so that you can complete a study of it within the time and with the resources to which you will have access (Bogdan and Biklen [1998] remind the beginning qualitative researcher that it is best to "think small" [p. 51]); (4) is one in which you are not directly involved. A researcher should not choose his or her own school, for example, because it is difficult to remain neutral and to assume the role of researcher with friends.

A review of the relevant literature at this step will help familiarize the researcher with theory in the area and with previous research designs and findings related to the problem. It will be most useful if you find related research that is *qualitative*. Although quantitative studies may provide background information on the topic, beginning qualitative researchers especially need to see how the qualitative paradigm has been used in research on relevant topics.

The choice of the research question is crucial because the question determines the design. Yin (1991) gives three standards that researchers can use to help them decide if qualitative methods are appropriate for their particular research question: (1) the phenomenon under investigation is contemporary; (2) the boundaries and context of the study are not distinct; (3) the researcher has little control over the phenomenon being studied. Using these criteria, you would determine that a problem such as violence in schools, for example, could be appropriately investigated with qualitative methodology.

After deciding that qualitative methodology is indeed appropriate, you next make decisions about the particular qualitative approach, the main data collection tools, setting for the study, the participants, size of sample, and the behaviors to study. A qualitative design, however, is flexible and may be changed as the researcher gets into the setting. Marshall and Rossman (1989) list three criteria for evaluating the qualitative design to be used to answer the research question: The first criterion is *informational adequacy*. That is, does the research plan maximize the possibilities that the researcher will understand the setting thoroughly, precisely, and accurately? Will the research strategy elicit the desired information? The second criterion is *efficiency*. Does the plan allow adequate data to be collected at the least cost in terms of time, access, and cost to participants? The third criterion to use is *ethical considerations*. Will the proposed method violate the participants' privacy or put them at risk? Will the procedure violate their human rights in any way? We will have more to say about ethics in a later section.

Choosing and Becoming Part of a Site

Guided by the research question, the qualitative investigator next selects a site for the study. Seek to gain access to a particular site or group of people in which you can study the topic, and then negotiate entry by adopting a role as either a full participant observer, just an observer, or some combination of the two. Some sites are very specific to the research question. For example, if you want to investigate college majors in gender studies and how they have developed, you must find universities that offer majors in gender studies.

Once the site is selected, the researcher has to get permission to conduct the study in that setting. It may take a long time from the first contacts with a site until final approval is given. Most school systems, for instance, have specific procedures they follow before giving approval to researchers. Bogdan and Biklen (1998) list some questions that the researcher should be prepared to answer: (1) What are you actually going to do? (2) Why us? (3) Will you be disruptive? (4) What are you going to do with the findings? (5) What will we get out of this? Negotiating entry, adopting a role, and developing and maintaining trust with the participants in a study are fairly complex topics, about which much has been written.

Following an initial period of becoming oriented to the site, learning about its members, and so forth, the investigator begins to focus the inquiry on salient aspects or issues by forming tentative (working) hypotheses or questions. These initial hypotheses or questions are subsequently refined (narrowed) as the data accumulate. Typically, during this stage the inquirer will continue to conduct literature reviews on the topic to deepen his or her understanding of the phenomena being investigated. Hypotheses are eventually confirmed and tested through a variety of procedures. The final stage is exiting from the site.

Sampling

Sampling is important in qualitative research just as it is in quantitative research. Qualitative researchers cannot observe everything about the group or site that might be relevant to the research problem, but they try to obtain a sample of observations believed to be *representative* of everything they could observe. Although the sample may be representative, it is not a random sample.

Qualitative researchers select *purposive* samples believed to be sufficient to provide maximum insight and understanding of what they are studying. They use their experience and knowledge to select a sample of participants that they believe can provide the relevant information about the topic or setting. Guba and Lincoln (1981, p. 276) write, "Sampling is almost never representative or random but purposive, intended to exploit competing views and fresh perspectives as fully as possible."

The qualitative researcher should first decide what in the situation is essential to a study of the problem. Let's say a qualitative study focuses on discipline in a school system. In this case, the researcher decides what personnel to interview (principals, assistant principals, teachers, coaches, students) and what settings (classroom, playground, cafeteria) to observe. The researcher must develop a plan to sample personnel and settings that in his or her judgment will provide an accurate picture of attitudes and disciplinary techniques employed in the school system.

Purposive Sampling

Several variations on purposive sampling are used in qualitative research:

1. **Comprehensive sampling.** In comprehensive sampling, every unit is included in the sample. For example, a study of physically disabled students in a high school would include all such students in the school. Comprehensive sampling is used when the number of units is small.

2. **Maximum variation sampling.** In maximum variation sampling, units are included that maximize differences on specified characteristics. For example, a study of American high school students might include students from schools that differ in location, characteristics of the students, parental involvement, and other factors. This type of sampling reveals differences, but may also identify commonalities across the units.

3. **Extreme case sampling.** Extreme case sampling selects units that are special or unusual. For example, you might choose to study an inner-city elementary school that has achieved exemplary reading and other achievement test scores. Such a study might identify practices, teaching methods, and student characteristics that may be relevant to their superior performance.

4. **Typical case sampling.** Typical case sampling selects units that are considered typical of the phenomenon to be studied. In a study of an elementary school, you would select a school considered typical rather than a very high-achieving school or a very low-achieving school.

5. **Homogeneous sampling.** Homogeneous sampling selects a subgroup that is considered homogeneous in attitudes, experiences, and so on. For example, you might choose only a sample of special education teachers from a population of teachers.

6. **Snowball or chain sampling.** Snowball or chain sampling occurs when the initially selected subjects suggest the names of others who would be appropriate for the sample. The latter might suggest others and so on. Such sampling occurs when potential respondents are not centrally located but scattered in different sites.

Size of Sample

Because of the depth and extent of the information sought in qualitative studies, purposive samples are typically small. How large should the sample be? There is no general rule about the number of participants to include in a qualitative study. Of course, practical considerations such as time, money, and availability of participants influence the size of the sample. But Lincoln and Guba (1985) state that the primary criterion of sample size is redundancy of information. Sampling should be terminated when no new information is forthcoming from new units (p. 202). This point is referred to as *data saturation*.

DATA COLLECTION METHODS

The next step is to choose the data collection method(s) that will be used. The most common data collection methods used in qualitative research are (1) observation (participant and nonparticipant) (2) interviewing, and (3) document analysis. The researcher may use one or more of these methods in a study.

Observation

Observation is the most basic method for obtaining data in qualitative research. It is a more global type of observation than the systematic observation used in quantitative research. The qualitative researcher's goal is a complete description of behavior in a specific natural setting rather than a numeric summary of occurrence or duration of observed behaviors. Qualitative observation usually takes place over an extended period of time and proceeds without any prior hypotheses.

The qualitative researcher may be a participant in the situation being observed or a nonparticipant. In **participant observation,** the observer actively participates and becomes an insider in the event being observed so that he or she experiences events in the same way as the participants. Anthropologists are participant observers when they conduct a study on a particular culture. The researcher's role as observer/researcher may or may not be known to the people being observed. Sociological researchers have pretended to join street gangs or pretended to be homeless in order to learn about such groups' feelings, relationships, and problems. In most educational research, however, it is difficult for the investigator to pretend to be a member of a group and play the same role as the subjects who are being studied. It might be possible for a young researcher to pretend to be a college freshman in order to gather data on the freshman experience, but could not become a participating member of a junior high school club. Wolcott (1992) writes that "most so-called participant observer studies in education warrant that label only in the sense that the researcher was physically present," because "researchers seldom become involved as genuine participants" (p. 20).

In other cases, researchers may interact with subjects enough to establish rapport but do not really become involved in the behaviors and activities of the group. Their status as observer/researcher is known to those under study. In this case, they are called *participant observers.* For example, a researcher could focus on studying a vocational training class for welfare recipients or an organization such as Alcoholics Anonymous. At the other extreme, the researcher observes without participating or taking any active part in the situation (**nonparticipant observation**).

The degree of participation is thus a continuum ranging from a complete participant at one end to a complete observer at the other. The observer must decide what degree of participation will provide the most appropriate data. It is easier to ask questions and record observations if members of the group know your purpose; furthermore, it may be more ethical to make people aware of what is going on. Being open, however, may present problems. Knowing they are being observed, group members may behave differently from the way they usually do, or they may not be truthful when answering questions. This impact of the observer on the participants being studied is called **observer effect** and can result in an inaccurate picture of the group and its interactions. There is a risk that the observer will destroy the very naturalness of the setting that he or she wants.

Another problem with observation as a data-gathering tool is the possible effect that the observer him- or herself might have on the results. **Observer bias** occurs when the observer's personal attitudes and values affect the observation and/or the interpretation of the observation. In participant observation, there may also be a problem of the observer's getting emotionally involved in the group and hence losing objectivity. The nonparticipant observer can be more objective and emotionally detached from the group. A major question with observation is the extent to which the observations of another researcher might be different.

Field Notes

The most common method of recording the data collected during observation is *field notes*. The researcher may make brief notes during the observation but then later expands his or her account of the observation as field notes. They contain what the researcher has seen and heard. Field notes have two components: (1) the *descriptive* part, which includes a complete description of the setting, the people and their reactions and interpersonal relationships, and accounts of events (who, when, what was done); and (2) the *reflective* part, which includes the observer's personal feelings or impressions about the events, comments on the research method, decisions and problems, records of ethical issues, and speculations about data analysis. Field notes may also include photographs and audio and video recordings.

The researcher's reflections are identified as *observer comments* ("OC") to distinguish them from the descriptive information. Exhibit 14.1 shows an excerpt from field notes collected as part of a study of students with disabilities in an urban high school.

The researcher's field notes present the data that will later be analyzed to provide an understanding of the research setting and the behavior of people within that setting. It can be said that the successful outcome of the study relies on detailed, accurate, and extensive field notes. Record everything you see, hear, or experience during the observation session. Observation sessions typically should last not more than one to two hours at a time; otherwise, so many data accumulate that it is difficult to record them all. Make the field notes as soon as possible following the observation, while the experience is still fresh in your mind. You may also use audio and video tapes to facilitate data collection. See Bogdan and Biklen's 1998 book for guidelines to writing field notes.

Date: March 24, 1980

Joe McCloud

11:00 a.m. to 12:30 p.m.

Westwood High

6th Set of Notes

THE FOURTH-PERIOD CLASS IN MARGE'S ROOM

I arrived at Westwood High at five minutes to eleven, the time Marge told me her fourth period started. I was dressed as usual: sport shirt, chino pants, and a Woolrich parka. The fourth period is the only time during the day when all the students who are in the "neurologically impaired/learning disability" program, better known as "Marge's program," come together. During the other periods, certain students in the program, two or three or four at most, come to her room for help with the work they are getting in other regular high school classes.

It was a warm, fortyish, promise of a spring day. There was a police patrol wagon, the kind that has benches in the back that are used for large busts, parked in the back of the big parking lot that is in front of the school. No one was sitting in it and I never heard its reason for being there. In the circular drive in front of the school was parked a United States Army car. It had insignias on the side and was a khaki color. As I walked from my car, a balding fortyish man in an Army uniform came out of the building and went to the car and sat down. Four boys and a girl also walked out of the school. All were white. They had on old dungarees and colored stenciled t-shirts with spring jackets over them. One of the boys, the tallest of the four, called out, "oink, oink, oink." This was done as he sighted the police vehicle in the back.

> O.C.: This was strange to me in that I didn't think that the kids were into "the police as pigs." Somehow I associated that with another time, the early 1970s. I'm going to have to come to grips with the assumptions I have about high school due to my own experience. Sometimes I feel like Westwood is entirely different from my high school and yet this police car incident reminded me of mine.

Classes were changing when I walked down the halls. As usual there was the boy with girl standing here and there by the lockers. There were three couples that I saw. There was the occasional shout. There were no teachers outside the doors.

> O.C.: The halls generally seem to be relatively unsupervised during class changes.

Two African American girls I remember walking down the hall together. They were tall and thin and had their hair elaborately braided with beads all through them. I stopped

▨ EXHIBIT 14.1
Example of Field Notes

Source: From *Qualitative Research for Education* (3rd ed., pp. 109–111), by R.C. Bogdan & S.K. Biklen, Boston: Allyn and Bacon.

by the office to tell Mr. Talbot's (the principal) secretary that I was in the building. She gave me a warm smile.

> O.C.: I feel quite comfortable in the school now. Somehow I feel like I belong. As I walk down the halls some teachers say hello. I have been going out of my way to say hello to kids that I pass. Twice I've been in a stare-down with kids passing in the hall. Saying, "How ya' doin'?" seems to disarm them.

I walked into Marge's class and she was standing in front of the room with more people than I had ever seen in the room save for her homeroom which is right after second period. She looked like she was talking to the class or was just about to start. She was dressed as she had been on my other visits-clean, neat, well-dressed but casual. Today she had on a striped blazer, a white blouse and dark slacks. She looked up at me smiled and said: "Oh, I have a lot more people here now than the last time."

> O.C.: This was in reference to my other visits during other periods when there are only a few students. She seems self-conscious about having such a small group of students to be responsible for. Perhaps she compares herself with the regular teachers who have classes of thirty or so.

There were two women in their late twenties sitting in the room. There was only one chair left. Marge said to me something like: "We have two visitors from the central office today. One is a vocational counselor and the other is a physical therapist," but I don't remember if those were the words. I felt embarrassed coming in late. I sat down in the only chair available next to one of the women from the central office. They had on skirts and carried their pocketbooks, much more dressed up than the teachers I've seen. They sat there and observed.

Alfred (Mr. Armstrong, the teacher's aide) walked around but when he stood in one place it was over by Phil and Jeff. Marge walked about near her desk during her talk which she started by saying to the class: "Now remember, tomorrow is a fieldtrip to the Rollway Company. We all meet in the usual place, by the bus, in front of the main entrance at 8:30. Mrs. Sharp wanted me to tell you that the tour of Rollway is not specifically for you. It's not like the trip to G.M. They took you to places where you were likely to be able to get jobs. Here, it's just a general tour that everybody goes on. Many of the jobs that you will see are not for you. Some are just for people with engineering degrees. You'd better wear comfortable shoes because you may be walking for two or three hours." Maxine and Mark said: "Ooh," in protest to the walking.

She paused and said in a demanding voice: "OK, any questions? You are all going to be there. (Pause) I want you to take a piece of paper and write down some questions so that you have things to ask at the plant." She began passing out paper and at this point Jason, who was sitting next to me, made a tutting sound of disgust and said: "We got to do this?" Marge said: "I know this is too easy for you, Jason." This was said in a sarcastic way but not like a strong putdown.

> O.C.: It was like sarcasm between two people who know each other well. Marge has known many of these kids for a few years. I have to explore the implications of that for her relations with them.

Interviews

The interview is one of the most widely used methods for obtaining qualitative data. Interviews are used to gather data on subjects' opinions, beliefs, and feelings about the situation in their own words. Interviews provide information that cannot be obtained through observation, or they can be used to verify the observation. The qualitative interview is typically more probing and open-ended and less structured than the interview used in quantitative research, but varies considerably in the way it is conducted. The structure of the interview follows the extent to which the questions to be asked are developed prior to the interview. At one extreme is the unstructured conversational type of interview where the questions arise from the situation. It is sometimes described as "a conversation with a purpose." The interview is not planned ahead of time; the researcher asks questions as the opportunity arises and then listens closely and uses the subjects' responses to decide on the next question. The subjects in the setting may not even realize they are being interviewed. At the other end of the continuum lies the more structured interview, scheduled for the specific purpose of getting certain information from the subjects. Each respondent is asked the same set of questions, but with some latitude in the sequence. Or both approaches may be used in the same study. One characteristic that all interview formats share is that the questions are open-ended and designed to reveal what is important to understand about the phenomenon under study (Maykut & Morehouse, 1994, p. 81).

An interview has the advantage of supplying large volumes of in-depth data rather quickly. Interviews provide insight on participants' perspectives, the meaning of events for the people involved, information about the site, and perhaps information on unanticipated issues. Interviews allow immediate follow-up and clarification of participants' responses. One disadvantage of the interview as a data-gathering tool is that interviewees may not be willing to share information or may even offer false information. Interviews require a great deal of time to conduct and later to transcribe the audio tapes or other notes. Interviewers need skill and practice to carry out a successful interview: they must be tactful, wellprepared (so that they know what questions to ask), and listen well. Careful listening is crucial to successful interviewing. Be on guard to eliminate any personal biases that could threaten the accuracy of the data collected.

The most efficient way to collect arranged interview data is to use a tape recorder. This is much less distracting than taking notes, and it also provides a verbatim record of the responses. Informal interviews in the field are reconstructed later and included in the field notes. A good source for additional information on interviewing is Maykut and Morehouse (1994, Chapter 7).

Focus Groups

Focus groups have become popular as a data-gathering tool in qualitative research. A focus group, which is like a group interview, typically centers on a particular issue; the trained interviewer elicits the views of the group members while noting interactions within the group. Focus groups are helpful because they bring several different perspectives into contact. The researcher gains insight into how the participants are thinking and why they are thinking as they do. Focus groups make more economical use of time and money than do individual interviews. And they are helpful when a researcher is studying a topic that is new or one for which little information is available. The topics and ideas expressed in the focus group can help the researcher to identify questions and other important aspects of the phenomenon to pursue in the study.

Focus groups typically consist of ten to twelve people. The group should be small enough that everyone can take part in the discussion, but large enough to provide diversity in perspective. Focus-group discussions usually need to last at least one hour and possibly two hours.

Documents

Qualitative researchers may also use written documents to gain an understanding of the phenomenon under study. These documents may be personal, such as autobiographies, diaries, and letters; official, such as files, reports, or minutes that have been prepared by observers of an event or setting; or documents of popular culture, such as books, films, and videos.

If a document is written by someone who has had firsthand experience with the phenomenon under study, it is considered a **primary source.** For example, researchers have used diaries and letters written by pioneer women to understand what life was like for such women in the early years of our country. A **secondary source** is a secondhand description written by someone who may have heard about an event from others, but did not directly experience it. You cannot assume that documents always provide accurate accounts of events or settings. Other sources of data should be used to corroborate the conclusions presented in the document.

Strategies Used in Qualitative Inquiry

Qualitative inquirers use a variety of procedures to confirm their developing insights or hypotheses and to ensure the trustworthiness of the data being gathered. Among these techniques are prolonged engagement at the site and persistent observation to provide sufficient scope and depth to observations. Other important aspects of the research procedure that contribute to the value of the research are

1. **Multiple methods of data collection.** A combination of data sources such as interviews, observations, and relevant documents and the use of different methods increase the likelihood that the phenomenon under study is being understood from various points of view. The use of multiple sources of data, multiple observers, and/or multiple methods is referred to as **triangulation.** In *data*

triangulation, the researcher investigates whether the data collected with one procedure or instrument confirm data collected using a different procedure or instrument. The researcher wants to find support for the observations and conclusions in more than one data source. Convergence of a major theme or pattern in the data from these various sources lends credibility to the findings. *Methods triangulation* uses more than one method (for example, ethnography and document analysis) in the study. The assumption is that the combination of methods results in better evidence.

To avoid the appearance of bias, researchers should show that they have looked for and explained any discrepant or contradictory data. Johnson and Christensen (2000, p. 212) describe the role of the researcher as a detective, examining each clue and attempting to rule out alternative explanations until the case is made "beyond a reasonable doubt."

2. **Building an audit trail.** To enhance the dependability of the study, a qualitative researcher often maintains an **audit trail** of materials that documents how the study was conducted, including what was done, when, and why. The audit trail contains the raw data gathered in interviews and observations, records of the inquirer's decisions about whom to interview or what to observe and why, files documenting how working hypotheses were developed from the raw data and subsequently refined and tested, the findings of the study, and so forth. Using the audit trail as a guide, an independent, third-party auditor examines the inquirer's study in order to attest to the dependability of procedures employed and to examine whether findings are confirmable—that is, whether they are logically derived from and grounded in the data that were collected (Schwandt & Halpern, 1988).

3. **Working with a team.** Even with multiple methods and an audit trail, qualitative research reported by an investigator working alone often comes under criticism for being biased. A researcher can increase the trustworthiness of the study if he or she can work with others. Several human instruments working together are usually better than one; furthermore, team members act as peer reviewers or "peer debriefers," keeping one another honest (Lincoln & Guba, 1985). A beginning researcher who must work alone on a dissertation can ask an outside person to be a debriefer; that is, the outsider can go through the researcher's audit trail periodically and point out bias when necessary.

4. **Member checks.** In member checks, the researcher solicits feedback from the participants themselves about the study's findings. Has the researcher accurately described and interpreted their experience? Feedback from the participants may help the researcher gain further insight and/or call attention to something that he or she missed. Furthermore, through member checking, the researcher demonstrates courtesy to the participants by letting them see what has been written about them.

These strategies are discussed in greater detail later in this chapter.

ETHICAL CONSIDERATIONS IN QUALITATIVE RESEARCH

Although we discuss ethical issues pertaining to educational research in Chapters 3 and 16, certain issues inherent in qualitative research require some attention here.

1. **Kind of information obtained.** One ethical issue may result from the lengthy and personal interaction that the qualitative researcher has with the subjects and the research site. The data collection methods involve personal interviews and observations of participants during a prolonged time at a site. Depending on the nature of the research, there is great likelihood of situations arising that present ethical dilemmas to the researcher. A researcher may come into unforeseen possession of knowledge about illegal activities, or in some cases may have actually participated in the illegal behavior. For example, a researcher studying a high school may learn about the use and sale of illegal drugs. An educational researcher investigating teaching styles may observe emotionally abusive teachers. What should a researcher do with such "guilty knowledge" (as it is sometimes called)? Do you have an ethical responsibility to report this information to the appropriate authorities? The researcher must decide whether his or her main responsibility is to the research study, to the participants, or to society as a whole. You must balance the benefit of continuing the study after acquiring such "guilty knowledge" against your responsibilities as a good citizen. One rule that researchers must always follow is that they are legally obligated (mandated) to report any evidence of child abuse.

2. **Researcher's relationship to participant.** After spending a great amount of time observing or interviewing, the relationship with the participants may gradually become less that of researcher and researched and more like friendship. Because the researcher is regarded as a friend, the participants trust him or her and may forget a research study is going on. Field researchers say they obtain their best data at this point, but at the same time are most ethically vulnerable (Langenbach, Vaughn, & Aagaard, 1994). Through such deception, Peshkin said, he "donned masks in order to remove the masks of those I wanted to observe and interview" (1984, p. 258). The reader is referred to Peshkin's account of his ethical concerns about the deceptive role he played during an eighteen-month study of a fundamentalist Christian school.

   Somewhat related are the issues of anonymity and confidentiality in qualitative research. Participants may expect and have a right to anonymity, but it can be problematic in qualitative research. The researcher cannot promise anonymity if, as is usually the case, he or she knows the names of the participants. If a researcher has promised confidentiality, then he or she must try to keep that promise if at all possible. Be aware, however, that your records can be subpoenaed if a court discovers that you may have evidence about criminal activity. For this reason, researchers who conduct sensitive research do not keep records that identify individuals unless absolutely necessary. In field notes, they can use false names or code numbers to keep track of what information came from whom without revealing identities.

The confidentiality issue may arise in educational research, as well. Let's say you have conducted a study of the teachers in a particular school and assured them confidentiality. At the end of the study, the principal asks you to see your data on one or more of the teachers. What would you do? Do you have a responsibility to the teacher(s) to whom you promised confidentiality, to the principal, or perhaps to the students who are exposed to this teacher?

3. **Consent.** Some qualitative research situations require consent and others may not. Informed consent means that the participants know (at least at a minimum) the purpose of the research, what will be required of them, and what harm they may receive from participating. If there is any question about the need for consent, check with the human subjects research committee at your university. One point that should be emphasized is that children cannot give informed consent. Children can assent, which means that they can agree to participate in a study, but they cannot give informed consent. Drew, Hardman, and Hart (1996) point out that *consent* is a legal term not generally considered appropriate to use with minors. Parental consent must be obtained from the parent or guardian. Even after obtaining legal consent from the parent, the researcher should still respect the wishes of a child by giving him or her the right to assent or refuse to participate. Providing consent for participation of minors is thus viewed as a shared decision.

4. **Harm.** One of the most basic concerns in research is that the participants must not be harmed. Participants must be protected not only from physical harm, but also from emotionally, psychologically, or socially adverse effects (National Commission for the Protection of Human Subjects, 1979, p. 5). Some types of qualitative research such as ethnography are vulnerable in terms of potential harm to subjects. An extreme example of violation of this ethical principle of "do no harm" was reported in a controversial new book by Tierney (November 2000). Tierney claims that anthropologists studying the Yanomami, a primitive South American tribe, in the 1960s introduced steel fishhooks and machetes that incited jealousy and violence among tribal members, and even more seriously, brought in deadly pathogens that caused epidemics resulting in suffering and slow genocide of the Yanomami. The American Anthropological Association has formed a task force to examine the serious charges brought forth in this book.

5. **Reciprocation.** Another issue about which the researcher should be concerned is the issue of reciprocity. The people in the research setting have given of themselves to help the researcher, and he or she is indebted. Qualitative researchers need to give participants something in return for their time, effort, cooperation, and just tolerating their extended presence. For example, assume a researcher has conducted a lengthy study of students' achievement, parental involvement, and the teachers in an elementary school. At the end of the study, it would be appropriate for the researcher and his or her team to give something back to the

school. They might offer to provide a written report, present the findings at a school or neighborhood meeting, give advice or assistance on other research projects at the school, or help with grant writing, and so forth. Marshall and Rossman (1995) write, "Of course, reciprocity should fit within the constraints of research and personal ethics, and within the constraints of maintaining one's role as a researcher" (p. 71).

6. **Getting permission to conduct research.** Like the quantitative researcher, the qualitative researcher must get approval for the project from his or her institution's Human Subjects Research Committee, especially if minors are included in the research. Beginning researchers should get a copy of the application form used at their institutions to see what questions they must answer. It is often more difficult for a qualitative researcher to inform the committee about the specifics of the research project, because in qualitative research you do not always know what is going to happen. The problem you think you are going to investigate may not be the one you actually end up studying. Qualitative research plans must be altered as you get the study underway, and unanticipated ethical issues may arise that you will need to resolve. Usually qualitative researchers inform the committee in a general way about the project. If it is necessary to change the focus or design of the study, then the researcher needs to get an amendment from the committee.

For further discussion of human subjects research, see Sales and Folkman *Ethics in Research with Human Participants* (2000), published by the American Psychological Association, and *Ethical Principles and Guidelines for the Protection of Human Subjects of Research* (National Commission, 1979). The latter, also known as the Belmont Report,★ is one of the most important documents for researchers in the United States. The Belmont Report identifies three fundamental principles that are particularly relevant to human subjects research:

1. **Respect for persons.** This is closely related to the Golden Rule, "Do unto others as you would have them do unto you." Respect for persons incorporates two ethical convictions: first, that individuals should be treated as autonomous agents; and second, that people with diminished autonomy are entitled to protection.
2. **Beneficence.** Beneficence means that researchers should not harm human subjects, and that studies should maximize possible benefits and minimize possible harms.
3. **Justice.** The principle of justice means essentially that the risks and benefits should be spread equitably across society. It is not fair, for example, if the burden of research is carried by poor people when everyone, rich and poor, can benefit from the results.

★You can find the Belmont Report at http://ohrp.osophs.dhhs.gov/humansubjects/guidance/belmont.htm.

TYPES OF QUALITATIVE RESEARCH

We will now look at a number of qualitative research approaches. It is important to remember that although these qualitative research approaches differ in context and participants, they overlap in many aspects. They all share the general characteristics described at the beginning of this chapter.

Naturalistic Observation

In **naturalistic observation,** the qualitative researcher simply observes and records events as they naturally occur. No attempt is made to alter the situation in any way, and because those being observed are not aware of the observation, their behavior does not change because of the researcher's presence.

A researcher who wants to study aggressive behavior in preschool children might choose naturalistic observation as the research method. The researcher could use a one-way mirror, a hidden camera, or some other unobtrusive technique to observe the children's behavior. On the playground, the researcher could observe from some distance so that his or her presence is not noticeable to the children. Simple naturalistic observation can take a great deal of time because you must wait for the behavior to occur naturally. For this reason, some researchers set up a contrived naturalistic situation to elicit the behavior to be observed. Although the setup is contrived, the researcher tries to maintain the naturalness of the situation and makes the observations in a way not noticeable to the subjects. Hartshorne, May, and Shuttleworth (1928) used naturalistic contrived observation in their classic study of classroom cheating (see Chapter 8).

Case Studies

Case studies and single-subject experiments (see Chapter 10) both study a single individual or a single, discrete social unit such as a family, club, social institution, community, or gang. However, single-subject experiments focus on a single behavior or a very limited number of behaviors, whereas case studies attempt to describe the subject's entire range of behaviors and the relationship of these behaviors to the subject's history and environment. In a single-subject experiment, the investigator introduces a specific treatment for the purpose of studying the effect of this treatment on the subject, whereas in a case study the investigator observes the subject's reaction to naturally occurring events.

In a case study the investigator attempts to examine an individual or unit in depth. The investigator tries to discover all the variables that are important in the history or development of the subject. The emphasis is on understanding why the individual does what he or she does and how behavior changes as the individual responds to the environment. This requires detailed study for a considerable period of time; that is, it is a longitudinal approach. The investigator gathers data about the subject's present state, past experiences, environment, and how these factors relate to one another.

Many case studies arise from endeavors to solve problems. Freud's well-known case studies began with his attempt to help his subjects solve their personality problems. As he probed deeply into the dynamics of his patients' personalities, he reasoned that the relationships he observed between them and their environments might also be characteristic of other individuals with similar problems. He published detailed accounts of his interviews with patients and his interpretations of their thoughts, dreams, and actions, on the assumption that far-reaching generalizations could be made from these studies.

The greatest advantage of a case study is the possibility of depth; it seeks to understand the whole child or the whole adult in the totality of that individual's environment. Not only the present actions of an individual but his or her past, environment, emotions, and thoughts can be probed. The researcher tries to determine *why* an individual behaves as he or she does, and not merely to record behavior. Case studies often provide an opportunity for an investigator to develop insight into basic aspects of human behavior. The intensive probing characteristic of this technique may lead to the discovery of previously unsuspected relationships.

Case studies are not limited to the study of individuals. Case studies are made of communities, institutions, and groups of individuals. A classic case study of a community was Lynd and Lynd's *Middletown* (1929), which described life in Muncie, Indiana, a typical average-size midwestern city. This first study was followed by *Middletown in Transition* in 1937. Another classic was Hollingshead's *Elmtown's Youth* (1949), which studied the life of adolescents in a small Illinois community. Other case studies have focused on communities ranging from the isolated mountain villages of Appalachia to life among ethnic and minority groups in inner sections of large cities.

Institutions such as churches, colleges, alternative schools, fraternal organizations, and businesses have been the focus of case studies. Case studies have been made of groups of individuals such as gays, drug addicts, delinquents, street gangs, migratory workers, CEOs, medical students, teachers, and many others. Members of religious groups such as the Amish, the Shakers, and various other denominations have been studied.

The case study permits an in-depth examination of factors that explain present status and that influence change over time. The advantages of the case study, however, are also its weaknesses. Although it can have depth, it inevitably lacks breadth. The dynamics of one individual or social unit may bear little relationship to the dynamics of others. In practice most case studies arise out of counseling or remedial efforts and therefore provide information on exceptional rather than representative individuals.

The opportunities for insights in a case study are also opportunities for subjectivity or even prejudice. The preconceptions of an investigator can determine which behaviors are observed and which are ignored, as well as the way in which the observations are interpreted.

The reputation of the case study approach has suffered because some investigators in the past have explained their observations in constructs that are impossible either to confirm or refute through empirical study. Because the extent to which case studies can produce valid generalizations is limited, their major usefulness is not as tools for testing hypotheses but rather in producing hypotheses, which can then be tested through more rigorous investigation. For example, the insights Jean Piaget gained in his famous case studies on the maturation of intellect provided useful hypotheses that have since been investigated through other methods.

In those instances when case studies result from attempts to learn about individuals in order to help them, the research aspects of the study take second place. However, case studies are also frequently conducted with the primary aim of gaining knowledge. Itard's classic case study on the "wild boy" of Aveyron (1962) was an effort to learn about the effects of civilization through studying (from documents) a boy who had grown up in isolation from civilization in eighteenth-century France. Piaget's case studies were conducted in order to learn about mental growth in children rather than to benefit the subjects involved.

Readers interested in doing a case study are referred to Merriam (1998) and Stake (1995).

Content or Document Analysis

Content or **document analysis** is a research method applied to written or visual materials for the purpose of identifying specified characteristics of the material. The materials analyzed can be textbooks, newspapers, speeches, television programs, advertisements, musical compositions, or any of a host of other types of documents. Content analysis is widely used in education. The following are some of the purposes of content analysis in educational research:

1. *To identify bias, prejudice, or propaganda in textbooks.* For example, a researcher might analyze high school history texts in a particular school district to see how often women are mentioned and how much discussion is given in each mention.

2. *To analyze types of errors in students' writings.* For example, you could look at students' written work to classify spelling or grammatical errors and their nature and frequency.

3. *To describe prevailing practices.* For example, you could identify the entrance requirements of Big Ten universities by analyzing their bulletins.

4. *To discover the level of difficulty of material in textbooks or other publications.* For example, you could ask, "What is the vocabulary level of the fourth-grade social studies textbooks in this district?"

5. *To discover the relative importance of, or interest in, certain topics.* For example, you might analyze popular educational research textbooks to see the coverage given to qualitative research.

Content analyses may be done in an emergent design framework. Or they may be done in a quantitative research framework with variables that are specified a priori and numbers that are generated to enable the researcher to draw conclusions about these specified variables. For example, Allen, Allen, and Sigler (1993) investigated gender-role stereotyping in one segment of children's literature, namely in books that had won the Caldecott Medal award. The purpose of the analysis was to determine if these books presented stereotypical or gender-dependent role behaviors to children through the characters in their text and pictures. They compared books from 1938–1940 and from 1986–1988 on eleven categories where gender-role stereotyping could occur, including the characters in text and picture, the occupation of the main characters, whether the characters were active or passive, indoor or outdoor, in traditional or nontraditional roles, and so on. They found a weak trend toward equal representation in seven of the eleven categories, although males still comprised the majority of the characters in each category. Males were characterized as active, outdoors, nontraditional, and in diverse occupations more often than females in both time periods. The researchers concluded that gender-role stereotyping has decreased, but it remains prevalent in each category of investigation.

The preceding study illustrates the steps involved in a content analysis:

1. *Specifying the phenomenon to be investigated* (such as gender-role stereotyping).

2. *Selecting the media from which the observations are to be made* (such as the Caldecott Medal books for specified time periods).

3. *Formulating exhaustive and mutually exclusive coding categories* so that the verbal or symbolic content can be counted (such as the eleven categories where gender-role stereotyping could occur).

4. *Deciding on the sampling plan to be used* in order to obtain a representative sample of the documents (such as the sample consisting of all the Caldecott winners for two 2-year periods). You might decide to look at three issues per week of a newspaper over a period of a year, for instance, or every issue of a weekly news-magazine for a year.

5. *Training the coders* so that they can consistently apply the coding scheme that has been developed and thus contribute to the reliability of the content analysis. Some coding is not so straightforward, but may require inferences about whether a minority group, for example, is being portrayed positively or negatively. Several coders should be able to code the documents using the scheme and obtain consistent results. If the interrater reliability is satisfactory, you can proceed to the next step. If it is less than satisfactory, the coders may be useful in revising the category definitions to make them clearer and more complete.

6. *Analyzing the data,* which may involve just the frequencies and percentages in the various categories. This step can be slow and time consuming. Fortunately, computers can now carry out a content analysis quickly and accurately. Most universities have image scanners that can read printed pages and transfer the text to electronic files. Then a computer program can be used to search through the scanned text and find words or phrases that meet specified criteria. You can obtain a listing of specified words, for example, and the frequency with which the words appear in the printed documents. Even more sophisticated computer programs, including ones that will be able to classify content and interpret

meaning of words according to the context, can be expected to become available as research continues into the area known as *artificial intelligence*.

An advantage of content analysis is that it is unobtrusive. The presence of the observer does not influence what is being observed. You do not need to enlist the cooperation of subjects or get permission to do the study. Another advantage of content analyses is that they are easily replicated.

Focused Interviews

A **focused interview** is a way of gathering qualitative data by asking individuals questions about their behavior. A focused interview is much more flexible and open in form than the survey interview discussed in Chapter 13. The respondents are free to answer in their own words, and can answer either briefly or at length. The questions asked may even vary from individual to individual. The responses are recorded by taking notes, either during the interview or immediately afterward, or with an audiotape.

For example, in a qualitative study designed to understand the persistence of black students at a predominantly white university, Kraft (1991) interviewed forty-three black undergraduate students about their perceptions of the academic experience, the bases of academic success, and why some black students attending a predominantly white university are more successful than others. Their responses indicated that the usual list of causal factors such as ability, effort, and task difficulty gives only a partial picture of how students assess academic performance. These students stressed the importance of minority students' beliefs about how they are perceived by faculty and student peers.

Focused interviews were also used by Kagan, Dennis, Igou, and Moore (1993) to examine the effects of a staff development program on the professional lives of four elementary teachers who participated in it. The program took experienced elementary teachers to a university college of education for two-year terms, during which they functioned as adjunct faculty. The teachers interviewed said that they did not learn radically new things in the program, but that it enabled them to clarify what they already knew about teaching and to recommit themselves to the role of career teacher. This qualitative research showed the potential of school-university partnerships for enhancing teachers' professional lives.

Ethnographic Research

Ethnography is the in-depth study of naturally occurring behavior within a culture or social group. It seeks to understand the relationship between culture and behavior. The ethnographic research method was developed by anthropologists (such as Margaret Mead) as a way of studying and describing human cultures. In Mead's classic study, *Coming of Age in Samoa* (1928), she studied adolescent girls in Samoa and analyzed the differences in development between Samoan and American girls. Anthropologists immerse themselves in the lives of the people they study, using primarily extended observation (participant and nonparticipant) and occasionally in-depth interviewing to gain clarification and more detailed information. The ethnographer undertakes the study without any a priori hypotheses, to avoid predetermining what is observed or what information is elicited from informants. The ethnographer explores and tests hypotheses, but the hypotheses evolve out of the fieldwork itself.

Ethnographers refer to the people from whom they gather information "informants" rather than participants, and they study "sites" rather than individuals.

Ethnographic research has advantages and disadvantages. The advantage is its observation of behavior in a real-life setting, the assumption being that human behavior can be fully understood only by knowing the setting in which it occurs. The main limitation is that the findings depend heavily on the particular researcher's observations and interpretations of the data. For example, researchers now suggest that Margaret Mead's interpretations of the data collected on the Samoan culture were completely wrong. Later research did not support her conclusions about the sexual behavior of young Samoan women, but found almost the exact opposite. Mead was criticized for spending too little time in Samoa, seeing only what she wanted to see, and accepting the responses of a few young girls at face value without corroboration from other sources (Freeman, 1983). Later in this chapter, we will discuss some strategies for enhancing the validity of interpretations made of qualitative data.

Spindler and Hammond (2000) describe some of the characteristics of good ethnography: (1) extended participation observation; (2) long time at the site (a year would be a short time for a community study); (3) collection of large volumes of material such as notes, artifacts, audio- and videotapes, and so on; and (4) openness, which means having no specific hypotheses or even highly specific categories of observation at the start of the study.

The term *ethnography* is used to refer to both the work of studying a culture and also the end product of the research. Ethnography has moved from anthropology to other disciplines, including education, where it is becoming a valuable tool in understanding the process of schooling. It has provided basic information on the nature of cultural transmission and the formal process of education that has resulted in insights and generalizations useful to educational practitioners (Chilcott, 1992). Ethnographic research on immigrant children and other minority populations in U.S. schools, for example, has helped educators understand these students' cultural backgrounds and the discontinuity that may exist between family and school culture that affects the success or failure of these diverse students in schools. Spindler and Hammond (2000) write that ethnography "can help teachers separate their personal cultural values from those of their students in order to see both themselves and their students more clearly," and to understand the voices of the "other" (p. 44).

Peshkin's work is an example of ethnographic research in education. In his 1991 work, *The Color of Strangers, the Color of Friends,* Peshkin presented a year-long, in-depth study of Riverview High School, a school in a working-class community in California with large numbers of students from different ethnic groups. He used participant observation and interviews to explore the role of ethnicity in this multiethnic school. Although Riverview had experienced ethnicity-based disorder and violence a few years earlier, Peshkin found the school characterized by ethnic peace. He described Riverview High School as a social success story—a place where strangers and friends were not sorted out on the basis of color. Social interactions that usually occur only within an ethnic group routinely took place across ethnic groups at Riverview. The students' level of academic success, however, did not match their success in social interactions. Peshkin found a persistently low level of academic success, especially among the black and Hispanic students.

In another ethnographic study, *The Imperfect Union: School Consolidation and Community Conflict* (1982), Peshkin focused on a midwestern rural school district that was resisting state-mandated consolidation. After thorough study of the school district and its history, Peshkin illustrated how, when viewed through the eyes of the people in the district, their behavior was quite reasonable and not at all "irrational" as had been suggested. That is what ethnographic research attempts to do—build a complete understanding of a group from the perspectives of the members of that group. Other ethnographic research has provided insights on immigrant children and ethnic minorities in our schools, special-needs children in schools, and teacher–pupil relationships in inner-city schools and other types of schools. Nozaki (2000) conducted an ethnographic study of Japanese children in an American school.

Methodology

Spradley (1980) identifies the sequence of steps making up the methodology of ethnographic research:

1. **Selecting an ethnographic project.** The scope of these projects can vary greatly, from studying a whole complex society, such as an Inuit hunting group in Alaska, to a single social situation or institution, such as an urban bar, a fraternity, or a school playground. The beginner would be wise to restrict the scope of his or her project to a single social situation so that it can be completed in a reasonable time. A social situation always has three components: a place, actors, and activities.

2. **Asking ethnographic questions.** The researcher needs to have questions in mind that will guide what he or she sees and hears and the collection of data.

3. **Collecting ethnographic data.** The researcher does fieldwork to find out the activities of the people, the physical characteristics of the situation, and what it feels like to be part of the situation. This step generally begins with an overview comprising broad descriptive observations. Then after looking at the data, you move on to more focused observations. Here you use participant observation, in-depth interviews, and so on to gather data.

4. **Making an ethnographic record.** This step includes taking field notes and photographs, making maps, and using any other appropriate means to record the observations.

5. **Analyzing ethnographic data.** The fieldwork is always followed by data analysis, which leads to new questions and new hypotheses, more data collection and field notes, and more analysis. The cycle continues until the project is completed.

6. **Writing the ethnography.** The ethnography should be written so that the culture or group is brought to life, making readers feel they understand the people and their way of life. The ethnographic report can range in length from several pages to a volume or two. You can greatly simplify this task by beginning the writing early as data accumulate instead of waiting until the end. The writing task will also be easier if, before writing, you read other well-written ethnographies.

Phenomenological Studies

The *phenomenological study* is designed to describe and interpret an experience by determining the *meaning* of the experience as perceived by the people who have participated in it. The assumption is that there are many ways of interpreting the same experience, and that the meaning of the experience to each person is what constitutes reality. This belief is characteristic of all qualitative studies, but the element that distinguishes phenomenology from other qualitative approaches is that the subjective experience is at the center of the inquiry. The central research question aims to determine the essence of the experience as "perceived by the participants." A phenomenological researcher who was asked to study, for example, the integration of special-needs children into a regular classroom would focus on asking what this experience means to the parties involved: the special-needs children, other students, and the teacher. Whether or not the integration plan is working is not the important issue; what matters is how the students and the teacher experience it. "Phenomenology . . . makes no judgment with respect to the reality status of experiences. It merely wants to understand how, through experience, all the events and objects of the world appear to the consciousness" (Giorgi, 1988).

The number of phenomenological studies in education has increased greatly in the past decade. The following examples of education topics have been studied by phenomenological researchers (Langenbach, Vaughn, & Aagaard, 1994, p. 155):

Coping styles of children

Being labeled "learning disabled"

The urban classroom

Children whose parents are unemployed

The anxious math student

The student athlete

Novice teachers

The schooling experience

Teaching neglected and abused children

Homework in the lives of children

Racial integration of an elementary school

Home schooling

The participants in a phenomenological study are chosen because they have had the experience being investigated and can share their thoughts and feelings about the experience. The distinguishing data collection method in a phenomenological study is the personal, unstructured interview. The interviews may be lengthy (one to two hours), and there may be more than one interview with each participant. The researcher typically interviews ten to twenty-five individuals who may come from a single site or different sites. Tape-recording the interviews facilitates the subsequent analysis.

Maykut and Morehouse (1994) write, "The human instrument is the only data collection instrument which is multifaceted enough and complex enough to capture the important elements of a human or human experience" (p. 27). Lincoln and Guba (1985) concur, stating that a human investigator can explore the idiosyncratic responses in ways that are not possible with any instrument that is constructed in advance of the study. Because of the importance of the interview in this research, it is critical that the investigator be a skilled interviewer. The questions used need to focus on meaning and be designed to elicit the "essence" of the experience from the perspective of the participants. The interviewer must be able to listen, prompt when necessary, and encourage subjects to expand and elaborate on their recollections of the experience.

From an analysis of the interview data, the researcher writes descriptions of the participants' experiences and how those experiences were perceived. In Chapter 15 we discuss analysis of qualitative data. From the analysis, the researcher derives an overall description of the general meaning of the experience.

For further discussion of phenomenological research, see the chapter by R. Hycner in Bryman and Burgess (1999, vol. 3, pp. 143–164).

Grounded Theory

The aim of a *grounded theory* study is to discover or build a theory in an area. This emphasis on theory distinguishes it from other qualitative approaches. Glaser and Strauss (1967) developed grounded theory as a way of formalizing the operations needed to develop theory from empirical data. This research approach focuses on gathering data about peoples' experiences in a particular context and then inductively building a theory "from the bottom up." The theory is grounded in the data, and the researcher has no preconceived ideas about what the theory will be. The desired theory is "conceptually dense"; that is, it presents many conceptual relationships that are stated as propositions pertaining to a particular context, situation, or experience.

In the role as the primary data-gathering instrument, the researcher asks questions about some event, experience, or social phenomenon. He or she collects data through observations and interviews, and then analyzes data by looking for similarities/differences among the participants' responses about the experience. After forming categories having similar units of meaning, the researcher looks for underlying themes and relationships among the categories. This analysis of the data results in insights, conditional propositions, and questions that are pursued through further data collection. The researcher constructs tentative theoretical statements about the relationships among constructs, and explores these theoretical propositions through further data collection, and so on. This cyclical process of testing the explanatory adequacy of the theoretical constructs by comparing with additional empirical data continues until the comparative analysis no longer contributes anything new (theoretical saturation). Thus through induction and verification techniques, the researcher progressively elaborates a general theoretical statement well grounded in the data. Generating the theory is not easy; it requires insight and understanding and, as indicated, many reviews of the data.

The personal open-ended interview is the primary method of data collection. The interviewer asks questions about what happened to individuals, why it happened, and what it means to them. Choose a sample where each individual has had the experience and can contribute to theory development. The study may include as many as twenty to twenty-five subjects who are interviewed on the topic until no new information is forthcoming (data saturation). To confirm or refute the theory that has developed, researchers sometimes interview another group that has had different experiences.

Grounded theory studies of a sociological nature have focused on victims of Alzheimer's disease and how families accommodate to the different stages, drug addiction in women, chronic illness, alcoholism, eating disorders, pain management, how families make decisions about placing members in a nursing home, and so on. A grounded theory study in education might focus on mainstreaming, mentoring new teachers, integrating minorities in private prep schools, classroom discipline, and many other topics. Readers who are interested in grounded theory methodology are referred to Strauss and Corbin (1998) and to Dey (1999).

Historical Research

Historical studies are oriented to the past rather than to the present and thus use different data collection methods from those used in other qualitative approaches. Historical research is included in qualitative research because of its emphasis on interpretation and its use of nonnumeric data. **Historical research** is the attempt to establish facts and arrive at conclusions concerning the past. The historian systematically and objectively locates, evaluates, and interprets evidence from which people can learn about the past. Based on the evidence gathered, conclusions are drawn regarding the past so as to increase knowledge of how and why past events occurred and the process by which the past became the present. The hoped-for result is increased understanding of the present and a more rational basis for making choices.

The historian operates under different handicaps from those of researchers in other fields. Control over treatment, measurement, and sampling is limited, and there is no opportunity for replication. As in descriptive and causal-comparative research, the independent, or treatment, variables are not controlled by the researcher. All the cautions in interpreting those studies also apply to historical research. However, in descriptive and ex post facto research, measurement can usually be controlled through deciding what measures will be administered as the dependent variable. Although historians have no choice concerning what documents, relics, records, and artifacts survive the passage of time, they do have some limited control over what questions they will ask of these sources and what measures they will apply to them. When interviewing witnesses of past events and when searching the historical record, researchers can decide what questions to ask and what is to be measured. But they can measure only those things that witnesses remember or the record contains. In descriptive and experimental research, investigators can attempt to control sampling; that is, they can decide for themselves whom they are going to study. Historians can study only those people for whom records and artifacts survive. If newspapers ignore a particular segment of a community and no other sources for that community exist, then historians cannot directly assess the contributions that particular segment of a population made to the life of that community. Another limitation impinging on historical researchers is that no assumption about the past can be made merely because no record can be found, nor can it be assumed, on the contrary, that a conspiracy of silence has distorted the historical record.

Primary and Secondary Sources

The historian classifies materials as *primary* and *secondary sources*. Primary sources are original documents, relics, remains, or artifacts. These are the direct outcomes of events or the records of eyewitnesses. Examples would be the minutes of a school board meeting, an unedited videotape of a basketball game, a collection of artwork completed by a third-grade class. In primary sources only the mind of the observer intrudes between the original event and the investigator. Note that the mind of the observer *does* come between the event and the record in each of our examples. Someone has decided what will and will not be recorded in the proceedings of the school board, when the camera is to be on or off and where it is to be focused during the basketball game, and which artwork is to be kept. In secondary sources the mind of a nonobserver also comes between the event and the user of the record. If a newspaper reporter has been present at a school board meeting, the published report is a primary source. If the reporter relies on the minutes of the meeting or an interview with a participant to prepare the report, then this report is a secondary source. Common examples of secondary sources are history books, articles in encyclopedias, and reviews of research. Historians seek to employ primary sources whenever possible.

External and Internal Criticism

Two ideas that have proved useful in evaluating historical sources are the concepts of external (or lower) criticism and internal (or higher) criticism. Basically, **external criticism** asks if the evidence under consideration is authentic and, depending on the nature of the study, may involve such techniques as authentication of signatures, chemical analysis of paint, or carbon dating of artifacts. Suppose a historian has a letter describing Massachusetts schools that is believed to have been written by Horace Mann. Using external criticism, the investigator would ask, Is the paper of the right age? Is the handwriting

Mann's? Are the point of view and the writing style consistent with Mann's other writings? After the authenticity of a piece of evidence has been established, the historical investigator proceeds to **internal criticism,** which requires evaluating the worth of the evidence—for instance, whether a document provides a true report of an event. Such a question can best be answered by comparing it with others that throw light on an event or provide further information about an event and the people or circumstances surrounding it. In the example, the investigator would ask, Is Mann's description of the schools unbiased? Does it agree with other contemporary descriptions of the schools?

Because historical research does have limitations, you could very well ask why it should be attempted. The fundamental reason is that there is no other way to investigate many questions. How else might you attempt to assess the effect of the Kent State shootings and other campus disorders in the spring of 1970?

An advantage of historical research, and sometimes a reason for using this approach, is that it is unobtrusive. The researcher is not physically involved in the situation studied. There is no danger of experimenter-subject interaction, nor is there any need to get the permission of school authorities for the research. The historian locates appropriate documents, gathers suitable data, and draws conclusions at a distance from the situation being studied. In addition, historical research may provide new perspectives to a crisis situation. The uninvolved nature of historical research may make it acceptable in an emotionally charged situation where other types of research would be impossible.

Because of its limitations, however, caution must be exercised in generalizing the results of historical research. Students who plan to do historical study should consult appropriate bibliographies and sources on historical methodology.*

■ VALIDITY AND RELIABILITY OF QUALITATIVE RESEARCH

Although the terms *validity* and *reliability* have most commonly been associated with quantitative research, the concepts of making valid inferences from data and the consistency of the data are also important issues in qualitative research. As you will see, qualitative researchers use different terms to apply to these criteria.

Validity/Credibility in Qualitative Research

The integrity of qualitative research depends on attending to the issue of validity. Validity in qualitative research concerns the accuracy or truthfulness of the findings. The term most frequently used by qualitative researchers to refer to this characteristic is **credibility.** How confident can you be in the researcher's observations, interpretations, and conclusions? Are they believable (credible)?

*See, for instance, *The Modern Researcher* (5th ed.) by J. Barzun and H.F. Graff (San Diego, CA: Harcourt Brace Jovanovich, (1992) and *Understanding History of Education* (2nd ed.), edited by R.R. Sherman (Cambridge, MA: Shenkman, 1984).

Credibility in qualitative research concerns the truthfulness of the inquiry's findings. Credibility or truth value involves how well the researcher has established confidence in the findings based on the research design, participants, and context. The researcher has an obligation to represent the realities of the research participants as accurately as possible and must provide assurances in the report that this obligation was met.

Hammersley (1992) noted that "an account is valid or true if it represents accurately those features of the phenomena that it is intended to describe, explain, or theorize" (p. 69). Krefting (1991) suggests that a qualitative study is considered credible when it "presents such accurate descriptions or interpretations of human experience that people who also share that experience would immediately recognize the description" (p. 215). The term *credibility* in qualitative research is analogous to internal validity in quantitative research.

Evidence of Credibility in Qualitative Research

A number of methods have been identified in the literature for enhancing the credibility (internal validity) of qualitative studies. These methods may be categorized according to five types of evidence: structural corroboration, consensus, referential or interpretive adequacy, theoretical adequacy, and control of bias.

Evidence Based on Structural Corroboration

Eisner (1998) defines **structural corroboration** as a "means through which multiple types of data are related to each other to support or contradict the interpretation and evaluation of a state of affairs" (p. 110). Structural corroboration uses different sources of data (data triangulation) and different methods (methods triangulation). When these different procedures or different data sources are in agreement, there is corroboration. For example, when interviews, related documents, and recollections of other participants produce the same description of an event or when a participant responds similarly to a question asked on three different occasions, one has evidence of credibility.

Evidence Based on Consensus

Validity based on **consensus** is defined as "agreement among competent others that the description, interpretation, evaluation, and thematics" are right (Eisner, 1998, p. 112). This type of validity is primarily demonstrated through two methods: *peer review* and *investigator triangulation*. In peer review, also called *peer debriefing,* the question is asked, "Given the evidence presented, is there consensus in the interpretation?" Colleagues or peers are provided with the raw data along with the researcher's interpretation or explanation. Discussions then determine whether the reviewer(s) considers the interpretation to be reasonable, given the evidence. Reviewers may identify problems in the interpretation and stress the need for additional data. Investigator triangulation involves having multiple researchers collect data independently and compare the collected data (Johnson & Christensen, 2000). The key questions here are "Did what was reported as taking place actually happen? Did the researcher accurately report what was seen and heard? If multiple investigators agree in their description of the context, in their description of events, and in their reporting of what was said, validity is enhanced. Using investigator triangulation makes it less likely that outside reviewers of the research will question the data.

Evidence Based on Referential or Interpretive Adequacy

Referential or **interpretive evidence** of validity refers to "accurately portraying the meaning attached by participants to what is being studied by the researcher" and "the degree to which the participants' viewpoints, thoughts, feelings, intentions, and experiences are accurately understood . . . and portrayed" (Johnson & Christensen, 2000, p. 209). Two primary strategies are used to enhance referential or interpretive adequacy: member checks and low-inference descriptors.

Member checks (participant feedback) ask the question "Do the people that were studied agree with what you have said about them?" At the end of the data collection period, the researcher may ask participants to review and critique field notes or tape recordings for accuracy and meaning. Or the researcher's sharing his or her interpretations of the data with the participants can help clear up miscommunication, identify inaccuracies, and help obtain additional useful data.

Using many **low-inference descriptors** such as verbatim or direct quotations helps the reader experience the participants' world. Using tape recorders or video cameras enables the researcher to use these descriptors. Thick, rich description also helps the research convey an understanding of the study's context.

Evidence Based on Theoretical Adequacy

Theoretical adequacy concerns the degree to which a theoretical explanation developed from the study fits the data and is credible (Johnson & Christensen, 2000, p. 210). There are three key strategies for promoting theoretical adequacy: extended fieldwork, theory triangulation, and pattern matching.

Extended fieldwork provides time for the researcher to observe a full range of activities in order to identify patterns and relationships and their typicality that will contribute to valid interpretations. An extended time in the research setting also enables the researcher to gain the participants' trust and thus to obtain more detailed and honest responses. Credibility is threatened by errors in data collection caused by participants providing socially acceptable responses or acting differently because of the researcher's presence. Use of extended fieldwork can reduce this possibility, because it provides the researcher more opportunities to check perspectives and allows informants to become accustomed to the researcher's presence.

Theory triangulation involves consideration of how the phenomenon under study might be explained by multiple theories. Considering different theories, the researcher may gain better insights.

Pattern matching involves making predictions based on theory and testing those predictions. Based on theory, the researcher predicts a certain pattern of results. Then the researcher determines the degree to which the patterns found in the data match the predicted pattern. If the predictions occur, the researcher has strong evidence to support his or her explanations.

Evidence Based on Control of Bias

Researcher bias is a source of invalidity in qualitative studies. Bias may result from selective observations, hearing only what one wants to hear, or allowing personal attitudes, preferences, and feelings to affect interpretation of data. Krefting (1991) writes, "Paradoxically, a major threat to the truth value of a qualitative study lies in the closeness of the relationship between the investigator and the informants that can develop during the prolonged contact required to establish credibility" (p. 219). The most common strategy to control for bias in qualitative studies is reflexivity. **Reflexivity** is the use of self-reflection to recognize one's own biases and to actively seek them out. Krefting (1991) suggests that the researcher keep a reflective journal that includes three types of information: a daily schedule with logistics of the study, a methods log where the researcher describes decisions and the rationale for them, and reflections of the researcher's thoughts, feelings, ideas, questions, concerns, problems, and frustrations. Denzin and Lincoln (1998) refer to a reflective account of the research process and the researcher's perspective as "an explicit statement about 'where the author is coming from'" and "the ethnographic version of truth in advertising" (p. 294). The researcher should refer to his or her journal reflections during the process of data analysis.

Another strategy used to control for bias is **negative case sampling,** where researchers intentionally seek examples that "disconfirm their expectations and explanations" (Johnson & Christensen, 2000, p. 207). Actively seeking information that is the opposite of what you expect makes it more difficult to ignore certain information. Table 14.1 summarizes the strategies used for enhancing credibility in qualitative studies.

Transferability/External Validity

Transferability is the degree to which the findings of a qualitative study can be applied or generalized to other contexts or to other groups. In quantitative research, the term *external validity* is used to refer to the generalizability of the findings. Qualitative inquirers argue that it is possible to apply qualitative findings to other people, settings, and times to the extent that they are *similar* to the people, settings, and times in the original study. Transferability of a set of findings to another context depends on the *similarity* or "goodness of fit" between the context of the study and other contexts. The transfer is made by the potential user of the findings, who must compare and decide on the similarity of the two contexts. This contrasts with quantitative research, where the original researcher makes generalizations. Although the qualitative researcher does not specify transferability, it is his or her responsibility to provide sufficiently rich, detailed, thick descriptions of the context so that potential users can make the necessary comparisons and judgments about similarity and hence transferability.

Be aware that there are threats to transferability, such as *selection effects* (the fact that the constructs being investigated are unique to a single group), *setting effects* (the fact that

Table 14.1 *Credibility/Validity in Qualitative Studies*	
CRITERION	STRATEGIES
Structural Corroboration	Methods triangulation
	Data triangulation
Consensus	Peer review
	Investigator triangulation
Referential/Interpretive Adequacy	Member check/respondent validation
	Low-inference descriptors
	Thick, rich description
Theoretical Adequacy	Theory triangulation
	Extended fieldwork
	Pattern matching
Control of Bias	Reflexivity
	Negative case/deviant case sampling

results may be a function of the specific context under investigation), and *history effects* (the fact that unique historical experiences of the participants may militate against comparisons) (Goetz & LeCompte 1993).

Dependability/Reliability

Qualitative researchers speak of *dependability* rather than *reliability*. Recall that reliability in quantitative research has to do with consistency of behavior, or the extent to which data and findings would be similar if the study were replicated. However, unlike quantitative research, where tight controls enhance replicability, qualitative studies expect variability, because the context of studies changes. Thus consistency is looked at as the extent to which variation can be tracked or explained. This is referred to as *dependability*. Some strategies to investigate dependability are using an audit trail, replication logic, stepwise replication, code-recoding, interrater comparisons, and triangulation.

1. One of the best ways to establish dependability is to use the *audit trail* that we discussed earlier in the chapter. Audit trails provide a mechanism by which others can determine how decisions were made and the uniqueness of the situation. The researcher must keep thorough notes and records of activities, and should keep data well organized and in a retrievable form. He or she should provide information on the sample of people studied, the selection process, contextual descriptions, methods of data collection, detailed field notes, tape-recordings, videotapes, and other descriptive material that can be reviewed by other people. After examining the data, the auditor can consider the findings, conclusions, and interpretations and can attest whether they are supported by the data. A complete presentation of procedures and results enables the reader to make a judgment about the replicability of the research within the limits of the natural context.

2. Replication logic, which involves conducting the study in multiple locations or with multiple groups, is suggested for determining dependability of a study (Johnson & Christensen, 2000). According to this logic, the more times a finding is found true with different sets of people or in different settings and time periods, the more confident the researcher can be in the conclusions.

3. Stepwise replication is another technique suggested for enhancing dependability. In this strategy, two investigators divide the data, analyze it independently, and then compare results.

4. A fourth method is the code-recode strategy: a researcher codes the data, leaves the analysis for a period of time, then comes back and recodes the data and compares the two sets of coded materials.

5. Because much qualitative research involves observation by multiple observers, some researchers suggest that interrater or interobserver agreement methods similar to those used in quantitative studies be used to enhance dependability. One way to obtain a measure of agreement among observers is to calculate the ratio of agreements to total agreements plus disagreements. In analyzing interview data, interrater reliability is also suggested for analysis of transcripts, field notes, and audio or video recordings.

6. Triangulation, which we have previously discussed, is also used to establish the dependability of qualitative studies.

Confirmability/Objectivity

Confirmability (or neutrality) in qualitative research is the same as the quantitative researcher's concept of objectivity. **Neutrality** is the extent to which the research is free of bias in the procedures and the interpretation of results. Because it may be impossible to achieve the levels of objectivity that quantitative studies strive for, qualitative researchers are concerned with whether the data they collect and the conclusions they draw would be confirmed by others investigating the same situation. Thus in qualitative studies, the focus shifts from the neutrality of the researcher to the confirmability of the data and interpretations.

The audit trail is the main strategy for demonstrating confirmability. By providing a complete audit trail, the researcher enables another researcher to arrive or not arrive at the same conclusions given the same data and context. Other strategies used to enhance confirmability include triangulation of methods, peer review, and reflexivity—all discussed earlier in this chapter. A summary of strategies to enhance dependability, transferability, and neutrality in qualitative studies is provided in Table 14.2.

It would be helpful to compare the terminology used in qualitative and quantitative research to refer to the standards just discussed. Table 14.3 summarizes and compares these terms.

In summary, support for validity and reliability of qualitative studies requires well-documented research and rich description. Mischler (1990) makes an interesting point when he suggests that the ultimate test of the worth of a qualitative study is whether

Table 14.2	*Other Standards in Qualitative Studies*
STANDARD	*STRATEGIES*
Dependability/Reliability	Audit trail
	Replication logic
	Stepwise replication
	Code-recode method
	Interrater comparisons
	Triangulation
Transferability/External validity	Thick, rich description
	Comparisons/Similarity
Neutrality/Objectivity	Audit trail
	Triangulation
	Peer review
	Reflexivity

Table 14.3	*Standards of Rigor for Research*	
QUALITATIVE	*QUANTITATIVE*	*ISSUE*
Credibility	Internal Validity	Truth value
Transferability	External Validity	Generalizability
Dependability	Reliability	Consistency
Confirmability	Objectivity	Neutrality

people believe the findings strongly enough to act on them. That is, do other researchers rely on the findings for their own work or do people outside of the research endeavor make decisions based on the findings? Two notable examples of studies that satisfy this criterion are William Perry's (1970) Harvard investigation of intellectual and ethical development during the college years. This study resulted in the formation of a useful epistemological theory and paved the way for many additional studies of adult thought and development. Belenky and associates' (1986) investigation of the intellectual development of women has stimulated a great deal of research. Their findings on gender differences in how knowledge is received and integrated has even influenced some women's colleges to reconstruct their college curriculum.

SUMMARY

Qualitative studies are a distinctive type of research in education and the social sciences that can produce vivid and richly detailed accounts of human experience. These studies are based on a fundamentally different approach to the study of social reality from that which underlies the standard quantitative approach to the study of education. One chooses a qualitative design because it is the appropriate method for investigating the problem. Qualitative inquiries demand a set of skills that are not readily learned by examining textbook accounts of methods. Becoming proficient in this approach to inquiry requires fieldwork experience in negotiating access to a site, developing a researcher role, establishing and maintaining trust with participants in the study, conducting and recording interviews and observations, managing data, and performing data analysis. Qualitative research requires a great deal of time and effort.

The major types of qualitative studies covered in this text include naturalistic observation, ethnography, case studies, document analysis, focused interviews, phenomenological studies, grounded theory studies, and historical research. The three most widely used qualitative data collection methods are observation, in-depth interviews, and documents.

Validity and reliability are important in qualitative as well as quantitative research. Qualitative researchers use the terms *credibility, transferability, dependability,* and *confirmability* instead of *internal validity, external validity, reliability,* and *objectivity,* respectively. A variety of methods are used to support the validity and reliability of qualitative data and its interpretation. Some of these are peer review, member checks, triangulation, maintaining an audit trail, seeking negative case evidence, and keeping a research journal.

REFERENCES

Allen, A.M., Allen, D.N., & Sigler, G. (1993). Changes in sex-role stereotyping in Caldecott Medal award picture books 1938–1988. *Journal of Research in Childhood Education, 7,* 67–73.

Belenky, M.F., Clinchy, B.M., Goldberger, N.R., & Tarule, J.M. (1986). *Women's ways of knowing: The development of self, voice, and mind.* New York: Basic Books.

Bogdan, R.C., & Biklen, S.K. (1998). *Qualitative research for education: An introduction to theory and methods* (3rd ed.). Boston: Allyn and Bacon.

Chilcott, J.H. (1992). Some contributions of anthropology to professional education. *Educational Researcher, 21*(2), 31–35.

Denzin, N.K., & Lincoln, Y.S. (1998). *Collecting and interpreting qualitative materials.* Thousand Oaks, CA: Sage.

Dey, I. (1999). *Grounding grounded theory: Guidelines for qualitative inquiry.* San Diego: Academic Press.

Drew, C.J., Hardman, M.L., & Hart, A.W. (1996). *Designing and conducting research.* Boston: Allyn and Bacon.

Eisner, E.W. (1998). *The enlightened eye: Qualitative inquiry and the enhancement of educational practice.* Upper Saddle River, NJ: Merrill/Prentice-Hall.

Freeman, D. (1983). *Margaret Mead and Samoa: The making and unmaking of an anthropological myth.* Cambridge, MA: Harvard University Press.

Geertz, C. (1980). Blurred genres: The refiguration of social thought. *American Scholar, 49,* 165–179.

Giorgi, A. (1988). Saybrook at a glance. *Saybrook Perspective,* Winter, (12).

Glaser, B.G., & Strauss, A.L. (1967). *The discovery of grounded theory.* Chicago: Aldine.

Goetz, J.P., & LeCompte, M.D. (1993). *Ethnography and qualitative design in educational research.* New York: Academic Press.

Guba, E.G., & Lincoln, Y.S. (1981). *Effective evaluation.* San Francisco: Jossey-Bass.

Hammersley, M. (1992). *What's wrong with ethnography? Methodological explorations.* London: Routledge.

Hartshorne, H., May, M.A., & Shuttleworth, F.K. (1928). *Studies in the organization of character.* New York: Macmillan.

Hollingshead, A.B. (1949). *Elmstown's youth.* New York: Wiley.

Hycner, R.H. (1999). Some guidelines for the phenomenological analysis of interview data. In A. Bryman & R.G. Burgess (Eds.), *Qualitative research* (vol. 3, pp. 143–164). Thousand Oaks, CA: Sage.

Itard, J.G. (1962). *The wild boy of Aveyron.* (G. Humphrey & M. Humphrey, Trans.). New York: Appleton.

Janesick, V.J. (1994). The dance of qualitative research design: Metaphor, methodolatry, and meaning. In N. Denzin & Y. Lincoln (Eds.), *Handbook of qualitative research* (pp. 209–219). Thousand Oaks, CA: Sage.

Johnson, B., & Christensen, L. (2000). *Educational research: Quantitative and qualitative approaches.* Boston: Allyn and Bacon.

Kagan, D.M., Dennis, M.B., Igou, M., & Moore, P. (1993). The experience of being a teacher in residence. *American Educational Research Journal, 30*(2), 426–443.

Kraft, C.L. (1991). What makes a successful black student on a predominantly white campus? *American Educational Research Journal, 28*(2), 423–443.

Krefting, L. (1991). Rigor in qualitative research: The assessment of trustworthiness. *The American Journal of Occupational Therapy, 45,* 214–222.

Lancy, D.F. (1993). *Qualitative research in education: An introduction to the major traditions.* White Plains, NY: Longman.

Langenbach, M., Vaughn, C., & Aagaard. (1994). *An introduction to educational research.* Boston: Allyn and Bacon.

Lincoln, Y.S., & Guba, E.G. (1985). *Naturalistic inquiry.* Beverly Hills, CA: Sage.

Lynd, R.S., & Lynd, H.M. (1929). *Middletown.* New York: Harcourt Brace.

Lynd, R.S., & Lynd, H.M. (1937). *Middletown in transition.* New York: Harcourt, Brace, and World.

Marshall, C. & Rossman, G.B. (1989). *Designing qualitative research.* Thousand Oaks, CA: Sage.

Marshall, C., & Rossman, G.B. (1995). *Designing qualitative research* (2nd ed). Thousand Oaks, CA: Sage.

Maykut, P., & Morehouse, R. (1994). *Beginning qualitative research.* Washington, DC: Falmer Press.

McCutcheon, G. (1981). On the interpretation of classroom observations. *Educational Researcher, 10,* 5–10.

Mead, M. (1928). *Coming of age in Samoa*. NY: William Morrow & Co.

Merriam, S.B. (1998). *Qualitative research and case study application in education*. San Francisco: Jossey-Bass.

Mischler, E.G. (1979). Meaning in context: Is there any other kind? *Harvard Educational Review, 49,* 2–10.

Mischler, E.G. (1990). Validation in inquiry-guided research: The role of exemplars in narrative studies. *Harvard Educational Review, 60,* 415–442.

National Commission for the Protection of Human Subjects of Biomedical and Behavioral Research. (1979). Ethical principles and guidelines for the protection of human subjects of research. The Belmont Report. Washington, DC: U.S. Government Printing Office.

Nozaki, Y. (2000). Essentializing dilemma and multiculturalist pedagogy: An ethnographic study of Japanese children in a U.S. school. *Anthropology and Education Journal, 31*(3), 355–380.

Perry, W.G. (1970). *Forms of intellectual and ethical development in the college years: A scheme*. New York: Holt, Rinehart, and Winston.

Peshkin, A. (1982). *The imperfect union: School consolidation and community conflict*. Chicago: University of Chicago Press.

Peshkin, A. (1984). Odd man out: The participant observer in an absolutist setting. *Sociology of Education, 57,* 254–264.

Peshkin, A. (1991). *The color of strangers, the color of friends: The play of ethnicity in school and community*. Chicago: University of Chicago Press.

Sales, B.D., & Folkman, S. (Eds.). (2000). *Ethics in research with human participants*. Washington, DC: American Psychological Association.

Schwandt, T.A., & Halpern, E.S. (1988). *Linking auditing and metaevaluation*. Beverly Hills, CA: Sage.

Spindler, G.D., & Hammond, L. (2000). The use of anthropological methods in educational research: Two perspectives. *Harvard Educational Review, 70*(1), 39–48.

Spradley, J.P. (1980). *Participant observation*. New York: Holt, Rinehart and Winston.

Stake, R.E. (1995). *The art of case study research*. Thousand Oaks, CA: Sage.

Strauss, A.L., & Corbin, J. (1998). *Basics of qualitative research: Techniques and procedures for developing grounded theory* (2nd ed). Thousand Oaks, CA: Sage.

Strauss, A.L., & Corbin, J. (Eds.). (1997). Grounded theory in practice. Thousand Oaks, CA: Sage.

Tierney, Patrick. (2000). *Darkness in El Dorado: How scientists and journalists devastated the Amazon*. New York: Norton.

Wolcott, H.F. (1992). Posturing in qualitative research. In M.D. LeCompte, W.L. Millroy, J. Preissle et al. *The handbook of qualitative research in education*. (pp. 3–53) New York: Academic Press.

Yin, R.K. (1991). *Applications of case study research*. Washington, DC: Cosmos Corporation.

KEY CONCEPTS

audit trail	inductive data analysis	qualitative inquiry
case study	internal criticism	quantitative research
concern for context	low-inference descriptor	referential adequacy
confirmability	member check	reflexivity
consensus	naturalistic observation	researcher bias
content (document) analysis	natural setting	researcher's relationship to
credibility	negative case sampling	participant
emergent design	neutrality	secondary source
ethnography	nonparticipant observation	structural corroboration
external criticism	observer bias	theoretical adequacy
focused interview	observer effect	transferability
historical research	participant observation	triangulation
human as instrument	peer debriefer	
hypothetico-deductive model	primary source	

EXERCISES

1. List four characteristics of qualitative research that distinguish it from quantitative research.

2. How do case studies differ from single-subject experiments?

3. Explain the concept of triangulation. How might it be used in a qualitative study on reading instruction in the elementary school?

4. Identify methods that qualitative researchers use to establish validity.

5. An investigator has a letter describing education in Britain in 1985. It is supposed to have been written by Prime Minister Margaret Thatcher.
   a. What question would be asked in external criticism?
   b. What question would be asked in internal criticism?

6. How are participants selected for a qualitative study?

7. What are the advantages and disadvantages of historical research as compared with other types of research?

8. Distinguish between participant and nonparticipant observation; give an example of each.

9. Compare the role of the hypothesis in qualitative and quantitative research.

10. Give an example of disguised participant observation.

11. What are field notes? What should they contain?

12. Suppose you want to determine the extent to which elementary school social studies textbooks are discussing the achievements of black Americans. How would you proceed to obtain data on this question?

13. What roles can a qualitative observer assume in a study?

14. Suggest a research question that could be answered best by using each of the following methods:
    a. Case study
    b. Ethnography
    c. Document analysis
    d. Phenomenological study

15. School systems in the United States are hiring an increasing number of social workers. You have been asked to gather data on what these social workers do and whether their presence in schools makes any difference for student achievement, student self-concept, discipline, and relations with parents. How would you design a qualitative study to answer this question? Indicate the method and the data-gathering procedure that you think would be most effective.

16. Assume you are going to prepare a qualitative research proposal for your research methods class or for a dissertation. List a question that you would like to investigate and then the qualitative method that would be most appropriate to use.

17. List some ethical concerns that may arise in qualitative research.

18. Why is external validity sometimes said to be weak in qualitative studies? How can it be enhanced?

19. What is the main difference between the interpretation of qualitative data and quantitative data?

20. What are the two main threats to the trustworthiness of observations in qualitative research?

ANSWERS

1. a. The nature of the data (qualitative is based on nonnumeric data)
    b. Qualitative research design evolves as research gets under way; no a priori hypotheses
    c. Type of data analysis
    d. Human instrument

2. Single-subject experiments focus on a single behavior or a very limited number of behaviors. The investigator introduces a specific treatment for the purpose of studying the effect of this treatment on the subject. A case study attempts to describe the subject's entire range of behavior as it occurs in a natural setting. The researcher observes the subject's behavior in relation to the influence of the physical, social, and psychological environment.

3. Triangulation is the use of multiple methods, data collection strategies, and/or multiple sources, in order to cross-validate information. The researcher would use different schools, different teachers, and collect data on reading instruction using different data collection methods, such as observations, interviews, and documents.

4. Prolonged engagement at the site; peer review; member checks; triangulation—the use of multiple observations, sources of data, and methods; periodic debriefing; and negative case sampling.

5. a. Was the letter really written by Margaret Thatcher?
    b. Does it accurately describe education in Britain in 1985?

6. Qualitative research uses purposive samples; subjects are selected because they can provide relevant information about the topic and setting investigated. A number of different strategies are used to get the sample of participants.

7. One advantage of historical research is the unlikelihood of researcher or experimental interaction effects confounding interpretation of findings. A historical perspective can deal with issues and past situations that cannot be handled experimentally. The main disadvantage is

the lack of experimental control, which makes unequivocal interpretation of data and generalization difficult. There is also the possibility of gathering inadequate or inaccurate information that is not verifiable.

8. In participant observation, the researcher actively participates in the group being studied. In nonparticipant observation, the researcher does not participate in any activity, but acts only as an observer. Examples will vary.

9. Qualitative researchers do not, typically, formulate hypotheses before the research and then proceed to test them. Hypotheses are formulated inductively as the research proceeds. Quantitative researchers, in contrast, formulate a hypothesis at the beginning of the research and then proceed deductively to identify what should be observed if the hypothesis is correct, then make the observations needed to test the hypothesis.

10. A researcher might take a job as a waitress or waiter in a neighborhood bar in order to study this particular social unit.

11. Field notes are the notes recorded in the field by a researcher doing a qualitative study. They consist of what the researcher sees or hears, or interpretations of observations. They have two components: descriptive (what the researcher sees and hears) and reflective (what the researcher thinks or feels).

12. A content analysis would be the appropriate research design. One would obtain a sample of widely used social studies textbooks and then set up categories and proceed to go through the books making counts of the number of times the achievements of black Americans are mentioned within each of the categories. The categories might be males, females, or they might involve the fields in which the achievements were made, such as music, science, literature, and so on.

13. The observer can be a participant observer who engages fully in the activities being studied, but is known to the group as a researcher. The researcher can be a nonparticipant observer, who observes but does not participate. In between these roles are combinations of the two extremes. The observer can also be a covert observer in which his or her identity is hidden from the group.

14. Answers will vary.

15. Answers will vary.

16. Answers will vary.

17. The researcher may face ethical dilemmas involving anonymity, confidentiality, what to do with "guilty knowledge," deception, and so on.

18. External validity concerns generalizability of the findings of research. Qualitative researchers refer to generalizability as *transferability*. It can be achieved in qualitative studies if the writer supplies thick, rich description so that readers can decide on the similarity of the two settings. But transferability (external validity) is not a major concern of the qualitative researcher.

19. Quantitative researchers use statistical tests as a basis for interpreting the data. Qualitative researchers analyze data inductively by organizing data into categories, identifying patterns and themes, and writing descriptive narratives.

20. Observer bias and observer effect

 ## INFOTRAC COLLEGE EDITION

Using the key word *grounded theory,* search for an article that used this approach in qualitative research (educational research, if possible). Why do you think grounded theory was the appropriate method to investigate this problem?

Chapter 15

Qualitative Research: Data Analysis and Reporting

After studying this chapter, the student will be able to:

1. Describe the general procedure followed in the analysis of qualitative data.

2. State the role of categories in qualitative data analysis.

3. Identify the most commonly used approaches to data analysis in qualitative research.

4. Specify the difference between data analysis and data interpretation.

5. Identify the components of a qualitative report.

6. State some of the criteria to use in evaluating a qualitative study.

The final activities in qualitative inquiry are analyzing and interpreting the data collected and presenting the results. Maykut and Morehouse (1994) state that data analysis is the heart of qualitative research and the process that most distinguishes qualitative from quantitative research. The challenge facing the researcher at this stage is to make sense of copious amounts of data and to construct a framework for communicating the essence of what the data reveal. Data analysis is a process whereby researchers systematically search and arrange the data in order to increase their understanding of the data and to enable them to present what they learned to others. As you will see, it is a process of making successive approximations toward the goal of describing and explaining the phenomenon under investigation.

ANALYZING DATA

Data analysis is a time-consuming and difficult process, because typically the researcher faces massive amounts of field notes, interview transcripts, reflections, and information from documents to examine and interpret. Analysis involves reducing and organizing the data, synthesizing, searching for significant patterns, and discovering what is important. The task can appear overwhelming, but becomes manageable when broken down into stages. Three steps are involved in data analysis: organizing the data, summarizing the data, and interpreting the data.

Organizing

The first step in analyzing qualitative data involves organizing the data. Bogdan and Biklen (1998) suggest that the researcher can actually begin some data analysis in the field, while collecting the data. You can begin to narrow the focus of the study, write observer comments, compare data with working hypotheses, and so on. The major task of organizing the large body of information begins, however, after you have completed data collection and have left the site.

Make sure that field notes, interview transcripts, audiotapes, observer comments, and other data are put into a readable form ready for analysis. We recommend that the data be typed. Maykut and Morehouse (1994) suggest that each page of data be marked to indicate the kind and source of the data and the page number of the particular data set. For example, the first page (1) of field notes from observing (O) at Central Middle School is coded O/CMS-1. Photocopy all data pages, and work from the copies. Always keep a backup copy of the original data.

The first thing to do in organizing is to reduce the data, which is done through a process called *coding*. Wiersma (1995) suggests that organizing through coding is analogous to getting ready for a rummage sale (p. 216): You sort the stuff for the sale into categories—housewares, clothing, furniture, books, and so on. You might further subdivide the categories: The clothing category would include children's clothing, teenagers' clothing, adults' clothing. Then each of these clothing categories could be further subdivided; for example, the children's clothing could be categorized as infants', toddlers', and school-age children's clothes; each of these categories could be further subdivided into boys' and girls' clothes.

Similarly, the field notes, transcripts, and other qualitative data are categorized. The most common approach is to read and reread all the data and sort them by looking for units of meaning—words, phrases, sentences, subjects' ways of thinking, behavior patterns, and events that seem to appear regularly and that seem important. Each unit of meaning should be understandable without any additional information. This classification of similar ideas, concepts, activities, themes, setting, and so on represents a **category.** You identify each unit of meaning (category) by choosing a word or phrase that describes the essence of the category; these words become the codes for the categories. The coding system facilitates further reviews of the data.

Developing coding categories enables the researcher to physically separate material bearing on a given topic from other material and is a crucial step in organizing the data. The goal is to come up with a set of categories that provide a reasonable reconstruction of the data that have been collected (Lincoln & Guba, 1985, p. 347). The categories should be internally consistent, but distinct from one another. The categories one investigator uses to organize qualitative data may not be the same categories another researcher would use to organize the same data. The researcher's interests and style and the research question influence to a great extent the categories chosen. Bogdan and Biklen (1998) suggest some coding categories that might be used:

1. *Setting/context codes.* These codes contain general information—on the setting, topic, subjects, and other materials—that places the study in a larger context. A study of an elementary school, for example, would place descriptive data about the school in this category.

2. *Definition of the situation codes.* These codes include data on how the subjects view the setting and their role in it. Data on how teachers really view their work ("love it" or "just surviving") would be put in this category.

3. *Perspectives held by subjects.* This category includes more specific ways of thinking that subjects may share, as well as their orientation toward particular aspects of a setting. Particular phrases that subjects use often reflect their perspectives.

4. *Subjects' ways of thinking about people and objects.* Subjects' understandings of each other, of outsiders, and of the objects in their world would be placed in this category. For example, teachers may have labels they apply to students, such as "achievers," "underachievers," or "troublemakers."

5. *Process codes.* These codes are words and phrases that enable you to categorize sequences of events, changes over time, or moving from one kind of status to another. For example, a teacher's description of the stages in his or her career would be put in this category.

6. *Activity codes.* These codes refer to regularly occurring kinds of behavior within a setting, such as assemblies, lunch, parent conferences, as well as informal behaviors such as students' "horsing around" or "rough housing."

7. *Event codes.* Event codes refer to particular activities in the subjects' lives that happen infrequently or only one time. The events may have happened prior to the research study. For example, a "student protest" or a "teacher strike" would be coded in this category.

8. *Strategy codes.* These refer to the methods, techniques, ploys, and other ways that subjects accomplish what they want and avoid what they don't want. Teachers, for example, employ strategies in teaching, to control students's behavior, or to get class assignments they want. Any comments teachers might make relevant to strategies would be placed in this category.

9. *Relationship and social structure codes.* This category includes regular patterns of behavior in a setting that describe the social structure. Any data about cliques, romances, friendships, enemies, and so on would be coded in this category.

10. *Methods codes.* This category includes the research procedures, methods, problems, and reflections to which the researcher refers during the inquiry.

See the Bodgan and Biklen text (1998) for a discussion and examples of data to include in each of the preceding coding categories.

The number of categories used will depend on the type of data collected, the focus of inquiry, and the researcher's analytic skills. If the number of categories is very large, collapse them into a manageable number. Bogdan and Biklen (1998) recommend using thirty to fifty categories, assigning each a code abbreviation or a number. Some writers put the list of coding categories in alphabetical order, which facilitates remembering the coding system.

Next go through all the data and mark each unit (paragraph or sentences) with the appropriate code. As the codes are developed, qualitative researchers can count the frequency with which these codes appear, which gives some insight into the importance of that category of meaning. Exhibit 15.1 shows field notes that have been coded. Notice that the marginal labels are category codes; other data that may be related to "teachers' work" would also be coded similarly and placed in that category.

After all the data are coded, place all paragraphs having the same coding categories together. You can do this manually by cutting with scissors according to the codes, and putting material with like codes together in a marked folder. Or you can do it using one of several computer programs. This classification simplifies further analysis, because you have similar material together and thus don't have to search through volumes of notes to find it.

Two strategies are widely used in qualitative data analysis: constant comparison and negative case analysis. Perhaps the best known strategy and the one described in the previous discussion is the **constant comparative method** that combines inductive category coding with simultaneous comparison of all units of meaning obtained (Glaser & Strauss, 1967). The researcher examines each new unit of meaning (topics or concepts) to determine its distinctive characteristics. Then compare categories and group them with similar categories. If there are no similar units of meaning, form a new category. Thus there

Fieldnotes

Vista City Elementary School Teachers' Lounge

Date: February 3, 1981

teachers' work

Then I went down to the teachers' lounge to see if anybody might hap-pen to be there. I was in luck. Jill Martin sat at the first table <u>correcting papers;</u> Kathy Thomas was also there walking around and smoking. I said, "Hi Jill, hi Kathy. Okay if I join you?" "Sure," Jill said. "You and your husband have been to China, right?" I said, "Yes Why?" Jill then turned to Kathy and said, "Have you studied China yet? Sari has slides that she can show." <u>Kathy said</u> to me that <u>she was going to study world communities, even though "they" had taken them out of the sixth-grade social studies curriculum "Now can you tell me who 'they' are?" I asked her. She said, "You know, 'them': 'they'."</u>

authority

autonomy

Both Jill and Kathy were upset at how they had mandated what the teachers could teach in their rooms. "They" turned out to be the central office who had communicated the state's revised sixth-grade social studies curriculum. The state has "taken out all the things that we think are important" from the curriculum and has substituted the theme of "economic geography" for the sixth-graders to study.

doing your own thing

Both Jill and Kathy think that "sixth-graders can't comprehend eco-nomic geography well," and think world communities of Africa and Asia are more important. They said they planned to teach what they wanted to anyway. Kathy said, "They'll come around one of these days." "Oh, Kathy, are you a rebel?" I asked. "No." she replied, "I'm just doing my own thing."

parents

After we chatted for a little while, Jill turned to me: <u>"You're interested in what concerns us. I guess one thing is parents."</u> She proceeded to describe a parent conference she had participated in yesterday after-noon with a child's parents and a child's psychiatrist. She said, "What really upsets me is how much responsibility they placed on me to change the child's behavior." They seemed to give lip service, she reported, to have "controls" come from the child when they said, "It's so difficult for parents to see that kids need to take responsibility for their actions."

parents

■ EXHIBIT 15.1
Coded Fieldnotes

Source: From *Qualitative Research for Education: An Introduction to Theory and Methods* (3rd ed.), p. 185, by R.C. Bogdan & S.K. Biklen, 1998, Boston: Allyn and Bacon.

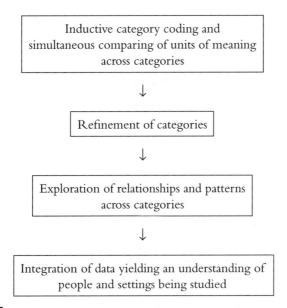

■ FIGURE 15.1

Constant Comparative Method of Data Analysis

Source: From *Beginning Qualitative Research,* (p. 135) by P. Maykut & R. Morehouse, 1994, Washington, DC: Falmer Press.

is a process of continuous refinement; initial categories may be changed, merged, or omitted; new categories are generated; and new relationships can be discovered (Goertz & LeCompte, 1993). Figure 15.1 illustrates the constant comparative method of data analysis.

See chapter 9 of Maykut and Morehouse (1994) for an excellent discussion of how to apply the constant comparative method of data analysis. Miles and Huberman (1994) is also a useful reference book for qualitative data analysis.

Another approach used in analysis is the **negative case analysis** and **discrepant data analysis.** Look for data that are negative or discrepant from the main body of data collected. Negative cases contradict the main category or pattern, and discrepant cases provide a different perspective on a category or pattern. This approach provides a counterbalance to a researcher's tendency to hold on to first impressions or hunches. Some researchers revise based on these instances; others go with the substantial accumulation of positive instances.

Summarizing

The next step is to summarize; here you begin to see what is in the data. Examine all entries with the same code, and then merge these categories into patterns by finding links and connections among categories. This process further integrates the data, and you can begin to make some statements about relationships and themes in the data. For example, when investigating classroom management in a large high school, you might first code the data into categories dealing with teachers' attitudes, students' attitudes, effect of certain techniques, descriptions of behavior, the setting, and so on. Then you would summarize by trying to find relationships among the categories.

Using Computers in Data Analysis

Several computer programs are available to aid in analyzing qualitative data. Kelle (1995) and Weitzman and Miles (1995) review some of the qualitative analysis programs available. Because technology changes so rapidly, it is not worthwhile to make a recommendation about a particular program here.

Using a computer saves an enormous amount of time in compiling and sorting data. For example, you can take a laptop computer into the field to write notes during observations. Computer programs exist to help with storing and organizing files and texts, inputting data from word processors, searching for words or categories, making counts of words and categories, and displaying information about aspects of the study.

Some writers in the field believe that computers are most beneficial to the experienced researcher. They believe that to really understand the data, beginning researchers need to "eyeball" and frequently re-examine the data, rather than depend on what the computer provides. An example of using the computer software called NUD★IST (Nonnumerical Unstructured Data Indexing Searching and Theory-Building) in a qualitative study can be found in Buston's article in Bryman and Burgess (1999, vol. 3, pp. 183–202).

Interpreting

In interpretation, the researcher goes beyond the descriptive data to extract meaning and insights from the data. You tell what you found that was important, why it is important, and what can be learned from it.

Interpreting involves reflecting about the words and acts of the study's participants, and abstracting important understandings from them. It is an inductive process, in which you make generalizations based on the connections and common aspects among the categories and patterns. You evaluate the plausibility of some of the hypotheses that have evolved during the analysis. Hypotheses are tested by going through the data again and searching for supporting data as well as negative or deviant cases.

Interpreting qualitative data is difficult, because there are no set rules to follow. The quality of the interpretation depends on the background, perspective, knowledge, and theoretical orientation of the researcher and the intellectual skills he or she brings to the task. Unlike quantitative research, there are no statistical tests of significance to facilitate interpretation of qualitative data. Patton (1990) makes an interesting comment on interpretation when he advises researchers to "make the obvious obvious, make the obvious dubious, and make the hidden obvious" (p. 423). That is, in interpreting qualitative data you confirm what you already know is supported by the data, you question what you think you know and eliminate misconceptions, and you illuminate new insights and important things that you didn't know but should.

Although interpretation is personal and proceeds without set rules, this does not mean that the qualitative researcher can rely strictly on personal feelings when interpreting the data. The interpretation cannot be just a figment of your imagination, but must be supported by the data. There are some guidelines to consider. Dey (1993) lists six questions you should ask to check on the quality of your data:

1. Are the data based on your own observation, or is it hearsay?

2. Is there corroboration by others of your observations?

3. In what circumstances was an observation made or reported?

4. How reliable are the people providing the data?

5. What motivations might have influenced a participant's report?

6. What biases might have influenced how an observation was made or reported?

REPORTING

The last step for the qualitative researcher is to write about what he or she saw, heard, and now understands about the phenomenon that was investigated. Reports of qualitative inquiry will, of course, vary in form depending on the nature of the publication in which they appear (for example, a paper prepared for the *American Educational Research Journal* will differ from a monograph or book-length study). It will be helpful to the student who is writing a qualitative report to look at journal articles to see how the reports are organized.

If you have written a good proposal prior to beginning the research, you already have information that can be used in the final report. For example, the proposal contains the problem statement and the methods section, which you can expand to include any further sampling and data collection procedures that were used. Qualitative reports generally include the following elements (or some variation of them):

Abstract

Introduction

Research design
    Steps to ensure trustworthiness (validity and reliability)

Methods
    Sample
    Data collection methods
    Data analysis procedures

Outcomes

Implications

References

Appendix

Next, each of these sections will be discussed briefly.

Abstract

An abstract is a very brief summary (100 to 200 words) of the major aspects of the qualitative inquiry: problem, design, methods, and outcomes. Concise abstracts are very helpful to readers who are conducting literature reviews.

Introduction

In the introduction, the writer states the purpose of the research study and provides the reader with some background of the problem and the need for the study. State the focus of inquiry as a question or a statement. Indicate how you became interested in the topic and how the question evolved. Present and discuss any relevant research in this section, because typically there is not a separate section for review of the literature.

Research Design

In the section on research design, explain the qualitative approach used and why you chose it to investigate the problem. Also discuss the steps taken to ensure trustworthiness of the study, such as triangulation, audit trail, member checks, and so forth. We discussed these procedures at length in Chapter 14.

Methods

In the methods section, you describe the research method that was followed to arrive at the findings. The reader should not have to wonder about what was done, to whom, or how it was done. Some aspects to cover in separate parts of the methods section are as follows.

Sample

In discussing the sample, the investigator describes the participants, how they were selected, and how entry was gained into the site; gives a detailed description of the site; and so on. Researchers generally use fictitious names of people and places to protect the privacy of the participants and the site.

Data Collection Methods

The section on data collection methods describes the methods used to gather the data (interviews, observation, document analysis, and so on) and explains why these methods were chosen. Because the *main* instrument in qualitative research is the human instrument, it is important that the writer give some personal or professional information about him- or herself that might be relevant to the inquiry. A complete discussion of the methodology is essential so that readers of the report can understand how the researcher reached conclusions, and can agree or disagree with them.

Data Analysis Procedures

The researcher should describe the approach taken in the analysis of the data. If you used the constant comparative procedure, for example, make this explicit.

Outcomes

The outcomes section contains the major findings or propositions relevant to the original focus of inquiry that are revealed in the data. Because of the massive amount of data in a qualitative inquiry, you cannot report everything you found. In fact, Wolcott (1990) has said that the real challenge for qualitative researchers is deciding what *not* to include in their reports. The researcher must rank the outcomes primarily on the basis of their relevance and significance. Use direct quotes and field note exerpts to illustrate the outcomes of the study and to help the reader to vicariously experience the research setting and to better understand how the conclusions were reached. Unlike quantitative research, this section also includes your interpretations of the data. You may also relate findings to the literature.

Implications

In the final section, you respond to the implicit question, So what? You discuss the meaning of the outcomes reported in the previous section and state major conclusions and implications of the study. You should relate the study to previous research and suggest directions for future research efforts.

References

A complete alphabetical listing of all works cited in the report is presented in the reference section of the report.

Appendix

The appendix includes interview schedules and other documentation that will help the reader understand the report.

WRITING QUALITATIVE RESEARCH REPORTS

Writing is extremely important in qualitative research. Qualitative reports are generally heavily narrative in form and contain rich descriptions of setting and context. This "thick description" is intended to place the reader vividly in the research setting so that the reader can follow the logical processes that the researcher went through in collecting the data. In contrast to the more technical and rigid style of quantitative reports, a qualitative report is more like a story, with very little, if any, technical language. Qualitative reports convey the participants' thoughts, feelings, and experiences in their own words as much as possible. Note that it is acceptable in qualitative reports for writers to refer to themselves in the first person, to distinguish their opinions from those of the participants.

Dey (1993) says that writing a qualitative report is like telling a story with a setting, characters, and a plot that unfolds toward some resolution. Dey provides six guidelines for writing the report:

1. Engage interest through description and dramatization.
2. Trace the evolution of the account.
3. Develop overall coherence.
4. Select key themes.
5. Use simple language.
6. Make concepts and connections explicit.

Qualitative reporting is illustrated in the following excerpt from a qualitative study of teacher relationships with at-risk students (Hughes, 1997):

> The research design began with the selection of four teachers to be primary subjects. Two of the teachers chosen are highly successful in working with at-risk students and the other two teachers have not been successful with at-risk students. . . .
>
> My first less successful (LS) teacher, Paul S., is a veteran teacher. Paul teaches eighth-grade social studies in a traditional style. A daily lesson begins with a 10- to 15-minute lecture and then the students are to complete a worksheet. Paul considers the book supplied by the school to be "too hard" for the students, so his curriculum is based on a series of worksheets that he writes or copies from printed curriculum. He describes his teaching style as "aided practice with minimal evaluations." He believes that students should be homogeneously grouped. This belief contradicts the district and school policy of heterogeneously grouped students in academic teams. He feels that because students are not grouped by levels, he is unable to teach effectively. Therefore, Paul gears his curriculum toward the low-performing students.
>
> SHERRY (researcher): How would you describe the effectiveness of your teaching style?
>
> PAUL: For what I have to work with, the attitudes and work habits, I think my teaching style is about the best we can do.
>
> The class sits in rows and the room has a very clean, neat appearance. The bulletin boards are covered with class schedules and administrative bulletins. On the front board hang discipline charts for each class period. The only posters that hang in the room are two computer-printed banners stating the district's theme for the academic year, "Let's Make It Happen!" These banners became somewhat ironic as I learned about Paul's methodology. Paul believes that "There isn't a way to have a successful class with these types of students." He also believes that if a student does not come to school with their "head on right," well-fed, well-rested, prepared for class, and open to learning, then that student should be removed from the classroom.

SHERRY: What disciplinary procedures achieve appropriate behavior in your classroom?

PAUL: Not that much works. Good teachers aren't in inner-city schools. . . .

PAUL: I have gone to a survival mode, what can I do to get through the day and eliminate damage control? Just survive.

The students interviewed showed little or no respect for either L.S. teacher. Students claimed that they and other students intentionally made fun of and acted defiant in the classroom of the two L.S. subjects.

SHERRY: What kinds of things did you do in his (Paul's) class?

STUDENT: Throw paper airplanes.

As this example illustrates, reports of qualitative studies present the natural language of the study's participants as drawn from interview data and observation, along with rich descriptions of the setting. The example continues with the researcher providing the reader with an account of a successful teacher of at-risk students:

Jane currently teaches eighth-grade social studies. Jane claims that there are "no typical days in her classroom." She does a variety of assignments including book work, reading maps, class discussions, and making three-dimensional models.

SHERRY: What do you consider your students' role to be in your classroom?

JANE: They are the workers and the learners; they need to be actively involved.

She is always very eager to try new and different idea. Jane's room was very organized and the place seemed almost like "home." Scattered throughout the room were big round tables that sat four students comfortably. In the front right corner of the room was the "living room." There was a couch, rocking chair, and a bookshelf filled with a variety of books. The walls were very decorative, and the room was covered with affirmative anecdotes or quotes, such as "We can work it out," and the positive consequences of her discipline management plan. During both observations, the agenda for the day and the instructions for the lesson were written in detail on the front board.

Jane is a very positive, upbeat person, and she emphasizes courtesy and respect in her classroom. She rewards students verbally, and also with personal attention. She gives a variety of rewards for perfect attendance, most improved, and good behavior. Jane enjoys being very involved and "hands-on" with students.

SHERRY: Why do you like Ms. Peterson's class?

STUDENT: Because she is nice to me.

SHERRY: Do you like social studies?

STUDENT: No, I just like Ms. Peterson.

(p. 83-97)

EVALUATING QUALITATIVE STUDIES

The following are some of the criteria used to evaluate qualitative reports:

1. Is the research question stated, and does the researcher make clear the conceptual and theoretical framework for the study?

2. Does the researcher show the relationship between the study and previous studies?

3. Does the researcher indicate how and why the participants were selected for the study and the extent to which they are representative of other participants in that setting?

4. Are the data collection methods explained so that the reader can judge if they were adequate? Does the researcher explain his or her role as participant observer or nonparticipant observer, interviewer, and so on?

5. Does the researcher explain the data analysis procedures used?

6. Are the strategies used to enhance the trustworthiness of the data (that is, triangulation and audit trail) described? Are competing hypotheses presented and discussed?

7. Are the descriptive data separate from the interpretations?

8. Is there evidence that the researcher maintained ethical standards?

9. Does the study answer the research question and suggest further questions for investigation? Does the researcher make explicit the theoretical significance of the study?

10. Does the report qualify any generalizations that were made, and does it help the reader see how what was learned might be transferred to another similar situation?

SUMMARY

Qualitative studies typically result in a massive amount of data. Analyzing the data is thus a tedious and time-consuming process. The first step in analysis is to organize the data by looking for words, phrases, and events that appear regularly and putting those with similar units of meaning into a category. One continues until one has a set of categories that provide a reasonable reconstruction of the data collected. Next one compares and tries to find connections and common themes among the categories. Interpretation is a highly personal activity in which the researcher explains the meaning of the data and why it is important.

Using thick, rich description, the qualitative researcher writes a narrative report of what was learned in the study. The exact format of the report depends on the nature of the report—whether it is a dissertation, journal article, or perhaps a presentation.

EXAMPLE OF A QUALITATIVE RESEARCH STUDY

The Alford (2000) article illustrates many aspects of qualitative research. Note the use of emergent design, lack of a priori hypotheses, unstructured interviews, and triangulation.

A Qualitative Study of the College Social Adjustment of Black Students from Lower Socioeconomic Communities

SCHEVALETTA M. ALFORD

Superficial gains made by Black students studying in the United States have created the illusion that college access and retention rates have improved. However, to support their education, commuter students from lower socioeconomic communities have developed coping skills that inhibit positive social adjustment. This article presents an examination of Black commuter-student relationships and associations.

Higher education enrollment rate of 3% for Black students has remained at a virtual standstill in recent years compared with enrollment rates of other minorities (Hollins, 1996). Yet, this slight increase has led some members of the United States government to assume that affirmative action programs are no longer necessary (Healy, 1998; Schmidt, 1997). Research also shows that Blacks are still behind in the struggle to stay in school although the first retention programs were originally designed for them (Ford, 1997, p. 36).

Some Black students, especially those from lower socioeconomic communities, leave college almost as quickly as they enter (Astin, 1988; Levine & Associates, 1990; Noel, Levitz, Saluri, & Associates, 1991). Studies examining attrition have attempted to explain the languid growth rate of numbers of Black students and poor retention of these students, pointing to weaknesses in their college preparation (cf. Astin, 1988, 1993; Browne-Miller, 1996). Other important factors influencing retention included the inability of students to reach and maintain college-level academic standards, incongruent personal and college goals, and lack of motivation or interest (cf. Astin, 1993; Tinto, 1987). Most of these explanations place the responsibility on the students; they blame the victim.

Fordham and Ogbu (1986) explained that many Black students come from personal environments that block them from attending college. Black students from the inner city who devote their time to their studies are considered to be "acting White." They are often ostracized by their peers. Therefore, when Blacks do attend college they are often socially excluded (cf. Fries-Britt, 1998; Mow & Nettles, 1990). Fleming (1984) describes academic environments that, although not outwardly hostile, provide little or no social support to Black students. Many of these students devise coping skills that allow them to function in the college academic environment. However, these skills do not always support the social adjustment of the students.

LITERATURE REVIEW

A review of the literature on college social adjustment points to the difficulties that students encounter as they attempt to become acquainted with college life (cf. Astin,

1993; Delworth, Hanson, & Associates, 1989; Pascarella & Terenzini, 1991). These studies have been primarily based on models that emphasize the lifestyles of residential students (cf. Huebner, 1989; Pascarella & Terenzini, 1991). Models of this type focus on factors within the college campus environment, (i.e., influences within the college community. However, increasing college costs and changing lifestyles have created the trend toward commuting).

As early as 1985, researchers found that 59 percent of the nation's students commuted (Stewart, Merrill, & Saluri, 1991). Black students are definitely included in this group.

Considering the rising college costs, it is very likely that this percentage has increased. Therefore, more studies are beginning to emphasize the examination of external factors that affect college adjustment (cf. Paul & Kelleher, 1995; Terenzini, Pascarella, & Blimling, 1996). Students who do not live in residence halls or within the confines of their colleges must make psychological shifts between their homes and their schools (Alford, 1998; Banning & Hughes, 1986).

Researchers

Astin (1988, 1993), Fleming (1984), Hurtado (1992), Neville, Heppner, and Wang (1997) have found that race, ethnicity, and socioeconomic factors further complicate student adjustment to college. For Black students from lower socioeconomic communities, developing and sustaining relationships with individuals who understand the college environment is an even greater challenge (Anderson, 1994; Dalton, 1989; Fleming, 1984; Gonchar, 1995; Jaynes & Williams, 1989; Tinto, 1987). If they are not extroverts, these students do not seek new associations (Fleming, 1984; Pascarella & Terenzini, 1991). Research shows that when students reside in communities in which values are noticeably different from those of their colleges, adjustment is significantly affected (cf. Astin, 1988; Gonchar, 1995; Malone, 1992).

Theoretical Underpinning

An underlying theory directly connected to college student adjustment comes from the work of Kurt Lewin (1936). According to Lewin, B = f (P, E); that is, an individual's behavior (B) is the result of the interaction (f) between the person (P) and the environment (E). Bronfenbrenner (1977) systematized Lewin's theory and created what is known as the ecological model. This organizing model can be used to understand the problems students encounter in adapting to different environments.

In the Bronfenbrenner model, the individual social relationships in which the student is involved are called microsystems. These include the relationships between the student and his or her family members, in-and-out of school friends, team members, and so forth. The confederation of microsystems is the student's mesosystem. The values held within the separate microsystems interact, overlap, and, at times, clash with one another.

When the values of the separate microsystems support one another, the mesosystem is harmonious. For example, if out-of-school peers, family members, and team members support college values, the mesosystem is harmonious. However, if the values in these units do not support college values, the student's mesosystem is dissonant. Thus, the ability of inner-city commuter students to stabilize relationships and values in their mesosystem might be difficult.

This difficulty directly affects college retention (Kuh & Whitt, 1988). The two other environmental influences of the Bronfenbrenner model are the exosystem and the macrosystem. The exosystem includes the sociopolitical and socioeconomic influences of the environments closest to the student, such as the community in which the student lives and attends college. Because this is an external environment, it exerts control over the mesosystem, which in turn affects the microsystems. The all-encompassing environment exerting indirect and, at times, direct influence on all the other systems is the macrosystem. This environment includes "cultural, social, political, legal, economic, religious, and educational values" (Bronfenbrenner, 1977) of a nation. The macrosystem suggests national standards for all aspects of life, from physical attractiveness to public policy (Muuss, 1996). It is most easily described as the sociopolitical climate of the nation. For example, as the number of conservative politicians has increased, the nation has become more conservative in its policies regarding affirmative action.

Because affirmative action initiatives are seen as liberal, they have been on the decline. This decline directly affects Black students from lower socioeconomic backgrounds because many of these students gained entrance to college through affirmative action programs. Therefore, we see the number of Black students enrolling in certain colleges decreasing as these programs disappear.

PURPOSE OF THE STUDY

I decided to conduct an exploratory study using the Bronfenbrenner model because of the need to better understand the factors affecting the retention of commuter students. The study focused on the methods used by these students to balance their mesosystems, examining the types of associations students made, why these associations developed, and whether the alliances had any impact on retention. The mesosystems consist of their home life, neighborhood peers, and college peers.

Qualitative and quantitative methodologies were used to thoroughly explore the types of associations that developed among the students (Stage & Associates, 1992). In this article I present a summary of the essential aspects of the qualitative data collected on the lower socioeconomic Black students who participated in the study and the analysis of that data. I also discuss the implication of the findings for counselors working with Black students who commute from lower socioeconomic communities to campuses.

METHOD

To understand the formation of relationships by Black commuter students the method used in this study was interviewing (Patton, 1990; Stage et al., 1992; Taylor & Bogdan, 1984). Anthropological methods have been cited as well suited for investigating college students because these methods provide "an insider's perspective on what is happening in the group's natural setting" (Stage et al., 1992, p. 17).

Interviews were conducted on two levels: focus group and individual. This allowed information gathered during the two types of interviews to be cross-referenced. It also served as an integral part of the triangulation process, a process using multiple methods to study an issue or phenomenon. This is a requirement of qualitative research methodology (cf. Patton, 1990; Stage et al., 1992). The final component of the triangulation was student counseling records. The records were examined to verify comments made during interviews. Data collected from group interviews, individual interviews, and counseling records served as the basis for triangulation.

Participants

Fifteen students were recruited from educational opportunity programs at two 4-year urban commuter colleges in the North Atlantic region of the United States, which includes states from Pennsylvania to Maine. These students responded positively to a request for individuals to discuss "friendships in and outside college." Although all of the students identified themselves as Black, 5 specified the Caribbean nations from which they had come. Counseling records showed that the 5 students arrived in the United States before they were 10 years old and that they lived in predominantly lower socioeconomic U.S. Caribbean communities for more than 10 years. A study by Waters (1996) showed that the cultural heritage of the Caribbean students might have influenced their attitudes and beliefs, and therefore, the national origins of these students were included in the profiles.

Three of the 5 Caribbean students were women, and the other 2 were men. Nine of the other students were women and 1 was a man. The students ranged in age from 18 to 30. Four students were 22, and only 1 was 30. Five of the students were freshmen; 4 were sophomores; 4 were juniors, and 2 were seniors. The following profiles provide essential facts about the lives of the students (pseudonyms have been used).

Edwena is a 22-year-old full-time sophomore from Jamaica. She is a single parent who has been assaulted by her daughter's father. She has lupus.

Lorraine is a 20-year-old sophomore separated from her husband. She has taken care of her delinquent teenage sister since the death of their mother.

Maureen is a 30-year-old senior employed full-time in an extremely high-risk job. She attends college part-time.

Caroline, a 22-year-old junior, lives at home with her disabled father and a number of tenants, most of whom are against Caroline's educational pursuits.

Claudia is a 24-year-old senior who lives with her mother and brother. Her brother is also attending college. Both children help their mother with expenses.

Ron, a 19-year-old first-year student, works on campus. He lives with his single mother and grandmother.

Art, a 20-year-old Trinidadian sophomore, works a tremendous amount of overtime for a courier service.

Raylone is a 19-year-old first-year student, who works full-time at a law firm. She lives with her grandmother and has many friends in her neighborhood.

Coline, a 22-year-old junior, lives with her mother and five siblings. She is actively involved in student government.

Naria is an 18-year-old first-year student, of South-Asian descent, born in Guyana. She lives with both parents and a large fictive family. She works full-time to contribute to the household.

Grandis is a popular 18-year-old Haitian first-year student, who resides with his parents and extended family. He works long hours.

Siniqua, a 24-year-old divorced mother of two, resides with her mother and sister and works part-time. Siniqua is a junior.

Kathy is a 22-year-old Jamaican junior who lives with her mother and four sisters, all of whom attend college.

Lindell, a 20-year-old sophomore who works 20 hours per week, seeks a new job that will give her more hours.

Tracy, an 18-year-old first-year student, is actively seeking employment other than her present baby-sitting.

Procedure

Using an interview protocol (see the Appendix), the researcher, an American-born Black woman, facilitated discussions among participants centering on friendships within the college and the community and the impact of those friendships on their progress through college. Each group interview was conducted with an independent observer (an American-born Black woman) present to verify that questions were asked in the same manner.

The group interviews lasted from 1½ hours to 2½ hours, whereas "individuals" lasted from a ½ hour to 2 hours. The interview protocol was the same for both group and individual interviews. Changes were made only when syntax was inappropriate.

Individuals were able to discuss issues in greater depth when interviewed alone than they were during group interviews. The individual discussions verified, clarified, and validated information obtained during group interviews. The candid discussions were taped and transcribed by a professional transcriber. The researcher also reviewed counseling and academic records for all student participants.

DATA ANALYSIS

A trained three-member team consisting of one American-born Black woman and two Caribbean-born Black women read the interview transcripts. The analysis was done on two levels. First, recurring responses to interview questions were identified as "sensitizing concepts or themes." The concepts served as a framework for the description of student adjustment. Second, common elements reflecting implicit beliefs and ideas, "indigenous concepts or themes," were identified.

For triangulation, counselor notes in student files were compared with the students' comments to learn whether themes and concepts identified reflected the students' lives. Thus, the three elements of triangulation were the two types of interviews, group and individual, and the counselor notes.

FINDINGS

The comments made during the interviews provided a gateway to understanding the method by which Black commuter students from lower socioeconomic communities managed their associations in and outside the college. Whether American-born or Caribbean-born, the Black students who participated in this study showed no clear differences in their behavior or attitude regarding their social environments. These relationships, or microsystems, were the social foundations of the lives of the students. The following are the most salient comments made by students that succinctly capture the ideas expressed by all the participants.

Limited Community Affiliation

Students in this study generally had very few friends in their neighborhoods. This situation existed because of self and parental imposed isolation. Some students explained that they never developed friendships in their communities. Edwena described her behavior in the following manner:

> I never had a lot of friends in the neighborhood. Actually none because I'm the type of a person that from school, I go home, right in the house and start reading my books. [My mother] used to try to force me and say, "Go outside and play with those kids." But sometimes I used to have like a phobia inside of me like I didn't want to be around them.

Kathy made the following comment:

> Well for me personally, I don't really have friends in my neighborhood. I wasn't born here—I grew up in Jamaica. It was something different. When I was growing up there, I had friends in my neighborhood. [In America] I never went to a school that was in my district, and I never even wanted to be surrounded by people [who] lived there. I always wanted to go places with new people.

The students had limited affiliations with their neighborhood peers whenever they had not lived in their neighborhoods from early childhood. Counseling records showed that these students had arrived in their new communities before the age of 10. However, the students usually had no friends because they were unable to continue friendships that had begun before moving into the new neighborhood. Students who lived in new neighborhoods within the same city or town were not permitted by their parents to return to old neighborhoods. As for the students from other countries, trips to their native countries were rare. For students who had continuously lived in the same neighborhood, a parent or parents had prevented them from developing neighborhood friendships. The following is a statement from Lorraine:

> When we [were] younger, she [my mother] was on public assistance, but she didn't want us to be that way. And, she never sent us to the neighborhood schools.

Maureen said,

> Everybody else bums, crack heads, you know, so my mother pushed us harder than I guess everybody else's mama did just to have a better life than what she had. I can't be around negative people, because that just brings me down, so I just leave them alone.

The few students who had friendships with "non-students" in their communities attempted to retain their friends. However, these students generally recognized differences between their personal responsibilities and values and those of their friends. Maintenance of these friendships was difficult and sometimes stressful, as described by Caroline:

> [Sometimes] I wish I didn't know so many people because people become . . . troublesome to you . . . like a nuisance. . . . [There are] times when I don't answer my phone. I just like let the answering machine pick up; I don't call people. I just stay to myself for a while and they don't understand that.

Ron said,

> These guys just—I don't know what's their problem. They are like party people. . . . [For] people around my neighborhood, it's just parties, party and hang out with each other. [These] people at home are usually bad for me.

A more verbal female student, Siniqua, described her community friends and explained the way in which she dealt with them:

> I told my mother; my friends are stupid! . . . I have learned now not to talk to certain people about school because . . . there's no interest there.

It was common for the students to end relationships with neighborhood friends because these associations interfered with their college work. Those who continued their relationships with individuals disinterested in college usually dropped out.

Limited College Associations

The students who developed associations with college peers usually described them as "limited." External responsibilities such as the care of siblings or their own children and work, often curtailed their associations. These activities, combined with academic requirements, prevented students from developing lasting friendships with their college peers. Caroline provided the following description of her situation:

> Well, I always had jobs. I had to because I have to take care of myself. . . . I mean, I just have to do it. It's like I rent from my father [who is disabled]. He doesn't put much pressure on me now because I don't make much money . . . but, you know, I still give him something.

At times, students overextended themselves in extracurricula activities. The negative effects on grades and personal responsibilities generally caused these students to separate from college peers. Coline described her situation in the following manner:

> They say "Oh you have leadership skills, and I want you to be my president." And, that's what happen to me. . . . So, I became president of . . . club when someone was leaving that semester. And even though [there were] other people around to help me with the club, I just said it was too much pressure on me at the time. And, I had other things that I wanted to concentrate on.

However, the students in this study commonly indicated that they established an alliance with people who served as resources, that is, people who were in some way useful. Siniqua presented one of the best examples. Her associations crossed racial and ethnic lines:

> She's Asian and if I don't have some information and she has it, she'll share what she's got with me. And, I'll share what I've got with her. . . . When we first started, we were separate. But now that the semester's going on. . . . [we] are starting to work together with what we do.

Kathy made this comment:

> I'm trying to assess myself now. . . . Let me use my resources of higher students, like juniors or seniors or people that I [know] that [are] in graduate school and use them and say: "Well what can I do to get myself on the better track to keep my grades up?"

They also explained what happened to people whom they did not find very helpful or useful. This statement from Maureen epitomizes the attitude:

> I'm moving forward, and if I have friends around me who are standing still, I gotta move *over* [emphasis in the original discussion] them because I feel I can come back 10 years from now, [and they're] gonna still be in that same spot. Eventually, you gotta keep on moving or else they're gonna bring you down with them.

CONCLUSION AND IMPLICATIONS

This article used elements of the Ecological Model developed by Bronfenbrenner (1977) as a framework to examine the methods by which students developed social relationships and to see whether these relationships supported college retention. Focusing on the micro- and macrosystems, an oral composite was constructed from the comments of Black commuter college students from lower socioeconomic communities. The essential points to be learned from the comments of the students were as follows:

1. Harmonious mesosystems were created by reducing the number of components. Often, the harmony was created by eliminating dissonate microsystems, that is, microsystems that did not support college completion. For participants in this study, neighborhood or community friendships were generally relinquished, especially if the friends did not attend college.

2. The students expanded their friendships, or microsystems, on an "as-needed" basis. Generally, they only sought alliances with college peers when the relationships supported college activities; thus, friendships with classmates rarely extended beyond the academic setting.

3. In addition, overwhelming external responsibilities hampered the development or continuation of the few friendships that these students made while attending school.

Individuals working with this population must recognize that many of these students may be commuting from neighborhoods where the activities of peers do not support college attendance (cf. Alford, 1998; Fries-Britt, 1998). Consequently, the Black students may not have friends in their communities. In addition, because they must commute, these students may not have the time or inclination to develop friendships with individuals at their colleges.

Because they have few or no friends in their communities or colleges or in any other setting, these students may have "impoverished mesosystems" (Muuss, 1996). Mesosystems of this type are the result of eliminating microsystems that create dissonance within the mesosystem. For example, the students may only associate with their parents and siblings, or siblings when parents were no longer around. They may confine relationships outside the immediate family to individuals with whom the students are intimately involved, such as their boy or girlfriends. By restricting their social relationships in this manner, these students may find it difficult to fit into other social settings. They may also encounter unusual complications when they attempt to correct problems that develop in these relationships.

Whether because of cultural values or necessitated by environmental factors, alienation or social isolation can become a way of life for Black commuter students that will eventually result in greater personal troubles. Counselors must recognize that dissonate or impoverished mesosystems not only affect present behavioral patterns of the students, but also have direct repercussions on future behaviors. Counselors must make special efforts to get Black commuter students involved in the college community. They can require students to participate in campus activities, some of which allow discussion directed toward self-exploration. Through these activities, students can examine the methods by which they interact with others. This will help the students to better understand why they have few, if any, associates outside their immediate family. Through recognizing the methods by which they relate to others, the students can also develop methods for change. This, in time, may lead to the development of mutually supportive relationships.

By helping Black commuter students from lower socioeconomic communities to develop their ability to negotiate relationships, counselors are helping them to establish interconnected microsystems. Through understanding the appropriate manner in which to handle each of their different microsystems, the students will be better able to function within the college community and in their neighborhoods. The harmony of the mesosystem will not be dependent on the connections between the internal and external school environments. It will be the result of the harmony created by the students' understanding of the differences and similarities of the microsystems. The work of counselors can greatly support this understanding. Through the personal creation of networks that are supportive of the college experience, many more Black commuter college students can remain in college until they graduate.

REFERENCES

Alford, S. (1998). The impact of inner-city values on student social adjustment in commuter colleges. *The NASPA Journal, 35,* 225–233.

Anderson, E. (1994, May). The code of the streets: Inner city Black community and the code of respect. *Atlantic Monthly, 273,* 80–83.

Astin, A.W. (1988). *Minorities in American higher education.* San Francisco: Jossey-Bass.

Astin, A.W. (1993). *What matters in college: Four critical years revisited.* San Francisco: Jossey-Bass.

Banning, J.H., & Hughes, B.M. (1986). Designing the campus environment with commuter students. *NASPA Journal, 24,* 17–24.

Bronfenbrenner, U. (1977, July). Toward an experimental ecology of human development. *American Psychologist,* 513–523.

Browne-Miller, A. (1996). *Shameful admissions: The losing battle to serve everyone in our universities.* San Francisco: Jossey-Bass.

Dalton, J.C. (1989). The influence of peer culture on college student values. *NASPA Journal, 26,* 180–186.

Delworth, U., Hanson, G.R., & Associates (1989). *Student services: A handbook for the profession* (2nd ed.). San Francisco: Jossey-Bass.

Fleming, J. (1984). *Blacks in college.* San Francisco: Jossey-Bass.

Ford, C. (1997). Holding on to what they've got. *Black Issues in Higher Education, 13,* 36–41.

Fordham, S., & Ogbu, J.U. (1986). Black students' school success: Coping with the burden of 'acting White.' *Urban Review, 18,* 176–206.

Fries-Britt, S. (1998). Moving beyond Black achiever isolation: Experiences of gifted Black collegians. *The Journal of Higher Education, 69,* 556–576.

Gonchar, N. (1995). Post-traumatic stress disorder among inner city commuter college students. *Journal of College Student Psychotherapy, 9,* 19–39.

Healy, P. (1998, November 13). Advocates of more money for colleges win key gubernatorial races, but many educators are disheartened by Washington State vote to end racial preferences. *The Chronicle of Higher Education,* pp. A29–A30.

Hollins, M.L., et al. (1996). National Center for Educational Statistics: *Enrollment in higher education: fall 1986 through fall 1994* (NCES 96-851). Washington, DC: U.S. Department of Education.

Huebner, L.A. (1989). Interaction of student and campus. In U. Delworth, G.R. Hanson, & Associates, *Student services: A handbook for the profession* (2nd ed.). San Francisco: Jossey-Bass.

Hurtado, S. (1992). The campus racial climate: Context for conflict. *The Journal of Higher Education 63,* 539–569.

Jaynes, G.D., & Williams, R.M., Jr. (1989). *A common destiny: Blacks and American society.* Washington, DC: National Academy.

Kuh, G.D., & Whitt, E.J. (1988). *The invisible tapestry: Culture in American colleges and universities* (Report No. 1). Ashe-Eric Higher Education.

Levine, A.L., & Associates. (1990). *Shaping higher education's future Demographic realities and opportunities 1990–2000.* San Francisco: Jossey-Bass.

Lewin, K. (1936). *Principles of topological psychology.* New York: McGraw-Hill.

Malone, R.M. (1992). Counseling the disadvantaged Black urban college student: A study of family support expectations. *NASPA Journal, 29,* 268–273.

Mow, S.L., & Nettles, M.T. (1990). Minority student access to, and persistence and performance in, college: A review of the trends and research literature. In J.C. Smart (Ed.), *Higher education: Handbook of theory and research* (Vol. 6, pp. 35–105). New York: Agathon.

Muuss, R.E. (1996). *Theories of adolescence* (6th ed.). New York: McGraw-Hill.

Nelville, H.A., Heppner, P.P., & Wang, L. (1997). Relations among racial identity attitudes, perceived stressors, and coping styles in African American college students. *Journal of Counseling & Development, 75,* 303–311.

Noel L., Levitz, R., Saluri, D., & Associates (1991). *Increasing student retention.* San Francisco: Jossey-Bass.

Paul, E.L., & Kelleher, M. (1995). Precollege concerns about losing and making friends in college: Implications for friendship satisfaction and self-esteem during the college transition. *Journal of College Student Development, 36,* 513–521.

Pascarella, E.T., & Terenzini, P.T. (1991). *How college affects students: Findings and insights from twenty years of research.* San Francisco: Jossey-Bass.

Patton, M. (1990). *Qualitative evaluation and research methods.* Newbury Park: Sage.

Schmidt, P. (1997, April 18). A Federal Appeals Court Upholds California Measure Barring Racial Preferences. *The Chronicle of Higher Education,* pp. A28–A29.

Stage, F.K., & Associates (1992). *Diverse methods for research and assessment of college students.* Alexandria, VA: American College Personnel Association.

Stewart, S.S., Merrill, M.C., & Saluri, D. (1991). Students who commute. In L. Noel, R. Levitz, D. Saluri, & Associates (Eds.), *Increasing student retention* (5th ed., pp. 162–182). San Francisco: Jossey-Bass. (Original work published 1985)

Taylor, S.J., & Bogdan, R. (1998). *Introduction to qualitative research methods: A guidebook and resource* (3rd ed.). New York: Wiley.

Terenzini, P.T., Pascarella, E.T., & Blimling, G.S. (1996). Students' out-of-class experiences and their influence on learning and cognitive development: A literature review. *Journal of College Student Development, 37*(2), 149–162.

Tinto, V. (1987). *Leaving College: Rethinking the causes and cures of student attrition.* Chicago: University of Chicago.

Waters, M. (1996). Ethnic and racial identities of second-generation Black immigrants in New York City. In A. Portes (Ed.), *The new second-generation* (pp. 171–196). New York: Russell Sage.

APPENDIX

Interview Protocol

1. Could you give me a general description or explanation of how you select your friends or the people with whom you associate?

1a. Would you say that you have used similar methods to select friends and associates here at school?

2. What would you consider the primary basis for most of the friendships? For example would you say that your friendships are based on socializing, academics, political views, race/ethnicity, personal issues . . . what?

2a. Explain why your friendships are based on this?

3. Are any of your friends here in the (Opportunity) Program at the college supportive?

3a. Describe the type of support you are getting from your friends here at this college?

4. Describe the type of support you get from people in your community, your acquaintances, the people you "hang out" with.

Note. *Since the time of the study, three of the students have withdrawn from their respective colleges, one requested a transfer, two have graduated, and all the others are enrolled full time.*

Schevaletta M. Alford is an assistant professor at John Jay College of Criminal Justice and a counselor and counseling coordinator for the Search for Education, Elevation, and Knowledge Program, both at the City University of New York. Correspondence regarding this article should be sent to Schevaletta M. Alford, John Jay College, 445 W. 59th St., New York, NY 10019-1199 (e-mail: smajj@cunyvm.cuny.edu).

REFERENCES

Alford, S.M. (2000). A qualitative study of college social adjustment of Black students from lower socioeconomic communities. *Journal of Multicultural Counseling and Development,* 28, 2–15.

Bogdan, R.C., & Biklen, S.K. (1998). *Qualitative research for education: An introduction to theory and methods* (3rd ed.). Boston: Allyn and Bacon.

Buston, K. (1999). NUD*IST in action: Its use and usefulness in a study of chronic illness in young people. In A. Bryman & R.G. Burgess, *Qualitative research* (Vol. 3, pp. 183–202). Thousand Oaks, CA: Sage.

Dey, I. (1993). *Qualitative data analysis.* New York: Routledge.

Glaser, B.G., & Strauss, A.L. (1967). *The discovery of grounded theory.* Chicago: Aldine.

Goertz, J.P., & LeCompte, M.D. (1993). *Ethnography and qualitative design in educational research.* New York: Academic Press.

Hughes, S. (1997). A study of teachers and their relationships with at-risk students. In T.S. Poetter, *Voices of inquiry in teacher education.* (pp. 83–97). Mahwah, NJ: Erlbaum.

Kelle, E. (Ed.). (1995). *Computer-aided qualitative analysis.* Thousand Oaks, CA: Sage.

Lincoln, Y.S., & Guba, E.G. (1985). *Naturalistic inquiry.* Beverly Hills, CA: Sage.

Maykut, P., & Morehouse, R. (1994). *Beginning qualitative research: A philosophic and practical guide.* Washington, DC: Falmer Press.

Miles, M.B., & Huberman, A.M. (1994). *Qualitative data analysis* (2nd ed.) Thousand Oaks, CA: Sage.

Patton, M.Q. (1990). *Qualitative evaluation and research methods* (2nd ed.). Newbury Park, CA: Sage.

Weitzman, E.A., & Miles, M.B. (1995). *Computer programs for qualitative data analysis.* Thousand Oaks, CA: Sage.

Wiersma, W. (1995). *Research methods in education: An introduction.* Boston: Allyn and Bacon.

Wolcott, H.F. (1990). *Writing up qualitative research.* Newbury Park, CA: Sage.

KEY CONCEPTS

category	discrepant data analysis
constant comparive method	negative case analysis

EXERCISES

1. Explain how data analysis in qualitative and quantitative studies differs.

2. Briefly describe the constant comparative method for analyzing qualitative data.

3. One of the criticisms of qualitative research is that it is subject to bias. Do you agree? What does the qualitative researcher do to rebut this kind of criticism?

4. Would you agree with a friend who believes a qualitative study would be easier for a disserta-

tion than a quantitative study? What are some differences you might point out?

5. How does a qualitative report differ from a report of quantitative research?

ANSWERS

1. One of the basic differences is that data analysis in qualitative research is inductive; it is a process of categorizing data that are in the form of words, synthesis, and finding meaning. Data analysis in quantitative research is deductive; it involves testing hypotheses using numerical data and statistical tests.

2. It is a process in which the researcher takes each new unit of meaning and compares it to other units of meaning (categories) and then groups it with categories that are similar. It is a way to reduce the data and make it more manageable and conducive to interpretation.

3. A number of procedures were discussed in the previous chapter that qualitative researchers use to contribute to a credible study. Among them are triangulation, audit trails, member checks,

and working with a team (using more than one human instrument is better than one).

4. Answers will vary. In some ways, qualitative research may be more difficult than quantitative research: The design is much less prescriptive and structured, data collection is time consuming, and data analysis is more tedious and involved. Writing a qualitative report is likely to take much more time than writing a quantitative report. One aspect that may make qualitative research easier for some is the lack of statistics.

5. A qualitative report is narrative in form, rich with descriptions, quotations, and so forth. One can use the first person, which is never used in quantitative reporting.

 INFOTRAC COLLEGE EDITION

Using the key words *data analysis* and *qualitative,* locate a qualitative inquiry and read the section describing data analysis. Did the researcher use the steps described in this chapter for organizing and interpreting the data? Did the data support the interpretations?

Chapter 16

Guidelines for Writing Research Proposals

After studying this chapter, the student will be able to:

1. Describe the components of a research proposal and why they are important.

2. Identify common weaknesses in quantitative research proposals.

3. Critique quantitative research proposals.

4. Select statistics appropriate for the questions being asked and the data involved.

5. Describe ethical and legal considerations in research.

6. Describe the role of an institutional review board.

7. Write a research proposal that meets the guidelines.

In most cases researchers will need to present their projects in organized written form at two stages: (1) the initial stage, which requires preparation of a research proposal to be presented to a professor or to a dissertation committee and (2) the final stage, a finished report of the results of the research. This chapter deals with the initial stage; Chapter 17 discusses the final stage.

WRITING A RESEARCH PROPOSAL

Writing the research proposal can be the most crucial and exciting step in the research process. At this stage the whole project crystallizes into concrete form. In the proposal, researchers demonstrate that they know what they are seeking and how they will recognize it and explain why the search is worthwhile. The researchers' inspirations and insights are translated into step-by-step plans for discovering new knowledge. The written proposal also permits others to evaluate the worth of the planned study and to make suggestions for improving it. The format may be the relatively informal outline offered by a student to satisfy the requirements of a research course, a formal thesis or dissertation proposal presented to a committee, or a funding request to a foundation or governmental agency.

Qualitative Research Proposal

There is no standard outline of categories or specific format for writing proposals for qualitative research; the format for a qualitative study depends on the specific study. Qualitative proposals are not as specific and detailed and thus not as long as quantitative ones, because researchers do not know for sure exactly what they will do until they get the study under way. Although the design is tentative, you should at least speculate about the following elements: the purpose and/or problem statement, the participants and setting, the methodology, the data collection methods, and any ethical issues that may arise.

You should also explain the potential significance of the study for theory or practice and why you chose the particular problem. Some writers suggest doing some preliminary data collection in the field before attempting to write the proposal. They maintain that this field experience helps a researcher see what he or she might be able to do, and ultimately to produce a better proposal. Needless to say, not all professors and dissertation committees agree with this unorthodox procedure. For further discussion of proposals for qualitative inquiry, see references such as Bogdan and Biklen (1998), Marshall and Rossman (1995), and Maykut and Morehouse (1994).

Quantitative Research Proposal

The following suggested outline for writing a quantitative research proposal contains the steps essential to formulate and propose a research study:

1. Introduction
   a. Statement of the problem
   b. Review of the literature
   c. Statement of the hypothesis(es)

2. Methodology
    a. Subjects
    b. Instruments
    c. Procedures

3. Analysis of data
    a. Data organization
    b. Statistical procedures

4. Significance of the study
    a. Implications
    b. Applications

5. Time schedule and budget
    a. Time schedule
    b. Budget

6. References

Although you need not follow this outline rigidly, it should provide a useful guide for writing any proposal, because all aspects listed here must be considered.

Introduction

A crucial part of a research proposal for quantitative research is the introduction to the proposed study. In the very first paragraph, state the research problem clearly and unambiguously. Then link the problem to the body of information available in the field and establish the importance of and the need for carrying out the research. Regardless of how tightly you formulate the design of the study and how well you select the statistical procedures, unless the introduction is written carefully and intelligently, other parts of the proposal will probably not receive serious consideration. It is not unusual for proposals to be turned down solely on the basis of a poor introduction, without much consideration being given to the proposed methodology and statistical design. So prepare this section with care, caution, and the aim of promoting the reader's interest in the problem.

The introduction to a research proposal should include (1) a statement of the problem, (2) a review of the literature, and (3) a statement of the hypotheses.

Statement of the Problem   State the problem clearly and directly very early in the introduction, ideally at the beginning of the first paragraph. The problem statement should imply a question about the relationship between specified variables. The statement can take interrogative form or can simply say, "The purpose of the study is to explore the relationship between . . . and . . ." You need not operationalize the variables at this point, only mention them in conceptual form. This section of the introduction should also include a brief description of the background of the problem and the potential significance of the study, although it is imperative to avoid the temptation to sell the importance of the topic before stating it. Two common errors to watch for are (1) beginning the introduction with an elaborate presentation of the background of a problem before you have clearly stated the problem itself, and (2) concentrating on a justification for the study at this point, burying the problem statement in the discussion or bringing it in only vaguely near the end. Another common error is to assume that the reader knows as much about the content of the question as you do. State the problem so that it can be understood by someone who is generally sophisticated but who is relatively uninformed concerning the area of the problem.

At an appropriate point in this section, define, in the way they will be used in the study, any terms that may not be familiar to the reader or to which you are ascribing special meanings. The specific limitations of the scope of the study and a foreshadowing of the hypothesis should close the section.

Review of the Literature   In the section on related literature, present what is currently known about the problem under consideration, thus setting the context for the questions or hypotheses of the proposed study. The literature review shows how the proposed research fits in with the existing body of knowledge. Include literature dealing with research on the variables of the proposed study as well as discussions of the theoretical background of the problem. The literature cited need not be exhaustive, but should contain the most pertinent related studies and show an awareness of promising current practices.

In this section, as author of the proposal, you demonstrate not only how you propose to proceed from the known to the unknown, but also how firm your grasp of the field and awareness of recent developments are. This does not mean that the review should be a tour de force of your erudition. Include only literature that clearly relates to the hypothesis of the study.

Organize the literature by topic. Topical organization points out to the reader what is known about various aspects of the study. Thus a complete picture of the background of the study is put together step by step. A pitfall to avoid in discussing related literature is to present a series of abstracts, one per paragraph. This offers the audience tedious reading and misses the opportunity for laying meaningful groundwork for the study. It is much better to organize by topic and to point out how the studies presented relate to the planned research.

Not all related studies need be discussed in detail. In reviewing several similar studies, you can describe the most important one, then simply state that the results were confirmed in similar studies that are mentioned but not described in detail. Enthusiastic beginning researchers often imagine their proposed study is unique and that no related research is available. This is very rarely the case. A thorough search almost always turns up several research papers related to at least some aspects of a proposed study. Even if there is no research in the field, there is usually literature of a theoretical or speculative nature that should be included as part of the background of a study. Of course, include theories and research results contrary to the stated hypothesis as well as those in agreement with it.

The related literature section should conclude with a discussion of the findings and their implications. Here you share the insights gained from your review of the literature and points out gaps in what is known about the topic, leading directly to the question you propose to investigate.

Statement of the Hypothesis(es)   The hypothesis should state concisely the expected relationship between the variables in the study. The research hypothesis is typically determined by the implications of the related research findings and the deductive logic of the underlying theory. The reader should be able to see the rationale for the hypothesis.

Some research, like surveys, may simply state the problem in question form. For example, How do the parents in the Monroe County School District feel about a longer school day? But most quantitative research states a hypothesis. It should probably be stated in operational form, but if this is not possible, it can be stated in conceptual terms followed by any operational definitions of the variables.

Methodology

In the methodology part of the proposal, the author shows *how* the study will be set up so that the research question will be answered or the hypothesized relationships will be observed, if in fact these relationships exist. Note that this section is written using future tense, because nothing has yet been done. If the methodology you describe in the proposal is actually the same as the method you eventually used in conducting the study, then you have a big section of the final report already written. It is only necessary to change the future tense of the proposal to the past tense used in the final report.

In previous chapters, we introduced appropriate research designs for different types of research. Select from among these research designs, experimental or otherwise, the one that best suits the question and/or hypothesis under consideration. For example, if you are to compare two methods of teaching chemistry, you are in fact raising an experimental question. This research problem requires at least two groups of subjects: experimental and control. If you also wish to investigate the interaction effect between methods of teaching chemistry and another variable—aptitude, for instance—the question, although still experimental, asks for a more sophisticated design than that of a two-group design. In this case you need to set up a factorial design with at least four groups for such a study.

In this methodology part of the proposal, the author includes a description of the proposed sampling procedures, methods of data collection, and instruments to be used. A convenient way of presenting the research methodology is to categorize all information regarding the design as (1) subjects, (2) instruments, or (3) procedures, as appropriate.

Subjects   The first step in identifying the subjects in a study is to describe the population of interest: Is the study concerned with college freshmen, dyslexic 6-year-olds, principals of elementary schools, and so forth? Then the author/researcher states the size of the sample and describes the procedure for drawing the sample from the population. If random selection is not possible, explain why you have adopted a particular procedure for sample selection and how well the sample used resembles the population of interest. A careful description of the subjects can help the reader of the proposal to determine if, in the reader's view, the results of the study can be generalized to the extent intended.

The following example describes the subjects in a proposal: "The children in this experiment all attend a public elementary school in the southeastern United States. Three intact classrooms will participate. There will be 17 children (11 boys and 6 girls) in kindergarten; 24 in second grade (13 boys and 11 girls); and 21 in fourth grade (10 boys and 11 girls). The children represent a variety of social, economic, and cultural backgrounds: Approximately one-third are African-Americans, a few are Asian-Americans, and the majority are European-Americans."

Instruments   The goal of a research project is to investigate relationships between constructs. However, because constructs are usually impossible to measure directly, you must select or develop indicators that will approximate them as well as possible. If an instrument is already established, the proposal should include reported evidence of its reliability and validity for the purpose of the study. In cases where the instruments are to be developed by the researcher, it is necessary to outline the procedure to be followed in developing them. This outline should include the steps that will be taken to obtain validity and reliability data on these instruments. If describing the reliability and validity procedures results in so much detail that it interrupts the continuity of the proposal, it is preferable to include this material in an appendix rather than in the text.

A description of the instrument might include, for example, "Students' prerecess and postrecess classroom behavior and their outdoor recess behavior will be observed daily for two months. A total of four observers, blind to the purpose of the study will be used: Three will be regular observers and one will be a rotating observer whose primary job is to be a reliability judge. Reliability will be measured with a kappa coefficient."

Procedures   In the procedures section the author describes the way in which the study will be set up so the hypothesized relationships can be observed, if these relationships in fact exist. In effect, you are saying, "*If* this hypothesis is true, *then* these results will be observed." By designing the study explicitly as an operation to permit the observation of the hypothesized relationships, you lay the foundation for the study. A careful description of the procedures of a study is a basic requirement of any research proposal. In survey research, the writing of this section is relatively simple, because the procedure merely involves sending out a questionnaire to be filled out and returned or conducting interviews. However, all the steps—that is, preparing the questionnaire or interview schedule, training the interviewers, giving them directions as to how to approach the subjects and how to perform the interview—should be listed and explained.

In experimental research, the procedures may be more complex. In this section the author should list the groups, specify step by step the manipulations planned for each one, and link each treatment to the proposed questions and hypotheses. These steps should be completely designated in operational form. By basing the procedures of the experiment on the hypotheses, you facilitate direct and unambiguous interpretation of results. You should also consider here the possibility of confounding variables—those variables that could account for criterion score differences that are not part of the independent variable. Specify in the procedures section how you propose to control for these variables. For example, you might control for student and teacher differences by randomly assigning students and teachers to the control and experimental groups. Make the time spent, physical setting, and facilities equivalent. In this section, include all the steps that operationally define the experimental and control treatments.

Also state any known limitations of the proposed methodology. The limitations are any factors that may negatively impact the results of the study or the generalizability of the results. Limitations may include size of the sample, selection of the subjects, the setting for the study, use of a pretest, length of the study, and so on.

Documents such as teaching or reading materials planned for an experiment need not be included in the main text of the proposal because discussion of such details usually interrupts continuity of the proposal. We recommend that the author place these documents in an appendix, describing them briefly but clearly in the procedures section. It is, however, essential to explain in this section any differences in the presentation of these materials to the different groups involved in the experiment.

After the section on procedures has been drafted, read it to verify that you have described all steps necessary to answer every question and test every hypothesis. You can check the completeness of this section with the question, Could the reader carry out this research by following the steps as described? If you can answer this question in the affirmative, this section is complete.

Analysis of Data

The next part of the research proposal describes the methods of handling and presenting data and outlines the statistical procedures to be used. Group this information in sections covering (1) data organization and (2) statistical procedures.

Data Organization   The presentation of the results of a research study can take different forms depending on the way the findings are organized. You must plan in advance for the arrangement of research results into an organized form. This is best done by reference to questions or hypotheses of the study. Planning in advance for the organization and presentation of data enables a researcher to determine whether the information being collected is relevant to the research questions. Those who bypass this step often find they have wasted considerable time and money in collecting irrelevant pieces of information.

Tables, figures, and charts are essential means for organizing and summarizing a whole set of data. While the research is in the planning stage, you should be able to picture how the data will be organized and presented in tabular form. At this stage you should list the bits of information that will be available for each subject, decide how you will present and summarize the information, and decide what statistical procedures to employ.

Statistical Procedures   The design of the study determines what statistical techniques should be employed, not vice versa. In other words, the researcher decides what design will permit observation of the hypothesized relationships, then selects the statistical procedure that fits the questions asked and the nature of the data involved. The researcher does not first select an appealing statistic and then design the study to fit that statistic.

The most commonly used statistical procedures have been described in earlier chapters. They are summarized for convenience in Table 16.1 ("Descriptive Statistics") and Table 16.2 ("Inferential Statistics"). Table 16.1 is designed to help identify the indexes that may be used to describe in summary form the data of a study. The appropriate statistical procedure is determined partly by the type of measurement scale characterizing the dependent variable. Therefore, the rows in the table are identified as "Interval," "Ordinal," and "Nominal." Columns (1), (2), and (3) list the various purposes descriptive statistics may serve. The most common uses of these statistics are the following:

1. To provide an index to describe a group or the difference between groups (measures of central location)

2. To provide an index to describe the variability of a group or differences in the variability of groups (measures of variability)

3. To locate an individual in a group (indexes of individual location)

4. To provide an index to describe the relationship of variables within a population (measures of correlation)

5. To describe how a set is divided into subsets

6. To describe the interaction among two or more variables in relation to a criterion (measures of interaction)

The required cell can be located by identifying the row and column heading appropriate to your study. Each cell is divided, and the section to use is determined by whether the study is concerned with one group or with more than one group. (Recall that you *may* choose a procedure for a lower scale of measurement but not the reverse; for example, you may use a median or a mode to describe interval data but may not use a mean to describe ordinal or nominal data.) In determining what type of scale to use in expressing the data, consider the advantages of each of three scales. Interval data provide more information than ordinal data, and ordinal data provide more information than nominal data. In making inferences, statistical tests of interval data are more "powerful" than tests of ordinal data; that is, you have a greater chance of rejecting a null hypothesis when you use interval measures than when you use ordinal measures. In the same manner, ordinal tests are more powerful than nominal measures. Therefore, when a choice is possible, prefer interval data to ordinal and ordinal data to nominal. For example, if you have interval data for the dependent variable and want an index to describe the difference between groups, Table 16.1 identifies the difference between two means as an appropriate statistic. (You could, if you chose, use difference between medians but this would be less powerful than the difference between means.)

If the study is inferential in nature, the researcher will proceed to test the statistical significance of the index selected. Table 16.2 lists appropriate statistics for this purpose.

Remember that a statistical procedure is selected on the basis of its appropriateness for answering the question involved in the study. Nothing is gained by using a complicated procedure when a simple one will do just as well. Statistics are to serve research, not to dominate it. We often tell our students, "Imagine you have gotten a fantastic grant for doing your study, but you are run over by a truck the very next day. Could a colleague pick up your proposal and actually conduct the study?" If you can honestly answer this question in the affirmative, the data analysis part of the proposal is complete.

Significance of the Study

Some researchers prefer to state the significance of the problem in the introduction to the proposal. Leaving this topic for a later section, however, provides the opportunity to re-

Table 16.1 *Descriptive Statistics*

PURPOSE OF THE STATISTIC

TYPE OF SCALE OF DEPENDENT VARIABLE	(1) CENTRAL TENDENCY		(2) VARIABILITY		(3) LOCATION	
	ONE GROUP	MORE THAN ONE GROUP	ONE GROUP	MORE THAN ONE GROUP	ONE GROUP	MORE THAN ONE GROUP
Interval	Mean	Difference between means	Standard deviation or variance	Difference between standard deviations or variances	z-Score, or other standard score	Difference between an individual's standard score in more than one distribution
Ordinal	Median	Difference between medians	Quartile deviation[a]	Difference between quartile deviations[a]	Percentile rank	Difference between an individual's percentile rank in more than one distribution
Nominal	Mode	Difference between modes	Range	Difference between ranges	Label or categorization	Label or categorization

PURPOSE OF THE STATISTIC

TYPE OF SCALE OF DEPENDENT VARIABLE	(4) CORRELATION		(5) SUBSETS		(6) INTERACTION	
	ONE GROUP	MORE THAN ONE GROUP	ONE GROUP	MORE THAN ONE GROUP	ONE GROUP	MORE THAN ONE GROUP
Interval	Pearson r	Difference in Pearson rs for same variables in two groups			Difference between observed cell means and expected cell means in factorial ANOVA (observed interaction)	Differences in observed interaction among groups
Ordinal	Spearman's rho or Kendall's tau[a] or W[a]	Difference in Spearman rhos Kendall's taus or Ws				
Nominal	point biserial correlation,[a] biserial correlation,[a] or phi coefficient	Difference in correlations for same variables in two groups	Proportion or percentage	Differences in proportions or percentages	Differences between observed cell frequencies and expected cell frequencies	Differences in observed interaction among groups

[a]This statistic is not described in this text but may be found in any number of statistics texts.

Table 16.2 *Inferential Statistics*

PURPOSE OF THE STATISTIC

TYPE OF SCALE OF DEPENDENT VARIABLE	(1) CENTRAL LOCATION		(2) VARIABILITY		(3) INDIVIDUAL LOCATION	
	ONE GROUP	MORE THAN ONE GROUP	ONE GROUP	MORE THAN ONE GROUP	ONE GROUP	MORE THAN ONE GROUP
Interval	Standard error of the mean	t-Test or one-way ANOVA		Bartlett's test[a] or t-test for homogeneity of variance;[a] F-max[a] statistics	Standard error of measurement[a]	Standard error of difference scores[a]
Ordinal	Standard error of median[a]	Median test, sign test,[a] Kruskal–Wallis one-way ANOVA,[a] or Friedman's test[a]				
Nominal						

PURPOSE OF THE STATISTIC

TYPE OF SCALE OF DEPENDENT VARIABLE	(4) CORRELATION		(5) SUBSETS		(6) INTERACTION	
	ONE GROUP	MORE THAN ONE GROUP	ONE GROUP	MORE THAN ONE GROUP	ONE GROUP	MORE THAN ONE GROUP
Interval	t-Test for Fisher's z transformation or F-test for linearity[a]	t-Test for Fisher's z transformation[a]			F-Test for multifactor ANOVA	F-Test for multifactor ANOVA
Ordinal	Test for Spearman's rho or Kendall's tau[a] or W[a]					
Nominal	Chi-square test for significance	Cochran's Q[a]	Chi-square or binomial test[a]	Chi-square or Fisher's exact test[a]	Log linear analysis[a]	Chi-square test for log linear analysis[a]

[a]This statistic is not described in this text but may be found in any number of statistics texts.

late it to both the background and the design of the study. This section is best handled in two stages: (1) implications and (2) applications.

Implications   Because the aim of research is to increase knowledge, the author of the proposal should show how his or her particular study will do this, by discussing what the results will contribute to theory and knowledge in the specific area to which the research question is related, and to what extent these results will be useful in solving problems and answering questions in the general field. Finally, you show how the results of the study will provide grounds for further research in the area. In addition, you may explain how your own experience and expertise, coupled with the facilities and goals of the institution where the study is being carried out, place you in a favorable position to solve the problem in question.

Applications   The author should be able to convince readers of the potential application of the findings to educational practice. This discussion should show how and to what extent educational practitioners could use the results to improve their work. To find the extent to which the study has application to educational practice, you may ask, Will the results of my study change anything in my field? Would my results help teachers, school counselors, principals, or other educators to improve their work? This aspect carries considerable weight in attracting research funds for carrying out the study. Many foundations evaluate research proposals on the basis of potential application to practice.

Time Schedule and Budget

All research should be planned with regard to the feasibility of carrying out the work. A proposal should conclude with a presentation of (1) schedule and (2) budget.

Time Schedule   The researcher needs to identify the sequence of stages necessary to complete the proposed research and to estimate the time needed to complete each stage. Dividing the project into manageable stages, then assigning a date to complete each stage helps systematize the project, enables you to estimate the effort that will be required to complete the entire project, and provides opportunities for periodically evaluating the development of the project.

Budget   Reviewing the previous sections of the proposal, the researcher now needs to determine the resources necessary to carry out the proposed research and make careful estimates of the costs of such things as supplies, travel expenses, duplicating, computer services, personnel, and consultant fees. If you are requesting external funding, most institutions have someone, such as a contract officer, to help plan the budget and fit it into the requirements of the anticipated funding agency.

References

In this section, the researcher must list the references that were cited in the literature review as well as any other sources cited in the development of the proposal. The reference list includes the full publication information for each entry, arranged in alphabetical order according to the senior author's last name. The APA format is the most popular one for listing references in journals, dissertations, and other research publications (*Publication Manual of the American Psychological Association,* 4th ed., pp. 174–222). Beginning researchers should become familiar with APA style.

CRITIQUING THE PROPOSAL

After completing the draft of a proposal, the author/researcher should go through it again carefully with a critical eye. It is also profitable to have colleagues read the proposal. Often someone else can identify weaknesses or omissions that are not evident to the author. In his work with the Research Advisory Committee of the USOE Cooperative Research Program, Smith (1963) identified six common weaknesses that the committee found in proposals submitted for funding.

1. *The problem is trivial.* Problems that are of only peripheral interest to educators or show little likelihood of adding to knowledge in education are not considered deserving of support. Smith (1963) gives as an example a plan to study an adult education program for library trustees and comments, "Not only is it of peripheral value to education and oriented toward action rather than research, but it is, to put it bluntly, a problem of little significance" (p. 282).

2. *The problem is not delimited.* The classic illustration by Good and Skates (1954) is a splendid example of this weakness. A letter written by a graduate student to the Commissioner of Education for Alaska indicated that the student had selected for his thesis the topic "The Teaching of English as Revealed in the Courses of Study of the English-Speaking Nations of the World." In the second paragraph, he asks the commissioner, "Do you know some interesting books on Alaska: her history, her economic problems, commerce, imports, exports, human relations, religion, etc.?"

   To produce a feasible proposal, you must focus the study. This is not to say that a study should never include a number of related variables. A researcher should attack those aspects of a problem that can reasonably be handled in a single study. A cluster of related variables can, and often should, be included in a study, but avoid unwieldy, overinclusive efforts.

3. *The objectives, hypotheses, or questions are too broadly stated.* Proposal writers are often tempted to state their objectives, hypotheses, or questions in broad, sweeping generalizations. In such cases one finds when reading the procedures section that the actual planned study is not capable of meeting the grand objectives set forth. Sometimes the objectives or hypotheses are stated in such broad, general terms that the reader must go to the procedures to discover what the study is really about. It seems obvious that the objectives and procedures should match; yet the Research Advisory Committee found that many proposals failed to meet this basic requirement.

4. *The procedures are lacking in detail.* Smith (1963) points out that "an investigator who omits more than he includes should not expect the committee to read procedural details between the lines. The committee lacks both the desire and the clairvoyance to do so" (p. 284). Remember, the procedures should be complete enough to allow for replication.

5. *A simple design is used to investigate a complex problem.* The design of a study should fit the problem. A simple comparison of the means of two groups is appropriate when a single variable is involved. More complex studies require more complex designs.

6. *Relevant variables are not considered or are lightly dismissed.* Failure to consider relevant extraneous variables is a serious error in a research proposal. The researcher should demonstrate that he or she is aware of such variables and explain how they will be handled in the design of the study.

THE IMPORTANCE OF COMPLETING THE PROPOSAL BEFORE COLLECTING DATA

In quantitative research a clear, well-stated, complete proposal indicates that the prospective researcher is actually ready to set the study in motion. It shows that the researcher knows what to do, why to do it, and how to do it. A prospective quantitative researcher who cannot produce a complete and coherent proposal is clearly not yet ready to proceed to the data-collecting stage of the project. Novice researchers are often inclined to say, "Let me collect my data now and decide what to do with it later."

Simultaneously collecting data and writing the proposal may seem to be a time-saving procedure, but that is seldom the case. Countless work-hours and thousands of dollars have been wasted in just that way. Until the proposal is formulated, you cannot be sure exactly what data you will need nor what will be the best way to handle this information in the light of the study's purpose. Researchers working under deadlines should set for themselves a date for completing the proposal well in advance of the target date for completing the entire project.

ETHICAL AND LEGAL CONSIDERATIONS

Strict adherence to ethical standards in planning and conducting both qualitative and quantitative research is most important. Researchers have obligations both to their subjects and to their profession. The proposal should state how informed consent, confidentiality, and other ethical issues will be handled. The proposed ethical standards for the American Educational Research Association (AERA) state that as educational researchers

> we should strive to maintain the integrity of our research, of our research community, and of all those with whom we have professional relations. We should pledge ourselves to do this by maintaining our own competence and that of people we induct into the field, by continually evaluating our research for its ethical and scientific adequacy and by conducting our internal and external relations according to the highest ethical standards. (American Educational Research Association, 1992, p. 23)

Obligation to Subjects

When employing human subjects in research, you must respect their rights, dignity, privacy, and sensitivities. Ten aspects of researchers' obligations to subjects are identified in the AERA proposed standards (American Educational Research Association, 1992, p. 24)

1. Participants, or their guardians, in a research study have the right to be informed about the likely risks involved in the research and of potential consequences for participants, and to give their informed consent before participating in research. Educational researchers should communicate the aims of the investigation as well as possible to informants and participants (and their guardians), and appropriate representatives of institutions, and keep them updated about any significant changes in the research program.

2. Honesty should characterize the relationship between researchers and participants and appropriate institutional representatives. Deception is discouraged; it should be used only when clearly necessary for scientific studies and should then be minimized. After the study the researchers should explain to the participants and institutional representatives the reasons for the deception.

3. Educational researchers should be sensitive to any locally established institutional policies or guidelines for conducting research.

4. Participants have the right to withdraw from the study at any time.

5. Educational researchers should exercise caution to ensure that there is no exploitation for personal gain of research populations or of institutional settings of research. Educational researchers should not use their influence over subordinates, students, or others to compel them to participate in research.

6. Researchers have a responsibility to be mindful of cultural, religious, gender, and other significant differences within the research population in the planning, conduct, and reporting of their research.

7. Researchers should carefully consider and minimize the use of research techniques that might have negative social consequences, e.g., negative sociometrics with young children or experimental interventions that might deprive students of important parts of the standard curriculum.

8. Educational researchers should be sensitive to the integrity of ongoing institutional activities and should alert appropriate institutional representatives of possible disturbances in such activities which may result from the conduct of the research.

9. Educational researchers should communicate their findings and the practical significance of their research in clear, straightforward, and appropriate language to relevant research populations, institutional representatives, and other stakeholders.

10. Informants and participants have a right to remain anonymous. This right should be respected when no clear understanding to the contrary has been

reached. Researchers are responsible for taking appropriate precautions to protect the confidentiality of both participants and data. Those being studied should be made aware of the capacities of the various data-gathering technologies to be used in the investigation so that they can make an informed decision about their participation. It should also be made clear to informants and participants that despite every effort made to preserve it, anonymity may be compromised. Secondary researchers should respect and maintain the anonymity established by primary researchers.

Obligation to the Profession

The researcher is also responsible to the consumers of research. Most research studies, in education as well as in other fields, are published in journals, monographs, books, and other media and are referred to and used by professionals in the field. You are morally obligated to plan a study in such a way that the findings obtained would not result in offering misleading information. Even more, you are obligated to report exactly and honestly what the findings were. Reporting research in a misleading way is a serious abuse of a researcher's responsibility to the profession. It is dismayingly easy to conduct research that becomes unintentionally deceptive. Kromrey (1993) pointed out,

> As researchers, we devote time and energy to the delineation of our theories, to the extent that our theories become much like our children. Consequently, much like tunnel-vision parents who can see no fault with their offspring, we convince ourselves that the empirical data would speak in favor of our theories if only we could analyze them "properly." From this perspective, our research efforts become directed toward supporting our theories rather than testing them (p. 25–26).

In a survey a researcher may inadvertently phrase questions in such a way as to elicit the answers sought. In conducting research someone may, without noticing, arrange things so that the experimental group has advantages the control group does not have that are not part of the independent variable. Before beginning the research, it is recommended that a trusted colleague go through the research plan to look for potential sources of misleading outcomes.

If the statistical analyses fail to support, or contradict, one's hypothesis, it is very tempting to suppose that a different statistical analysis would have "come out right." It is important to select the most appropriate statistical analysis before conducting a study, and then derive conclusions from those statistics. It is also important to report the results of *all* statistical analyses, not just those that are statistically significant. For example, if you test fifty hypotheses, and find that two are statistically significant, reporting only those two implies that they were unlikely to be a function of chance—when actually two statistically significant results in fifty are very likely to be a function of chance.

With computers it is very easy to search through the data for subsets of the sample in which one's hypotheses are confirmed despite retained null hypotheses for the total sample. You may, for example, discover what you seek among sixth-grade girls with

Spanish surnames. It is appropriate to plan statistical contrasts between treatments, between sexes, between grade levels, and between ethnic groups before conducting a study. However, the results of unplanned post hoc analyses of subgroups can lead to misleading conclusions.

Legal Obligations

Researchers' obligations to human subjects are not only incorporated into the professional ethics statements of professional organizations such as AERA (1992) and the American Psychological Association (Sales & Folkman, 2000), but they have also been incorporated into federal regulations. Prior to 1974, there were several infamous studies in which researchers placed subjects at definite risk in order to conduct their study. One of the most heinous (critiqued by Jones, 1982) was the Tuskegee syphilis experiment, begun in 1932 in Tuskegee, Alabama, to study the progression of the disease without treatment. Later, when penicillin was discovered, subjects were not treated because they were part of the control group in a comparative study of the treatment. Stanley Milgram's research (1963) on reaction to authority deceived participants into administering "electric shocks" of up to 450 volts to accomplices who acted as though they were in pain. Laud Humphrey's (1970) study of homosexuality was another controversial study because of its deception and gross invasion of privacy.

Studies such as these prompted the government to set down a unified set of regulations for research. In 1974, the federal government passed legislation that applies to all research performed by or under the general supervision of institutions receiving federal research funds. The National Research Act of 1974 requires that, to ensure protection of participants, all proposed research involving human subjects be reviewed and approved by an authorized board before the study begins.

Three major areas related to protection of participants are (1) protection of the human subjects from harm (physical or mental), (2) respect for subjects' right to know the nature and purpose of the study and their right to give or withhold consent to participate (the right of informed consent), and (3) respect for subjects' privacy. One stipulation of the law is that colleges and universities engaging in research with human subjects have an **institutional review board** (**IRB**) that must approve each proposal and certify that the research will be conducted in accordance with the law. These boards, usually referred to as human subjects review boards, require researchers to complete a lengthy form that provides a summary of the purpose and procedures of the proposed project and specific information about possible risks to subjects. Exhibit 16.1 lists the questions that the researcher must answer in a "Summary Safeguard Statement."

If the members of the review board are satisfied that the research will not place subjects at risk, they sign the approval form. Failure to follow all the procedures almost guarantees that the research will not be approved. Exhibit 16.2 shows an example of the form used by the Human Subjects Review Committee at Indiana University, Bloomington, to indicate *approval* of the project.

BLOOMINGTON CAMPUS COMMITTEE for the PROTECTION OF HUMAN SUBJECTS

SUMMARY SAFEGUARD STATEMENT

Project Title (if you wish to use a different title in the consent statement than is listed on page 3, explain here).

A. Briefly describe, in lay terms, the general nature and purpose of the proposed research, and where the study will take place. If student research, indicate whether for a course, thesis, dissertation, or independent research. If the study is only for a course, please review the Student Research Policy to ascertain if this project requires HSC review.

B. Describe how subjects will be recruited, how many (or estimate) subjects will be involved in the research, and how much time will be required of them. List specific eligibility requirements for subjects (or describe screening procedures), including those criteria that would exclude otherwise acceptable subjects. If your study uses only male or female subjects, explain why. For NIH-funded research only, address the inclusion of women, minorities and children in the research. Disclose any relationship between researcher and subjects - such as, teacher/student; superintendent/ principal/teacher; employer/employee.

C. Check appropriate box for type of vulnerable subject population involved when investigation specifically studies:

☐ minors (under age 18), ☐ fetuses, ☐ pregnant women, ☐ persons with mental disabilities, ☐ prisoners, ☐ persons with physical disabilities, ☐ economically or educational disadvantaged, ☐ other vulnerable population.

If any of the above are used, state the necessity for doing so. Please indicate the approximate age range of the minors to be involved.

D. List all procedures to be used on human subjects or describe what subjects will do. If done during regular class time, explain what non-participants will do. If you are taping, explain that here. *Asterisk* those you consider experimental. For those asterisked procedures, describe the usual method(s), if any, that were considered and why they were not used.

E. State the potential risks - for example, physical, psychological, financial, social, legal or other - connected with the proposed procedures.

F. Describe methods for preserving confidentiality. How will data be recorded and stored, with or without identifiers? If identifiers are used describe the type: names, job titles, number code, etc. How long are identifiers kept? If coding system is used, is there a link back to the subject's ID? If yes, where is the code list stored in relation to data and when is the code list destroyed? How will reports be written, in aggregate terms, or will individual responses be described? Will subjects be identified in reports? Briefly describe how risks to subjects are reasonable in relation to anticipated benefits. Describe procedures for protecting against, or minimizing, potential risks. Assess their likely effectiveness. Describe disposition of tapes/films at the end of the study. If tapes are to be kept, indicate for how long and describe future uses of tapes.

EXHIBIT 16.1

Bloomington Campus Committee for the Protection of Human Subjects Summary Safeguard Statement

SUMMARY SAFEGUARD STATEMENT (continued)

G. What, if any, benefit is to be gained by the subject? In the event of monetary gain, include all payment arrangements (amount of payment and the proposed method of disbursement), including reimbursement of expenses. If class credit will be given, list the amount and the value as it relates to the total points needed for an A. List alternative ways to earn the same amount of credit. If merchandise or a service is given, indicate the value. Explain the amount of partial payment/class credit if the subject withdraws prior to completion of the study.

H. What information may accrue to science or society in general as a result of this work?

I. Coinvestigators, . . . , Cooperating Institutions. If there are multiple investigators, please indicate only one person on the Documentation of Review and Approval . . . as the principal investigator; others should be designated as coinvestigators here. **Coinvestigators . . . should sign here. . . .** If you are working with another institution, please include a letter of cooperation from that institution.

EXHIBIT 16.1
Continued

INDIANA UNIVERSITY
BLOOMINGTON CAMPUS COMMITTEE FOR THE PROTECTION OF HUMAN SUBJECTS

DOCUMENTATION OF REVIEW AND APPROVAL
of
Research Project Utilizing Human Subjects

Protocol # _____

TITLE OF PROJECT _____

PROJECT DURATION - START DATE_____ END DATE _____

PRIN. INVESTIGATOR _____ SCHOOL/DEPARTMENT _____

ADDRESS _____ E-MAIL _____ PHONE_____

RANK: Faculty __ Res. Scientist __ Post-Doc __ Staff __ Student: undergrad __ masters __ PhD/EdD __

If PI's rank is *OTHER* than faculty, name of faculty overseeing the research (SPONSOR) _____

_____

SPONSOR'S E-MAIL & CAMPUS ADDRESS _____ PHONE _____

FUNDING AGENCY _____ APPL. DEADLINE _____

AGENCY PROJECT # _____ New _____ Continuation _____

EXHIBIT 16.2
Indiana University Bloomington Campus Committee for the Protection of Human Subjects
Documentation of Review and Approval of Research Project Utilizing Human Subjects

DOCUMENTATION OF REVIEW AND APPROVAL
of
Research Project Utilizing Human Subjects (continued)

As the principal investigator, my signature testifies that I pledge to conform to the following:

As one engaged in investigation utilizing human subjects, I acknowledge the rights and welfare of the human subjects involved.

I acknowledge my responsibility as an investigator to secure the informed consent of the subject by explaining the procedures, in so far as possible, and by describing the risks as weighed against the potential benefits of the investigation.

I assure the Committee that all procedures performed under the project will be conducted in accordance with those Federal regulations and University policies which govern research involving human subjects. **Any deviation from the project (e.g., change in principal investigator, research methodology, subject recruitment procedures, etc.) will be submitted to the Committee in the form of an amendment for its approval prior to implementation.**

PRINCIPAL INVESTIGATOR

_____   _____   _____
(typed/printed name)   (signature)   (date)

As the faculty sponsor, my signature testifies that I have reviewed this application and that I will oversee the research in its entirety.

FACULTY SPONSOR

_____   _____   _____
(typed/printed name)   (signature)   (date)

****

CAMPUS LEVEL REVIEW

This protocol for the use of human subjects has been reviewed and approved by the Indiana University/Bloomington Campus Committee for the Protection of Human Subjects.

____ Exempt Review¶# ____,   ____ Exempt ¶# ____ with signed/documentation of consent,

____Expedited Review,   ____ Full Review,   ____ Not Approved,   ____ Withdrawn

_____   _____
Chairperson/Agent IUB Committee   Date

logged in ts _____ approval logged _____ copy to PI _____ notice to agency _____

EXHIBIT 16.2
Continued

Protecting Subjects from Harm

For research that is funded by the Department of Health and Human Services and that involves human subjects outside the exempted categories (see p. 511), the federal regulations require a determination of whether the subjects will be placed "at risk" by the research procedures. If the researcher can demonstrate that the physical, mental, and social risks involved in the proposed project are no greater than those encountered "in daily life or during the performance of routine physical or psychological examinations or tests," the subjects are not considered "at risk." If the subjects are "at risk," then the researcher must be able to argue that (1) the value of the knowledge that is likely to be gained exceeds the potential harms; (2) all subjects will be fully informed of the risks in the procedures, and the voluntary and written consent of each subject will be obtained; and (3) appropriate medical or other support services will be available to subjects who participate in the research. If these conditions are met, the IRB will usually approve the proposed work. Typically, there is no appeal procedure from an IRB.

Obtaining Informed Consent

Another stipulation of the National Research Act is that the researcher must obtain **informed consent** from research participants. Consent should be (1) voluntary, (2) informed, and (3) given by a competent individual. Obtaining consent is more than simply having a potential research participant sign a form. An informed consent statement has two purposes: (1) to enable potential research subjects to make an informed choice as to their participation in the study, and (2) to document their decision to participate. To make an informed choice, potential subjects must understand the purpose of the study, the procedures, the risks, and benefits of the project, as well as the obligations of both the participants and the researcher. Informed consent is documented by the use of a written consent form approved by the institution's IRB and signed by the subject or the subject's legally authorized representative.

In some cases, it may be argued, prior knowledge of the purposes of the study would bias the results. For such cases it is still important to maintain the voluntary nature of participation even if the purposes are not fully or accurately presented prior to the procedures. In cases where it is important not to discuss the purpose before the procedure, a full explanation should be provided to all subjects after the completion of the procedures. Coercion of subjects and fraudulent explanations of purpose are prohibited by virtually every professional code of ethical standards.

The obtaining of informed consent from people who are not considered capable of representing themselves is problematic. If their competence limits their ability to give consent, researchers should obtain these individuals' *assent* to participate and the *consent* for their participation from their guardians. Researchers facing this problem are advised to consult with the chair of their IRB or with the legal counsel of their institution or organization. The Office for Protection from Research Risks in the Department of Health and Human Services is usually willing to consult on these matters and may be able to provide current information on legal rulings relevant to various groups.

Right to Privacy

Respect for **privacy** and confidentiality is at the heart of the conduct of ethical research with human participants. Folkman (2000) distinguishes between these two terms as follows: "Whereas *privacy* refers to a person's interest in controlling other people's access to information about himself or herself, **confidentiality** refers to the right to maintain private information divulged in the course of a professional relationship with a researcher" (p. 49). There is broad professional agreement that all subjects have an inherent right to privacy. If the researcher does not need to collect the individual's name and other identifying information, it is recommended that the information not be collected. If it is necessary to collect the data for follow-up or other purposes, then it is the researcher's responsibility to provide secure storage for that information and to control access to it. In general, it is recommended that only the principal researcher and those staff members who must know individual data for work-related purposes have access to them. If students or colleagues are to be given access to the data or if it is to be placed in an archive, then it is the responsibility of the principal researcher to remove all personal identifying information from those files.

For research funded by the Department of Health and Human Services, the investigator must provide assurance for the secure storage and maintenance of all names and other identifying information. If the research project collects any personally incriminating or socially damaging information, this obligation is even more important. Failure to keep information of this type secure could lead to sanctions under the federal regulations (disqualification from further grant support) or to civil suits for personal damages.

Present regulations limit the federal regulations to those projects funded by grants from the Department of Health and Human Services and provide several broad **categorical exemptions** from the regulations. The five major categorical exemptions as set forth in the federal document, ***Protection of Human Subjects,*** (1993) are as follows:

(1) Research conducted in established or commonly accepted educational settings, involving normal educational practices, such as (i) research on regular and special education instructional strategies, or (ii) research on the effectiveness of or the comparison among instructional techniques, curricula, or classroom management methods.

(2) Research involving the use of educational tests (cognitive, diagnostic, aptitude, achievement), survey procedures, interview procedures or observation of public behavior, unless: (i) Information obtained is recorded in such a manner that human subjects can be identified, directly or through identifiers linked to the subjects; and (ii) any disclosure of the human subjects' responses outside the research could reasonably place the subjects at risk of criminal or civil liability or be damaging to the subjects' financial standing, employability, or reputation.

(3) Research involving the use of educational tests (cognitive, diagnostic, aptitude, achievement), survey procedures, interview procedures, or observation of public behavior that is not exempt under paragraph (b)(2) of this section, if: (i) The human subjects are elected or appointed public officials or candidates for public office; or (ii) federal statute(s) require(s) without exception that the confidentiality of the personally identifiable information will be maintained throughout the research and thereafter.

(4) Research, involving the collection or study of existing data, documents, records, pathological specimens, or diagnostic specimens, if these sources are publicly available or if the

information is recorded by the investigator in such a manner that subjects cannot be identified, directly or through identifiers linked to the subjects.

(5) Research and demonstration projects which are conducted by or subject to the approval of department or agency heads, and which are designed to study, evaluate, or otherwise examine:

(i) Public benefit or service programs; (ii) procedures for obtaining benefits or services
under those programs; (iii) possible changes in or alternatives to those programs or procedures; or (iv) possible changes in methods or levels of payment for benefits or services
under those programs. (pp. 293–294)

While these regulations exempt much of educational research from direct federal regulations, the IRBs remain in place, and institutions may elect to continue regulations that are
more restrictive in character or broader in scope than the federal regulations. There has been
some informal pressure for institutions to continue the broader regulations. The researcher
should plan to consult his or her IRB to determine institutional rules and policies.

There are a number of publications in the educational and psychological literature on
ethics in research. The American Psychological Association (APA) recently published a
book, *Ethics in Research with Human Participants* (2000), edited by Sales and Folkman. The
Ethical Standards of the American Educational Research Association (AERA) was published in
1992. The Belmont Report, *Ethical Principles and Guidelines for the Protection of Human
Subjects of Research* (National Commission for the Protection of Human Subjects, 1979)
is another statement of basic ethical principles and guidelines for the conduct of research
with human subjects.

SUMMARY

A research proposal is a step-by-step plan for discovering new knowledge. It is at this
stage that the researcher's inspiration and insights crystallize into concrete form. The following categories of information should be included in a quantitative research proposal.

First, a clear statement of the problem, accompanied by unambiguous definitions of
terms, should be made early in the proposal.

Second, a review of pertinent literature should follow. A good review of literature
shows what is so far known about the problem and lays the foundation for stating hypotheses regarding relationships between variables under consideration. In addition, this
part should be written with the aim of providing a foundation for interpreting results.

Third, in the discussion of methodology that follows the introductory section, methods for subject selection, methods of data collection, observational procedures, and measurement techniques should all be described with sufficient detail so that a reader could
carry out the research by following the proposed steps exactly as the original writer of
the proposal would.

Fourth, the next part of the research proposal describes the procedures to be used for
data presentation, such as tables, figures, and charts, and introduces the statistical techniques that will be used for data analysis.

Fifth, a discussion of the potential significance of the study should follow. Here the
researcher should attempt to show how the findings will increase knowledge and what

the results will mean to theory and research in the field of interest. A discussion of the applications of the findings to practice is helpful to readers who wish to assess the significance of the proposed research.

Sixth, the final section of the proposal contains the time schedule and estimated budget of the study. This information is useful to readers in making an overall evaluation of the proposal.

Proposals for qualitative research do not follow a fixed format, but they should provide general information about the purpose of the study, a rationale, a description of subjects and setting, the methodology and data collection procedures, and significance.

A matter of considerable importance in planning research is the observation of ethical standards. Subjects must have the right of informed consent, they must be protected from harm, and their privacy must be respected.

REFERENCES

American Educational Research Association. (1992). Ethical standards of the AERA. *Educational Researcher, 21*(7), 23–26.

American Psychological Association. (1994). *Publication manual of the American Psychological Association* (4th ed.). Washington, DC: American Psychological Association.

Bogdan, R.C., & Biklen, S.K. (1998). *Qualitative research in education* (2nd ed.). Boston: Allyn and Bacon.

Ethical Principles of Psychologists and Code of Conduct. In B. Sales & S. Folkman (Eds.), *Ethics in research with human participants* (pp. 129–160). Washington, DC: American Psychological Association.

Folkman, S. (2000). Privacy and confidentiality. In B. Sales & S. Folkman (Eds.), *Ethics in research with human participants* (pp. 49–59). Washington, DC: American Psychological Association.

Good, C.V., & Skates, D.E. (1954). *Methods of research* (pp. 82–83). New York: Appleton.

Humphreys, L. (1970). *The teahouse trade: Impersonal sex in public places.* Chicago: Aldine-Atherton.

Jones, J.H. (1982). *Bad blood: The Tuskegee syphilis experiment.* New York: Free Press.

Kromrey, J.D. (1993). Ethics and data analysis. *Educational Researcher, 22*(4), 24–27.

Marshall, C., & Rossman, G.B. (1995). *Designing qualitative research* (2nd ed.). Thousand Oaks, CA: Sage.

Maykut, P., & Morehouse, R. (1994). *Beginning qualitative research.* Washington, DC: Falmer Press.

Milgram, S. (1963). Behavioral study of obedience. *Journal of Abnormal and Social Psychology, 67,* 371–378.

National Commission for the Protection of Human Subjects of Biomedical and Behavioral Research. (1979). *Ethical principles and guidelines for the protection of human subjects of research.* The Belmont Report. Washington, DC: U.S. Government Printing Office.

Public Welfare (1993). Protection of human subjects. 45 C.F.R. 546. 101

Sales, B.D., & Folkman, S. (2000). *Ethics in research with human participants.* Washington, DC: American Psychological Association.

Smith, G.R. (1963). A critique of proposals submitted to the cooperative research program. In J.A. Culbertson & S.P. Hencly (Eds.), *Educational research: New perspectives* (chap. 17). Danville, IL: Interstate Publishers and Printers.

KEY CONCEPTS

categorical exemptions	informed consent	privacy
confidentiality	institutional review board (IRB)	

EXERCISES

1. What are the basic components of a quantitative research proposal?

2. How does a qualitative research proposal differ from a quantitative one?

3. At what point in the proposal should a clear statement of the problem be made?

4. Rewrite the following hypotheses, operationalizing all variables:
   a. Children who learn reading by the whole-language approach read better than those taught by a traditional approach.
   b. High school students who score above the top quartile of the XYZ Mechanical Aptitude Test make better mechanics.
   c. Scores on the math subtest of the SRA Achievement Test for smart seventh-grade students who have been instructed with the new math approach for one year will exceed scores of smart seventh-grade students who have been instructed with a traditional approach.

5. What are some confounding variables that may affect differences of mean achievement scores between classes of the same grade level? How could you control for these variables in your proposed procedures?

6. What is the appropriate statistic for measuring correlation if the scale of the variables are nominal?

7. What measure of central tendency is appropriate for interval data?

8. For what types of data is ANOVA appropriate?

9. What is the function of an institutional review board?

10. How might some research results be affected by subjects' knowledge of the purpose of the research? How is the requirement of informed consent met in these circumstances?

11. What precautions should be taken to ensure confidentiality of responses and subjects' privacy in research projects?

12. List some common faults to avoid in preparing a quantitative research proposal.

13. Read about one of the infamous studies mentioned in this chapter (Milgram, Humphrey, Tuskegee study, etc.), and list the ethical principles that were violated.

14. Assume that in your qualitative study of teaching styles, you observed a teacher who was emotionally abusive to students. What would you do? Should you report this observation to the building principal?

ANSWERS

1. Introduction, methodology, analysis of data, significance of the study, and time schedule and budget

2. A qualitative proposal is not as specific as a quantitative one because qualitative research evolves as the study gets underway.

3. In the first paragraph of the introduction

4. a. Third-graders who learned reading in first and second grade by the whole-language approach will score higher on the California Reading Test than third-graders who learned to read using a basal reading approach.

   b. Juniors and seniors who scored above the top quartile of the XYZ Mechanical Aptitude Test before becoming apprentices will be rated more highly by supervisors after one year in a mechanics apprenticeship program than those scoring below the top quartile.

   c. Scores on the math subtest of the SRA Achievement Test of seventh-graders with IQs above 115 on the WISC who have been instructed with the new math approach for one year will exceed scores of similar students who have been instructed with the traditional approach.

5. Different average ability levels, physical class environments, teachers, and types and amount of materials are some factors. One can control for some of these variables by pretesting for ability level, selecting classes with similar environments, and training teachers to certain levels of competence. Using large numbers of classes randomly assigned to conditions offers a different type of control.

6. Phi coefficient

7. The mean

8. Nominal-independent variables and interval-dependent variables

9. The institutional review board determines if the subjects in a proposed experiment are at risk under federal and institutional guidelines, determines if benefits outweigh the risks, then grants or does not grant approval for the research to proceed.

10. Knowing that an unusual or experimental treatment is being used can influence subjects' psychological state and/or expectancy, which may detract from or otherwise influence the actual treatment effects. The subjects in such circumstances should be told that they will be informed of the purpose of the study when it is completed.

11. Subjects should not have to identify themselves unless necessary and should not be identified as individuals in the public report of the study unless they have given their consent.

12. Some possibilities include the following: The problem is trivial. The problem is not delimited. The objectives, hypotheses, or questions are too broadly stated. The procedures are lacking in detail. A simple design is proposed for a complex problem. Relevant variables are not considered.

13. Answers will vary.

14. This incident presents an ethical dilemma. Did you promise confidentiality? Does the benefit that may come from the study outweigh the possible harm to students if this behavior is not reported and is allowed to continue?

 ## INFOTRAC COLLEGE EDITION

Using the key words, *ethics* and *research,* locate a quantitative or qualitative research article in which there were ethical concerns. How did the researcher deal with these ethical issues?

Chapter 17

Analyzing, Interpreting, and Reporting Results of Quantitative Research

INSTRUCTIONAL OBJECTIVES

After studying this chapter, the student will be able to:

1. List points that should be included in a checklist for evaluating quantitative research reports.

2. List principles that the researcher should keep in mind when interpreting results that were anticipated.

3. Distinguish between statistical significance and practical significance.

4. List principles that the researcher should keep in mind when interpreting unanticipated results.

5. Explain the various circumstances that might result in the retention of a null hypothesis.

6. List some principles of interpretation that the researcher should keep in mind when the null hypothesis has been retained.

7. Write appropriate titles for a dissertation or other quantitative research report.

8 Describe the nature of the content to include in each section of a thesis or dissertation.

9 State the procedure to follow when preparing a research article for a professional journal.

10 State the procedure to follow when preparing a paper to be read at a professional conference.

INTERPRETING AND REPORTING QUANTITATIVE RESEARCH

Once the proposal has been accepted, the researcher can begin to collect and analyze the data. When hypothesis-testing research is set in motion, it is important that the study be carried out exactly as planned. This rule has ethical as well as practical implications.

To illustrate the ethical implications, suppose that Mr. Williams, a language teacher, has developed, with a great expenditure of time and effort, a system of teaching French that he believes greatly superior to existing methods. To test the efficacy of this method, he establishes an experimental group taught by his method and a control group taught by another method. He devises a series of weekly French achievement tests to serve as the dependent variable. Suppose he discovers in the first few weeks that the mean test scores for the two groups are almost identical. Having a big investment in his own method, he finds it hard to believe that it is no better than the other, so he decides to sit in on the two classes to see what has "gone wrong." He discovers that the experimental group seems to show much greater knowledge and appreciation of French life and culture. Because he is determined to find a difference between scores, he decides to change his dependent variable to scores on tests on French life and culture.

Such a change would be unethical. Given two random groups, one can always find through chance alone a superiority in either group if one looks long enough. If the experimental group had not appeared superior on French life and culture, it might have been superior in verbal fluency, listening skills, on-task behavior, or some other variable. The language teacher *must* carry out the experiment as planned and not change the dependent variable. The investigator should report the evidence suggesting a relationship between method and appreciation of French life and culture, but should make it clear to readers that this relationship was not hypothesized and therefore could easily have been a function of chance. It is unethical to abandon independent or dependent variables that do not seem to be "working out," or to add promising new ones.

Adding new variables is also unwise from a practical standpoint. Such a tactic can confuse the results of a hypothesis-testing study and obscure the meaning of the results. Researchers are often tempted to add interesting new variables that crop up in their study. However, the theoretical base for interpreting these variables has not been laid, and again the best advice to researchers is to leave them for later studies.

Of course, this caveat only applies to research in which predetermined hypotheses are being tested. In qualitative research the hypotheses emerge as the study proceeds and are redefined when appropriate. Also, in descriptive research—such as developmental studies and trend analyses that do not begin with a hypothesis—there is no reason why a researcher should not add variables when appropriate.

WRITING THE FINAL REPORT

Following data analysis, the researcher is ready to write the final report. A research project is of little value unless the findings can be communicated to others. Writing the final report is not as difficult a task as a beginning researcher might think. Much of the writing, such as the introduction, review of literature, and methodology has already been done in the initial proposal. Only minor revisions and a switch to the past tense should be needed on these preliminary sections. At this point, the researcher's major task is to present the findings, discuss the findings, and draw conclusions. We now briefly discuss each of these tasks.

The Results

This section presents the results of the statistical analyses of the data. A recommended technique for presenting the results is to organize findings around the hypotheses; that is, the researcher restates the first hypothesis and presents findings concerning it, then repeats this procedure for each hypothesis in turn. Note that he or she does *not* interpret or discuss the results at this point, but merely presents the findings. This section of the final report is thus relatively brief.

To facilitate comprehension, tables and figures are typically used to present the findings. Tables and figures present the numbers and statistics more clearly and more concisely than is possible if the same information is presented in text form. A *table* shows the quantitative data organized in rows and columns. A *figure* shows the data in diagram or graphical form. Well-constructed tables and figures should "stand alone"; readers should be able to understand them without having to refer to the text.

The first table in the report usually summarizes the descriptive statistics, such as means, standard deviations, correlations, percentages, and so on. Later tables present the results of applying inferential statistics and tests of significance to the data. Name the calculated statistic, give the degrees of freedom, and give the probability level at which the statistic was significant (or not significant). Use a summary table, for example, to present the results of an analysis of variance. Most style manuals such as the *Publication Manual* (American Psychological Association, 1994) provide examples of commonly used types of tables and figures and instructions for their construction. Computer software has greatly simplified the task of preparing tables and figures for research papers.

When writing the results section, the researcher refers to each table and each figure by number and comments on the most important and interesting finding in each. Use present tense when pointing out the significant aspects of a table or figure. The following example was taken from a journal article: "Table 2 shows the descriptive statistics for prerecess inattention measures for the three groups. Kindergarteners were less attentive during the long, compared to the short, confinement period. Table 3 shows the analyses of the recess data with a grade $\times$ gender $\times$ condition repeated measures ANOVA. Main effects were observed for grade, $F (2, 56) = 4.92, p < .0005$, and for gender, $F (1, 56) = 10.26, p < .0001$" (Pellegrini, Huberty, & Jones, p. 853, 1995).

The Discussion

A beginning researcher will probably find the discussion section the most difficult but also the most rewarding to write. This section is more difficult because there is no standard format for the content; you must use insight and original thinking to provide an explanation and interpretation of the results that you presented in the previous section. Be ready to provide the answer to the original research question. First discuss how the results support or fail to support the hypotheses of the study. In this *interpretation,* you must deal not only with expected results, but also occasionally with unexpected or negative results. We now provide some guidelines for interpreting various results.

Interpreting Expected Results

Researchers are understandably pleased when the results of a study fit into the previously constructed framework and interpretation can proceed as expected. The study has "worked," and there is agreement between rationale and results. Only a few words of caution need apply in **interpreting expected results:**

1. *Do not make interpretations that go beyond the information.* This injunction may seem patently obvious, but researchers often get so excited when results are as expected that they draw conclusions that do not have a valid basis in the data. Even published research sometimes offers more interpretations than the data warrant.

2. *Do not forget the limitations of the study.* These limitations, of course, should have been previously identified in the study—limitations inherent in the less-than-perfect reliability and validity of the instruments, limitations caused by the restriction in sampling, the internal validity problems, and so forth.

3. *Ethics require that the researcher report internal-validity problems that could account for the results.* If, despite the researcher's best efforts, the nonexperimental variables were particularly benign for the experimental group and those for the control group were particularly malign, these conditions must be reported and taken into account in interpreting results. (For example, despite random assignment of teachers to groups, the experimental group may have mostly experienced teachers and the control group may have mostly inexperienced teachers.)

4. *Remember that statistical significance means only that for the appropriate degrees of freedom, the results are unlikely to be a function of chance.* **Practical and statistical significance** have very different meanings. Statistical significance does not mean that the results are significant in the generally accepted meaning of the word—

that is, important, meaningful, or momentous. Do not assume that statistical significance guarantees momentous import to your findings.

Suppose that two equivalent groups have been subjected to two different systems of learning spelling over a 2-year period. Those using System A show a mean gain equivalent of 2.15 years of growth on standardized tests during the experiment, whereas those using System B show a gain of 2.20 in the same period. If the groups are large and/or if the differences within groups are small, the differences between the means would be statistically significant. But a difference of half a month over a two-year period is relatively meaningless in practical terms. If System B is more expensive in terms of student time, teacher time, or materials, teachers would be unwise to adopt it simply because it produced statistically significantly greater gains than System A. If, in contrast, System B is less expensive, teachers would be inclined to favor it because its results are so similar to those of System A in practical terms.

The potential importance or meaningfulness of results must be established in the proposal before the study begins. A study is not important if it does not add meaningful information to the existing body of knowledge, no matter how statistically significant the results may be.

Interpreting Negative Results

Researchers who find negative results, results opposite to those hypothesized, often develop sudden revelations concerning the shortcomings of their study. Their interpretation of results reads like a confession. The instruments were inadequate for measuring the variables involved, the sample was too small and was so unrepresentative that results cannot be validly generalized to a meaningful target population, and so on. Hindsight reveals internal-validity problems that explain why the study did not come out as it "should have."

Of course, any or all of these things could be true, and the shortcomings of any study should be reported no matter what the results. However, research is always a venture into the unknown, so there is no ultimate "should be." An investigator predicts the expected results of a study on the basis of theory, deduction, experiences, and the results of previous research. If these are so conclusive that there can be absolutely no doubt as to the results of this study, then the study is pointless in the first place.

When you undertake a study, you implicitly state that the outcome is a matter of conjecture, not a matter of certainty. When you complete your proposal, it is understood that you declare you will impartially seek to determine the true state of affairs with the best instruments and procedures available to use for that purpose. Therefore, you are obliged to accept and interpret your data no matter how the data stand. When the results contradict the theoretical rationale of the study, the discussion section of your report should include a reconsideration of the original theory in light of the findings. Researchers are often reluctant to present and interpret data that conflict with previous research or with well-established theory. However, it may be that their results are right and previous results wrong. The progress of the science of education will be retarded if investigators are reluctant to report findings that disagree with those reported in earlier studies.

Contradictory results indicate that a question is not settled and may stimulate further research. Additional research or theory formation may eventually reconcile seemingly contradictory results. Theory is tentative and should not deter investigators from giving a straightforward interpretation of what was found.

Reconsideration of the theoretical base of a study belongs in the discussion section. One must *not* go back and rewrite the related literature and hypothesis sections of the report.

Interpreting Results When the Null Hypothesis Is Retained

Because a null hypothesis may be retained for a variety of reasons, **interpreting** a **retained null hypotheses** can be particularly difficult. A retained null hypothesis may occur because

1. The null hypothesis is, in fact, true. There may be no relationship between variables. The experimental treatment may be no more effective than the control treatment.

2. The null hypothesis is false, but internal-validity problems contaminated the investigation so badly that the actual relationship between variables could not be observed.

3. The null hypothesis is false, but the research design lacked the power to reject it.

Any of these states of affairs may be the case, but the investigator does not know which is true and therefore should not claim any one of them as the explanation for the results.

It is incorrect to present a retained null hypothesis as evidence of no relationship between variables. A retained null hypothesis must be interpreted as lack of evidence for either the truth or falsity of the hypothesis. A widely used toothpaste commercial stated that tests show a particular toothpaste to be unsurpassed in reducing tooth decay. Interpreting the term *unsurpassed* to mean "no significant difference," we can imagine a test in which a very small number of subjects were used and/or numerous internal validity problems were present. If a retained null hypothesis is the desired result of an experiment, it is remarkably easy to arrange for such an outcome.

There is a danger that investigators who become too enamored of their experimental hypothesis may be tempted to explain away a retained null hypothesis. They cite internal validity problems and declare that the results would certainly have been significant if only those unanticipated problems had not ruined the experiment. Of course, one should report all internal-validity problems that arise in a study, but one should not use them to explain away disappointing results. One may suggest additional research, planned in such a way as to avoid the internal validity-problems encountered, but still one must report a retained null hypothesis as lack of evidence and no more.

Recall from Chapter 7 that the *power* of an experiment refers to the statistical ability to reject a null hypothesis when it is, in fact, false. This power is a function of the size of the sample, the heterogeneity of subjects with reference to the dependent variable, the reliability of the measuring instruments used, and the nature of the statistical procedure used to test the hypothesis, as well as effect size. Researchers should take these factors into account when planning an experiment. The power of an experiment should be considered in planning the study. It must not be brought in at the end of a study to explain away lack of statistical significance. For example, one should not say, "The results would have been statistically significant if the sample had been larger."

With rare exceptions, the only legitimate interpretation of a retained null hypothesis is that "sufficient evidence for a conclusion has not been observed." Of course, if you are studying a small population and can do a complete census of that population, a retained null hypothesis can legitimately be interpreted as a lack of relationship between variables within that particular population. A retained null hypothesis also acquires credibility if you can show that the study was free of internal validity problems and had sufficient power to reject the null hypothesis with a relatively trivial effect size.

Interpreting Unhypothesized (Serendipitous) Relationships

We emphasized earlier that a researcher should not abandon a hypothesis during the conduct of a study in order to pursue more promising avenues that present themselves during the course of the study. This does not mean that you should ignore any unhypothesized relationships that you may observe in conducting a study. On the contrary, you should record and analyze them with the same rigor you employ in pursuing hypothesized relationships. Throughout the history of science, such **serendipitous discoveries** have often proved important. However, such findings should always be viewed with more suspicion than findings directly related to the hypothesis, because there is a relatively great possibility that a spurious unhypothesized relationship will appear in a study. Such relationships should be reported, but they should be considered incidental to the main thrust of the investigation. Before they can be employed as the basis for conclusions, they should be made the subject of a later study specifically designed to investigate them.

In the discussion section, it is very important that the researcher point out the specific *implications* of the research. The results may support or not support relevant theoretical positions. You may explain how the theory should be modified and may suggest further studies that would logically follow. Also, discuss how the results fit in with previous research findings. Lastly, give some attention to stating the possible *application* of the findings to educational practice. The sections on implications and applications of the results are often not sufficiently developed because the writer assumes these will be as obvious to the reader as they are to the investigators. In fact, in the conduct of the study the investigators probably gained insights into the problem that are deeper than those most of their readers can be assumed to have. Therefore, researchers' interpretations should be more meaningful than those that readers might make for themselves.

Conclusions and Summary

The conclusions and summary sections together form the capstone of the report.

Conclusions

In the conclusions section, the researcher tells what the research findings really mean in conceptual terms. The conclusions indicated by the research findings should be limited to those that have direct support in the research findings. Researchers are often tempted to conclude too much. The hypotheses provide a convenient framework for stating conclusions; that is, indicate in this section whether the findings support the hypotheses. It is important to distinguish between *results* and *conclusions*. Results are direct observations summarized and integrated by the statistical analysis, such as a comparison of two group means. A conclusion is an inference based on the results, expressed in terms of the study's hypothesis, such as one group's treatment being more effective than the other group's. For example, a study might result in the observation that the mean spelling test scores of students taught spelling by Method A is significantly higher than the mean of students taught by Method B. The conclusion that Method A is more effective than Method B is not a direct result of the study but rather is an inference based on the results of the study.

Summary

Because the summary will be more widely read than other sections of the report, its wording must be particularly clear and concise. The summary usually includes a brief restatement of the problem(s), the main features of the methods, and the most important findings. On completing a draft of this section, check it carefully to determine whether it gives a concise but reasonably complete description of the study and its findings. Also check to ascertain that no information has been introduced here that was not included in the appropriate preceding sections. It is a good idea to have a colleague read the conclusions section to see if you are communicating as well as you intended.

▮ PUTTING IT ALL TOGETHER

We have looked at the major components of a formal quantitative research project. In this section, we give some general suggestions to follow in the organization and presentation of various types of written reports. For specific rules on style and format, consult a style manual.

Because busy professionals will read the report, it should be as concise and as logically organized as possible. Anecdotes, stories of personal experiences, and argumentative discourses are out of place in a quantitative research report. This does not mean the report must be dull and pedantic. If the researcher has approached the study with enthusiasm, this spirit tends to be conveyed between the lines.

And because the purpose of the report is to present the research rather than the personality of the author, keep the tone impersonal. In keeping with this, first-person pronouns are never used. Thus, you would *not* write, "I randomly assigned subjects to the two treatment groups," but rather "Subjects were randomly assigned to the two treatment groups." Despite a natural enthusiasm about the importance of the work, the author should not brag about it but should leave its evaluation to readers and to posterity.

A formal and uniform method of presenting research reports has evolved. Although at first glance these formalities may seem inhibiting, in practice they serve a useful purpose. It is important to have research reports arranged in such a way that readers know exactly where to find those specific parts they may be seeking. Otherwise time is lost seeking relevant information. In addition, the presence of an established format eliminates the need for devising one's own. As this topic is discussed, it will be seen that the established format follows logically the steps in a research project presented in earlier chapters.

A research report may be presented as (1) a thesis or dissertation, (2) a journal article, or (3) a conference paper. A different approach is required in each of these cases.

The Thesis or Dissertation

Most universities have a preferred **style manual** that describes in detail the form the university requires. For students who are free to choose, several style manuals are listed at the end of this chapter. Once a manual has been chosen, the entire report should be styled according to its recommendations.

The following outline lists the sequence and general components described in most style manuals:

1. Preliminary pages
   a. Title page·
   b. Acceptance page
   c. Acknowledgments or preface
   d. Table of contents
   e. List of tables
   f. List of figures
2. Text
   a. Introduction
      (1) Statement of the problem and rationale for the study
      (2) Statement of the hypotheses
      (3) Definitions of terms
      (4) Related literature
   b. Methods
      (1) Subjects
      (2) Procedures
      (3) Instruments
   c. Results
      (1) Presentation of data
      (2) Analysis of data
   d. Discussion
      (1) Interpretation of findings
      (2) Implications
      (3) Applications
   e. Conclusions and summary
      (1) Conclusions
      (2) Summary

3. Supplementary pages
   a. References
   b. Appendixes
   c. Vita (if required)
   d. Abstract

Preliminary Pages

The preparation of the preliminary pages is largely a matter of following the rules of the style manual. However, one aspect of these pages that needs additional explanation at this point is the title of the study itself.

The title should describe, as briefly as possible, the specific nature of the study. A rule-of-thumb states that a title should have no more than twelve to fifteen words. For example, consider (1) a study of culturally disadvantaged children that compares the reading readiness of those who have participated in a Project Head Start program with that of a matched group of children with no formal preschool experience, and (2) the title, "A Comparison of Reading Readiness Test Scores of Disadvantaged Children Who Have Attended Head Start Classes for Six Weeks or More with Similar Children with No Preschool Experience." Although this title does convey what the study is about, it is too long. Such phrases as "a comparison of," "a study of," and "an investigation into" are usually superfluous. Furthermore, most prospective readers will know that Project Head Start is a preschool experience designed for culturally disadvantaged children. However, to go to the other extreme by providing a title that is too brief or too vague to convey the nature of the study is a much more serious mistake. With vague or overly brief titles, a prospective reader must search out the article to determine what it is about. Titles such as "Head Start and Readiness" or "Reading among the Disadvantaged" illustrate this shortcoming. *The title should identify the major variables and the populations of interest.* The operational definitions of the major variables and the description of the samples need not be included in the title.

Because correct titling will ensure correct indexing, a useful strategy is for researchers first to decide under what key words they want their studies to be indexed, working from there to a concise title. In addition, the title should, if possible, begin, not with an article (a, an, the) but with a key word, and a fanciful part should be relegated to subtitle because bibliographers often cut off the subtitle or alphabetize under the article (the, a), ensuring real confusion or loss to searchers. In our example, the important key words for indexing would be *reading readiness* and *Project Head Start.* So an appropriate title might be "Reading Readiness of Project Head Start and Non–Head Start Children." This title is reasonably brief, yet it gives the prospective reader a valid indication of what the study is about.

Avoid at all costs emotion-laden titles, such as "We Must Expand the Head Start Program" or "Don't Let the Disadvantaged Become Poor Readers." The prospective reader will not expect research findings under such titles but rather armchair articles attempting to sell a point of view.

Text

The main body of the dissertation includes the introduction; sections on methods and results; the discussion of results; and the conclusions and summary. Each of these sections is typically a chapter in the dissertation. We have already familiarized you with the writing of these sections; no further discussion is needed.

Supplementary Pages

References

The reference list must include all sources mentioned in the text. Most universities insist that *only* these be listed, but a few ask that pertinent references not specifically mentioned also be listed. The style manual previously selected will give complete details on the method of listing references. It is important to follow these rules rigorously and completely. In fact, it is good strategy to learn them before carrying out the search through the literature for the proposal. By listing each reference in the correct form as it is encountered, you can avoid the extra time involved in finding the references again in order to have them in complete form for the bibliography. List them on cards or enter them in your computer so you can file them in alphabetical order.

Appendixes

The appendixes contain pertinent materials that are not important enough to include in the body of the report but may be of value to some readers. Such materials may include complete copies of locally devised tests or questionnaires together with the instructions and scoring keys for such instruments, item analysis data for measurements used, verbatim instructions to subjects, and tables that are very long or of only minor importance to the study.

Vita

The authors of research reports are sometimes asked to include brief accounts of their training, experience, professional memberships, and previous contributions.

Abstract

Most institutions require a separate abstract of the dissertation, which should include a definitive statement of the problem and concise descriptions of the research methods, major findings, conclusions, and implications. The abstract must be limited in length (typically 600 words or less). Number the abstract pages separately and place them either at the very beginning or the very end of the dissertation.

The Journal Article

In preparing a research article for publication in a journal, a good first step is to look through your bibliography to determine which journal has published the greatest amount of work in your area of interest. Information concerning the procedure for submission of manuscripts is usually on the inside of a journal's front cover. Many journals specify which style manual should be used (for example, the *Publication Manual of the American Psychological Association,* fourth edition, 1994). If a manual is not specified, you can determine the preferred style, method of referencing, and so on from looking at the articles included in a recent issue of the journal. A research article follows the same general outline as a dissertation, but must be much shorter. A thesis or dissertation functions to demonstrate a student's competence and requires a full setting forth of the related research, complete description of the procedures, complete tabulation of results, and reflective elaboration. The journal article, in contrast, requires only communication of the author's contribution to knowledge. For the sake of economy of journal space and readers' time, the article must be concise. The section on related literature contains only those results and arguments that provide the basis for the problem. The general statement of the problem is given in one paragraph, or possibly even omitted, in which case the article would begin with the hypothesis. The procedures section is also presented very briefly, although all the information needed to replicate the experiment should be included if at all possible. The results section is of greatest interest to the reader and therefore represents a greater proportion of the article than it would in a dissertation. Only the most important findings should be discussed in any detail.

A brief cover letter should accompany the manuscript. The editor usually sends the author a postcard acknowledging receipt of the manuscript and circulates copies of it among the appropriate members of the editorial board for review. From this point considerable time usually elapses before the author is informed whether the article has been accepted (six weeks is probably typical). After an article is accepted, it is usually many months before it appears in print. When a manuscript is rejected by a journal, the rejection notice is usually accompanied by a statement of the reasons for this rejection. A rejection by one journal does not necessarily mean that the article is unworthy of publication. A number of factors—such as competition for space, changes in editorial policy, or bias of reviewers—can influence the decision on publication. An article that has been rejected by one journal may be revised and submitted to another. Many articles make the rounds of several journals before finding a home. It is not ethical, however, to submit an article to more than one journal at a time.

The Professional Convention Paper

Many researchers find that hearing papers read at professional conventions is a good way to keep up to date in their field. The reason for this is that there is a great lapse of time between the completion of a research project and its appearance in print. This time lag is often so long that professional journals have sometimes been described as being archival in nature.

Papers presented ("read") at professional meetings are prepared in much the same manner as journal articles. They are not necessarily always reports of completed research but may be progress reports of ongoing projects. A read paper is less formal than a journal article and can usually be more precisely geared to its audience. The audience can generally be expected to be familiar with details of related research and methods of measurement.

The paper is frequently organized as follows:

1. Direct statement of the hypothesis

2. Brief description of the procedures

3. Findings, conclusions, and implications
   The time allowed for reading a paper is usually quite brief, frequently less than 30 minutes. Therefore, the paper should focus on the most important aspects of one's study. A convenient rule of thumb is to allow 2½ to 3 minutes for each page of double-spaced typed copy.

   If figures or tables will assist in the presentation, copies should be available for the audience. Some speakers also distribute copies of the text of their paper to the audience. However, because the audience reads the paper silently more rapidly than the author can read it aloud, there may be a gap in attention. It is preferable to have copies of a complete description of the study available for people who request it after the paper is presented.

Poster Session Presentations

Professional conventions often include poster sessions. Poster presenters are assigned a bulletin board (typically $4' \times 8'$) in a designated room and a designated time frame, typically 1–1½ hours. The author mounts the presentation on the bulletin board and stands by it during the designated time. Those interested in the presentation will inspect it and may ask the presenter about it. Only a brief review of the study can fit onto the bulletin board, so only the abstract and highlights can be presented in this format. The presenter should have available the details needed to answer any questions that may be asked. Presenters often choose to have copies of the complete report available for those who request them.

CHECKLIST FOR EVALUATING QUANTITATIVE RESEARCH REPORTS

The following checklist should be useful for evaluating your own quantitative research reports and the reports of others. It brings together many of the topics presented in this text.

Title
> Is the title brief but informative?
> Does the title make clear the population of interest and the major variables?
> Have vague, ambiguous, and emotion-laden terms been avoided?

Statement of the Problem
> Have the variables of interest been identified?
> Has the theoretical foundation for the study been developed?
> Is the problem clearly stated?
> Is there a justification or rationale for the study?

Related Literature
> Is the related literature relevant and sufficient?
> Are the connections between the present study and the previous research and theory made clear?

Hypotheses
> Are the hypotheses explicit?
> Do the hypotheses follow logically from the statement of the problem?

Subjects
> Is the population of interest defined?
> Is the method for selecting the sample explicit?
> Does the sampling allow for generalization to the population of interest?

Procedures
> Are the procedures described well enough to allow replication of the study?
> Do the procedures include appropriate operational definitions of the independent variables?
> Do the procedures provide sufficient control for internal validity?
> Do the procedures provide sufficient control for external validity?

Instruments
> Are the instruments adequately described?
> Is information on the validity and reliability of the instruments provided?
> Are the instruments appropriate operational definitions of the dependent variables?

Analysis of the Data
> Are the descriptive statistics used appropriate for summarizing the data?
> Are the inferential statistics used appropriate for testing the hypotheses?
> Have the statistics been interpreted appropriately?
> Are the statistics appropriate for the level of measurement of the data?

Results
> Are the results of all hypothesis tests presented?
> Are the statistics interpreted correctly?
> Are the results clearly presented?
> Are tables and figures used appropriately?

Discussion
> Is there a clear interpretation of the results?
> Does the author present implications of the study results?
> Are the implications presented based on the results of the study, not on what the author hoped or expected to be true?
> Are appropriate applications discussed?
> Do the applications follow logically from the results of the study?
> Are the connections between the results and theory and existing literature shown?
> Are there suggestions for future research?

Conclusions

Are the conclusions clearly presented?

Do the conclusions follow logically from the results of the study?

Has the author avoided reaching conclusions that are not directly supported by the outcomes of the study?

Summary

Is the summary clear, concise, and sufficiently complete?

STYLE MANUALS

The following are widely used manuals detailing general form and style for theses and dissertations:

American Psychological Association. (1994). *Publication manual of the American Psychological Association* (4th ed.). Washington, DC: American Psychological Association.

Campbell, W.G., & Ballou, S.V. (1990). *Form and style: Theses, reports, term papers* (8th ed.). Boston: Houghton Mifflin.

Turabian, K. (1996). *A manual for writers of term papers, theses, and dissertations* (6th ed.). Chicago: University of Chicago Press.

University of Chicago Press. (1993). *The Chicago manual of style* (14th ed.). Chicago: University of Chicago Press.

SUMMARY

Researchers communicate the results of their investigations in written reports. They communicate what question was investigated, why and how it was investigated, and what was found. The research report may take the form of a thesis or dissertation, journal article, or presentation at a professional meeting.

The main text of a report of quantitative research includes introduction, method, results, discussion, and conclusions/summary. Following the text is a list of references that indicates *all* the sources cited in the report and *only* those sources. The researcher follows standard guidelines for writing each of these sections. Probably the most difficult section to write is the discussion, because here the researcher must explain the findings.

Interpreting the results of a study is a straightforward task if, in the proposal, the researcher has laid a proper foundation for the research. The following cautions should be kept in mind:

1. Interpretation should be strictly based on the data derived from the study.

2. Internal- and external-validity problems and other limitations of the study should be considered.

3. Conclusions must be presented as probability statements rather than as facts.

Negative results deserve the same respect and interpretation as do positive results. A retained null hypothesis is interpreted as indication of insufficient evidence and no more. Unhypothesized results deserve attention as sources of future hypotheses.

Formal procedures have been developed for preparing dissertations, journal articles, and papers. Researchers need to familiarize themselves with the style manual required at a university or journal and follow it in the preparation of the final manuscript. The most popular format for educational research reports is the APA *Publication Manual* (fourth ed., 1994).

REFERENCE

Pellegrini, A.D., Huberty, P.D., & Jones, I. (1995). The effect of recess timing on children's playground and classroom behaviors. *American Educational Research Journal, 32,* 845–864.

KEY CONCEPTS

interpreting expected results

interpreting retained null hypotheses

interpreting serendipitous discoveries

practical and statistical significance

style manual

EXERCISES

1. Indicate in which section of a journal article reporting quantitative research (introduction, methods, results, discussion) the following statements would belong:

    a. "Subjects were first-grade students in three schools located in the same rural district of a state in the Far West. Students were predominantly lower- to lower-middle-class Anglo Americans, with a few Hispanics."

    b. "The purpose of this research is to examine the effects of implementing two reading programs in comparable first-grade classes during one school year."

    c. "All first-graders were pretested on the Peabody Picture Vocabulary Test and the Woodcock Reading Mastery Test."

    d. "Students using Program A tended to perform least well relative to Program B students on Passage Comprehension, while surpassing them on Word Attack. One possible explanation lies in the students' previous experiences with the tasks required by the different reading comprehension testing formats."

    e. "Results of the ANOVA performed on the overall sample ($n = 184$) were significant, $F(4, 176) = 5.89, p < .001$."

    f. "There is a need to continue this study over time, replicate it elsewhere, and to experiment with combinations of the two reading programs and other strategies."

2. Indicate whether the format of the following statements written for a journal article is correct or incorrect. If incorrect, tell why and rewrite the statement using acceptable format.

    a. "I administered a pretest to both groups of subjects."

b. "The means of the pretest and posttest for the two groups are summarized in the following table and the interaction is shown in the graph below."

c. "The experimental group will be shown a series of films designed to change attitudes toward smoking."

d. "Recently, a study at Indiana State evaluated the Reading Recovery Program in comparison to three alternative programs in four Indiana school districts."

e. "Groups of mothers were randomly assigned to one of four interview discussion groups ($n = 5$) held in a quiet setting within the school."

3. What is the difference between results and conclusions?

4. Explain the difference between statistical significance of the results and the significance of the study.

5. What states of affairs can lead to a retained null hypothesis in a quantitative study?

6. Decide whether each of the following titles is acceptable or unacceptable for quantitative research and give reasons for your choices:

a. "Grade-Point Average and Driver Education"

b. "The Effects of Individualized Tutoring by Sixth-Grade Students Three Times a Week on Reading Performance of Below-Average Second-Grade Readers"

c. "Children Should Be Taught through Discovery Learning!"

d. "Relationship between Personality Characteristics and Attitudes toward Achievement of Good and Poor Readers"

7. What are the differences in format for research reported in dissertation form, in journal form, and in a paper to be read at a conference?

8. Should one discuss research results that do not agree with one's hypothesis?

9. For the following situations, indicate whether you would report your research in a journal article or in a paper at a professional meeting.

a. A progress report of an incomplete but ongoing research project.

b. Your goal is to communicate to the widest possible audience in the field.

c. You wish to avoid the time lag in communicating results.

10. A researcher reported the following: "Achievement test scores for 36 subjects working under tangible incentives were mean = 72.0 and standard deviation = 10.9 on Test 1 and mean = 76.0 with a SD = 9.7 on Test 2. Combined average = 74.0, SD = 10.3. Scores for 34 subjects working under intangible incentives were mean = 68.0 with SD = 8.5 on Test 1 and mean = 70.0 with SD = 10.2 on Test 2. Combined average for intangible incentive group = 69.0 with SD = 9.3." Show how the researcher could use a table to present these findings so that they could be more readily comprehended by readers.

ANSWERS

1. a. Methods
   b. Introduction
   c. Methods
   d. Discussion
   e. Findings
   f. Discussion

2. a. Incorrect, personal pronouns are not used in research reports: "A pretest was administered to both groups of subjects."
   b. Incorrect, tables and figures are always referred to by number: "The means of the pre- and posttests for the two groups are

summarized in Table 1 and the interaction is shown in Figure 1."

c. Incorrect, use past tense when writing the methods section: "The experimental group was shown a series of films designed to change attitudes toward smoking."

d. Incorrect, no name or date is given for the reference to the research reported: "Smith and Green (1999) evaluated the Reading Recovery Program in comparison to three alternative programs in four Indiana school districts."

e. Correct

3. A result is a direct observation. A conclusion is an inference based on results.

4. Statistical significance means only that the results are not likely to be a function of chance; the significance of the study is determined by the importance of the findings in regard to theory testing or practical implications.

5. A retained null hypothesis could result from the null hypothesis's actually being true in nature; or it could result from contamination by internal-validity problems that obscure treatment effects, from lack of statistical power of the design used in the study, or from inability of the instruments to measure accurately the effects of treatment on the dependent variable.

6. a. Unacceptable; no statement of relationship is given
   b. Unacceptable; too wordy

c. Unacceptable; emotion-laden titles are not appropriate for research articles

d. Acceptable; meets criteria for title

7. Dissertation form is the most formal and detailed in presentation; it follows the specifics of a particular style manual. The journal article is a more concise presentation, with a brief statement of problem, related literature, and methodology; a greater proportion of the article is devoted to major results and a discussion of their significance. A paper that is to be read at a conference is the most informal; geared to its audience, it states the hypothesis, briefly describes the procedure, and emphasizes the most important findings.

8. Yes. Results contrary to one's expectations are as legitimate as any other results and should be interpreted as such.

9. a. Paper at a professional meeting
   b. Journal article
   c. Paper

10. Answers will vary. The following is simply a suggestion.

		Test	
Incentive	1	2	Combined
Tangible (*n* = 36)			
M	72.0	76.0	74.0
SD	10.9	9.7	10.3
Intangible (*n* = 34)			
M	68.0	70.0	69.0
SD	8.5	10.2	9.3

 ## INFOTRAC COLLEGE EDITION

Search InfoTrac to find a research article on a topic you are interested in knowing more about. Does it have all the sections we discussed in this chapter? Evaluate the article using the criteria presented.

APPENDIX

Table A.1   Areas of the Normal Curve

(1) z	(2) AREA BETWEEN THE MEAN AND z	(3) AREA BEYOND z	(1) z	(2) AREA BETWEEN THE MEAN AND z	(3) AREA BEYOND z
0.00	.0000	.5000	0.35	.1368	.3632
0.01	.0040	.4960	0.36	.1406	.3594
0.02	.0080	.4920	0.37	.1443	.3557
0.03	.0120	.4880	0.38	.1480	.3520
0.04	.0160	.4840	0.39	.1517	.3483
0.05	.0199	.4801	0.40	.1554	.3446
0.06	.0239	.4761	0.41	.1591	.3409
0.07	.0279	.4721	0.42	.1628	.3372
0.08	.0319	.4681	0.43	.1664	.3336
0.09	.0359	.4641	0.44	.1700	.3300
0.10	.0398	.4602	0.45	.1736	.3264
0.11	.0438	.4562	0.46	.1772	.3228
0.12	.0478	.4522	0.47	.1808	.3192
0.13	.0517	.4483	0.48	.1844	.3156
0.14	.0557	.4443	0.49	.1879	.3121
0.15	.0596	.4404	0.50	.1915	.3085
0.16	.0636	.4364	0.51	.1950	.3050
0.17	.0675	.4325	0.52	.1985	.3015
0.18	.0714	.4286	0.53	.2019	.2981
0.19	.0753	.4247	0.54	.2054	.2946
0.20	.0793	.4207	0.55	.2088	.2912
0.21	.0832	.4168	0.56	.2123	.2877
0.22	.0871	.4129	0.57	.2157	.2843
0.23	.0910	.4090	0.58	.2190	.2810
0.24	.0948	.4052	0.59	.2224	.2776
0.25	.0987	.4013	0.60	.2257	.2743
0.26	.1026	.3974	0.61	.2291	.2709
0.27	.1064	.3936	0.62	.2324	.2676
0.28	.1103	.3897	0.63	.2357	.2643
0.29	.1141	.3859	0.64	.2389	.2611
0.30	.1179	.3821	0.65	.2422	.2578
0.31	.1217	.3783	0.66	.2454	.2546
0.32	.1255	.3745	0.67	.2486	.2514
0.33	.1293	.3707	0.68	.2517	.2483
0.34	.1331	.3669	0.69	.2549	.2451

Table A.1	Areas of the Normal Curve (cont.)					
(1) z	(2) AREA BETWEEN THE MEAN AND z	(3) AREA BEYOND z	(1) z	(2) AREA BETWEEN THE MEAN AND z	(3) AREA BEYOND z
0.70	.2580	.2420	1.05	.3531	.1469
0.71	.2611	.2389	1.06	.3554	.1446
0.72	.2642	.2358	1.07	.3577	.1423
0.73	.2673	.2327	1.08	.3599	.1401
0.74	.2704	.2296	1.09	.3621	.1379
0.75	.2734	.2266	1.10	.3643	.1357
0.76	.2764	.2236	1.11	.3665	.1335
0.77	.2794	.2206	1.12	.3686	.1314
0.78	.2823	.2177	1.13	.3708	.1292
0.79	.2852	.2148	1.14	.3729	.1271
0.80	.2881	.2119	1.15	.3749	.1251
0.81	.2910	.2090	1.16	.3770	.1230
0.82	.2939	.2061	1.17	.3790	.1210
0.83	.2967	.2033	1.18	.3810	.1190
0.84	.2995	.2005	1.19	.3830	.1170
0.85	.3023	.1977	1.20	.3849	.1151
0.86	.3051	.1949	1.21	.3869	.1131
0.87	.3078	.1922	1.22	.3888	.1112
0.88	.3106	.1894	1.23	.3907	.1093
0.89	.3133	.1867	1.24	.3925	.1075
0.90	.3159	.1841	1.25	.3944	.1056
0.91	.3186	.1814	1.26	.3962	.1038
0.92	.3212	.1788	1.27	.3980	.1020
0.93	.3238	.1762	1.28	.3997	.1003
0.94	.3264	.1736	1.29	.4015	.0985
0.95	.3289	.1711	1.30	.4032	.0968
0.96	.3315	.1685	1.31	.4049	.0951
0.97	.3340	.1660	1.32	.4066	.0934
0.98	.3365	.1635	1.33	.4082	.0918
0.99	.3389	.1611	1.34	.4099	.0901
1.00	.3413	.1587	1.35	.4115	.0885
1.01	.3438	.1562	1.36	.4131	.0869
1.02	.3461	.1539	1.37	.4147	.0853
1.03	.3485	.1515	1.38	.4162	.0838
1.04	.3508	.1492	1.39	.4177	.0823

Table A.1   Areas of the Normal Curve (cont.)

(1) z	(2) AREA BETWEEN THE MEAN AND z	(3) AREA BEYOND z	(1) z	(2) AREA BETWEEN THE MEAN AND z	(3) AREA BEYOND z
1.40	.4192	.0808	1.75	.4599	.0401
1.41	.4207	.0793	1.76	.4608	.0392
1.42	.4222	.0778	1.77	.4616	.0384
1.43	.4236	.0764	1.78	.4625	.0375
1.44	.4251	.0749	1.79	.4633	.0367
1.45	.4265	.0735	1.80	.4641	.0359
1.46	.4279	.0721	1.81	.4649	.0351
1.47	.4292	.0708	1.82	.4656	.0344
1.48	.4306	.0694	1.83	.4664	.0336
1.49	.4319	.0681	1.84	.4671	.0329
1.50	.4332	.0668	1.85	.4678	.0322
1.51	.4345	.0655	1.86	.4686	.0314
1.52	.4357	.0643	1.87	.4693	.0307
1.53	.4370	.0630	1.88	.4699	.0301
1.54	.4382	.0618	1.89	.4706	.0294
1.55	.4394	.0606	1.90	.4713	.0287
1.56	.4406	.0594	1.91	.4719	.0281
1.57	.4418	.0582	1.92	.4726	.0274
1.58	.4429	.0571	1.93	.4732	.0268
1.59	.4441	.0559	1.94	.4738	.0262
1.60	.4452	.0548	1.95	.4744	.0256
1.61	.4463	.0537	1.96	.4750	.0250
1.62	.4474	.0526	1.97	.4756	.0244
1.63	.4484	.0516	1.98	.4761	.0239
1.64	.4495	.0505	1.99	.4767	.0233
1.65	.4505	.0495	2.00	.4772	.0228
1.66	.4515	.0485	2.01	.4778	.0222
1.67	.4525	.0475	2.02	.4783	.0217
1.68	.4535	.0465	2.03	.4788	.0212
1.69	.4545	.0455	2.04	.4793	.0207
1.70	.4554	.0446	2.05	.4798	.0202
1.71	.4564	.0436	2.06	.4803	.0197
1.72	.4573	.0427	2.07	.4808	.0192
1.73	.4582	.0418	2.08	.4812	.0188
1.74	.4591	.0409	2.09	.4817	.0183

Table A.1 Areas of the Normal Curve (cont.)

(1) z	(2) AREA BETWEEN THE MEAN AND z	(3) AREA BEYOND z	(1) z	(2) AREA BETWEEN THE MEAN AND z	(3) AREA BEYOND z
2.10	.4821	.0179	2.45	.4929	.0071
2.11	.4826	.0174	2.46	.4931	.0069
2.12	.4830	.0170	2.47	.4932	.0068
2.13	.4834	.0166	2.48	.4934	.0066
2.14	.4838	.0162	2.49	.4936	.0064
2.15	.4842	.0158	2.50	.4938	.0062
2.16	.4846	.0154	2.51	.4940	.0060
2.17	.4850	.0150	2.52	.4941	.0059
2.18	.4854	.0146	2.53	.4943	.0057
2.19	.4857	.0143	2.54	.4945	.0055
2.20	.4861	.0139	2.55	.4946	.0054
2.21	.4864	.0136	2.56	.4948	.0052
2.22	.4868	.0132	2.57	.4949	.0051
2.23	.4871	.0129	2.58	.4951	.0049
2.24	.4875	.0125	2.59	.4952	.0048
2.25	.4878	.0122	2.60	.4953	.0047
2.26	.4881	.0119	2.61	.4955	.0045
2.27	.4884	.0116	2.62	.4956	.0044
2.28	.4887	.0113	2.63	.4957	.0043
2.29	.4890	.0110	2.64	.4959	.0041
2.30	.4893	.0107	2.65	.4960	.0040
2.31	.4896	.0104	2.66	.4961	.0039
2.32	.4898	.0102	2.67	.4962	.0038
2.33	.4901	.0099	2.68	.4963	.0037
2.34	.4904	.0096	2.69	.4964	.0036
2.35	.4906	.0094	2.70	.4965	.0035
2.36	.4909	.0091	2.71	.4966	.0034
2.37	.4911	.0089	2.72	.4967	.0033
2.38	.4913	.0087	2.73	.4968	.0032
2.39	.4916	.0084	2.74	.4969	.0031
2.40	.4918	.0082	2.75	.4970	.0030
2.41	.4920	.0080	2.76	.4971	.0029
2.42	.4922	.0078	2.77	.4972	.0028
2.43	.4925	.0075	2.78	.4973	.0027
2.44	.4927	.0073	2.79	.4974	.0026

Table A.1   Areas of the Normal Curve (cont.)

(1) z	(2) AREA BETWEEN THE MEAN AND z	(3) AREA BEYOND z	(1) z	(2) AREA BETWEEN THE MEAN AND z	(3) AREA BEYOND z
2.80	.4974	.0026	3.10	.4990	.0010
2.81	.4975	.0025	3.11	.4991	.0009
2.82	.4976	.0023	3.12	.4991	.0009
2.83	.4977	.0024	3.13	.4991	.0009
2.84	.4977	.0023	3.14	.4992	.0008
2.85	.4978	.0022	3.15	.4992	.0008
2.86	.4979	.0021	3.16	.4992	.0008
2.87	.4979	.0021	3.17	.4992	.0008
2.88	.4980	.0020	3.18	.4993	.0007
2.89	.4981	.0019	3.19	.4993	.0007
2.90	.4981	.0019	3.20	.4993	.0007
2.91	.4982	.0018	3.21	.4993	.0007
2.92	.4982	.0018	3.22	.4994	.0006
2.93	.4983	.0017	3.23	.4994	.0006
2.94	.4984	.0016	3.24	.4994	.0006
2.95	.4984	.0016	3.30	.4995	.0005
2.96	.4985	.0015	3.40	.4997	.0003
2.97	.4985	.0015	3.50	.4998	.0002
2.98	.4986	.0014	3.60	.4998	.0002
2.99	.4986	.0014	3.70	.4999	.0001
3.00	.4987	.0013	3.90	.49995	.00005
3.01	.4987	.0013	4.00	.49997	.00003
3.20	.4987	.0013	4.50	.4999966	.0000034
3.03	.4988	.0012	5.00	.4999997	.0000003
3.04	.4988	.0012	5.50	.499999981	.000000019
3.05	.4989	.0011	6.00	.499999999	.000000001
3.06	.4989	.0011			
3.07	.4989	.0011			
3.08	.4990	.0010			
3.09	.4990	.0010			

Table A.2 Table of t-Values

	LEVEL OF SIGNIFICANCE FOR A DIRECTIONAL (ONE-TAILED) TEST					
	.10	.05	.025	.01	.005	.0005
	LEVEL OF SIGNIFICANCE FOR A NONDIRECTIONAL (TWO-TAILED) TEST					
df	.20	.10	.05	.02	.01	.001
1	3.078	6.314	12.706	31.821	63.657	636.619
2	1.886	2.920	4.303	6.965	9.925	31.598
3	1.638	2.353	3.182	4.541	5.841	12.941
4	1.533	2.132	2.776	3.747	4.604	8.610
5	1.476	2.015	2.571	3.365	4.032	6.859
6	1.440	1.943	2.447	3.143	3.707	5.959
7	1.415	1.895	2.365	2.998	3.499	5.405
8	1.397	1.860	2.306	2.896	3.355	5.041
9	1.383	1.833	2.262	2.821	3.250	4.781
10	1.372	1.812	2.228	2.764	3.169	4.587
11	1.363	1.796	2.201	2.718	3.106	4.437
12	1.356	1.782	2.179	2.681	3.055	4.318
13	1.350	1.771	2.160	2.650	3.012	4.221
14	1.345	1.761	2.145	2.624	2.977	4.140
15	1.341	1.753	2.131	2.602	2.947	4.073
16	1.337	1.746	2.120	2.583	2.921	4.015
17	1.333	1.740	2.110	2.567	2.898	3.965
18	1.330	1.734	2.101	2.552	2.878	3.922
19	1.328	1.729	2.093	2.539	2.861	3.883
20	1.325	1.725	2.086	2.528	2.845	3.850
21	1.323	1.721	2.080	2.518	2.831	3.819
22	1.321	1.717	2.074	2.508	2.819	3.792
23	1.319	1.714	2.069	2.500	2.807	3.767
24	1.318	1.711	2.064	2.492	2.797	3.745
25	1.316	1.708	2.060	2.485	2.787	3.725
26	1.315	1.706	2.056	2.479	2.779	3.707
27	1.314	1.703	2.052	2.473	2.771	3.690
28	1.313	1.701	2.048	2.467	2.763	3.674
29	1.311	1.699	2.045	2.462	2.756	3.659
30	1.310	1.697	2.042	2.457	2.750	3.646
40	1.303	1.684	2.021	2.423	2.704	3.551
60	1.296	1.671	2.000	2.390	2.660	3.460
120	1.289	1.658	1.980	2.358	2.617	3.373
∞	1.282	1.645	1.960	2.326	2.576	3.291

Source: Table A-2 is taken from Table III of Fisher and Yates, *Statistical Tables for Biological, Agricultural, and Medical Research,* published by Longman Group UK Ltd., 1974.

Table A.3 The 5 (Roman Type) and 1 (Boldface Type) Percent Points for the F Distribution

DENOMINATOR

N₁ DEGREES OF FREEDOM FOR NUMERATOR

df = N₁	1	2	3	4	5	6	7	8	9	10	11	12	14	16	20	24	30	40	50	75	100	200	500	∞
1	161	200	216	225	230	234	237	239	241	242	243	244	245	246	248	249	250	251	252	253	253	254	254	254
	4,052	**4,999**	**5,403**	**5,625**	**5,764**	**5,859**	**5,928**	**5,981**	**6,022**	**6,056**	**6,082**	**6,106**	**6,142**	**6,169**	**6,208**	**6,234**	**6,258**	**6,286**	**6,302**	**6,323**	**6,334**	**6,352**	**6,361**	**6,366**
2	18.51	19.00	19.16	19.25	19.30	19.33	19.36	19.37	19.38	19.39	19.40	19.41	19.42	19.43	19.44	19.45	19.46	19.47	19.47	19.48	19.49	19.49	19.50	19.50
	98.49	**99.00**	**99.17**	**99.25**	**99.30**	**99.33**	**99.34**	**99.36**	**99.38**	**99.40**	**99.41**	**99.42**	**99.43**	**99.44**	**99.45**	**99.46**	**99.47**	**99.48**	**99.48**	**99.49**	**99.49**	**99.49**	**99.50**	**99.50**
3	10.13	9.55	9.28	9.12	9.01	8.94	8.88	8.84	8.81	8.78	8.76	8.74	8.71	8.69	8.66	8.64	8.62	8.60	8.58	8.57	8.56	8.54	8.54	8.53
	34.12	**30.82**	**29.46**	**28.71**	**28.24**	**27.91**	**27.67**	**27.49**	**27.34**	**27.23**	**27.13**	**27.05**	**26.92**	**26.83**	**26.69**	**26.60**	**26.50**	**26.41**	**26.35**	**26.27**	**26.23**	**26.18**	**26.14**	**26.12**
4	7.71	6.94	6.59	6.39	6.26	6.16	6.09	6.04	6.00	5.96	5.93	5.91	5.87	5.84	5.80	5.77	5.74	5.71	5.70	5.68	5.66	5.65	5.64	5.63
	21.20	**18.00**	**16.69**	**15.98**	**15.52**	**15.21**	**14.98**	**14.80**	**14.66**	**14.54**	**14.45**	**14.37**	**14.24**	**14.15**	**14.02**	**13.93**	**13.83**	**13.74**	**13.69**	**13.61**	**13.57**	**13.52**	**13.48**	**13.46**
5	6.61	5.79	5.41	5.19	5.05	4.95	4.88	4.82	4.78	4.74	4.70	4.68	4.64	4.60	4.56	4.53	4.50	4.46	4.44	4.42	4.40	4.38	4.37	4.36
	16.26	**13.27**	**12.06**	**11.39**	**10.97**	**10.67**	**10.45**	**10.27**	**10.15**	**10.05**	**9.96**	**9.89**	**9.77**	**9.68**	**9.55**	**9.47**	**9.38**	**9.29**	**9.24**	**9.17**	**9.13**	**9.07**	**9.04**	**9.02**
6	5.99	5.14	4.76	4.53	4.39	4.28	4.21	4.15	4.10	4.06	4.03	4.00	3.96	3.92	3.87	3.84	3.81	3.77	3.75	3.72	3.71	3.69	3.68	3.67
	13.74	**10.92**	**9.78**	**9.15**	**8.75**	**8.47**	**8.26**	**8.10**	**7.98**	**7.87**	**7.79**	**7.72**	**7.60**	**7.52**	**7.39**	**7.31**	**7.23**	**7.14**	**7.09**	**7.02**	**6.99**	**6.94**	**6.90**	**6.88**
7	5.59	4.74	4.35	4.12	3.97	3.87	3.79	3.73	3.68	3.63	3.60	3.57	3.52	3.49	3.44	3.41	3.38	3.34	3.32	3.29	3.28	3.25	3.24	3.23
	12.25	**9.55**	**8.45**	**7.85**	**7.46**	**7.19**	**7.00**	**6.84**	**6.71**	**6.62**	**6.54**	**6.47**	**6.35**	**6.27**	**6.15**	**6.07**	**5.98**	**5.90**	**5.85**	**5.78**	**5.75**	**5.70**	**5.67**	**5.65**
8	5.32	4.46	4.07	3.84	3.69	3.58	3.50	3.44	3.39	3.34	3.31	3.28	3.23	3.20	3.15	3.12	3.08	3.05	3.03	3.00	2.98	2.96	2.94	2.93
	11.26	**8.65**	**7.59**	**7.01**	**6.63**	**6.37**	**6.19**	**6.03**	**5.91**	**5.82**	**5.74**	**5.67**	**5.56**	**5.48**	**5.36**	**5.28**	**5.20**	**5.11**	**5.06**	**5.00**	**4.96**	**4.91**	**4.88**	**4.86**
9	5.12	4.26	3.86	3.63	3.48	3.37	3.29	3.23	3.18	3.13	3.10	3.07	3.02	2.98	2.93	2.90	2.86	2.82	2.80	2.77	2.76	2.73	2.72	2.71
	10.56	**8.02**	**6.99**	**6.42**	**6.06**	**5.80**	**5.62**	**5.47**	**5.35**	**5.26**	**5.18**	**5.11**	**5.00**	**4.92**	**4.80**	**4.73**	**4.64**	**4.56**	**4.51**	**4.45**	**4.41**	**4.36**	**4.33**	**4.31**
10	4.96	4.10	3.71	3.48	3.33	3.22	3.14	3.07	3.02	2.97	2.94	2.91	2.86	2.82	2.77	2.74	2.70	2.67	2.64	2.61	2.59	2.56	2.55	2.54
	10.04	**7.56**	**6.55**	**5.99**	**5.64**	**5.39**	**5.21**	**5.06**	**4.95**	**4.85**	**4.78**	**4.71**	**4.60**	**4.52**	**4.41**	**4.33**	**4.25**	**4.17**	**4.12**	**4.05**	**4.01**	**3.96**	**3.93**	**3.91**
11	4.84	3.98	3.59	3.36	3.20	3.09	3.01	2.95	2.90	2.86	2.82	2.79	2.74	2.70	2.65	2.61	2.57	2.53	2.50	2.47	2.45	2.42	2.41	2.40
	9.65	**7.20**	**6.22**	**5.67**	**5.32**	**5.07**	**4.88**	**4.74**	**4.63**	**4.54**	**4.46**	**4.40**	**4.29**	**4.21**	**4.10**	**4.02**	**3.94**	**3.86**	**3.80**	**3.74**	**3.70**	**3.66**	**3.62**	**3.60**
12	4.75	3.88	3.49	3.26	3.11	3.00	2.92	2.85	2.80	2.76	2.72	2.69	2.64	2.60	2.54	2.50	2.46	2.42	2.40	2.36	2.35	2.32	2.31	2.30
	9.33	**6.93**	**5.95**	**5.41**	**5.06**	**4.82**	**4.65**	**4.50**	**4.39**	**4.30**	**4.22**	**4.16**	**4.05**	**3.98**	**3.86**	**3.78**	**3.70**	**3.61**	**3.56**	**3.49**	**3.46**	**3.41**	**3.38**	**3.36**
13	4.67	3.80	3.41	3.18	3.02	2.92	2.84	2.77	2.72	2.67	2.63	2.60	2.55	2.51	2.46	2.42	2.38	2.34	2.32	2.28	2.26	2.24	2.22	2.21
	9.07	**6.70**	**5.74**	**5.20**	**4.86**	**4.62**	**4.44**	**4.30**	**4.19**	**4.10**	**4.02**	**3.96**	**3.85**	**3.78**	**3.67**	**3.59**	**3.51**	**3.42**	**3.37**	**3.30**	**3.27**	**3.21**	**3.18**	**3.16**

Table A.3 The 5 (Roman Type) and 1 (Boldface Type) Percent Points for the F Distribution (cont.)

DENOMINATOR

N_1 DEGREES OF FREEDOM FOR NUMERATOR

df = n_1	1	2	3	4	5	6	7	8	9	10	11	12	14	16	20	24	30	40	50	75	100	200	500	∞
14	4.60	3.74	3.34	3.11	2.96	2.85	2.77	2.70	2.65	2.60	2.56	2.53	2.48	2.44	2.39	2.35	2.31	2.27	2.24	2.21	2.19	2.16	2.14	2.13
	8.86	**6.51**	**5.56**	**5.03**	**4.69**	**4.46**	**4.28**	**4.14**	**4.03**	**3.94**	**3.86**	**3.80**	**3.70**	**3.62**	**3.51**	**3.43**	**3.34**	**3.26**	**3.21**	**3.14**	**3.11**	**3.06**	**3.02**	**3.00**
15	4.54	3.68	3.29	3.06	2.90	2.79	2.70	2.64	2.59	2.55	2.51	2.48	2.43	2.39	2.33	2.29	2.25	2.21	2.18	2.15	2.12	2.10	2.08	2.07
	8.68	**6.36**	**5.42**	**4.89**	**4.56**	**4.32**	**4.14**	**4.00**	**3.89**	**3.80**	**3.73**	**3.67**	**3.56**	**3.48**	**3.36**	**3.29**	**3.20**	**3.12**	**3.07**	**3.00**	**2.97**	**2.92**	**2.89**	**2.87**
16	4.49	3.63	3.24	3.01	2.85	2.74	2.66	2.59	2.54	2.49	2.45	2.42	2.37	2.33	2.28	2.24	2.20	2.16	2.13	2.09	2.07	2.04	2.02	2.01
	8.53	**6.23**	**5.29**	**4.77**	**4.44**	**4.20**	**4.03**	**3.89**	**3.78**	**3.69**	**3.61**	**3.55**	**3.45**	**3.37**	**3.25**	**3.18**	**3.10**	**3.01**	**2.96**	**2.89**	**2.86**	**2.80**	**2.77**	**2.75**
17	4.45	3.59	3.20	2.96	2.81	2.70	2.62	2.55	2.50	2.45	2.41	2.38	2.33	2.29	2.23	2.19	2.15	2.11	2.08	2.04	2.02	1.99	1.97	1.96
	8.40	**6.11**	**5.18**	**4.67**	**4.34**	**4.10**	**3.93**	**3.79**	**3.68**	**3.59**	**3.52**	**3.45**	**3.35**	**3.27**	**3.16**	**3.08**	**3.00**	**2.92**	**2.86**	**2.79**	**2.76**	**2.70**	**2.67**	**2.65**
18	4.41	3.55	3.16	2.93	2.77	2.66	2.58	2.51	2.46	2.41	2.37	2.34	2.29	2.25	2.19	2.15	2.11	2.07	2.04	2.00	1.98	1.95	1.93	1.92
	8.28	**6.01**	**5.09**	**4.58**	**4.25**	**4.01**	**3.85**	**3.71**	**3.60**	**3.51**	**3.44**	**3.37**	**3.27**	**3.19**	**3.07**	**3.00**	**2.91**	**2.83**	**2.78**	**2.71**	**2.68**	**2.62**	**2.59**	**2.57**
19	4.38	3.52	3.13	2.90	2.74	2.63	2.55	2.48	2.43	2.38	2.34	2.31	2.26	2.21	2.15	2.11	2.07	2.02	2.00	1.96	1.94	1.91	1.90	1.88
	8.18	**5.93**	**5.01**	**4.50**	**4.17**	**3.94**	**3.77**	**3.63**	**3.52**	**3.43**	**3.36**	**3.30**	**3.19**	**3.12**	**3.00**	**2.92**	**2.84**	**2.76**	**2.70**	**2.63**	**2.60**	**2.54**	**2.51**	**2.49**
20	4.35	3.49	3.10	2.87	2.71	2.60	2.52	2.45	2.40	2.35	2.31	2.28	2.23	2.18	2.12	2.08	2.04	1.99	1.96	1.92	1.90	1.87	1.85	1.84
	8.10	**5.85**	**4.94**	**4.43**	**4.10**	**3.87**	**3.71**	**3.56**	**3.45**	**3.37**	**3.30**	**3.23**	**3.13**	**3.05**	**2.94**	**2.86**	**2.77**	**2.69**	**2.63**	**2.56**	**2.53**	**2.47**	**2.44**	**2.42**
21	4.32	3.47	3.07	2.84	2.68	2.57	2.49	2.42	2.37	2.32	2.28	2.25	2.20	2.15	2.09	2.05	2.00	1.96	1.93	1.89	1.87	1.84	1.82	1.81
	8.02	**5.78**	**4.87**	**4.37**	**4.04**	**3.81**	**3.65**	**3.51**	**3.40**	**3.31**	**3.24**	**3.17**	**3.07**	**2.99**	**2.88**	**2.80**	**2.72**	**2.63**	**2.58**	**2.51**	**2.47**	**2.42**	**2.38**	**2.36**
22	4.30	3.44	3.05	2.82	2.66	2.55	2.47	2.40	2.35	2.30	2.26	2.23	2.18	2.13	2.07	2.03	1.98	1.93	1.91	1.87	1.84	1.81	1.80	1.78
	7.94	**5.72**	**4.82**	**4.31**	**3.99**	**3.76**	**3.59**	**3.45**	**3.35**	**3.26**	**3.18**	**3.12**	**3.02**	**2.94**	**2.83**	**2.75**	**2.67**	**2.58**	**2.53**	**2.46**	**2.42**	**2.37**	**2.33**	**2.31**
23	4.28	3.42	3.03	2.80	2.64	2.53	2.45	2.38	2.32	2.28	2.24	2.20	2.14	2.10	2.04	2.00	1.96	1.91	1.88	1.84	1.82	1.79	1.77	1.76
	7.88	**5.66**	**4.76**	**4.26**	**3.94**	**3.71**	**3.54**	**3.41**	**3.30**	**3.21**	**3.14**	**3.07**	**2.97**	**2.89**	**2.78**	**2.70**	**2.62**	**2.53**	**2.48**	**2.41**	**2.37**	**2.32**	**2.28**	**2.26**
24	4.26	3.40	3.01	2.78	2.62	2.51	2.43	2.36	2.30	2.26	2.22	2.18	2.13	2.09	2.02	1.98	1.94	1.89	1.86	1.82	1.80	1.76	1.74	1.73
	7.82	**5.61**	**4.72**	**4.22**	**3.90**	**3.67**	**3.50**	**3.36**	**3.25**	**3.17**	**3.09**	**3.03**	**2.93**	**2.85**	**2.74**	**2.66**	**2.58**	**2.49**	**2.44**	**2.36**	**2.33**	**2.27**	**2.23**	**2.21**
25	4.24	3.38	2.99	2.76	2.60	2.49	2.41	2.34	2.28	2.24	2.20	2.16	2.11	2.06	2.00	1.96	1.92	1.87	1.84	1.80	1.77	1.74	1.72	1.71
	7.77	**5.57**	**4.68**	**4.18**	**3.86**	**3.63**	**3.46**	**3.32**	**3.21**	**3.13**	**3.05**	**2.99**	**2.89**	**2.81**	**2.70**	**2.62**	**2.54**	**2.45**	**2.40**	**2.32**	**2.29**	**2.23**	**2.19**	**2.17**
26	4.22	3.37	2.98	2.74	2.59	2.47	2.39	2.32	2.27	2.22	2.18	2.15	2.10	2.05	1.99	1.95	1.90	1.85	1.82	1.78	1.76	1.72	1.70	1.69
	7.72	**5.53**	**4.64**	**4.14**	**3.82**	**3.59**	**3.42**	**3.29**	**3.17**	**3.09**	**3.02**	**2.96**	**2.86**	**2.77**	**2.66**	**2.58**	**2.50**	**2.41**	**2.36**	**2.28**	**2.25**	**2.19**	**2.15**	**2.13**

Table A.3 The 5 (Roman Type) and 1 (Boldface Type) Percent Points for the F Distribution (cont.)

DENOMINATOR

N_1 DEGREES OF FREEDOM FOR NUMERATOR

df = n_1	1	2	3	4	5	6	7	8	9	10	11	12	14	16	20	24	30	40	50	75	100	200	500	∞
27	4.21	3.35	2.96	2.73	2.57	2.46	2.37	2.30	2.25	2.20	2.16	2.13	2.08	2.03	1.97	1.93	1.88	1.84	1.80	1.76	1.74	1.71	1.68	1.67
	7.68	**5.49**	**4.60**	**4.11**	**3.79**	**3.56**	**3.39**	**3.26**	**3.14**	**3.06**	**2.98**	**2.93**	**2.83**	**2.74**	**2.63**	**2.55**	**2.47**	**2.38**	**2.33**	**2.25**	**2.21**	**2.16**	**2.12**	**2.10**
28	4.20	3.34	2.95	2.71	2.56	2.44	2.36	2.29	2.24	2.19	2.15	2.12	2.06	2.02	1.96	1.91	1.87	1.81	1.78	1.75	1.72	1.69	1.67	1.65
	7.64	**5.45**	**4.57**	**4.07**	**3.76**	**3.53**	**3.36**	**3.23**	**3.11**	**3.03**	**2.95**	**2.90**	**2.80**	**2.71**	**2.60**	**2.52**	**2.44**	**2.35**	**2.30**	**2.22**	**2.18**	**2.13**	**2.09**	**2.06**
29	4.18	3.33	2.93	2.70	2.54	2.43	2.35	2.28	2.22	2.18	2.14	2.10	2.05	2.00	1.94	1.90	1.85	1.80	1.77	1.73	1.71	1.68	1.65	1.64
	7.60	**5.42**	**4.54**	**4.04**	**3.73**	**3.50**	**3.33**	**3.20**	**3.08**	**3.00**	**2.92**	**2.87**	**2.77**	**2.68**	**2.57**	**2.49**	**2.41**	**2.32**	**2.27**	**2.19**	**2.15**	**2.10**	**2.06**	**2.03**
30	4.17	3.32	2.92	2.69	2.53	2.42	2.34	2.27	2.21	2.16	2.12	2.09	2.04	1.99	1.93	1.89	1.84	1.79	1.76	1.72	1.69	1.66	1.64	1.62
	7.56	**5.39**	**4.51**	**4.02**	**3.70**	**3.47**	**3.30**	**3.17**	**3.06**	**2.98**	**2.90**	**2.84**	**2.74**	**2.66**	**2.55**	**2.47**	**2.38**	**2.29**	**2.24**	**2.16**	**2.13**	**2.07**	**2.03**	**2.01**
32	4.15	3.30	2.90	2.67	2.51	2.40	2.32	2.25	2.19	2.14	2.10	2.07	2.02	1.97	1.91	1.86	1.82	1.76	1.74	1.69	1.67	1.64	1.61	1.59
	7.50	**5.34**	**4.46**	**3.97**	**3.66**	**3.42**	**3.25**	**3.12**	**3.01**	**2.94**	**2.86**	**2.80**	**2.70**	**2.62**	**2.51**	**2.42**	**2.34**	**2.25**	**2.20**	**2.12**	**2.08**	**2.02**	**1.98**	**1.96**
34	4.13	3.28	2.88	2.65	2.49	2.38	2.30	2.23	2.17	2.12	2.08	2.05	2.00	1.95	1.89	1.84	1.80	1.74	1.71	1.67	1.64	1.61	1.59	1.57
	7.44	**5.29**	**4.42**	**3.93**	**3.61**	**3.38**	**3.21**	**3.08**	**2.97**	**2.89**	**2.82**	**2.76**	**2.66**	**2.58**	**2.47**	**2.38**	**2.30**	**2.21**	**2.15**	**2.08**	**2.04**	**1.98**	**1.94**	**1.91**
36	4.11	3.26	2.86	2.63	2.48	2.36	2.28	2.21	2.15	2.10	2.06	2.03	1.98	1.93	1.87	1.82	1.78	1.72	1.69	1.65	1.62	1.59	1.56	1.55
	7.39	**5.25**	**4.38**	**3.89**	**3.58**	**3.35**	**3.18**	**3.04**	**2.94**	**2.86**	**2.78**	**2.72**	**2.62**	**2.54**	**2.43**	**2.35**	**2.26**	**2.17**	**2.12**	**2.04**	**2.00**	**1.94**	**1.90**	**1.87**
38	4.10	3.25	2.85	2.62	2.46	2.35	2.26	2.19	2.14	2.09	2.05	2.02	1.96	1.92	1.85	1.80	1.76	1.71	1.67	1.63	1.60	1.57	1.54	1.53
	7.35	**5.21**	**4.34**	**3.86**	**3.54**	**3.32**	**3.15**	**3.02**	**2.91**	**2.82**	**2.75**	**2.69**	**2.59**	**2.51**	**2.40**	**2.32**	**2.22**	**2.14**	**2.08**	**2.00**	**1.97**	**1.90**	**1.86**	**1.84**
40	4.08	3.23	2.84	2.61	2.45	2.34	2.25	2.18	2.12	2.07	2.04	2.00	1.95	1.90	1.84	1.79	1.74	1.69	1.66	1.61	1.59	1.55	1.53	1.51
	7.31	**5.18**	**4.31**	**3.83**	**3.51**	**3.29**	**3.12**	**2.99**	**2.88**	**2.80**	**2.73**	**2.66**	**2.56**	**2.49**	**2.37**	**2.29**	**2.20**	**2.11**	**2.05**	**1.97**	**1.94**	**1.88**	**1.84**	**1.81**
42	4.07	3.22	2.83	2.59	2.44	2.32	2.24	2.17	2.11	2.06	2.02	1.99	1.94	1.89	1.82	1.78	1.73	1.68	1.64	1.60	1.57	1.54	1.51	1.49
	7.27	**5.15**	**4.29**	**3.80**	**3.49**	**3.26**	**3.10**	**2.96**	**2.86**	**2.77**	**2.70**	**2.64**	**2.54**	**2.46**	**2.35**	**2.26**	**2.17**	**2.08**	**2.02**	**1.94**	**1.91**	**1.85**	**1.80**	**1.78**
44	4.06	3.21	2.82	2.58	2.43	2.31	2.23	2.16	2.10	2.05	2.01	1.98	1.92	1.88	1.81	1.76	1.72	1.66	1.63	1.58	1.56	1.52	1.50	1.48
	7.24	**5.12**	**4.26**	**3.78**	**3.46**	**3.24**	**3.07**	**2.94**	**2.84**	**2.75**	**2.68**	**2.62**	**2.52**	**2.44**	**2.32**	**2.24**	**2.15**	**2.06**	**2.00**	**1.92**	**1.88**	**1.82**	**1.78**	**1.75**
46	4.05	3.20	2.81	2.57	2.42	2.30	2.22	2.14	2.09	2.04	2.00	1.97	1.91	1.87	1.80	1.76	1.71	1.65	1.62	1.57	1.54	1.51	1.48	1.46
	7.21	**5.10**	**4.24**	**3.76**	**3.44**	**3.22**	**3.05**	**2.92**	**2.82**	**2.73**	**2.66**	**2.60**	**2.50**	**2.42**	**2.30**	**2.22**	**2.13**	**2.04**	**1.98**	**1.90**	**1.86**	**1.80**	**1.76**	**1.72**
48	4.04	3.19	2.80	2.56	2.41	2.30	2.21	2.14	2.08	2.03	1.99	1.96	1.90	1.86	1.79	1.74	1.70	1.64	1.61	1.56	1.53	1.50	1.47	1.45
	7.19	**5.08**	**4.22**	**3.74**	**3.42**	**3.20**	**3.04**	**2.90**	**2.80**	**2.71**	**2.64**	**2.58**	**2.48**	**2.40**	**2.28**	**2.20**	**2.11**	**2.02**	**1.96**	**1.88**	**1.84**	**1.78**	**1.73**	**1.70**

Table A.3 The 5 (Roman Type) and 1 (Boldface Type) Percent Points for the F Distribution (cont.)

DENOMINATOR df = n_1	N_1 DEGREES OF FREEDOM FOR NUMERATOR																							
	1	2	3	4	5	6	7	8	9	10	11	12	14	16	20	24	30	40	50	75	100	200	500	∞
50	4.03	3.18	2.79	2.56	2.40	2.29	2.20	2.13	2.07	2.02	1.98	1.95	1.90	1.85	1.78	1.74	1.69	1.63	1.60	1.55	1.52	1.48	1.46	1.44
	7.17	**5.06**	**4.20**	**3.72**	**3.41**	**3.18**	**3.02**	**2.88**	**2.78**	**2.70**	**2.62**	**2.56**	**2.46**	**2.39**	**2.26**	**2.18**	**2.10**	**2.00**	**1.94**	**1.86**	**1.82**	**1.76**	**1.71**	**1.68**
55	4.02	3.17	2.78	2.54	2.38	2.27	2.18	2.11	2.05	2.00	1.97	1.93	1.88	1.83	1.76	1.72	1.67	1.61	1.58	1.52	1.50	1.46	1.43	1.41
	7.12	**5.01**	**4.16**	**3.68**	**3.37**	**3.15**	**2.98**	**2.85**	**2.75**	**2.66**	**2.59**	**2.53**	**2.43**	**2.35**	**2.23**	**2.15**	**2.06**	**1.96**	**1.90**	**1.82**	**1.78**	**1.71**	**1.66**	**1.64**
60	4.00	3.15	2.76	2.52	2.37	2.25	2.17	2.10	2.04	1.99	1.95	1.92	1.86	1.81	1.75	1.70	1.65	1.59	1.56	1.50	1.48	1.44	1.41	1.39
	7.08	**4.98**	**4.13**	**3.65**	**3.34**	**3.12**	**2.95**	**2.82**	**2.72**	**2.63**	**2.56**	**2.50**	**2.40**	**2.32**	**2.20**	**2.12**	**2.03**	**1.93**	**1.87**	**1.79**	**1.74**	**1.68**	**1.63**	**1.60**
65	3.99	3.14	2.75	2.51	2.36	2.24	2.15	2.08	2.02	1.98	1.94	1.90	1.85	1.80	1.73	1.68	1.63	1.57	1.54	1.49	1.46	1.42	1.39	1.37
	7.04	**4.95**	**4.10**	**3.62**	**3.31**	**3.09**	**2.93**	**2.79**	**2.70**	**2.61**	**2.54**	**2.47**	**2.37**	**2.30**	**2.18**	**2.09**	**2.00**	**1.90**	**1.84**	**1.76**	**1.71**	**1.64**	**1.60**	**1.56**
70	3.98	3.13	2.74	2.50	2.35	2.23	2.14	2.07	2.01	1.97	1.93	1.89	1.84	1.79	1.72	1.67	1.62	1.56	1.53	1.47	1.45	1.40	1.37	1.35
	7.01	**4.92**	**4.08**	**3.60**	**3.29**	**3.07**	**2.91**	**2.77**	**2.67**	**2.59**	**2.51**	**2.45**	**2.35**	**2.28**	**2.15**	**2.07**	**1.98**	**1.88**	**1.82**	**1.74**	**1.69**	**1.62**	**1.56**	**1.53**
80	3.96	3.11	2.72	2.48	2.33	2.21	2.12	2.05	1.99	1.95	1.91	1.88	1.82	1.77	1.70	1.65	1.60	1.54	1.51	1.45	1.42	1.38	1.35	1.32
	6.96	**4.88**	**4.04**	**3.56**	**3.25**	**3.04**	**2.87**	**2.74**	**2.64**	**2.55**	**2.48**	**2.41**	**2.32**	**2.24**	**2.11**	**2.03**	**1.94**	**1.84**	**1.78**	**1.70**	**1.65**	**1.57**	**1.52**	**1.49**
100	3.94	3.09	2.70	2.46	2.30	2.19	2.10	2.03	1.97	1.92	1.88	1.85	1.79	1.75	1.68	1.63	1.57	1.51	1.48	1.42	1.39	1.34	1.30	1.28
	6.90	**4.82**	**3.98**	**3.51**	**3.20**	**2.99**	**2.82**	**2.69**	**2.59**	**2.51**	**2.43**	**2.36**	**2.26**	**2.19**	**2.06**	**1.98**	**1.89**	**1.79**	**1.73**	**1.64**	**1.59**	**1.51**	**1.46**	**1.43**
125	3.92	3.07	2.68	2.44	2.29	2.17	2.08	2.01	1.95	1.90	1.86	1.83	1.77	1.72	1.65	1.60	1.55	1.49	1.45	1.39	1.36	1.31	1.27	1.25
	6.84	**4.78**	**3.94**	**3.47**	**3.17**	**2.95**	**2.79**	**2.65**	**2.56**	**2.47**	**2.40**	**2.33**	**2.23**	**2.15**	**2.03**	**1.94**	**1.85**	**1.75**	**1.68**	**1.59**	**1.54**	**1.46**	**1.40**	**1.37**
150	3.91	3.06	2.67	2.43	2.27	2.16	2.07	2.00	1.94	1.89	1.85	1.82	1.76	1.71	1.64	1.59	1.54	1.47	1.44	1.37	1.34	1.29	1.25	1.22
	6.81	**4.75**	**3.91**	**3.44**	**3.14**	**2.92**	**2.76**	**2.62**	**2.53**	**2.44**	**2.37**	**2.30**	**2.20**	**2.12**	**2.00**	**1.91**	**1.83**	**1.72**	**1.66**	**1.56**	**1.51**	**1.43**	**1.37**	**1.33**
200	3.89	3.04	2.65	2.41	2.26	2.14	2.05	1.98	1.92	1.87	1.83	1.80	1.74	1.69	1.62	1.57	1.52	1.45	1.42	1.35	1.32	1.26	1.22	1.19
	6.76	**4.71**	**3.88**	**3.41**	**3.11**	**2.90**	**2.73**	**2.60**	**2.50**	**2.41**	**2.34**	**2.28**	**2.17**	**2.09**	**1.97**	**1.88**	**1.79**	**1.69**	**1.62**	**1.53**	**1.48**	**1.39**	**1.33**	**1.28**
400	3.86	3.02	2.62	2.39	2.23	2.12	2.03	1.96	1.90	1.85	1.81	1.78	1.72	1.67	1.60	1.54	1.49	1.42	1.38	1.32	1.28	1.22	1.16	1.13
	6.70	**4.66**	**3.83**	**3.36**	**3.06**	**2.85**	**2.69**	**2.55**	**2.46**	**2.37**	**2.29**	**2.23**	**2.12**	**2.04**	**1.92**	**1.84**	**1.74**	**1.64**	**1.57**	**1.47**	**1.42**	**1.32**	**1.24**	**1.19**
1000	3.85	3.00	2.61	2.38	2.22	2.10	2.02	1.95	1.89	1.84	1.80	1.76	1.70	1.65	1.58	1.53	1.47	1.41	1.36	1.30	1.26	1.19	1.13	1.08
	6.66	**4.62**	**3.80**	**3.34**	**3.04**	**2.82**	**2.66**	**2.53**	**2.43**	**2.34**	**2.26**	**2.20**	**2.09**	**2.01**	**1.89**	**1.81**	**1.71**	**1.61**	**1.54**	**1.44**	**1.38**	**1.28**	**1.19**	**1.11**
∞	3.84	2.99	2.60	2.37	2.21	2.09	2.01	1.94	1.88	1.83	1.79	1.75	1.69	1.64	1.57	1.52	1.46	1.40	1.35	1.28	1.24	1.17	1.11	1.00
	6.64	**4.60**	**3.78**	**3.32**	**3.02**	**2.80**	**2.64**	**2.51**	**2.41**	**2.32**	**2.24**	**2.18**	**2.07**	**1.99**	**1.87**	**1.79**	**1.69**	**1.59**	**1.52**	**1.41**	**1.36**	**1.25**	**1.15**	**1.00**

Source: Reprinted by permission from *Statistical Methods*, 8th ed., by George W. Snedecor and William G. Cochran. Copyright © 1980 by Iowa State University Press, Ames, Iowa 50010.

Table A.4 Table of χ^2

df	.99	.98	.95	.90	.80	.70	.50	.30	.20	.10	.05	.02	.01	.001
1	.000157	.000628	.00393	.0158	.0642	.148	.455	1.074	1.642	2.706	3.841	5.412	6.635	10.827
2	.0201	.0404	.103	.211	.446	.713	1.386	2.408	3.219	4.605	5.991	7.824	9.210	13.815
3	.115	.185	.352	.584	1.005	1.424	2.366	3.665	4.642	6.251	7.815	9.837	11.345	16.266
4	.297	.429	.711	1.064	1.649	2.195	3.357	4.878	5.989	7.779	9.488	11.668	13.277	18.467
5	.554	.752	1.145	1.610	2.343	3.000	4.351	6.064	7.289	9.236	11.070	13.388	15.086	20.515
6	.872	1.134	1.635	2.204	3.070	3.828	5.348	7.231	8.558	10.645	12.592	15.033	16.812	22.457
7	1.239	1.564	2.167	2.833	3.822	4.671	6.346	8.383	9.803	12.017	14.067	16.622	18.475	24.322
8	1.646	2.032	2.733	3.490	4.594	5.527	7.344	9.524	11.030	13.362	15.507	18.168	20.090	26.125
9	2.088	2.532	3.325	4.168	5.380	6.393	8.343	10.656	12.242	14.684	16.919	19.679	21.666	27.877
10	2.558	3.059	3.940	4.865	6.179	7.267	9.342	11.781	13.442	15.987	18.307	21.161	23.209	29.588
11	3.053	3.609	4.575	5.578	6.989	8.148	10.341	12.899	14.631	17.275	19.675	22.618	24.725	31.264
12	3.571	4.178	5.226	6.304	7.807	9.034	11.340	14.011	15.812	18.549	21.026	24.054	26.217	32.909
13	4.107	4.765	5.892	7.042	8.634	9.926	12.340	15.119	16.985	19.812	22.362	25.472	27.688	34.528
14	4.660	5.368	6.571	7.790	9.467	10.821	13.339	16.222	18.151	21.064	23.685	26.873	29.141	36.123
15	5.229	5.985	7.261	8.547	10.307	11.721	14.339	17.322	19.311	22.307	24.996	28.259	30.578	37.697

Table A.4 Table of χ^2 (cont.)

df	.99	.98	.95	.90	.80	.70	.50	.30	.20	.10	.05	.02	.01	.001
16	5.812	6.614	7.962	9.312	11.152	12.624	15.338	18.418	20.465	23.542	26.296	29.633	32.000	39.252
17	6.408	7.255	8.672	10.085	12.002	13.531	16.338	19.511	21.615	24.769	27.587	30.995	33.409	40.790
18	7.015	7.906	9.390	10.865	12.857	14.440	17.338	20.601	22.760	25.989	28.869	32.346	34.805	42.312
19	7.633	8.567	10.117	11.651	13.716	15.352	18.338	21.689	23.900	27.204	30.144	33.687	36.191	43.820
20	8.260	9.237	10.851	12.443	14.578	16.266	19.337	22.775	25.038	28.412	31.410	35.020	37.566	45.315
21	8.897	9.915	11.591	13.240	15.445	17.182	20.337	23.858	26.171	29.615	32.671	36.343	38.932	46.797
22	9.542	10.600	12.338	14.041	16.314	18.101	21.337	24.939	27.301	30.813	33.924	37.659	40.289	48.268
23	10.196	11.293	13.091	14.848	17.187	19.021	22.337	26.018	28.429	32.007	35.172	38.968	41.638	49.728
24	10.856	11.992	13.848	15.659	18.062	19.943	23.337	27.096	29.553	33.196	36.415	40.270	42.980	51.179
25	11.524	12.697	14.611	16.473	18.940	20.867	24.337	28.172	30.675	34.382	37.652	41.566	44.314	52.620
26	12.198	13.409	15.379	17.292	19.820	21.792	25.336	29.246	31.795	35.563	38.885	42.856	45.642	54.052
27	12.879	14.125	16.151	18.114	20.703	22.719	26.336	30.319	32.912	36.741	40.113	44.140	46.963	55.476
28	13.565	14.847	16.928	18.939	21.588	23.647	27.336	31.391	34.027	37.916	41.337	45.419	43.278	56.893
29	14.256	15.574	17.708	19.768	22.475	24.577	28.336	32.461	35.139	39.087	42.557	46.693	49.588	58.302
30	14.953	16.306	18.493	20.599	23.364	25.508	29.336	33.530	36.250	40.256	43.773	47.962	50.892	59.703

Source: Taken from Table IV of Fisher and Yates: *Statistical Tables for Biological, Agricultural and Medical Research*, published by Longman Group UK Ltd., 1974.

Table A.5   *Critical Values of the Pearson Product Moment Correlation Coefficient*

	LEVEL OF SIGNIFICANCE FOR A DIRECTIONAL (ONE-TAILED) TEST				
	.05	.025	.01	.005	.0005
	LEVEL OF SIGNIFICANCE FOR A NONDIRECTIONAL (TWO-TAILED) TEST				
df = N − 2	.10	.05	.02	.01	.001
1	.9877	.9969	.9995	.9999	1.0000
2	.9000	.9500	.9800	.9900	.9990
3	.8054	.8783	.9343	.9587	.9912
4	.7293	.8114	.8822	.9172	.9741
5	.6694	.7545	.8329	.8745	.9507
6	.6215	.7067	.7887	.8343	.9249
7	.5822	.6664	.7498	.7977	.8982
8	.5494	.6319	.7155	.7646	.8721
9	.5214	.6021	.6851	.7348	.8471
10	.4973	.5760	.6581	.7079	.8233
11	.4762	.5529	.6339	.6835	.8010
12	.4575	.5324	.6120	.6614	.7800
13	.4409	.5139	.5923	.6411	.7603
14	.4259	.4973	.5742	.6226	.7420
15	.4124	.4821	.5577	.6055	.7246
16	.4000	.4683	.5425	.5897	.7084
17	.3887	.4555	.5285	.5751	.6932
18	.3783	.4438	.5155	.5614	.6787
19	.3687	.4329	.5034	.5487	.6652
20	.3598	.4227	.4921	.5368	.6524
25	.3233	.3809	.4451	.4869	.5974
30	.2960	.3494	.4093	.4487	.5541
35	.2746	.3246	.3810	.4182	.5189
40	.2573	.3044	.3578	.3932	.4896
45	.2428	.2875	.3384	.3721	.4648
50	.2306	.2732	.3218	.3541	.4433
60	.2108	.2500	.2948	.3248	.4078
70	.1954	.2319	.2737	.3017	.3799
80	.1829	.2172	.2565	.2830	.3568
90	.1726	.2050	.2422	.2673	.3375
100	.1638	.1946	.2301	.2540	.3211

Source: Table A.5 is taken from Table VII of Fisher and Yates, *Statistical Tables for Biological, Agricultural, and Medical Research*, published by Longman Group UK Ltd., 1974.

Table A.6 *Table of Random Numbers*

ROW	00000 01234	00000 56789	11111 01234	11111 56789	22222 01234	22222 56789	33333 01234	33333 56789
					COLUMN NUMBER			
					1st Thousand			
00	23157	54859	01837	25993	76249	70886	95230	36744
01	05545	55043	10537	43508	90611	83744	10962	21343
02	14871	60350	32404	36223	50051	00322	11543	80834
03	38976	74951	94051	75853	78805	90194	32428	71695
04	97312	61718	99755	30870	94251	25841	54882	10513
05	11742	69381	44339	30872	32797	33118	22647	06850
06	43361	28859	11016	45623	93009	00499	43640	74036
07	93806	20478	38268	04491	55751	18932	58475	52571
08	49540	13181	08429	84187	69538	29661	77738	09527
09	36769	72633	37948	21569	41959	68670	45274	83880
10	07092	52392	24627	12067	06558	45344	67338	45320
11	43310	01081	44863	80307	52555	16148	89742	94647
12	61570	06360	06173	63775	63148	95123	35017	46993
13	31352	83799	10779	18941	31579	76448	62584	86919
14	57048	86526	27795	93692	90529	56546	35065	32254
15	09243	44200	68721	07137	30729	75756	09298	27650
16	97957	35018	40894	88329	52230	82521	22532	61587
17	93732	59570	43781	98885	56671	66826	95996	44569
18	72621	11225	00922	68264	35666	59434	71687	58167
19	61020	74418	45371	20794	95917	37866	99536	19378
20	97839	85474	33055	91718	45473	54144	22034	23000
21	89160	97192	22232	90637	35055	45489	88438	16361
22	25966	88220	62871	79265	02823	52862	84919	54883
23	81443	31719	05049	54806	74690	07567	65017	16543
24	11322	54931	42362	34386	08624	97687	46245	23245

Table A.6   *Table of Random Numbers* (cont.)

ROW	00000 01234	00000 56789	11111 01234	11111 56789	22222 01234	22222 56789	33333 01234	33333 56789
						COLUMN NUMBER		
				2nd Thousand				
00	64755	83885	84122	25920	17696	15655	95045	95947
01	10302	52289	77436	34430	38112	49067	07348	23328
02	71017	98495	51308	50374	66591	02887	53765	69149
03	60012	55605	88410	34879	79655	90169	78800	03666
04	37330	94656	49161	42802	48274	54755	44553	65090
05	47869	87001	31591	12273	60626	12822	34691	61212
06	38040	42737	64167	89578	39323	49324	88434	38706
07	73508	30908	83054	80078	86669	30295	56460	45336
08	32623	46474	84061	04324	20628	37319	32356	43969
09	97591	99549	36630	35106	62069	92975	95320	57734
10	74012	31955	59790	96982	66224	24015	96749	07589
11	56754	26457	13351	05014	90966	33674	69096	33488
12	49800	49908	54831	21998	08528	26372	92923	65026
13	43584	89647	24878	56670	00221	50193	99591	62377
14	16653	79664	60325	71301	35742	83636	73058	87229
15	48502	69055	65322	58748	31446	80237	31252	96367
16	96765	54692	36316	86230	48296	38352	23816	64094
17	38923	61550	80357	81784	23444	12463	33992	28128
18	77958	81694	25225	05587	51073	01070	60218	61961
19	17928	28065	25586	08771	02641	85064	65796	48170
20	94036	85978	02318	04499	41054	10531	87431	21596
21	47460	60479	56230	48417	14372	85167	27558	00368
22	47856	56088	51992	82439	40644	17170	13463	18288
23	57616	34653	92298	62018	10375	76515	62986	90756
24	08300	92704	66752	66610	57188	79107	54222	22013

Table A.6 *Table of Random Numbers (cont.)*

ROW	00000 01234	00000 56789	11111 01234	11111 56789	22222 01234	22222 56789	33333 01234	33333 56789
				3rd Thousand				
00	89221	02362	65787	74733	51272	30213	92441	39651
01	04005	99818	63918	29032	94012	42363	01261	10650
02	98546	38066	50856	75045	40645	22841	53254	44125
03	41719	84401	59226	01314	54581	40398	49988	65579
04	28733	72489	00785	25843	24613	49797	85567	84471
05	65213	83927	77762	03086	80742	24395	68476	83792
06	65553	12678	90906	90466	43670	26217	69900	31205
07	05668	69080	73029	85746	58332	78231	45986	92998
08	39202	99718	49757	79519	27387	76373	47262	91612
09	64592	32254	45879	29431	38320	05981	18067	87137
10	07513	48792	47314	83660	68907	05336	82579	91582
11	86593	68501	56638	99800	82839	35148	56541	07232
12	83735	22599	97977	81248	36838	99560	32410	67614
13	08595	21826	54655	08204	87990	17033	56258	05384
14	41273	27149	44293	69458	16828	63962	15864	35431
15	00473	75908	56238	12242	72631	76314	47252	06347
16	86131	53789	81383	07868	89132	96182	07009	86432
17	33849	78359	08402	03586	03176	88663	08018	22546
18	61870	41657	07468	08612	98083	97349	20775	45091
19	43898	65923	25078	86129	78491	97653	91500	80786
20	29939	39123	04548	45985	60952	06641	28726	46473
21	38505	85555	14388	55077	18657	94887	67831	70819
22	31824	38431	67125	25511	72044	11562	53279	82268
23	91430	03767	13561	15597	06750	92552	02391	38753
24	38635	68976	25498	97526	96458	03805	04116	63514

Table A.6   *Table of Random Numbers (cont.)*

ROW	00000 01234	00000 56789	11111 01234	11111 56789	22222 01234	22222 56789	33333 01234	33333 56789
				4th Thousand				
00	02490	54122	27944	39364	94239	72074	11679	54082
01	11967	36469	60627	83701	09253	30208	01385	37482
02	48256	83465	49699	24079	05403	35154	39613	03136
03	27246	73080	21481	23536	04881	89977	49484	93071
04	32532	77265	72430	70722	86529	18457	92657	10011
05	66757	98955	92375	93431	43204	55825	45443	69265
06	11266	34545	76505	97746	34668	26999	26742	97516
07	17872	39142	45561	80146	93137	48924	64257	59284
08	62561	30365	03408	14754	51798	08133	61010	97730
09	62796	30779	35497	70501	30105	08133	00997	91970
10	75510	21771	04339	33660	42757	62223	87565	48468
11	87439	01691	63517	26590	44437	07217	98706	39032
12	97742	02621	10748	78803	38337	65226	92149	59051
13	98811	06001	21571	02875	21828	83912	85188	61624
14	51264	01852	64607	92553	29004	26695	78583	62998
15	40239	93376	10419	68610	49120	02941	80035	99317
16	26936	59186	51667	27645	46329	44681	94190	66647
17	88502	11716	98299	40974	42394	62200	69094	81646
18	63499	38093	25593	61995	79867	80569	01023	38374
19	36379	81206	03317	78710	73828	31083	60509	44091
20	93801	22322	47479	57017	59334	30647	43061	26660
21	29856	87120	56311	50053	25365	81265	22414	02431
22	97720	87931	88265	13050	71017	15177	06957	92919
23	85237	09105	74601	46377	59938	15647	34177	92753
24	75746	75268	31727	95773	72364	87324	36879	06802

Table A.6 *Table of Random Numbers (cont.)*

	COLUMN NUMBER							
ROW	00000 01234	00000 56789	11111 01234	11111 56789	22222 01234	22222 56789	33333 01234	33333 56789
				5th Thousand				
00	29935	06971	63175	52579	10478	89379	61428	21363
01	15114	07126	51890	77787	75510	13103	42942	48111
02	03870	43225	10589	87629	22039	94124	38127	65022
03	79390	39188	40756	45269	65959	20640	14284	22960
04	30035	06915	79196	54428	64819	52314	48721	81594
05	29039	99861	28759	79802	68531	39198	38137	24373
06	78196	08108	24107	49777	09599	43569	84820	94956
07	15847	85493	91442	91351	80130	73752	21539	10986
08	36614	62248	49194	97209	92587	92053	41021	80064
09	40549	54884	91465	43862	35541	44466	88894	74180
10	40878	08997	14286	09982	90308	78007	51587	16658
11	10229	49282	41173	31468	59455	18756	08908	06660
12	15918	76787	30624	25928	44124	25088	31137	71614
13	13403	18796	49909	94404	64979	41462	18155	98335
14	66523	94596	74908	90271	10009	98648	17640	68909
15	91665	36469	68343	17870	25975	04662	21272	50620
16	67415	87515	08207	73729	73201	57593	96917	69699
17	76527	96996	23724	33448	63392	32394	60887	90617
18	19815	47789	74348	17147	10954	34355	81194	54407
19	25592	53587	76384	72575	84347	68918	05739	57222
20	55902	45539	63646	31609	95999	82887	40666	66692
21	02470	58376	79794	22482	42423	96162	47491	17264
22	18630	53263	13319	97619	35859	12350	14632	87659
23	89673	38230	16063	92007	59503	38402	76450	33333
24	62986	67364	06595	17427	84623	14565	82860	57300

Source: Kendall, M. G., and B. B. Smith (1938). Randomness and random sampling numbers. *Journal of the Royal Statistical Society, 101,* 164–166. Reproduced by permission of the Royal Statistical Society, London.

GLOSSARY

ABAB design A single-subject experimental design in which baseline measurements of the target behavior are made (A) followed by a treatment (B), and then a second baseline measurement (A) and a second treatment (B).

abstract A brief summary of the contents of a document.

accessible population The population of subjects that is accessible to the researcher for a study, and the one to which the findings can be generalized.

accidental sampling A non-probability sampling technique that simply uses conveniently available subjects without regard to how well the sample represents the population of interest.

achievement test A measure of the extent to which a person has acquired certain information or skills, often as a result of specific instruction.

active independent variable An independent variable created through active manipulation in the course of an experiment. Active independent variables are characteristic of experimental research.

agreement coefficient The percentage of persons for whom the same decision (mastery or nonmastery) is made on two administrations of a *criterion-referenced test*. Used as an index of reliability for criterion-referenced tests.

alpha coefficient See **Cronbach alpha.**

alternate-form (estimate of reliability) See **equivalent-form.**

analysis of covariance (ANCOVA) A statistical technique that provides partial statistical control for one or more variables, removing their influence from the comparison of groups on the dependent variable.

analysis of variance (ANOVA) An inferential statistical test used for experimental designs with more than one independent variable or more than two levels of an independent variable.

applied research Research that aims to solve an immediate practical problem.

aptitude test A test that measures general abilities or characteristics believed to indicate a person's ability to learn a future task or to achieve in a particular area.

attitude scale A measure of the degree of favorableness or unfavorableness a subject has toward a group, institution, construct, or object.

attribute independent variable An independent variable on which subjects differ before a study begins. Attribute independent variables are characteristics of ex post facto research.

audit trail A qualitative researcher's documentation of how a study was conducted, including what was done, when, and why. It allows an independent auditor to examine the study from beginning to end and judge the trustworthiness of the outcome.

baseline Measures of the dependent variable taken prior to the introduction of the treatment in a time-series experimental design and used as the standard of comparison.

basic research   Research that aims to obtain empirical data that can be used to formulate, expand, or evaluate theory rather than to solve a practical problem.

biased sample   A sample in which certain elements in the parent population are systematically under- or overrepresented.

Boolean search   Named after the nineteenth-century mathematician George Boole, a search allowing the inclusion or exclusion of documents through the use of Boolean operators such as AND, NOT, and OR in the query.

canonical correlation   A statistical procedure for determining the relationship between several independent variables and more than one dependent variable.

case study   A qualitative examination of a single individual, group, event, or institution.

categorical variables   Variables that differ in kind, not in degree or amount.

causal–comparative research   See **ex post facto research.**

causal relationship   A relationship in which changes in one variable produce changes in another variable.

ceiling effect   An effect that occurs when the performance range on a measure is so restricted on the upper end that subjects cannot perform to their maximum ability.

census   A survey that includes the entire population of interest.

central tendency (measures of)   Averages such as mean, median, and mode, commonly used to summarize the data in a frequency distribution.

change score   The difference between subjects' pre- and postexperimental scores on the dependent variable(s).

checklist   A type of survey question that presents a number of possible answers, of which respondents are asked to check those that apply.

chi-square(χ^2) An inferential statistic that compares the frequencies of nominal measures actually observed in a study with frequencies expected under a null (chance) hypothesis.

CIJE (*Current Index to Journals in Education*)   ERIC monthly journal that indexes articles from more than 700 journals by subject, author, and journal and includes abstracts of these articles.

closed-ended question   A question followed by a fixed set of alternative responses from which the respondent chooses.

cluster sampling   A probability sampling technique that randomly selects intact groups (clusters) such as classrooms or voting precincts and then includes every element in each of the selected cluster in the sample.

coding   A process of organizing qualitative data that results in data reduction. It helps the researcher see what is in the data.

coefficient alpha   See **Cronbach alpha.**

coefficient of correlation   See **correlation coefficient.**

coefficient of determination   The square of the correlation coefficient. It indicates the percentage of variance in one variable in common with another variable.

cohort study   A longitudinal survey study in which a specific population is studied by taking different random samples from the population at various points in time.

common cause   A variable that accounts for differences in both the assumed independent and dependent variables.

comparison group   The group in a study that receives no treatment or a treatment different from the treatment received by the experimental group.

computer search   Using a computer to locate information in databases.

concurrent validity   See **criterion-related validity evidence.**

confirmability   The extent to which qualitative research is free of bias in the procedures and interpretation of results. It is the extent to which the data and the conclusions drawn would be confirmed by others investigating the same situation. Also called *neutrality*.

confounding variable   An uncontrolled extraneous variable whose effects on the dependent variable may incorrectly be attributed to the independent variable.

consequential validity   The extent to which a test is free of adverse consequences on individuals or groups that are caused by problems such as construct underrepresentation or construct irrelevant variance.

constant   A characteristic that takes on the same value for all individuals in a study; contrasts with *variable*.

constant comparison   A method of analyzing qualitative data that combines inductive category coding and simultaneous comparison of such units of meaning. Similar units of meaning are grouped together.

constitutive definition   A definition in which a word is defined by using other words.

construct   An abstraction at a higher level than a concept used to explain, interpret, and summarize observations and to form part of the conceptual content of a theory.

construct–irrelevant variance   The effect on test scores from processes that are extraneous to the construct being measured. It affects the validity of the test. For example, reading ability may affect performance on a math test.

construct underrepresentation   A term that is applied to assessment that is too narrow and fails to include important dimensions of the construct. It threatens the validity of the assessment.

content evidence (of validity)   Evidence based on the degree to which the items of a test representatively sample an intended content domain. Determined mainly by logical analysis.

contingency question   A survey question whose answer depends on the answer to a previous question.

continuous variable   A variable, the measure of which can take an infinite number of points within a range.

contrived observation   Observation of subjects in a prearranged simulation.

control   Steps taken by the researcher to remove the effects of any variable(s) other than the independent variable that might influence the dependent variable.

control group   The group in a study that does not receive the experimental treatment; it is compared with the experimental group to determine the effects of the treatment.

convergent evidence   Evidence for test validity based on the relationship to other measures intended to assess a similar construct. It shows that the intended construct is being measured.

correlation   A technique for determining the covariation between sets of scores; paired scores may vary directly (increase or decrease together) or vary inversely (as one increases, the other decreases).

correlational research   Research that attempts to determine the extent and the direction of the relationship between two or more variables.

correlation coefficient   A statistic that shows the degree of relationship between two variables; its value ranges between -1.00 and $+1.00$.

correlation matrix   A table that shows the coefficients of correlation between every measure and every other measure.

counterbalanced design   An experimental design in which the effects of order are controlled by having all groups receive all treatments, but in a different order.

credibility   In qualitative research, the accuracy or truthfulness of the findings from a study.

criterion-referenced test   An instrument that measures an individual's level of mastery of a predefined content or skill domain.

criterion-related validity evidence The degree to which scores on an instrument are related to other indicators of the same thing (the criterion). If the criterion scores are collected at the same point in time, the correlation is evidence of *concurrent validity.* If the criterion scores are collected at a later time, the resulting correlation between scores and criterion is evidence of *predictive validity.*

Cronbach alpha An internal-consistency reliability coefficient that measures the extent to which the scores of the individual items agree with one another. It is especially useful for attitude scales or essay tests.

cross-sectional survey A survey in which data are collected at one point in time from a specified population.

crosstabulation A table showing how frequently various combinations of two or more categorical variables occur, from which one can "see" the relationship (if any) between the variables.

cross-validation The process of validating a prediction equation based on one group by using it with a different group.

cumulative frequency The number of cases in a distribution with scores equal to or less than a given score.

curvilinear relationship A correlational relationship where a scattergram of the paired scores is better described by a curve than by a straight line. For example, if high scores on Y were paired with average scores on X and low scores on Y were paired with both high and low scores on X, the relationship would be curvilinear.

data saturation In qualitative research, the point at which no new information is forthcoming from additional participants or settings. Also called *redundancy.*

deduction Beginning with general premises or already known facts and deriving specific logical conclusions.

deductive hypothesis A hypothesis derived by deduction from a theory.

degrees of freedom (df) The number of observations free to vary around a constant parameter. Each inferential statistic has a defined procedure for calculating its degrees of freedom, which are used to determine the appropriate critical values in statistical tables for determining the probabilities of observed statistics.

dependability In qualitative research, the consistency or stability of the results; the extent to which the same general results would occur with different sets of people or in different settings and time periods.

dependent variable A variable that is a consequence of or dependent on an antecedent (independent) variable; also called the *outcome* or *effect variable.*

descriptive research Research that asks questions about the nature, incidence, or distribution of variables; it involves describing but not manipulating variables.

descriptive statistics Techniques for organizing, summarizing, and describing observations.

developmental study Investigation of how children change as they mature and respond to their environment.

dichotomous variable A categorical variable that has only two classes.

differential selection Creating experimental and control groups in such a way that they differ before treatment; an internal-validity problem.

directional hypothesis A hypothesis that specifies the direction of the expected findings—that is, whether a "greater than" or "less than" result is expected.

directional test (one-tailed test) A statistical test of a hypothesis that only states that the population parameter is greater than or less than the value of the parameter specified in the null hypothesis.

direct observation Observation of subjects to record the frequency and duration of behaviors falling within predetermined categories.

discriminant analysis A correlational procedure using a number of predictor variables to predict membership in categorical dependent variables.

discriminant evidence Evidence for test validity based on the relationship between the test scores and measures of purportedly different constructs. It shows that the wrong construct is not being measured.

documentary analysis The systematic examination of documents to investigate specific topics or themes.

double-barreled question A single-survey question that actually asks two questions in one.

double-blind experiment An experiment in which neither the observers nor the subjects know which is the experimental group and which is the control group.

double-dipped sample A sample drawn from the nonrespondents to a survey, who are then interviewed to determine if they differ significantly from respondents.

dummy variable A categorical variable that has been recoded as a binary variable for entry into a multiple regression. For example, gender could be coded as 1 or 0.

ecological validity The extent to which the findings from an experiment are independent of a particular research setting and can be generalized to other settings.

effect size The difference between experimental and control groups, divided by the standard deviation of the control group.

emergent design A design typical of qualitative research in which an initial problem or sampling strategy is changed or refined as data are collected and analyzed.

equivalent-form (estimate of reliability) Reliability assessment procedure correlating the scores of the same subjects on two tests that are as similar as possible in content, difficulty, length, format, and so on.

ERIC system Supported by the U.S. Department of Education's Office of Educational Research and Improvement, the Educational Resources Information Center (ERIC) is a national information system that collects, preserves, and organizes educational information and makes this information available to the public. The ERIC system maintains the ERIC database, the world's largest source of published and unpublished education information.

error of central tendency A tendency for a rater to avoid extreme scale positions, rating all individuals near the middle of the scale.

error of severity A tendency to rate all subjects too low.

ethnography A form of qualitative research that aims for a holistic picture of a cultural group; it uses in-depth interviewing and prolonged participant observation.

experimental design A plan for an experiment that specifies what independent variables will be applied, the number of levels of each, how subjects are assigned to groups, and the dependent variable.

experimental group The group in a research study that receives the experimental treatment.

experimental mortality Attrition of subjects during a study. An internal-validity problem if attrition is not the same for experimental and control groups.

experimental operational definition A definition stated in terms of the steps taken to produce certain experimental conditions.

experimental research Research in which the investigator manipulates one or more independent variables (the treatment) and observes the effect on one or more dependent variables.

experimenter bias The effects of the experimenter's attitudes, behavior, and expectancies on the behavior of the subjects in an experiment.

ex post facto research A type of research that attempts to determine the causes for, or the consequences of, differences that already exist in groups of individuals. Also called *causal-comparative research*.

external criticism   Evaluation of the authenticity of a document or other concrete evidence in historical research.

external validity   The extent to which the findings of a particular study can be generalized to other subjects, other settings, and/or other operational definitions of the variables.

external validity of operations   The extent to which the operational definitions employed and the manner in which a study is conducted truly represent the variables of the study.

extraneous variable   An uncontrolled variable that may affect the dependent variable of a study; its effect may be mistakenly attributed to the independent variable of the study.

factor   An underlying construct accounting for the covariation among a larger number of variables.

factor analysis   A statistical procedure for analyzing the intercorrelations among three or more measures that reduces the set to a smaller number of underlying factors.

factorial design   An experimental design that investigates two or more independent variables at the same time, in order to study their effects singly and/or in interaction with each other.

field experiment   An experiment conducted in a naturally occurring environment.

field notes   The researcher's reflections and the written records of observations and conversations made during a qualitative research project.

field testing   A process of testing a research instrument with a small number of persons, in order to identify ambiguities or other problems before the final form is prepared.

floor effect   An effect that occurs when the performance range of a measure is so restricted at the lower end that subjects cannot show their ability to perform. Occurs when the task is too difficult for the subjects.

focus group   A data-gathering tool in which a researcher interviews a small group of people to obtain different perspectives on a particular issue.

focus of inquiry   In qualitative research, the initial topic (problem) that a researcher pursues. It may be presented in the form of a question or a statement.

focused interview   A qualitative research data-gathering technique employing open and flexible questions that respondents are free to answer in their own words.

follow-up study   An investigation of subsequent development of subjects after a specified treatment or program.

frequency distribution   A tabular representation of the scores obtained by a group of individuals.

F-test   A statistical procedure used for testing hypotheses about differences among two or more means, and for other purposes.

generosity error   A tendency for a rater to give every subject the benefit of the doubt and, when uncertain, to give high ratings.

grounded theory   Theory derived inductively from the data collected in a natural setting rather than from a priori ideas or theorems.

halo effect   The tendency for a rater's general impression of a subject to influence the rating given for specific aspects or behaviors of the subject.

Hawthorne effect   An effect on the dependent variable resulting from the treatment group's knowledge that the members are participating in an experiment.

histogram   A graph in which the frequency distribution of scores is represented by vertical bars.

historical research   A systematic attempt to establish facts and arrive at conclusions about the past.

history (an internal validity problem)   Events or conditions other than the independent variable that produce changes in the dependent variable.

homogeneous group   A set of subjects who are the same or similar on a relevant variable.

homogeneous selection   Employing subjects that are as alike as possible in regard to relevant characteristics, to reduce the influence of extraneous variables.

human instrument   The investigator as the means of data gathering in qualitative inquiry.

hypothesis   A tentative proposition suggested as a solution to a problem; a statement of the researcher's expectations about the relationship among the variables of a study.

hypothesis test   Collection of observations to determine whether these observations confirm or fail to confirm a hypothesized relationship.

imperfect induction   The process of inferring from a sample of a group to what is characteristic of the whole group.

implementation threat   A threat to the internal validity of a study resulting from possible variations in implementing the treatment.

independent variable   A variable that is antecedent to the dependent variable; also called the *experimental* or *treatment variable.*

induction   Gaining knowledge through systematic study and observation of specific facts or episodes and then arriving at generalized conclusions.

inductive analysis   A process of beginning with observations (data) and then proceeding to hypothesis formation and refinement and finally to theory.

inductive hypothesis   A hypothesis derived through generalization from observation.

inferential statistics   Procedures that permit one to make tentative generalizations from sample data to the population from which the sample was drawn.

informed consent, right to   The right of a subject in a research study to know the nature and purpose of the study and to give or withhold consent to participate.

institutional review board (IRB)   A committee that determines whether proposed research meets federal and other legal and ethical standards.

instrument   A device for operationally defining a variable.

instrumentation threat   The possibility that results of a study are caused by variations in the way instruments are used to operationally define the variables; a threat to internal validity.

interaction   The outcome of a factorial experiment when the effects of one independent variable on a dependent variable change at different levels of the second independent variable.

internal-consistency   Reliability assessment procedure measuring the extent to which items of a test (or subtest or scale) are positively intercorrelated and thus all measure the same construct or trait; the extent to which a test measures only one characteristic.

internal criticism   Evaluation of the truthfulness of a document in historical research.

internal structure evidence (of validity)   Evidence based on an analysis of the internal structure of a test; it looks at the intercorrelations among test items to determine whether the test is measuring a single construct and whether the interrelationships conform to the theory behind the construct being measured.

internal validity   The extent to which observed differences on the dependent variable in an experiment are the result of the independent variable, not of some uncontrolled extraneous variable or variables.

Internet   An interconnected system of computer networks allowing for information sharing.

interrater reliability   The extent to which two or more observers produce similar quantitative results when observing the same individual during the same time period.

interval scale   A scale of measurement that orders objects or events and has points equidistant from one another.

interview   Oral questioning of a subject.

interviewer bias   A bias that occurs in interviews when the interviewer verbally or nonverbally rewards the subject's correct responses or negatively reinforces wrong responses.

interview schedule   A document used by an interviewer that contains the instructions, the questions in a fixed order, and any transition phrases.

inventory   A collection of statements to which subjects respond by indicating whether the statement describes them or not; used in assessing personality.

item analysis   Analysis of a test determining for each item the number and proportion of correct responses and the correlation of scores on that item with total test scores.

John Henry effect   An effect that occurs when the control group performs above its usual average when it perceives itself in competition with an experimental group that is using a new method or procedure.

known-groups techniques   A method for determining the validity of a measure by seeing whether groups known to differ on the construct also differ on the measure itself.

Kuder-Richardson formulas   Formulas for determining the internal-consistency reliability (homogeneity) of an instrument from a single administration and without splitting the test into halves.

laboratory experiment   An experiment conducted in a highly controlled environment.

law of the single independent variable   Rule stating that to unambiguously determine the effect of an independent variable on a dependent variable, the independent variable must be the only difference between the experimental and control groups before the dependent variable is measured.

level of significance   The largest probability of error acceptable for rejection of the null hypothesis. Often $p = .05$ or $p = .01$ in educational research.

Likert scale   A measurement scale consisting of a series of statements followed by five response categories, typically ranging from "strongly agree" to "strongly disagree."

Likert-type item   A statement similar to those in a Likert scale, where the response options are on a continuum from "strongly agree" to "strongly disagree."

linear relationship   A correlational relationship where the plotted points in a scattergram of the paired scores fit around a straight line.

longitudinal survey   A survey in which data are collected several times over an extended period of time.

low-inference descriptor   Verbatim or direct quotations from the participants in qualitative research that help a reader experience the participants' world.

main effect   The effect that an independent variable has on the dependent variable in a factorial experiment irrespective of the influence of the other independent variables.

manipulated variable   The variable that is systematically altered by an experimental researcher in order to observe the effect on a dependent variable.

margin of error   An estimate of the extent to which sample results are likely to deviate from the population value.

matching   Identifying pairs of subjects who are as alike as possible before a study begins.

maturation   A threat to internal validity from factors that occur as a result of the passage of time. In addition to the experimental treatment, factors such as growing older, hungrier, more fatigued, or less motivated may influence performance on the dependent variable and thus threaten internal validity.

maximum variation sampling   A sampling technique widely used in qualitative inquiry in which a researcher attempts to understand a phenomenon by seeking out people or settings that represent the greatest difference in that phenomenon.

mean   A measure of central tendency for a distribution of interval data; the sum of the scores divided by the number of scores in the distribution; the arithmetic average.

median   The point in a distribution below which are 50 percent of the scores (the 50th percentile); used with ordinal or interval data.

measured operational definition   A definition stated in terms of the operations used by researchers to measure the concept.

member check   A process in which a qualitative researcher asks the participants in a study whether he or she has accurately and realistically described their experience. The participant feedback contributes to the trustworthiness of qualitative inquiry.

Mental Measurements Yearbooks   Serial publication listing tests available, with descriptions and critical reviews of these tests.

meta-analysis   The systematic combination of quantitative data from a number of studies investigating the relationship between the same variables. A weighted average of effect sizes.

mode   The score that occurs most frequently in a distribution of scores; used with nominal, ordinal, interval or ratio data.

mortality   A threat to internal validity that occurs when some participants drop out of a study before it is completed.

multifactor analysis of variance   An analysis of variance with more than one independent variable.

multiple-baseline design   An experiment in which several dependent variable baseline measures are done for a single subject, and then treatments designed to change dependent variables are instituted at different times for each dependent variable. It is also used to determine the effects of the same treatment instituted at different times for different subjects.

multiple correlation   The correlation between a set of predictors and a single dependent variable. The extent of relationship is indicated by the multiple correlation coefficient (R).

multiple prediction   The prediction of a criterion using two or more predictor variables in combination. Each predictor is weighted in proportion to its contribution to prediction accuracy. The equation showing the weights assigned to each predictor is the *multiple prediction equation*.

naturalistic inquiry   The study of subjects in their normal environment without predetermined hypotheses.

naturalistic observation   Studying people in their natural setting, preferably without the subjects being aware that they are being observed.

natural setting   An environment for research in which activities occur in the ordinary course of events as opposed to an environment in which events are contrived or manipulated for the purpose of the research.

negative-case sampling   A strategy used to control for bias in qualitative research, in which researchers intentionally seek examples and information that disconfirm their expectations.

negative correlation   A correlation with high scores on one variable associated with low scores on the other variable.

negatively skewed curve   A polygon showing many scores piled up at the high (right) end and the lower scores spread out toward the left (low) end; the tail of the curve extends to the left.

nominal scale   A scale of measurement that classifies objects or individuals into categories that are qualitatively but not quantitatively different.

nondirectional hypothesis   A hypothesis that states a relationship between variables will be observed but does not specify the direction of the expected findings.

nondirectional test (two-tailed test)   A statistical test that takes into account differences in either direction (greater or less than) from the value specified in the null hypothesis; the null hypothesis is rejected if the difference is large enough in *either* tail of a sampling distribution of the statistic.

nonparticipant observation   A research method in which the observer does not participate in the situation being studied but is only an observer.

nonprobability sampling   Sampling through other than random selection.

nonresponse   A situation in which people receive a survey but fail to return the completed instrument.

normal curve   A hypothetical symmetrical, bell-shaped distribution of scores used as a model for many naturally occurring distributions and for many statistical tests.

norm-referenced test   A test that enables one to compare an individual's performance with the performance of others who have taken the test.

null hypothesis   A hypothesis that states there is no effect, no difference, or no relationship between variables; it is a negation of the research hypothesis—hence one that the researcher hopes to reject.

observer bias   An effect that occurs when the observer's personal attitudes and values affect the observation and/or the interpretation of the observation. Can especially be a problem in qualitative research.

observer effect   The impact that an observer has on a study's participants so that they behave differently from the way they normally would. It destroys the naturalness and results in an inaccurate picture of a situation.

observer participant   An observer who interacts with subjects enough to establish rapport but does not really become involved in the behavior or activities of the group. The person's status as an observer/researcher is known to the group.

one-tailed test   See **directional test.**

open-ended question   A question that doesn't have fixed response alternatives but allows the respondent to respond as he or she chooses.

operational definition   A definition that specifies the procedure or operation to be followed in producing or measuring a concept.

ordinal scale   A scale of measurement that rank-orders objects and events according to the extent to which they possess the characteristic of interest, but the distance between points cannot be assumed to be equal.

panel study   A longitudinal survey study in which data are gathered from the same sample of people at different points in time.

parallel-form   See **equivalent-form.**

parameter   A characteristic of a population, such as the population mean (μ) or the population standard deviation (σ).

parsimony principle   The principle that states that other things being equal, the simplest explanation of a phenomenon is preferred over a more complicated explanation.

partial control   Some but not complete control over relevant extraneous variables.

partial correlation   A statistical procedure for describing the relationship between two variables, with the correlation between these variables and a third variable removed.

participant observation   A research method in which the researcher becomes a part of and participates in the activities of the group or situation being studied.

path analysis   A statistical procedure for investigating the causal relationships among correlated variables.

Pearson product moment coefficient (Pearson r)   An index of correlation for interval or ratio data; it is the mean of paired z-score products of the two variables.

peer debriefers   Members of a qualitative research team who check one another's work and look for evidence of bias. They act to keep one another honest.

performance assessment   A type of assessment that requires subjects to show what they know by performing specified tasks rather than by filling out a paper and pencil instrument.

phenomenological approach   A philosophy of research that focuses on understanding the meaning events have for people in particular situations. It underlies qualitative research.

phenomenology   A type of qualitative research designed to gain an understanding of how participants experience and give meaning to an event, concept, or phonomenon.

phi coefficient   A correlation coefficient for use when both variables are measured on a nominal scale.

pilot study   A trial run with a few subjects to assess the appropriateness and practicability of the procedures and data-collecting instruments.

placebo   A chemically inert or neutral material given to subjects in an experiment to make them believe they are receiving a drug or experimental treatment.

polygon   A graph showing scores and frequency of scores by connecting the intersections of each of the scores and the frequencies.

population   The larger group to which a researcher wishes to generalize; it includes *all* members of a defined class of people, events, or objects.

population validity   How well a sample represents a population; the extent to which the results of a study can be generalized from the sample to a population of interest.

positive correlation   A correlation with high scores on one variable associated with high scores on the other variable, and low scores associated with low scores.

positively skewed distribution   A polygon showing many scores piled up at or near the low (left) end and higher scores spread out toward the high (right) end; the tail extends to the right.

positivism   A philosophy of research characterized by objective inquiry based on measurable variables; believes that science should be primarily concerned with the explanation and the prediction of observable events. It underlies quantitative research.

power   The ability of a significance test to find significant differences when differences truly exist; the ability to avoid making a Type II error.

power calculation   A mathematical procedure for determining the sample size needed to reject the null hypothesis at a given level of significance with a given effect size.

predictive validity   See **criterion-related validity evidence.**

predictor   A variable from which predictions are made in a prediction study.

preexperimental research   Experimental designs with little or no control of extraneous variables and therefore little internal validity.

pretest sensitization   The effect of a pretest on subjects that causes them to respond differently to the treatment from the way they would without the pretest.

primary source   Original documents, relics, remains, or the records of an eyewitness used in historical research.

probability sampling   Sampling employing random selection, which means that every element in the population has a non-zero chance of being selected.

probe   A follow-up question used during an interview to elicit clearer and more complete responses from the interviewee.

projective technique   A method for assessing personality by analyzing subjects' responses to ambiguous material.

purposive sampling   A nonprobability sampling technique in which subjects judged to be representative of the population are included in the sample.

qualitative research   A generic term for a variety of research approaches that study phenomena in their natural settings, without predetermined hypotheses.

quantitative research   Inquiry employing operational definitions to generate numeric data to answer predetermined hypotheses or questions.

quasi-experimental research   Research in which the investigator can control the treatment and the measurement of the dependent variable but cannot control assignment of the subjects to treatment.

questionnaire   An instrument in which respondents provide written responses to questions or mark items that indicate their responses.

quota sampling   A nonprobability sampling technique that determines the size of each relevant subgroup in the population and then nonrandomly selects subjects to produce a sample in which the proportion of each subgroup is the same in the sample as it is in the population.

random assignment (randomization)   Assigning members of a sample to experimental or control groups through a chance procedure.

randomized matching   A procedure in which subjects are first paired (matched) on relevant variables, and then a chance procedure is used to assign one member of each pair to the experimental group and the other to the control group.

random sample   A sample selected by a chance procedure so that every member of the population has an equal probability of being selected.

random selection   The process of selecting a sample by chance means, so that every member of the population has an equal probability of being included.

range   A nominal measure of dispersion; the difference between the highest and lowest scores plus 1 unit of measure.

ranking item   A type of survey question that asks respondents to indicate the order of their preference among a number of options.

ratio scale   A scale of measurement that provides a true zero point as well as equal intervals.

referential accuracy (or interpretive accuracy)   A term used in qualitative research to refer to the degree to which participants' viewpoints, thoughts, feelings, and experiences are accurately understood.

reflexivity   Qualitative researchers' use of self-reflection to recognize and actively look for their own biases.

regression (statistical)   The statistical tendency for extreme scores on the first measurement to move closer to the mean on a second measurement.

regression threat   The internal-validity problem that arises when results in a study are caused by a tendency for groups selected on the basis of extreme scores, to move (regress) toward the average on subsequent measures, regardless of the experimental treatment.

reliability   The extent to which a measure yields consistent results; the extent to which scores are free of random error.

replication logic   A process in which one conducts a qualitative study in multiple locations or with multiple groups in order to assess the dependability of the findings.

research proposal   A step-by-step plan for conducting and completing a research study.

response process evidence (of validity)   Evidence about what a test measures obtained by looking at the mental processes and skills that subjects use when responding to the items on a test.

response set   A habitual way of responding that is independent of the content of a particular survey or test item, as when a subject always checks "undecided" regardless of the statement.

reverse causality   An alternative hypothesis stating that the supposed dependent variable is in actuality the independent variable (Y causes X, not X causes Y).

RIE (Resources in Education)   ERIC monthly journal that indexes U.S. government-sponsored research and fugitive or ephemeral materials and provides abstracts of these documents.

sample   A group selected from a population for observation in a study.

sample survey   A survey done on only a portion (a sample) of a population, often using a questionnaire or interview.

sampling error The difference between a sample statistic and a population parameter.

scale A continuum, usually having quantitative units, that measures the extent to which individuals exhibit certain traits or characteristics.

scattergram A figure using plotted points to represent the intersection of individuals' paired X and Y scores; used to show the relationship between the X and Y variables.

scholastic aptitude test A test that measures abilities that are predictive of success in academic tasks.

scientific approach A way of seeking knowledge that involves both inductive and deductive reasoning to develop hypotheses that are then subjected to rigorous and objective testing.

search engine The software that searches an index of Internet Web pages and returns matches.

secondary source Secondhand information, such as a description of a historical event written by someone other than an eyewitness.

selection-maturation interaction An internal-validity problem created when subjects are selected in such a way that the experimental and control groups mature at different rates.

semantic differential scale A method of assessing subjects' attitudes by having them mark points on a continuum between bipolar adjectives.

single-subject research An experiment with only one subject or intact group.

snowball sampling A sampling procedure used in qualitative research that occurs when the initially selected subjects suggest the names of others who would be appropriate for the sample, and the latter suggest others and so on. Also called *chain sampling*.

social desirability bias A bias that occurs in interviews when subjects give responses to enhance their image rather than honest responses.

Social Science Citation Index A periodic journal; its citation index enables users to start with an older article on a topic of interest, then identify more recent works that cite that original work in their bibliographies or footnotes. It enables the researcher to locate updated research and find retractions and corrections. Its corporate index identifies the institutional source of published works. Its permuterm index identifies interconnections in article titles.

Solomon four-group design An experimental design that involves random assignment of subjects to each of four groups; two groups are pretested, two are not; one of the pretested and one of the nonpretested groups receive the treatment, and all four groups are posttested.

Solomon three-group design An experimental design in which subjects are randomly assigned to three groups: (A) pretest plus treatment, (B) pretest plus no treatment, or (C) no pretest plus treatment.

Spearman-Brown formula A statistical procedure employing the correlation between split-halves of a test to estimate the reliability of the whole test.

Spearman rho An index of correlation for use with ordinal data.

split-half reliability A type of internal-consistency reliability obtained by artificially splitting a test into two halves and correlating individuals' scores on the two half tests.

spurious result An apparent relationship between variables that is not genuine.

standard deviation A measure of the extent to which individual scores deviate from the mean of the distribution; the square root of the variance; a measure of dispersion used with interval data.

standard error of estimate A measure of the expected difference between predicted scores and actual scores.

standard error of measurement An index of the amount of measurement error in test scores; theoretically, the standard deviation of the distribution of observed scores around an individual's true score.

standard error of the mean   The standard deviation of sampling errors of the mean; indicates how much the means of random samples drawn from a single population can be expected to differ through chance alone.

standardized test   A test with specified content, prescribed directions for administering and scoring, norms, and reliability and validity information derived from administration to representative samples.

standard score   A transformed score expressed in terms of the number of standard deviation units the score is above or below the mean; standard scores have a mean and standard deviation set to some arbitrary standard. For example, a *z*-score has a mean of 0 and standard deviation of 1; *T*-scores use a mean of 50 and a standard deviation of 10.

static group comparison   A preexperimental design that involves at least two nonequivalent groups; one receives a treatment and both are posttested. Provides little or no control.

statistic   A characteristic of a sample.

statistical equivalence   Condition occurring when any difference between groups is a function of chance alone; random assignment of subjects to groups results in statistically equivalent groups.

statistically significant result   A result that has less than a previously specified probability of being a function of chance.

stepwise replication   A process in which two investigators divide the data from a qualitative inquiry, analyze it independently, and then compare results. A way of checking on the dependability of the research.

stratified sampling   A probability sampling technique that first divides a population into subgroups by relevant variables such as age, social status, or education and then randomly selects subjects from each subgroup.

structural corroboration   The use of different sources of qualitative data and different methods to see if there is agreement (corroboration) in the description and interpretation of a state of affairs.

style manual   A book detailing form and style for theses, dissertations, and other formal written works.

subject   A person in a study.

subject descriptors   A controlled vocabulary list of terms and phrases. Descriptors, also called *subject headings,* are standardized terms used in indexes and catalogs to describe the content of a document indexed. Controlled vocabularies are often arranged with broader, narrower, and related terms, as in the ERIC thesaurus, which provides the searcher with an idea of the relationships of terms and concepts.

summated rating scale   A scale that arrives at a person's total score by finding the sum of the weighted responses made to all the items in the scale. See **Likert scale.**

survey   Study of a sample to investigate the incidence and distribution of variables.

symmetrical distribution   A distribution that can be represented by a polygon whose right side is a mirror image of its left side.

systematic sampling   A probability sampling in which every *k*th element of the population list is selected for the sample.

target population   The total group (population) to which the researcher would like to generalize the results of a study.

test   A systematic procedure for measuring a sample of behavior presumed to represent an educational or psychological characteristic.

test of significance   A statistical test used to determine whether the obtained results are likely to be a function of chance. Used to assess the credibility of the null hypothesis.

test-retest reliability   A measure of reliability obtained by correlating scores from two administrations of the same measure to the same subjects.

theory   A set of interrelated propositions or hypotheses that presents an explanation of some phenomenon.

thick description   A term used in qualitative research that refers to descriptions that are written to create vivid images of the setting and behaviors being observed.

time-series design   An experiment in which dependent variable measures are made several times before and after treatment.

transferability   In qualitative research, the degree to which the findings of a study can be generalized to other contexts or to other groups.

trend study   A longitudinal survey in which data are gathered from different samples of a general population at different points in time to investigate changes over time.

triangulation   Confirming data using multiple data-gathering procedures or multiple sources of data; used in qualitative research.

true experimental design   An experimental design in which the researcher controls the treatment and uses randomization to assign subjects to treatments.

T-score   A standard score with a mean of 50 and a standard deviation of 10.

t-test   A statistical procedure for testing hypotheses concerning the difference between two means; also used for other purposes.

two-tailed test   See **nondirectional test.**

Type I error   The error that occurs when a researcher rejects a null hypothesis that is in fact true.

Type II error   The error that occurs when a researcher fails to reject a null hypothesis that is in fact false.

validity (of measurement)   The extent to which a measure actually taps the underlying concept that it purports to measure.

variability   The dispersion or spread in a distribution of scores.

variable   A representation of a construct that takes on a range of values. For example, height, reading test score, aptitude, and gender are variables.

variance   The mean of squared deviation scores; an interval measure of dispersion of scores around the mean.

World Wide Web   The use of graphical user interfaces and hypertext links to access information on the Internet. Also, the complete set of documents residing on the Internet that can be accessed through the Web.

z-score   A standard score that indicates how far a score is above or below the mean score in terms of standard deviation units.

CREDITS

INDEX